Memoir of the Life of Admiral Sir Edward Codrington

ADMIRAL SIR EDWARD CODRINGTON.

VOL. II.

LONDON: PRINTED BY
SPOTTISWOODE AND CO, NEW-STREET SQUARE
AND PARLIAMENT STREET

BATTLE OF NAVARIN, OCTOBER 20, 1827.

See page 71

Genos, 74

Capitan Bey's ship, 86
(Turkish Admiral)

Egyptian, 24

Asia, 84
(Vice-Admiral
Sir E. Codrington)

Hind, 6

Moharem Bey's ship, 62
(Egyptian Admiral)

Egyptian, 28

MEMOIR OF THE LIFE

OF

ADMIRAL SIR EDWARD CODRINGTON.

WITH SELECTIONS

FROM

HIS PUBLIC AND PRIVATE CORRESPONDENCE.

EDITED BY HIS DAUGHTER

LADY BOURCHIER.

WITH PORTRAITS AND OTHER ILLUSTRATIONS.

IN TWO VOLUMES.

VOL. II.

LONDON:

LONGMANS, GREEN, AND CO.

1873.

CONTENTS

OF

THE SECOND VOLUME.

———◆———

CHAPTER I.

(September 22 to October 16, 1827.)

CHAPTER II.

(October 16 to 24.)

CHAPTER III.

(October 25 to December 29)

REFERENCES FOR APPENDIX.

ILLUSTRATIONS TO THE SECOND VOLUME.

MEMOIR

OF

ADMIRAL SIR EDWARD CODRINGTON.

CHAPTER I.

By the arrival of the French Admiral before Navarin on the 21st of September whilst a portion of the Turkish fleet was still outside the harbour, not only was the force under Sir Edward Codrington increased, but instead of the isolated and critical responsibility of the English squadron, a joint action of the Allies was partially secured.

Although the Russian squadron was still absent, yet Sir Edward Codrington and Admiral De Rigny at once commenced proceedings, and in an interview with Ibrahim Pacha, declared the determination of the Allied Courts to carry out the Treaty, and the necessity imposed on the Admirals to enforce the armistice referred to in their instructions.

From Admirals Sir E. Codrington and Count de Rigny to his Highness Ibrahim Pacha.

(5)   Before Navarin : September 22, 1827.

As Your Highness appears to have entertained some doubt of the perfect harmony which exists among the three Allied Powers, I must inform you that, Admiral Codrington having communicated to me the letter which he had the honour to address to Your Highness, during a calm which detained me at some miles from this place, we have thought proper to transmit to you a second copy of it in French, and signed by us both.

&c., &c., &c.,

DE RIGNY.

We have the honour to inform Your Highness, that in consequence of a Treaty signed at London, between England, France and Russia, the Allied Powers have agreed to unite their forces for the purpose of preventing the transport of any troops, arms, or warlike stores to any part of the continent of Greece, or of the islands.   This measure has been adopted, as much for the interest of the Grand Signior himself, as for the benefit of all nations trading in the Archipelago; and the Allied Powers have taken the humane precaution of sending a very strong force to prevent all possible opposition on the part of the Turkish commanders, whose resistance would not only bring with it their own destruction, but would also be very hurtful to the interests of his Highness.

It would be as painful to us, as it would also be to our respective sovereigns, whose great desire it is to spare the effusion of blood, to be compelled to use force on this occasion.   We earnestly beg you not to oppose a resolution, the execution of which it is not in your power to resist; for we must not conceal from you that, although it is our desire to put an end to this cruel war by conciliatory means, our orders are such that we must proceed to the last extremity rather than forego the object for the accomplishment of which our sovereigns are allied.   If then, on this occasion, a single gun is fired against our flags it will be fatal to the Ottoman fleet.

The undersigned have the honour, &c.,

EDWARD CODRINGTON, Vice-Admiral, &c.
H. DE RIGNY, Rear-Admiral, &c.

From Admiral De Rigny to Sir E. C.

'Syrène,' Navarin : ce 23 septembre 1827.

MONSIEUR L'AMIRAL,—Je viens d'avoir une conférence particulière avec Méhémet * Ali. Je n'ai pas voulu en avoir une publique, parce que je crois très à propos que nous fassions ensemble cette démarche en présence d'Ibrahim, du Capitan Bey, et de Tahir Pacha.   Je ne doute pas que la résolution d'Ibrahim Pacha soit de ne pas sortir : il a fait donner cette nuit l'ordre à sa flotte de rentrer, mais je sais que cet ordre avait été provoqué par l'Amiral turc, qui est dehors.   Il paraît que d'après quelques paroles du Capitaine Hamilton, il craignait qu'on ne mît obstacle à la rentrée de cette partie de la flotte ; et son inquiétude s'accroît par cette circonstance que c'est la flotte de Constantinople qui est ainsi exposée, et que cela pourrait paraître une combinaison concertée entre nous et lui. Il veut expédier une goëlette à son père,

* [*Sic.*] An evident mistake for Ibrahim Pacha.

et un courrier à Constantinople, et tout suspendre jusqu'à de nouveaux ordres : c'est donc une suspension d'armes de fait ; il demande alors, si les Grecs, rencontrant cette goëlette, nous permettrions qu'ils l'arrêtassent—puisque vous exigez de moi que je n'aille pas à Hydra, ne devez-vous pas exiger des Grecs qu'ils s'abstiennent de leur côté de toutes hostilités ? Dans cette circonstance, Monsieur l'Amiral, je vous prie d'entrer ; je crois que nous aurons un résultat passable ; si non, nous emploierions les grands moyens Mais au moins nous aurons épuisé tous ceux de la persuasion.

Mr. Cradock vous donnera plus de détails, auxquels j'ajouterai, aussitôt que vous paraîtrez, ceux que j'aurai pu encore recueillir. Je pense que vous approuverez que j'ai prié le Capitaine du 'Dartemoute' de vous porter cette lettre. Je vous prie d'agréer de nouveau ma haute considération.

Le C^{tre}-Amiral

H. DE RIGNY.

From Sir E. C. to the Admiralty.

'Asia,' off Navarin   September 25, 1827.

SIR,—On the 19th of September, still finding myself without the aid of Rear-Admiral De Rigny, I sent the enclosed documents* (Nos. 1 and 2) into the port of Navarin. After receiving the report (No. 3) made by Captain Baillie Hamilton, who was employed by Captain Fellowes to execute this service, I sent in the note (No. 4) with the extracts therein mentioned. On the 22nd, on being joined by Rear-Admiral De Rigny, we agreed to take advantage of Ibrahim Pacha having expressed doubts of the truth of our union, to send in the letter (No. 5) ; and the Rear-Admiral acceded to my request, that he would support it by going into Navarin himself, accompanied by Lieut.-Colonel Cradock. At 6 in the evening Colonel Cradock returned in the ' Dartmouth ' to strengthen the Rear-Admiral's opinion that I should have a personal interview with the Pacha. Accordingly the ' Asia ' obtained an anchorage here yesterday evening ; and it was agreed that the whole of the Turkish ships should also come in to prevent a suspicion of collusion

---

* ENCLOSURE No. 1.

No. 1. Letter to the Turkish Admiral

2. Note to the Austrian Commander.

3 Captain Baillie Hamilton's report.

4. Note to Ibrahim Pacha

5. Joint letter from the English and French Admirals.

6 Letter from Sir E. C to Ibrahim Pacha, September 24.

7. Mr Dyer's memorandum of the Conference with Ibrahim.

arising from the circumstance of the Egyptian division not having yet put to sea. Upon the 'Asia' anchoring I sent the letter (No. 6), and this morning saluted the Pacha with 19 guns, which was returned with equal number. At 9 A.M. to-day I received an invitation to attend the Pacha, according to my letter; and I have now to inform you, for the information of his Royal Highness, of the result. It is agreed that the Turco-Egyptian fleet shall remain in the port of Navarin, and there suspend hostilities until the Pacha can receive from Constantinople and Alexandria orders consequent on his representation of the communications which we have made to him—first, of our orders and the necessity we are under of enforcing them to the utmost necessity; and secondly, of his finding it impossible to resist them without the sacrifice of the whole expedition under his command. It will not be deemed necessary that I should attempt to detail a discussion of about three hours, in the presence of the whole Turco-Egyptian chiefs, by which this arrangement was brought about. It will, I trust, suffice that the result should have been an armistice *in fact*, as far as this great expedition is concerned, which the Porte itself has peremptorily refused, for a period of about a month, whilst the Greeks are still at liberty to profit during that interval for improving their internal condition. I have communicated this despatch to Mr. Stratford Canning.

I have, &c.,
EDWARD CODRINGTON.

A letter identical with this in substance was written to Mr. Stratford Canning at Constantinople, as well as to Lord Dudley in England.

P.S.—As the circumstance of Rear-Admiral De Rigny's not having joined me with his squadron until the Turkish fleet was actually out of the harbour and waiting only for the Egyptian division, may otherwise leave an unfavourable impression, I think it incumbent on me to say that I have derived the greatest possible benefit from his personal support and assistance, and that he has contributed greatly to the establishment of the present favourable state of affairs.

E. C.

From Sir E. Codrington to Ibrahim Pacha.

H.B.M.'s ship 'Asia,' at Navarin: September 24, 1827.

SIR,—As I am come into this port, to explain the orders under which I am acting, and the necessity I am under of obeying them to the fullest extent, whatever may be the consequences, it is my wish that I may be permitted to do so in the presence of all the principal chiefs commanding in the Turkish expedition.

&c., &c., &c.,

To his Highness Ibrahim Pacha, EDWARD CODRINGTON.
&c., &c., &c.

Memorandum of the Conference at Navarin, September 25, 1827, with Ibrahim Pacha.

Vice-Admiral Sir Edward Codrington having entered the port of Navarin on the 24th September, 1827, with the intention of having a conference with Ibrahim Pacha, the next morning was appointed by Ibrahim for receiving Sir Edward, as well as Rear-Admiral De Rigny, who had likewise entered Navarin at the same time with the English admiral.

On the 25th, at 10 A.M., Sir E. Codrington landed, accompanied by Captain Curzon, of the 'Asia,' Lieutenant Dilke, his flag-lieutenant; Mr. Dyer, his secretary; the Honourable Colonel Cradock, and Mr. Codrington, midshipman; and joining the French admiral on the beach, who was accompanied by some of his officers, they proceeded together to the tent of Ibrahim Pacha. All the Turkish and Egyptian chiefs, with the exception of Tahir Pacha, who was said to be unwell, were ranged on one side, and the officers of the French and English squadrons took their seats on the other.

After the introduction and usual Turkish compliments had passed, the Admirals began by informing Ibrahim that, in consequence of a treaty which had been signed by England, France and Russia, it became their imperative duty to intercept every supply sent by sea of men, arms, &c., destined against Greece, and coming from Turkey or Africa in general; and in order to show the perfect frankness which they wished to use in all their relations with him, they read to him, in extenso, those parts of their instructions which were applicable to the case in point.

Ibrahim replied that the Admirals must be aware that he was a soldier, like themselves, and that to obey orders was as imperative a duty to him as to them; that his orders were to attack Hydra, and that he must put them in execution; that it was his part to act and not to negotiate, and that he must refer them to the Grand Signior for any diplomatic arrangement.

The Admirals answered that they were aware what must be the feelings of a brave man under such circumstances,

and that they congratulated him on having a force opposed
to him which it was impossible to resist. They reminded
him that if he put to sea in defiance of their amicable warning, they must carry their instructions into execution, and
that if he resisted by force, the total destruction of his fleet
must follow; and that it would be an act of madness which
the Sultan could not applaud. The Admirals said that perhaps if they regarded their feelings as mere military men,
his obstinacy would only afford them a means of distinction
which they might wish; but in the present friendly relations
between the Allies and the Turks, they would deeply deplore
any circumstance which could tend to compromise the good
terms which subsisted. It was the sincere wish of the three
Governments, and their positive instruction, to avoid whatever might tend to a rupture; and that it was with this view
at heart that they had come thither to open his eyes to the
situation in which he stood; that they wished to make this
declaration before an assembly of his chiefs, in order that
no doubt might be entertained as to the real intentions of
the Admirals; that no distrust might be generated amongst
his officers with regard to the communications of the Admirals with himself.

Ibrahim then replied that he acknowledged the weight of
what he had heard—it was true that when his orders had
been sent to him from Constantinople, the actual state of
affairs, and the risk of a collision with the combined fleet,
had not been foreseen. He would therefore take upon himself
to suspend all operations of the land and sea forces forming
the expedition from Alexandria till he received answers
from Constantinople and Alexandria by couriers, which he
would immediately despatch; until that period the expedition should remain stationary at Navarin. He, at the same
time, asked permission to send two despatch vessels, one to
Alexandria and the other to Previsa, which was immediately
granted. The Admirals offered even to send a vessel with
them to ensure their safety; but this, he said, would compromise the dignity of the Turkish flag.

The Admirals then said that his promise satisfied them,
and that they would trust to his word of honour as they expected that he would trust to theirs. Ibrahim put his hand
upon his heart and said that it was sacred; but added, ' when
I have promised this, I must say that I cannot think it just
you should impose this obligation on me, and allow the
Greeks to prosecute hostilities.' The Admirals answered that
it was not a parallel case, for that the Greeks had accepted
the mediation of the Allies, and that the Turks had not. Sir

E. Codrington then said that, to prove to Ibrahim the fairness with which he wished to act, in consequence of information he had received of Lord Cochrane's intention to excite an insurrection beyond the actual theatre of war, he would himself put a stop to his proceedings.

The conference here ended, and the Admirals re-embarked. Next morning (the 26th) Mr. Abro, the Pacha's interpreter, came on board the 'Asia,' and told Sir Edward Codrington that Ibrahim had received intelligence in the interval, of Lord Cochrane having made a descent upon Patras; that his first impulse had been to cut his cables, break the armistice, and sail in the night, but that fortunately he had thought better of it; and that he came on board from the Pacha to request permission to send a part of his fleet to Patras. This was peremptorily refused, and it was agreed that, if the Pacha still showed a disposition to assert a right to reinforce Patras, that Mr. Abro should return on board; but if, on the contrary, the Pacha acquiesced in the prohibition of the Admiral according to the arrangement of the day before, that no further communication was necessary. Mr. Abro did not return, and on the same night the 'Asia' and 'Syrène' put to sea.

Ibrahim wished, after the conference, and more particularly when he had pledged his word of honour to observe the armistice, to talk on other subjects not connected with the treaty, &c.; but Sir Edward Codrington said to the dragoman (Abro) : 'I wish to understand before the conversation ends, whether his Highness fully comprehends all that has been communicated from me and Admiral De Rigny to you;' to which he replied 'Yes, fully.'

HENRY S. DYER, Secretary to Vice-Admiral
Sir Edward Codrington, K.C.B.
HOBART CRADOCK, Lieut.-Colonel.
EDWD. CURZON, Captain of H.M.S. 'Asia.'

From Admiral De Rigny to the Comte de Guilleminot.

(*Translation.*)

'Syrène,' Navarin . September 26, 1827.

MONSIEUR LE COMTE,—I have the honour to inform your Excellency that I arrived before Modon and Navarin September 21. Thirty-two ships of the Turkish fleet, of which three were ships of the line, seven frigates, the rest brigs and corvettes, were cruising off the entrance to the harbour. These ships were evidently filled with troops; eighty other vessels of all kinds were within the harbour.

One English corvette and two brigs, in search of their Admiral, were with us at the time; one had on board Mr.
Cradock. The same day at noon we saw the English ships
which had been becalmed to the westward. The following
day we joined them in the presence of the same Turkish
ships. I went on board the 'Asia' to confer with Admiral
Codrington. He told me that while cruising near Hydra, .
he learnt, on meeting with a Greek vessel, that the Turkish
fleet had arrived on September 7 at Navarin, and that they
were hastening the embarkation of troops for the expedition
to Hydra; that this meeting had made him decide to repair to Modon; and that he had sent forward his cutter to
give notice of his intention, but that, a strong north wind
coming on unexpectedly, this information had not been able
to reach its destination. On seeing the Turkish fleet make
such hasty preparations, he had thought proper to address,
in his own name, to the Turkish Admiral commanding the
ships outside the harbour, a letter, which had been carried
by an English officer to the Capitan Bey; but he having
refused to open it, saying that he was under the orders of
Ibrahim, and that to him the letter must be addressed, the
same letter was then taken to Navarin, and given to
Ibrahim. It appears that, on reading this letter, written in
English, which the dragoman of the Pacha does not understand very well, Ibrahim expressed some doubt on its being
the unanimous opinion of the three chiefs of the Allied
Squadron—the more so, that at the date of its being written
the French ships were not within sight of Navarin. Admiral Codrington having communicated to me the report of
the British officer whom he had sent to Ibrahim, and having
informed me that he had despatched the 'Dartmouth' frigate
to Navarin, I proposed to Sir Edward Codrington, in order
to give to the step which he had taken that character of
concert which might appear to be wanting to it in the eyes
of the Turkish chieftains, that the same letter which he had
written should be translated into French and sent again to
Ibrahim Pacha, signed by us both, under the form hereunto
annexed. In order to act in this matter with greater effect,
it was agreed between Sir Edward Codrington and me, that
I should go myself to Navarin, and, after an interview with
Ibrahim, at which I should point out to him that the
menaces mentioned in that letter would certainly and speedily
be carried into execution, I should let the English Admiral
know if I saw any necessity for his coming to join me in a
final appeal. I anchored at Navarin on the 22nd, and immediately forwarded to Ibrahim the letter agreed upon, requesting him to appoint a place of meeting, which was fixed

for the following morning at whatever hour I should choose. At 8 o'clock I was in his tent: he was there alone with Tahir Pacha, who commanded one of the two divisions of the fleet at Constantinople. When Ibrahim, who was desirous of a private interview, made a sign to Tahir Pacha to withdraw, the latter made him repeat it, and testified some displeasure; his distrust was evident. At this interview with Ibrahim Pacha, he did not attempt to conceal his embarrassment. He found himself in the same position at Navarin as his father was at Alexandria. The eyes of the Turks were upon him; and these conferences, rather of a confidential nature, excite in them feelings of jealousy towards the Egyptians. I forcibly depicted to him the results of the obstinacy of the Sultan: I told him the total destruction of the Ottoman fleets would be the consequence of it. I then learnt, that although he had not had, either from the Porte or from his father, any order relative to the circumstances which had lately taken place, he knew on August 13, by a messenger from England and Trieste, that the Treaty was signed; that he had for a long time expected his fleet, always hoping that he should have time to settle matters at Hydra before we could throw any obstacles in his way; that this fleet being now arrived, he had hurried on his preparations, and that on the 21st the two last divisions of his fleet were ready, the troops embarked—when, at the moment he thought of attaining his object, and of giving a mortal blow to the Greeks, he found himself arrested in his progress by an obstacle which he knew to be insurmountable. That he was about to send couriers to his father and to Constantinople with the summons which had been addressed to him; that he would order those divisions to return which were outside the port; and on this subject he expressed some astonishment at what the British officer who had been sent to him had said of opposition which might even be made to their return to port. He was most anxious to be informed on this point. This matter not having been discussed by Admiral Codrington and myself, I replied that it was not probable that, while I was talking to him, there should exist an idea of preventing the return of his division; but that I could assure him, in my own name as well as in that of Sir Edward Codrington, that his fleet would not be permitted by us to take any outward direction excepting only that of Alexandria. With regard to sending these couriers, I told him that he would do well to await the arrival of the British Admiral, whom a contrary wind at this moment prevented from approaching the port; that the courier's vessel might be taken by the Greeks. 'So then,' cried he with some warmth, 'whilst you require of me to suspend all operations, you allow the Greeks to do as they wish; that is not just.' I answered him, that the obstinacy of the Grand Signior, in not accepting a mediation which it was his interest to have done, might, although there was no change in our desire for peace, effect a change nevertheless in the nature of the means to be employed, &c. His situation, he said, was too embarrassing; he could not escape from it until he received fresh orders. 'It is a most unfortunate thing for me that you did not make this demand at Alexandria when the fleet was there; all would now have been settled.' He then turned to the subject of the fortified places, under the supposition of the evacuation by him of the Morea. 'Never,' said he, 'will the Grand Signior consent to give back the fortified places to the Greeks; he would rather die under the ruins of Constantinople.' 'There is no question of the fortified places,' said I; 'that will be decided at a future time. What is required at present is to obtain an armistice, either with the consent of the Porte or by force, which will compel the Porte to treat. In establishing it *de facto*, you may perhaps save the Ottoman empire; you will at least save your father and your inheritance. Your father is old, and much burdened with cares. Reflect. Egypt with its riches is of much more value than the Morea, of which you are making a desert.'

Doubtless Ibrahim would wish to withdraw himself from the difficult position in which he finds himself—one word from his father would decide him; but in the presence of the Turkish fleet and its chieftains, he is exposed to their distrust, which has been roused ever since the interview with the officer sent to him by the British Admiral; that officer, pursuing his written instructions, which he held in his hand, turned the conversation on Egypt, on the desire which was felt to respect his father's interests, &c. &c., expressions which, although suppressed or modified by his Dragoman, had nevertheless been understood by one of the persons present (Tahir Pacha), and interpreted and spread about as the result of an understanding between him and us. One circumstance has given to this jealousy a more serious character. Tahir Pacha, incensed at what passed yesterday, retired on board his ship, and refuses to leave it. Ibrahim has sent me his confidential dragoman to acquaint me with this occurrence, which appears to occupy his attention much. Thus, at the point where matters are now arrived, the object would appear for the moment gained, as far as regards the terms of the second instructions, which require, '*that the measures to be adopted against the Ottoman marine should not*

*degenerate into hostilities, and that the armistice at sea, which
the Porte might not concede de jure, should be established de
facto;'* for I repeat, there is no doubt that Ibrahim does not
wish to commit himself without receiving further orders from
the Porte, which I am inclined to believe he would not obey
if his father advised him otherwise. His hundred and odd
vessels which have re-entered Navarin can never sail out
again in a body; the expedition against Hydra has failed
and become impossible, as much from the nature of the
obstacles thrown in its way, as from the jealousies which
have arisen between the Turks and the Egyptians. We may
be quite sure that Ibrahim will wait until the return of the
couriers. If, on the contrary, in spite of the repeated summons, or even after the return of the couriers, he resolves to
pursue the orders he has received to destroy Hydra, we cannot fail to meet with him in the Archipelago; we recover the
advantage which we should have enjoyed if we had possessed
the power of acting before his fleet had entered Navarin,
and by compelling him to return to Egypt with his fleet
entire, or dispersed, great progress would be made in the
business. In order to effect this, it is only necessary to watch
his fleet by two or three brigs, of which one would always
remain off the islands of 'Sapienza, and to have the ships
always ready to unite at the first intelligence, and to close
every other passage except that of Alexandria for the Egyptians, and that of the Dardanelles for the fleet of Constantinople. At that point we shall have exhausted all indirect
means, we shall have pursued the spirit and letter of the
instructions; in any case I do not now think that, should
we meet this large squadron at sea, it would oppose any resistance to the notification which would be made to it, the
more so that we shall then be joined by the Russian squadron. On the 24th I sailed out of Navarin to meet Admiral
Codrington; and the same evening, and at the same time
with the Turkish division, which was re-entering, we cast
anchor at Navarin with the intention of making on the following day, personally to Ibrahim, when surrounded by the chiefs
of his fleet, a public notification, reserving at the same time
for himself alone, and in consideration of the personal situation of his father, communications of a confidential character.
On the 25th, at 10 o'clock in the morning, Sir Edward
Codrington and myself, accompanied by Mons. Achille Rouen,
first Secretary of Embassy, by Mr. Cradock, attached to the
British Mission, and by some French and English officers,
repaired to the tent of Ibrahim Pacha, where we found him
surrounded by his principal officers. After the usual com-

pliments, we stated to him, each in turn, in English and in French (the replies being all made in French), the orders with which we were charged, in consequence of the refusal of the Porte to accept the mediation. Some paragraphs of the second instruction to the Admirals were then read to him, terminating with a formal declaration to establish *de facto* an armistice, and to destroy any Ottoman vessels which should break it. After having listened with the utmost attention and coolness to our declarations, the Pacha replied, ' that as a servant of the Sublime Porte he had received orders to press the war in the Morea, and to terminate it by a decisive attack upon Hydra; that he had no authority to listen to communications such as we had made to him, nor to act upon his own responsibility. That, however, the orders of the Porte not having foreseen the extraordinary case which presented itself, he should forthwith send couriers to Constantinople and into Egypt, and that till their return he gave his word that his fleet should not quit Navarin, however hard it was upon him to be thus arrested just at the moment when all was settled, because the force of his expedition, as we ourselves saw, was too strong for the Greeks to resist. That ' if his Sovereign, who was the best judge of his real interests, still maintained in force his first orders, he should obey them whatever might be the result of the unequal struggle in which he should be engaged.' As his couriers were to go by sea and in his vessels, he asked if, while we required a suspension of hostilities on his part, we would leave it in the power of the Greeks to attack his vessels? Upon this we proposed to him to allow his vessels to be accompanied by one of ours; but he did not appear to be pleased with this proposal, which might be considered as derogatory to him; and he preferred to risk meeting with the enemy, from which, on the other hand, we could not secure him, since the Greek pirates, acting on all sides without order and without license, always dispersed at our approach, and by that means escaped us. One may see, in this complicated situation, the confusion which results from that article of the instructions which treats of an understanding to be concerted with the Greeks, when we find there neither government nor individuals with whom to act in the present state of disorganisation of this country. It is very desirable that the respective ministers and ambassadors should also consider attentively this side of the question, on which we find great difficulties. To reply as well as possible to some observations, which were not wanting in justice, and speaking in the sense of a communication from the ambas-

sadors, dated September 4, which I received yesterday, relative to the限iits within which the Greek navy must confine its operations, we said to Ibrahim, that 'having been
informed that Lord Cochrane purposed proceeding towards
the coasts of Albania, with the view of exciting a revolt
there, it was the intention of Admiral Codrington to oppose
at once any attempt of this kind (such attempt being made
in the Ionian Sea) as tending to enlarge the theatre of war,
as long as there existed any armistice either temporary or
definitive.' I will not enter into a detail of the objections
and arguments which he put forward in addition, when, after
his promise had been given, the conference ceased to be
official; but I cannot refrain from remarking that all that
Ibrahim said shows an understanding and good sense very
superior to what is generally seen, and to the education
which he must have received. He was especially anxious to
refute all that had been published in the papers respecting
his pretended cruelties, and we, who have been on the spot,
must confess that exaggeration has been as busy there as
elsewhere. Such is then at present, as I observed above, the
situation of affairs. The Turkish fleet, consisting of near
126 vessels, of which there are 4 ships of the line, 4 frigates
of 60 guns, 14 frigates of 40, 29 corvettes, 37 brigs, &c., remains inactive in Navarin. If it attempts to quit the port
in consequence of any fresh orders from Constantinople,
which Ibrahim cannot receive for twenty-one days at least,
we shall meet with them in the Archipelago, and all return
to the Morea will be cut off. Some very confidential communications on the part of Ibrahim Pacha give me reason to
believe that he will secretly give us notice when he is about
to come out; and I think I can affirm beforehand that a demonstration will suffice to send back this formidable expedition to Egypt and the Dardanelles. I must not omit to
mention here that, with the consent of Mr. Cradock, I have
informed Ibrahim of what had been concerted at Cairo with
his father, and also that the letter of Mehemet Ali addressed
to his son (of which I was the bearer on my return from
Egypt, where I discussed with the Pacha all the supposed
cases which have since been realised), has determined the
latter to follow that course which I have stated it to be my
opinion that he will pursue. Such has been, and such without doubt will be, the result of measures concerted between
Sir Edward Codrington and myself.

One work remains even more difficult than that which we
have already accomplished, even supposing it to be necessary
to follow up that work in a short time by the employment of

force—it is to annihilate, if possible, that piracy which has become so inveterate among the Greeks. It will not be heard perhaps without a feeling of surprise, that at the very moment when the squadrons of the Allied Powers are on the point of engaging in a contest with the Turks in favour of the Greeks, merchant vessels, English and French, are carried off from the coasts of Syria to Egina, seized upon and pillaged, because, under the pretext of a right of search so unfortunately conceded, the Greek pirates, caring little for the fate of their country, have no other object in view than to make a livelihood by piracy, and to bear away to Hydra their plunder, converted, by the greatest abuse, into lawful prize. It would be shameful, it would even be ridiculous, to suffer any longer the existence of such abuses; but it is necessary to act with vigour and adopt decisive measures. I know of none others than those I have so often proposed to employ.

I beg your Excellency, &c.,
DE RIGNY.

From H. J. Codrington to his sister Jane.

H.M.S. 'Asia,' Navarin Harbour : September 25, 1827.

DEAR JANE,—Yesterday the 'Asia' and 'Philomel' with the 'Sirène,' French admiral, anchored in here to communicate with Ibrahim Pacha. The entrance at the south end is narrow enough to render working in inconvenient for a large ship; but the water there is deep and the bottom clear. The harbour is formed by a long, rocky island (Sphacteria) running along the coast in a bight just to the north of Modon. The island itself seems quite unproductive, and, except a Turkish guard, there is nobody on it. The entrance to the southward is very fine, though not so striking as many others. The northern entrance I hear is too narrow and shallow for anything larger than brigs or boats. The harbour is large and, I think, very commodious, but I'll tell you more about it by-and-bye. At present it is full of Turks, large and small. Well, this morning we went on shore to visit Ibrahim; the party were as follows : English—Admiral, Captain Curzon, Lieutenant Dilke, Colonel Cradock, Mr. Dyer, and myself. French- -Admiral De Rigny, his captain, a secretary of legation, and a captain of a schooner. Lord Ingestrie went with us also. We pulled on shore and landed just underneath his tent; which, with several others belonging to people of consequence, was pitched on the top of a little bank rising from the beach to the northward of the

town. His tent or tents, for it was a continuation of them,
was green.   Though the place was pretty level, they had
collected a great number of large stones which they stowed
as close to each other as possible on the ground through
these two tents, which opened into one.   Over these stones,
in the inner tent, a sort of rough platform was made by
laying boards on them, and *on* these boards was the Pacha's
sofa, with its embroidered velvet cushions and a mattress
with gold fringes.   Under the inner tent, and just over this
sofa, was a sort of small pavilion or tent, the strings of
which interfered very much with my cocked hat.   Around
the sofa and on the platform were ranged arm-chairs.   As
we came into the tent, he bowed, but did not *rise* off the sofa.
Father came to on the said sofa, close alongside him; and
the French Admiral brought up also, on the sofa, under
father's lee.   *We* were ranged round in their front rather on
the right; and on the left, and behind him, were ranged his
officers, pachas, beys, &c., and attendants.   They first began
with the ceremony of introduction; which, as there were a
good number of us on each side, was proportionably long. . . .
At length, however, I got settled, and began to look round
me again; this tent also was open, and from his sofa he
looked down over the whole harbour, and really the sight
was beautiful, covered as it was by the ships, and boats of
all sorts continually passing to and fro.   His tent was *outside* the walls of Navarin; and indeed what force he had
with him appeared to be outside of the town.   Altogether I
thought he had chosen the coolest and most convenient place
to pitch his tent on that could be found.   But, to return
thither.   He is a man of about 40 years old, not at all good-
looking, but with heavy features, very much marked with
the small-pox, and as fat as a porpoise.   Though I had no
opportunity of seeing his height (as he was on his sofa, lying
down or sitting the whole time), I should not think him
more than five feet seven inches.   He was *for a Pacha*
plainly dressed I think, particularly as his followers and
officers were covered with gold and embroidery; and for a
Turk, I think his manners were very good indeed.   The conversation first began about the weather and such common-
place things, for I learnt (from the interpreter) he does not
talk of business till *after coffee.*   A short time after we were
seated, the Pacha took his 'gem-adorned chibouque,' and
father and De Rigny also had each one, and I never saw
such *beautiful* ones before.   The mouth-pieces were, of course,
of the purest and largest amber, and the upper and lower
parts of the stem were studded with diamonds and other

precious stones. The stem itself was at least ten feet long.
Then they brought in a small cup of coffee for each of us,
and, what I believe is a great favour, it *was sweetened*. The
cups were of china, and about the size of three thimbles.
They had no handles, but as the Turks take their coffee very
hot, they place these said cups in a sort of filagree stand of
silver or gold; which is very necessary, as from the heat
of the coffee it would otherwise be impossible to handle
them. These being removed with great caution by the
attendants, business was entered upon before everybody, so
that *his* officers might also understand the whole. It was
carried on through an interpreter, who continued standing
the whole time. Father spoke most, I should say nearly all;
and it was by the interpreter translated from his French or
English into Turkish. I cannot tell you *all* they talked
about, for I can't remember it; but I was very much interested in it the whole time. At length, they settled that he
should not proceed in the war any further till he had received fresh instructions from Constantinople, in answer to
the representations which he was going to send thither of
the state of affairs and of the impossibility of his moving
any way without being sunk by our fleet. This will take
about twenty days, which time, I believe, we are to take advantage of by sending the 'Genoa' and 'Albion' to refit at
Malta. I must say I was very much surprised by the clear-
ness and ability with which father's arguments were carried
on, and the good sense which Ibrahim showed. On his
being told that in the event of his attempting to come out
we must drive him into the harbour again, and if he resisted,
sink him; he said that, like us, he was under positive orders,
which as a subject of the Porte he must execute, though in
the attempt he were certain of destruction; and that a few
years would not make much difference in his life now. Father
answered that, as the *two* parties had such positive orders
(which evidently could not both be complied with) the execution of them would depend on the relative force of the two
parties, for whichever would prove strongest must necessarily,
in honour, enforce their orders; and, he added, that without
doubt we were at present the strongest, and would, by the
arrival of the Russians (who were hourly expected) be much
stronger. In fact, after some more such palaver, the business
was arranged. Ibrahim gave in to reason, *as slowly as a Turk
among Turks* could; he rallied several times, and once said, as
a *dernier* effort, 'Nous n'avons d'autre marchandise abord de
nos vaisseaux que les balles et la poudre à canon;' which little
M. de Bigny quickly answered by ' Et nous les avons aussi;

and we can exchange some with you and *give you good weight too!'* This, with a little humbug about their regret at having to destroy, without reason, so many brave men (pointing to the Turkish officers), backed by a little quiet flattery to soften their wounded pride, opened their eyes to conviction. Ibrahim found that however decided *he* might *show himself*, the admirals could not, and would not, swerve from their orders and instructions, extracts from which were, before everybody, read to him and translated. When they had finished business, he with a smile said that though they had transacted all the matters of service, &c., yet he requested them to stay and ' talk jokingly over things in general;' and so, *on they did talk*; with some occasional *fishing* on his part, and questions about *us*, and the *Greeks*, and *Lord Cochrane*, &c. However, father quite brought him up with a round turn once; for on his depreciating very much the Greeks in every way, and affecting to despise them, saying that there never was a Greek worth anything; he answered, that his Highness ought to abstain from undervaluing those men whom he had been such a time attempting to conquer; for that by so doing he must lower in our estimation the talents and abilities of himself and those brave men (pointing to the Turkish officers) who had made several campaigns with him without effecting their object. This was a regular pull-er, and he made no answer; but as soon as he recovered, changed the subject. In spite of the regular custom of Turks (trying to keep the muscles of the face immovable so as not to let observers see what is passing within), I could clearly make out that he was quite taken aback, and that he found he had unadvisedly got himself into a scrape. Indeed, the pride of his heart had led him too far; for, were the Greeks what he represents them, the Sultan would never have sent an armament of three 74's, 18 frigates and small vessels, in all 120 sail or more, against them now, and this not for the first time. Has he not been beaten several times by them? Have not the forts of Napoli, Athens, Tripolitza, Navarin, Corinth, and many others, successively fallen by the arms of the Greeks? Has not the whole force of the Turkish Empire been continually employed against them since the breaking out of the rebellion in 1821? and, as yet, very little is done by such an overwhelming force to warrant Ibrahim's boast? Throughout the whole conference I could see that there were many things that would never have been said on either side, had it not been for the sake of the Turkish pachas being present. As for instance, though Ibrahim said, ' I am the Porte's soldier; whatever they order I must execute, and if they order me out of the harbour I *must go*, though it be to certain death;' yet I am sure he never would have gone out. As it was, he only sent the *Turkish* division out the other day. I am certain that if the Porte should even now order him to proceed, he would send the Turks out but not budge with his Egyptians. What would be the use of the Pacha of Egypt having all his fleet sunk or destroyed on account of the obstinacy of the Sultan!

I must add that the humbug of palaver was not confined to the *Turkish* side only. Ibrahim made the following remark at the end of the *joking* conversation, viz., that he took in most English and French papers, and yet never did he see one in favour of the *Turks;* he saw by them that the *Greeks* were always successful everywhere, and the Turks always massacring, but the Greeks never! Now he said he could disprove them all, for he had several hundred Greek villages under his Government, now very quiet, and those Greeks near him fed and provided by him. In short, his account of affairs is very different from the general one. The right line I suspect is between both. He also remarked that, if Greece was to pay the Porte any sum of money, England or the allies must be guarantees for it; or perhaps (laughing) the English *would give them another loan.*

Altogether I liked him pretty well, and was very much pleased with my forenoon, for we were upwards of three hours there. It has given me a much better opinion of him than I had before, though, of course, we only saw the fair side of the picture.

When I first began this letter I did not intend to talk about politics; but as there was nothing but said politics at the interview, and I was so led on from one thing to another, I could not help it. Indeed, I am glad I have done so, for I find father has said nothing about it, trusting to me; so that you must take this disjointed epistle for an account of the whole; and you must excuse me if it is neither legible nor intelligible, as I am now in the greatest hurry.

Your affectionate brother,
H. J. C.

From Sir Frederick Adam to Sir E. C.

(*Extract.*)

Corfù: September 21, 1827.*

Our Government are by this time informed by Mr. S. Canning, from Constantinople, of the determination of the Sultan

* Received September 25.

Map of the
WEST COAST
of
GREECE

Nautic Miles

ACARNANIA

Ithaca

Petala

Kursolari I.

Mesolonghi

Gulf of Patras

Patras

C.Kalogria C.Papa

Cephalonia

Poros

C. Skala

Manoladha

C.Tornese

P.Trepito

Zante

Zante

Gulf of
Gastuni

C.Geraka

P.Kastro

C.Kieri

C.Katakolo

M

O

R

E

A

Gulf of

Arkadia

Arkadia

Filiatro

Prodano

Navarin

Gulf
Kalamata
or
Coron

Modon

Sapienza

Coron

Kabrera

C.Gallo

Merlera

Sidari

Albania

Corfu

Corfu

C.Bianco

Island of
CORFU

E Waller

to use every effort to carry on the war vigorously by land, and in a very few days they must know of the arrival of the Egyptian fleet and reinforcements at Navarin, for I communicated the information given me by Lord Ingestrie; and they, with their allies, will have taken their determination, and will give their orders. I hope these orders may be in time. It is quite true, or at least highly probable, that the war by land on the part of the Turks will die of exhaustion in the course of a twelvemonth, if their operations by sea are interrupted, and if *Austria be prevented from carrying supplies*: but in the mean time this land war, while it can remain in a state of vigour, will go nigh to having exterminated the Greeks, to have deprived them of all possession of the country,—and then where is the object of the Treaty?

Sir E. C. to Mr. Stratford Canning.

'Asia,' in the port of Navarin : September 25, 1827.

DEAR SIR,—On the 23rd I received your letter of the 11th, with your official letter of the 8th September, enclosing the mem. of the 10th, the Protocol, &c. I need not say how much I am gratified by finding I had anticipated your private wishes, as well as the decision of yourself respecting neutrals carrying Turkish property contraband of war. Admiral De Rigny tells me the Austrian schooner of war which was in the port when we first reached it, did not accompany the expedition, but was the bearer of despatches for Ibrahim; that he fell in with her on her way from hence, when watching his movements; and that, when questioned if I was off this port, and if the Turkish ships were within it, he said '*no*' to the latter question, and replied to the former that he saw *some large ships which he supposed to be Turks*. As he had sailed from this port after our having shown ourselves close to it with our colours flying, and several days after the whole expedition was anchored, this is somewhat barefaced; and shows how little officers of that nation, in these seas, can be trusted; whilst their whole conduct belies the statement of the Court of Vienna being equally anxious with the Allies for the fulfilment of the Treaty.

That the absence of my colleague at such an important moment is hardly to be accounted for, and was very near producing a collision between myself and the Turkish Commander is not to be denied. But it is incumbent on me to say that, since his arrival at so fortunate a juncture, he has done everything I could possibly wish, and has greatly promoted the object of our Governments. He has approved of all my proceedings previous to his arrival, although certainly very different from his own at that period; and whenever he has suggested an opinion as to what we should do, to which I showed a dissent, he has readily yielded the point at once. In fact the sea is not his element.

Although the result of our joint interview with Ibrahim and his chiefs to-day will be all that you may absolutely require, I could wish that Colonel Cradock, or one of the by-standers, would give you the detail of what passed; for it is a task which, as being a principal actor, and having to study my words and those of my colleague, as well as the interpretation of them, and the effect they produced, it is quite out of my power to perform. And yet if fully described, it might enable you to form an early judgment of the course which things are likely to take eventually. I can only say that I am more than satisfied with the progress which we have thus far made. And I do sincerely believe that we have disposed all the chiefs of the expedition to feel sincerely desirous of receiving orders to accede to our proposals. My letters to Lord Dudley and the Lord High Admiral will go to Corfu at the same time that this starts for Smyrna. Admiral De Rigny will also write to Mr. Bogos, as will Colonel Cradock to Mr. Salt, by a French vessel which the Admiral proposes to send there, at the same time that the Turkish vessel goes on the same errand to Mehemet Ali. I intend sending such an order by the 'Philomel' to the neighbourhood of Cape Papa, as will stop Lord Cochrane's meditated embarkation of General Church's troops until I can proceed there myself to put an end to his ill-timed expedition altogether. I begged Colonel Cradock, whom I requested to accompany Admiral De Rigny into Navarin, would endeavour to see the letter from Mehemet Ali to Ibrahim. The Admiral first showed the letter to Colonel C. and then delivered it himself to Ibrahim, who was much affected by it. You will be glad, as I am, to find that there was no insincerity in this; and at the same time lament, with me, that my colleague should lay himself open to such general suspicion.

I remain, &c.,
EDWARD CODRINGTON.

Sir E. C. to Mr. S. Canning.

'Asia,' in the port of Navarin: September 25, 1827.

DEAR SIR,—Although my public letter will tell you all that is essential, I cannot help offering you my congratulations on the issue thus far of our intercourse with the Turco-Egyptian commanders. The arrival of M. De Rigny and his squadron was certainly very opportune; and the assistance which I derived from his opinions and his knowledge of the parties, of material use in producing, what I am sanguine enough to consider, the present prosperous state of affairs here. It will probably be a month before Ibrahim can receive his answers; and during that time he is bound to remain inactive. Even if he should then have an order to make the meditated attack, the season will have become more likely to defeat his purpose, and even to destroy some of the ships of which his fleet is composed; whilst we, as I trust, by the arrival of the Russian squadron, and by having our own ships replenished and re-supplied with stores of which they are deficient, shall become more fit to profit by their increased difficulties. I am glad you have taken into consideration the conduct of the Austrian vessels. The letter which I had prepared for the commander of the schooner which was in this port when we arrived, M. De Rigny will take with him to Milo where he proposes placing his ships of the line for the interval, that he may deliver it to some other Austrian captain, or to Count Dandolo himself. Since we have been in the harbour that flag has not been exhibited, although the transports must be somewhere in the fleet. I intend to profit by the opportunity, and to send the 'Genoa' and the 'Albion' to Malta for such supplies as they may require. But I shall find too much to do with Lord Cochrane and the Greeks to admit of the 'Asia' going into port, until the fate of the Turkish fleet is decided on one way or the other.

Believe me, my dear Sir, very truly and sincerely yours,

EDWD. CODRINGTON.

Sir E. C. to Mr. S. Canning.

September 26, 1827.

. . . . .

What with the despatches, the piracies, and the claim for regular convoys and extra convoys, I assure you the ships under my orders are more harassed than they used to be in the height of war. Most of the captains are obliged to have their linen washed on board like the ships' companies, and they are often upon the ship's provisions also. I have now sent Spencer to hunt in the Gulf of Coron for poultry, &c., for the fleet as well as himself. Adam has always his fears of the effect of Capo d'Istria's arrival. I confess, I have on the contrary an opinion that it is the only thing we can look forward to, as a means of settling the country. If he obtain a Swiss army of some 4,000 or 5,000 men to support his government, he will be able to put down the Capitani, the curse of the country. And as to fears of Russian influence, surely *free* Greece will neither require her support nor submit to her despotism. Time will be gained at all events, and the ' march of intellect ' will have had its effect. Besides, —as I enforced in the private ear of Ibrahim's interpreter yesterday,—the having so dexterously got Russia into the treaty, must prevent her assumption of more than an equal influence with the Allied Powers.

I remain, &c.,
EDWD. CODRINGTON.

I must still add to this, that it is evident by what passed yesterday in reference to the private communications which Mehemet Ali held with Colonel Cradock, that Ibrahim had had instruction from his father : for he has done precisely all that the father said he would do upon our making to him the representations which we did according to the father's suggestion.

From Sir E. C. to H. Salt, Esq., H.M. Consul-General
at Alexandria.

'Asia,' at Navarin : September 26, 1827.

SIR,—As Colonel Cradock is giving you a substantial account of the state of affairs, I have only to catch a hurried moment and acknowledge your letters of August 21 and 22. I trust Mehemet Ali will be convinced that we have done our utmost to save his fleet from that inevitable destruction which would attend the Sultan's persevering in his proposed attack on Hydra, or any other part of Greece.

I have, &c.,
EDWD. CODRINGTON.

Sir E. C. to Lady C.

In the port of Navarin : September 26.

Harry will tell you all our interesting story, and will do it better than I could do : because *I* was employed in producing and watching final effects of paramount importance. The position in which I have been, and still am, is singular, and I may say unparalleled. Here we are, now, De Rigny and myself, surrounded by above 120 vessels in their own port, whom we are forcing into obedience to the allies, in direct contradiction of the orders of a Sovereign whose slightest disapprobation deprives his subjects of their heads. To a by-stander the scene must have been highly interesting, and I trust Harry will so paint it to you. I cannot read his letter, if I wished it, I am so harassed with business : for what time I can spare I would rather devote to you this way. I should tell you that Ibrahim has agreed to send to the Porte and to his father for orders, after they know of our decision, to prevent by force his proceeding to execute the orders he is at present under, and of his inability to resist without sacrificing his fleet, &c. And he is in the meantime to remain here in suspension of all hostility. De Rigny has done everything I wished or could wish since his arrival ; and has certainly been of great use in bringing about the present favourable appearances. He does not, however, like the sea, and cannot imagine blockading ; and he will, I am sure, proceed again to Smyrna, after seeing his big ships into Milo, where they are to stay during the interval of suspension.

From Sir E. C. to Lord Dudley.

'Asia,' off Navarin : September 27, 1827.

My Lord,—The accompanying letters from Mr. Salt reached me this morning by the 'Pelorus.' Added to what I sent off last night for Corfu, they will give your Lordship such an insight into the state of affairs in Egypt, as may enable you to give me decisive instructions as to the line of conduct I am to pursue under the circumstances therein anticipated. The dragoman of Ibrahim Bey came to me again yesterday evening, when I was about to quit the port of Navarin, to say that his Highness had received information of Lord Cochrane, with several Greek vessels of war, lying off Patras with the intention of operating against that and the other fortresses thereabout : and that his Highness expected that I would either obstruct him myself or allow him to send a Turkish force competent to do so. Admiral De Rigny had received the visit of the dragoman previously, and consequently followed him to the 'Asia.' Much art was employed by the dragoman, by making some part of what he had to say private information, and the other part official communication from his master, to induce us to relax from our decision of the preceding day. Advantage was taken of my voluntary intention of not suffering Lord Cochrane to excite a rising at a distance, to show that it was equally just that I should do so in the Gulf of Lepanto. We met this

by a reference to our Instruction, and the refusal of the
Porte whilst the Greeks accepted our mediation : which
naturally led to a partiality to which the Porte could not
with reason object, and to which she must now succumb,
whether she liked it or not.   At length, after an hour's discussion, and the dragoman finding that nothing could shake
our resolution, he took his leave, letting us understand that
if he did not shortly return or send, the Pacha did not propose making any further communication.   Accordingly,
having waited until there was merely sufficient daylight to
effect it, we weighed our anchor and joined the ships off the
harbour's mouth, where I had collected them by signal, ready
to proceed to that extremity which, judging by the description which the dragoman gave at one time of the irritation
of the Pacha, I thought would probably become necessary.

I have, &c.,

EDWD. CODRINGTON.

From Sir E. C. to Admiral De Rigny.

'Asia' : September 27—5 P.M.

MY DEAR ADMIRAL,—I fear it is quite impossible for us to
stop the impertinent and ill-timed observations of which we
have all to complain in turn.   Upon hearing that the Greeks
accused each of our Courts individually of intending to deceive
them, and to subject them to the Turks, and shortly afterwards that the Treaty itself was not intended to be carried
into effect, I wrote a letter and addressed it to Mavrocordato,
Zarini, or Tricoupi, whom I knew to be then at Poros, to say
that I should myself be soon there with my squadron in proof
of English sincerity ; that French sincerity was most strongly
exemplified by the reduction by the French of the time limited
for the Porte's answer, from thirty to fifteen days ; and that
Russian sincerity was still more clearly exemplified than either,
by Mr. Timoni being sent to authorise us to act for Russia, in
the absence of Count Heiden and his squadron.   I put the
stronger term to this latter because of there being then no
news of the Russian squadron having even arrived in England.   I shall always be ready to declare by word, as I have
done in my letters, that in all our conferences I have found
in you the greatest cordiality ; that we have never been at
issue upon any one point of public service, and that I have
derived from your counsel and assistance all the support I
could desire.*   I think you may rely upon what we have done

---

* Sir E. C., after personal communication with Admiral De Rigny, and
after the joint action towards Ibrahim in the Conference for the Armistice
of September 25. had full confidence in the support of his colleague.

here within these few days in unison for removing all such reports as you mention from the minds of either of our ministers at Constantinople, or those of any other on whom they have made any impression. I have courts-martial to form, which must keep my ships here together to-morrow and perhaps the next day; and in the meantime the 'Albion,' 'Genoa,' and 'Cambrian' will provision the small vessels, in readiness to go themselves to Malta. They will return from Malta, show themselves 'en passant,' and catch me at Zante or near it, where I propose watching Lord Cochrane's movements, and seeing at the same time that the Turks do not slip out to attack him. I think it might lull the fleet in Navarin into quiet if your ships were to show themselves here a few days longer, taking the first strong northerly wind for going to Milo as you propose, at dark, when their movements are not seen from Navarin. I shall keep one, and probably two vessels hereabout, to see that all goes on well. I will return the Protocol when I have had time to look it over, which I have not had yet.

Believe me, my dear Admiral,
Very sincerely yours,
EDWD. CODRINGTON.

Sir E. C. to Mr. S. Canning.

'Asia,' off Navarin : September 29, 1827.

DEAR SIR,—I have nothing material to add to my last letter, because things remain in Navarin just as they were when I wrote them. On the next day I received letters from Mr. Salt for Lord Dudley, of which I conclude you have either copies or the substance ; and I sent them off to Corfù at once, in hopes of being in time to accompany those of the preceding day, with one from myself of which I will enclose an extract. Although the discussion referred to produced no result, it will show you that Ibrahim was ready with this 'ruse de guerre' to improve on the agreement he had entered into ; and that he had only so bound himself because he could do no better. The other enclosures will explain themselves. The Rear-Admiral was so uncomfortable that I was glad to be able to soothe him.* I am not surprised at your being anxious upon the subject of his joining me. The chance of wind admitting of my closing with the Turkish fleet, as I was under all sail endeavouring to do after making the signal to prepare for battle, might have brought me to

---

* See letter of September 27 to Admiral De Rigny.

the extremity I was obliged to contemplate, an hour before
his arrival. As it turned out, the wind which advanced him
retarded me at the same time. I trust we shall henceforth
manage our rendezvous better. In the meantime, I have the
pleasure of assuring you that nothing can have been more
cordial than all our personal communications, and that I
have found in him everything I could wish on this most
trying and important occasion. The 'Genoa' and 'Albion'
are just gone to Malta, to be ready to return here in a fortnight; and the French ships will go to Milo for the same
purpose, where they have a store-ship.

I shall keep the sea between this and Corfù, where if
opportunity offer I may have an interview with Sir F. Adam;
and I shall thus watch the movements of Lord Cochrane and
of the Navarin fleet at the same time.

I remain, &c.,

EDWD. CODRINGTON.

It will be seen that this watchfulness on the part of
Sir E. C. saved Greece from calamity, and the alliance
of the three Powers from ridicule or worse.

Sir E. C. to Lady C.

Navarin: September 30, 1827.

The more I look into what I have done, the more I
am satisfied with my conduct. It may be vanity, it may be
blindness; but it is at all events a very agreeable contemplation, and thus I impart it to you. It is said, 'Il n'y a point
de héros pour son valet de chambre.' You, in my case, represent my valet de chambre; for you are behind my scenes,
and know all the contrivances by which I get through my
part of the great drama we are now performing; nor am I
afraid of letting your scrutinizing eye *peer* into the inner-
most recesses of the very complicated machinery upon which
our success depends. My colleague is, or rather was in a
quandary, for I have helped him out of it. He himself must
account in the best way he can for not coming to sea sooner;
viz., by his not receiving my letters and so forth; without
telling the world that neither I nor the commodore of his
own ships of the line knew where to send to him if they had
had the means. It seems that the news of the Alexandria
fleet sailing, and my leaving Vourla for the Greek coast in
preparation for preventing its acting, reached Constantinople
at the same time: that the tone of the Reis Effendi was
therefore more mild, and the anxiety of Mr. S. Canning
more strong; the one fearing the loss of his fleet, the other

that a war might be brought on by me for want of the support of the French ships. Mr. S. Canning, under these circumstances, and hearing from me that I knew not De Rigny's
plans or movements, mentioned his anxiety to Count Guilleminot; and referred, I fancy, at the same time, to reports
prevailing at Smyrna, 'that my said colleague and myself
were upon bad terms.' A letter from the Count reached De
R. three days ago upon this subject after I had experienced
in him perfect concord and cordiality, which he communicated to me. I therefore wrote him a letter, to say that I
had found this in all our conferences, and that I derived
great benefit from his counsel and assistance; and that I
should be always ready to repeat this, as I had already
written it in my public letters lately. I further sanctioned
his showing my letter or making any use of it he pleased,
and he is more than contented. The report will, however,
do him good. He has now so arranged, that if himself
absent, his ships will obey my wishes at any time; and I
have no doubt of all going on well, even if we should not
have the aid of the Russians. In preparation for this latter
event, and for the termination of the armistice, I have
written to Count Heiden at Malta; and have sent ' Genoa,'
' Albion,' and ' Cambrian' there, to get such provisions and
other supplies as will prepare them for keeping the sea until
the fleet is disposed of. I shall continue at sea, or in one of
the Ionian Islands, where I can best watch Cochrane, and
keep up a communication with Adam, and shall return
here on or about October 14. If, as I expect, we should
have merely to convoy the ships of this fleet to Alexandria and the Dardanelles, I shall wish very much that you
were with me. Harry and I have done so before during
this cruise, when with our *large fleet!* of three sail of the
line and a frigate, we were performing evolutions as a
practice, and I could have wished for you on more than one
occasion since; for example, when sailing in the midst of the
Turkish fleet, when standing into the port of Navarin, tacking
round their ships, and coming to an anchor as if the ' Asia '
were a small frigate, in the centre of their whole force and
in front of Ibrahim's tent; and when coming out just before
dark under every stitch of lofty sail, with the band serenad-
ing a beautiful young moon, in one of the loveliest evenings
I ever enjoyed! It was a scene altogether of peculiar interest, from the variety of extraordinary and important
circumstances which so closely preceded our coming out of
that magnificent harbour. The whole affair is almost too
much mixed up with self for me to detail it, even if I were

competent to do so.   But to those who, not being principals,
could attend to the working of the minor wheels, the story
of what passed in the three or four days to which I refer,
including the interview with the Pacha, would be well worth
the relation.

From Sir E. C. to H.R.H. the Duke of Clarence.

Off Navarin: September 30, 1827.

SIR,—I find it difficult to give Your R. H. all the information upon the subject of discipline to which a sense of duty
prompts me, without appearing to throw reflections which
might be deemed invidious.   But it is due to myself to say,
that I have found a falling off in this respect since I was last
employed, which has quite astounded me.   I am at a loss to
comprehend how the service was carried on at all, under such
circumstances as have been represented to me : and I am
quite sure, that if I had not succeeded in producing a better
system we could not have executed the duties which we have
now to perform.   I would rather refer Your R. H. for particulars to such captains as have served on this station, and
who are equally aware of the causes and their effects, than
enter further myself on details with which I am not personally
acquainted.   My remarks on the severity of some of the
punishments in the quarterly returns, were met by the absolute necessity of it for restoring that discipline which I
insisted upon having established.   The frequency of petty
officers being struck by private men, seems to have originated
in an idea of a positive right to do so if the former lifted
their hands first ; whilst the want of proper support left no
other alternative for getting the common routine of duty
performed.   This naturally led to inferior men becoming
petty officers ; and this is the only way in which I can
account for so many of that class having been subject to
corporal punishment.   In mustering the ships I felt it requisite to comment upon this practice, and to desire that no
man, subject by his conduct to such treatment, should continue to be so rated.   This produced the question of what
was to be done, when there were no others equal to the duty ?
And this, Sir, brings me to the system of manning ships
referred to in my letter of the 17th inst., which prevailed
before Your R. H. entered on your high office ; of which the
'Asia' has been the victim ; which Your R. H. has had
the wisdom to change ; and which I trust will never again
be permitted to drive from the Navy the flower of English
seamen.

Had Your R. H.'s circular of the 19th June 1827 been

in force when the 'Asia' was fitting out, she would have
been one of the best manned ships that ever went to sea;
whereas she is now as inferior in the quality of her men as
she is deficient in number for the guns she has to fight. Not
having met with any satisfactory consideration to the observations I offered during our outfit, I did not wish to say all I
might in my late public letter; but the enclosed explanation
of our provision for battle, will put Your R. H. at once into
possession of my present feelings, as to what may be expected of the 'Asia' if she should be called upon to force
the Turkish fleet to the point required by the Treaty.

October 3.

I have now had a still stronger practical proof of the error
in sending the 'Asia' out with a crew so little proportioned
to her armament. A great disparity in numerical force
between mine and that to which I expected to find myself
actively opposed, as shown by my official letter, with the
common chances even of random shot taken into consideration, might have produced consequences extremely fatal on
this very critical occasion.

Fortunately, the Asia's appearance in battle array, with
the danger of passing such a broadside, and the bold and
determined countenance of her supporters, the 'Dartmouth,'
'Talbot,' and 'Zebra,' awed our opponents into a submission
which was entirely beyond my most sanguine expectations,
but which I hope I may now consider as a presage of our
future success. To what further trials, however, we may yet
be exposed in this novel and arduous business, I am not
bold enough to attempt to calculate. Thus far I may consider myself as favoured to the utmost by fortune; and
before the opposite side of the wheel turn uppermost, I trust
I shall be joined again by the 'Genoa' and 'Albion,' so
replenished and refitted as to make me more independent of
her favour. Your R. H. will observe in the punishment
reports of this ship, and I believe in that of most others,
that the great majority of culprits are marines. This
betokens some error in the management of that corps generally; and what has just been discovered in this ship may
lead to a general improvement. We find that the sergeant-
major has been selling liquor to the marines, and that he has
apparently had the purser's steward's mate, if not another,
in partnership with him. As he frequently brought marines
to the quarter-deck for drunkenness, he was not suspected,
and even fifty lashes would not bring those who it turns out
had bought of him, to confess the source of their supply. I

shall order this man before a court-martial, on which occasion
the whole scene will be perhaps more fully developed. But I
beg leave to suggest to Your R. H., that instead of appointing
sergeants and corporals, according to the roster, or rota,
suitable selections should be made for all ships going abroad,
and more particularly for the flag-ships, from which promotions are to be made into the smaller ones.

I have, &c.,
EDWD. CODRINGTON.

From H.R.H. the Duke of Clarence to Sir E. C.

Bushey House: November 4, 1827.

DEAR SIR,—Your confidential of 30th September is what
it ought to be from a Commander-in-Chief to a person in
my situation. You and I ought to know *when* and *where* to
be prudent, and to write and talk with confidence. I served
a whole peace, and therefore by experience am aware, unless
the officer in command, and particularly abroad, is exceedingly attentive, the discipline is very improperly relaxed.
The respect due from the fore-mast men to the petty officers
has never been properly defined; and I now trust the order
so properly issued respecting the non-punishment of petty
officers and the badges worn, will make that class of useful,
and I hope in future respectable, men be considered and
looked up to.

You know I never approved of our ships in peace having
a different complement from war; and as fast as I have the
power so will I send you men to complete the whole squadron. The 'Warspite' will have joined you.

I admire your public despatches and approve altogether of
your conduct. I trust all the captains and commanders will
follow your excellent example in zeal and ability.

The following letters relate to the attempt of Ibrahim
to relieve Patras during the absence of the allied squadrons from Navarin.

From Sir E. C. to the Secretary of Admiralty.

'Asia,' in the Gulf of Lepanto: October 2, 1827.*

SIR,—Yesterday, while at anchor at Zante Roads, in com-
pany with the 'Talbot' and 'Zebra,' at about 4 P.M., the
'Dartmouth' hove in sight and made the signal that the
Turkish fleet was putting to sea from Navarin. The weather

* Received at Admiralty, October 27, 1827.

was so bad, with thunderstorms, heavy rains, light and variable winds, that it was with difficulty this ship was got under
way. About 8 P.M. Captain Fellows came on board and
reported that it was a division of the fleet only,* consisting of
one double-banked frigate, six other frigates, nine corvettes,
nineteen brigs, and four Austrian vessels under convoy, and
that they were steering N.W. The 'Asia,' with the before-
named ships in company,† being placed for the purpose, the
Turkish fleet was discovered coming down at midnight; and
she was between them and the entrance of the Gulf of Lepanto in the morning at daylight. I directed the Honourable
Captain Spencer, of the 'Talbot' to inform the Turkish
Admiral that their coming out of Navarin was a breach of
parole; that I should not allow him to proceed; and that if
he permitted a single gun to be fired at the English flag, I
would destroy his whole fleet, if I could. Upon this he
brought to; and whilst the two frigates and brig were turning back the advanced ships, the second in command, Hallil
Bey (the Reala Bey) a Rear-Admiral, came on board. Although he admitted that he was present with the other
chiefs in Ibrahim's tent when he bound himself in honour
not to send any of his ships out of port without the joint
permission of Rear-Admiral De Rigny and myself, he pretended to believe I had given my consent to a division of
them going to Patras.‡ I told him that having broken their
words of honour, I would put no faith in either Ibrahim or
any one of them hereafter; and if they did not turn about
willingly I would make them. As the interpreter seemed to
shuffle, and be afraid to explain in its full force what I had
said, I wrote a letter, of which I enclose a copy, and sent it
by one of the lieutenants of the 'Asia' to Mustapha, the
Petrona Bey,§ and a Vice-Admiral commanding the division.

* OTTOMAN FORCE—1ST DIVISION.		† ENGLISH FORCE.	
	Guns.		Guns.
1 Frigate (flag)	52	Asia	84
1 Frigate (flag)	54	Dartmouth	42
1 Frigate	58	Talbot	28
1 Frigate	52	Zebra	18
1 Frigate	52		
1 Frigate	52		
1 Frigate	44		
9 Corvettes	22 to 28		
19 Brigs	14 to 22		

‡ The Dragoman came on purpose to ask this on September 26, and was
positively refused by Admiral De Rigny and myself.
§ The third in command is called 'the Petrona,' and his ship so named
after his office.

In about an hour and a half I received an answer, of which I enclose a translation. Upon the receipt of this answer, the 'Asia' filled her main topsail and fired a gun; when the Turkish fleet, by a signal from their Admiral, filled and made sail also towards Navarin.

I have, &c.,
EDWD. CODRINGTON.

From Sir E. C. to Mustapha Bey.

His Britannic Majesty's Ship 'Asia,'
off the mouth of the Gulf of Lepanto : October 2, 1827.

SIR,—His Highness Ibrahim Pacha gave his word of honour to the French Admiral and myself, in the presence of his chiefs and by their consent, that none of the ships of the Turkish fleet should leave the port of Navarin without our permission. He has forfeited that word of honour, and I will not again trust the word of honour of him or any chief under his command. The ships now here under the command of Mustapha Bey shall not re-enter the port of Navarin, or any port in Europe on this side of the Dardanelles.

To His Excellency Mustapha Bey, &c.

From Sir E. C. to the Admiralty.

'Asia,' at Zante : October 4, 1827.*

SIR,—When proceeding as mentioned in my letter of the 2nd instant, a division of Turkish ships (as per margin),† two bearing flags at the main, the rest carrying pendants, came round the north end of Zante, and joined the rest of the fleet. The 'Asia' was at this time considerably advanced in the S.E., looking out for any support that might be coming, and preparing to take a position in the mouth of Navarin for obstructing the entrance of the fleet. Upon observing the Petrona Bey to bear up with his division, and seeing symptoms in the other division, evidently commanded by Ibrahim Pacha in person, of making sail towards Patras, I

---

* Received at Admiralty, October 27.

† OTTOMAN FORCE—SECOND DIVISION.

Double-banked Frigate—60 guns	. Ibrahim Pacha.
Double-banked Frigate—60 guns	. Moharem Bey.
Frigate of 50 guns . . .	. Tahir Pacha.
4 corvettes—22 and 28 guns.	
7 brigs—14 to 22 guns.	

directed Captain Curzon to bear up also, and beat to quarters, with the intention of doing the best I could with such a disparity of force, in fulfilment of the orders and instructions under which I am acting. On approaching the body of the fleet I observed a communication taking place between the Admirals, and therefore hove to to see what effect might be produced by the letter I had written to Petrona Bey. About 6 P.M. the whole fleet made sail towards Navarin, although the wind was then fair for Patras.*

The night afterwards became very threatening, the wind light and variable, and a swell rising, &c. I therefore anchored at the mouth of this bay, in company with the 'Talbot,' having detached the 'Zebra' towards Navarin for any ships which might be there to come to our assistance, leaving the 'Dartmouth' outside to watch the motions of the fleet. The 'Talbot' was short of water, and entirely destitute of fuel, and the officers generally of the detachment in want of stock and refreshments. Of these we have received a partial supply; and as soon as there shall be a sufficient breeze to command the ship against the swell which still prevails, I shall again proceed in execution of my instructions.

I wish it to be made known to his Royal Highness the Lord High Admiral, that there are seven Austrian merchant vessels in this fleet laden with supplies; and that an Austrian corvette called the 'Caroline,' and one, if not two, different men-of-war schooners have been frequently at Navarin, and, according to the private information of Admiral De Rigny, have been the constant carriers of the Turkish despatches. Two of these transport vessels having chosen not to hoist their colours when the Turkish ships did, until guns were fired at them from the 'Asia,' I have taken away their papers to show proof of the Austrian proceedings.

I have, &c.,
EDWD. CODRINGTON.

Sir E. C. to Lady C.

October 2—4 P.M.

These Turks won't fight with *us*, whatever they may do with others. Yesterday evening, when lying in Zante, the

---

* TOTAL OF THE TWO OTTOMAN DIVISIONS WHEN THEY UNITED.

3 Double-banked frigates	. . . 172
7 Frigates	. . 370
13 Corvettes	. . 312
26 Brigs	. . 416
49	1270 guns.

'Dartmouth' came from her station off Navarin, with the signal that the Turkish fleet had put to sea; and by the time variable light winds, heavy rain, and thunder storms would let us get fairly under way, Captain Fellowes was on board to tell me it was a division of forty-seven sail coming to Patras.   We got sight of them at midnight; and at daybreak in the morning they saw us just betwixt them and their entrance into the Gulf.   Boats passed between the two Bey Admirals; and I sent Spencer in the 'Talbot' to say that I would not suffer them to pass, and that if they fired a shot at the British flag I would destroy the whole fleet, if I could.   The Rear-Admiral then came to me to explain, when I told him that before they broke their word I esteemed the Turks, and wished to save them as much as possible, but *now* that I looked for an opportunity of punishing them, and that whenever I found one I would do it severely.   As the interpreter he brought was afraid to give what I said its full strength, I *acted* the *brag* so as to impress the Bey, in their way, with my determination; and he was right glad to get out of the ship again to communicate with his superior.   He pressed hard to go to Patras, and lied terribly as to what had passed at Navarin upon that subject.   I therefore wrote to his chief ' that I would not consent to his re-entering Navarin or any port in Europe on this side of the Dardanelles.' To this he has sent an answer, 'that he will not oppose me, and that he will go to Navarin for orders;' with a shuffle about my having given permission.   I then filled the 'Asia's' main topsail and fired a gun, and he made his fleet fill also, by signal; and thus we are now jogging on towards the place we came from.   As the French look-out frigate, the ' Armide,' went for De Rigny at the same time that the ' Dartmouth' came to me, I hope we shall find him off Navarin.   My friends the ' Genoa' and ' Albion' will not stay at Malta longer than they can help; but I can hardly afford to send anything for them.   Colonel Cradock, attached to the Paris Embassy, has been my messmate for about a week, and is likely so to continue.   I find him sensible, well-informed, and agreeable.

Off Zante : —9 P.M. October 3.

This is very curious work.   We saw thirteen additional ships yesterday evening at a distance, which prove to be Ibrahim and two other full Admirals, one of which I take to be Tahir Bey.   Upon their joining the others this afternoon the latter bore up, and I thought the whole were pushing for Patras.   I therefore bore up also to see what could be done ; and I must say our fellows again received the beat to quarters with great cheerfulness. However, after a consultation, in which my letter was no doubt made known to Ibrahim, the whole hauled to the wind, as if decided on pursuing their way towards Navarin. This being the case, I felt myself too happy to let them alone ; and as it suited my purpose to come here and get something to eat for us all, I made it a matter of delicacy that they should go on without any further threat on my part, and I can easily join them in the morning. The ' Dartmouth ' is watching them, and will call me out if they bear up for Patras. It is impossible for me to judge of their final intentions; and with such a disparity of force it is best for me to say no more of mine, until De Rigny or my own ships come to my support. We 'Asias' shall all have a good and quiet night's sleep at all events, whilst the Turks are assailed by thunder storms and very ugly weather. And so I must finish, with my ' God bless you and yours !'

Zante : October 4.

We have had a very quiet night in spite of thunder, rain, &c. When we anchored the sky seemed to be charged with Pandora's box, and I think my friend Ibrahim must have been a little troubled by its contents—although in all this sort of weather we have lately had, there have been no strong squalls of wind. And now I must wind up by telling you, there is no reason to think we shall have any fighting. There certainly was a probability of something two days ago, but the young ones have now given up all hopes, and you may as well, therefore, give up any fears that may have tormented you. And so once more, at ease or in difficulty, believe me your affectionately devoted,

E. C.

From H. J. Codrington (Midshipman) to his Mother.

' Asia,' Zante : October 4, 1827.

We arrived here from Navarin on the 1st, the Turks having promised not to do anything for twenty days. . . . . Both squadrons had dispersed, leaving the ' Dartmouth ' and a French frigate off Navarin. The French Admiral went to Cervi, near Cerigo, and we came to this place with the ' Talbot ' and ' Zebra.' But as it turned out, the Turks seeing us go away, thought the coast clear, and came out. On the evening of the 2nd we were lying here, the rain pouring in bucketfuls, when the ' Dartmouth ' hove in sight with the signal up that they were ' out of port.' When we had got our boats in, and given the people their supper, it was dark, and we had to beat out of Zante Bay with light and very variable winds, closer to several merchantmen than they liked, with the rain pouring incessantly in a way that defied everything to keep it out.

When we got out we stood off and on Zante, or between Zante and the mainland, till 12, when the Turks hove in sight, coming down before the wind (which was to the southward) for the Gulf of Patras. Having stuck to them all night, we found ourselves ('Asia,' 'Dartmouth,' 'Talbot,' and 'Zebra') in the presence of half or two-thirds of the Turkish fleet! At 6 o'clock we beat to quarters and got all clear for action. Father then sent a message to the Admiral of the Turkish squadron to say, that if the ships tried to enter the Gulf they would be fired into, and if they fired a shot at the British flag, he would immediately sink the ships so offending. And seeing that several of the Turks were slow in heaving to, he accelerated their motions by despatching several very efficient messengers to them in the shape of 32-pound shot across their bows. It is astonishing how plain all guns, from the musket to the 68-pounder, can talk, particularly a long 32-pounder, one may well say that it *speaks volumes!* In this case the summons was very well understood and instantly obeyed; and afterwards the Turkish Rear-Admiral, the second in command, came on board, and being asked on what pretence they had broken their word by coming out of Navarin, he replied that when they were in Navarin their intention was to go to Hydra; and that though they had given us a promise not to go out of port for that purpose, that yet they did not extend it to any other place. Now it so happens that though we thought at the time that Hydra was their object, yet their promise was *not to go out of Navarin*, in fact to *suspend operations for twenty days*. After a little talk, at the end of which Father gave his ultimatum, that as Ibrahim and his chiefs had broken their word of honour with him, he would neither let them go into Navarin nor any other port this side of the Dardanelles—they, in number 7 frigates, 9 corvettes, 22 brigs, turned tail—and there were we, three ships and a brig, driving them back, like a huntsman and the whippers in and the hounds. It was a very pretty and curious sight. At dusk we popped in here with 'Talbot' to get some provisions, leaving 'Dartmouth' to watch the Turks; and this morning they are out of sight, I suppose gone to the south, as we wished them. The fact is they had not the slightest idea of seeing any of us here, and thought most likely they would have time to get past the Castles in the Gulf of Lepanto (or Corinth) before we started from Corfù, where I think *they guessed* we were. But by the French Admiral being at Cervi, he would be enabled to stop anything going to Hydra, and by our being here we have stopped this expedition. Fancy 'Asia,' 'Dartmouth,' 'Talbot,' and 'Zebra' drawn up in line ahead across the entrance of the Gulf of Patras, saying to the Turkish fleet, '*Thus far*, and *no farther!*' Had it been a finer day the sight would have been beautiful. As it is, since we have been in sight of Zante it has, with very short interruptions, been raining continually. I have never seen any decks so magnificent as ours when clear! Mind there is not in the main and lower decks *one* bulkhead or cabin up, the deck is perfectly clear, and standing aft and looking forward they appear most formidable batteries! They are quite magnificent.

From Sir E. C. to the Admiralty.

'Asia,' off Cape Papa: October 6, 1827.*

SIR,—On the morning of the 4th inst., after writing my letter to you whilst lying in Zante Bay, I learned by communication with the 'Dartmouth,' that a considerable part of the Turkish fleet had stood towards Patras. As soon, therefore, as there was wind enough to command the ship, the 'Asia' weighed and made sail in that direction. The weather was very variable and squally, and it was not until 6 P.M. that we had approached Cape Papa, where we saw most of the largest Turkish ships at anchor, and the rest of the fleet endeavouring to join them. It was evident to me, that this was a sly trick on the part of the Turkish commander to send supplies into Patras, in defiance of the second agreement of the Petrona Bey made with me the day preceding. It was observed, that the vessels still working up for an anchorage, directly contrary to their usual custom would not show their colours to us in passing. Shot fired near them not producing the effect of either making them hoist their colours, or bring to, several shots were fired at them from this ship and from the 'Dartmouth;' and thus a large division of the vessels carrying the supplies, was prevented joining the admirals and the rest at anchor. Shortly after dark the weather became extremely bad; violent squalls from different quarters, with lightning and heavy rain confined our attention to the preservation of our own ships. At daylight it blew a hurricane, and we put before the wind under bare poles, in order to shelter under the lee

* Received at Admiralty October 27.

of Zante. At this time from twenty-five to thirty sail were seen under the same circumstances far ahead, between Zante and Cephalonia, and the rest of the fleet in a state of general dispersion. So soon as the gale abated, I endeavoured to work back and ascertain if any ships were still left in a position to send supplies into the Gulf of Lepanto; and at 9 P.M. gained an anchorage under Cape Papa, in company with some fifteen sail of Turkish and Austrian vessels including a frigate and corvette and two or three other vessels of war, besides the 'Dartmouth,' 'Talbot,' and 'Philomel,' which latter sloop hove in sight yesterday morning. This morning the captain of the Turkish frigate came on board with his Italian pilot, who said that they were returning to Navarin on the night of the 3rd inst. until nine o'clock, when Ibrahim Pacha, in a thick squall, made the signal to bear up, and that they anchored the next morning under Cape Papa at four o'clock. They remained there, being prevented going higher up by the contrary wind, until five P.M., when hearing some guns in the offing (our firing at the vessels which would not show their colours), Ibrahim made the signal and they got under way, but were dispersed by a gale of wind on the night of the 4th; that Ibrahim was on board a Leghorn-built frigate, double-banked, but *never hoisted his flag, although all the signals* were made from his ship. The two admirals, with flags at the main, were Tahir Pacha and Moharem Bey. I informed the captain of this frigate, who asked me permission to go to Patras with supplies, which he states to have been the known intention of Ibrahim in bearing up in the night of the 3rd, that I would not permit him, repeating to him what I had said to the Petrona Bey; and I gave it to him in writing as the only means, as he thought, of preventing his having his head cut off on his return to Turkey. Trusting that the French frigate 'Armide' will have reached Rear-Admiral De Rigny so as to enable him to be by this time off Navarin, and perhaps with him some of the ships under my immediate orders, I shall probably delay hereabout so as to baffle any other attempt to send supplies into this Gulf.

I have, &c.,
EDWARD CODRINGTON.

Zante, October 10, 1827.

P.S.—On Sunday the 7th I proceeded nearer to Patras and turned away two Austrian vessels which were pressing towards that place, notwithstanding the warning they had; and we brought away also a Turkish brig, which landed about twenty men at Vassaladi, the fort commanding the entrance to Missolunghi, in spite of the guns from this ship, the 'Dartmouth,' and 'Talbot.' These vessels being towed as far as Cape Tornese were then directed to follow the Turkish fleet; and on the night of the 8th we anchored in this bay where we have since been—completing our water.

5 P.M. The 'Alacrity' has just joined me from Corfù, with an account that the landing at Petalà was by a party of mere pirates: and that she showed her colours this morning to seven sail of Russian vessels of war to the westward of this island. I have sent the 'Talbot' with a letter to request Count Heiden will have the goodness to meet me off Navarin.

EDWARD CODRINGTON.

Sir E. C. to Lady C.

October 6, 1827.

We anchored under Cape Papa where we are now, at 9 P.M. last night; in company with 'Dartmouth,' 'Talbot,' and 'Philomel,' and a division of Turks of some 15, including a large frigate, a corvette, and 3 or 4 smaller vessels of war. Cape Papa is at the entrance of the Gulf of Patras, which is at the entrance of the Gulf of Lepanto. My last letter left me on the 3rd at Zante, whilst Ibrahim and his fleet we supposed to be obediently working *towards* Navarin. It seems that in the night, inspired by the *dirty* weather, the *dirty dog* edged away for Patras, and was stopped by a violent wind down the Gulf from proceeding beyond this Cape, where we saw him and his admirals, &c., at anchor, after we had approached in chase to intercept his movements. There was evidently trick in this; for none of the vessels we passed would hoist their colours (although as their general rule they keep them at all times flying), until they had several shot right at them. By thus detaining a considerable number of these vessels with the supplies, we separated them from the fleet; and the frequent fire of this ship, and the 'Dartmouth,' and the 'Talbot,' was an earnest to Ibrahim of the spirit in which we were now acting since the failure of his word.

Whatever may have been the cause, the effect was his weighing at and after dark, with all those around him; being exposed, like ourselves, during the night to weather which made it enough for each to look out for ourselves; and being at length obliged, like us, to put before a hurricane for shelter. By 8 A.M. yesterday (the 5th) the wind abated. We then saw some 25 sail down to leeward betwixt Zante and Cephalonia, at too great distance to know what they were; and nearly as many more scattered about in all directions. These, like me, imagined that the chief himself might still be within the gulf; and we therefore all made to the same point, for the same purpose. Accordingly, I found the 'Asia' surrounded by them this morning; and they are now all under way, obeying my directions to proceed towards Alexandria. The captain of the frigate, who came on board this morning to ask my leave to go to Patras, told me that Ibrahim made a signal in the night to bear up for that place, and was stopped by the wind, as above, &c. That the two flags at the main were those of Moharem Bey and Tahir Pacha; that Ibrahim hoisted no flag, but yet made all the signals. Thus we have again by activity and spirit, defeated the object of the Turks, and fulfilled the instructions emanating from the Treaty: and we have shown that there is no solid foundation for the prevalent belief in either Turkish honour or Turkish bravery.

Spencer is gone to bed until my dinner-hour of 3 P.M., having been up the last two nights; the 'Asia,' 'Dartmouth,' and 'Philomel' having gained their anchorage we have all had a real good snooze. I cannot describe the luxury of hearing the rain last night pour down over my head after the lightning, without a breath of wind to call up the people, the preceding night having called every one of us on deck. Late last night the 'Hinde,' cutter, brought me your letters to 25th September. In proportion as I myself am made happy by good accounts of you to so late a date, I am annoyed at your being so long in getting similar accounts of me. You will find it is neither my fault nor Hal's, for we have never missed an opportunity. Nor has there been any need of pumping; for we have had plenty to write about, as my official letters alone would show you. I have no doubt that those alone will be found very interesting, from the variety of events which have occurred, and are still occurring every day suddenly and unexpectedly.

Sir E. C. to Lady C.

October 7.

I told you in my last I had been so far very fortunate: I may again say the same; for the many difficulties to which I have been exposed have turned to my personal credit. We 'Asia,' 'Dartmouth,' 'Talbot,' and latterly the 'Philomel, have driven off Ibrahim and his four admirals, &c., &c., &c., amounting to fifty-seven sail (but excluding his three ships of the line, which, I conclude, were left at Navarin as not sea-worthy), and have prevented his succeeding in the object for which he broke his word, not certainly without firing guns, but without producing hostilities; an effect for which the Allied Governments had prepared twelve ships of the line, besides frigates, &c. I staid behind in this Gulf of Patras, to prevent supplies being landed slyly in small quantities. Accordingly, seeing a brig anchor of Missolunghi and send off a boat full of men, we have just cut her cable, and are taking her out to sea, short of her boat and the crew in her, with her cargo of flour. From one or the other of us she has received several shot through her sails and hull, but none have been killed. The captain asked if his head was to be cut off, and seemed well pleased with the negative, which he immediately communicated to the others. ·

We have all in turn (except Dilke) been watching a corps of Albanians marching along in regular order. Smith was the longest of all, helped on by Harry, who was himself half an hour in finding out they were *pelicans*; all books of travels relate this sort of thing, but nobody believes it until they are convinced by their own experience of the similarity in appearance. I must also record another curiosity which I never saw before, that is a lunar rainbow on the night of the 5th, extremely perfect. The red and orange rays were very discernible.

From H. J. Codrington to his Mother.

'Asia,' off Navarin: October 18.

. . . . . .

At dusk on the 4th it came on to blow very fresh out of the Gulf, and, after having furled all the sails, we were obliged to bear up again for the mouth of the gulf till it moderated. At daylight we were at the entrance of the gulf, 'Dartmouth,' 'Talbot,' and 'Philomel' in company, but only one or two stray Turks to be seen. 'Philomel' told us Lord Cochrane and the steamer with several Greek brigs had been in the Gulf of Lepanto, and that Lord Cochrane had left it, but the steamer, &c., had burnt nine vessels, either belonging to or in pay of the Turks, amongst them some Austrian merchantmen, who had just landed some corn for the Turks, and whose masters were at the Turkish camp getting their money. She also told us that when she was running down during the night, the Turkish fleet had come down before the wind under a very heavy press of sail, and passed her in great confusion, running right out of the gulf at a devil of a rate; and, on taking a careful look from our mast-head, we did see half of them to leeward very much dispersed. That evening (October 5) we anchored near Cape Papa among a few Turks, whom we sent off next morning (6th). The captain of one said that most likely if we did not let him go to Patras Ibrahim would cut his head off for not getting there, and the poor man was very disconsolate for some time. So that there was very good reason for those fellows so obstinately persisting the day before. On the 7th we weighed and ran up the gulf a little higher past Cape Papa, turned a few more Turkish and Austrian brigs, &c., out, had a good look at Missolunghi, &c., and a glimpse at Patras. Missolunghi is built on a perfect flat at the foot of some very high hills running N.W. and S.E. about; on the shore of the gulf it is surrounded on the land side by low and impassable marshes, except on one front, which is fortified, if I may so call it, by a ditch and wall, neither in good repair. Report says there were sixty pieces of cannon mounted in the town. Towards the sea no vessel bigger than a small boat could come within several miles of it, on account of the shoals and sand banks which form the lagoons, or lakes, between it and the sea. From the entrance of the banks to the town there are only one or two canals, or passages, for even boats, which passages are serpentine and very difficult to find; as to the lagoons themselves, they are of too soft a bottom to be fordable, but too sticky a one to be navigable for anything but flat-bottomed boats. There are also several tiers of banks above water between the outer one or entrance, and the town, with only a few passages, and those difficult to find. One of the outer entrances (the chief one) is guarded by a small fort called Vassiladi, which has only two narrow passages to it, although the great passage into the gates is close under its guns. We saw it (in 1825 or 1826, when in the Naiad) taken from the Greeks by the Turks, by means of their flat-bottomed gunboats which they built at Patras, towed over to the lakes, and got in at a smaller entrance out of shot. At one time there were upwards of twenty of these, some with two and some with three guns, firing at this fort. It was taken in consequence of the magazine being blown up by a shell. In consequence of its loss the Greeks could no longer victual Missolunghi from the sea, as that passage by the fort was the only one that could admit loaded boats. As to the town, while we were at anchor off it in 'the Naiad' we regularly saw them begin every evening at nine o'clock, firing into and bombarding it, and once or twice saw a general assault, always at night, and invariably repulsed. It was certainly very beautiful, and amused the first watch very much. During the day they were generally very inactive, except when either party fired a chance gun; then it was immediately answered and re-answered for five minutes, when they left off. This happened five or six times a day. Latterly, I believe, the Turks had nearly fifty large flat-bottomed gun-boats on the lakes against the town. Before its fall the garrison had eaten nothing but sea-weed for four days. Then they made their last desperate sally; part escaped, part were repulsed, and the Turks immediately storming the town, the garrison being so much weakened, were driven from the batteries to the armed houses, where, finding there was no chance of escape, *they ultimately blew up themselves and children*. But, to return to present time, the red flag was waving on the little fort, and, having taken out a brig which was at anchor near the fort, and which had a boat with her officers on shore, we commenced beating out, taking in tow several Austrian brigs, &c., which still hovered round. . . . On the 13th, in the morning, we fell in with the Russian squadron (4 sail of the line, 2 frigates, and 1 corvette); and subsequently with the French squadron. In the evening the French squadron (two sail of the line, two frigates, &c.), went to Zante, and we, Russians in company, continued our route to Navarin. The same day two Turkish corvettes came from Ibrahim, who was at Navarin, to enquire after part of his fleet, and to ask leave to go to Patras, which was refused. It was curious to observe how the Turks kept clear of the Russian ships and got under our lee. When the Russians came near them they bore up and ran to the side of us, for they did not like their looks. The Russian ships are very clean, and, I think, in very good order. Many of their officers speak good English, and several of them served as volunteers in the English navy during the war. Count Heiden is the Russian Rear-Admiral, his flag-ship is 'the Azoff.' They all have their names on their sterns, appear quite new, and, their copper being new, is of a beautiful dark rose colour, which very much improves the appearance of the ships. Since our arrival we have been cruising about as usual, waiting for the French, who arrived here yesterday.

From Sir Frederick Adam to Sir E. C.

Corfù : October 8, 1827.

MY DEAR CODRINGTON,—   .   .   .   .   .
I am very anxious to hear what has been the result of your bold, decided measures, and that the return to Navarin has

been prevented. If you meet the French squadron in time
I am confident you will prevent their returning to that port;
I even anticipate this result if you don't fall in with aid. It
has given me great pleasure and a sensible gratification to
hear of your little force commanding and directing one so
superior; and I admire the decision which produced this
result. I hope, however, very soon to learn how this has
terminated.

From Sir E. C. to Sir Frederick Adam.

Zante: October 10, 1827.

Knowing that I have had this work to perform with such
a small force, the good folks at home will be anxious for
further news; and will partake of my satisfaction in having
defeated Ibrahim's object without actual hostilities, and in
this arrival of the Russian ships preventing my being again
placed in a similar extremity. The 14th was the day fixed
for De Rigny and myself re-joining off Navarin when we
still relied on Ibrahim's promise; therefore we are sure to
assemble there all together in readiness to act decisively.

I am glad Lord C. has given up his projects in Albania.
He might have had pretty pickings out of this fleet after the
late gale, if he had had anything hanging about for such a
purpose. I dare say that he is gone back to Poros; as the
time for which his men were entered is nearly out, and they
won't serve without being regularly paid up.

As to my having steamers, you may judge of the encouragement I have to ask for such aid, when I tell you I
am allowed 20 men for manning the tenders which take 65;
that we are so over-armed in proportion to our men, that
being now several short, we could only put 9 men to a 32-
pounder if we were to fight the whole; and that having
about 2,000 fathoms of one-sized rope in wear as lifts and
braces, always liable to go from being always relied upon for
supporting the yards, we have some 85 fathoms to replace
them as our full allowance. This is economy with a
vengeance, but I trust our new master will order it in a more
un-Secretarial manner.

10 p.m.

I have just got your note of the 8th by the steamer. I
assure you my good friend I know the value of your good
opinion of my conduct and prize your expression of it accordingly. We certainly put a good face on it, and I suspect
Ibrahim thought we had been joined by some of our friends,
by his bolting away as he did, after having sacrificed his

honour in order to effect his purpose. If De R. got to Navarin in time, he will have shut the door on Ibrahim of course: but if not, we can now force him into our measures without difficulty.

P.S.—Stovin tells me the Turkish fleet have got into Navarin. I fear De Rigny again changed his mind, and did not go to Cervi to water, as he settled to do, but went away to Milo or Poros; or else he must have got back in time to stop them.

Yours, with great regard,

EDWD. CODRINGTON.

Sir E. C. to Lady C.

Zante : October 9, 9 P.M.

The 'Alacrity' came here this evening from Corfù having shown her colours to seven sail of Russian ships-of-war on the other side of this island. This is a good bit of news for you as well as me, for it will show you that I shall now have ample means of doing what is required, and that my anxiety will be greatly diminished: as you know what sort of man Adam is and that his good opinion is well worth having, I will enclose a note I received from him last night. It was impossible for *me* to prevent the fleet getting back to Navarin as there were always some devils hanging back for Patras, and at the last we were obliged to use both shot and the tow-rope to effect our purpose. It is of no consequence, except that the job would certainly have been more complete. However, I may fairly say to *you* that if my masters are not contented with me they are very unreasonable.

October 9 (after hearing the news of Mr. Canning's death).

I admired him as much as most people out of his personal circle, but I cannot forget the blots in his political conduct, blots which the good arising from the change of system he was about establishing would certainly have wiped off, but which at this early period it is quite impossible to forget. . . . . . However, he is a very severe loss to us just now, and it is lamentable that he should not have lived to see the benefits of his late measures.

From Sir Frederick Adam to Lady C.

Corfù : October 14, 1827.

Although I send the latest accounts of the Admiral from himself, you must, my dear Madam, submit to receiving this also, that I may congratulate you, as I do most sincerely, on Codrington's brilliant achievement, for such I must consider his late encounters with the promise-breaking Turkish fleet. The Admiral's whole conduct has been a fine specimen of prompt, bold, and manly decision, has done him great honour, and added to the character of the noble service to which he belongs. Fifty three against four, and the four obliging their opponents to comply with their demand! it has really done me good. I am national enough to be pleased too, that this important service has been accomplished by the English squadron alone: this may be called narrow-minded, but I am Englishman enough to have such narrow-minded feelings.

With great truth, your very sincere, &c.,

F. ADAM.

From General Ponsonby to Sir E. C.

Malta: October 21, 1827.

MY DEAR ADMIRAL,—Again let me congratulate you on the success of your late operations (at Patras) which could not have succeeded except by the greatest decision in most critical circumstances,—and by this decision the peace of the world is still maintained.

From Sir E. C. to the Admiralty.*

'Asia,' at Zante: October 10, 1827.

SIR,—I have more than once had to complain of the irregular conduct of Lord Cochrane. You will now inform his Royal Highness the Lord High Admiral that I received a letter from his Excellency Lieutenant-General Sir Frederick Adam on the 23rd of last month, stating that information had reached him of a Greek squadron under his Lordship having on board a considerable body of troops said to be under the command of General Church, being about to make an attack on some parts of the Albanian provinces to the north of the Gulf of Prevesa. Agreeing with Sir F. Adam, and my opinion being sanctioned by that of Rear-Admiral De Rigny, that it was requisite to restrain the Greek forces from exciting revolt in parts not hitherto the theatre of war, I immediately sent the 'Philomel' to wherever Lord Cochrane might be, with directions to Commander, Lord Viscount Ingestrie, to make known to the commanders of the expedition that I considered it my duty in the present state of affairs to prevent such a measure being carried into exe-cution; and that I should shortly present myself in that neighbourhood. The 'Philomel' joined me off Cape Pupa

* Received October 27.

on the 5th inst.; and Lord Ingestrie reported that upon his showing the order to Lord Cochrane his Lordship promised to guide himself by the spirit of it. Lord Ingestrie then passed into the Gulf of Lepanto where he made a similar communication to General Church, who equally expressed his decision to attend to it. That general was at Vostitza on the 4th inst., meditating the blockade of Patras by land. Yesterday, I received another despatch from Sir Frederick Adam, reporting to me the occupation of the Island of Petala by a part of Lord Cochrane's force, and requiring the assistance of a frigate. As the 'Ariadne' must have reached Corfù very soon after the date of this last letter, and as I hear the 'Hellas,' with a steamer in tow, was seen on September 28, off 'Cephalonia,' steering to the southward, I trust the Lord High Commissioner will have had sufficient means of restoring that island to its former state of neutrality.

I have, &c.,

EDWD. CODRINGTON.

From Sir E. C. to Sir Henry Wellesley.

'Asia,' Zante · October 11, 1827.

MY DEAR SIR HENRY,—As your son will have told you of our proceedings and of his being a party to them in this ship, I need only say that we have brought Turkish honour and Turkish valour to a discount: there have been two occasions in which I thought it impossible they could yield without fighting for it; but they nevertheless, after forfeiting their word of honour to effect their purpose of giving supplies to Patras, &c., gave up that purpose rather than encounter the broadside of this ship, supported by the little 'Dartmouth' frigate, the lesser 'Talbot' with her carronades, and the 'Zebra' brig. As we were to avoid hostilities, it is a satisfaction to me to have effected the object with such a modicum of the force prepared for that service by the Allied Governments, without going to such an extremity. I fear Admiral De Rigny did not get back to Navarin in time to prevent Ibrahim and his fleet re-entering that port. However, there his Highness's expedition will terminate its hostile career, I think, since the Russian squadron is announced to me as being now off this island. I hear a report of the 'Sultan' having been at direct variance with his divan, and having quitted them and joined his army at Scutari, where he is building another seraglio. The Greeks, instead of aiding their own cause, are mostly employed in piracies at sea and on shore: and whenever the affair is

settled with the Turks, we shall have an endless work to
perform in bringing the Greeks to anything like regularity.
If Capo d'Istria come with some 3,000 or 4,000 Swiss to
support his government, things may do well,—but so long
as the Capitani are to continue their sway, so long will vice
prevail over patriotism and even common honesty.

Very sincerely yours,

EDWD. CODRINGTON.

From Sir E. C. to Mr. S. Canning, Constantinople.

' Asia,' off Navarin : October 14, 1827.

SIR,—I had the honour of addressing Your Excellency on
the 29th of last month by the ' Dryad,' which ship proceeded
to Smyrna. The enclosed copies of letters to the Admiralty,*
and of one to his Excellency Sir Henry Wellesley,† will
afford you all the information of our proceedings since that
date. The Russian squadron, consisting of four sail of the
line, three frigates, and a corvette, joined company yesterday
morning off Zante, and are now proceeding with me towards
Navarin.   Rear-Admiral De Rigny also joined company
yesterday with part of his squadron, but went into Zante
with them for the purpose of getting refreshments.   It
appears that when off Cerigo proceeding to Cervi, ' La
Provence' ran aboard ' le Scipion' in the night, by which
accident both ships were disabled, the one losing her mainmast and the other her bowsprit.   Whilst remaining at
Cervi the mainmast was taken out of ' la Provence ' and
put into ' le Scipion,' which will make the latter ship
effective. ' la Provence ' is ordered to Toulon.   It is very
creditable to Admiral De Rigny's squadron to have effected
this very difficult operation.   It is, however, much to be
lamented that such an accident should have prevented the
French squadron coming off Navarin during the time that
Ibrahim's fleet was at sea, as we could then have given it
what direction we pleased.   Upon Admiral De Rigny's return I shall consult with him and Count Heiden as to the
propriety of forcing Ibrahim to come out and proceed to
Turkey.

I have, &c.,

EDWD. CODRINGTON.

* Relative to the affair at Patras.
† Relative to Austrian vessels.

From Sir E. C. to Mr. S. Canning.

'Asia,' off Navarin: October 14, 1827.

DEAR SIR,—Yesterday, at the moment of being joined by the Russian squadron, I received by the 'Brisk' your letters of the 28th and 29th September, with their enclosures. Although, from the want of a correct understanding of Admiral De Rigny's plans and rendezvous, and from my being unable to detach a vessel to make known my sudden movements after the Turkish fleet, I was put into a very critical situation, and felt myself called upon to state the difficulties I had to contend with, it becomes me to assure you that my colleague would have gladly co-operated with me from the first, with the same zeal and cordiality which I have found in him since our meeting. The only vessels which knew of my coming this way were driven by a gale of wind beyond Candia; and when the 'Cambrian' came as far as Sapienza in search of me, I was carried by a current as far as the Strophades. For all the extraordinary events which have attended Ibrahim's breach of faith I refer you to my letters to his Royal Highness the Lord High Admiral, of which I have sent you copies with my official letter. I was always of opinion that something was meditated in the neighbourhood of Patras, before the avowed attack on Hydra; I therefore placed myself at Zante, where I could be ready for any small detachments from this port, as well as to watch the motions of Lord Cochrane. I did not, however, feel any doubt of Ibrahim's ostensibly fulfilling his engagement, any more than did Admiral De Rigny; or I should not have sent my squadron into Malta to refit. That the service which was thrown upon me by this violation of good faith was arduous and critical, will be evident to you on the perusal of my narrative; and that by the gallant and able support of the little band which I had with me, I was enabled to defeat the purpose for which Ibrahim sacrificed his honour, I shall consider as one of the most fortunate circumstances of my professional life. I reckoned on being back here in time to prevent the re-entry of the fleet; but that very wind which favoured my first object, by dividing and dispersing them, detained me off Missolunghi so long that I could only hope for that measure being effected by the arrival of the French or Russian squadron. When Admiral De Rigny returns from Zante, I shall confer with him and Count Heiden as to taking measures for forcing Ibrahim's return to

Egypt. He is now less entitled to delicacy on our part; and if he before stood in awe of the 'Asia' singly, he may be very ready to yield obedience to the ten sail of the line united.

From Sir E. C. to Mr. S. Canning

'Asia,' off Navarin : October 14, 1827.

DEAR SIR,—I have written you such a private letter as I think you will find no difficulty in showing to your colleagues. In that I have touched upon Admiral DeRigny's not joining me, in such a way as I hope will make all smooth as far as concerns his sincerity. He does not, however, understand service in our way of performing it, and seems to incline much more to the diplomatic. After asking about his ships going away from hence when ours did, and being advised by me to let them remain here three or four days, and then profit by a strong northerly wind to let them get away in the night when they would not be seen, he took them off the next day in sight of the Turks, and of an Austrian vessel of war, which of course gave notice of his movements. When off Cerigo, two of his ships ran foul of each other, by which both were disabled, until (much to their credit) they transferred the mainmast of the one to the other in Cervi Bay. The 'Armide' carried him the news of Ibrahim's breach of faith at the same time that the 'Dartmouth' came to me; but there he remained, and only joined me yesterday; whereby, besides leaving me unsupported to prevent the success of Ibrahim's treachery, he lost the opportunity which his coming directly here with his other two ships of the line, his own large frigate, and the 'Armide,' &c., would have given him, of preventing the return of the Turkish expedition into Navarin; and conducting them, as in that case we should be now doing, back to their own ports. He joined me yesterday at the same time as Count Heiden; and though I proposed we should have a conference as soon as the wind should moderate, he proposed going to Zante, *if I had no objection*, for stock for his officers. I offered to share mine with him, but he said all his officers were in the same destitution; and, as he still clung to it, and said he would not be a whole day absent, I could not but consent. Such is the man, and I therefore mention it to you. But at the same time he is quite ready to act as I wish when present with me; and, though delays and difficulties will arise, I doubt not but we shall come out pretty well in the end. Count Heiden was on board the 'Asia' to-day, and is to dine with me to-morrow. He appears to be all I could wish; like one of our service, eager to act under my orders as he is directed by his instructions to do, whether the French commander do the same or not; and his ships are apparently in good service-like order. He says, but for being ordered to rendezvous at Messina (and then Zante) he should have been here a fortnight sooner. He will write to propose Malta hereafter, instead of Messina. At the moment of his joining there were two Turkish corvettes coming to ask me after seven missing vessels, *three of which they openly said were Austrians.* I told them I knew nothing of their vessels, and upon their asking to go to the Gulf of Patras, and getting from me a flat refusal, they went away from Navarin, and of course made known the arrival of the Russian squadron. To-day we have shown ourselves close enough for Ibrahim to see their colours, and I imagine it was a sight to him not of the most agreeable description. Captain Hamilton has got your letters to him, and is gone to make a visit to Pedro Bay at Maina. Admiral De Rigny talked to me about his letter on piracy and gave me a copy of it, some time after he had received your answer to Count Guilleminot upon its contents. Thinking we had then quite enough upon our hands here, I did not enter much into the subject. I may say at once to you that I by no means agree to his plan of having a tribunal at Syra, a plan originating in his wish to favour the Catholics there, whom he considered under his immediate protection. So soon as the actual warfare ceases, I apprehend some regular consular agents will be appointed; and their signatures at the seat of Government may perhaps be a good countersign to the documents furnished by the executives. I am told that the eagerness on the part of the said executives for these condemnations arises from their receiving a twentieth part themselves, which they account for as they please. I have used, and must use, strong language to these people, and must take strong measures also: or the delay in completing the object of the Treaty may almost annihilate our commerce in these seas.

Tuesday, 16th, 10 A.M.

As Rear-Admiral De Rigny is not yet returned from Zante, and as it is important that the arrival of the Russian squadron should be known by you and your colleagues, I will send my letters, and those of Count Heiden off at once. Whenever you suspect a reason for having another vessel at Tenedos, after you may have despatched the 'Rifleman,' you will of course let me hear of it.

Believe me, &c.,
EDWD. CODRINGTON.

P.S.—Sir F. Stovin believes that the line of limitation being extended to Arta might interfere with the supply of cattle to the Ionian Islands; but I shall shortly have Sir F. Adam's official answer to this question.

October 16, 3 P.M.

Since I enclosed my letter this morning, an Austrian corvette, which I have no doubt is the 'Carolina,' made such a push for Modon that I directed the 'Dartmouth' and 'Talbot' to endeavour to stop her, and bring her to me. I think they will be too late. The 'Cambrian' is now under signal to stop two Austrian schooners doing the same thing; but to say that if charged with despatches for Ibrahim or the Turks, they may go. I wish to commit them to the fact, but not to prevent a communication which possibly may occasion the retirement of the expedition to Turkey. Count Heiden and I have agreed upon a note to Ibrahim, which we proposed having signed by Commodore Milius, if Mons. De Rigny should not return in time, and then sending it in with the hope of stopping him in laying waste the country as he is now doing.

Your very obedient servant,
EDWD. CODRINGTON.

From Sir E. C. to Lady C.

Off Navarin : October 15, 1827.

On the 13th, when close to the southward of Zante, we were joined by both the French and Russian squadrons. It seems that two of the former, the 'Provence' and 'Scipion,' ran foul of each other off Cerigo, that the mainmast of the former was transferred to the latter in Cervi Bay,* a job which does them great credit, and that the 'Provence' is gone to Toulon. The Russians seem to be in good service-like condition, well managed, and very desirous of going hand in hand with us in everything. Count Heiden is quite like one of us, candid, hearty, and eager to act under my orders. Our visit yesterday made us well-acquainted, and as he dines with me to-day, we shall henceforth fully understand one another. I think to-morrow will bring my own two friends from Malta ('Genoa' and 'Albion') and De Rigny back from Zante, where he went on the 13th with his squadron, to get some grub. I offered to share mine with him, having already sent him two sheep and twelve fowls; but as he pressed the point, I did not like to offer any objection to his

* NOTE BY SIR E C.—' De Rigny remained there after "l'Armide" had joined him, in order to see this operation.'

going, ill-timed as it was. I must say that now, after having done what excites the approbation of all hands, I feel some-what proud of my mixed and most extraordinary command. The whole history will be better detailed by others than by myself; for I have not time for more than my actual duty claims, except this little relaxation with you. It is altogether so curious : we have at this minute a Greek brig-of-war in company which brought me letters, and a Turk watching our movements, in addition to our own three flags. Sir G. Don calls the Treaty the tricolour treaty, which I think not inappropriate.

*From Lord Dudley to Sir E. C.**

F. O. : November 5, 1827.

MY DEAR SIR EDWARD,—An Ionian messenger goes to-day, and though it is not my business to communicate with you officially, yet I may be allowed to tell you as a friend how much I am gratified by the spirit and ability you have shown in the late transactions with the Turks.

If this affair is speedily and satisfactorily terminated, you will have contributed your full share to that result.

We are on the tiptoe of expectation for accounts of the effect produced at Constantinople by the communication from Ibrahim Pacha. Upon that depends the turn subsequent events are to take.

Believe me, ever most truly yours,

DUDLEY.

Lord Dudley was Secretary of State for Foreign Affairs : there was no hesitation in expressing approval of the execution by force of a portion of the Treaty, when it had been successful, without a battle. But the account of this bold act of personal and naval respon-sibility, maintained by cannon shot against so superior a force—this first instalment of active hostility—was never published, either from ministerial fear, or from some anti-professional influence at the Admiralty. And so, the gallantry called forth by this almost unique episode, and the success resulting from the moral effect of that gallant bearing, have remained even to this time almost unknown to the English public. It is, however,

* After receiving the account of the encounter with the Turkish fleet off Patras on October 4.

such acts as these that awaken the warm sympathy of Englishmen, and the public acknowledgment of which forms the best incitement to their imitation.

It seemed as if those in England responsible for the Treaty, did not dare to show to the world that its execution against the will of Turkey involved actual hostility. This affair of Patras was a warning—a practical measure of war, sure to culminate in something more serious when the time. might come for enforcing upon the Turkish and Egyptian forces a full compliance with the Treaty. Meanwhile, the warm cordiality of Lord Dudley became checked, and this was the last expression of it. No more private letters were received from him, and the next communication from his Lordship was the official·despatch containing the 'Queries.'

CHAPTER II.

THE following warning from Admiral De Rigny to the French officers in the Turkish fleet was supposed to have been given some time before, when if done it might have had a very advantageous effect.

From Admiral De Rigny to 'Messrs. Letellier, Bompard, et autres Officiers français à bord de la Flotte turque.'

Syrène : le 15 octobre 1827.

MESSIEURS,—La situation dans laquelle vous voyez les flottes ottomanes blocquées dans le port de Navarin, la circonstance du manque de parole de S.A. Ibrahim Pacha, qui s'était engagé à une suspension d'armes provisoire, doit vous indiquer que désormais vous pouvez vous trouver en face de votre pavillon. Vous savez les chances que vous courez, et en vous sommant de quitter le service turc au moment où la flotte ottomane s'est placée dans une situation agressive dont elle doit courir les chances, je vous donne un avis que vous ne devez pas négliger si vous êtes restés Français.

J'ai l'honneur, etc.,
DE RIGNY.

Order by Sir E. C.

Given on board the ' Asia,' off Navarin : October 16, 1827.

WHEREAS, I have received information that a part of the army of Ibrahim Pacha, in direct breach of the agreement which he made with Rear-Admiral De Rigny and myself on September 25 last, has advanced into the plain of Kalamata, where it is ravaging the country, destroying the habitations, and burning the olive and other fruit trees ; and that it is likely to force the pass of Varga for the purpose of going to Maina—you are hereby directed to proceed in the ship you command towards Varga, put yourself in communication

with the Greeks, and use your utmost endeavours not only
to defend them against these barbarities, but to drive back
the army of the Pacha within the lines of Navarin.

EDWARD CODRINGTON.

To G. W. Hamilton, C.B.,
Captain of H. M. Ship 'Cambrian.'

*From the English, French, and Russian Admirals to His
Highness Ibrahim Pacha.*

À bord du vaisseau de S.M.B. 'Asia,' le 17 octobre 1827.

ALTESSE,—Des informations très-positives, qui nous arrivent de toutes parts, nous annoncent que de nombreux dé-
tachemens de votre armée parcourent dans différens sens la
partie occidentale de la Morée; qu'ils dévastent, détruisent,
brûlent, arrachent les arbres, les vignes, toutes les produc-
tions végétales; qu'ils se hâtent enfin de faire de cette contrée un véritable désert.

Nous apprenons de plus, qu'une expédition est préparée
contre les districts de Maina, et que déjà des forces avancent
dans cette direction.

Tous ces actes de violence extrême se passent sous les yeux
pour ainsi dire, et au mépris de l'armistice que Votre Altesse
s'est engagée sous sa parole d'honneur d'observer fidèlement
jusqu'au retour de ses courriers—armistice en faveur duquel
la rentrée de sa flotte à Navarin lui fut accordée le 26 septembre dernier.

Les soussignés se voient dans la pénible obligation de
vous déclarer aujourd'hui qu'une pareille conduite de votre
part, une violation aussi étrange de vos engagemens, vous
placent, Monsieur, hors la loi des nations, et au dehors des
Traités existans entre leurs Cours et la Porte ottomane.

Il y a plus; les soussignés considèrent les dévastations qui
se commettent dans ce moment même par vos ordres, comme
directement contraires aux intérêts de votre souverain, qui
pourroit perdre, en raison de ces dévastations, les avantages
réels que le Traité de Londres lui assure sur la Grèce.

Les soussignés demandent à Votre Altesse une réponse
catégorique et prompte à la présente notification, et ils lui
laissent à prévoir les conséquences immédiates d'un refus ou
d'une tergiversation.

EDWD. CODRINGTON, Vice-Admiral.
LE COMTE DE HEIDEN, Contre-Amiral.
H. DE RIGNY, Contre-Amiral.

From Colonel Cradock to Sir E. C.

H.M.S. 'Dartmouth,' off Navarin: October 18, 1827.

Sir,—In compliance with your desire I proceeded to Navarin with the letter for Ibrahim Pacha from the three Admirals. On entering the Port, Captain Fellowes sent an officer on board the ship bearing the flag of Mucharem Bey, with a request that Mr. Abro, Ibrahim Pacha's interpreter, might be informed of my wish to see him. The officer brought back word that Ibrahim was absent they knew not where, and that Mr. Abro was at Modon, at two hours' distance, but that a messenger should be sent to him, and that he would probably come to Navarin that evening or early the next day. At 10 o'clock this morning Mr. Abro came on board the 'Dartmouth.' I told him that I had a letter signed by the three Admirals which I was directed to deliver to the Pacha. Mr. Abro replied that Ibrahim was not at Navarin. I asked him whether it was not probable that the Pacha might return were he informed that a person had arrived with a letter of great importance from the Admirals, and who wished to present it personally; or, that if he would find me a horse and accompany me, that I would proceed to wherever the Pacha might be, provided it was within a day's distance. Mr. Abro replied that unfortunately there was no means whatever of forwarding the letter to His Highness, as his movements had been kept a profound secret, and that nobody knew where he was. On Mr. Abro giving me his honour of this, I proposed to Captain Fellowes to return to the squadron, and I enclose herewith to Your Excellency the letter with which you entrusted me.

I have, &c.,

HOBART CRADOCK.

Sir E. C. to Lady C.

October 17.

We have sent in a paper to Ibrahim by which we hope to stop his ravaging the country, as he is now doing in mere spite; and at the same time giving him an opening for any fresh proposal which he may have to make, now that he has probably had an answer from his father. We are now assembled in full force. . . . . It is said Ibrahim is very sulky in consequence of being foiled so unexpectedly in the object for which he sacrificed his word of honour; and well he may, for he has heretofore prided himself in his character for both courage and honour, as the Turks understand the latter at least; and I have certainly exposed his want of both, with an inferiority of force which removes all excuse. *He* was probably instructed to avoid war as strongly as *I* was, but I presume he had orders which he was bound to execute at all risks, or else he would not have broken faith; and in this we were equally under the responsibility of originating a war, when peace was the object in view. It is my good fortune to have escaped that extremity; and yet to have effected that with one ship of the line, which was destined to have been performed by twelve.

Now, is not this enough of myself? I think it may do for the present at all events, if I add, that both Harry and myself are quite well. However, you will have more of me from others, for I shall send you the flattering expressions of Sir Frederick Adam, who did not then know the worst which befell me; and of Sir Frederick Ponsonby, another soldier of the same right sort, who knew only the first act of the drama.

I like my new colleague (Admiral Heiden) much; he is a straightforward sort of fellow, and ready, perhaps too ready, to go all lengths. He says if he had not had such positive orders to go to Messina, and had gone to Malta instead, he would have been here a fortnight sooner. He was only three days at Portsmouth; went there unprepared and unknowing his destination, and had to get provisions, &c., for the voyage. Messina ! of all places, the last for the purpose. He has now written to propose Malta.

P.S.—Our letter to Ibrahim is brought back unopened, his lying dragoman saying nobody knows where he is gone. I dare say he will be found to-morrow, if the wind favour our running into an anchorage alongside his ships.

Sir E. C. to Lady Emily Ponsonby at Malta.

Off Navarin: October 18, 1827.

Many thanks, my dear Lady Emily, for your kind chatty note, which accompanied that of the 8th from Ponsonby. The expressions of approbation which I have received from him and from Adam, as coming from men who have none of that which is so well understood by the vulgar word *humbug* about them, are very agreeable to me, and I trust they will have no reason to think otherwise of my subsequent proceedings. My Russian colleague is more of my sort than the other, and is desirous of being always with me and going hand in hand with me on all occasions. De Rigny is quite as much so when we are together, but he has none of that endurance which became the character of our profession in the late war, and which is wanted for the present service. This it is which leads to his being out of the way at particular times when his presence is much wanted, and which brings on him the character of insincerity. However, I might easily have had a worse colleague, and I doubt not, since we now understand each other, we shall get through the business very well.

From Sir E. C. to G. Glaraki, Secretary to Provisional Government of Greece.

'Asia,' off Navarin   October 18, 1827.

SIR,—In answer to your three letters of September 24, last, I shall begin by saying that, as I believe the owners of the 'Achilles' to be much more in fault than the people whom they send to sea for the purpose of committing piracies, instead of doing what they wish I will do my utmost to have the ship destroyed, and to make them responsible for all the damage she has done.

Next, as to the conduct of Captain Lambessi. As his conduct in plundering the 'Kitty' English brig of her cargo, is much more blameable than the conduct of the master of the 'Kitty,' instead of suffering that vessel to be carried before your tribunal, she is already set at liberty : and if the Greek Government and the Greek tribunal had an honest and upright sense of justice, they would punish the Greek captains for such infamous conduct.

You claim from me this vessel as the right of your nation, and you call upon me for justice and humanity in favour of public robbers, against my own countrymen who have not been proved to have committed any offence, and whose commerce it is my duty to protect. And you then talk to me about the rights of a nation whose subjects, under the protection of their government, are committing piracies upon the commerce of the three Allied Powers which are making enormous sacrifices for them. I deny all claim on the part of such a Government, and on the part of a nation that submits to be so governed. I now hear of an Ionian vessel, part of whose cargo was condemned by your tribunal, being plundered at Egina of the remainder by express orders from you, in the name of the Greek Government. When other important matters admit of it, I will give my attention more particularly to these abuses. In the meantime I must inform you that I shall consider you and the individual members composing the present Provisional Government of Greece, as personally responsible for this outrage; and my future applications will be made to the legislative body. With respect to the news contained in the postscript of your letter, I can inform you that if I had not, with only the 'Asia,' 'Dartmouth,' 'Talbot,' and 'Zebra,' placed myself between the whole Turkish fleet and the entrance to the Gulf of Patras, both Captain Hastings and Captain Thomas, the only people whom I hear of opposing their enemy, would have been entirely destroyed; and had those Greek cruisers which have been seizing English vessels even as far as the Island of Maritimo, been as much disposed to make war against the Turks, they might have made prizes from the scattered Turco-Egyptian fleet, which would have been a source of both profit and honour.

From Captain Hamilton to Sir E. Codrington.

(*Extract.*)

H.M.S. 'Cambrian,' Kitries: October 18, 1827.

I have the honour of informing you that I arrived here yesterday morning in company with the Russian frigate 'Constantine,' the captain of which ship had placed himself under my orders. On entering the gulf, we observed by clouds of fire and smoke, that the work of devastation was still going on. The ships were anchored off the pass of Ancyro, and a joint letter from myself and the Russian captain was despatched to the Turkish commander, a copy of which I enclose; the Russian and English officers, the bearers of it, were not allowed to proceed to head-quarters, nor have we yet received any answer. In the afternoon we, the two captains, went on shore to the Greek quarters, and were received with the greatest enthusiasm. The distress of the inhabitants driven from the plain is shocking! women and children dying every moment of absolute starvation, and hardly any having better food than boiled grass! I have promised to send a small quantity of bread to the caves in the mountains, where these unfortunate wretches have taken refuge. It is supposed that if Ibrahim remained in Greece, more than a third of its inhabitants will die of absolute starvation.

Protocol of the three Admirals.
(*Translation.*)

Off Navarin : October 18, 1827.

The Admirals commanding the squadrons of the three Powers which signed the Treaty of London, having met before Navarin for the purpose of concerting the means of effecting the object specified in .the said Treaty, viz., an armistice de facto between the Turks and the Greeks, have set forth in the present protocol the result of their conference.

Considering that after the provisional suspension of hostilities to which Ibrahim Pacha consented,·in his conference of the 25th of September last with the English and French Admirals, acting likewise in the name of the Russian Admiral, the said Pacha did the very next day violate the engagement, by causing his fleet to come out with a view to its proceeding to another point in the Morea :

Considering that, since the return of that fleet to Navarin in consequence of a second requisition addressed to Ibrahim by Admiral Codrington who had met him near Patras, the troops of this Pacha have not ceased carrying on a species of warfare more destructive and exterminating than before, putting women and children to the sword, burning habitations, and tearing up trees by the roots, in order to complete the devastation of the country :

Considering that, with a view of putting a stop to atrocities which exceed all that has hitherto taken place, the means of persuasion and conciliation, the representations made to the Turkish Chiefs, and the advice given to Mehemet Ali and his son have been treated as mockeries, whilst they might, with one word, have suspended the course of so many barbarities:

Considering that there only remains to the commanders of the allied squadrons the choice between three modes of fulfilling the intentions of their respective Courts, namely:

1st. The continuing throughout the whole of the winter a blockade, difficult, expensive, and perhaps useless, since a storm may disperse the squadrons and afford to Ibrahim the facility of conveying his destroying army to different points of the Morea and the islands ;

2ndly. The uniting the allied squadrons in Navarin itself, and securing by this permanent presence the inaction of the Ottoman fleets; but which mode alone leads to no termination, since the Porte persists in not changing its system ; .

3rdly. The proceeding to take a position with the squadrons in Navarin, in order to renew to Ibrahim propositions which, entering into the spirit of the Treaty, were evidently to the advantage of the Porte itself:

After having taken these three modes into consideration, we have unanimously agreed that this third mode may, without effusion of blood and without hostilities, but simply by the imposing presence of the squadrons, produce a determination leading to the desired object:

We have in consequence adopted it, and set it forth in the present protocol.

Signed by the English, French, and Russian Admirals.

October 18, 1827.

The following notes relating to circumstances immediately preceding the Battle of Navarin, were written down by me some years later from my father's dictation. They were all read over by him, and authenticated by his own corrections.*—JANE B.

Upon leaving Zante after the affair off Patras, I was joined by the Russian squadron. Count Heiden took the earliest moment to visit me on board the 'Asia,' bringing with him Mons. Katakasi, a diplomatist. I saw at once that the Count was a plain-sailing, open-hearted man; which inspired me with a desire to communicate openly and frankly with him upon the duties we had to perform. He spoke very good English, though mixed up with French whenever he found a word in that language more expressive of his meaning. But, before proceeding further, I asked him whether I was to treat his companion with the some confidence with which I proposed to treat himself: to this he replied in the affirmative, and our discussion was pursued on that understanding. I note this now, because on a subsequent occasion, when more intimate with the Count, I expressed my surprise that he, as a sailor, should bring a diplomatist with him to talk over such matters with a brother sailor. He told me that this man, being sent officially with him to make his report to the Emperor, felt himself quite out of his element in having to deal only with sailors. His observation was, 'Que peut-on faire avec ces marins anglais?' and that he (Heiden) had told him that he was quite sure he would find

* Note by Sir E. C., on the manuscript.—' Written down from Sir E. C.'s dictation in October 1838, by J. B. C.'

me candid and open in communication, without interposing
any difficulties; that he brought him on board on the first
occasion to give him an early proof of it, and that on their
return to 'Azoff,' he (Katakasi) repeatedly expressed his astonishment at my free communication on all the subjects of
our discussion, and at my seeming to have no concealment,
no arrière-pensée, whatever. It was, I think, the following
day that we were joined by Admiral de Rigny. He was
considerably junior to Count Heiden, although bearing the
same rank as Rear-Admiral; and wishing to get them upon
good terms with each other, I so expressed myself as to hint
the propriety of his calling upon Count Heiden. I think I
proposed that we should go together: he evaded this at
once by expressing a wish to go to Zante for stock, if I had
no objection to it, as he was very much in want of provisions
for his table: I told him that I believed we had got everything that was to be had there; and that I was very willing
to share it with him, which I could the more readily do, as
our own ships coming from Malta would certainly bring me
a sufficiency of everything. But he still pressed his object
so pertinaciously that, in spite of my strong objections to it,
at a moment when it was material that the three squadrons
should be united and prepared to act in concert, I could no
longer resist it without exciting an unpleasant feeling. This
was an augury of the difficulty I contemplated in uniting
the three divisions as one squadron. Upon the return of
Count De Rigny and the junction of the French and English ships of the line (the former reduced to three by an
accident which happened near Cervi Bay),* it became requisite
to form an order of sailing in two lines. My object was to .
keep the French and Russians, who evidently bore no good
will to each other, as much separated as possible. In this
wish each of my colleagues seemed to share, De Rigny
being well pleased with my proposal, that the French ships
should take station astern of the English in the weather line,
while Count Heiden seemed equally gratified with my plan
that his four line-of-battle ships and his large frigates should
continue in one complete division by themselves, forming the
lee line. I found myself hampered by this jealousy in all
my communications, lest I should seem to give a preference
to one over the other. The two chiefs readily met at dinner,
or otherwise, on board the 'Asia,' but neither of them
seemed disposed to make a visit to the other on board his
own ship. In occasionally drawing up records of our pro-

* It was repaired in Cervi Bay.

ceedings to be signed by each, the paper being in the first instance placed before me for my signature, was put down on the table by me without presenting it preferably to either, and I observed that whichever first took hold of it put his signature next, without acknowledging in the other any superiority ; De Rigny thus putting himself upon an equality with Heiden, although the other was much the oldest rear-admiral of the two.

The object of the Allied Powers was to prevent Ibrahim pursuing his barbarities in Greece. On the union of the three squadrons off Navarin, I found that he was then ravaging the Morea by means of that army which he was bound by the Convention not to employ. This was made known to me by deputations from the Morea, and verified by Captain Hamilton, whom I sent there on purpose to ascertain the fact. A letter upon this was addressed to Ibrahim, signed by myself and colleagues, warning him of the consequences of such breach of honour. This letter was entrusted to Colonel Cradock, and sent in in the ' Dartmouth ' frigate. Colonel Cradock was told upon landing, by Ibrahim's own dragoman, that nobody knew where Ibrahim was to be found, not even he himself being aware of it, and that no other person could open the letter or act upon it, even if they were apprised of its contents. Colonel C. told the dragoman that such was my anxiety that Ibrahim should have this letter, that if he was within a ride of 48 hours and they would give him a horse, he would gladly undertake the journey. But the dragoman persisted that no one knew where he was, and Colonel Cradock had no alternative but to return on board with the letter. What was to be done? some decisive step became necessary. We had been carried away by currents in a calm, and on other occasions had been driven out of sight of Navarin by gales of wind, so as to make effectual blockade impracticable; and if, whilst so driven off, the Ottoman fleet had put to sea in order to pursue their great object of destroying Hydra or any other place, and we had fallen in with them at sea, a battle must have ensued, even according to the very wording of our instructions. Under these circumstances, and considering that Ibrahim had submitted to be driven back from off Patras by a small portion of the force which I then had at my disposal, I felt myself justified in concluding that the imposing spectacle of the whole Allied Squadrons (that force which the Government had deemed ample for the purpose) anchored in the Bay of Navarin, where we could be eye-witnesses of his proceedings, and ready to punish any infraction of his agreement, would awe Ibrahim at once into submission, and thus obtain without bloodshed *the objects of the Treaty*. In the Egyptian squadron Monsr Letellier and several French officers were embarked as naval instructors for their management. Admiral de Rigny, at my request, had written to the principal, warning him that a battle might possibly arise, and that if they were found opposed to their own flag the consequences to them might be very serious, and he therefore advised them to retire from their situations; and although he received in answer a promise that they would do so, he did not feel confident of that result. According to the plan brought out by the ' Dartmouth,' the whole Ottoman forces were anchored in the form of a compact horse-shoe in the entrance portion of the harbour, so as to have the assistance of the batteries; the principal limb being that on the right hand going in, which was occupied by the largest ships. Those ships were anchored as near to each other as they could be in safety; the next in size filling up the intervals, the corvettes and smaller vessels forming a sort of third line, in readiness to direct their fire through any openings that might be left. Three fire-vessels on one ·side and two on the other occupied the entrance part of this horse-shoe, leaving no space for the Allied Squadrons but the passage between them leading directly into the middle of the horse-shoe, where it was contemplated we must necessarily anchor. Admiral de Rigny had received information that this well-concerted position had been preparing, under the direction of Letellier, for four or five days, every one of the Turkish ships having springs on her cables for giving their broadsides the most advantageous direction. The whole scheme was evident to me on the first inspection of it; but being precluded from showing any evidence of hostility, I could not defeat their object by breaking a way between the upper end of their line and the shore, and thus taking them in reverse, as I otherwise should have done: feeling obliged to avoid all appearance of suspicion, and to proceed to the inner part of the horse-shoe which they had prepared for us. The head of the principal line was formed by four double Egyptian frigates, the fourth bearing the flag of Moharem Bey. The next in succession was the principal Turkish division under the Capitan Bey, whose flag was in an 84-gun ship, next to Moharem Bey, forming the fifth ship in that line; next to her was another Turkish ship of the line, and, with two or three frigates intervening, there was a third Turkish ship of .the line in the bight of the horse-shoe.

Having therefore made up my own mind that there was no other means but this of effecting *the object of the Treaty,* my next business was to bring my colleagues to the same conclusion; and the question for my consideration was how to bring this matter about. I had found Count Heiden as ready in every instance to meet my wishes as if he had been an officer of our own navy. With my other colleague the case was very different. In our intercourse at Nauplia, he had shown a rooted dislike to the Greeks and a leaning towards the Egyptians, with whom he had long been in friendly intercourse. I had also found in him so pertinacious an adherence to such details as were suggested by himself, that in order to ensure his yielding to me whatever I considered essential, I embraced every opportunity of giving way to him in matters of *minor* importance. The situation in which I now found myself respecting him was one of great difficulty. Any hesitation or backwardness on the part of either of my colleagues in following me into the Port, would have been our destruction. In order, therefore, to ensure and rely upon the cordial support of Count De Rigny, my object was to lead him, as if of himself, to the same conclusion which the above circumstances had produced in me. I relied upon the wearisome nature of the blockade service for giving me this opportunity, and my hopes were realised shortly afterwards. Upon Admiral De Rigny coming on board one morning to make me a friendly visit, I adverted to the difficult and harassing prospect before us of a winter blockade; and this brought us to the point at once. He treated the blockade as a thing impossible to be continued, and considered the attempt to execute it as tantamount to giving up the object of the Treaty; since Ibrahim could move his army in any direction he pleased, even if he did not take advantage of our occasional absence to put to sea with his fleet. I expressed my accordance in this, suggesting at the same time the strong censure which would be thrown upon us for the failure, however unjust it might be; and then put the direct question of—'Does any remedy occur to you?' After a little consideration he said, 'None—except going into the port and anchoring in company with the Ottoman Fleet.' I then asked him if he had thought of this before, and had weighed all the consequences; candidly telling him that I had been for some time persuaded that it was our only means of preventing the barbarities of Ibrahim and effecting the objects of the Treaty. He said, No; that the suggestion

arose out of our present conversation, and that if I approved
of it, he was ready to join me in carrying it into execution
at once. I pointed out to him the possible consequences if
the measure should be disapproved of by our Governments; warning him that though the principal portion of
censure would fall upon me, he was sure to obtain his share
from his own Government; adding, that I thought he had
better go on board and sleep upon it before he entirely made
up his mind. He said, No; it was not requisite; that he saw
all the consequences, and was perfectly ready. He staid with
me about an hour; when, finding him apparently quite steady
to his purpose, I said: 'If your mind is as much made up as
it appears to be, I will at once make the signal for Count
Heiden and hear what he has to say about it.' To this he
acceded; and upon the plan being communicated to the
Count, he frankly signified his full approval, and his readiness to take whatever part I might point out. This determination being settled, I became strongly impressed with the
great difficulty—in preparing for the contingency of a battle—
in preventing the possible ill-effects of the jealousy evinced
by my Allies towards each other, and the consequent liability
to failure from want of union. I therefore resisted their
desire that I should at once indicate to them the positions I
intended them to take, begging them to return to their ships
and to leave me to consider that matter undisturbed. My
plan had been made at the time of the measure having first
occurred to me, from a consideration of the position of the
Ottoman fleet as pointed out in a sketch taken on board the
'Dartmouth' when I sent her in with Colonel Cradock.
This plan I now determined to pursue; but I had some
doubts how to make it palatable to my colleagues. As soon
as they were gone—being left alone in my cabin with Colonel
Cradock—I ejaculated: 'Now comes my difficulty! how am
I to ensure the cordial co-operation of these two people;
seeing that there is such a rooted jealousy between them that
they would as lief be engaged with each other as with the
Ottoman Forces?' Colonel Cradock then said to me: 'I
think, sir, you said when you were looking over the plan
made in the 'Dartmouth,' that you had made up your mind
how the Allied fleets should be placed in the bay if such a
measure should become necessary?' I said: 'Yes; and I
see no reason for altering the opinion I then formed, now
that the determination is made. I should go in in the order
of sailing, for two reasons—first, because we can be equally
prepared for defence if attacked; and secondly, because it
will remove all objection to my leading in in the 'Asia,' as I

certainly shall do. My plan is, that De Rigny in his double frigate, followed by his three ships of the line, shall anchor abreast of the four Egyptian double frigates, which form the head of the principal Ottoman line on the right hand of the Bay; that the English squadron shall take station next to them, each of us having our own frigates abreast of us on the opposite line of the Ottoman fleet; and that the Russian squadron shall have the bight of the Bay to themselves; . thus placing the English division in both lines between the French and Russian ships, so as to prevent any unpleasant occurrence taking place between them : but this gives two of the Ottoman ships of the line to the English division, and the remaining one to Count Heiden, whilst it gives the French division only the four double frigates-; and this, I suspect, will excite jealousy on the part of De Rigny.' ' Sir,' said Cradock, ' as Admiral De Rigny by your desire has had a correspondence with the French officers employed in the Egyptian squadron, warning them of the contingency of their being opposed in battle to the French flag, and advising them to retire immediately—cannot you satisfy Admiral De Rigny by pointing out to him the probability of his ensuring their retirement by anchoring as you propose ?— whereas, on the contrary, if any part of the Russian squadron were so placed, it would produce a contrary effect and secure to the Ottoman division the benefit of their assistance ?' ' Thank ye,' said I, ' you have relieved me at once from my difficulty '—and I then drew out the order to my two col- leagues, which was subsequently carried into execution.

Instructions as to the Manner of Placing the Combined Fleet in the Port of Navarin.

'Asia,' off Navarin : October 19, 1827.

It appears that the Egyptian ships in which the French officers are embarked, are those most to the south-east; it is, therefore, my wish that his Excellency Rear-Admiral Chevalier de Rigny should place his squadron abreast of them. As the next in succession appears to be a ship of the line with a flag at the main, I propose placing the 'Asia' abreast of her, with the ' Genoa' and ' Albion' next to the 'Asia ,' and I wish that his Excellency Rear-Admiral Count Heiden will have the goodness to place his squadron next in succession to the British ships of the line. The Russian frigates in this case can occupy the Turkish ships next in succession to the Russian ships of the line ; the English frigates forming alongside such Turkish vessels as may be on the western side of the harbour abreast of the British ships of the line; and the French frigates forming in the same manner, so as to occupy the Turkish frigates, &c. abreast of the French ships of the line. If time permits, before any hostility is committed by the Turkish fleet, the ships are to moor with springs on the ring of each anchor. No gun is to be fired from the combined fleet without a signal being made for that purpose, unless shot be fired from any of the Turkish ships; in which case the ships so firing are to be destroyed immediately. The corvettes and the brigs, are under the direction of Captain Fellowes of the 'Dartmouth,' to remove the fire-vessels into such a position as will prevent their being able to injure any of the combined fleet. In case of a regular battle ensuing and creating any of that confusion which must naturally arise from it, it is to be observed, that, in the words of Lord Nelson, 'No captain can do very wrong who places his ship alongside that of an enemy.'

EDWD. CODRINGTON, Vice-Admiral.

From Sir E. C. to the President and Members of the Legislative Body of the Greek Nation.

'Asia,' off Navarin: October 19, 1827.

GENTLEMEN,—The conduct of the Provisional Government of Greece, and of the Marine Tribunal, has been so unjust and so injurious to the commerce of the Allied Powers, and they have so entirely falsified the promises they made to me, that I shall decline writing to them henceforth, and must beg to communicate with you instead. In consequence of a direct breach of the word of honour given me by Ibrahim Pacha, I found myself with only two small frigates and a brig opposed to the whole of the Turco-Egyptian force at the entrance of the Gulf of Patras. I well knew the Pacha's object was to destroy the vessels commanded by Captains Hastings and Thomas, and the others with them in the Gulf of Lepanto; and as that was the only Greek force which I knew of being employed against their enemy, I determined to run all risks with the very inferior force I had with me to secure their protection. I had the good fortune of being successful in saving those brave men from destruction. Judge, Gentlemen, under these circumstances, what are my feelings that in the meantime the boasting Hydriotes, Spezziots, Ipsariotes, &c., have been plundering the ships of all nations, even at the distance of Malta and Maritimo: and that ar-

rangements have been forming for distant and useless enter-
prises : and judge of my indignation at finding that their so
cruising has been under the sanction of your Provisional
Government. If the sums which have been expended in
fitting out these corsairs had been laid out for the purpose
of attacking the Turks, honour and profit would have attended
it, for the Turkish fleet has been dispersed over these seas ;
and the wretched people of Kalamata and that neighbourhood
would not be living upon boiled grass, as Captain Hamilton,
whom I sent to prevent the advance of the Turkish army,
informs me they are now doing. I have only time to add at
present, that the united fleet of the Allied Powers is about
to enter the port of Navarin, for the purpose of preventing any
further operations on the part of the Egyptian expedition.

I am, &c.,

EDWD. CODRINGTON.

Sir E. C. to Lady C.

October 19, 7 P.M.

Well, this day has gone by with all preparation and no
fight. The wind was not strong enough to carry us in, and
we must now take the chance of what to-morrow produces.
I have given out my Instructions, which seem to please my
two colleagues, each being content with the part allotted to
him, and my own squadron appear to be so perfectly up to
the mark, that they will think it a pity if it all end in smoke.
Such is, however, my own expectation, although the Turks
have apparently made every preparation to receive us. The
French officers who were in the Egyptian ships have retired,
according to De Rigny's advice, except Letellier the chief,
-and are now embarked in an Austrian merchant brig. This
Ibrahim, who boasted to us his humanity and complained
of being called in the newspapers the ' Sanguinary Ibrahim,'
is ravaging the whole country; and Hamilton, whom I sent
to drive back his army near Kalamata, tells me that some of
the poor houseless wretches in the country which he has
desolated, are living upon boiled grass ! God bless you and
yours, say I; a sentiment I may I hope repeat and repeat
again.   Yours, E. C.

The following day, however, did not go by with ' no
fight'—the crisis had come, and the 20th of October
was a day of fate to many: a full and complete detail of
its circumstances and results is furnished by the following collection of official and private letters.

The OTTOMAN FORCE consisted of:—

    3 line-of-battle ships.
    4 double-banked frigates.
  13 frigates.
  30 corvettes.
  28 brigs.
    6 fire brigs.
    5 schooners.
    (exclusive of 41 transports.)

  89

35,000 Egyptian troops in the Morea, 4,000 of whom came with the above ships, as stated by the Secretary to the Capitana Bey.

The ALLIED FORCE consisted of:—

ENGLISH.

    3 line-of-battle ships.
    4 frigates.
    4 brigs.
    1 cutter.

FRENCH.
    3 line-of-battle ships.
    1 double-banked frigate.
    1 frigate.
    2 cutters.

RUSSIAN.
    4 line-of-battle ships.
    4 frigates.

  24 ships of war.

From Sir E. C. to the Admiralty.

H.M.S 'Asia,' in the port of Navarin : October 21, 1827.

SIR,—I have the honour of informing his Royal Highness the Lord High Admiral that my colleagues, Count Heiden and the Chevalier De Rigny, having agreed with me that we should come into this port, in order to induce Ibrahim Pacha to discontinue the brutal war of extermination which he has been carrying on since his return here from his failure in the Gulf of Patras, the combined squadrons passed the batteries, in order to take up their anchorage, at about 2 o'clock yesterday afternoon.

The Turkish ships were moored in the form of a crescent, with springs on their cables, the larger ones presenting their broadsides towards the centre, the smaller ones, in succession, within them, filling up the intervals.

The combined fleet was formed in the order of sailing in

two columns; the British and French forming the weather
or starboard line, and the Russian the lee line.

The 'Asia' led in, followed by the 'Genoa' and 'Albion,'
and anchored close alongside a ship of the line bearing the
flag of the Capitana Bey, another ship of the line, and a
large double-banked frigate; each thus having their proper
opponent in the front line of the Turkish fleet. The four
ships to windward, part of the Egyptian squadron, were
allotted to the squadron of Rear-Admiral De Rigny; and
those to leeward, in the bight of the crescent, were to mark
the stations of the whole Russian squadron, the ships of their
line closing those of the English line, and being followed up
by their own frigates.

The French frigate 'Armide' was directed to place herself
alongside the outermost frigate on the left-hand entering the harbour; and the 'Cambrian,' 'Glasgow,' and
'Talbot' next to her, and abreast of the 'Asia,' 'Genoa,' and
'Albion.'   The 'Dartmouth' and the 'Musquito,' the
'Rose,' the 'Brisk,' and the 'Philomel' were to look
after six fire-vessels at the entrance of the harbour. I gave
orders that no gun should be fired unless guns were first
fired by the Turks; and those orders were strictly observed.
The three English ships were accordingly permitted to pass
the batteries and to moor, as they did with great rapidity,
without any act of open hostility, although there was evident
preparation for it in all the Turkish ships; but upon the
'Dartmouth' sending a boat to one of the fire-vessels, Lieutenant G. W. H. Fitz Roy and several of her crew were shot
with musketry. This produced a defensive fire of musketry
from the 'Dartmouth' and 'la Syrène,' bearing the flag of
Rear-Admiral De Rigny; that was succeeded by a cannon-
shot at the Rear-Admiral from one of the Egyptian ships,
which of course brought on a return; and thus very shortly
afterwards the battle became general. The 'Asia,' although
placed alongside the ship of the Capitana Bey, was even
nearer to that of Moharem Bey, the commander of the
Egyptian ships; and since his ships did not fire at the 'Asia,'
although the action was begun to windward, neither did the
'Asia' fire at her. The latter, indeed, sent a message 'that
he would not fire at all,' and therefore no hostility took
place betwixt our two ships for some time after the 'Asia'
had returned the fire of the Capitana Bey. In the meantime, however, our excellent pilot, Mr. Peter Mitchell, who
went to interpret to Moharem my desire to avoid bloodshed,
was killed by his people in our boat alongside. Whether with
or without his orders I know not, but his ship soon after-

wards fired into the 'Asia,' and was consequently effectually destroyed by the 'Asia's' fire, sharing the same fate as his brother-admiral on the starboard side, and falling to leeward a mere wreck. These ships being out of the way, the 'Asia' became exposed to a raking fire from vessels in the second and third line, which carried away her mizenmast by the board, disabled some of her guns, and killed and wounded some of her crew. This narration of the proceedings of the 'Asia' would probably be equally applicable to most of the other ships of the fleet. The manner in which the 'Genoa' and 'Albion' took their stations was beautiful; and the conduct of my brother-admirals, Count Heiden and the Chevalier De Rigny, throughout, was admirable and highly exemplary.

Captain Fellowes executed the part allotted to him perfectly; and with the able assistance of his little but brave detachment, saved the 'Syrène' from being burnt by the fire-vessels. And the 'Cambrian,' 'Glasgow,' and 'Talbot,' following the fine example of Capitaine Hugon, of the 'Armide,' who was opposed to the leading frigate of that line, effectually destroyed their opponents, and also silenced the batteries. This bloody and destructive battle was continued with unabated fury for four hours, and the scene of wreck and devastation which presented itself at its termination was such as has been seldom before witnessed. As each ship of our opponents became effectually disabled, such of her crew as could escape from her endeavoured to set her on fire; and it is wonderful how we avoided the effects of their successive and awful explosions.

It is impossible for me to say too much for the able and zealous assistance which I derived from Captain Curzon thoughout this long and arduous contest; nor can I say more than it deserves for the conduct of Commander Baynes and the officers and crew of the 'Asia' for the perfection with which the fire of their guns was directed; each vessel in turn to which her broadside was directed, became a complete wreck.

His Royal Highness will be aware that so complete a victory by a few, however perfect, against an excessive number, however individually inferior, cannot be acquired but at a considerable sacrifice of life; accordingly I have to lament the loss of Captain Bathurst of the 'Genoa,' whose example on this occasion is well worthy the imitation of his survivors.

Captain Bell commanding the Royal Marines of the 'Asia,' an excellent officer, was killed early in the action in the steady performance of his duty; and I have to mourn the death of Mr. William Smith the master, admired for the zeal and ability with which he executed his duty, and beloved by all for his private qualities as a man. Mr. Henry S. Dyer, my secretary, having received a severe contusion from a splinter, I am deprived temporarily of his valuable assistance in collecting and keeping up the general returns and communications of the squadrons; I shall therefore retain in my office Mr. E. I. T. White, his first clerk, whom I have nominated to succeed the Purser of the 'Brisk.' I feel much personal obligation to the Hon. Lieut.-Col. Cradock for his readiness during the heat of the battle in carrying my orders and messages to the different quarters after my aides-de-camp were disabled; but I will beg permission to refer his Royal Highness for further particulars of this sort to the details of the killed and wounded; a subject which it is painful for me to dwell upon when I contemplate, as I do with extreme sorrow, the extent of our loss. I console myself with the reflection that the measure which produced the battle was absolutely necessary for obtaining the results contemplated by the Treaty, and that it was brought on entirely by our opponents.

When I found that the boasted Ottoman's word of honour was made a sacrifice to wanton, savage devastation; and that a base advantage was taken of our reliance upon Ibrahim's good faith, I own I felt a desire to punish the offenders. But it was my duty to refrain, and refrain I did; and I can assure his Royal Highness that I would still have avoided this disastrous extremity if other means had been open to me. The 'Asia,' 'Genoa,' and 'Albion' have each suffered so much, that it is my intention to send them to England as soon as they shall have received at Malta the necessary repairs for their voyage. The 'Talbot' being closely engaged with a double-banked frigate, has also suffered considerably, as well as others of the smaller vessels; but I hope their defects are not more than can be made good at Malta. The loss of men in the Turco-Egyptian ships must have been immense, as his Royal Highness will see by the accompanying list obtained from the secretary of the Capitana Bey, which includes that of two out of the three ships to which the English division was opposed. Captain Curzon having preferred continuing to assist me in the 'Asia,' I have given the charge of my despatches to Commander Lord Viscount Ingestrie, who, besides having a brilliant share in the action, is well competent to give his Royal Highness the Lord High Admiral any further particulars he may require.

I enclose for his Royal Highness's further information a

letter from Captain Hamilton* descriptive of the proceedings of Ibrahim Pacha, and the misery of the country which he has devastated; a protocol of a conference which I had with my colleagues;† and the plan and order for entering the port, which I gave out in consequence.‡

I have, &c.,

EDWD. CODRINGTON, Vice-Admiral.

Memorandum written by Sir E. C.

By Admiral Codrington sending in the 'Dartmouth' frigate with a letter from the three Admirals to warn Ibrahim Pacha of the consequences to himself of his continuing to devastate the country contrary to his agreement, he obtained a correct knowledge of the position of the Ottoman ships and of their preparation for battle. But as he wished to effect the object of the Treaty without bloodshed, if possible, he avoided every appearance of hostility, and anchored his ships within the crescent formed by the Ottoman ships instead of forcing an opening through the fire-vessels which closed the horns of the crescent with the shore as he could easily have done, and then taking them in reverse where they were unprepared. With the view also of not showing any suspicion that the Turks would fire on his squadron, he did not form the line of battle, but preserved the usual order of sailing in two lines. He allotted to the French division the four Egyptian double frigates which were the four first ships on the right hand. But the only one which reached the position indicated by him was the 'Syrène' double frigate, bearing Count De Rigny's flag, and she became placed between the first and second instead of engaging the first only, in consequence of the first cannon-shot fired by the Turks cutting her cable in two the moment she was about to let go her anchor. The two French ships of the line, 'le Scipion' and 'le Trident,' anchored nearer the entrance of the harbour, and eventually engaged the batteries. But the 'Scipion' being set on fire by one of the fire-vessels, was saved from being burnt by the English boats commanded in person by Captain Davies of the 'Rose,' under the orders of Captain Fellowes of the 'Dartmouth,' and the boats afterwards saved the 'Syrène' in the same manner. The third of the Egyptian ships not being occupied as intended by one of the French ships, continued to fire into the 'Asia's' larboard side all the time she was engaged on the starboard side with a Turkish 84 and a double frigate, having a cor-

* See page 60.   † Page 61.   ‡ Page 68.

vette and a brig keeping up a raking fire into her stern. The sternmost ship of the French, the 'Breslau,' 74, kept her course into the bay, and eventually anchored close to and greatly assisted the 'Azoff,' bearing the flag of Count Heiden.   The fourth Egyptian ship, bearing the flag of Moharem Bey, the brother-in-law of Ibrahim Pacha, did not open her fire for about three-quarters of an hour, by which time the 'Asia' had destroyed her starboard side opponents, and had sprung or turned her larboard broadside towards the third Egyptian ship, which was still firing at her   At this moment the ship of Moharem began to fire also ; and in about ten minutes the 'Asia's' fire destroyed them both; the one was driven ashore dismasted, and the other was blown up.   The 'Asia' then had to spring her broadside round again to destroy the corvettes and brigs which had been raking her during the whole time of the battle unopposed by anything except the little 'Hind' cutter, and by which vessels she had lost her mizenmast and been much cut up about the stern.   During this period the third Egyptian ship continued burning ; and the wind then being in a direct line from her, and the smoke greatly increasing, it appeared to the fleet as if she had fallen on board and set fire to the 'Asia.' This produced a temporary cessation in that part of the battle, in order if possible to send boats to her assistance, when the Egyptian ship suddenly blew up, and the 'Asia' was seen uninjured by the explosion ; the Admiral was observed still on the poop, where he had taken his station during the battle.   The feelings of the crews contiguous were then expressed by three hearty cheers, and the battle recommenced. Of the ships engaged by Admiral De Rigny, one was sunk and the other blew up ; and of those around Count Heiden there was a similar destruction.

Letter sent by the three Admirals to the Turkish Commanders at Navarin.

(Translation.)

Navarin : October 21, 1827.

As the squadrons of the Allied Powers did not enter Navarin with an hostile intention, but only to renew to the Commanders of the Turkish fleet propositions which were to the advantage of the Grand Signior himself, it is not our intention to destroy what ships of the Ottoman navy may yet remain, now that so signal a vengeance has been taken for the first cannon-shot which has been ventured to be fired on the Allied flags.

No. 1.

No. 2.

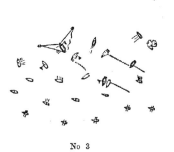

No 3

No 4

We send, therefore, one of the Turkish captains, fallen into our hands as a prisoner, to make known to Ibrahim Pacha, Moharem Bey, Tahir Pacha, and Capitana Bey, as well as to all the other Turkish chiefs, that if one single musket or cannon-shot be again fired on a ship or boat of the Allied Powers, we shall immediately destroy all the remaining vessels, as well as the forts of Navarin; and that we shall consider such new act of hostility as a formal decla-ration of the Porte against the three Allied Powers, of which the Grand Signior and his Pachas must suffer the terrible consequences.

But if the Turkish chiefs, acknowledging the aggression they have committed by commencing the firing, abstain from any act of hostility, we shall resume those terms of good understanding which they have themselves interrupted. In this case, they will have the white flag hoisted on all the forts before the end of this day.

We demand a categorical answer, without evasions, before sunset.

Signed by the English, French, and Russian Admirals.

From Sir E. C. to Lady C.

October 20, 10 P.M.

Well, my dear, the Turks have fought, and fought well too; and we have annihilated their fleet. But it has cost us dear. We have lost poor Smith, Captain Bell (R.M.), and many good men. I was *slued round* more than once, and Harry has a slight wound which will ensure him his pro-motion directly he has served his time. He wants to write to you himself, but I wish to keep him quiet that he may not get the least fever, and I do not think I shall let him. He was sound asleep when I went down to see him, in one of the cockpit cabins, where he is better off until I can get something like a cabin. Little Hanmer Bunbury has lost an arm, but will do well. Harry told me a delightful anecdote of him: he had some water given him, and hearing a poor sufferer call anxiously for water, he gave it to him directly. Now, my dear, don't fancy anything more than I tell you. *I* am entirely unhurt; but the 'Asia' is quite a wreck, having had her full allowance of the work. Our men fired beautifully; my two colleagues and the brave men they commanded behaved admirably; and nothing could exceed the style in which my own ships went into action. I went to see poor Bathurst just now, and take leave of him, for he cannot live! The delight of the poor fellow upon my telling him that his ship took up her station as well as a ship could do, was gratifying to me. I have yet no list of the killed and wounded, but I fear it is considerable, and that there will be some difficulty in obtaining it, without delaying the despatch for England.

October 21, 1827.

I will not pass this anniversary, my dear Jane, without assuring you that your dear Harry is as well as it is possible to be. He is such a favourite that he never wants a friend to talk with him; and he seems to have spun a very long yarn for you into the bargain. He laments being kept down below and losing the magnificent explosions to which these Turks are constantly treating us, by blowing up all their crippled ships in succession: but he is so well as he is, that I will not let him be moved until I can have a berth in my cabin for him. If I can, I will get you copies of the public documents relative to this (as I trust I may follow the example of others in calling it) very splendid victory. But as I was in too excited a state to profit by lying down last night, I must quit my pen for my pillow; where my heart will equally say, as my pen does, may God bless you and yours!—E. C.

October 23, 1 p m.

Our dear boy is doing quite well. His good temper would assuage a fever if he had one—but he has not the least: he reads whenever he is not, Pacha-like, giving audience. It is worth such a wound to have been in such a glorious battle. Write a line to Will. by Ingestrie, if he is able to see you on this way. The 'Dartmouth,' which takes him to Ancona, will wait and bring you back from thence.

God bless you, again!
E. C.

From Lady C. to Sir E. C.

Florence · November 6.

God bless you! and God bless our dear boy! I will write to-morrow; at present I only add this line to Jane's letter to let you see I have survived the joy and pride your noble and gallant conduct and, above all, your safety, has given. I hope and believe from all you say that our dear Hal. is going on well. Once more, God bless you both!

From Lady C. to Sir E. C.

Florence : November 12.

Now that the first and indescribable sensations on reading
your account of the battle you have passed through have a
little subsided, I must try to write to you in a little more
collected manner than I could have done before.   That we
are all full of *joy* and *pride* and *thankfulness* you may well
suppose; but I believe the *latter* predominates in *me*, who
am more given to fear than to hope for those dear to me,
under such appalling circumstances ! How is it possible that
for *four* hours you should have been exposed to so tremendous
a fire (as Lord Ingestrie writes to me) on the poop and yet be
untouched.   And shall I not be grateful to that Power who has
protected you through such imminent danger ? I am indeed,
both for that and the narrower escape of our dear Harry.
Alas, I grieve that he has been wounded at all; but when I
think how very near he was to destruction, how many there
are who, although spared the extremest evil, are yet much
more severe sufferers than he is, I am *full of thankfulness* for
that blessing too.   All other joys appear to me dull and
insipid compared to the grateful happiness arising from the
safety of two such valued beings after such terrific scenes
of destruction as you were surrounded by.   Once more let
me relieve my still overflowing heart by devoutly thanking
God for your preservation.

It was, I think, on the 5th November that the news
of the Battle of Navarin reached Florence; and it was
towards evening that we saw the Ambassador's carriage
drive quickly across the large open space of Santa Maria
and stop at our door.   Having lately had the news of
the encounter at Patras, we were strung up to anxious
expectation as to what might come next.   But when we
found he had, on getting out, sent his carriage away,
fear took the upper hand, and with it the foreboding
that he was come to comfort us under evil tidings. My
mother and I stood transfixed with suspense till Lord
Burghersh entered with his beaming, kindly face, ex-
claiming, ' I have the best possible news for you!'
He spent two hours with us, eagerly conning over all
the details in the letters ; and it was not till he left
us that my mother found relief in tears, and in the

burst of gratitude that sent her on her knees to pour
out her fervent thanksgiving.—J. B.

From Lord Burghersh, Ambassador at Florence, to Sir E.
Codrington.

November 6, 1827

MY DEAR SIR EDWARD,—I give you my most hearty congratulations on your triumphant exploits.   I admire you
beyond measure; you have achieved one of the great things
in the annals of our country.   Immediately upon the receipt
of your letter I went to Lady Codrington, and I did my best
to break the news of your son's wound, and to diminish the
alarms she would feel at the first mention of such an event.
I hope I in some measure succeeded; but it is impossible to
describe the scene, between the joy at your triumphs and
your escape, and yet the feel of the danger both yourself
and the darling boy had been exposed to.   I wish you had
Force sufficient to appear immediately off the Dardanelles, if
it were only to send a *friendly message*.   When I was with
Duckworth, if instead of going to the Islands of Prota we
had gone to within gun-shot of the seraglio, we should have
made peace by the alarm created, without further expenditure of powder.

Yours most sincerely,
BURGHERSH.

No more private letters passed at this time.   The
'Dartmouth' took the despatches announcing the battle
to Ancona, from whence Lord Ingestrie carried them
overland to England.   Lady Codrington and her three
daughters left Florence; and after a severe journey,
crossing the snow-covered Apennines, they sailed in the
'Dartmouth' from Ancona on the 19th; a very trying
passage of nine days, with every variety of foul wind,
head sea, and dead calm, to aggravate and prolong their
anxiety, brought them to Malta at last on the 28th November.   On entering the harbour Lady C. saw there
the Navarin ships, and among them the 'Asia,' with
nothing above her deck, the wounded masts having been
removed, and the Admiral's blue flag flying on a boat's
mast.

In the Admiral's house she found her son going about on crutches, and her husband just recovered from a sharp attack of illness that had followed upon the anxious days spent on the coast and inside the Bay of Navarin.

On the 20th October Sir Edward Codrington had taken up his station on the poop, which afforded him a commanding position for watching all the parts of the battle; he only left it once, and it was to go forward and endeavour to get a view, round the smoke, of some portion of Capitan Bey's ship, so as to see whether she was still in the same position, and the 'Asia's' fire rightly directed to her. It was while standing at the knight-head that Mr. Lewis, the boatswain, to whom he was speaking, was killed close beside him. Indeed, as he afterwards said, it seemed as if every man he spoke to was to be killed before him. On the poop, Mr. Smith, the master, was in conversation with him when struck down and killed by a shot; and a shot shattered the head of Capt. Bell, of the marines, while standing very near him on the quarter-deck. Towards the close of the battle he went below for a few minutes to see his wounded boy. He had not seen him disabled, and when he first missed him from his station, he was afraid to ask what had become of him—whether he was alive, or not? He himself, though a tall man standing in that exposed position, and remaining at one time the only individual on deck, all others having been either disabled or sent below by him with orders,—was never wounded; but he had several wonderfully narrow escapes. He was of course in uniform, but wearing instead of his cocked hat a round hat which afforded better shade to his eyes; this hat was pierced right through the upper part of both sides, by a bullet which left two distinct holes, but did not actually touch his head. The same thing happened to his coat sleeve, which he habitually wore rather loose, and which, just above the wrist, had two holes from a bullet which pierced it without wounding his arm. On one occasion his watch was the means of saving his life: he wore it, not in the waistcoat pocket as at the present day, but according to the custom of his own day, in a fob, with a broad ribbon and one seal depending from it. A ball struck the watch in his fob, indented its gold sides and broke its works, and *left him uninjured!* Indeed, he seemed to bear a charmed life, for Tahir Pacha afterwards told Mr. Kerigan and others on board His Majesty's ship 'Blonde,' that he had himself during the battle directed a company of riflemen to take aim at the English Admiral and shoot him if they could. During the latter part of the battle, after the 'Asia' had conquered her chief opponent, and suffered much herself from others while doing so, he continued walking up and down on the poop from side to side of the ship.* The Asia's mizen-mast, which had been badly wounded, fell with all the wreck of sails and rigging hanging about it, right aft over the poop; and the Admiral in his short turns up and down had only just passed from the spot where it fell, in time to save him from being crushed under it in its fall.

From Sir E. C. to Admiral De Rigny.

Navarin: October 23, 1827.

SIR,—When Your Excellency did me the honour of voluntarily placing yourself and the French squadron under my command, you gave me a right to judge, in that situation, by making me, in a great degree, responsible for it. I take advantage, then, of that right to say that I contemplated your way of leading your squadron into battle, on the 20th, with the greatest pleasure; that nothing can exceed the good management of the ships under your especial direction; and that my having had you under my orders in that bloody and destructive engagement will be one of the proudest events of my whole professional life. Although it was my wish to avoid entering into any particular detail, the general expressions of the captains of the British ships who were near the 'Armide' call upon me to say that the conduct of Captain Hugon entitles him to the marked consideration of Your Excellency.

A letter was addressed by Sir Edward to the Russian Admiral in nearly similar terms.

* On stooping his head under the awning rolled up, a shot passed through its folds.

Count Heiden having read the letter which Captain Maude gave him from the Admiral, expressed his highest satisfaction, and said that it was in itself a reward as great as any he could receive from his own sovereign.*

From Admiral Heiden to Sir E. C.

(Extract.)

'Azoff,' dans la baie de Valette, le 8 novembre 1827.

MONSIEUR L'AMIRAL,—La lettre obligeante et trop flatteuse qu'elle a bien voulu m'adresser après le combat du $\frac{8}{20}$ octobre, est un document qui restera à jamais gravé dans mon cœur, et sera l'héritage de mes fils.   Qui n'aurait pas fait son devoir, Monsieur l'Amiral, dans cette mémorable journée, ayant sous les yeux l'exemple de sang-froid et de bravoure déterminée offert par l''Asie,' où flottait votre noble pavillon?

La journée la plus heureuse de ma vie a été celle où j'ai pu me montrer comme marin, scruté par un amiral anglais, —les héros de la mer, et les plus généreux des alliés comme des ennemis.

From Sir E. C. to H.R.H. Duke of Clarence.

'Asia,' in Navarin: October 21, 1827.

SIR,—Since we were unavoidably forced into collision with the Turkish fleet, Your Royal Highness may not object to receive my congratulations on the ships under my orders having done their duty admirably on the occasion.   It would have done Your Royal Highness's heart good to have seen the tremendous effect of the 'Asia's' guns.   They were worked with a precision which looked like mere exercise; and yet, as the state of the ship and the casualties evince, there were causes to disturb men less trained than they are. The Capitana Bey's ship, according to his secretary's account, lost 650 men killed out of 850.†   Her hull had the appearance of being tasted by the adze preparatory to being docked.   I really believe all the ships did their duty equally well.   The lamented death of Captain Bathurst has enabled me to promote Captain Davies, of the 'Rose,' a man whose merits, since I have had this command, have entitled him to the best rewards of the service.   If Lord Ingestrie had also

* In the port of Navarin—after the battle: written down by Captain Curzon.

† The badly wounded were left to die.

been without other protection, I should have promoted him, in payment of a debt I owe him for having sunk a fire-vessel which he was charged to dispose of, by so well directed a fire that she could hardly make any opposition. But Captain Anson, whom I have so often employed on important services, and who never makes a difficulty, has equally served his commander's time, and has equal claims that I should recommend him to the consideration of Your Royal Highness.

My friend Spencer, in the little 'Talbot,' silenced the guns of a large frigate, single-handed; and it was not in default of opposition on the part of the Turks, for they fought with their characteristic obstinacy, and were prepared with more ability than they have in general credit for. It seems that our decision to remove the fire-ships defeated their plans, and precipitated the battle, which was intended to have been commenced at midnight, by an attempt to destroy our ships by means of these very fire-vessels. In consequence of the desire expressed by Your Royal Highness, in your late letter of September 2nd, I have decided on putting Lieutenant Edwardes to act in the 'Gannet,' and I have given the commander's commission, consequent on the death of Captain Bathurst, to my Flag-lieutenant Thomas Dilke, an officer for whose zeal and attention to his duty I will refer Your Royal Highness to Captain Robert Spencer. The two lieutenant vacancies which I am entitled to fill up, I shall give to the two mates of the 'Asia,' whom Captain Curzon recommends as having the strongest claims. This has been my guide in all the appointments I have hitherto made; and Your Royal Highness may rely upon my continuing to reward merit, as far as in me lies, so long as I hold a command. The defects of the 'Asia' are very considerable certainly; but as they are principally above water, I trust it will not be necessary to prevent her return to me. She was the great lion of the Mediterranean before this action, and her appearance henceforth will have a good effect upon whatever service she may be destined to perform. If manned up to her full power, certainly her long 32-pounders on the main-deck would tell in action. But the ship would be better at sea for having them changed to the medium 32-pounders; and she might then have similar guns on the quarter-deck and forecastle, instead of 42-pounder carronades, which, besides being of different calibre, are so likely to be upset in quick firing, as ours were on the 20th. I cannot conclude this letter better than by assuring Your Royal Highness that I have not exaggerated in the smallest degree the able and gallant support which I have mentioned in my public letter my having received from my colleagues. The casualties of each of their flag-ships show how large a share *they* had in the action. Their followers were enveloped in smoke; and the light breeze which brought *us* in, was diminished almost to a calm by the general cannonade which ensued. They were, however, extremely useful in relieving us eventually from the more distant but galling fire in the rear, as well as occupying the batteries. The conduct of Captain Hugon, of the ' Armide,' has gained him the admiration of all who witnessed it. The wounds, in general, are of a very serious nature; but whatever can be done by ability and by kindness of attention, the poor sufferers will find in Doctor Liddell, whose superior I have never met with in the service. Sir Henry Bunbury's son has lost an arm, and my son has a shot now in his thigh, and another passed through the calf of his leg, and his collar-bone was dislocated; but I am happy to say both are doing as well as possible. The different ships are adjusting themselves as well as their means admit of, and as soon as the wind favours us, we shall proceed to Malta. Ever since the battle, in day and night, the Turks have continued to set fire to their disabled ships; and at the moment my despatches close, which will be whenever Count Heiden sends me his, I will give Your Royal Highness a comparative list of what they were, and what has been their fate.

I have, &c.,
Edward Codrington.

The ' Hind' cutter was tender to the 'Asia'; she was about 150 tons, and had a crew of about 30 men, and was commanded by Lieut. John Robb, detached from the 'Asia' for that purpose. Having been absent on a mission, she came in sight of the squadron just as they were running into the bay; and observing the firing begin, and being without any orders as to any particular position, her gallant commander placed her as near as he could on the inshore side of the flag-ship. In this central position, the cutter was exposed not only to the shot especially directed to her, but also to those which were fired at the 'Asia' herself with which she was in a line, from the inner and as yet unengaged lines of the double horseshoe. In the course of the battle the little vessel was hit by twenty three round shot,—no wonder she got the name in the fleet of ' His majesty's line-of-battle cutter!' Mr. Dumaresque and Mr. Lee, midshipmen, each lost a leg, and others were severely wounded. At one time, while the surgeon was below, about to perform an amputation, there was a call —'All hands to repel boarders'— and the surgeon had to leave his patients, and join the rest in 'repelling boarders.'

From Henry Codrington, Midshipman, to his brother, Captain William Codrington.

Malta: November.

. . . Next day (19th) the 'Dartmouth' came out, having made a sketch of the position of the Turks. It was certainly a very strong one indeed. It was executed by a renegade Frenchman by name Letellier, who had been in the French service. There had been, indeed, many French officers in the Turco-Egyptian fleet, but the whole had retired to some neutral in the harbour, sending a note to De Rigny signed with their names as a witness. Letellier, after having signed his, returned on board Ibrahim's ship, and was in her when it commenced. What became of him is not known. He had persuaded Ibrahim that the French ships, knowing the French officers were in the fleet, would not fight against their country-men, and that there would only be ourselves and the Russians to look after, and that he, Letellier, would place the Turkish fleet in a situation where they might easily destroy us. So he placed them in a long semicircle round the south end of the harbour in three lines; the outer line composed of three line-of-battle ships, five double-banked Egyptian frigates 64 guns each, and 15 Turkish frigates about 50 guns. The next line consisted of 26 heavy corvettes, about 24 guns each, so placed that abreast of every opening in the first line there should be a corvette. Behind them were the brigs about 20 guns each: there were also four or five schooners and about 40 transports and merchantmen behind the lines. Now the way he wanted us to go in was evidently to place ourselves in the centre of this sort of semicircle or circle I may say, for some brigs which were anchored in the entrance to wind-ward of the fleet, and of which about three were fire-brigs, nearly completed the round. He had judged, and correctly too, that the allied fleet would come in with a wind which would place them when anchored to leeward of the fire-brigs; and though he expected and wished us to anchor within his circle, yet he did not think we would have anchored so close to his own line as to render its position less formidable.   T have no doubt that he intended us to collect in the focus of his circle and so be an easy prey to him. During the action a man (Arab) swam on board of the ' Philomel ' from a fire-brig which she sank in two broadsides, and among other things said that it was quite a mistake the action beginning then, for that it was to be put off to 12 at night, when the fire-brigs were to cut their cables and run down on fire among us (supposed in the focus) whilst the double line was peppering us. The truth of this I cannot swear to, but it looked very like it, for they were prepared for action, springs ready, tompkins out, &c., yet let several ships anchor, when this mistake, as it is called, took place. Had we gone in as enemies, the best way would have been for us to anchor in line inside and along his line of corvettes or brigs on the east side, turning adrift or running down the transports and other small fry ; then we should have had one side of the circle only to engage and our shot have reached the other. But in this meditating, peacemaking, diplomatique style we were obliged to go in as friends, and therefore the position to be taken up was this. The line-of-battle ships, counting the ' Syrène ' 60, French Admiral, as one, were to anchor along-side of the line on the east side, while the frigates were to take the other side as per plan. By this means each ship of the circle being closely employed, the plan was rendered in a measure abortive.

The ' Asia ' had 8 round shot in her bowsprit, 18 in fore-mast, 25 mainmast, mizen-mast dowsed, standing and run-ning rigging cut to pieces, lower yards useless, &c., and 125 round shot in the hull, besides quantities of grape, canister, and musket shot, &c. I believe no round shot penetrated her side in the lower deck, and none through the main deck ; there are several shot which have nearly penetrated and even pushed in the inner plank, but I think none got regularly through, except on the upper deck and through ports, &c. She is a regular fine ironsider, and really I am excessively pleased with her in every way.

I had nearly forgotten to tell you how astonished I was at the coolness and intrepidity shown by all the men during the action ; for my part, I was hopping about here and there and everywhere, hurrying them on, for I had not that cool way at all ; but devil a bit would they hurry, and they went on in a way that actually made me stare. My father says that he never saw any ship's fire equal to ours from our main and lower decks in precision and steadiness. As to the upper deck, the breachings of the carronades (42) stretched and the guns capsized, and the men, as I said above, were sent

down to work the main deck ones. Having never seen anything of the sort before,* I can make no comparisons; but I
must say that the splinters, &c., in the cabin were quite
wonderful : some of the bulkheads had been left up and the
stern railing also, pieces of which the shot sent in in quantities, killing and wounding many men. Had all the cabin
guns been mounted and manned, the slaughter would have
been great; but four were not, as we had not men enough
for them. Three of father's double-barrelled guns and my
little single one, were lying lashed together under the sofa,
and a shot came in and literally dashed them to pieces tearing even the double barrels into two : I mean dividing the
barrels from each other, and, excepting one, breaking them
to pieces. Some of the pieces went on to the poop—how, God
knows. Altogether the crash was quite terrible in the
cabin.

A piece of the small upright bars of the iron stern railing
of the Admiral's cabin (which had by mistake been left up)
was struck by a shot and sent edgeways quite through the
calf of my right leg, as I was looking aft; it grazed the shin
bone on the inside, and, turning clear of it, passed through,
tearing a little of the muscle out; the iron must have been
about an inch square. In the thigh of the same leg, a little
above the knee, a musket ball, or small canister of that size,
went in and took a bend clear of the bone, and the deuce
knows where it is gone. It must be in, but as it has given
me no annoyance and has all but healed up, I am quite content. Then I had a splinter which struck my left collar-
bone, and luckily, instead of breaking it, only dislocated it,
making a yellow place as big as my two hands put together,
but except the bruise, that gave me no pain, and is now all
right. I was struck in several other places by splinters, but
they were too small to hurt. I went down to the cockpit
about the middle of the action. On going down the ladder
(tarpaulin and grating being lifted) I found myself almost in
the dark and in an atmosphere which was as hot, though not
so pure, as many an oven. On the chests, &c., the men's
mess tables had been laid, and over them beds ; on these lay
the wounded, some too bad to speak, others groaning and
crying out with the agony they were in. Some (generally
the least hurt) calling out lustily for the doctor. 'Oh!
doctor, my dear doctor, do come here, I'm bleeding to death,'
&c., and some saying it was their turn, &c. I managed to
feel my way to an unoccupied berth amidships, alongside a

* He was just nineteen.

poor fellow who had been severely wounded, and I think we made a pretty quiet pair, except occasional, nay frequent, calls for water, of which, owing to my excessive thirst, I must have drunk a great deal, besides what I poured on the bandage which had just been put on my wound, which felt as if it was on fire and devilish uncomfortable : the water felt like ice to it, and relieved it a great deal.* When the doctor came to overhaul me he found the upper wound in my thigh, which I had not complained of before, thinking it only a scratch (not having cut off my trousers), for I found that the pain of the one diminished or concealed the pain of the other. The probing of the upper one was not painful, but the ball had so buried itself with a turn that it could not be found. The lower one was very painful, for the finger being much more satisfactory than the probe, the doctor had made his meet, thus satisfying himself that nothing was in. This did bring me to the 'vocative case.' I was then removed into a cockpit cabin, and remained there two or three days, during which time the inflammation was completely subdued by poultices, and I was comparatively easy. After I had found my berth and got my eyes accustomed to the light, or what little of it there was, I began to look around me, and a disagreeable sight it was. Had not I known that father was on deck and in such immediate danger, I might have given you some very fine reflections upon honour and glory, &c., well suited to time and place ; but my thoughts were more on deck than below, and the only thought I had of that nature was that I had had quite enough of honour and glory for the occasion, and would be an interesting object to boot ! However, when all was over, I thought, and think now, that I was a very lucky fellow to get off as I did, taking everything into consideration.

Sir E. C. to Mr. Bethell.

In the port of Navarin : October 23, 1827.

You will soon know more particulars, my dear Bethell, by the newspapers ; I can only say now that we have had a desperate battle and have annihilated the Turco-Egyptian fleet. It has cost us dear,—very dear : but the moral effect will have much marked influence. My dear Harry is wounded,

---

* Doctor Liddell, who was very fond of him (they had been together for three years in the 'Naiad'), seeing him there, asked what was the matter, and wanted to attend to him : he answered that it was not much, and he would rather wait and take his turn with the others.

and severely wounded too, but is doing quite well, and will, I am sure, go on so, owing to absence of all fever, and a placidity of temper which is quite lovely. The balls out of a canister shot disabled several of them at once. He has one now in his thigh, and had another through the calf of his leg on the same side, and his collar-bone was dislocated. But his wounds are flesh wounds, and his flesh is wholesome, and the air is delightfully temperate. Bunbury's little boy has lost his arm short of the elbow, but is also doing well. But I cannot bear to dwell on this part of the business. It requires me to look round and see the devastation of our treacherous opponents to rouse back my feelings to the glory of the victory we have gained, and the fine example we have given them of the effects of their baseness. I was twisted round two or three times, and find several splinter scratches and bruises on different parts of my body. I am worn down, but upon the whole may say I am well. The load of responsibility which I have had has been lightened by the good conduct of my colleagues, and in battle they acted admirably. W. Fitzroy has lost a son. We have seventy-five killed and wounded in the 'Asia,' lost our mizen mast by the board, and though we have saved our mainmast, the ship is a mere wreck. You should go and see her as soon as she arrives at Portsmouth. The fire of this ship was quite beautiful, and does high honour to Curzon and the officers. Tell Fane Blair is quite well, and, like the rest of us, did his duty admirably. Of about sixty vessels of war and others amounting to about 120, not less than fifty-three of the former are destroyed. The Turks themselves have burned all they could since the action, God knows why, as we were content with having made them mere wrecks. We have had some thirty-seven beautiful explosions. The scene has been the same night and day since the battle on the 20th. It would not have been so well on the 21st, as the French were now with us.—E. C.

General Order.

'Asia,' in the port of Navarin : October 24, 1827.

Before the united squadrons remove from the theatre in which they have gained so complete a victory, the Vice-Admiral Commander-in-Chief is desirous of making known to the whole of the officers, seamen, and marines employed in them, the high sense which he has of their gallant and steady conduct on the 20th inst. He is persuaded that there is no instance of the fleet of any one country showing more complete union of spirit and of action than was exhibited by the squadrons of the three Allied Powers together in this bloody and destructive battle. He attributes to the bright example set by his gallant colleagues the Rear-Admirals, the able and cordial support which the ships of the several squadrons gave to each other during the heat and confusion of the battle. Such union of spirit and of purpose, such coolness and bravery under fire, and such consequent precision in the use of their guns, ensured a victory over the well-prepared arrangements of greatly superior numbers; and the whole Turkish and Egyptian fleets have paid the penalty of their treacherous breach of faith. The boasted Ibrahim Pacha promised not to quit Navarin or oppose the Allied Fleet, and basely broke his word. The Allied Commanders promised to destroy the Turkish and Egyptian fleets if a single gun was fired at either of their flags, and with the assistance of the brave men whom they had the satisfaction of commanding, they have performed their promise to the very letter. Out of a fleet composed of sixty men-of-war, there remain only one frigate, and fifteen smaller vessels in a state ever to be again put to sea.

Such a victory cannot be gained without a great sacrifice of life; and the Commander-in-Chief has to deplore the loss of many of the best and bravest men which the fleet contained. The consolation is, that they died in the service of their country, and in the cause of suffering humanity.

The Commander-in-Chief returns his most cordial thanks to his noble colleagues, the two Rear-Admirals, for the able manner in which they directed the movements of their squadrons; and to the captains, commanders, officers, seamen, and royal marines, who so faithfully obeyed their orders, and so bravely completed the destruction of their opponents.

EDWARD CODRINGTON, Vice-Admiral.

CHAPTER III.

The combined fleets left Navarin on the 25th October,
and reached Malta on the 3rd November. It was a great
relief to the Admiral when his disabled ships got safe
past the forts at the mouth of the harbour; and the
comparative rest of those few days' sail came to him as
a needful benefit. The excitement, anxiety, and responsibility of the previous period had told upon him,
and caused an attack of illness which lasted some days
after his arrival at Malta. He did not, however, desist
from work, even on the passage there, as the following
letters will show.

From Sir E. C. to H.R.H. the Duke of Clarence.

'Asia,' on her way from Navarin to Malta: October 26, 1827.

Sir,—I had the satisfaction of getting the whole fleet out
of Navarin yesterday. The light air with which we started,
and the uncertainty whether the batteries would attempt to
impede us, upon being becalmed as we were between them,
made it an anxious moment. The Turks saw that we were
prepared for the worst, and did not attempt to interrupt the
crippled ships or exchange a single shot with those which
were directed to cover us by bringing up the rear; and by
the assistance of such boats as could be collected by the fleet,
we cleared the harbour and gained an offing before dark.
With night came on lightning, and heavy squalls from all
points of the compass, torrents of rain, &c., with a directly
contrary wind. I was very apprehensive of the consequences
to masts fished and rigged in such a scramble, but I do not
observe a difference in any of the ships of either squadron
this morning. Thus, Sir, Your Royal Highness has a detail
up to the time I am now writing, according to the principle
which has and will continue to guide me—to tell ' the truth,
the whole truth, and nothing but the truth.' And now that
the excitement arising from the ' rage of battle ' has some-

what subsided; now that the ambition which covets distinction is lulled into quiescence, and now that those feelings
of poignant regret for the brave companions who have suffered or are still suffering, are assuaged by the calm reflection
that they are a sacrifice to the good of their country, we may
reasonably hope that our judgment will not be warped in
reviewing the battle of the 20th and contemplating its consequences. Having proved this base and boasting Ibrahim
to be wanting in courage as well as in honour, I was certainly disposed to doubt a resistance by the fleet at Navarin.
It seems, however, that the renegade Letellier, who but a
few days before signed and sent to Admiral De Rigny a joint
submission to his directions, induced Ibrahim as well as
some of his own countrymen, to believe that the French
squadron would not join us in the attack; and that by his
proposed plan we should be effectually destroyed. Accordingly, his plan was carried into execution on the 8th and
9th, as I have endeavoured to describe it in my public letter,
by the help of the documents which accompany it. If we
could have gone in openly as enemies, we might have easily
crossed the head of their line, anchored amongst the small
vessels, and taken their principal line in reverse; but being
avowedly and actually desirous of avoiding collision, and
being obliged to attribute the same feeling to them, we could
only anchor in that part of the harbour which their well-
concerted plan left vacant for us. Letellier, however, had
underestimated our power. For, from the time the 'Asia's'
broadside returned the fire of the Capitan Bey's ship—an 84
—she received little injury from her, though galled all the
while by the ships within her. All these were as speedily
silenced in turn as the 'Asia's' guns could be brought to
bear on them.

I should observe, Sir, that we did not begin with any one
of them. I had told Moharem Bey that I would not fire
unless he did, in reply to his message that he would not;
but that if any one gun were fired from any of the Turkish
ships at either of the Allied flags, I would destroy the whole
Turkish fleet. His ship did not keep his promise, for which
she received condign punishment. The 'Asia' and the other
ships which I have the honour to command effectually kept
mine; and my purpose of preventing the transmission of
supplies by sea has been thereby fully answered. As I wish
'nothing to extenuate or set down aught in malice,' I will
do Moharem the justice to say that I believe his crew fired
without his orders; for they killed our pilot in our boat
whilst his captain was speaking to my flag-lieutenant on

the gangway. However, the period during which his neutrality was preserved, was sufficient for the 'Asia' to get rid of her two starboard opponents; and as his fire opened upon us just as we had sprung the 'Asia' to return the fire of the double tier frigate next beyond him, we were enabled to pay them both off at the same time.

Till now, neither Captain Curzon nor I could tell where the shot which most injured us came from. But as these two front line ships were cleared away, we found that some corvettes and brigs had been all the while raking us through the intervals; and I verily believe they did us more mischief than any of our more regular opponents. All these, however, like their predecessors, quitted their positions either by design or by their cables being shot through, and added to the mass that ran aground abreast of us. Although the firing had now nearly ceased in our neighbourhood—nearly six o'clock—we found a new and an awful danger in the surrounding vessels on fire. The burning fragments of the double frigate on the other side of Moharem Bey's ship, still at her anchorage about a cable's length from us when she exploded, fell all about us; but we had already wetted the decks and booms, and we escaped without taking fire. If Moharem had begun to fire earlier, we should have been put to great difficulty, for we had quite as much to do as could be performed by our numbers in keeping the guns on one side constantly at work, firing occasionally some of the opposite ones, and veering either cable, and hauling in either spring as most wanted to defend us against other ships. For this purpose I was obliged to send marines and everybody else, even from the carronades in the cabin, to assist on the main and lower deck; and I can assure Your Royal Highness I had a strong practical example of that deficiency of numbers for such an occasion which I mentioned in a former letter. It is quite impossible for me to say too much in favour of the conduct of both officers and men under such circumstances. I do not, however, doubt that all the other ships which had the opportunity of taking up the stations allotted to them, had quite as much to do and did it quite as well. And if all, not only of the English but of the Allied ships also, had been able to place themselves as we did, there would still have been a full allowance of opponent guns for each—since, according to Mons. Bompard, one of the French officers who had retired at Admiral De Rigny's summons, there were in all 81 vessels in the Turkish fleet carrying guns and pendants or flags, whereas our number was only 23, besides the 'Hind' tender and two similar-sized French

tenders, which would have been more useful if they had remained outside. The fact is, Sir, that after the battle was
fairly begun, the wind fell so light and the smoke became so
dense, that neither of the French ships of the line could close
with the ships between the ' Syrène ' and the ' Asia,' the
' Scipion ' having been set on fire by one of the Turkish fire-
vessels in the attempt; and that all the Russian ships, except
the ' Azoff,' carrying Count Heiden's flag, were thrown into
the same difficulty.

' L'Armide,' French frigate, and our little ' Talbot,' coming
in early, were enabled to choose, as they did highly to their
honour. The ' Cambrian ' and the ' Glasgow ' were delayed
by the latter being sent to meet Captain Hamilton with the
orders, on his way from the pass of Amyro, near Kalamata,
where I had sent him to check the brutalities of Ibrahim's
army; and it is much to their credit that they could get in in
time to silence the batteries and relieve their friends already
requiring their assistance. I may mention to Your Royal Highness that Captain Hamilton's appearance at Amyro checked
the advance of the 5,000 of Ibrahim's army destined to ravage
Maina, thus breaking in a second instance his agreement
with us; and that upon hearing the cannonade the whole
returned towards Navarin. If I did not know the interest
which Your Royal Highness takes in all naval operations, I
should fear tiring you with this detail. However, I will now
proceed to submit my opinion on the consequences of this
late battle. Sir, I think the first great effect will be, that the
Sultan, finding that by the loss of his fleet he has no longer
the means of continuing the war, will now accede to the
proposed armistice; and that the second will be the Russians
relinquishing an intention, which I dare say is now in the
progress of execution, of marching their army towards Constantinople. For the only grounds on which Russia could
take such a step (inconsistent with the Treaty, which appears
to me to have very ably put a curb on this disposition) must
be the persevering resistance of the Porte. Another effect
will be Ibrahim's army being put to great difficulty in trans-
porting supplies, and I trust consequently ceasing that cruel
system which may lead to their own destruction; and another of no small importance— strongly aided by the joint
measures of my colleagues and myself, the Greek resources
being turned from the general plunder of commerce, against
their own enemy. As to Mehemet or Mohammed Ali, who
has been trying to commit England to support him against
the Porte, as I fully believe only with the view of inducing
the Sultan to reward his sham fidelity by giving him Da-

mascus and Syria, I shall not be surprised if he lose his head as a just reward for his base hypocrisy. I hope, at all events, that the conduct of Ibrahim at sea and on shore will not be forgotten whenever the question of tribute and compensation for Turkish property within the limits of regenerated Greece be taken into consideration. The Turks having not only refused the mediation, but having set at defiance the power of the Allies to enforce it, may well be made to pay the penalty of their resistance—a resistance, moreover, solely prolonged for the purpose of vengeful brutality. Two Greeks swam on board the 'Asia' with manacles on their legs; others have been found chained to floating pieces of wreck; and we hear of numbers being purposely left with the dead and the dying, previous to the whole being blown up together. I should observe, Sir, that these poor wretches were kept as galley slaves, and not as prisoners of war. We have also received some Englishmen and some Americans, *who say* that they were seduced to go on board the Turkish ships to work in fitting them, and at last were put in irons and forced to come to sea in them. *They say* they were put in the tops during the action; that there are no surgeons in the Turkish ships, and that if a man be wounded they let him alone to bleed to death.

Before I close this letter I wish to explain to Your Royal Highness one part of the manœuvre on bearing up for our stations, which may seem to require elucidation. The Egyptian ships, which formed the head of the principal line, had had French officers in them, who, it was presumed, would not act in opposition to Admiral De Rigny; and I therefore placed the French squadron as their opponents in the line, whilst by this means I gained the superior flag and the largest ships for the English squadron. The Rear-Admiral observed and joked me upon this, but I claimed it as my right. It would have been more regular under these circumstances to have allowed him to lead in; but I am sure Your Royal Highness will not disapprove of my having sacrificed a little simplicity in the evolution for the sake of giving to myself, to Captains Bathurst and Ommanney, the opportunity of showing conspicuously how the ships should take their stations, an opportunity which was admirably embraced by both those gallant officers.

By giving the above reason for this arrangement, I escaped the appearance of giving either of my colleagues that superiority over the other, which, with all my attention to it, I could never catch a symptom of either of them seeming to feel or to acknowledge, ready as they both showed themselves to put themselves and their squadrons under my command. I take the liberty of enclosing a plan, giving more correctly the form of the Harbour of Navarin, done by my son whilst sitting up in his cot, for his amusement.

I have, &c.,

EDWD. CODRINGTON.

From Sir E. C. to the Admiralty.

'Asia,' at Malta : November 6, 1827.

SIR,—I have the honour to inform his Royal Highness the Lord High Admiral that, although no direct answer was received to the joint letter from myself and the Russian and French Admirals, dated the 21st of October last, to Ibrahim Pacha and the other chiefs at Navarin, Tahir Pacha, who came on board the 'Asia' (and who was the only one of them who would not attend the conference at Navarin when Ibrahim Pacha pledged himself to an armistice which he evidently intended to break), assured me that, as far as the remaining ships were concerned, no further hostilities should be committed, but that he had no control over the forts and land forces. The allied squadrons, however, left Navarin on the 25th, without a gun being fired at them.

Sir E. C. to Doctor Wollaston.

'Asia,' on her way to Malta, from Navarin · October 29, 1827.

That I frequently have wished you here with me, my dear Wollaston, is true, because you would have seen extraordinary sights. I cannot say I wished for you in the late destructive battle, however, because I neither expected to escape its effects myself, nor that anyone about me would be so fortunate. And although many who read of it may wish they *had seen* it, their taste differs much from mine if they wish actually *to be* in anything of the sort. To this ship individually it was an astounding encounter. I adopted the largest ship in the Turkish fleet for her particular opponent, directing the 'Genoa' and 'Albion' to support her to the northward, and the four French ships (three of the line and De Rigny himself in a large double-tier frigate) to occupy the four Egyptian (three being double-tier) frigates to the southward, forming the head of the Turkish line. Although not intending to oppose the English squadron to the headmost ships, I did not like the French to lead; and therefore so arranged the manœuvre that we should not only lead in, but be opposed to the strongest ships. However, the evolution was still very plain and simple, and if we had had

a little more wind would have been executed precisely. We
were under the further disadvantage of being obliged to suppose that none of the Turkish vessels would fire upon us, and
consequently to anchor in the position they had left open to
us, as it now turns out, under the plan of the French renegade Letellier, who made the Turks, or rather Ibrahim,
believe that the French would not act with us, and that we
should therefore be effectually destroyed by the concentrated
fire which would thus be brought upon us. We succeeded
in getting the 'Asia' moored with great rapidity in her
proper station, as did the 'Genoa' and 'Albion' after her
in succession. De Rigny, in the 'Syrène,' attained his place
also betwixt number 1 and number 2; but the wind
dying away, the battle raging, and the smoke enveloping
the whole space, the three French ships of the line could not
reach their stations, and were bothered in the middle of the
crescent, where, at first, their attention was devoted to the
batteries, and, at last, to vessels in the inner lines, which
had been galling the 'Syrène' and the 'Asia' all the time of
the action. This gave the 'Asia' two front-line opponents
(double-tier frigates) on the larboard side, whilst on the starboard side she had her proper antagonist, an 84, carrying
the Capitana Bey's flag at the main, and a (not sure if
double) frigate in the second line, astern of her. If these
had all begun at the same time, we should have been much
more cut up than we are; but, luckily, we had time to silence
those on the starboard side, by a fire which would not have
disgraced Woolwich practice, before Moharem Bey, scarcely
our length from us, (or rather his crew) opened their fire;
and we were at that moment springing the ship round to
bring the larboard guns to bear on the ship next beyond
him, about a cable's length from us, so that we could finish
both at the same time. Moharem's ship went off in a shattered state, and ran aground, where she subsequently lost
her masts by the board; the other appeared at one time
about to sink; but she eventually blew up, and so covered
the 'Asia' with the burning embers that our friends believed
that she too was on fire. It was hard to find ourselves still
galled by the corvettes and small fry, raking us as they had
done during the whole battle, without our knowing where
the shot came from. However, the moment these rascals
felt the effect of our getting our broadside sprung round to
them, away they went and joined a mass about the ship of
Moharem Bey, aground. The 'Albion' was still firing when
dark came on; and thenceforward, during the whole night,
we were entertained with most beautiful though awful explo-

sions. The morning presented us with a scene of horror and
disaster which it is impossible to describe.   Besides the
wrecks lining the beach all round the harbour, the water was
covered with floating spars, upon which were multitudes of
poor wretches, calling for help in various languages, amidst
their dead and dying fellow-sufferers.   Some that could swim
to us did so, and amongst them were Greeks with manacles
on their legs.   But boat we could produce none to assist
them.   It is shocking to reflect upon the number of Greeks,
as well as wounded Turks, which must have been wantonly
destroyed by their burning their vessels as they did, to the
number of about 30 (37), including those which took fire
during the battle.   I could not learn their motive for this;
and fearing that many Greeks in chains were thus barba-
rously destroyed with them, they were informed that, having
sufficiently punished them for firing upon us, I had no wish
to do them further injury.   Still, however, the burning went
on, and havoc seemed to be the order of the day.   At length
Tahir Bey, who was the only one not present when Ibrahim
pledged his word of honour to us not to move by land or sea
until he had fresh orders from the Sultan, came on board the
'Asia.'   I explained to him all that had passed from the
beginning, and he admitted that they had only themselves to
blame.   It was evident to me that the Egyptians and Turks
were not upon terms, and that something had taken place
betwixt him and Ibrahim, although he would not betray it.
I felt for him very much, because he seemed to me to feel
for his country, and to be in danger of losing his head, owing
to Ibrahim's base misrepresentations; and at the end of a
second visit he claimed my future friendship, if ever we
should meet again.   I sent home a rough plan of the port
and the position of the ships, which Spencer can show you,
with other documents that perhaps will not be made public.
I fear I cannot get you one done to accompany this,
although Harry is sitting up in his cot now at work on this
subject.   This said dear fellow is doing as well as possible,
although his wounds are very severe.   The thing which
passed through the calf of his right leg was about a large inch
in diameter, and square, as if it had been cut off an iron
rail; a similar one is now in the right thigh, and I cannot
guess what it was which struck him so as to knock his collar-
bone out of joint.   The latter is in its place, and the other
wounds are going on very favourably.   He has no fever, and
between times he sings and whistles as usual.   Little Hanmer Bunbury has lost his right arm up to the elbow; but has
just eaten a very good dinner in an arm-chair beside me, and

moves into the stern-walk to look at anything passing. I have written to Genoa, but fear the father and mother will hear the news before they get my letter. Pray remember me kindly to our friends in Walbrook Buildings. . . . I have had my worries, and anxieties, and disappointments, as well as our friend Brunel; and have felt short, very short, of means to perform my undertaking. But I have brought it, as I trust, to a good result at last, as you may tell him I trust he will his. And I hope he and I may both live to see as many tunnels in different parts of England as the Turks have unceremoniously made through H.M.S. 'Asia.' The frigate 'Dartmouth,' which is gone to Ancona with my despatches, will, I expect, bring the poor, anxious mother and daughters to join us at Malta, where, as I shall be without a flag-ship, I must remain until the 'Asia' returns from England.

Yours with great and sincere regard,
EDWARD CODRINGTON.

· From Sir Frederick Adam.
Corfù : October 30, 1827.

MY DEAR CODRINGTON,—I congratulate you with all my heart on your glorious achievement, which has indeed finished your operations in a way not to 'disparage their commencement.' That you should have been forced to come to this extremity is to be regretted, but the way in which you have conducted it fully comes up to my anticipations of what you would do if obliged to act. Your official letter is admirable in its way, as your conduct has been as a naval commander; and you may rely on my sincerity and truth when I tell you that I look upon your whole arrangements and conduct with the sincerest admiration.

Poor Lady Codrington will suffer the misery of suspense where those so dear to her were involved in so much peril. I envy her, however, all her brighter feelings, when she knows the truth. Well may she be proud of you, my good and gallant and able friend.

I am delighted to find that both your colleagues have behaved so admirably. De Rigny seems to have been most brilliant, as well as the 'Armide.' Lord Ingestrie gave me a sketch of the action. The stubborn fellows (the Turks) seem to have shown great courage.

Mehemet Ali, on the 1st of November, said to Captain Peter Richards, of H.M.S. 'Pelorus,' at Alexandria,—

'The Sultan has ordered Ibrahim to put out and attack

Hydra in spite of your admiral. He will not move however till I write to him, which will be in a few days;' and added, with a laugh, 'there must be an engagement at sea, but it will be nothing; a few of the first will be destroyed, and the others will turn back : this is necessary to convince every one you are in earnest.' *

From Sir Frederick Adam to Sir E. C.

Corfù : November 28, 1827.

Your account of the battle is very interesting and very excellently told too; the praises you meet with are really no more than you deserve, and *I feel* that *you* deserve them so much the more because there is so rare an absence of egotism in the way in which you relate your operations, and in the manly and handsome way in which you give credit to others. Your description in your private letter to me is quite graphic. Count Heiden's letter is a true (as it is a most eloquent) exposition of his real feelings, and I have not a doubt that he is as straightforward and as fine a fellow as you represent him to be. Lord Dudley's note (of September) is very satisfactory indeed, and the principle of lightening responsibility is a wholesome one, as it is also a new one amongst Ministers. I have no doubt you will be approved; for besides that they must have been prepared for 'hostile collision' from what occurred near Patras, the hostility was not of your bringing on. There is another view : they, the Allies, are quite serious in their intentions; they must feel that nothing short of some such lesson as you have given, would work on the Sultan; nothing else would convince him that there is unity and union between the contracting parties to the Treaty : and possibly this event (your victory) may prevent what of all things is to be deprecated, the Russians attacking the Turks.

Lord Granville, in his last letter to me, says, in answer to one of mine of 14th October :—

'Sir E. Codrington has acted † with a decision and firmness most creditable to him, and well calculated to impress not only on those who were the immediate objects of coercion, but upon the Divan also and upon the Pacha of Egypt, that we are in earnest in the prosecution of our object. The French Ministers are highly satisfied with our Admiral's energetic conduct, and only regret that Admiral De Rigny had not the opportunity of co-operating in the vigorous measures of Sir E. Codrington.' Now your measures on the *4th October*

---

* This must have been before the Pacha knew of the event of October 20. —NOTE by Sir E. C., on Capt. Richards' memorandum.

† At Patras.

might have brought on an action—they are approved of; and it was no more your conduct on the 20*th* that did bring on an action than the same conduct *might* have done so earlier.

The following anecdotes relating to the Battle of Navarin were written down by me at a later period, from my Father's dictation.—J. B.

At the time that the 'Asia's' mizen-mast was shot away which I think was entirely done by the corvettes and brigs, which formed a sort of third line or division, I happened fortunately to be walking forward, by which means I escaped being touched by either the ropes or spars. Of the two men then in the top one was considerably hurt, and they both fell overboard, but both scrambled in again by means of the rigging. The vessels of this third line did us considerable mischief whilst we were occupied by the other two sets of larger vessels to which we were exposed. It was just about the time when we were employed springing the ship's broadside towards them; for which purpose, and to avoid their being unnecessarily exposed, I had sent down both Captain Curzon and Commander Baynes to direct the use of the springs upon the lower deck, being then myself the only person remaining upon either the poop or quarter-deck. Seeing that the object of getting the starboard broadside to bear was not likely to be successful, and wanting some person to carry a message down to Captain Curzon on the subject, I was calling out in great anxiety, ' Is there no one within hearing of me that can carry a message ? ' when a person, with whose figure I was not acquainted and whose face was all over blood, came limping towards me, saying, ' He could.' I explained to him what I wanted done with the springs, asking him if he fully understood and could carry that message to Captain Curzon ; he answered quickly in the affirmative, and away he went with great alacrity. He returned speedily, and asked me if I had any further commands; upon which I again sent him with a similar message respecting veering the cable, which he delivered with the same intelligence and alacrity. Upon observing to Captain Curzon, the following morning, that I had fallen in with important assistance at a time of great need from a person with whom I was perfectly unacquainted, he explained to me that the man was his new clerk, Cyrus Wakeham, whom he had lately received from the ' Seringapatam ;' upon which I begged he might be sent to me that I might thank him for his conduct. He came into the cabin, limping with so much difficulty that I was induced to ask him if he was not wounded, to which he answered, 'Slightly.' I then enquired what the surgeon said about it, when he told me he had been several times to the sick bay, but always found him occupied with others worse wounded than himself, and who seemed to have superior claims on his assistance. Upon this I desired Captain C. to go forward to the sick bay with him, himself, and let me know what the surgeon said about it. It turned out that he had several severe wounds, that from that moment he was obliged to take to his cot, where he remained until he was sent with others of the ship to Haslar Hospital, from whence he was only discharged in the following autumn. It is worth notice, that when put into his cot, he occupied himself in writing a descriptive poem on the Battle, and also a song for the amusement of the ship's company; and I subsequently learned that he was the principal writer of those effusions in prose and verse in the ' North Georgia Gazette,' to which Captain Parry attributes so much of the cheerful endurance of the ' Hecla's' ship's company when fixed in the ice. Notwithstanding all his claims, as here specified, and his having been two voyages to the North Pole, my utmost exertions could not procure him promotion to a purser's warrant until the 9th of January, 1835!!

Returning from that episode to the period when we had just succeeded in destroying the corvettes and brigs which formed our third batch of opponents, an alarm was given that one of the Egyptian frigates right ahead, and then on fire, was coming right down upon us. It was a question whether it was most safe to slip from our anchors and expose ourselves to a similar danger elsewhere, or to remain where we were. We were so completely enveloped in smoke from this frigate, that to De Rigny, who was to windward of us, and to Heiden, who was down to leeward, and indeed to the whole of the ships of our line, the 'Asia' appeared to have taken fire. This caused a cessation of firing in those parts where the battle still raged, and an endeavour to get boats to send to our assistance;—when by the sudden explosion of the frigate, which proved to have still remained at her anchors, and by the blaze by which it was accompanied, the 'Asia' was discovered to be clear of that immediate danger. Upon this a cheering along the line took place, followed by a renewal of the action by those ships whose firing had only for the moment been checked by a contemplation of the 'Asia's' imminent peril.

At the time when the Egyptian frigate above mentioned as being on fire appeared to be fast approaching us—an appearance created by the rapidly increasing smoke — I

had placed myself at the fore part of the poop, anxiously
watching the space of water between us, and steadily resisting
Captain Curzon's urgent desire to slip the cables, until the
diminution of that space should make the danger of collision
too imminent for longer delaying that measure, for which
immediate preparation had been arranged. I myself, in
common with Captain Curzon and others, believed the frigate
on fire to be adrift from her anchors; but I relied upon the
'Asia,' having still the foremast, mainmast, and all the gear
standing, driving out of her way whenever the diminution of
that space should in my judgment render the slipping the
cables a preferable expedient. Captain Curzon had also
urged my quitting the position I had taken, that I might not
be exposed to the pieces of falling timber the explosion would
occasion, which I had resisted on account of not losing my
watchfulness of the space of water by which the two vessels
were separated, which was to be the guide for my decision.
At this moment, the explosion taking place, showed the expediency of his precautionary advice, from the firebrands and
other pieces of wood, and even of men, which fell on different
parts of the deck. It was for the double purpose of seeing
the situation of the conflicting squadrons, and showing that
I myself remained in a condition to continue the duties of
my office, that I then placed myself conspicuously on a cuddy
which had been erected on the after part of the poop, when
the cheering before mentioned immediately took place.

The fire was so thick upon the 'Asia' in the early part of the
action, that Captain Curzon was under the impression that we
were fired upon by friends as well as foes. Our position certainly exposed us to this, by the contiguity of the two parts of
the horseshoe form in which the two squadrons were anchored,
and the different positions in which the broadsides of the different ships in those lines were directed. The smoke at this
time being so thick that the people at the guns could no
longer see our immediate opponents, their fire being rightly
directed to the position of our opponents was only known by
my seeing their mastheads, and confidence was placed in this
proper direction of our fire, from the guns being run out in
the same position in which they had been placed in the
beginning of the battle. At length, upon the masts of the
Turkish Admiral's ship falling, and his fire ceasing, in my
anxiety to ascertain that we were not firing into each other,
I tried to make the general signal to cease firing; but as fast
as the flags could be attempted to be shown, either the men
hoisting them were killed, or the means by which the signals

were to be displayed were shot away. I then tried to despatch a boat with this object, when it was found that we had no boat that would swim; an attempt by hailing to get one from the 'Genoa' was equally unsuccessful, and I was obliged to give up the attempt and leave things to take their course.

My first visitor at the close of the action was Count Heiden. After our mutual congratulations, he expressed the great desire he had felt to lose no time in making known to me the gallant conduct of Captain La Bretonnière, in placing the 'Breslau' so as to relieve the 'Azoff' from a considerable portion of the enemy's fire, by which she was entirely surrounded. This was highly creditable to the feelings of the Count, considering the jealousy between the men of those two nations. When I expressed a wish to see Captain La Bretonnière to thank him, I was told that he was too severely wounded to be able to come. .

The next person that came on board was Count De Rigny, who said he had hurried on board under great anxiety to express the satisfaction he felt in reporting to me that not only his own ship, but also the 'Scipion,' had been saved from being burnt by the able and gallant conduct of Captain Davies of the 'Rose,' and the boats of the English squadron. The next was Captain Spencer, who had come on board to describe to me how much he owed to Le Capitaine Hugon of 'l'Armide,' for having placed his ship between the 'Talbot' and an Ottoman frigate that was raking her (the 'Talbot' being engaged at the time with a double frigate on her broadside); adding, that upon the before-mentioned frigate striking her colours to 'l'Armide,' Capitaine Hugon hoisted the French and English colours jointly over the Turkish, showing the English the higher of the two. I begged Captain Spencer would immediately bring Capitaine Hugon to me, that I might thank him for his conduct. He had hardly, however, got into his boat before Hugon himself appeared. He expressed himself highly gratified by the terms in which I had spoken of the conduct of 'l'Armide;' and said that without reference to his own proceedings, he was coming on board to describe to me the admirable conduct of Captain Davies, who, after saving the other ships by towing off the fire-vessels, had moved the 'Rose' from the position in which she had first anchored, and placed her between 'l'Armide' and another Ottoman frigate, by which she had been exposed to a raking fire similar to that from which 'l'Armide' had relieved the 'Talbot.' These circumstances induced me to prefer Captain Davies to the

rank of Post-Captain in the vacancy made by Commodore
Bathurst, who died about 3 A.M. the following morning.*

On the evening of the battle I had a visit from Tahir
Pacha,† the Commander of the Turkish division, the immediate object of which I have never clearly understood; it
probably was to lead me to apprehend that being under
Ibrahim's orders he had no choice but to act as he did, and
to make the best excuse for his having done so, in order to
prevent further ill-consequences. Our interpreter being a
very inferior one, made the difficulty of explanation so much
the greater. I told him that I had taken sufficient satisfaction for the insult offered to the Allied flags, and that if
they were contented with the result, I was. I observed
strongly on the breach of word and honour shown by Ibrahim
and his chiefs, in attempting to enter the Gulf of Lepanto
after the agreement he had made with me in their presence
to make no movement with either the troops or ships for at
least twenty days; that as he himself (Tahir Pacha) did not
attend that meeting as all the other chiefs did, I acquitted
him of being a party to it, and should therefore place reliance upon whatever he might have to say to me. I said
that I understood his reason was disapproval of the conduct
of Ibrahim; to which he seemed to assent, by saying he was
not upon terms of open communication with him. I told
him that the letter I was then writing was intended to warn
Ibrahim that if he attempted anything further against the
shipping, I should consider it as a declaration of war on his
part; that I should open a fire upon his camp immediately,
and destroy as many of the Ottoman people and the Ottoman
vessels as I possibly could. I also explained to him, that
previous to coming into the harbour I had written a letter to
Ibrahim warning him of his having already broken his promise by his expedition to the Gulf of Lepanto, and again by
the conduct he was then pursuing by the exterminating
system of his army in the Morea; that if he did not desist,
I should feel myself called upon to *enforce* a strict obedience
to the convention agreed upon. I expressed a wish that he
himself would take this letter in, that I might be sure of its
being delivered, by which means all further bloodshed might
be prevented. He repeated that he was not upon terms to

* Le Baron Milius, captain of ' le Scipion,' also came on board the ' Asia '
after the battle of Navarin, and said to Sir E. C., ' Je viens faire mon compliment au brave des braves. Ah ! que cela a été beau ! Si jamais je dois
encore combattre, j'espère que ce sera sous vos ordres pour bien apprendre
à faire mon devoir.'

† See in Appendix, a curious account by Tahir Pacha himself. Also
H J C.'s account of Tahir Pacha.

have any personal communication with Ibrahim, but that he should certainly hold himself bound to deliver the letter if I desired him to do so; and he took charge of it accordingly.* During the time of his short visit, I remarked three explosions of the Ottoman vessels, and I asked him what it meant—repeating that having sufficiently avenged the insult offered, it was not our doing, and that it must be the act of some of the Ottoman people, and that I wished he would take measures to prevent it. Upon this point he did not seem willing to give a candid explanation, and I was therefore led to believe that it was an act done by his order, or at all events with his sanction.

On the second visit of Tahir, which I think was on the following morning, he told me that he had taken means to have the letter safely delivered to Ibrahim. Upon some further conversation respecting the explosions of the Ottoman vessels still continuing, and the cruelty probably inflicted on the wounded, who were still on board of them; and my professing a desire to do anything he could point out to prevent any further continuance of them, and calling his attention to the 'Cambrian' frigate under sail near the vessels aground with a flag of truce at her mast head, sent there by me for that express purpose, he signified to me that if I would recall the frigate and send a boat it would be more likely to have the effect desired; with which I immediately complied. He then left the ship, apparently much satisfied with our interviews. We supposed him not to understand any language but his own, and spoke of him and his visit openly upon that supposition. But Captain Curzon, who attended him out of the ship, having observed aloud 'that he appeared to be a very fine fellow, and that he pitied him from his heart,' was surprised by his saying in return, 'I thank you.'

Although I thought that the chastisement that Ibrahim had brought upon his fleet, and the warning I had sent him through Tahir Pacha, would prevent any further act of hostility on his part, it was advisable to prepare for the worst. I therefore placed the 'Cambrian' and 'Glasgow' frigates with the 'Trident' and 'Provence' French ships of the line which remained uninjured, opposite Ibrahim's camp, with orders to open their fire upon it in case of any gun being fired from the forts upon the crippled ships whilst quitting the harbour. When we first weighed anchor we had a light favourable breeze, which diminished to almost a calm with light flaws of wind in a contrary direction at the moment when the

* See letter, p. 76.

whole of us were passing the narrows. This occasioned considerable confusion by obliging the ships to risk their getting aground on either side, which probably would have taken place but for the assistance of the boats of the squadron to those who were most in want of it. The extraordinary appearance of the ships under their jury rigging, contrived according to their different necessities and the means they had of providing for their sea voyage—all heaped together in the very entrance of the harbour—and the anxiety lest the forts should open their fire upon them in that condition, made it a moment of extreme anxiety which will not easily be erased from my memory ; but it would form a beautiful subject for such a painter as Vandervelde.

This chivalrous zeal to afford help to each other— and chivalrous eagerness in each to give public acknowledgment of the help received from another—was one of the most unalloyed pleasures attending this day of trial and danger. It showed how fortunate the Commander-in-chief was in the instruments placed within his hands to work with. Even his own captains were most of them unknown to him before he came to his command ; but he was not unknown to them by character, and his frank and loyal bearing had quickly won their confidence.

Whatever might be the reciprocal prejudices of the two Rear-Admirals, both the Russians and the French had confidence in the English ; and all combined to support their leader with heart and hand. English, French, and Russian ships came to each other's assistance as circumstances called for it; and brave men who had done their own duty nobly, delighted to proclaim the merits of their companions in arms, and the aid they had received from them. It was a happy contrast in that respect to the difficulties Lord Howe had to contend with in *his* day of glory and of trial; and forcibly recalled the words written by Sir E. C. to his wife on the 1st June, 1812 :—

' Here is the anniversary of the glorious and ever-memorable 1st June. Eighteen years have elapsed since the day of that grand battle. And if the captains of that day *had done their duty as they do now*, it would still keep its preeminence over all the subsequent victories of Nelson himself,

because there was no Cadiz to take shelter in, and the whole
might probably have entered Spithead together, captors and
captured forming one grand spectacle.'

*A letter from Mr. Thomas Kerigan (of H.M.S. 'Blonde') to Sir
Edward Codrington.*

March 26, 1845.

DEAR SIR,—I feel much pleasure in giving you the substance of the conversation which took place at the gun-room
table of the ' Blonde,' shortly after our arrival at Constantinople in June, 1829.

Tahir Pacha, the Turkish Vice-Admiral, and the *second*
in command, came on board the 'Blonde,' attended by
several officers, and took a minute survey of the ship. . . .
After completing the object of his mission he came into the
gun-room, and took a seat at our table; he was very com-
municative, and entered largely into the particulars relating
to the Battle of Navarin. . . . He then talked of the
battle, and of the distinguished prowess of the English
Admiral, who, *tall as a mast*, was conspicuous in all parts of
his flag-ship, directing the operations of the most sanguinary and destructive battle that had taken place for *many
ages* between two hostile fleets. At one time, as the
English Admiral stood upon the poop, taller than the
mizen mast, (I use the very words as reduced to English
by our interpreter,) I directed a company of riflemen to
take a deliberate aim at him, and put an end to the
dreadful conflict by shooting him through the head or
heart, telling them that it was the only hope of salvation
which was open to us. 'Destroy the English Admiral and
the day is ours; for when he falls his ships will surrender
and not fire another gun.' Well, my riflemen fired at the
English Admiral; they took a deliberate aim at him, the
same as if they were only firing at a target; but, like a
target, a pillar, he stood firm and untouched; and, though
taller than the mizen-mast, noble, goodly, and erect,—a fine
man (here the Pacha raised his hand high above his head),
the best marksmen in the fleet were not able to strike him;
he was proof against all their shots. But it was the will of
God that he should be saved from my sharp-shooters; it
was God alone that saved him; and shortly after I was a
prisoner on board his flag-ship. But he appeared so mild and
benignant, so calm, cool, and collected, that in his presence
I forgot the enemy, and looked upon him at once as my con-
queror and my friend. He is *not* the enemy of our country,
though he destroyed twenty-eight of our ships, and sacrificed

nearly 11,000 of our best seamen.   But the English Admiral
is not to be blamed for all this destructive waste and
slaughter; he is a great and good man; it was the will of
God that we should suffer a grievous loss; he was favoured
by Heaven, and God armed his hands for battle, and prepared his heart for a great victory over the fleets of Turkey
and Egypt.

The above is a *verbatim* statement of what Tahir Pacha
said relative to you and to the ever-memorable Battle of
Navarin.   THOMAS KERIGAN.

The following notes, though twelve years out of date,
will not, I think, be considered out of place, from the
interesting account they give of one of the prominent
actors in the Battle of Navarin.

*Notes written by Captain Henry Codrington of his meeting
with Tahir Pacha in 1838–9.*

H.M.S. 'Talbot,' at Smyrna.

I was present at an entertainment given in honour of
Tahir Pacha, then on his way through Smyrna from Constantinople to take possession of his Government of the
Pachalic of Aidin to which he had just been appointed.
(Smyrna is in the Pachalic of Aidin.)   One of the bystanders
informed him of my name, upon which he desired me to be
sent for from the other side of the room and presented to
him.   He received me with great kindness and cordiality of
manner, asked me if I was the son of Sir Edward Codrington,
and on my saying that I was, he replied that he always
considered him as one of his greatest friends to whom he
was under great obligation.   He then took me by the hand,
saying, ' Come and sit down with me, we must have some
conversation together :' he then led me out of that crowded
room into the next, which happening to be equally full, he
led me on to a third room which was more quiet and with
several vacant sofas.   Taking possession of one, he made me
sit down alongside him, his friend and man of business (Mr.
Kune I think is his name) being also close to us, and
occasionally joining in conversation, and explaining when
our deficient Italian put us at fault.   He understood Italian
very well, and spoke it passably himself.

English and French he did not speak, and professed not to
understand.   He enquired much after my father, asked how
and where he was, and what he was doing now, &c., &c.; he
spoke of his kindness to him on board the ' Asia ' after the
battle of Navarin, and said how greatly he considered him-

self indebted to him, and how much he admired his character. He asked if I was going to Constantinople. I said I was not going immediately, though probably a short time hence the ship I commanded might be sent to be stationed there. 'Well,' said he, 'my house is at Balta Liman (on the Bosphorus close above Constantinople), and I hope to see you there: and,' added he, 'if I knew when you would be at Constantinople I would go there to receive you.' This certainly sounded rather Eastern and allegorical, for the Pacha of the Province Aidin to go all the way to Constantinople to receive the captain of a foreign 'donkey' frigate, as I well knew the difference of value in Turkey and Turkish estimation of Pachas and captains of donkey frigates: but the future showed that whatever verbiage there was in this, his kindness was real, and shown at Constantinople as well as at Smyrna. The conversation continued for some time on various topics, old Tahir expressing himself (for a Turk) rather freely, as if conscious of being individually in a position sufficiently secure, and in times improved enough, to allow of his doing so. Besides natural shrewdness and habit of observation, his remarks showed considerable acquaintance with the men and names of the day, and the changes consequent on the modification of the old *régime* that was going on. He evidently had a good head, and, for a Turk, was a man of business; but there was a coldness in his grey eye, and an expression of decision and hardness of character in his countenance, which, in spite of all his kindness to me personally, gave me the idea that there might be some foundation for the prevailing reports of his sternness and occasional violence and cruelty. On my rising to take leave of him, I said something civil about not wishing to obtrude longer upon him, or take up more of his time from others whom he might wish to see; and I thanked him for the kindness with which he had received me. Before I had quite finished, he interrupted me, and taking my hand in one of his, he patted me on the shoulder with the other, saying, 'Figlio di Codrington figlio mio.' One or two days afterwards he went on to Aidin. I was much pleased with his manner and kindness to me as my father's son; and having, luckily, a print of my father, I sent it to Tahir as a souvenir of one who had always had a very high esteem for him, Tahir. In the meantime, for I don't exactly know which was done first, he had ordered his man of business to present me a horse,—a very nice little Turkish horse that had belonged to himself, as a mark of his friendship for me. He also, after receiving the print, wrote a kind letter of thanks to me.

In the winter of 1840, when the 'Talbot' was at Constantinople, I again met old Tahir, and several times called on him in his own house at Balta Liman. He was now out of office, but as stately in person and as vigorous in mind as ever. He subsequently visited me on board the 'Talbot,' but declined all salutes or honours. On my first visit to his house, while we were sitting with pipes and coffee in his morning room, he suddenly rose, and taking me by the hand, led me through one or two rooms till he came to one which, with other European furniture, had pictures hung up round it; then leading me up to one, he pointed it out to my notice. It was a picture in oils of the Battle of Navarin!!! I was astonished at this; for it seemed extraordinary that he, one of the commanders of a beaten fleet, beaten too in the act of their dirty work, should thus seek to perpetuate the glory of his opponents, and thus keep before his own eyes such a record of the disgrace and humiliation of his country's arms. The explanation is, perhaps, that these people do not feel the bond of nationality as we do. The personal character of an individual, with them, as with us, is of great consequence to himself, or may be so, as it materially affects his prospects in life besides touching his personal honour; but if there is in their imagination such a thing as a national character, it has no connection with the individual personally.

Tahir was not implicated in the Turkish breach of faith which preceded the battle, nor responsible for the mismanagement by which they brought it on; but he felt that like a brave man he had done his duty, and fought with courage and honour in the greatest battle that had occurred for years; and that in fact the Battle of Navarin did him, Tahir, personally much credit. To a man who, like him, had by turns been in the service of most of the Mussulman states—a soldier of fortune seeking the means of rising in life—the nationality of the calamity that destroyed his fleet was but a name. With us the national character and that of the individual are so closely interwoven, that anything affecting the credit of his country is of the greatest moment to the individual citizen. He considers himself in some degree as one of its guardians, and he would resent personally anything to the disparagement of his country, nationally.

Tell an Englishman his sovereign is no better than he or she ought to be; that his countrymen are a set of rogues, or his country a faithless one,—and he will knock you down. Tell a Turk the same, and he will say, Allah! Kerim! A Turk has no country: an Englishman has, and it is his own.

I also saw in Tahir's house prints of several other national engagements, including the First of June, Lord Howe's victory : one of those of the First of June was a rare one that I had not seen before. At Smyrna he had his young son with him, a nice-looking, modest lad (he was not allowed to sit in his father's presence), and he seemed pleased when at Constantinople I asked for him again, and I saw him. Old Tahir can make a joke now and then. One day, standing together by the block of stone placed near the Giant's Landing-place (or landing-place of the Giant's Mountain) where the Russian auxiliary army had been encamped, he pointed to it and said, 'You, England and France, placed that mountain there.' Not imagining a joke in his grave eye and face, I replied that I had heard the Russians had placed it there. 'Well,' said he, 'was it not the conduct of England and France that brought the Russians here ?' I felt that I could not say it really was not. He was then, in 1840, still an active, energetic man; and one day in his garden, after a cup of coffee, he suddenly called for his horses, and starting off at full speed, he led me a very sharp burst as hard as we could go, galloping by winding narrow paths up the face of the steep hills that overhung his house. I was glad, and the horses too, when we reached his farm at the top. The character attributed to him at Constantinople is that of a good, active officer, but too harsh and severe for the present day.

H. J. CODRINGTON.

The letters of hearty congratulation received by Sir E. C. on the victory of Navarin are far too numerous for insertion; they came from admirals, generals, and other friends well capable of forming a judgment on the subject, and were much valued by him. I have inserted a very few of these cordial and gratifying testimonials ; and have refrained from adding more for fear of overburdening the text with them.

From Admiral Sir John Gore to Sir E. C.

November 12, 1827.

MY DEAR CODRINGTON,—I must leave you to the dictates of your own feelings to render justice to ours towards you and yours upon the first intimation of your great and most unparalleled victory over the Turco-Egyptian fleet in Navarin harbour. To say that we congratulate you, however sincere, sounds *cold*, and not to convey an iota of our sentiments. We are all alive to all that you and dear Lady C. can enjoy on such an occasion, and we fully participate in it *all*. We rejoice with *you* and we unite in the national exultation that the navy have clearly manifested being in its full vigour after thirteen years of peace. There can be but one sentiment on such an event, and *we* all feel proud that our friend has achieved it. May you live long in happiness to enjoy the honours so nobly won! Your official letter is perfect—you have left nothing unsaid nor anything to unsay. You came, you saw, you conquered; and you, by yourself, you, set a noble example which all will be proud to follow when you and I are returned to our native dust. And let the consequences or results of this merited chastisement be as it may, you can only feel the proud consciousness that you have fulfilled your duty amidst dangers and awful scenes never before witnessed!

Your loss has been severe in officers, but when the nature of the action is considered, the cross-fire you must have been exposed to, and the number of deliberately pointed guns fired from batteries and vessels unoccupied by your ships, I am only surprised that it was not greater, deplorable as it is. I can fancy the effect of 'Asia's' broadside in such a situation, and you had a fine opportunity of experiencing all the advantages of your round stern over 'Genoa's' old-fashioned one. I have no chart to give an idea of Navarin, and thereby enable me to judge completely of your own and the adversary's position. Could you send me a sketch, however rough? Sir George Montagu will be pleased to see such; and note the direction of the wind when you entered. 'Warspite' (William Parker) is on the way to join you, but I conclude that all your ships will be replaced. I propose to go to London to-morrow to learn the sentiments of the Admiralty upon the rewards for such services. They are cold and close, but I will see the Lord High Admiral if I can. He so highly applauded all your conduct previous to this brilliant service, that he cannot fail to extol it now. Dear Lady C., how anxious I am to hear of her after this excitement of her noble soul. Her proud feeling that her husband has won the day, and under circumstances so peculiarly novel—a British Admiral leading a confederated fleet of Russians, French, and English against Turks and Egyptians, to victory so entirely perfect! We all unite, my dear friend, in *shouts* of admiration and most sincere good wishes to you on this great event; may it please God to bless you with many years of health to enjoy the result.

Believe me your faithfully-attached friend,
JOHN GORE.

Whitehall: November 13, 1827.

The King has been pleased to nominate and appoint Vice-Admiral Sir Edward Codrington, Knight Commander of the Most Honourable Military Order of the Bath, to be a Knight Grand Cross of the said Most Honourable Military Order.

The King has also been pleased to nominate and appoint the undermentioned officers in the Royal Navy to be Companions of the said Most Honourable Military Order of the Bath, viz.,

> Captain John Ackworth Ommanney,
>   ,,   the Hon. J. A. Maude.
>   ,,   the Hon. Frederick Spencer.
>   ,,   Edward Curzon.
> Commander John Norman Campbell.
>   ,,   Richard Dickinson.
>   ,,   George Bohun Martin.
>   ,,   Lewis Davies.
>   ,,   the Hon. William Anson.
>   ,,   the Lord Viscount Ingestrie.
>   ,,   Robert Lambert Baynes.

From H.R.H. the Duke of Clarence to Sir E. C.

Admiralty: November 19, 1827.

DEAR SIR,—In the first place, I am to congratulate you on the splendid victory you have obtained, and rejoice you are quite well. I admire your perfect conduct on the day of battle, and most highly appreciate the exertions of all ranks under your orders.

This will be delivered to you by our common friend, Sir John Gore, who proceeds, with the approbation and the perfect knowledge of the Cabinet, to obtain a complete and satisfactory explanation to certain questions which his Majesty's confidential servants have thought it their duty to put to you respecting the cause of your going into Navarin Bay, and the commencement of the firing. Last night a messenger was despatched from the Earl Dudley with the very queries which you will, I make no doubt, so satisfactorily answer through Sir John Gore. I mention this fact because the Cabinet sent him off in such a hurry that there was no time to inform me, who was, being Sunday, out of town at Bushy, or otherwise I should most certainly have written.

> Ever believe me, dear Sir,
> Yours most sincerely,
> WILLIAM.

P.S.—By the mail coach of this evening I send down to Captain Bridgeman, of the 'Rattlesnake,' your Insignia of the Bath, and the crosses of the C. B.'s for the various Captains and Commanders who had the honour and happiness of serving under, and sharing with you the glory of the 20th of October last.

By the same conveyance I venture to send a sword from myself, which I trust you will accept as a small token of my admiration of your conduct in Navarin Bay.

From H.R.H. the Duke of Clarence to Sir E. C.

Bushy House: December 2, 1827.

Dear Sir,—I am to acknowledge yours of 9th August at Vourla, &c. . . . . You were perfectly right in proceeding off Navarin with the squadron. I make no doubt you will always do your duty. . . . . Having now answered all your letters except that which relates to your Action, I now enter on this interesting and glorious event. I could have wished, either by the messenger who preceded Sir John Gore, or by that Admiral, to have written at once. But I really had not time. Not being in the Cabinet, I can only look at the business as a sea officer, and I do therefore, *from the bottom of my heart*, congratulate you on the event. The 'Asia's' fire speaks for itself—the Capitana Bey's ship a perfect wreck, with 650 killed out of 850 ! I rejoice *all* did their duty. Everybody must lament poor Bathurst. I altogether approve of Captain Davies's promotion. I have, of course, promoted Lord Ingestrie. Anson is also a Captain, and all the commanders in the ships of the line are, or will be, made Captains, as will those in the sloops . . . . I approve entirely of the two mates of the 'Asia' being made Lieutenants. I am confident *you* will ever reward *merit*. I trust the 'Asia' will be able to continue your flagship.

I rejoice your colleagues have so well done their duty. Capitaine Hugon in ' L'Armide ' has eminently shone. Your gallant son has been most seriously wounded, but I trust in God by this time he is quite well again. You must have had plenty to do to refit the ships so far as to return to Malta, where, thank God, we know they are safe arrived. I understand from Lord Ingestrie the Turkish, Egyptian, and Tunisian squadrons hardly exist.

I have now answered your letters, and have to add the King of France has nominated you a Grand Cross of the Order of St. Louis ; Captain Fellowes a Knight Commander of the Legion of Honour, and all the captains and commanders who were actually in the command of ships and vessels of the British during the action in Navarin to be Knights of St. Louis. I suppose we shall hear shortly of similar honours to yourself and the gallant *fine* fellows under your command from the Emperor of Russia. On every account I must and shall be anxious to hear from you after the arrival at Malta of Sir John Gore. For the present, adieu, and ever believe me,

Dear Sir, yours sincerely,
WILLIAM.

From H.R.H. the Duke of Clarence to Sir E. C.

Admiralty: December 7, 1827.

DEAR SIR,—This morning brought me yours of October 26th, between Navarin and Malta, and your letter of November 17th from Malta.

In answer to your first and most important letter, I shall begin by observing how sincerely I do rejoice at the whole fleet having got out of Navarin without any damage, and that equally the ensuing gale did not any damage. Your remarks are just, that the passions of men will be up in great events, and you write your first letter, *then cool.* I understand your reason for taking up your anchoring ground as you did: the pilot *may* have been killed contrary to orders. I can easily conceive the surrounding vessels on fire were very dangerous; the wetting of the decks and beams was very judicious; your contest, from the numbers of the enemy, must have been severe. I clearly understand you must have felt the shortness of complement on board the 'Asia'; the enemy were clearly numerous. The 'Talbot' and 'L'Armide' did indeed their duty; I make no doubt the 'Cambrian' and 'Glasgow' did all they could. As for the consequences of your victory I will not venture an opinion. I hope *you* are *right* and *I*, therefore, *wrong*; but I am more inclined to believe in *war* than *peace.* You were very wise in placing the French opposite to the Egyptians. I trust with all my heart your son is quite recovered.

God bless you both, and ever believe me, dear Sir,

Yours truly,
WILLIAM.

From Sir John Gore to Sir E. C.

November 14, 1827.

MY DEAR CODRINGTON,—In my letter of Monday I purposed to make my bow of congratulation to the Lord High Admiral upon your brilliant victory under his Royal Highness's administration. I did so yesterday, and was well received and most truly gratified by the unmeasured terms of approbation he (the Duke of Clarence) expressed on the whole of your conduct, and the admirable manner you have secured yourself from being made a political 'cat's paw,' by identifying the French and Russians so completely in the cause.

'As I have nothing to do with political considerations, and only look to the conduct of the navy, when I sent Codrington's despatches to the King I requested that the Grand Cross of the Bath should be sent to him at once; and as the case is entirely novel, and sloops of war have fought with ships of the line, I have promoted all the commanders, the senior officer of each rank in every ship, and, contrary to the routine, I have given the vacancies in the Marines to the officers on the spot. But, to effect this, I have been obliged to fight a battle to overcome the obstinate prejudices which exist in that Boardroom of which you can form no idea— yes, you can, from their treatment of you respecting the Signal Committee; but I conquered, and will again, in order to do justice.'

He then told me that Ministers are thrown on their backs by your splendid achievement in chastening the faithless Mussulman; that they could not imagine the probability of such results, and that he had a personal altercation almost amounting to open quarrel with Mr. Canning for sending the 'Genoa' and 'Albion' to you, and that 'Warspite' is now on her way to you unknown to the Cabinet (*ex officio*). 'I told Mr. C., presiding as I do over the navy, it is my duty to preserve its importance, and I will not suffer a risk of its disgrace. If your object is peace, send such a force as will command it, not one to invite hostilities. It is strange that Sir George C. sided with Canning against my opinion, and no man was more astonished at the arrival of Codrington's despatch than him. But they shall not catch me asleep. I have ordered "Revenge," "Ocean," and "Wellesley" to sail as soon as possible to replace the ships coming home. The consequences of this victory to the navy must be most beneficial and lasting, and it is my duty to see justice done to all who aided in its achievement.'

'Your Royal Highness has enhanced the value of your approbation by the promptness of the rewards.'

'Yes, in that consists the advantage of my not being a Cabinet Minister. I, like the Duke of York, have only to look to my own duty, without waiting the cold calculation of political considerations. Ministers would gladly shelter themselves from the odium of the nation by throwing the blame on Codrington; but he has done his duty nobly. I will uphold him. And he has placed himself above their disapprobation by linking Count Heiden and Admiral De Rigny to his car.'

This is the substance (if not verbatim) of our conversation on the subject.

I long for a chart of the port and the position of the fleets —*all* the ships. Cannot dear Harry send me one? I was delighted to hear from the Duke, Spencer, and Will, that on the 23rd said Harry was doing quite well, and that you were not under any anxiety about him. I read a copy of the Duke's letter to Mrs. Bathurst. It is manly, beautiful, and most truly benevolent; so that in all respects he has done, and is doing, well on this great and *glorious occasion!* And now again, my good friend, let me congratulate you on all these results, and the honourable commendation I hear from all persons of your whole conduct. It was truly gratifying to me yesterday in London to hear but one sentiment respecting *your conduct*—though the policy which led to it is very loudly execrated as likely to produce incalculable results. Sir George Montagu is delighted, and commands Geena and me to communicate to you his highest sentiments of admiration and congratulation. The voice of the nation will doubtless be expressed in Parliament, and yourself and subordinates receive the high meed of your valour.

From Sir Isambard Brunel to Captain W. Codrington.

November 17, 1827.

One of the most extraordinary circumstances of the late achievement of your worthy father is that of his being the first British commander who has commanded a French fleet, and where the French have shown a cordiality and devotedness which reflects the highest credit on both; most particularly on your father for having directed everything with so much regard towards the different parties.

That he is safe and well after this, is for his friends a most delightful reflection, and in this feeling no one is more sincere than

Yours truly,

M. I. BRUNEL.

On the Allied fleets separating for repair and refit after the battle of Navarin, it was arranged with Admiral de Rigny, who was to remain at Smyrna, that he should undertake the duties in the Archipelago, and especially the watching the ports of Navarin, Modon, &c., in the Morea.

The refittal of the Russian squadron occupied the main attention and resources of Malta Dockyard; the English squadron, which reached that port on the 3rd November, was afterwards sent to England, as the quickest means of refit and return.

There remained at Malta no disposable vessel for the Admiral's flag, which was temporarily hoisted on board a 28-gun frigate then under repair.

But, although at Malta, this was no idle time for Sir E. Codrington. Every available vessel had been dispersed for the protection of British subjects in the Ottoman ports against possible fanatical outbreaks; Greek piracy required immediate and decided measures for its suppression, with or without the consent of Count Capo d'Istrias, the President of Greece, who was on the point of arrival.

The slowness and inefficiency of communication at that time are shown by the fact that the affair of Patras, the Battle of Navarin, and the subsequent arrival of the English fleet at Malta on the 3rd November, all took place before the receipt from London of the Protocol and Instructions of 15th October, by which a final answer was obtained to questions of importance put by Sir E. C. to Mr. S. Canning in August.

These Instructions of October 15th are printed in the Appendix.* They were in answer to, and confirmation of, the previous views and corresponding acts undertaken by Sir E. C. on his own responsibility, as

* See Appendix.

to preventing or facilitating particular movements of the
Ottoman ships between their own ports, whether in
Greece, Egypt, or Turkey.   Yet in a subsequent part
of this memoir will be seen a declaration of the Government, that he who originated them did not understand
or obey them.—W. J. C.

From Sir E. C. to Earl Dudley.

'Asia,' in Malta harbour : November 8, 1827.

Your private letter of October 16* proved excellent medi-
cine to me, my good friend, early this morning in my sick
bed.   I knocked up just before our arrival here on the 3rd.
You will find that we maritime diplomatists are rather rapid
in our proceedings, and that we have already advanced in
anticipation of your instructions as well as those which we
get from Constantinople.   Thus it is, you will say, with
people whose only dragoman are cannon shot; and I will
say, this is the way with people who have confidence in the
due support of their employers, and who see the advantage
of their boldly undertaking at once that which they feel must
be done eventually.   Had we waited in a blockade for further
instructions, the base and brutal Ibrahim would have devastated the Morea whilst we were looking on.   He cannot do
more; and if he should, it will be at his own eventual cost.
But when I can give myself to this part of the subject, I
propose submitting to Mr. S. Canning my opinion that a
warning to the Porte and to the Pacha of Egypt of certain
consequences, will alter his system.   We can turn the tables
on him, I think, and his provisions will not last him long, even
if the Greeks should not enter upon that harassing warfare
which I am trying to press upon them.   I hope the strong
measures which the horrid conduct which Greek cruisers
have lately pursued under the encouragement of the present
venal Provisional Government obliged myself and my colleagues to have recourse to, will have the effect we expect of
leading the legislative body to change the individuals composing it, without even waiting for Capo d'Istrias.   For without putting their power aside no good could arise, and Greece
would be quite ruined before the final arrangements could be
entered into.   I am sanguine enough to think that the
victory of October 20, instead of creating a war, will prove
the only means of preserving peace.   Here again you will
smile at my maritime diplomacy.   First, the Turk will succumb and accede to the Treaty; secondly, the Russians will

* See page 460, Vol. I.

have no excuse for not stopping their meditated march on
Constantinople, which I imagine them to be now actually
beginning, and submitting to the silken bonds by which that
Treaty has so ably tied them down; and thirdly, the Greeks
will, by our present power to watch them, be obliged to act
on their own coast, and enter into some sort of trade instead
of living by piracy; and during this process a better class of
men will probably come forward. I will not enter into the
story of the battle, since I have detailed all that concerns it
in my official letters so fully. I consider it merely what the
pugilists would term a 'turn up,' arising from our suddenly
entering the antagonists' quarters uninvited, and whilst they
were in the act of training; but I will say before the best of
them, that it would not have disparaged the loftiest stage
and the finest ring which could have been collected in
Europe.

From Sir E. C. to Mr. S. Canning.

'Asia,' at Malta: November 12, 1827.

DEAR SIR,—From the time of the 'Rifleman' having
joined my flag with your despatches, I have been so unwell
I could do no more than get through the daily demands
which have been made upon me; demands, indeed, which to
a man in health would have been very agreeable, as they
have arisen out of our late success.   .   .   .   .
By these last you will see that I have never lost sight of the
subject of piracy, although I have not had time to form
speculative opinions upon it, or have been able to aid you
with my sentiments as much as I could wish; I assure you
it has not been for want of disposition to do so, but merely
owing to that multiplicity of demands upon me (even when
I had to manage the treacherous Ibrahim singlehanded), that
the day was not long enough for me to work through its
duties. You will see that Mehemet Ali, as well as his *worthy*
son, has been playing a game both with the French and ourselves.   .   .   .   .   .
It is clear to me that he wished to be able to tell the Porte,
that he had been assured of English support in case of his
throwing off his allegiance, in order thereby to obtain Damascus and Syria, and to be put, as Mr. Salt termed it, at
the head of the Mussulman world. Upon the subject of the
French officers, I cannot do better than refer Your Excellency to the communications which Admiral de Rigny will
have made to Count Guilleminot.

I am convinced that the attack and resistance of the
Turco-Egyptian fleet was owing to the renegade Letellier

having persuaded Ibrahim that the French squadron would not co-operate with us; and that by his plan of placing us in the centre of their fire, we should be effectually destroyed.

. . . .

The venal composition of the present Provisional Government of Greece naturally gave rise to the fresh intrigue of Colocotroni and other Capitani. The language openly held in all personal communications wherever we went, as to the consequences to the parties eventually, had probably prevented the success of all those attempts; and the influence which the late battle has given us will preponderate still more decisively hereafter. You will see by the strong measures we have felt ourselves called upon to adopt, that we dreaded consequences beyond the contemplation of your letters, unless a stop were put at once to the proceedings therein practised.

I am, &c.,
EDWD. CODRINGTON.

From Sir E. C. to Mr. S. Canning.
(*Confidential.*)

'Asia,' at Malta : November 12, 1827.

DEAR SIR,—I have been so ill since the receipt of your letter by the 'Rifleman,' that I could not till now send her back to you as I wished for the chance of her being wanted. By this time the conduct of the Sultan must be decided; but I send the 'Rifleman,' nevertheless, for my own satisfaction, and for the chance of getting late despatches that way from you. If there be no occasion for her stay, you will oblige me by not detaining her.

De Rigny is quite cured of any predilection he may have had for the Egyptians; and well he may, for nothing can be more clear than that Mehemet Ali has long been playing him off to his private purposes. The opinions contained in his letters, of which you have sent me copies, are similar to those he has always expressed to me. And that wily chief seems to have worked in the same manner upon Mr. Salt, and even Colonel Cradock, who could hardly believe in his treachery until it became too glaring. Perhaps if I had had a personal communication with him, I might have felt the same confidence; but I could never be persuaded that Hydra was the sole object of such preparations; and even if I had not found it requisite to watch Lord Cochrane's movements, I should still have kept in the neighbourhood of Zante. However, as it was that over-reliance on the good faith of

Ibrahim which induced De Rigny to let him see the French squadron quit Navarin, instead of going away in some dark night as I proposed, and which consequently led to the battle from which I expect so much eventual good, I have no reason to complain of it. After he heard of the Turks being out, he still remained at Cervi with his two sound ships of the line, and his own and another frigate, instead of coming away at once as he should have done. And yet, upon learning from Bompard the detail of Ibrahim's plans about going from Patras to Hydra, he himself observed: 'So that if any one ship, even a frigate, had been off Navarin when you drove him from Patras, he would not have attempted to re-enter that port.' I give you this merely to make you aware of everything, but not to lessen De Rigny in your eyes; for his conduct in the battle, and on all occasions when present with me, has been as able and as cordial as possible. You will see that the urgency of the case obliges us in many instances to anticipate instructions from you as well as from home. Before explanations can be given, the mischief would be done. I have now an order, or rather a power, to detain Lord Cochrane's schooner, which I shall announce both to him and to the Greek legislative body, that we may avoid the necessity of it.

I feel confident that the strong line I have taken respecting the conduct of the Greeks will make them give their exertions a more proper direction at sea, and leave our commerce more unrestrained. Malta has been almost blockaded of late by the Greek vessels of war, and the Ionian Islands much in the same state. These vessels have been under regular license from the Provisional Government, who share a twentieth of the condemnations. With respect to Protocols, you will see that in one important instance—my decision to place the fleet in Navarin with the Turks—my colleagues supported me by a regular document of that sort. But separated as we must necessarily be, it is not possible for us in general to adopt that proceeding. We are obliged to act on the spur of the moment as the occasion requires: and though we cannot pledge each other to our measures thus separately entered upon, they are undertaken upon a previous concert as to contingencies.

Believe me, &c.,

EDWD. CODRINGTON.

Extract of a letter from Sir E. C. to the Admiralty.

'Asia,' at Malta : November 16, 1827.

The Tunisian Admiral, who was with the fleet at Navarin, sent me word that he had had no intention to take part in any hostility against us,* and that he hoped I would permit him to return to Tunis, in a brig, the only remaining vessel of his squadron. I acceded immediately to this, assuring him that I had only acted in self-defence ; and that having amply punished the perfidy of Ibrahim Pacha, I should consider the battle as a mere casual event to be attributed to the misconduct of that individual, and as not likely to interrupt the amity which before prevailed betwixt England and the several Ottoman Powers. I am in hopes that this circumstance being made known by the Tunisian Admiral will prevent any brutality on the part of the populace in any of the Mussulman States.

I have, &c.,

EDWD. CODRINGTON.

At the N.W. corner of the island of Candia there rises from the sea a small rocky island named Grabusa or Carabusa, 200 or 300 feet in height and perhaps half a mile across. The greater part has a high perpendicular and impracticable cliff for its coast, whilst at another smaller portion of the island the ground rises in a steep grassy and stony slope from low rocks up to the fort, which crowns the available space at the top. The anchorage is bad from its small size and rocky bottom : it is formed by the shelter between this island and the mainland, and by a dangerous reef of rocks which bars the effect of sea. But it well answered the purpose of a refuge for pirates in their small vessels—and of this class, description, and occupation were at that time many of the so-called Greek men-of-war—the vessels anchored below, and their plunder was sent up to the castle, which nominally was supposed to be in possession of the Greek Government, and hoisted its flag. This nest of piracy, the head-quarters of villains, who not only plundered vessels but committed all sorts of crimes upon the crews, had to be destroyed ; and the duty was entrusted to Commodore Sir T. Staines, lately arrived from England in H.M.S. 'Isis,' by an

---

* On the subsequent taking of Carabusa there were found in a cask letters from the Bey of Tunis to his Admiral at Navarin, enjoining him to do his utmost to destroy the Allied ships; and the Bey of Tunis was informed pointedly of the discovery of these instructions.

order to destroy the fortress, with all vessels and boats of
whatever description belonging to it, and to carry to Malta
in irons for trial all persons who might be likely to be iden-
tified as principals in the piracies committed.—W. J. C.

At this period of difficulty, the English Admiral was
left by his Government without further information or
instructions than could be obtained from a despatch
containing 'Queries' as to the cause of the Battle of
Navarin.

On the 4th December, 1827, a small merchant brig
under sail was seen trying to reach the Island of Malta,
and attempting a well-known signal of 'wishing to
speak the Admiral ;' and when, after some difficulty,
she had gained the anchorage, Vice-Admiral Sir John
Gore, an old and intimate friend of Sir E. Codrington,
who had been sent by the Government through France,
and had embarked in this brig at Marseilles, placed the
following despatch in the hands of Sir E. C.

*From Earl Dudley to His Royal Highness the Lord High
Admiral, K.G. (sent to Sir E. C.).*

Foreign Office : November 17, 1827.*

SIR,—His Majesty's confidential servants have had under
mature consideration the despatch from Sir Edward Codrington of October 21, which, together with its several enclosures, has been transmitted to me by Your Royal Highness's command.   They entirely concur with Your Royal
Highness in recognising the great skill and distinguished
bravery displayed by His Majesty's naval forces on October
20, as well as the ability of Sir Edward Codrington in maintaining that perfect harmony and good understanding with
the admirals commanding the Allied forces, which became
the guarantee of their cordial and gallant co-operation in
the hour of trial at Navarin.   Whilst, however, His Majesty's
Government are happy to make this acknowledgment, it is
impossible not to lament the loss of life with which this
severe conflict has been attended ; and it is their duty to
consider the circumstances of this case with reference to the
instructions under which Sir E. Codrington was acting,
marked as they were by an anxious desire to avoid, except

Received December 4.

in the last extremity, any act of hostility. In this view of
the question there are some points of great importance, upon
which the despatches hitherto received from the Admiral do
not convey that full explanation which His Majesty's Government deem it essential to obtain; the omission of which
they ascribe solely to the circumstances under which those
despatches were written, and to the Admiral's anxiety to
transmit the earliest intelligence of the important event that
had occurred.

The points respecting which further explanation is considered to be necessary are those adverted to in the following
Queries :—

1. Is the memorandum transmitted in Sir Edward Codrington's despatch of September 25 (Enclosure No. 7) the
only written document in which there is any specification of
the conditions of the armistice agreed upon with Ibrahim
Pacha?

2. Was that memorandum communicated to Ibrahim
Pacha, or to any officer of the Turkish forces who had been
present at the conference at which the armistice was agreed
to?

3. It being stated in Sir Edward Codrington's memorandum that the armistice was to take effect by sea and land,
was there any article or any understanding in respect to the
forces and districts to be included in it, or as to the period
and mode of its termination?

4. Was there any mode agreed upon for denouncing the
armistice by either party on receipt of the answer from Constantinople?

5. On October 18, when the protocol was signed, had any
answer been received from Constantinople; and, if so, was
the nature of that answer known to the admirals when they
agreed to the protocol?

6. It having been alleged in the answer of Patrona Bey,
when he was turned back with the forces under his command
on his way to Patras, that Ibrahim Pacha did not consider
the armistice as precluding him from making that movement, was any explanation entered into between the return
of Patrona Bey to Navarin and October 20 for clearing up
that difference of construction of the armistice?

7. Was any step taken by Sir Edward Codrington, after
the conclusion of the armistice, and before the entrance of
the combined fleets into Navarin, to remonstrate against
the hostilities carried on by the forces of Ibrahim Pacha by
land?

8. Was any communication made to the admiral com-

manding the Ottoman fleet in Navarin, as to the object of
the movement of October 20, before it was carried into
effect ?

9. If the second mode of proceeding mentioned in the
protocol of October 18 had been adopted, would it not, on
the one hand, have effectually obviated all the risks pointed
out as objections to the first mode ; and, on the other hand,
as effectually secured, so far as the naval forces in Navarin
were concerned, the main object of the instructions of July
12, namely, ' the interruption of all supplies of arms, ammunition, &c., to the Turkish forces' in Greece, without incurring the same danger of collision as was apprehended
from the third ?

10. With respect to the third mode of proceeding, what
were the propositions referred to therein, as intended to be
made to Ibrahim Pacha ?

His Majesty's Government confidently expect that the explanations which they thus require, will enable them completely to vindicate, whenever they may be called in question,
the grounds upon which Sir Edward Codrington acted at
Navarin.—I have the honour to be, with the highest respect,
Sir, Your Royal Highness's most obedient humble servant,
DUDLEY.

Answers to 'Queries.'

From Sir E. Codrington to the Admiralty.

'Asia,' at Malta: December 9, 1827.

SIR,—On the 4th inst. I received your letter of the 18th
November with the enclosure of the 17th from the Earl of
Dudley, which his Royal Highness, the Lord High Admiral,
was pleased to entrust to the care of Vice-Admiral Sir John
Gore.   By these letters I am commanded 'to give such
further explanations as may occur to me as necessary for
putting his Royal Highness and his Majesty's Government
in full possession of all the circumstances and motives on my
part which led to the battle of Navarin, and with particular
explanations of points stated in Lord Dudley's letter.'

I propose, therefore, in the first place taking these latter
points seriatim :

First Query. ' Is the memorandum transmitted in Sir E.
Codrington's despatch of the 25th September (EnclosureNo.7)
the only written document in which there is any specification
of the conditions of the armistice agreed upon with Ibrahim
Pacha ? '

Answer.   There was no written agreement between

Ibrahim and the Admirals. I was given to understand that it was not customary with this people to put such things down in writing; but also because their word given in the presence of witnesses is supposed to be sacred. On this account I demanded that the interview which Ibrahim required with me might take place in the presence of all his chiefs; and I for the same reason took with me several of my officers, as did also Rear-Admiral de Rigny. I likewise took on shore with me as interpreter, a gentleman of Malta, but did not insist on his admission when told it would offend.

I spoke in English, which the Pacha's dragoman showed he well understood by repeating the sense of what I said in French to the full satisfaction of Admiral de Rigny, and which he then transferred to the Pacha and his chiefs in the Turkish language, without the least hesitation. And it was the conviction of the bystanders, who watched his manner and the effect my observations thus translated had upon the auditors, that they were given faithfully.

Second Query.—'Was that memorandum communicated to Ibrahim Pacha, or any officer of the Turkish forces who had been present at the conference at which the armistice was agreed to?'

Answer.—The dragoman was always asked if he clearly understood what we said, to which he replied in the affirmative; and we were all convinced, by watching him and his auditors, that he did so. When off Patras, I asked the Reala Bey, who came on board the 'Asia,' if he was not present at the interview, and he answered that he was; and when I then told him he was therefore as bad as Ibrahim himself in breaking his word of honour, he excused himself by saying that he understood I had given leave on the 26th. And further, upon the dragoman being asked if what passed at this conference was as binding as if committed to paper, he replied that his Highness Ibrahim's word was considered as his bond, and therefore it might be as much relied upon as a written treaty. And, upon my desiring at the close of our conference that this question might be put to the Pacha, the dragoman objected that it would be an affront to doubt it. I nevertheless made a point of it, and it was therefore put, and replied to by Ibrahim in the affirmative.

Third Query.—'It being stated in Sir E. Codrington's memorandum that the armistice was to take effect by sea and land, was there any article or any understanding in respect to the forces and districts to be included in it, or as to the period and mode of its termination?'

Answer.—The armistice by sea and land thus agreed upon

referred only to the ships and troops forming the expedition then at Navarin. It was to remain inactive at Navarin until Ibrahim should receive answers from Constantinople and Alexandria to the communications he was to make of what had passed at our conference. Upon my asking how long the answers might be coming, it was stated that twenty days was the shortest period; and it was agreed that Ibrahim should make known to us, through our ships off the port, his receiving those answers. At this time the Turkish part of the fleet was outside the harbour, and I acceded to Ibrahim's request that I would allow them to come in (lest, as he said, suspicion of his inclination to follow our wishes should arise from the Egyptian ships alone being in the port) on account of his disposition to bind himself by the armistice.

Fourth Query.—'Was there any mode agreed upon for denouncing the armistice by either party on receipt of the answers from Constantinople?'

Answer.—Ibrahim was to make known his receipt of answers to his communications, and whether, by those answers, our proposals were or were not acceded to.

Fifth Query.—'On the 18th October, when the Protocol was signed, had any answer been received from Constantinople; and, if so, was the nature of that answer known to the Admirals when they agreed to the Protocol?'

Answer.—I have no means of knowing whether any answers were received or not. No notification as agreed upon, of any such answers being received, was made to us.

Sixth Query.—'It having been alleged in the answer of Patrona Bey, when he was turned back with the forces under his command on his way to Patras, that Ibrahim Pacha did not consider the armistice as precluding him from making that movement, was any explanation entered into between the return of Patrona Bey to Navarin and the 20th October, for clearing up that difference of construction of the armistice?'

Answer.—No explanation was entered into, because I felt sure that Ibrahim had misstated the fact designedly. On the 26th September, when the 'Asia' and 'Sirène' were about to quit Navarin, betwixt two and three o'clock Ibrahim's dragoman came to me from the Pacha to say that he had received information of Lord Cochrane having made a descent upon Patras, and to ask if I would give him leave to send a force competent to beat him off.* Admiral de Rigny was present at this interview on board the 'Asia,' and we both replied that on no account whatever could we permit such a thing, as being directly contrary to that part

---

* There was no truth in this.

of our orders which we had read at the preceding day's conference. The dragoman argued that I had myself promised
to prevent Lord Cochrane's proceedings. I said that this
intention referred to a meditated expedition to a part beyond
the present theatre of war; and that, the Greeks having
accepted our mediation, I had no authority for interfering
with their operations in any part within the present theatre
of war. I then enquired if I was to consider the armistice
still as binding; to which the dragoman, in conclusion, said
that if the Pacha had any further objection to urge he would
return to announce it; and that if he did not return in about
an hour, we were to conclude that the agreement remained
as settled the preceding day. We waited until almost dark,
and, the dragoman not having returned, the 'Asia' and
'Sirène' went out of the harbour.

Seventh Query.—'Was any step taken by Sir Edward
Codrington after the conclusion of the armistice, and before
the entrance of the combined fleet into Navarin, to remonstrate against the hostilities carried on by the forces of
Ibrahim Pacha by land?'

Answer.—Yes; as the accompanying document clearly
shows. But Ibrahim, consistently with his other conduct,
made his dragoman swear that he did not know where to
find him, and that there were no means whatever of sending
him the letter. (See Lieutenant-Colonel Cradock's report.)*

Eighth Query.—'Was any communication made to the
Admiral commanding the Ottoman fleet in Navarin, as to
the object of the movement of the 20th October, before it
was carried into effect?'

Answer.—None. Because the commander of the Ottoman
fleet had refused to receive my letter of the 19th September,
alleging that he had no authority to receive any such communications, and that they must pass through Ibrahim himself. Accordingly, Ibrahim, who was then passing in his boat,
received the letter himself from Captain Baillie Hamilton,
although not addressed to him.

Ninth Query.—'If the second mode of proceeding mentioned in the Protocol of 18th October had been adopted,
would it not, on the one hand, have effectually obviated all
the risks pointed out as objections to the first mode; and, on
the other hand, as effectually secured, so far as the naval
forces in Navarin were concerned, the main object of the
Instructions of the 12th July; namely, "The interruption
of all supplies of arms, ammunition, &c., to the Turkish

* Page 57.
K 2

forces in Greece," without incurring the same danger of collision as was apprehended from the third?'

Answer.—The third mode of proceeding having in contemplation the renewing the propositions, was less likely to 'degenerate into hostilities' than the second; but as Ibrahim had determined to receive no communications from us while without the port, and as we considered an effectual blockade of Navarin during the winter as physically impossible, we adopted the plan of entering the port as the only means of fulfilling the object of the Treaty. I may here state that when before Navarin in the middle of September, we were at one time carried as far to the northward as the Strophadia Islands; and at another time, in a strong wind, aided by a southerly current, below the Gulf of Coron; and there is no anchorage whatever upon any part of the neighbouring coast. There is no safety for any larger vessel than a sloop of war in Modon or under Sapienza, where the 'Columbine' was lost.

Tenth Query.—'With respect to the third mode of proceeding, what were the propositions referred to therein as intended to be made to Ibrahim Pacha?'

Answer.—The propositions referred to were, that the expedition should return to Alexandria or the Dardanelles, and not operate further in Greece or the islands; and we were prepared to guarantee the safe return of any or all the forces at Ibrahim's disposal, if he consented to abandon the country.

I am induced to think the answers which I have thus given to the queries put by Lord Dudley, will be satisfactory to the Government, as showing that I had no other means of effecting the purpose of the Treaty than by anchoring in the port of Navarin.

But I will beg leave to trespass further upon the time of His Royal Highness the Lord High Admiral, by adverting in the first place to that part of the second instruction emanating from the Treaty, which says: 'Should this hypothesis be realised you will be informed thereof directly by the King's ambassador at Constantinople, who is instructed to correspond with you, &c. The informations which you may receive and the directions which may accompany them, to which you will be pleased to conform, will be concerted between the three ambassadors; and the proceedings and arrangements which these ambassadors shall have pointed out, as well as those which circumstances may have rendered necessary, must be arranged between you and the French and Russian commanders.'

Now, upon weighing the possible, if not probable, effect of carrying this Instruction into execution, I wrote on the 11th August to Mr. Stratford Canning :—' Neither of us* can make out how we are by force to prevent the Turks, if obstinate, from pursuing any line of conduct which we are instructed to oppose, without committing hostility. Surely it must be like a blockade—if an attempt be made to force it, by force only can that attempt be resisted.'

To this he replied in a *confidential* letter dated 19th August, 1827: ' I agree with you in thinking that any loss or imminent danger occurring to His Highness's fleet is more likely to soften than to rivet his determination. In speaking of " collision " in a former letter, I only meant that the decisive moment as to war will be that in which he first learns by experience that we mean to enforce, if necessary by cannon shot, the armistice which it is the object of the Treaty to establish, with or without him, as the case may be. This I imagine to be the true meaning of the second Instruction addressed to you and your colleagues. You are not to take part with either of the belligerents, but you are to interpose your forces between them, and to keep the peace with your speaking-trumpet, if possible, but, in case of necessity, with that which is used for the maintenance of a blockade against friends as well as foes—I mean force.'

And in another confidential letter dated 1st September, 1827, he further replied: ' On the subject of *collision*, for instance, we agree that, although the measures to be executed by you are not to be adopted in a hostile spirit, and although it is clearly the intention of the Allied Governments to avoid, if possible, anything that may bring on war, yet the prevention of supplies, as stated in your Instructions, is ultimately to be enforced, if necessary, and when all other means are exhausted, by cannon shot.'

These documents will show that it was my duty to execute the Treaty, by persuasion if I could, but if not, by the employment of actual force, and that force is defined by Mr. S. Canning to be—*cannon shot.*

In all my subsequent proceedings, detailed with a scrupulous minuteness, His Royal Highness will observe that I used my utmost endeavours to avoid the collision contemplated in the Treaty. My first letter received by Ibrahim in Navarin, urging consent to the mediation, goes to establish this point; for, if the expedition had put to sea, and he had refused to return with it to Africa upon my representation,

* Meaning Admiral de Rigny and myself.

it is evident I must, according to my instructions, have employed the force under my command to effect it, without waiting for his first making an attack upon any of the Allied ships. Even if a blockade could have been made effectual, we must have come to this extremity whenever a want of provisions might oblige the Ottoman fleet to put to sea. But in the meantime the whole Peloponnesus would have been ravaged by the vengeful Ibrahim and his army; and its unopposing and unoffending inhabitants reduced to that misery, to prevent which was the prominent object of this important Treaty. This conduct of Ibrahim was first made known to me by deputies bringing letters from Armyro, translations of which, with other papers, accompany this.

In order further to show that I have made it my object throughout to avoid collision with the Ottoman fleet, and not to let my interruption of the supplies of men, arms, vessels, and warlike stores, degenerate into hostilities, I have enclosed copies of papers referring to this particular head; in all of which His Royal Highness the Lord High Admiral, and his Majesty's Government, will observe that caution on this point has been my prominent principle.

Even when a division of the Navarin fleet was met with going to Patras in breach of the armistice, and when so favourable an opportunity was afforded for professional distinction, I refrained as much as possible from coming into actual collision. The same evidence of determination to execute the object of the Treaty which prevented collision on the above occasion, enabled me to deter Ibrahim himself, with almost his whole fleet, from forcing the passage which it was my duty to intercept.

I may now be permitted, in closing this letter, to repeat that, according to the concurrent testimony of all the pilots and all the officers whose local experience established the soundness of their opinions, a blockade of the port of Navarin was physically impracticable.

That so long as the Allied Fleet remained without the port, Ibrahim continued to practise uninterrupted that barbarous and exterminating warfare which the Treaty was formed to prevent.

That, therefore, the object of the Allied Powers could only be accomplished by our actually entering the port of Navarin, and, by means of the imposing presence of the squadrons, inducing Ibrahim to send back the expeditionary force to Alexandria or the Dardanelles.

I have, &c., &c.,
EDWD. CODRINGTON.

From Captain Fellowes to Sir E. C.

Malta: December 11, 1827.

Sir,—Having been called upon by you to furnish a statement of the immediate causes which led to the commencement
of the action of Navarin, on the 20th October, 1827, I have
the honour to state for your information, that, in pursuance
of your instructions of the 19th October, I anchored
H. M.'s ship under my command betwixt the brûlot and the
first ship (double-banked) on the eastern side of the harbour.
While in the act of furling sails, a Turkish boat pulled past
the 'Dartmouth,' in the greatest hurry, and went on board
the brûlot. On perceiving them occupied in preparing their
train, and from our being so very near, I felt it absolutely
necessary that immediate steps should be taken to prevent
the destruction of the fleet, which, from their manner of proceeding, seemed inevitable. I accordingly sent the pinnace
with the first lieutenant, directing him to explain to them
that if they remained quiet no harm was intended; but, as
their position was one of great danger to us, I wished them
to quit the vessel in their boats, or to remove her further
in shore out of our way. As our boat left the ship, perceiving
one of our midshipmen with his sword drawn, I desired him
to sheath it; and that the men in the boat might perfectly
understand, I called out from the gangway, in the hearing of
the ship's company, 'Recollect, Sir, that no act of hostility
is to be attempted by us *on any account.*' When the boat
reached the quarter of the vessel, and was in the act of laying
in the oars, the coxswain was shot dead, although the first
lieutenant had made signs to the Turkish commander that
no violence was intended, which he even repeated after the
man had been shot close by him. This shot was followed up
by several others, fired through the after ports, killing and
wounding others of the boat's crew. At the same moment
we observed part of the Turkish crew ignite the train forward; upon which I despatched Lieutenant Fitzroy in the
cutter for the purpose of towing her clear of this ship; in
executing of which he met a boat conveying the crew of
the burning fire-vessel towards the shore, who immediately
opened a fire of musketry upon him by which he was killed.
On observing this, I ordered the marines to cover the retreat
of the boats, which were again sent to tow the vessel, then
in flames, clear of us. Almost at the same instant, two shots
were fired from an Egyptian corvette in shore, one of which
passed close over the gangway, and the other we observed

strike the 'Sirène,' bearing the flag of Rear-Admiral de
Rigny, then in the act of anchoring. Thus, from the aggression on the part of the Turks, commenced the action ; nor
could forbearance on ours have been exceeded, or your particular instruction to avoid hostility more fully complied
with.

I have the honour to be, Sir,
Your most obedient humble Servant,
THOMAS FELLOWES, Captain.

Sir John Gore's Report to the Lord High Admiral.

After carefully perusing all the documents, and attending
to all the parole circumstances relating to the entrance of
the allied fleet into the harbour on October 20, 1827, it
appears to me that the measure was indispensable for the
fulfilment of the Treaty and the obedience to Sir E. Codrington's instructions founded thereon.

On September 25 Ibrahim Pacha, surrounded by all his
chiefs, received Vice-Admiral Sir E. Codrington and R. A.
de Rigny, with their respective suites, and, in a solemn
divan, agreed to a suspension of hostilities *by sea and land*
until he should receive instructions from Constantinople and
Alexandria, of which he pledged himself to inform Sir E. C.

On the 26th Ibrahim sent his dragoman (Arbro) to the
Allied admirals, and obtained a further declaration respecting the intent and object of the treaty of the previous day's
conference. Notwithstanding which, a few days after, he
put to sea with part of his fleet, and attempted to get to
Patras, but was foiled by the firmness and address of Sir
E. C. (who, trusting to the protestation of honour of Ibrahim
Pacha, was left with the 'Asia' 84, 'Dartmouth' 42, 'Talbot' 28, and 'Zebra' 18 only) ; and was obliged to return to
Navarin. On this occasion, a further explanation of the
treaty and extent of the armistice was given to the Capitana
Bey who commanded the Turkish fleet, and who was second
in command under Ibrahim Pacha.

The Allied squadrons reassembled before Navarin about
the time Sir E. C. was led to expect that answers would be
received from Constantinople and Alexandria, and of which
Ibrahim Pacha had promised to inform him ; but no intimation was conveyed to him that such answers had been received,
though the brig which went to Alexandria on September 27
returned to Navarin on October 16. On the contrary, he
was informed from various authorities that Ibrahim Pacha
was at the head of part of his army devastating the Morea
and committing all those cruelties and atrocities which it

was the object of the Treaty of London and the instructions
of Sir E. C. to prevent. Consequently, on October 17, the
Allied admirals wrote a letter to Ibrahim Pacha calling on
him to desist, and sent it into Navarin by the Hon. Lieutenant-Colonel Cradock in H.M.S. 'Dartmouth.' This letter
was returned unopened, the Turkish admiral and Arbro the
dragoman declaring repeatedly upon their honour that they
did not know where Ibrahim was, and that *no person had
authority* to open any letter, or to *give any reply!* The
Allied admirals were thus cut off from all means of communication so as to suppress such acts of barbarity on the part
of the Turco-Egyptian forces; and as the season was too far
advanced to admit of blockading Navarin which is entirely
impracticable during the winter, and as in personal conference with Ibrahim it was found they could amicably
arrange the most essential objects of the Treaty of London,
it was determined to take the Allied fleets into Navarin, and
there demand an interview with the Pacha and by conference prevail on him to retire to the Dardanelles and
Alexandria with his forces. It was ascertained that the
Turco-Egyptian fleet was moored in a very strong position
with fire-vessels at each extremity, and in every way prepared for offence and defence, even to having springs on
their cables. A corresponding caution was required on the
part of the Allies; and under the entire breach of confidence
in Ibrahim Pacha, it would have been an act of indiscretion
almost amounting to insanity for the Allied admirals to have
come into Navarin to hold such conference with less than
their entire force prepared for battle. In doing so, to evince
that the intentions of Sir E. C. were not hostile, see his
letters to Mr. S. Canning of August 11* and 24, his general
orders to his captains of September 8,† his letter to Rear-
Admiral Count Heiden of September 30, and his letter to
Ibrahim Pacha of October 17,‡ which was returned to him
unopened, whereon the Allied admirals decided to proceed
into Navarin and obtain a conference, and propose an amicable return of the Turco-Egyptian forces to the Dardanelles
and Alexandria.

As the known want of discipline and extreme carelessness
of the Turks on board their ships rendered the situation of
the fire-vessels dangerous to the Allied fleet in the position
it was intended to take up, Captain Fellowes, of the 'Dartmouth,' was directed to move them to leeward, and within
their own fleet, and in a manner as little offensive as the
circumstances would admit of. In going in, Count Heiden

---

* Pages 415 and 432.   † Page 451 in Vol. I.   ‡ Page 56 in Vol. II.

requested permission to prepare to anchor his squadron by
the stern. Sir E. C. replied, 'No, for it will bear the appearance of premeditated hostility;' and on Captain Curzon
wishing to haul the 'Asia's' ports flat against the side, as
for battle, Sir E. C. forbid it, saying at the same time, 'We
must not put on a hostile appearance, but be in all respects
prepared to act if required.' So soon as the 'Asia' was
moored and the sails furled, the watch was called to square
the yards, and the band was mustered on the poop to play.
The furniture was not moved out of the admiral's cabin (in
consequence most of it was destroyed by shot), nor was the
drum beat to quarters until the firing was commenced by
the Egyptian corvette. A fire of musketry from an Egyptian fire-vessel on the 'Dartmouth's' boat first called attention; it was followed by three shots from an Egyptian corvette—one passed over the 'Dartmouth's' gangway, another
struck the French admiral's ship amidships and killed two
men, a third cut her cable the moment she had anchored
and obliged them to let go a second anchor! It had been
repeatedly urged to Ibrahim Pacha and his chiefs that the
first shot fired at either of the Allied flags would be considered a
declaration of hostilities; consequently, upon this outrage, a
general battle ensued.

The Turkish officer who went on board the 'Asia' as she
entered the harbour, sent by the Capitana Bey to 'request
Sir E. C. would not come in with such a force as Ibrahim
Pacha was not there to receive him,' went direct from the
'Asia' to the shore; he was met on landing by numerous
chiefs, and was seen to run swiftly up the hill, followed by
them all, to a tent; soon after which a *red flag was hoisted at
the tent and a gun fired—unshotted.* On this signal, a boat
was sent from the Capitana Bey to the Egyptian admiral's
ship, and to the fire-vessel close to the 'Dartmouth;' and
on Captain Fellowes seeing them preparing the train, he
sent his first lieutenant in the pinnace to request they
would desist; and, observing the midshipman in the boat
draw his sword, he called out, 'Put up your sword, sir, and
make no hostile demonstration whatever,' and the lieutenant
in the boat made every sign he could imagine of pacific intentions. Nevertheless, as the boat approached, the coxswain
and one of the crew were shot dead from the quarter ports,
and the midshipman was killed going up the side, and fell
across the gunwale. Seeing this, and that the vessel was
in flames, Captain Fellowes sent Lieutenant Fitzroy in a
cutter (not armed) to tow the fire-vessel clear of the Allied
fleet. On crossing her bow, the cutter met the boat full of

the retiring crew, who opened a fire of pistols, whereby Lieutenant Fitzroy and several of the cutter's crew were killed and wounded. At this moment, ' la Sirène,' Mons. de Rigny's flagship, passed close and fired some muskets, as did the ' Dartmouth,' to cover the boats, and at the same time the corvette as before mentioned laying close to the *place where* the Turkish officers had *landed*, commenced the fire. At this period, only the ' Asia,' ' Genoa,' and ' Dartmouth' had anchored; the ' Albion' received two broadsides before she anchored, and every Turkish ship and Egyptian ship and vessel had opened their fire before either of the French ships of the line had anchored, so that the ' Breslau' did not see her proper station.

From these facts it is manifest that hostilities did not commence with the Allies; and it may reasonably be presumed that the battle was premeditated by Ibrahim Pacha, under the advice of the French renegado Le Tellier, and that hoisting the red flag and firing the gun at Ibrahim's tent was the signal to engage, as a similar act occurred previous to the battle of Algiers.   Having carefully perused all the extensive correspondence which Sir E. Codrington has maintained with Sir S. Canning, the Earl Dudley, Viscount Granville, Mr. Consul Salt, and his colleagues, since the first moment he received the Treaty and his instructions for its fulfilment, it is impossible for me not to be surprised and to feel admiration at the dispassionate, enlightened, and extensive view he has taken of the whole, and the manner in which he has by anticipation adopted the intentions of His Majesty's Government in carrying into effect so extraordinary, unprecedented, and arduous a duty: nor has he evinced less ability in the manner in which he has preserved unanimity among his associates, who are all in good humour with each other, and join in almost enthusiastic admiration of the chief who has directed and led them.

J. GORE.

From Lord Ingestrie to Sir E. C.

71 Lower Grosvenor Street: November 20, 1827.

MY DEAR SIR,—You will see how magnificently the Duke has behaved to us all, for it is all his doing and nobody else's. Since my arrival I have been catechised pretty copiously in all quarters. The whole affair seems to have occasioned the greatest degree of surprise, and to none more than to His Majesty's Ministers. I am told they do not like it, and think that you have been precipitate and so forth; and, as it has always been, when an odious thing was to be accomplished, have wished to throw the whole onus on the shoulders of the executive department. I am glad of it, for I know you will come triumphant from all their mean insinuations. I find that the transactions of September 25, and the subsequent ones of October 2 and 3, are only known to those in office, and consequently to the world it appears somewhat strange. People at large exonerate you, but question, as I have always done, the policy of the Treaty; and I hope the Ministers will get a good rattling shake. They had me before the Cabinet and asked me a string of questions, the whole tendency of which was to make me let something inadvertently drop, which would imply that sufficient provocation had not been given you to act as you did. It struck me that they wished to make out that Ibrahim was entitled to proceed how he liked by land, and seemed to forget his gross violation of faith by sea, entirely.

I answered them in a fearless manner, by a simple affirmative or negative. I am considerably hurt at the unhandsome manner I conceive they have used towards you and myself—I say to you, for I think it most unjust that a pack of questions should be put without allowing me to refer to the transactions relative to *Patras* at all; and to me, for it makes me, an eye-witness, appear to have been guilty either of gross stupidity or want of observation. Of course I could only answer such questions as were put to me, and that I did in the most straightforward manner I could. You cannot conceive the fuss that is made in this town about the whole affair. We unresponsible people receive our share of the credit that accrues to you *nemine dissentiente* as far as the action itself goes.

Who the deuce would ever have thought of my being a C.B.! I have insisted with your soldier son on being allowed to present you with your G.C.B. insignia, and you will confer an additional obligation on me by pocketing the affront from a paltry post-captain. With every wish to your health, honour, and happiness,

I am yours gratefully,
INGESTRIE.

These, with a few questions as to who fired the first gun, &c., and concerning the death of Mitchel, the resources of Ibrahim, &c., are as near as I can recollect the questions and answers. I enclose them, for it will be satisfactory to me to know how you approve of my answers.

1. Did you understand that by the armistice Ibrahim was restricted by land as well as by sea?

Ans. Certainly, in my opinion. Ibrahim's own impression was most decidedly that his ships were not to move, from the circumstance of his asking leave to send a ship with the despatches.

2. Did any communication take place after the return of the Egyptian fleet to Navarin, between Ibrahim and the Admirals of the combined fleet, previously to the action?

Ans. Being absent on other duties I cannot say, but I believe there was some.

3. Did the 'Dartmouth' carry any letter in, or was she there only for the purpose of reconnoitring, and how long was she there?

Ans. She was there a whole night; the former part of the question I cannot answer.

4. What was the general impression in the fleet as to whether there would be an action or not?

Ans. My own was that there would be none, and I think that was the most general opinion.

5. Had the Admiral any other means of knowing that atrocities were committed on the part of Ibrahim except by Captain Hamilton?

Ans. Yes; by what means I know not, but it was a current fact before Captain H. left the fleet for Kitries, after which the letter was written.

6. Was it the general impression in the fleet that those atrocities were committed?

Ans. Nobody doubted it.

7. Did the forts fire at you going in?

Ans. No; they fired a blank gun after a boat had been to the Admiral, to tell him he must not come in, who answered that he was come to give and not to receive orders.

8. Had the boat from the 'Dartmouth' a flag of truce up when she was fired into? *

Ans. No.

9. What was she sent for?

Ans. She went to desire the brûlot to move from a position which rendered the situation of the fleet precarious; her orders were to avoid committing any hostility.

10. Was any signal made from the 'Asia' for commencing the engagement?

Ans. I saw none; but after the first gun, the firing became general.

* Not customary except between belligerents.

From Sir E. C. to Admiral Sir George Cockburn, Admiralty.

Malta: December 10, 1827.

MY DEAR COCKBURN,—Many thanks for your congratulations. It is very flattering to me to have received such strong approbation of my conduct from so many of my brother officers, as well as from my countrymen in general; and when these are added to the commendation of the Lord High Admiral, and the distinction bestowed on me by my King, I need not, and shall not, be uneasy as to what may be said by politicians. All I will say further on this point is, that the more my conduct is scrutinised the more I shall be satisfied, provided I am given the opportunity of explaining myself. My excellent son is nearly well, and as merry and as happy, whether on his crutches or steering his wheel-chair through the doorways of this large house, as if he had escaped unhurt, as I did. By the way, it is not easy to account for my escape upon examining my coat. There is a hole through the two parts of my sleeve without the bit being torn through, which Dr. Liddell thinks must have been a musket-ball, or a piece of their extraordinary langridge; and yet it only produced a scratch, of which I was not sensible at the time, and which never required even a piece of sticking plaister, although the mark is still there. The other results were caused by splinters, which merely pulled me round rudely. But I have no doubt of my watch and seal having saved me from what would, but for their nobly sacrificing themselves for their master, have proved a severe contusion. On putting my hand up, in consequence of the blow, I caught the piece of rail which occasioned it and threw it overboard. How one's pen is led on! I had no intention of entering upon this history when I began; and you must attribute it to yourself for mentioning *my escape* in your letter. I think all our friend Gore will have to tell the Government, added to the mass of which my despatch is composed, will tire them of requiring explanations from me. They will show at least that I have no wish to conceal anything. And I have sent Fellowes also with this view; as, besides being the immediate cause of precipitating the battle, which no doubt was to have been begun by the Turks at midnight, he, having been sent twice into Navarin with letters, can further explain all the verbal instructions which accompanied the order under which we acted. Lady Codrington is of too anxious a nature not to fidget about the mission of John Gore; and like him, has hardly yet

ceased to be surprised at my treating it so lightly. The fact
is, I have always looked forward to such a contingency, and
it has taken them unawares. What has been often said of
success, I say of approbation. I cannot be sure of obtaining
it; but, as far as my ability can reach, I will take care to
deserve it. As I can hardly now except the wounded son, I
may say Lady C. and her children are all well. She desires
her kind regards to be joined with those of

, Yours most sincerely,

EDWD. CODRINGTON.

From Sir E. C. to H.R.H. the Duke of Clarence.

Malta : December 10, 1827.

SIR,—I fear Your Royal Highness will be tired of the sight
of letters from me; but I cannot let my friend Sir J. Gore
return without adding to the mass of papers which accompany him the expression of my cordial thanks for the sword
which Your Royal Highness has sent me by the 'Rattlesnake.' I consider that sword as a very valuable addition
to the other splendid proofs of your approbation of my conduct in and relating to the battle of Navarin; and I shall
never put it to my side without inward feelings of pride
that I should have been deemed worthy of so distinguished
a mark of Your Royal Highness's kindness. I have further
to thank Your Royal Highness for having chosen as the
medium of your late communications a brother officer of high
rank and distinction; whose mind is sure to be directed to
the attainment of a just and upright view of the business
in which he is engaged, and whose warm and honest heart
is guided by the sincerest friendship for me personally.
Events may perhaps by this time have removed from the
Cabinet those fears for the consequences of the Treaty which
they do not appear to have contemplated. My conduct as
an officer is not to be judged by those events, whatever they
may be; but I may repeat to Your Royal Highness the
opinion which I took the liberty of offering shortly after the
battle, that it is more likely to produce a good than a bad
effect upon the future proceedings of the Sultan. It appears
to me by Mr. Croker's letter of the 13th November that
Your Royal Highness would have readily bestowed some
additional honour upon those officers named therein who
were already Companions of the Bath. I am therefore led
to mention a suggestion of General Ponsonby, that they
should be made Knights Commanders of St. Michael and St.
George. He thinks that making this a military order, and

thus giving it to officers for conduct in battle within these seas, will enhance the value of the Order.   Honoured as I am with the Grand Cross of the Bath, I trust it will not be thought that by mentioning this suggestion I am seeking only to make my own distinction permanent, although I am aware that such an arrangement would naturally follow his Majesty's adoption of it.   In such case, I feel it incumbent on me to request that the name of Captain Curzon may be joined with those of Captains Hamilton and Fellowes. There is one other point which I am induced to advert to, as it may be turned to Parliamentary account in the discussion of the battle of Navarin with some flippant debater. The island of Sphacteria by which the harbour is formed, is admitted by Treaty to belong to the Ionian States; and as it has been admitted that the Turks have no right to sail in the Ionian waters without first obtaining permission, the port of Navarin itself appears to belong more to the Ionian States than to the possessors of the adjacent coast.   I am sure Your Royal Highness will now be glad to be released; and I will trouble you no further at present than to receive my assurances that I am, with the most unfeigned respect, Your Royal Highness's very grateful and obedient servant,
EDWD. CODRINGTON.

From Sir E. C. to H.R.H. the Duke of Clarence.
- Malta. December 18, 1827.

SIR,—Although I think my letter replying to the queries contained in the letter of Lord Dudley will be sufficient to remove any idea of my not having conducted myself according to my instructions, I take the liberty of addressing to Your Royal Highness some further observations arising from the communications made to me verbally by Sir John Gore, and from his notes taken when in conversation with Sir George Cockburn just before his departure.   The report made by Captain Fellowes will remove all doubts as to how the battle was brought on.   But as I wish that there should be no ground for supposing I have a desire to withhold anything whatever relating to its origin, I have requested Captain Fellowes himself will accompany Sir John Gore to England.   It will be evident to Your Royal Highness that if I had intended to begin hostilities I should not have done so with musketry, but by firing our broadsides into those fire-vessels as we proceeded towards our anchorage.   It is equally evident, that instead of placing the Allied fleets where I did, exposed to the fire of both the principal lines of the Ottoman fleet, and to the fire-vessels also, I should have passed betwixt the Egyptian division and the shore, and have attacked them on that side, on which they were probably unprepared. But I sacrificed this advantage to give proof of my desire to preserve peace at all hazards; and I objected to Count Heiden's wish to have a cable out of the 'Azoff's' stern, as I did to Captain Curzon's wish of hauling up the 'Asia's' lower-deck ports beyond their level, as indicative of hostile intentions. In fact, so little did I expect a battle, that after the 'Asia' was moored and the sails furled, the watch had been piped to secure yards, and the band was mustering on the poop, when the firing at the 'Dartmouth's' boat took place; and then the drum was again beat to quarters.

Men without professional knowledge may consider our going in prepared for battle as evidence of hostile intention. I might beg leave respectfully to refer them to your Royal Highness as to the duty of captains on such occasions. But a very sufficient reply to such a supposition will be found in the Instructions to Captains, page 79, article 17; which says: 'In time of peace he is not to approach a ship of war of any foreign power without having the ship so far prepared for battle, that in case of aggression he may be immediately ready to defend himself,' &c. I am free to say that this very preparation, and the answers I gave to the Turkish officer who desired me to wait the pleasure of Ibrahim Pacha (he who chose not to be found when required to receive the joint letter of my colleagues and myself), were well calculated to have prevented hostilities, if that wily chief had not previously directed an attack to be made on us, according to the plan of the renegade Letellier. With respect to my desiring that the fire-vessels should be removed, I consider that measure as a precaution under any circumstances indispensably necessary for the safety of the fleet, and as a probable means of preventing the execution of hostility previously concerted, had there been sufficient time to effect it; for, according to the concurrent testimony of several Greeks and English who were forcibly detained in the Ottoman fleet, as well as that of a Turk saved from the fire-vessel which was sunk by the 'Philomel,' the setting fire to those vessels at midnight and dropping them down upon the Allied fleet was the meditated signal for a general attack.

As to my designating the Turks 'enemies,' your Royal Highness will excuse my observing on the inconsistency of those who object to that single word at the end of a sentence—and quoted from Lord Nelson—and who pass over the early part of the sentence, which runs 'in case of a regular battle ensuing,' &c. I am almost ashamed to have addressed answers to such observations as the above to your Royal Highness personally, who have been pleased to view my conduct in the late important battle with so much favor, and so much generosity. It has been my pride, my ambition, to deserve that confidence of which your Royal Highness had always given me so many proofs; and after such gratifying marks of the gracious approbation of my Sovereign and of your Royal Highness, whose professional judgment cannot be questioned, I might well rest contented, without combating the unreasonable objections of persons entirely uninformed. But my character is no longer merely my own. I feel now bound to prove that I am not unworthy the spontaneous, the generous patronage which his Majesty and your Royal Highness have given me. I hope, therefore, I may be excused for having entered more into detail upon the subject of my own conduct, than I should otherwise have considered necessary, in order to justify such unbounded kindness on the part of my Sovereign and of your Royal Highness. And I beg to assure your Royal Highness that if I had no other motive for the zealous fulfilment of my instructions, this very kindness would insure my devotion to the important duties with which I have the honor of being intrusted.

I cannot sufficiently express how sensible I am of his Majesty's most gracious consideration of my services, in bestowing upon me the Grand Cross of the Bath; and of the gracious recommendation of your Royal Highness that I should be honored with this most valuable distinction. Nor have I words to convey to your Royal Highness the joyous, the grateful feelings of the officers and men under my command, for that high approbation, those liberal promotions, and those honorable distinctions, with which your Royal Highness has been graciously pleased to mark their brave and exemplary conduct in the battle of Navarin.

I have the honor to be, with the greatest respect, your Royal Highness's very grateful and obedient

EDWD. CODRINGTON.

It may have been right to ask for full explanation from Sir E. Codrington of the cause of the battle, and to send for that purpose a distinguished naval officer and intimate friend. Yet these official queries, and the doubts thus thrown on the conduct of the English Admiral, left the future in uncertainty, both as to the Treaty itself and the measures to be taken under it.   The English Government—Lord Goderich being Prime Minister—surprised by a hostile result for which they ought to have prepared themselves by their knowledge of the affair of Patras, and the country by the publication of it, was weak in nerve, weak in Parliament, and was in face of a strong opposition, particularly in regard to the foreign policy of their late chief, Mr. Canning.   This Ministry resigned in December, 1827, before the meeting of Parliament, and was succeeded by that of the Duke of Wellington.—W. J. C.

Sir E. Codrington had received from his own sovereign the Grand Cross of the Bath; and there was no hesitation in France and Russia as to the approval of the sovereigns of those countries.   The King of France conferred upon Sir E. C. the Grand Cross of the Military Order of St. Louis; and he had the rare honour of wearing the second class of the Military Order of St. George, conferred upon him by an autograph letter from the Emperor Nicolas: Count Heiden was also desired, if an English ship were not available, to offer any Russian line-of-battle ship for the flag of the English Commander-in-Chief.   ' Vous mettriez à sa disposition tous ceux de votre escadre, et vous l'assureriez que l'Empereur regarderait sa présence sur un de nos bâtimens comme un véritable honneur pour la marine russe.'

Sir E. C. said to Count Heiden: 'I can never forget the rare compliment of offering me permission to hoist my flag in one of the Russian ships.'

From the Emperor of Russia.

St. Pétersbourg, le 8 novembre 1827.

MONSIEUR LE VICE-AMIRAL CODRINGTON,—Vous venez de remporter une victoire dont l'Europe civilisée doit vous être doublement reconnaissante.   La mémorable bataille de Navarin et les manœuvres hardies qui l'ont précédée, ne donnent pas seulement au monde la mesure du zèle de trois grandes Puissances pour une cause dont leur désintéressement relève encore le noble caractère; elles prouvent

aussi ce que peut la fermeté contre le nombre, et une
valeur habilement dirigée contre un courage aveugle, quelles
que soient les forces dont il s'appuye. Votre nom appartient
désormais à la postérité. Je croirais affaiblir par des éloges
la gloire qui l'environne, mais j'éprouve le besoin de vous
offrir une marque éclatante de la gratitude et de l'estime
que vous inspirez à la Russie. C'est dans cette vue que je
vous envoye ci-joint l'ordre militaire de St.-George.

La marine russe s'honore d'avoir obtenu votre suffrage
devant Navarin, et pour moi j'ai le plus vif plaisir à vous
assurer des sentimens de considération que je vous porte.

                                        NICOLAS.

À M. le Vice-Amiral Codrington.*

From Sir E. C. to H.R.H. the Duke of Clarence.

.   Malta: December 15, 1827.

SIR,—Although I conclude the situation of affairs at Constantinople is known to his Majesty's government, I have
thought it well worth while to direct that a courier should
be sent from Genoa to Paris with the information of the
ambassadors having demanded their passports; so that Lord
Granville may forward it by express if no such information
has passed through the capital.   The Porte has refused the
passports, and the general tranquillity of the people indicates
peace rather than war; and notwithstanding any contrary
appearances, I still retain the opinion I first submitted to
your Royal Highness and have since repeated, that the
battle of Navarin is more likely to preserve peace than to
create war. The Reis Effendi received the account with perfect calmness, as an event which he expected; observing
'This is what you call friendship, occasioning the Sultan the
loss of a million and a half of pounds sterling, and the lives
of betwixt eight and nine thousand of his subjects.'   I hear
Tahir, and several other Turks, slipped away in the night
from Navarin, in the corvette in which he had hoisted his
flag, and is arrived at Constantinople, and that at the first
moment of learning of the destruction of his fleet the Sultan
ordered Pera to be surrounded by his troops and to be given
up to butchery; that the Divan under the influence of the
Capitan Pacha had the heads taken off those who were to
have carried this measure into execution, and thus stopped
it, whilst the Internuncio sat up with the Sultan all night,

* To this gracious kindness Sir E C. returned a grateful and suitable
answer.

and at length succeeded in dissuading him from this brutality.   I believe letters are coming in a French vessel to me
from Mr. S. Canning, but I have not had a line from him
since he knew of the battle.   However, the measure of
demanding the passports I rather think was previously determined on, in case of the Porte continuing obstinate, as the
only one which could force a decision.

December 17.

A gale of wind directly into the harbour has prevented
any vessel getting out since I began this letter, and I myself
have been too ill to close my despatches; but I trust I am
now sufficiently convalescent to continue my duties.   I give
your Royal Highness the above *reports* of what is passing,
without being able to place any reliance upon them.

The 'Asia' will be ready to sail, jury-rigged, in a few days,
and I intend that she and the 'Albion' should go together.
It would take more time, and be, I imagine, more expensive,
to repair her here, or I should not subject myself to the inconvenience occasioned by her absence.   The divers report
a notch in her gripe, I apprehend just where the stem is
scarfed to the keel, which would endanger a cable being
caught in it.   I have put some of the mates lately promoted,
to join the 'Asia' upon an understanding that they are not
to remain in her.   There are several lieutenants on the station whom I wish to have in the 'Asia,' on account of their
good conduct, if your Royal Highness will give me that indulgence, as an encouragement of that zeal and spirit which
is conspicuous on this station.

In a private letter from Captain Richards, of the 'Pelorus,'
he mentions the Pacha of Egypt having said, on November
1, before he had heard of the battle : 'The Sultan has ordered
Ibrahim to put out and attack Hydra in spite of your admiral; he will not move, however, till I write to him, which
will be in a few days;' (and he added with a laugh) : 'There
must be an engagement at sea, but it will be nothing; a few
of the first will be destroyed, and the others will turn back;
this is necessary to convince everyone that you are in earnest.'
All that I have yet heard since the loss of the Ottoman fleet
became known, convinces me that if we carry the business
in which we are engaged with a high hand, particularly now
that the whole race are so humbled, the result of the Treaty
will be satisfactory.   But I trust your Royal Highness will
excuse my saying that it behoves any government to support
their own instructions.   Had they done so, they would perhaps have avoided an attack which a contrary conduct would
seem to invite.

From Sir E. C. to Vice-Admiral De Rigny.

Malta: December 17, 1827.

MY DEAR ADMIRAL,—I most sincerely congratulate you upon your promotion, as announced to me in your letter of the 7th of this month by the 'Jasper,' and it will always be a great pleasure to me to reflect that I have been so fortunate as to have under my command, an officer who, besides exhibiting such conspicuous gallantry, has entitled himself in so many other ways to my great esteem and regard. If I do not immediately answer your official communication of His Most Christian Majesty having honored me with the Grand Cross of St. Louis, it is because I must undergo the form of asking my own Sovereign's permission to wear it. It is best, perhaps, to wait until I get an answer to this request, which I have immediately made, for myself and my brethren in arms. Your news of what is passing at Constantinople, is very interesting. In spite of warlike appearances, I still retain my opinion that the battle of Navarin will have inclined the Sultan to yield to circumstances. I hear that since the arrival of Tahir at the capital, provisions have been sent to Ibrahim. This shows that if Lord Cochrane and his fleet had blockaded Navarin instead of going to Scio, the army in the Morea would have been reduced to great extremity. But it seems his Lordship wanted to be Grand Master of the Islands of the Archipelago under the banner of Christ !!! De Heiden has expressed to Mons. de Ribeaupierre the same opinion you have, that the Russians can only act under the Treaty. Sir Thomas Staines will have by this time made known to you my plan for destroying the principal establishment at Carabusa; and he will consult you on the subject. I have not received a line from Mr. S. Canning since the news of the battle reached him. I quite agree with you, that if we are to pass the Dardanelles, we must have the assistance of troops to take the castle on *one* side, if not both. But by the time we have done that, this ferocious Sultan will have lost his head. For his brutal subjects must revenge themselves on somebody for their losses; and I hope they will not find it quite as easy to get at yours or mine, as that of their own *most sublime master.*

I have still got the 'Asia' and 'Albion' here, in case of a pressing demand for ships, but I shall send them off with the next easterly wind. For if such ships are wanted, the news from Mr. S. Canning arriving in London, will induce our Lord High Admiral to send me others in their places. If the Greeks will not blockade Navarin, and endeavour to starve

Ibrahim's army, we must try what we can do ourselves; for upon that depends the conduct of the Porte. If that army is able to continue its ravages, the Sultan will be contented, and will remain sulky; but if he finds it loses ground daily, he will perhaps come to his senses.

Believe me, &c.,
EDWD. CODRINGTON.

I have received the most unqualified approbation of my Sovereign and of his Royal Highness the Lord High Admiral; but our ministers, like yours, not being able to foresee the consequences of the battle, are in a fright, and don't know how to defend their own Treaty. My last letter will open their eyes.

From Sir E. C. to the Admiralty.

'Asia,' at Malta: December 20, 1827.

SIR,—On my first arrival off Navarin on the 12th September last, I found the Ottoman army had taken regular possession of the Islands of Sphacteria and Sapienza which are component parts of the Ionian States; the first forming the harbour of Navarin, the last that of Modon. On Sphacteria, Ibrahim Pacha had placed a considerable body of troops, and he had erected batteries at the S.E. end, in order to command the entrance. In contemplating an effectual blockade of the port, the means of so doing by taking possession of this island, did not escape me: it was, however, quite evident that the attempt would have been resisted, and that it could not have been enforced without that open hostility which it was my desire to avoid; whilst I felt justified in expecting that no opposition would have been offered to the whole Allied squadron combined, by that same force which had relinquished the most important object of relieving Patras, when the 'Asia' was supported by only the 'Dartmouth,' 'Talbot,' and 'Zebra.' In order to fulfil the second instruction emanating from the Treaty under the circumstances of the Sultan still obstinately refusing the mediation, whilst Ibrahim Pacha is endeavouring to destroy the whole Peloponnesus,—I beg to submit to his Royal Highness the Lord High Admiral, the propriety of now claiming possession of those two islands, and enforcing that claim against any resistance that may be offered; as the most effectual and prompt way of paralysing the future movements of the whole Ottoman army now ravaging the country.

I have, &c.,
EDWD. CODRINGTON.

From Sir E. C. to His Royal Highness the Duke of Clarence.

Malta: December 20, 1827.

SIR,—The reports of our Ambassadors having actually quitted Constantinople, indicate that continued obstinacy in the Sultan which will make it requisite for us to draw more strictly the line of opposition to his measures. I have therefore made the proposal contained in my public letter of this day's date, a duplicate of which I intend sending open through Sir Frederick Adam, that he may, if he think proper, make any observations of his own on it to the Colonial Secretary of State. The paucity of troops in these parts just now, may occasion hesitation. But even if Ibrahim should offer resistance, and boldly justify this breach of neutrality in taking possession of Ionian territory, I do not think his opposition could be effectual; and the occupation of those islands by any troops of ours, could only be temporary, since he could not retain either Navarin or Modon under such circumstances.

I take this opportunity of requesting that your Royal Highness would be pleased to let my friend Ingestrie succeed to the little 'Talbot' upon Captain Spencer's paying her off, as he is desirous of doing at the proper period, unless some other professional arrangement should have been made for him. His heart is at present in the service; he performs his duty zealously and ably in every respect, and he will do credit to himself by persevering in it through that period which so many who have his prospects waste in the idleness and dissipation of our attractive metropolis. I am still without a line from Mr. S. Canning since he heard of our battle. The island of Corfu will scarcely afford the accommodation which I understand he and Count Guilleminot intend seeking in it. Your Royal Highness will see that if the Greeks had closely blockaded Navarin and Modon, instead of attacking Scio, which they will not be able to obtain possession of even if they get the fortress, Ibrahim's army would have been much straitened for supplies.

I have, &c.,

EDWD. CODRINGTON.

Sir E. C. to Sir Frederick Adam.
(Extract.)

December 22, 1827.

I have endeavoured all along, my dear Adam, to keep you apprised, not only of my conduct, but of the motives by which that conduct was guided; because I considered you a sound judge in your public capacity of what that conduct ought to be, and in your private situation as a friend who would give me your opinion candidly, whether I performed my task right or wrong. Your commendation, my good friend, is almost too strong for me to speak of it in such terms as my heart inclines; but I may assure you, at all events, of that heart being fully sensible of the value of such commendation coming from such a quarter. I imagine I have used a stronger expression than outwardly the case justifies, as to the feeling of Ministers, or rather, perhaps, some of the Ministers: for you quote my words, 'finding fault,' in your letter this minute received. I believe I should speak more correctly if I were to say that from not knowing their own case, and being ignorant how to support their own treaty from not having contemplated consequences, they '*wish* to find fault' with me in order to relieve their own shoulders. Dudley's last despatch leads me to except him individually; but he is so indolent and indifferent, that he is but a broken reed. I fear you will be puzzled to make out the very rough sketches which I sent you by 'Warspite;' but I am confident that J. Gore presenting himself with the documents he has in charge, accompanied by Fellowes to explain how the action was brought on, these said Ministers will see that attempting to censure me will only the more expose them to that turn-out which it seems to be their whole object to avoid. . . The fact is, that though outwardly I am required to answer the 'Queries' merely to give information, I know, confidentially, that the question of recalling me *was agitated*. The confidence I have of my having done right, would have made me indifferent to this, as I am to what has passed openly. But I never can be indifferent to the manly conduct of the Duke of Clarence, in deciding at once as he judged right; nor to the promptness of the King in giving, at his brother's request, joint proofs to the country of their unqualified approbation. When I add to these, my dear Adam, the encomiums of most of my distinguished brother officers, of which some of my *family secretaries* are now writing for you two or three specimens; and when I add to them the opinions of yourself, Ponsonby, and Stovin, jointly with those of my coadjutors on the 20th October, I feel that I am fully rewarded for a whole life of such anxiety as I have been undergoing for some few months.

From Sir E. C. to Mr. S. Canning.

Malta: December 28, 1827.

Vice-Admiral Sir John Gore arrived here on the 4th Dec., (being chosen by the Lord High Admiral as being one of my intimate friends) with certain queries on the part of the Government, and returned by way of Marseilles with my replies on the 11th. The nature of those queries shows that the Ministers, for want of the master-mind which planned the Treaty, do not know how to defend it and its consequences; and they have good reason, I believe, for expecting a very strong opposition to it in Parliament. I have said I shall wait here for the next despatches; and it is evident that I must now have further instructions as to my future proceedings. Here also I am in expectation of Count Capo d'Istrias, with whom I must concert future operations respecting the Greeks; and therefore here I must remain, even if I had a suitable ship to bear my flag. The 'Asia' and 'Albion' are now ready to proceed to England under jury-masts, whenever the wind may suit; and the 'Warspite' is in the Ionian seas, looking out for the Count, to bring him here. Now, under these circumstances, and the preference which this place affords in all respects to Corfu, I cannot resist pressing your coming to Malta. . . . . I assure you, after having acted with you on so important an occasion, and so very confidentially, I should regret extremely the loss of any opportunity of repeating personally the satisfaction I have derived from your candid manner of conducting our communications.

But I will not let my letter go without my sincere thanks for your kind congratulations. The prompt and liberal proofs I have had of the unqualified approbation of the King and our illustrious Lord High Admiral, have filled the squadron under my command with an enthusiasm which appears to be loudly echoed by our brethren at home. In fact I am amply rewarded by the commendations which I have received from many of the most distinguished officers, not only of my own, but of the military service also.

Believe me, &c.,

EDWD. CODRINGTON.

From Sir E. C. to H.R.H. the Duke of Clarence.

. Malta : December 29, 1827.

SIR,—   .   .   .   .   .   .

Captain Cotton of the ' Zebra ' has written to me in strong lamentation, that his officers and himself should not share in the consideration which your Royal Highness has shown so bountifully towards the rest of the gallant fellows who supported me off Patras, and who had the good fortune to be with me at Navarin.   However I felt it right to let Mr. S. Canning know of the former affair,—if I could have anticipated the subsequent resistance of the same fleet to the whole force of the allied squadrons, I certainly should not have parted with the ' Zebra.'   I cannot recall time and circumstances, and put Captain Cotton where I wished to have seen him.   But I can say with truth, judging from the enterprise he has shown against the pirates, his boldly placing his little brig abreast of the ' Asia ' to aid in resisting the progress of the Turkish forces, and his spirited control of an Austrian corvette whose captain wanted to enter Navarin, before my return there, are satisfactory proofs that had the ' Zebra ' been with us in the action he would not have been behind his friends in deserving the rewards by which they have been distinguished.

From Admiral De Rigny to Sir E. C.*

Vourla, 21 décembre 1827.

MY DEAR ADMIRAL,—L' ' Isis ' vient d'arriver et m'a remis vos lettres du 29 novembre et 3 décembre. Je pense que vous avez reçu des nouvelles d'Angleterre qui vous auront confirmé que notre décision à Navarin a été très-approuvée par les Gouvernemens : peut-être pensait-on alors que cela ferait céder la Porte. Mais quand on va savoir que nos Ambassadeurs sont partis, il faudra bien qu'on reconnaisse que les Turcs n'auraient pas fléchi devant les notes diplomatiques, puisqu'ils résistent aux notes des canons. Je pense que nous serons peut-être obligés de passer les Dardanelles, pour nous trouver aussi de notre côté à Constantinople, si les Russes veuillent y aller du leur. Les Turcs préparent un supplément de canons à Ténédos, et aux châteaux d'Europe et d'Asie. Un de nos officiers, *prize-master* d'un brick pirate, a été forcé par le mauvais tems de relâcher à *Nauplia*, et avait dix-neuf matelots avec lui : ils ont été

_ * Received at Malta.

attaqués par quatre barques portant plus de 190 hommes.
Neuf Français ont été tués en se défendant : l'officier, quoique grièvement blessé, s'est traîné jusqu'à la cabine où il
avait préparé les poudres ; il cria alors aux Français qui
pouvaient se jeter à la mer, de le faire ; et se fit sauter, lui
et plus de 80 Grecs qui étaient à bord.   Quatre Français se
sont échappés, l'un avec les deux jambes cassées, les autres
plus ou moins meurtris.   Ce qu'il y a de remarquable, c'est
que le lieutenant avait concerté ce plan avec son *quartier-
maître*, et que celui-ci avait juré de l'exécuter, s'il était le
survivant : il ne voulait point se sauver et sauta ; c'est lui
qui eut les jambes fracassées.   Il est arrivé à terre sans
savoir comment : les trois autres s'étaient jetés à l'eau quand
on le leur avait commandé.   C'est un trait hautement re-
commandable.

On a trouvé 71 cadavres grecs le lendemain matin sur le
rivage.   Tous étaient des Candiotes étrangers à l'île, dont
les habitans se sont au contraire bien comportés vers le
Français.

Une canonière de Cochrane, commandée par un Anglais
(Derby), a été les chercher à Stampalie, et les a remis à notre
Consul à Santorin.

Je pense que M. Canning part demain pour Corfù ; M.
Guilleminot après-demain.

CHAPTER IV.

AMONGST the papers of Sir Edward Codrington relating to this period, there is a mass of correspondence, private and public, with England, with Admiral De Rigny, and with naval officers detached to the various Mediterranean ports.

Unfortunately the letters of Sir E. C. to his intimate friend Sir John Gore in England, have been destroyed; many letters from Sir John Gore are therefore inserted as giving details of interest closely connected with the position of Sir E. C. in the Mediterranean.

These, and the publication of the Duke of Wellington's Memoranda and Despatches, vol. iv.—1871, bring into distinct light the difficulties under which the duty of naval Commander-in-Chief was carried on, affected as his position was shown to be, by the absence of all professional and personal consideration, and by political hostility to the Treaty.

The absence of Sir E. Codrington from the Levant was caused by two circumstances:—

First. His flag-ship, the 'Asia,' had not returned from England. It is not simply the hoisting of a flag that converts another captain's ship into a flag-ship: it may entail the displacement of the captain from his own cabins, and the necessary reception of a flag-lieutenant and secretary, with the staff and space for office work, and records; or, that the admiral invites himself to be the private guest of the captain.

Secondly. Malta was the station for the arrival and refittal of the ships of the squadron, and of the direct packet communication with England, from whence Sir E. C. might well expect those fresh instructions which (as now seen by the Wellington Memoranda published in 1871) were under preparation and discussion by the Government at home. But no communication as to the line of policy to be adopted, no assistance, no information was given to Sir E. Codrington consequent upon the altered circumstances of the execution of the Treaty.—W. J. C.

From Admiral De Rigny.*
(Extract.)

'Trident,' à Vourla : 17 janvier, 1828.

DEAR ADMIRAL,—Quelqu'inquiétude règne à Smirne ; il y a quelques jours un Grec a blessé un Turc dans la rue ; le Pacha lui a fait couper la tête.

Nos marchands et les vôtres se sont constitués en opposition avec la médiation : ils sont excités par les feseurs de gazette. . . . . . Le Pacha m'a fait prier de venir à Smirne les jours qui suivront le départ des Consuls, pour aider à calmer les esprits inquiets. J'aurais bien désiré que les trois Ambassadeurs se fussent réunis à Malte ou à Corfou, et je les y aurais immédiatement suivis. Mon intention dans tous les cas était d'aller à Malte ; mais j'apprends que M. S. Canning a dit au capitaine de l' 'Alacrity' qu'il vous priait de venir à Corfou, de sorte que je ne sais où vous trouver. Je suis bien pressé de savoir ce qu'on aura résolu dans nos Cours ; mon opinion serait d'attendre ce qui sera décidé avant de rien faire, et si j'apprends que vous avez quitté Malte pour Corfou, je pense d'aller vous y faire une visite.

H. DE RIGNY.

Sir E. C. to the Admiralty.

Malta : January 6, 1828.
(Extract.)

His Excellency Mr. S. Canning left Vourla in the 'Dryad' on the 23rd of last month for Corfu, and the French Ambassadors sailed on the same day in the 'Armide.' By an Austrian merchant vessel which arrived this day from Constantinople, information has been received of the Russian Ambassador having passed the Dardanelles on December 21 for Vourla.

* In answer to Sir E. C.'s letters of 17th and 19th December, 1827.

The 'Galatea' arrived here yesterday, having visited Algiers, Tunis, and Tripoli, at all which Regencies the most perfect tranquillity prevailed.

I have, &c.,
E. CODRINGTON.

*From General Sir George Murray to Sir E. C.**

Royal Hospital, Dublin : November 12, 1827.

MY DEAR SIR EDWARD,—I cannot refuse myself the pleasure of offering you my congratulations upon your victory at Navarin. It appears to me to have been achieved with the characteristic skill and gallantry of the British navy, and in a manner that will both uphold their fame and add to your own already well-established reputation. And if these results are desirable and valuable at any time, they are doubly important, in a national point of view, when they are connected with an action in which the British Fleet has been combined with those of other Powers. The British flag, under your guidance, has been placed in its proper station opposite the main force of the enemy, and in the point which was to determine the issue of the battle.

I will not take up your time by entering into any political speculations connected with this important event: the first point of view in which it presents itself to me, is that of a triumph honorable to yourself and to the navy, and gained in the cause of humanity. I am sorry to observe in the list of those severely wounded a young gentleman of your name. I should be most sincerely sorry if your victory were to be accompanied by any cause of private grief.

Believe me always, my dear Sir Edward,

Very sincerely yours,
GEORGE MURRAY.

Sir E. C. to Lieut.-General Sir George Murray, G.C.B.

January 6, 1828.

MY DEAR SIR GEORGE,—While certain of the newspapers, indirectly under the guidance of a political party struggling for favour, are cavilling at my conduct without knowing what that conduct has been or the instructions by which it was guided, it is very highly gratifying to me to receive the approbation of so distinguished an officer as yourself, whose opinion outweighs that of all the mere politicians in England. Having foreseen the probability of being so assailed by one

* Received and answered January 6.

or the other party for whatever might take place in so complicated a service, I think my assailants, like the Turks themselves, will in the end turn out to be my best friends. For the more the whole business is investigated, and the more I am brought before the public, the more I shall be satisfied. As an officer I must bear and forbear, and, as you know, we are never sure that we have done our duty until our masters tell us so. But in the full conviction of having acted strictly according to the Treaty and the instructions emanating from it, I court that publicity which I cannot with propriety obtain without being charged with obtrusion. The affair off Patras *should* be published, in justice to the gallant few by whom I was supported on that trying occasion. Situated as I then was, others may well doubt, as I did at the time, whether the object of the Treaty should supersede the probable destruction of a portion of the naval force. Had I been a mere diplomatist, I might have decided on a line of conduct which, as a military man, I did not think would have become me. Success, it seems, led to my justification. But how are those who approve of such a risk as that, to disapprove of my approaching the Ottoman fleet with the whole of that force which they allotted to me, as ' by its display to cause their wish to be respected?' I have entered thus much into this subject, my dear Sir George, because I wish to show you that your prompt and valuable approbation has not been mistimed or misplaced. I consider it due to the good opinion of yourself and many of the most distinguished of my brother officers who have favoured me with their commendations, to show that they have not misplaced their confidence. The great and so honorably unasked support which I have received from His Majesty and our illustrious Lord High Admiral, would have made me quite indifferent as to all that could be said by our mere politicians, but for the principle which has such a strong hold of me, of justifying to the public the favorable notice which they have taken of my proceedings. I will close this subject by venturing an opinion which I adopted upon the close of the battle of Navarin, that the whole object of the Treaty is more likely to be gained than to be compromised by that event. My son's wounds, severe as they were, are all healed, and he can walk upright without crutches. He is specially included in the liberal distinctions which the Emperor of Russia has bestowed upon us.

Believe me, &c.,

Edwd. Codrington.

From Sir John Gore to Captain W. C. at Malta.

January 5, 1828.

For all news, &c., &c., I refer you to Captain Fellowes who has been in London for the last fortnight, and heard the opinions of all people, *pour et contre*, the cause and effect of Navarin. I had been interrogated by all the former Ministers, and had related all that I had heard on the subject, and replied to the questions asked me, and one from Lord Dudley. I enclose an answer I thought it right to write to him, and I sent it through Cockburn, who showed it to the Lord High Admiral before he sealed it. He told me two days after: ' I sent it because you desired me to do so, but it is of no moment in explaining the weak points over which we are likely to stumble.' I replied: ' I cannot see any obstacle to those who are willing to be convinced '—as was the case with the Duke of Wellington, with whom I was closeted two hours, which concluded with : ' I am very much obliged to you for all this information. I shall ask the Duke of Clarence for your report which the King has told me of; and unless it appears that Sir E. C. has done something outrageous, we will take care of him. I will send for you if I require further explanation on any point.' I referred him to Fellowes, and desired F. to call on the Duke. He saw him, but he could not enter on the question. Since then the meeting of Parliament has developed the public feeling, and the approbation that has been expressed almost by acclamation, cannot but be highly satisfactory and gratifying to you all, as it has been to us. The speech alone staggered us, as you will see by the enclosed letter from your uncle it did him. What could be meant by it ? On the 14th we shall understand it better. Mr. Hobhouse's motion will be carried even should Ministers oppose it. If Sir G. C. and J. W. C. oppose it, they will offend the King and the Lord High Admiral; and then, and what then ? Changes may chance to take place. The present Lord Privy Seal had put himself at the head of the declaimers against Navarin, and had prepared a morsel of eloquence to last two hours, and a reply of one and a half. After he had taken his seat as Lord Keeper, a noble Earl, a friend of your father's, met him (and I relate it from his Lordship's tongue) : ' So, E., you have taken office under W., but what is become of your speech and reply ?' 'Oh, I am quite satisfied on that point; I have read all the papers and Sir John Gore's report, and find that I was in the dark, as the Ministers were before he returned.'

So that this arch-opponent is to become the champion! The *on dit* is that the Turk has demanded the recall of your father and Mr. S. C., and the payment of 1,000,000*l.*, which it is thought will be a cheap purchase of peace, and that the acknowledgment of an error is more honorable than to persist in it; but I maintain that the slightest sacrifice of honor will be the dearest tribute that we can pay. Lord Strangford is certainly to go to Constantinople as our Ambassador Extraordinary to negotiate peace, in order to prevent the Russian army marching into Turkey, and the Austrian and Prussian armies opposing them. If these take place, who will predict what the result will be? If Ministers are obliged to yield to political necessity, they will not fail to do ample justice to your father. He has no longer a weak, timid man to rely on, but a noble-souled, high-minded man, who knows and can face all that is due to an officer who has ably and amply fulfilled his duty; and in his hands your father's honor is safe, while at the same time he is strongly upheld by the two highest personages in the realm; and under this impression I think your father may feel secure and quietly abide the evil, yielding to its pressure as necessity, should it reach him, of which fact I very strongly doubt. Yet in private life, as on the quarter-deck, I like to look out for squalls, and be prepared for them in order that I may not be crippled or overset when they reach me. I shall rejoice through life that I was made an active medium in the business, and though desired to 'keep out of the way of being asked questions,' I have not chosen to make myself passive. I have, therefore, clearly explained all the facts whenever I had an opportunity to do so, to those where they would be of consequence to your father; and I have furnished your uncle Bethell with all the papers, in order that he might put them into the hands of his own and your father's friends. The ships and troops about to proceed to the Mediterranean will afford your father a scope for action beyond the powers of the little 'Talbot,' and place the distinguished banner of Navarin in a more suitable sphere.

From Sir John Gore to Sir E. C.

January 6, 1828.

MY DEAR FRIEND,—My letter to Lady C. of the 26th will have informed you of my being about to start from Toulon, which I did at 11 A.M. on that day, and notwithstanding Captain Fellowes knocking up and obliging me to stop a day at Troyes, and various little accidents to the carriage which required repairs, all which detained us at least 24 hours, we arrived at Boulogne on the 2nd at 2 P.M. I hired the 'Royal George' steamer, and sailed at 9 A.M.; wind S.S.W., mild and gentle. At 10 we were taken aback with a violent gale at N.E.; we struggled all night and were drenched with spray. I landed at 4 A.M. with my despatches only, leaving Fellowes, Louis, carriage, &c., &c., on board; stept into a hack chaise at Dover at a quarter before 6, and got out at the Admiralty at 12. Thus you see I lost no time. All were as much surprised as pleased to see me, for they had counted on the 15 day quarantine (*N.B.*—I overtook Lieut. Pardoe at Lyons, and got back my despatches).

Well, I was handed up to the Sanctum, and your letter eagerly opened and read by J. W. C., commenting as he went; but I had previously told G. C. that all was right and well. So soon as the Lord High Admiral knew I was there, he sent for me and would not let me out of his sight; even took me to luncheon with the Duchess, &c.

He insisted upon having all the papers and reading them himself (aloud to me) before they were copied for the Cabinet Ministers; he was much pleased, and when he read your letters to himself he was *gratified*. 'Now let me see what *you* say,' and read my report, a copy of which I sent you, aloud to me. When ended he said, 'Thank you for this,' folding it up and placing it in the King's box (so marked). 'These letters I will read to the King to-morrow morning; now sit down, Gore, and let me hear all you have to say,' which was followed by 10,000 questions. At two, 'Come, I will not let you out of my sight; come to the Duchess, she has a déjeuner to-day, and a ball in the evening, at which you must appear.' At 5 o'clock, seeing me dead tired, and learning that I had not been in bed for seven nights, he said, 'Then go home and remain quiet to-morrow, for I shall be with the King; and be ready to come if he sends for you; but be here on Friday at 12 o'clock, when I shall be back from Woolwich.' I am thus prolix that you may judge how keenly interested he is on the *whole subject*; and I rejoice to say is *perfectly* satisfied. On my way downstairs I sent for G. C., who was then equally well satisfied with all your reply, and my recapitulation of my report. Fellowes did not reach London until late at night. On Thursday morning he was closely interrogated, and on stating that Cradock would not part with your letter of 18th October, but took it on board, *off they flew*; 'this destroys all—overthrows the foundation of Gore's report, and puts us as much in the wrong as ever; but for this, all was as clear as day,' &c., &c. !! Fellowes went to Bath that

night.   When I went to London next day, I found the flame
in G. C.'s mind raging and increased by J. W. C. discovering
that you had not replied to the query, Why did you not adopt
the second article of the Protocol instead of the third ?   The
Duke of C. said, 'Before I say anything more to you, go to
Lord Dudley and Huskisson, and come to me after.'   The two
Ministers repeated Croker's objection.   'I really think the
question is fully answered, nor can I imagine how Sir E. C.
could say more.'   I saw them again yesterday; the same
objections and queries — the same question except that
Lord D. asked me 'why you did not anchor further off from
the Turks?'   'Because, my lord, the water is too deep, and
if Sir E. C. had taken a distant position, not only the Turks,
but the French and Russians, and many of his own people
would have thought he was afraid.   Rest assured, Lord D.,
that he could do no otherwise than he did, and that the more
it is investigated, the clearer it will prove.   Respecting Col.
Cradock's not delivering the letter to the dragoman on the
18th, he and every one else was convinced that Ibrahim was
on the spot, and that the cause of his absence was subterfuge
to gain time, he being well aware that at that advanced season
the fleets were likely to be dispersed and would not rejoin.'
It is impossible for me to relate all that was said, but such
is the substance.   Fellowes and I are desired to be ready to
attend the Houses of Parliament; but there is *no* question
that the present Ministers will not be on the Treasury bench :
—who will, is a mystery (and the same sort of change is about
to take place in France); I wish, my dear C., I could fancy
as much *good will* to do honour to the gallantry and conduct
you have displayed, as there is to cavil at the latter.   If they
could they would throw you overboard, and save themselves ;
but you are above their reach, and you are upheld by the two
highest powers in the Realm.   Therefore, 'keep your temper,' and rest assured that I shall neither slumber nor sleep
in your cause.   I am advised to be silent—but I will not—
and your friends shall know how to defend you, and those
who are not so shall be ignorant for me.

From Sir Frederick Adam to Sir E. C.

Corfû : January 8, 1828.

I return your answers to the queries.   They are perfectly
satisfactory to me, and I have not a doubt the event will
prove them equally so to the ministers, who had better have
shown no diffidence, as they *must* defend you, and their
sending out Sir John Gore only tends to embarrass *their* de-

fence—it strengthens yours.   The Turk's is a stubborn
and dogged refusal to hear anything of the Treaty, and we
must (in my opinion) carry it through.   In my next I will
give you some of my thoughts on this subject, as to the manner how; but we must use force without war unless attacked.
The letters from Sir James Saumarez, Penrose, and Sir W.
Hotham are admirable, and such opinions, from such men,
more than repay you for any *doubts* which politicians may,
for their own convenience, have entertained.   There can be
nothing more satisfactory, too, than the behaviour of the Duke
of Clarence and the King, and Spencer's account of the former
is full proof that His Royal Highness's feelings are sincere as
strong.

Your next letters will be *most interesting*, as they will give
me an account of the effect of Sir John Gore's return.   I am
delighted at the good accounts of your son.   You must all
come up in a body, that we too may have a share in receiving
the heroes of Navarin as they deserve.

Ever, my dear C., yours truly,
FREDERICK ADAM.

From General Sir Frederick Ponsonby.

1828.

MY DEAR ADMIRAL,—I have had a letter from Lord
Bathurst, in which are these words :—'I see nothing in what
Sir E. Codrington has done at Navarin which the July Treaty
does not warrant.   I know not how a hostile Treaty can be
executed without committing acts of hostility.   It is they
who framed the Treaty, and not they who execute it, are responsible.'

On January 14, 1828, the strong but necessary
measure for suppressing piracy was adopted by orders
from home, of preventing any armed vessel bearing the
Greek flag from putting to sea, except those belonging
to the Government of Greece.

Sir E. C. to Sir Frederick Adam, Corfù.

Malta : January 15, 1828.

Whether it be the fascinating power of Capo d'Istrias
merely, or the more fascinating effect of plain truth, time will
discover; but I certainly am induced to give credit to his
intending to act quite as I would desire in his capacity of

Head of the Greek Government, if he should accept that
important office. I do really believe him sincere, my dear
Adam, mainly because I am persuaded it is his interest, in
every point of view in which I can contemplate him, to be
so; and circumstances which he has detailed to me, and also
to Count de Heiden, would, I think, dispose you that way
also. His brother wrote him, amongst other things, that
Mr. S. Canning mentioned there being reports of his dislike
to England, and to her having influence in the cause of
Greek independence. He read me his brother's letter, or at
least what he stated to be the letter, which he had in his
hand, and also his answer, which I hope you, jointly with
Mr. S. Canning, will see. One point, which I think very
important in disproving this supposition, I must mention, as
I do not recollect if it was in the letter or not; and, moreover, it is a curious matter of history. First, I should relate
an anecdote which he gave us the day before he received his
brother's letter. When Minister in Switzerland he signed a
Treaty, entered into by Swartzenburg, directly contrary to
his Emperor's (Alexander) orders; and that this *coup de tête*,
as he termed it, led to his going to Petersburg. Alexander
was at first angry, but when the effect was explained he said
with kindness, ' Ce n'est pas en Suisse mais à Pétersbourg
que vous me servirez.' I cannot sufficiently detail the particulars; but the object was to establish the *integrity and independence of Switzerland.* He has lived in that country on
account of the freedom of its institutions, &c., and, by the
way, I may observe that he gave us, in his agreeable manner,
a short history of that country, which we listened to with
great delight. However, upon his being closeted with the
Emperor as a preliminary to his taking office, he begged to
make one condition. His Imperial Majesty drew up, and the
other observed that it was merely personal to himself. He then
said that, as a native of the Ionian Islands, he hoped his Majesty would promise never to consent to any other than Great
Britain having dominion over them. The promise was given,
and eventually kept in the most honorable manner. In the
Congress Lord Castlereagh *wanted to give Austria those islands.*
Alexander said his consent depended upon Count Capo
d'Istrias. The rest urged, and the Count continued inflexible;
nor would he put his name to any of the other arrangements
in the name of Russia, until this matter was conceded to him.
This must be known to the Duke of Wellington and many
others now living, as the Count observed : and, if true, surely,
my good friend, we are justified in believing what I must
say has been long evident to me, that the Head of the Greek

Government, meaning to establish the independence of that country, must rely principally upon England. Without waiting to sound me, he at once stated that the only guide he looked to was the Treaty, which the Allies had agreed to execute, and which they had full power to enforce; that he conceived any variation from it on his part would be fatal, as would also any difference amongst the Allies; and that he would not take the office proposed to him, but under its guarantee: that he would not accept even pecuniary aid, upon which success in the first instance depends, from *one* of the three; and he pressed upon Count de Heiden, as well as me, the necessity of his having near him the support of one of the vessels of war of each, that all observers might thereby see that he was supported in all his proceedings by the three Powers. He dwells upon this evidence of union in support of the Treaty, as his mainstay: and so, of course, do I; and so must we all. I pointed out the impossibility of his accepting the Presidency unless Lord Cochrane and General Church were made dependent upon his authority; for he did not appear to me quite as much impressed with this evil of independence in them, as I thought necessary; although his decision to exact certain conditions before he accept his office, would eventually have led to my proposal, that he should call an assembly of the people to diminish this power in them to act as they may think proper without even making known to the Government what they are going to do. His plan will hasten the retreat of Lord C., which the Count and I agree in thinking the best thing for Greece which can happen. He is strong with me in this point.

Memorandum by Sir E. C., written at Malta.

January, 1828.

I was ordered to send a vessel to bring Count Capo d'Istrias from Ancona; and concluding by this that it was the object of the English government to establish an English influence over him, I devoted the 'Warspite,' 74, to this service, directing Captain Parker to bring him to Malta, at which place I considered myself bound to await fresh orders from home consequent on the battle of Navarin. Upon the Count's arrival, and our meeting at the Admiralty House, I asked him as a preliminary to anything further, 'how long he proposed to stay at Malta;' to which he answered with a particular expression, which gave me to understand that he came there against his will instead of going direct to Greece — 'I came here by your Excellency's command, and am entirely at your Excellency's mercy.' I said, 'Your Excellency is very anxious, no doubt, to get to Greece?' He replied, 'Most certainly, having come for that sole purpose.' I then said I was as anxious to get him to Greece as he was to find himself there; and in his presence asked Captain Parker how soon the 'Warspite' could be got ready to take him; to which Captain P. answered that he feared the ship could not be ready that evening, but she would by ten o'clock the next morning. I immediately told Count C. that at ten o'clock the following morning the 'Warspite' would be entirely at his disposal; and 'I now beg leave to repeat my question, how long your Excellency proposes staying at Malta?' He seemed very much taken by surprise, and said he hoped I should not think two or three days too long. Upon this I explained that being myself tied down to Malta, and considering it material that we should have a personal intercourse in preference to a long epistolary correspondence, in order to understand each other, I had thought it absolutely necessary to bring him to Malta in the first instance, though not with any wish to delay his ultimate destination; that, as he had decided not to go away immediately, I would request him to dine with me that evening and become acquainted with my family, and that I hoped he would give me as much of his company as he could during his stay; and we would begin our business to-morrow morning. He showed himself full of anecdote and information, and made himself extremely agreeable to the whole of the party assembled to meet him, with all of whom he left the impression of his being a complete man of the world, very clever, and very entertaining. On the following morning the Count came to the Admiralty House to talk over with me the affairs of Greece according to appointment. I said I was ready to listen to anything he had to propose; to which he replied that as I had brought him there he expected to hear what I had to say first. I then said: 'I will be quite plain with you, in order that no misunderstanding may arise between us. I am no philanthropist, nor am I the least of a Philhellenist; I set no particular value upon either Greeks or Turks, and have no personal feeling towards either. I am guided solely by my duty as an English officer; and my duty in this case is pointed out by the Treaty of London and my instructions emanating from it, which I am determined to fulfil to the utmost: which instructions lead me to lean towards the Greeks and from the Turks under present circumstances. So long as your Excellency acts according to that Treaty I am your warmest and sincerest friend; from the moment that you swerve from it I am your bitterest enemy.' 'Well,' said the Count, 'that is quite candid, and I will act towards you in the same manner, with equal desire to fulfil the object of the Treaty, which, as you know, has brought me to this country.'

From Sir E. C. to H.R.H. the Duke of Clarence.

Malta: January 18, 1828.

SIR,—In addition to your Royal Highness's letter of December 2, I have since received your letters of November 4 and December 7. It is impossible for me to peruse these letters without repeating again and again the great satisfaction which I derive from your Royal Highness's approbation of my conduct. I may truly say it enables me to do my duty not only more cheerfully but more effectually; and I am sure that all those who can fully contemplate the important concerns in which the naval commander-in-chief on this station will have to take a part, will see the necessity of lightening his load of responsibility as much as possible. The arrival of Count Capo d'Istrias, who is gone on in the 'Warspite' after four days' stay here, seems to me to open a prospect of great eventual benefit. In spite of the prejudice against him for having been a Minister in Russia, and of the caution I have had against his fascinating conversation, I feel great reliance upon his pursuing that line of conduct which our Government would desire. He at once detailed his plans to me without reserve, upon finding that instead of delaying his arrival in Greece, as he had imagined, I was most anxious to expedite it. He has not accepted the post to which he is nominated, as yet, because he wishes to exact certain concessions preparatory, which I agree with him in thinking necessary. He was nominated by the same meeting which gave Lord Cochrane power to act independently of the government at sea, and General Church by land. I have urged his calling a meeting of the people to revise this system; for if he and I should agree in any measure, Lord Cochrane may act in direct opposition to it, either knowingly or otherwise; since he may do what he thinks proper without previous communication with the government. Lord C. has at present, moreover, authority from the government to collect revenue from the islands for the ·use of the navy, which he deputes to a Swiss, M. D., and your Royal Highness may infer from this that such power might, with more benefit to the public good, remain in the hands of the president. It is said that the Count's arrival will be the signal for his Lordship's resignation, which, when it is considered that he has already cost the Greeks an expenditure of above a million sterling, appears to me a consummation devoutly to be wished. The confidence with which your Royal Highness has been pleased to honor me, leads me to commit opinions which otherwise I ought in prudence not to anticipate. I venture, therefore, to say at this early period, that I believe Count Capo d'Istrias honestly bent upon guiding himself strictly according to the object of the Allies, and, like me, making the Treaty the law by which he will guide his conduct. I say this with the more confidence because he stated it openly to me and gave his reasons, before he had heard my sentiments upon any part of those operations in which we may be jointly employed. I am much mistaken if the benefit of his arrival, as regards piracy, is not made evident in the course of the coming summer; for he is not only desirous of facilitating the commerce of other Powers, but extremely anxious for re-establishing a turn for trade amongst the Greeks themselves, both as a source of revenue and an occupation of men who now join in piratical expeditions because no other means of support lie open to them.   The great difficulty we shall have to contend with, is the conduct of the Austrian navy under ——. I fear I shall not be able by this opportunity to reply officially to the complaint of Prince Metternich on this head, because it will require the examination of a large mass of papers to expose to your Royal Highness's view the whole of the circumstances and the object of the parties; for although I write all my own letters, I want the assistance of my secretary to collect facts and extracts with which my memory will not furnish me, and he and his first clerk are both at present unwell.   In the meantime, I beg leave to guard your Royal Highness against the machinations of the Austrian agents; who besides cloaking their own misconduct under complaints against me, seem desirous of impeding the execution of the Treaty by every little contrivance they can think of for their own exclusive benefit.

The ' Brisk' has just brought me information from Alexandria of the arrival there on the 27th and 28th of December, of the fleet collected at Navarin, including all those which have arrived from different places up to the 19th December, when they left that port.   Captain Keith writes that the line-of-battle ship, full of sick and wounded, which left Navarin with the others, parted company two days afterwards in a gale of wind, and has not been since heard of, and it is supposed she foundered, as many of her shot-holes were merely covered with canvas.

I have the honor to be, Sir, with the greatest respect, your Royal Highness's very faithful and obedient servant,

EDWD. CODRINGTON.

From Sir E. C. to Sir F. Adam, at Corfù.

Malta: January 19, 1828.

MY DEAR ADAM,—Your letter of the 14th has just reached me by the 'Weazle,' in company with the officials about Cradock's mission, and the letter of Mr. S. Canning, who seems to have been put in a quandary by my mention of the expected arrival here of his colleagues. I was so wrong as to Count Guilleminot, that when off here in the commencement of a very violent gale of N.W. wind, when the devil himself would have been glad to get into port, the frigate would not bear up and come here; and I think she must be gone by the Faro of Messina. Had I thought it of importance, I should not have mentioned the subject, as I did not mean more than to add some little inducement for him to come here. I only knew that the French Consul here (M. Miège) felt sure Guilleminot would call here in his way, and that Count de Heiden has still the same persuasion as to Mons. de Ribeaupierre, as each might naturally call in their way to Toulon. De Rigny hints his own coming as a possible case, in a letter to me; and as I was writing to Mr. S. C. at the same time, and was thus led to conclude we should all meet here, I mentioned it to him. I still think it very odd that either of them should pass Malta without stopping, unless they would thereby have lost a strong fair wind. And indeed I am surprised that the whole of them should not have assembled here in the first instance, ready to receive further instructions from home, and to instruct us further how to act in consequence.

It is odd at this moment of increased importance, and when I know there is a readiness to find fault with me, that I should be left without any guide for my conduct. Instead of any instruction, I get a long diplomatic tirade of a complaint coming from Prince Metternich about my conduct to Austrians, which a letter sent by me to Mr. Croker would have in the most part explained, and of which letter he had acknowledged the receipt. I have had several more letters lately from his illustrious master, all in the same approving and encouraging style. Cradock will have the 'Galatea' to take him first to you and then to Alexandria.

I should have been glad to have seen you, and also Mr. S.
C., but it is quite impossible for me to leave Malta until I
have answers to the papers sent home by Gore, and some instructions for my future conduct. I shall still be ready to
do, at all times, whatever the service clearly requires; but
it is as due to the Government as it is to myself personally,
that I should avoid adopting any decisive proceedings until
they themselves now signify their sentiments.

I don't see why this feeling should have prevented Mr. S.
C. 'touching upon any question of politics,' as he says, 'con-
ceiving, from my last letter, that I do not consider myself
in a situation to enter thereon with advantage until the receipt
of further instructions from home.' No one can be surprised
at my being unwilling to adopt any line purely my own, subject to the censure of people ready to supersede me by sending out ——, as the 'John Bull' asserts—an assertion which
accounts to me for his having been closeted with Huskisson upon my subject for five hours, and for his having
'found difficulty in defending the line I had pursued. Our
latest news from England was in the 'Galignani' of December 19.

Pray collect all particulars resulting from our late battle;
whether Tahir went away by order or without, &c. Your
mission pleases me much. We had this object, about which
Ibrahim would not receive communications. After his fleet
was destroyed, he courted communication with the commander of a French schooner. If he accede now to your
proposal, it will be owing to the loss of his fleet; if he resist,
the same loss puts him and his army at our mercy. Thus
good must, in one or the other way, be the consequence of
the battle of Navarin.

Yours truly,
EDWD. CODRINGTON.

At this time, while recording these matters, I look
back to those days of early youth with wonder, to think
how quietly all this labour was got through, and how
little all these troubles and perturbations were allowed
to darken our daily life. My father's usual custom was
to work steadily all the morning in his office room; and
when he came among us in the latter hours of the day,
it was apparently with a mind disengaged from care, and
ready to enter into the enjoyment of the hour, whatever
it happened to be.

His habits of regularity were a great help to him :

I never in my life remember to have seen him either sitting unemployed, or doing anything *in a hurry.* The one was the consequence of the other.

From Sir E. C. to Mr. S. Canning.

Malta: January 20, 1828.

DEAR SIR,—Your letter of the 14th reached me yesterday by the 'Weazle.' I lament having mentioned anything of your colleagues at all, since it seems to have created uneasiness on your part. I only gave the convictions of Mons. Miège, the Consul here, and of Count de Heiden, upon which my own was formed. The latter still thinks Mons. de Ribeaupierre will come here. Count Guilleminot, I suspect, was in a French frigate which when off here several days ago, in the beginning of a severe gale from the N.W., persevered in keeping the sea, although she would have saved distance by sheltering here. I therefore return the despatch brought by the 'Weazle.' I have directed the 'Galatea,' which was sent out only to visit the Regencies and see if all was quiet there, to take Colonel Cradock, first to meet Sir Frederick Adam, and then to Alexandria. Admiral De Rigny merely mentioned the probability of his coming here, but I think it is material that we should meet to combine further operations, and he knows that he would find Count de Heiden and myself both within this port; but of the movements of the parties positively, I know nothing more than I have mentioned. By means of the steamboat, no doubt you can ensure communication with England by messengers, in the surest and best manner; but I doubt Corfù being the fittest point for general rendezvous. I hope you do not mistake any expression from me as of unwillingness to act politically in any way which you may advise. I certainly am not desirous of taking upon myself the responsibility of any new line of operation consequent on your leaving Constantinople, when the opportunity offers for my being instructed by those who seem to have been ready to saddle me with the natural results of the Treaty, under what I think still a mistaken notion of what these results will be. I shall not, however, hesitate, in the interim, in undertaking anything which either you or I myself may deem advantageous to the public service. The mission now directed to be adopted shows the propriety of my looking for further instructions from home. I was here interrupted by letters from Alexandria in the 'Brisk.' I enclose an extract from that of Captain Keith, of the 'Philomel,' with a list of the ships from Navarin, which arrived from Alexandria, under Moharem Bey. I should observe that this list includes all that arrived there from the time of the battle until the time of their sailing on the 19th December, either from the Dardanelles, Prevesa, Patras, Modon, or elsewhere.

Believe me, &c.,
EDWARD CODRINGTON.

From Sir E. C. to the Admiralty.

'Talbot,' at Malta: January 21, 1828.*

SIR,—I have this minute received the accompanying letters from Captain Richards, of the 'Pelorus,' and Mr. Consul Barker, all brought in the 'Pelorus' by Captain Richards himself.† And although some of them are of an old date, and I conclude the substance of them has been communicated to the Earl Dudley, they contain matters of such interest that I think it right to place them before H.R.H. the Lord High Admiral. To these I will add a letter which I received yesterday from the Honorable Captain Keith, of the 'Philomel,' written since the departure of the 'Pelorus;' as it contains a somewhat more circumstantial account of the vessels from Navarin.

I should observe that the list includes all those vessels which were sent there subsequent to the battle, and those which could be collected from Modon, Patras, Prevesa, &c. On January 15, I received by the packet Mr. Barrow's letter of November 27, and on the 19th I received, by way of Corfù, his *secret* letter of December 21. In compliance with these letters, I have ordered Captain Sir Charles Sullivan to take the Honorable Lieutenant-Colonel Cradock upon the mission therein mentioned, not having any other suitable ship ready for the purpose, and deeming that mission to be of the greatest importance at this particular juncture.

I have, &c.,
EDWD. CODRINGTON.

* Acknowledged February 18, 1828.

† List of enclosures in Admiralty letter, January 21, 1828 :—
Two letters from Mr. Consul Barker, dated November 28 and December 26, 1827.
Two letters from Commander Richards of the 'Pelorus,' dated November 4, 1827, and January 21, 1828.
A letter from Honorable Commander Keith of the 'Philomel,' dated January 7, 1828,
giving accounts of the arrival of the remains of the Egyptian fleet from Navarin, having the sick and wounded and many Greek slaves on board, the ships in a wretched state, the line-of-battle ship missing.

Memorandum—W. J. C.

This question of Greek slaves—and their transmission with the wounded men and the remains of the Turkish fleet from Navarin to Alexandria, is a history worthy of the attention of men of all professions.   Sir E. Codrington, in this letter, reported to his Government the movement immediately he heard of it—for he knew that the departure of these ships was an advantage to Greece; and he was ordered to facilitate—not to arrest—the departure of any Turkish ships, serviceable or unserviceable, from the Morea.   But a question of ' slavery' and the 'Greek slaves' was as usual taken up in Parliament; and Mr. Huskisson, Secretary for the Colonies, being questioned on March 5, in the House of Commons, made a Government explanation, stating that 'renewed instructions,' &c., had been 'sent out to our Admiral.'

No such instructions, however, were sent.   And on April 3, on another discussion in Parliament, Mr. Peel said that ' in forty-eight hours after the news arrived communications were made to the British Admiral.'

Now for the facts : this account, dated January 21, and sent home by Sir E. C. himself, is acknowledged by Government on February 18.

No notice is taken of it to Sir E. C. till the despatch from Lord Dudley of March 18, one whole month later.

And there is now seen in ' Despatches and Memoranda of the Duke of Wellington,' page 336, a letter from Mr. Huskisson to the Duke of Wellington, dated April 6, 1828, with these words :—' In the draft to Codrington, I have adverted to the Greek slaves in a manner which I hope will meet your approbation.   You will see that I assume that a despatch has been already written by Dudley to our Consul at Alexandria to try to get them back by a strong appeal to the Pacha of Egypt.   Such an appeal should be made to him in the most forcible terms, as he values the protection and friendship of this country.   I think something to this effect should be sent off immediately, dated at least a fortnight back, when Peel strongly urged it in the Cabinet, and I understood it was settled.   We shall otherwise not stand well in Parliament on this point.

' Yours very truly,
'W. Huskisson.'

From Sir E. C. to H.R.H. the Duke of Clarence.

Malta: January 21, 1828.

SIR,—In my letter of yesterday and the day before, I have touched upon the conduct of ships under the flag of Austria. This is a subject of so much importance at the present moment that I am induced to revert to it, and to suggest to your Royal Highness how much it is connected with the mission of Colonel Cradock, the good effect of which seems to be relied upon by His Majesty's Ministers. It is made evident, by the complaint of Prince Metternich, that the Austrians will continue to supply the Turkish army with the means of prolonging their stay in Greece, under the plea of our not having a belligerent right to blockade, and of the Greeks neither having the right nor the power to blockade effectually. Now, a pretty strong interruption as far as locality admits, of that part of the coast in which Ibrahim's army is established, would, in my opinion, at once decide his wish to retire. This is the first and perhaps the most important consideration as to the liberation of Greece. But as we may still have great difficulty in bringing the Sultan to a decision, and as that decision may depend upon the conduct of the Pacha of Egypt, I beg leave to suggest that the threat of a blockade of Alexandria would have more effect upon him than any negotiation whatever. His coffers are now extremely reduced, and his means of replenishing them, upon which alone his power depends, are the sale of his produce to foreign merchants, and his external trade in general. I am persuaded that there is no more truth in him than in Ibrahim, and that neither of them will keep any agreement longer than it may suit their personal object; and I believe they will both be more attracted by the boons which they may exact from the Sultan in the present state of his affairs, than from any benefits that can be offered to them by England. I am thus entering upon matters beyond the line of my immediate duty; but I am led by the confidence and the kindness which I receive from your Royal Highness, to venture upon speculative opinions and anticipations which otherwise I might find it prudent to withhold. I had imagined that the Sultan would have acceded upon hearing the fate of his fleet, for I did not reckon upon his indulging in an obstinacy which can only lead to his own injury. Having carried his temper thus far, it is difficult to say to what extent it may go. But I cannot help thinking that if he should still persevere, and should exclude us from that commerce which we have partaken of in common with other nations, it will become the Allies to prevent Austria from grasping it to herself as a consequence of her having supported underhand that resistance to the Treaty which the Emperor had avowed a wish to promote. A blockade of the Turkish and Egyptian ports, until the Sultan should relax, would soon produce the desired effect, and would in the end prove the least detriment to general commerce and the best economy to the Allied Powers. At this late period it is not very necessary to add anything to the statement which I sent home by Sir John Gore, in justification of my own conduct. But I shall never cease wishing to make the ground of that justification as strong as possible, in order that Your Royal Highness may be the more strongly satisfied with the kindness which you have shown me. I enclose a statement of Captain Richards, of Mehemet Ali himself having said, that Ibrahim had orders to obey his former orders in spite of me; so that sooner or later a battle must have ensued. I feel justified, therefore, in retaining my opinion that entering the port of Navarin offered the only hope of executing the Treaty without hostility, whilst it would at once check that brutal warfare which Ibrahim was pursuing uninterruptedly in the Morea. This warfare is referred to moreover in the enclosed extract from a letter of Mr. Stratford Canning accompanying the Protocol of the Ambassadors. And, in reference to the conduct of Austrian vessels, I may observe that the fifth Protocol itself points out that 'Les commandans des deux escadres ne peuvent permettre aux bâtimens neutres d'introduire dans la Grèce des secours destinés aux Turcs,' &c. This refers to merchant vessels particularly; and transfers my term of vessels of His Imperial Majesty, by which I meant those under his flag, into 'bâtimens de guerre,' in the same spirit which pervades the two letters he has written me, copies of which I presume he has sent to Prince Metternich.

I have, &c.,
EDWD. CODRINGTON.

The following extract is inserted as a specimen of the kindly consideration for the comfort of officers, which, in Admiral Codrington's view of the right mode of carrying on the service, had a claim upon the attention of a Commander-in-Chief:—

Sir E. C. to Sir Thomas Staines.
(Extract.)

Malta: January 15, 1828.

Bridgeman and all married men should leave the address of their wives, that I may write of them when perhaps they cannot write themselves; and with this view I will beg you to name them as being well, if so, or otherwise, in your communications.

From H.R.H. the Duke of Clarence to Sir E. C.

Admiralty. February 5, 1828.

DEAR SIR,—I am to acknowledge yours of 28th November; two of 10th December; of 20th and 26th December; and of 6th January, and various enclosures. I conceive the King's Speech, which I enclose, the complete and manly declaration of the Duke of Wellington, the perfect concurrence in your conduct from the Marquis of Lansdowne and Viscount Goderich, and the unqualified approbation in the House of Commons, will entirely satisfy your mind. The letter from the Emperor of Russia, together with the honors conferred on you by the King of France and his Russian Imperial Majesty, must convince you of the opinion of the Allied Powers. The new Government is hardly enough fixed for me to talk on the subject of Orders, but I will the moment I can with effect. I am sorry to say there seems doubt as to the positive fact of the Island of Sphacteria being *ours.*

.   .   .   .

I have now seen the ' Genoa' at Plymouth, the 'Asia,' the 'Albion,' and the 'Rose' at Portsmouth, and shall pay another visit to the 'Asia' before she returns to the Mediterranean.   .   .   .   .   .   .

I will not venture an opinion on war or peace. The new Ministry must act before an idea can be estimated. After the vacations we may see what will be done. More at present I cannot say. I hope the 'Asia' will not be long before she is again ready for sea.

I remain, dear Sir, yours truly,
WILLIAM.

Extract from the King's Speech, January 29, 1828.

'In the course of the measures adopted with a view to carry into effect the object of the Treaty, a collision, wholly unexpected by His Majesty, took place in the port of Navarin, between the fleets of the Contracting Powers and that of the Ottoman Porte. Notwithstanding the valour displayed by the combined fleet, His Majesty laments that this conflict should have occurred with the naval force of an ancient ally: but he still entertains a confident hope, that this untoward event will not be followed by further hostilities, and will not impede that amicable adjustment of the existing differences between the Porte and the Greeks, to which it is so manifestly their common interest to accede.'

In the debate which ensued Lord Holland said:—

' I cannot but lament the use of the word " untoward," as applied to the battle of Navarin. If the phrase means to say, that the battle of Navarin is an obstacle to their independence,* I cannot agree to its propriety or justice ; I think that even now, it has furthered and promoted the emancipation of Greece. I look upon it as a step, and a great step, to the pacification of Europe.'

Duke of Wellington:—

'There is one other subject to which, with your lordships' permission, I shall briefly address myself: I mean the sense in which the word "untoward" has been used. It was intended by "untoward" to convey, that the event referred to was unexpected—was unfortunate. The sense in which the word was used was this : in the treaty, which is not yet before the House, and which cannot, therefore, regularly come under discussion, though all of us have read it, it is mentioned as one stipulation, that the execution of it, if possible, shall not lead to hostilities : and, therefore, when the execution of it *did* lead to hostilities, it was a consequence which the Government did not anticipate, and which it has, therefore, a right to call " untoward." But, in making this statement, do I make the slightest charge, do I cast the least imputation upon the gallant officer who commanded at Navarin? Certainly not. That gallant officer, in doing as he has done, discharged what he felt to be his duty to his country. His Majesty's Government have taken that gallant officer's conduct into consideration, and have acquitted him of all blame: and therefore, it would ill become me to cast the slightest imputation on the distinguished action he performed. My Lords, it should be recollected, that the gallant Admiral was placed in a situation of great delicacy as well as difficulty. He was placed in the command of a combined squadron, in

* Speaking of the Greeks.

n 2

conjunction with two foreign Admirals: and his conduct was such, that they placed the most implicit confidence in him, and allowed him to lead them to victory.   My Lords, I should feel myself unworthy of the situation which I hold in His Majesty's councils, if I thought myself capable of uttering a single syllable against that gallant Admiral, admiring as I do the intrepid bravery with which he conducted himself in a moment of much danger and difficulty.'

Earl Grey:—

'I perfectly agree with the noble Earl (Eldon) who has spoken from the cross bench, in looking upon the battle of Navarin as a most unfortunate event; but in saying this, I mean not to impute the slightest blame to the gallant officer who achieved that victory, so much to his own honour and the character of his country.   I have been long and well acquainted with that gallant officer (Sir Edward Codrington), and I can venture to assure your Lordships that a better, a braver, or a more skilful officer does not exist.   I agree perfectly with the noble Duke, in thinking we ought not to look with too critical an eye at the conduct of an officer placed in a situation of such delicacy and difficulty as Sir Edward Codrington was; and who, in acting as he has done, felt that he was doing his best for the honour and interests of his country.'

Marquis of Lansdowne:—

'All I feel it necessary to declare at the present moment is, that if blame attaches anywhere it does not rest with Sir Edward Codrington.   I concur with the noble Duke, and with other noble Lords who have spoken on the subject, that the battle of Navarin was an unfortunate circumstance, as every circumstance must be considered which is attended by great destruction of human life.   But, my Lords, I am not ashamed to say, it would be quite absurd and childish to expect that an armed interference could take place without some risk of war—without some chance of those hostilities which I entirely agree with the noble Duke in thinking it would be the wish of every man to avoid if possible.   But, my Lords, let me repeat, that if blame rests anywhere, it will be very easy to satisfy your Lordships and the country, that it does not rest with the gallant Admiral whose name has been so frequently mentioned this evening—but not mentioned without deserved praise and honour—but with those who concluded the treaties which placed him in a situation in which, I contend, he exercised a sound discretion as to what was due to his country, and who risked his life in maintaining untarnished the honor of her flag. My Lords, I agree with my noble friend in regretting the unlucky selection of the word " untoward;" and much as I was desirous that the Address should pass unanimously, I should have felt it my duty to oppose it, if the gallant Duke had not declared that, in the sense in which it was used, there was not even a remote hint of disapprobation intended against the gallant officer. When all the documents on this subject shall be laid before your Lordships, it will appear that the gallant officer was necessarily entrusted with a large discretion, which I contend was well and fairly exercised; and in justice to the gallant officer himself, I trust that the whole of the documents in the possession of Government on this subject will be laid before your Lordships. When the intelligence of the transaction first reached Government, it was found that further information respecting it was wanting. Immediate steps being taken for the purpose, that information was supplied; and being supplied, it was seen that the gallant Admiral was entitled to the warm approbation of the Government and the country.'

Viscount Goderich:—

' My Lords, I agree with what has fallen from my noble friend, the noble Duke at the head of the Government, as well as from the noble Marquis, respecting the conduct of the gallant officer, Sir Edward Codrington. He was placed in circumstances of no ordinary difficulty, and in my opinion, my Lords, he acted with sound discretion, and discharged his duty with consummate skill and courage. Whenever that transaction may become the subject of discussion before your Lordships, I shall be prepared to support the gallant Admiral, not merely on the principle that it is the duty of a Government to support those whom it employs to execute its orders, but from my deep and firm conviction that he was justified in the course he took; and that, in that course, he neither tarnished his own fame nor sullied the honor of his country.'

Earl Dudley:—

' With respect to the affair at Navarin, he entirely concurred with what had fallen from the noble Duke, and with every noble Lord who had mentioned the name of Sir Edward Codrington—upon whom it was not his intention to cast the slightest imputation.'

House of Commons, Jan. 29, 1828. Mr. Brougham:—

'But I do enter my protest and dissent in the strongest manner against one clause in the Speech—which protest and dissent I trust to hear re-echoed and affirmed from one end of the kingdom to the other. I allude, Sir, to the manner in which the late glorious, brilliant, and immortal achievement of the British navy is spoken of as matter of lamentation only. As matter of lamentation! This is the first time in the course of my experience that I have ever seen men anxiously come forward to take an early, an uncalled-for, an improper, and I say an unfair opportunity of expressing concern and regret at the victorious achievements of the arms of their countrymen. I, however, cannot conceive how censure can be cast upon the chief in that engagement, after he has been covered with honors, which are only less estimable than the fame and glory which he has achieved in the service of his country. Wholly concurring in the sentiment, that it would be greatly for the benefit of Greece if peace were restored, and believing that this victory will mainly contribute to the attainment of that object, I greatly rejoice in the event.'

Lord Althorp:—

'I agree entirely with my honorable and learned friend (Mr. Brougham), so far as we are informed of the circumstances —that the battle of Navarin was a necessary consequence of the Treaty which the Allies had contracted to carry into effect. I agree, too, most fully, in the protest of my honorable and learned friend, against those expressions in the Speech from the Throne which seem to cast censure upon the gallant Admiral who commanded at Navarin. It would, indeed, be hard upon naval officers if they were employed in highly delicate, as well as important, duties, and afterwards had blame insinuated against them, without the clearest proof that cause for such blame existed.'

Lord Palmerston:—

'It was therefore a collision entirely unexpected by this Government. The expressions so employed have not been meant as any reflection on the conduct of the English Admiral who commanded in that engagement.'

Lord John Russell:—

'With respect to the affairs of Greece and Turkey, I was glad to hear the noble Lord opposite make the declaration he did, because it relieves me from the apprehension that any blame was intended to attach to the excellent Admiral who fought the glorious battle of Navarin. But I must add that if no blame was intended to attach, the words chosen in allusion to him are the most unfortunate I ever heard. It is my decided opinion that that glorious victory was a necessary consequence of the Treaty of London; and it is also my opinion that it was as honest a victory as was ever gained by the arms of any Power from the beginning of the world.'

Lord Morpeth :—

'Ministers might have chosen many other epithets with reference to a victory which had filled with joy the heart of every lover of freedom. The selection of the word "untoward" was injudicious and unjust; it is the most injurious and shabby epithet which could have been supplied by the researches of Ministers into the English language.'

Lord Palmerston:—

'It is impossible to deny that in that sense of the word, the battle of Navarin was an "untoward event." But as far as relates to the character of the country, and to the reputation and fame of its arms, no human being can suppose that the epithet "untoward" was applied in that sense in his Majesty's Speech. In no fair construction of the passage does it imply any censure on the gallant Admiral who commanded the Allied fleet on that day of arduous but splendid success.'

Sir F. Burdett :—

'As to the battle of Navarin, so far from thinking it an "untoward event," I regard it as one of the most fortunate circumstances that could have happened, highly creditable to the character of the country, and calculated to raise it in the estimation of the civilised world. I cordially approve of the Treaty, and cannot help expressing my regret that the Ministry which had the vigour to strike this blow of foreign policy, had not the vigour afterwards to support itself. The Treaty was dictated by sound policy, and carried into effect with ability by the gallant Admiral and his fleet in the performance of their perilous duty. That achievement stands far beyond the reach of any vote in this House.'

From Sir John Gore to Sir E. C.

February 10, 1828.

You will hear and read that all question respecting Navarin is at an end; that the highest and most *unquestionable* approbation of your conduct has been expressed; but that *Thanks* are not, under political considerations, thought advisable. Mr. Hobhouse intends to urge them, and, it is supposed, will be negatived by the previous question, as peace and conciliations of all kinds are universally and most anxiously sought for. Therefore, I wish, for your sake, that he would not urge his motion; for, as the approbation is so perfect, and as the Duke of Wellington knows and feels all that is due to an officer who has so nobly fulfilled his duty as you have done, I would rather trust to his honorable high-mindedness than to Mr. Hobhouse's zeal, and patiently abide the issue of negotiation; for if peace is perfectly re-established while you are in command, I can have no doubt that your services will then be amply rewarded; but not till then. I cannot convey to you an adequate idea of the dread which still exists of war; and the Duke of Wellington told me, ' If we can but preserve peace I see nothing to be afraid of; but war now will be the destruction of all Europe.' Every breath that indicates hostility is deprecated.

Sir E. C. to Admiral De Rigny.

Malta: February 8, 1828.

My dear Admiral,—The enclosed copy of my letter to our Lord High Admiral* will tell you my sentiments as to what we should now do respecting Turkey. I think if Smyrna or Alexandria were not included in a blockade with the rest of the Ottoman ports, the Sultan would still continue sulky; and dissatisfaction, by long continuance, would eventually ' degenerate into hostilities.' But if we were at once to declare a blockade of *all* the ports of the Sultan and the dependencies, he *must* yield of necessity to any terms we might choose to impose on him. Colonel Cradock is again gone to the Viceroy of Egypt. I do not approve of asking terms which, I think, I have the right and the power to dictate. My plan would have been to complain loudly against the insult and the aggression offered to us at Navarin; and to demand, by way of satisfaction, the Sultan's acceding to the

* See Appendix.

proposed armistice immediately; and I would blockade all the ports until I gained my object. In this case it would become the interest, not only of the French and English merchants who now remain under Turkish protection, but that of the Austrians also, to assist in bringing the Porte to our terms, and we well know that all these persons take interest as their only guide.

Mr. S. Canning has not informed me of his latest communications with the Reis Effendi, and seems to withhold his sentiments on the present state of affairs; and our Ministers do the same. This is very diplomatic, but very unfair, as I think. In the meantime that we are thus left without instructions how to act under the new order of our relations with the Porte, English vessels at Constantinople have had their cargoes of corn taken from them with nothing but a mere *promise* to pay less than it cost the owners, and some of the people have been bastinadoed into the bargain. I shall shortly have the documents on which to make a representation, which I think must wake our superiors out of their present supineness. I should like to have the account given by Mons. Bompard, which must be correct. I think you must have found his journal a very interesting document.*

From Admiral De Rigny.
(*Extract.*)

15 février.

DEAR ADMIRAL,— .   .   .   .   .   .
Les Turcs se réjouissent fort du changement de ministère dans nos pays. Je crois que Sultan Mohammed veut absolument essayer ses troupes contre la Russie.

Sir E. C. to the Primates of the Island of Scio.

H.B.M.S. 'Talbot,' at Malta: February 11, 1828.

GENTLEMEN,—In reply to your letter of the 28th of last December, requesting the assistance of the Allied fleet in defending the Greek forces at Scio against an attack from the Turkish ships, I have only to inform you that, as the expedition to that island was made against our injunctions, and appears to me to have been undertaken much more to gratify private interests than to promote the welfare of the Greek people in general, I do not consider it as our duty to comply with your request. You, Gentlemen, must know as well as I do that if the resources wasted on this occasion

* See Appendix.

had been employed in favor of the Morea, the army of Ibrahim Pacha would have suffered a similar fate to that of his fleet, and Greece would not have had the additional reproach which has been brought upon her by the misconduct of the Sciotes themselves in this ill-advised expedition.

I am, &c.,

EDWARD CODRINGTON.

From H.R.H. the Duke of Clarence to Sir E. C.

Admiralty: February 17, 1828.*

DEAR SIR,—I am to acknowledge yours of January 18 and 21, from Malta. Both in my *public* and *private* situation I consider the matter of Navarin completely set at rest, and for *yourself* in the most *favorable* manner possible. I do not conceive you will have anything more to do with Lord Cochrane, as his lordship is now in London. You were right in sending Count Capodistrias to Greece, and I hope he may not play false to Great Britain. I therefore cannot caution you too much to be constantly on your guard respecting this individual. I wish most heartily piracy may be fairly put down by the Greek Government. Count Dandolo I cannot know. But he is, like yourself, obliged to obey the orders he receives. I recommend towards the Austrian navy firmness but much coolness on your part. Recollect we are in close alliance with *Austria*, and particularly on the subject of *Portugal*. I shall be anxious to see events—how they arise—and the utmost deliberation and steady conduct are requisite. I am extremely glad the 'Galatea' was not sailed, and has, therefore, been sent to carry Lieutenant-Colonel Cradock. I do not think the fleet from Navarin will return there again.

You and I differ widely. I never thought the Sultan would act otherwise than he has, because he must be aware it is not to the interest of either Great Britain or France to permit *Russia* to be in *possession of Constantinople*. However false the Divan may be, or however treacherous the Pacha of Egypt and Ibrahim may be, they do not want for *abilities*. It is for the Cabinet of the Duke of Wellington to determine with the Allies what ought to be done. *I can only obey the instructions I receive.* I say nothing more on the subject of Navarin, because I conceive the public mind here for ever at rest. You ought, with your friends, to be most perfectly satisfied; and *I* once more repeat you were *fully* authorised by your instructions to strike the blow you did in Navarin,

* Received April 7.

and the *whole of Europe* has *amply* and *honorably* done you justice.

God bless you, and ever believe me, dear Sir,

Yours most truly,

WILLIAM.*

From Admiral De Rigny to Sir E. C.
(*Extract.*)

'Trident,' ce 9 février 1828.

DEAR ADMIRAL,—   .   .   .   .
J'ai envoyé l' 'Iphigénie' et un brick devant Navarin, pour empêcher des vivres d'y arriver; mais les petits bâteaux ioniens font ce trafic plus facilement; les Présidens pourraient peut-être y mettre obstacle.

Sir E. C. to the President and the Members of the Legislative Body of the Greek Government.

H.B.M. ship 'Talbot,' at Malta: February 11, 1828.

GENTLEMEN,—I have had the honour of receiving your letter of November 30, 1827, in which you request an extension of the limits fixed upon as the range for the Greek cruisers, and in which you point out how necessary it is to make allowance for the present condition of the Greek people. It is well to claim every consideration for errors committed by a people so situated; but the misconduct of the persons forming your Provisional Government towards the Powers which have allied themselves for the disinterested purpose of effecting the welfare of their countrymen, admits of no excuse whatever—allows not of the least palliation. Greek corsairs under the signature of Mr. Glaraki, the secretary to the Provisional Government, instead of acting against the Ottoman forces, have interrupted and plundered our vessels pursuing regular and lawful commerce, even on the coast of Malta and Sicily. Our vessels so seized and so plundered have been declared lawful prizes by a tribunal not guided by law or equity and nominated by the same Provisional Government whose members share a twentieth part of the booty, whilst pirates and the owners of the pirate vessels are suffered to continue ther depredations unpunished. Seeing, therefore, that little good was to be expected from the Greek armed vessels, under such circumstances it became the duty of the admirals commanding the Allied squadrons to limit as much as possible their power to do mischief. I have thought it

* NOTE BY SIR E. C. UPON THE LETTER.—'His Royal Highness told Sir John Gore he objected strongly to the word "untoward."—E. C.'

right to say this much, Gentlemen, in explanation. With regard to the required extension of the limits, I am sure it will give great pleasure to my colleagues and myself to find ourselves enabled by the more regular proceedings of the Greek vessels of war, to attend to your wishes in that and in every other respect. If, therefore, the Count Capodistrias should assume the presidency, I shall readily propose to my colleagues to take the subject into their consideration; and in the meantime I can venture to assure you that they will not deal harshly with any of your vessels which may be honestly communicating with Greek troops in the parts you mention even beyond the prescribed limitation.

However, Gentlemen, if Count Capodistrias should unfortunately despair of bringing the Greek people into those habits of regularity and social order which alone can obtain their admission into the great compact of civil society, and you should continue to the members of your present Provisional Government the power which they have so disgracefully abused, I must warn you that I shall not cease to act upon the principle that the more their conduct is kept under restraint the better for the people over whom they hold authority.   I am, &c.,

EDWD. CODRINGTON.

Captain Hamilton, in H.M.'s ship 'Cambrian,' was on his way to England, after an arduous service of six years on the coasts of Greece and in the Levant. He had orders to call at Carabusa* for the purpose of assisting in the attack and destruction of the pirate vessels. These vessels at anchor could be reached by the fire of ships passing along the outer side of the dangerous reef of rocks forming the small harbour. The 'Isis' and 'Cambrian' therefore stood in under sail, giving their fire as they passed; but on tacking to stand out, the two ships ran foul of each other: the 'Cambrian' was thus thrown upon the reef. Every effort was made to move her, but without success; she went to pieces on the rocks, and it may well be said-that the 'Cambrian' died in the service of that country which had so long benefited by the humanity, the energy, and the discretion of her commander, Capt. Gawen Hamilton.—W. J. C.

* Carabusa or Grabusa.

From Sir E. C. to the Admiralty.

'Talbot,' at Malta: February 13, 1828.*

SIR,—The accompanying documents, whilst they make known to his Royal Highness the Lord High Admiral the destruction of eleven pirate vessels at Carabusa, will also inform him of the unfortunate but accidental wreck of the 'Cambrian' in the operation.   However lamentable the termination of the career of a ship remarkable for a long course of important duties, I consider it a source of particular gratulation that our country may still benefit by the future services of her distinguished captain, and that of the officers and crew who have been trained under his example.

The whole arrangement, as well as the execution of this enterprise, does great credit to Commodore Sir Thomas Staines and the officers and men employed in it.

I trust that its taking place upon the arrival of Count Capodistrias will facilitate his turning the Greek armed vessels to better account than heretofore, and leading the inhabitants of the coast to re-establish commercial intercourse with each other.   Amongst the vessels employed on this occasion, his Royal Highness will observe that the 'Zebra' was conducted by Commander Cotton with his usual devotion to the duties of his station.   His assistance of the 'Cambrian' was the last act of his zealous exertion.   He was shortly afterwards seized with a brain fever, of which he died on the night of the 11th inst.

I have, &c.,
EDWD. CODRINGTON.

From Captain Gawen Hamilton to Sir E. C.

Malta: February 12, 1828.†

DEAR SIR,—I had little idea, when I wrote to you from Cerigo, that my next letter was to be from a strange ship, with the painful intelligence of the total loss of the 'Cambrian' off Grabusa.   I was to have left the station that night, and indeed went on board the Commodore to take leave, when he informed me that it was his intention to pass along the reef in succession, and fire on the shipping.   I will not at present enter into particulars, indeed, could not, except as to what relates to myself.   I had longed, with presentiment of misfortune, to leave the Archipelago; but the less I agreed with the opinion of my superior, the

---

* Received April 1.   † Received same day at Malta.

more I felt it a duty to second by every means whatever he thought proper to do. This feeling I expressed to Captain Parker in a private letter, when I begged provisions to be sent to enable me to go off Grabusa.

Nothing could be finer than the conduct of my ship's company. They worked as silently, as well, in a ship beating heavily on a rock and every instant in expectation of her going over, in a dark and tempestuous night, as they ever did in presence of an admiral. The squadron did all they could for us; Bridgman ran down on our weather beam, and brought up in a dangerous situation with two anchors. He then came to me; nor could I by entreaties or orders engage him to leave the ship until my simple duty was performed. No lives were lost; for which I am most thankful to God. The masts went in time to prevent the ship from going further than her beam. Cotton also remained with me to the last. I will hasten to finish these heart-rending details, —his reason is gone. . . My tears will not allow me to dwell on this subject.

I am, dear Sir,
Yours faithfully,
G. W. HAMILTON.

Sir E. C. to Captain Sir Thomas Staines.

Malta: February 12, 1828.

The 'Rattlesnake' gave me your letters about Carabusa this morning, and the 'Zebra' has brought in the dead body of poor Cotton this afternoon—he died last night. This is a sad case; and the loss of the 'Cambrian' is certainly a very lamentable event. We must, however, look to the other side of the picture, and feel rejoiced at the destruction of the nest of pirates which have so long outraged humanity. The vessels which you have sent with some of the 'Cambrian's' crew, will not be released, you may depend upon it. Their coming in here does not prevent our destroying them, according to Lord Bathurst, and the order of Sir H. Neale grounded on it.

From Sir E. C. to H.R.H. the Duke of Clarence.

Malta: February 20, 1828.

Sir,—Although it does not become me to notice the reports that are generated by the self-interest of people in this part of the world, even when they apply to me individually, I feel it right to counteract such as may be detrimental to the public service on which I am employed. I hear that it

has been industriously circulated at Smyrna, that Admiral
De Rigny has disavowed being a willing party to the Allied
fleet being taken into the harbour of Navarin. I have no
wish to shrink from my full share of that measure; and
thinking of it as I still do, and as I am persuaded even those
who cavil at it will do by-and-bye, I would gladly take the
whole upon myself, as I should necessarily have done if the
whole fleet had been British. But it is due to my colleague
to show, that he acted on that occasion with as much candour and sincerity as he did with judgment and bravery in
the battle which followed it. I had fully considered the
subject, and made up my mind on the absolute necessity of
this measure, when Admiral De Rigny himself upon coming
into the 'Asia's' cabin threw out the suggestion; and after
discussing it more fully together, I sent for Count De Heiden,
and the determination was fully made. Thus your Royal
Highness has the whole account of this affair, and will, I
trust, feel as much satisfied as I am of Admiral De Riguy's
uprightness on the occasion. He is much more likely to
have taken the credit of originating the measure. But as a
specimen of the sincerity with which he is guided in his conduct towards me, I enclose an extract from a letter which I
have lately received from him, which I think it will be agreeable to your Royal Highness to read.

Your very faithful and obedient servant,

EDWD. CODRINGTON.

Sir E. C. to Hon. Captain Maude, H.M.S. 'Glasgow.'

'Talbot,' at Malta : March 2, 1828.

SIR,—I received your letters of February 2 and 8 by the
'Oxta' Russian brig of war yesterday. Although the
Viceroy of Egypt has given you his word that the supplies
mentioned in your letter are not destined for the Morea, I
wish you to watch as narrowly as you can the movements of
the force by which it is accompanied. And as my instruction
of September 8, 1827, respecting such supplies, was confined
to frigates, I now enclose a general order which you will
give out to any of the sloops with which you may communicate. In the event of supplies of this sort hereafter leaving
the Turkish or Egyptian coasts, you will not only yourself
endeavour to prevent their reaching their destination, but
you will make the circumstance known to Commander Sir
Thomas Staines, or the senior officer in the Levant, as
speedily as possible.

I am, &c.,

EDWD. CODRINGTON.

*From Sir E. C. to the Admiralty.**

'Talbot,' at Malta: February 5, 1828.†

Sir,—I have the honour of placing before H.R.H. the
Lord High Admiral the copy of a letter from Vice-Admiral
le Chevalier De Rigny to the French Minister of Marine.‡
I feel strongly the justice of my colleague's observation that
it would have been better that the Ambassadors should have
given us the benefit of their advice and opinions, if not their
instructions, before they determined on separating so entirely
from each other as well as from the scene of action ; and I
could also have wished that we should have been informed of
the tone in which they announced the effect of the battle of
Navarin to the Porte, as well as the cause to which they
attributed it. H.R.H. will not fail to observe the difficulty
in which we are placed by this absence of instructions at a
moment when such aid appears to be more than ever requisite. Looking to the doubts which have been evinced by
the ' Queries ' put to me by Earl Dudley as to the propriety of my conduct when acting, as I did then, and do still,
firmly believe, in the full spirit of the Treaty and according
to my instructions emanating from it, I am not desirous of
exceeding the bounds of my prescribed duty. But the generous confidence which I have met with from H.R.H. induces
me nevertheless to submit such opinions for his consideration
as may appear to me useful to the great object of establishing peace in the Levant and restoring commerce to its natural
course. In the absence, then, of the above-mentioned information, I do not hesitate saying, that I think satisfaction
should have been immediately demanded for the insult offered
to our flags and the injury done to the fleet on that occasion.
Under a conviction that such a measure would have induced
the Sultan to accede to the mediation, I am led to conclude
by his present resistance that the Ambassadors acted differently. Be that as it may, in order now to bring the Porte
to assent to the object of the Treaty, and to put an end at
once to the state of discontent and irritation in which the
Sultan seems disposed to indulge, I beg leave to submit to
H.R.H. my opinion, that we should immediately adopt as
strict a blockade as possible of all the Ottoman ports. I do

* Note by Sir E. C. on the letter.—'No answer was ever made either
by the Foreign Office or the Admiralty to the proposals or the request for
instructions contained in this letter.'
† Acknowledged April 3.
‡ Note by Sir E. C. on the letter.—'This letter was sent to the
Cabinet without loss of time, as mentioned in the Duke of Clarence's letter
of March 2.'

not agree with Admiral De Rigny in excluding Smyrna.   I observed nothing like British feeling in the merchants of that place, even before the signature of the Treaty ; and I am convinced that those who now remain there, whether nominally French or English, will find their interest in becoming decidedly Turkish, thereby obtaining the exclusive privileges which will be given to them and others being no parties to the object of the Allies and forwarding the views of the Porte.   Neither would I exclude Alexandria, unless the Hon. Colonel Cradock should be more successful in his mission than I am prepared to expect.   For upon these places no doubt the Sultan mainly relies for those resources which enable him to persevere in his present resistance, and in his probable intention of letting things continue on their present discordant footing.   Deprived of them he must give way at once; and as his irritation will then not have been of long duration, so will it require but a short period to reconcile him to a new arrangement of which he will shortly feel the pecuniary and permanent benefit.

As to the question of piracy, I certainly am not quite as much of my colleague's opinion as he seems to imagine owing perhaps to not having expressed any dissent when we have cursorily touched on the subject.   I have found it important on some occasions to lead him from his own to my sentiments, when it appeared to me that such change was for the good of the service we had jointly to perform ; and I have therefore at all times avoided showing a discordance of opinion when not absolutely called for.   Perhaps his desire of promoting the interests of Catholic Syra induces him to think that place better for general purposes than it appears to me to be.   The port itself is objectionable for vessels of war ; and I think that all such tribunals as he refers to should be at the seat of government or at the port most contiguous to it.   But under the present circumstances it is right that measures of this sort, and indeed all others referring to the conduct of the Greeks, should be concerted in the first instance with Count Capodistrias, for I am persuaded he will cordially join us in putting down a system which must impede, in every step he may take, his progress towards establishing anything like social order in the distracted country over which he is invited to preside.

I have, &c.,

EDWD. CODRINGTON.

P.S.—Vice-Admiral Count de Heiden having favoured me with his remarks on the propositions of Vice-Admiral Che-

valier De Rigny, I have the honour of adding them also for
the information of H.R.H. the Lord High Admiral.

It is with much pleasure that I insert this spontaneous
expression of Admiral De Rigny's manly determination
to stand by his leader and colleague.   In behalf of his
friend he certainly shows no hesitation, no vacillation
of purpose ; and the absence of all parade about it
enhances the value of the act itself.

From Admiral De Rigny to Sir E. C.*
(Extract.)
'Trident,' ce 9 janvier 1828.

La même gazette dit que vous êtes rappelé à Londres.
S'il en était ainsi, je demanderais mon rappel, et j'irais aussi
à Londres partager avec vous une responsabilité commune.
Je prépare, en attendant, quelques pages à ce sujet, et que je
vous communiquerais d'avance, si l'occasion venait de les
publier.

Agréez la nouvelle assurance de mes sentimens très-dé-
voués, et mes vœux pour cette nouvelle année.

H. DE RIGNY.

From Sir E. C. to his Royal Highness the Duke of Clarence.
(Private.)
Malta : February 26, 1828.

SIR, ...
I cannot resist the pleasure of adverting to the assurance which Sir John Gore has given me† of your Royal
Highness being fully satisfied with my answers to the queries
with which he was charged.   I am, and shall ever continue
to be, most anxious to secure your Royal Highness's approbation ; not, as I confidently believe, with reference to any
worldly advantage to myself, but because I am sure I shall not
have it without being entitled to it.   I well know that, placed
as I am, I must continue liable to the censure and abuse of
politicians, as may best suit their party purposes.   I will
not say I am indifferent to such censure; nor can I deny
that certain feelings of indignation do occasionally arise in
my breast, when I read that the flag which I have strenuously
endeavoured to uphold has been tarnished in my hands.   But
the conviction that truth must in the end prevail over misrepresentation, and that I serve under the just protection
of your Royal Highness, restores my submission, and excites

* Received February 18, sent to Admiralty February 20.
† Referring to Sir John Gore's letter of January 6, 1828.

fresh desire in me to pursue with devotion the arduous duties with which I am entrusted. I understand that —— joined with —— in thinking that Colonel Cradock's bringing back our letter to Ibrahim 'overthrew all Sir John Gore's report, &c.' I lament, on my brother officer's own account, that he should not have found this merely political objection removed by the explanation of the other chiefs having before refused to receive such communications. As to Lord Dudley's enquiry ' why I anchored the ships so near the Turkish line,' I could answer his lordship effectually by telling him it was to deter them from meditated hostility on their part, by that bold countenance when supported by ten sail of the line which the Government deemed ample for the purpose, which his lordship-admired so much when I was opposed to nearly the same force off Patras with a mere tithe of the number. It is difficult, at such a distance, to combat objections such as these. I trust I have fully answered all the doubts openly expressed; and I feel myself capable of combating all objections to my proceedings from first to last, which are fairly put to me, come from whom they may. But I cannot help saying to your Royal Highness, that I think it somewhat unfair that persons seeming to have authority, should let slip doubts and insinuations which give rise to torrents of coarse abuse on the part of public writers, hardly admissible in describing acknowledged criminality. In —— Magazine I am depicted as a disgrace to his Majesty's service, quoting as a fact a statement in the —— which was fabricated for mere party purpose. Amongst the papers which accompany my official letters there is one which contains two autograph passages of the Sultan : Count Capodistrias and others consider one of these as establishing the acknowledgment of the Turks being the aggressors on the 20th of October. To me the ' trahison' appears to refer particularly to the fire-vessel not merely having begun the action, but having begun it at a wrong moment instead of waiting until midnight. But at all events, when this is coupled with the admission of the Viceroy of Egypt, that the Sultan had ordered Ibrahim to use force in resistance of the Allies, I think there remains no doubt of the impossibility on my part of avoiding hostilities. I regret being thus led on to occupy so much of the valuable time of your Royal Highness in my desire to show that I am not unworthy the kindness of which I am most sensible; but I rely upon a further extension of that kindness, in attributing it to the real motive by which I am actuated.

I have, &c.,

EDWD. CODRINGTON.

Sir E. C. to His Royal Highness the Duke of Clarence.

'Talbot,' at Malta: February 26, 1828

SIR,—I received the accompanying documents yesterday from Count Capodistrias. I have shown the originals in the Turkish language to Monsieur Chabert, late first dragoman to the English embassy, and he has verified the handwriting and signature of the letters which accompanied the protocol, &c. As this protocol does not appear to have been transmitted by any other means, and as it may give a more complete insight into the disposition of the Ottoman Porte than has yet reached our Government, I propose sending it by way of Marseilles immediately; and as His Majesty's Ministers may not wish it to be made public, I have thought it best to address it to your Royal Highness personally. I beg leave also to draw your Royal Highness's particular attention to the state of Greece as depicted by Count Capodistrias. It is evident that the most effectual, as well as, eventually, the most economical way of carrying into effect that part of the Treaty of 6th July last which relates to Greece itself, will be the enabling the President to establish a sufficient force by land and sea to maintain his authority against the Primate and Capitani, by whom all the resources of the country are now grasped for their own corrupt purposes. If the sum now required by the Count should be granted to him, whilst there is an enthusiastic desire to support his authority, and whilst we are engaged in a united effort to put down piracy and to turn the minds of the people towards regular commercial intercourse, he will be enabled, in all probability, to collect a revenue more than sufficient to cover the requisite expenditure.

I cannot help observing to your Royal Highness on the importance of assisting Count Capodistrias at this moment of his first entering upon his arduous office, and when he is cordially endeavouring to establish strong measures for the security of commerce in the Levant. I have reason to believe that piracy is practised to a great extent by renegadoes of other nations in the character of Greeks and under the Greek flag. If so, we may reasonably infer that as its success with those in whom it originated led others to follow their example, so the suppression of it among the Greeks will lead to a discontinuance of it by the people of other nations. The finances of the Sultan do not at present appear to be in a very flourishing state; and so long as he continues to resist the Treaty they must continue to deteriorate. But the contest of expense now carried on by the Allies may, by a well-timed support of the arrangements meditated and promulgated by the President, be shortly transferred to the Greek Government. For the revenue of Greece, relieved from the oppression of the Turks and of their own still more unprincipled chiefs, may be justly expected to increase in proportion as that of their opponents is diminished. I am therefore induced respectfully to submit my opinion, that compliance with the urgent request of Count Capodistrias for present pecuniary assistance, would facilitate the object of the Allied Powers declared by the Treaty of London.

I have, &c.,
EDWD. CODRINGTON.

From Sir E. C. to H.R.H. the Duke of Clarence.

Malta: February 28, 1828.

SIR,—

If His Majesty's Government should accede to the request made by Capodistrias for pecuniary assistance, I am persuaded they will find it the cheapest mode of executing the Treaty, and of suppressing piracy. Without money to create an immediate armed support of his authority whilst the enthusiasm prevails, the Capitani will again make head, by means of that intrigue which has before been successful and which the agents of the Porte will assist; and if we also supinely allow the Sultan to carry on his commercial communications under the deception of the Austrian flag, there will be no end to the present disturbed state of affairs. I have been wrong in my expectation that the Porte would succumb after the battle of Navarin; but I certainly reckoned on some decisive measures being adopted to enforce it. I should inform your Royal Highness that Mr. S. Canning told Captain Hamilton that the battle made no difference as to the Ambassadors leaving Constantinople; on the contrary, that their observations were never so well attended to as after that news was received. I was not aware, moreover, until lately, of a religious feeling in the Turks against surrendering any part of their possessions. Their Koran seems only to admit of their having it taken from them by force. In fact, I believe that to this day they carry on the farce of *permitting Christian governments to perform their functions, as a mere indulgence of their Sultan.* And when certain British senators are dwelling upon the destruction of human life by the battle of Navarin, and lauding the tender government of this said Sultan, they should be reminded of his having ordered the massacre of 150,000 of his subjects whom he thought liable to oppose his new system, besides the cold-blooded destruction of 30,000 at Scio. I enclose an account of the forces under Ibrahim Pacha, procured by Captain Hamilton; but I cannot rely upon its correctness. There cannot be a greater instance of cruelty than sending the ship of the line to founder with such a load of wounded, &c., on board.

I have, &c.,

EDWD. CODRINGTON.

From H.R.H. the Duke of Clarence to Sir E. C.

Admiralty : April 1, 1828.

DEAR SIR,—I am to acknowledge your two letters of 26th and one of February 28, and various enclosures, most of which I have forwarded to Lord Dudley. The letters I of course keep to myself.

Not being in the Cabinet, I must leave the policy of assisting Greece with money to the King's Ministers.

I never expected the immediate or quiet submission of the Sultan, and, therefore, after the signature of the Treaty of London, I recommended to you to be fully prepared for the worst.

I can only repeat, your conduct before and in the action of Navarin appears to me correct and perfect. I consider this transaction as entirely over, and you ought to banish it from your mind, except the pleasant recollection of having done your duty ably. I cannot look into futurity, and must wait events. Negotiations must of necessity be going on, and I am confident you will obey the instructions you will receive from the King's confidential servants.

I remain, dear Sir,

Yours most truly,

WILLIAM.

From Admiral De Rigny to Sir E. C.
(Extract.)

À Milo, 6 avril 1828.

J'ai lu avec bien du plaisir ce qu'a dit au Parlement le Marquis de Lansdowne : toutes ces intrigues ministérielles ont dû vous donner beaucoup d'ennuis ; mais je pense qu'elles sont jugées à leur valeur, et qu'il vous est facile, avec l'appui du Duc de Clarence et de vos amis au Parlement, de ne plus vous en inquiéter.

Je regrette quelquefois qu'on ne m'ait pas attaqué dans nos chambres, pour que nous puissions combattre encore ensemble.

Attendons, puisqu'il le faut, ce qui sera décidé; mais donnez-moi toujours votre opinion, pour le but commun, et dans les choses sur lesquelles je puis être plus à l'aise que vous pour agir.

Votre très-dévoué
De Rigny.

From Captain Maude to Sir E. C.

H.M.S. 'Glasgow,' Alexandria : February 6, 1828.

My dear Sir,—I shall not apologise for troubling you with a few lines, because I know it will be satisfactory to you to hear that the Pacha has received me most graciously, and, as you had anticipated, with greater marks of respect than ever. He condescended to invite me to dine with him the day on which I paid my first visit. On the 4th inst. I had a long interesting conversation with His Highness. The Navarin business he calls an unfortunate affair, the result of which he had anticipated fifteen days before the news of the battle reached him. He has heard that Colonel Cradock is on his way to this place, and concludes he is charged with a mission. He said, if he comes with another proposal to withdraw the Egyptian troops from the Morea, that it will not be in his power to comply with such a request. He does not quite assent to the Porte's political measures, but as a Turk he must unavoidably act in concert with the wishes of the Grand Seignior ; were he to do otherwise he would lose the reputation he has gained since he has been Viceroy of Egypt. I have, however, been told that, were he protected by the Allied Powers, something might be done to induce him to relinquish his command in the Morea. He is in great poverty, and seems quite sensible of his own weakness unless time be given him to re-establish his commerce, without which he is fully aware he cannot possibly exist. He says that the Porte will never agree to the terms of the Treaty without being compelled to it by force of arms, as it is contrary to the Mahometan religion for the Government to give up their control over a subject or yield one inch of territory unless driven to do so by superior force. He made allusions to the total impossibility of the Greeks governing themselves, and said as much, that, could the Porte be assured the Allies would make themselves responsible for the good conduct of the Government, less objection would be raised against the

Treaty of London. He is manifestly doing all in his power, by erecting batteries and bringing troops from Cairo, to protect himself against any sudden invasion. On hearing that Colonel Cradock had actually embarked for Alexandria, I was induced to request His Highness to postpone his journey to Cairo; he has consented to remain on the spot until the ' Galatea's' arrival.

I have the honour, &c.,
J. A. MAUDE.

CHAPTER V.

THE following letters give information as to Ibrahim Pacha in the Morea, and Mehemet Ali at Alexandria; and the attempt made to persuade them to a compliance with the Treaty.

From Captain W. J. C. to Mr. Bethell* in England.

H.M.S. 'Galatea,' Zante : January 28, 1828.

DEAR UNCLE,—Orders came out from England to send Cradock to Alexandria, to see what effect *peaceable* conversation would have with Mehemet Ali, in inducing him to remain neutral in regard to the Greek war ; at the same time Sir Frederick Adam is hourly expected here, in order to go to Ibrahim Pacha, to see what his sentiments are on this head. On the 25th we were off Navarin—to me, and many others, of course, a most interesting place. A boat was sent in, in which I was a passenger. We passed the forts, which we found all ready with their ramrods and spunges out, &c. We went into a kind of landing-place, where soon were collected groups of Turks and others, and finding Sir F. Adam was not there, we had little more to say. Ibrahim was at Modon with the troops, which seem all to have left Navarin. There is an old line-of-battle ship, the 'Asia's' opponent, brought up near the town, and forming a kind of floating battery close to the others. She is tremendously knocked about, with a large hole amidships, and her bows riddled, with no masts standing. An Austrian merchant schooner, a corvette, ashore, wreck from the action, and a Turkish brig at the entrance of the harbour, with several Ionian vessels, small craft, was all that was to be seen, except now and then a mast sticking up out of the water. The said Navarin is, however, a most magnificent harbour and bay, with room enough for any number of fleets, and capable of being made very strong. From Navarin we worked up against the N.W. wind to Zante, where we anchored yesterday. Sir Frederick Adam is expected in 'Wolf' every hour ; and I hope we all go

* Sir E. C.'s brother.

together to Ibrahim at Modon. I then go on with Cradock in
'Galatea' to Alexandria. Ibrahim seems to have turned civil
to us. The packet boat to Cerigo was taken by a vessel from
Modon, and plundered. Ibrahim, on hearing of its being our
boat, sent for the plunderer, caused him to give up everything,
and then had the fellow's head cut off. The army of the Turks
is certainly supplied with provisions by the Ionian boats from
Zante, Cefalonia, Corfu, &c. A great profit to the islands,
and consequently winked at by their Governments. I do not
believe there is much hope of the success of this mission to
Alexandria; it is probable they will both say that they are
not free agents. Then, I suppose, at last must come the only
effective means of bringing the Pacha of Egypt to reason—
a blockade of Alexandria. Four frigates, about 8 corvettes,
and 9 or 10 brigs-of-war, arrived at Alexandria from Navarin
about three weeks ago. Several brigs and corvettes have
been collected since the action, from different parts, Turkish
possessions in the Morea. The frigates all much damaged;
a line-of-battle ship that was in the action, having some of
her shot-holes only stopped with canvas, sailed in company,
but was lost sight of in a gale of wind, and supposed to be
gone down as she had not arrived at Alexandria some time
afterwards. In case of war with the Porte, the Pacha of
Egypt is to have (great object of his ambition) the two
additional Pachalicks of Syria and Damascus.

Your affectionate

W. J. C.

From Captain W. J. C. to Mr. Bethell.

Modon: February 2, 1828

DEAR UNCLE,—On the 30th we sailed for Navarin, which
we looked into, having in company the 'Wolf' sloop, 'Weazle'
brig, and a Russian brig; there was nothing there but an
Austrian merchant vessel, and a Turkish merchant brig.
The 'Asia's' opponent was brought up from the other end
of the bay, and anchored close to the town as an additional
means of defence. She was terribly cut up in her hull, and
all her masts gone. We got to this place the day before
yesterday, sent a message requesting an interview with
Ibrahim, which was appointed for ten o'clock yesterday.
Accordingly, the Lord High Commissioner and his two
aides-de-camp (one being myself, *pro tem.*), with a variety of
captains and others, walked up from the shore, escorted by

a guard of honour of Egyptians with black faces and all brickdust-coloured clothes, looking just like reddish monkeys. They had all arms, however, and a drum and a fife besides; this was our attendant music up to the small house in which Ibrahim resides. The town of Modon is small, but has a port and a small mole; the fort runs towards the sea, and forms a small anchorage for boats; behind the town rises an ascent, on the top of which is a small wooden-built octagon dignified by the name of the Kiosk, where the said chief resides, from whence he overlooks his camp on the declivity of the hill on each side of him to the north and south. We had two guardians to prevent anyone touching us and our touching anyone, in order to be kept out of quarantine. We were all introduced to Ibrahim; I was not by name, but as aide-de-camp to Sir F. A. There was nothing in the room but a sofa on which he sat on his velvet carpet, apparently with no legs; a butcher-like fellow with a red cap on, very much marked with the small-pox, with a cunning look about his eye, but of the most ordinary appearance altogether. He was, as he always is, very plainly dressed. When they wished to proceed to business, I was sorry to find we were all turned out but Sir Frederick Adam, his private secretary, and Sir C. Sullivan. Sir Frederick's object was to persuade him to evacuate the Morea, or at all events to be willing to do so. Ibrahim at first said that he was merely, as his father, a general in the service of the Porte; but after a long conversation of two hours, the result was that he would obey any order that he might receive from his father Mehemet Ali at Alexandria. This is something, though I am afraid not much, gained. He sends a letter to his father by us to-day, which most probably contains the contrary of what he has said to Sir F. There is no actual want in the camp here; we saw geese and turkeys going about; these might be Ibrahim's, but there were also plenty of dogs and some horses, which shows they are not actually starving. In the morning there was a grand review (Friday being their Sunday) on the beach; we could see it pretty well, though some way off, from the ships. Having found out when on shore that *all* the troops he had in his camp at Modon were out, we made their numbers amount to between 5,000 and 7,000 men. They have all musquets, and are drilled in the European way. They formed columns and lines; and if things are to be taken by comparison, they are beautiful compared to any regular force that the Greeks have; but if compared to any European nation, very lamentable by way of troops. The cavalry was at Calamata; I do not suppose above 1,000 or

1,500; as they told us, 10,000; but having asserted that their
infantry present here was 30,000, and it is only 6,000, we
may well deduct from their other account. Arbro, the interpreter, began the subject of Patras with Sir F. Adam again,
saying that it was not right in the English Admiral calling
his Highness a man who had broken his word of honour, &c.,
&c.,—but was stopped by Sir F. Adam saying, that whatever
his personal respect and friendship might be towards his
Highness, he could allow no one, 'qui que ce soit,' to cast
imputations against the perfect good faith and honour which
governed the conduct of a British Admiral and Commander-
in-chief, and moreover a particular private friend of his;
that the subject was now past, and one for history; that
Colonel Cradock, who was present on board the 'Asia'
'quand vous, Mr. Arbro, avez eu la conversation à ce sujet
avec l'Amiral Codrington,' was then on board H.M.S.
'Galatea,' and Mr. Arbro must know as well as he (Sir F.
Adam) the result of that conversation. This was what is
called clapping a stopper on his mouth. A grand salute was
fired for Sir F. Adam by all the ships when he landed. The
Turkish fort also saluted with the same number of guns, 19,
two of which (to seaward, luckily) were shotted.

While the conference was going on we wandered about,
accompanied by one or two Corsicans who had come to teach
the troops French drilling; they would not let us go into the
fort without permission, which we did not ask, and they
were also rather jealous of our getting near their camp. I
went into one or two of the officers' houses, who were very
civil, giving us coffee, &c. The Pacha of Modon is a good-
looking man, who was also very civil to us. His was much
the most pleasing expression of any we saw there. The
colonels of regiments, supposed to be 4,000 each, were presented to Sir Frederick, very handsomely dressed and in
uniform. Sir Frederick Adam had some private information
of Ibrahim wishing to leave the Morea, which was the cause
of orders from home to have the interview. I believe the
best foundation for this idea is that he has sent his *harem* to
Egypt. Ibrahim's letter is now on board, and with a fair wind
we shall be off to-day for Carabusa, and then Alexandria.
From thence, after Cradock has done his business, in about
a week come back to Corfù, and thence to Malta.

Yours,

W. J. CODRINGTON.

From Captain W. J. C. to Mr. Bethell.

Alexandria : February 12, 1828.

DEAR UNCLE,—Cradock had his conference yesterday morning with the Pacha of Egypt. The result is he must wait until he hears from Constantinople the determination of the Porte with regard to the proposed neutrality on his part. He said that he could not possibly take such a step without the permission of the Porte : it would be an actual declaration of independence. The Tartar, with his despatch, goes to-morrow; he has pressed on the Porte the necessity of not exposing his resources and army to destruction. Cradock is to be here, or wait here, for the answer to arrive in thirty days. I was introduced to Mehemet Ali as the son of the Admiral; he had known of our coming and was not at all surprised, and perfectly gentleman-like. He is fifty-seven years old, with rather an agreeable countenance, and a quick intelligent eye. There are four frigates, seven corvettes, and twenty-four brigs of war here, the greatest part of which are ready for use; and this morning sailed part of a convoy with corn for Candia,* but which will find its way to the Morea.

From Captain W. J. C. to Mr. Bethell.

Malta (in quarantine): April 8, 1828.

MY DEAR UNCLE,—You will have received some account from Alexandria. The answer of the Pacha to Cradock's mission is nothing decided, as indeed might be easily fore-seen. A kind of temptation to independence is offered to a governor by wishing him to do an act of disobedience to his Government; no guarantee is held out in case he draws upon himself the anger of the Porte, but plenty of threats, unsupported by any appearance of force, are loaded upon him to oblige him to commit the said act of rebellion; how could anyone think the Pacha fool enough to do what was desired of him now, when he knows that it would always be time enough when those threats of blockade. &c., were being put into execution? Why commit himself with the Porte (who, in case of his willing withdrawal of his troops from the Morea, would declare him a rebel) when he has no offer of support or mediation, against a war which would be carried on against him? The Pacha is no fool; he has also the fate of Ali Pacha before him. The Sultan's declaration of a man

* Candia was a Turkish island, and excluded from the operations of the Allies.

being a traitor, has the Pope's power of excommunication of olden time against a Catholic; it then becomes a duty in any good Mussulman to do all he can to destroy him, and in Egypt such people would not be found wanting, nor others who would be glad of it to try for his place. The Pacha knows well enough that, were an army to be sent from Turkey to Egypt to punish him for an act of independence, England would not send an army to stop it. There is no doubt that Ibrahim would be very glad to quit the Morea, either to return to Alexandria or to march into Roumelia to join the army under the Seraschier Pacha. Various interceptions of despatches from Constantinople to Ibrahim show this; Mehemet Ali, however, ordered him to remain where he was, and thus obtained very great credit for zeal with the Porte. The Porte stipulated to send him provisions of which he was in much want, from Albania, and Patras, and then by sea. Mehemet Ali, no doubt, must see that by Ibrahim's leaving the Morea he would do much towards strengthening the independence of Greece; but I should think another reason might have its effect on him—that of seeing his troops, and indeed his best troops, removed to a greater distance from him, and more under the eye of the Porte. This feeling must also have had its weight in producing so *disinterested* an order as that conveyed to Ibrahim. If Government would but give decided instructions as to a blockade of the Morea, his army could not then remain at Modon; and, if he goes to Roumelia, it seems to me an immense point gained, if the Treaty of July 6 is really to be carried into effect in spirit as well as wording. The result of Cradock's mission is a verbal answer from the Pacha's confidential interpreter at Alexandria to this effect: 'That if the Morea is blockaded, a line of communication for the forwarding convoys of provisions will be established from Albania and Patras down to Athens; that Ibrahim's army will thus be well supplied with all necessaries; that, this being the case, it would be much to the advantage of the Allies that he should be permitted to receive provisions by sea at Navarin or Modon.' In short, this seems something like laughing at us; and indeed it is not without reason that he might do so, if our actions were judged by this last mission. I do not think the Pacha will ever declare himself independent of the Porte, even if obliged by circumstances to do anything contrary to the wishes of his Government. I think he would take any opportunity of making the *amende* rather than be declared a rebel. Besides, he has actually all the independence he can wish, everything except the name, and latterly the necessity of the expense of the Greek war. When anything disagreeable comes to him he refers to his being dependent on the Porte, &c., &c.; but when he chooses does what he likes. In commercial treaties the same ; the Porte is the *scapegoat* for disagreeable arrangements, and he either grants them or refuses them at his own convenience in this manner. He is certainly a very clever man; has overcome all the prejudices which a Turk imbibes from his childhood; has established schools for other branches of knowledge than the Koran, manufactures of cotton and silk, foundry of cannon, and manufacture of small arms: these are all at Cairo, the superintendents are generally French, the workmen all are Arabs. The said manufactures are, however, a great expense to him, and do not return him anything; but, in case of a war, he might perhaps derive advantage enough from them to compensate for their present expense. Yours, W. J. Codrington.

From Sir E. C. to Count Capodistrias.

(*Private.*)

Malta : March 3, 1828.

My dear Count,—I am very much obliged to you for the intercepted correspondence to Ibrahim, copies of which I have sent to England with other documents mentioned in my public letter to you; they are very interesting to me, and I think will be so to our Lord High Admiral. I assure you I have strengthened your claim for some pecuniary assistance as much as I could; feeling as I do its absolute necessity at the moment, and the great advantage which would be eventually, and indeed I may say speedily, derived from it. I am more than ever impressed with the ill effect of wasting the resources of Greece upon such expeditions as those of Scio and Candia. Had the expense of those measures been devoted to gaining ground in the Morea, you would soon have derived the revenue which that country is capable of producing. The mission of Colonel Cradock will not produce any result, as it appears to me. Neither the Viceroy nor his son Ibrahim will openly defy the Sultan's power; and they will only hold out appearances of doing so to gain time. The Treaty has been laid before our Parliament, and by this time I dare say there has been a full discussion of its merits. The word *untoward*, which admits of more than one meaning, was introduced into the King's Speech as applied to the battle of Navarin; and it brought out a discussion on my conduct, in which I had the praise of all

sides, including the Ministers who used it. The French boast,
with reason, of their king having avoided throwing any doubts
on his approbation. I have given copies of the Turkish protocol both to Count de Heiden and the Chevalier de Rigny.
I regret that the affair of Carabusa was not executed according
to your wishes. If you could assure us of the four vessels
which came from thence with the crew of the 'Cambrian' being
used for the Government, and that they could in no case return
into the possession of those owners who, though concerned in
the piracies, might claim them, I think we might find reason
for placing them at your disposal. I shall be very glad to do
so, if I can feel myself justified in it.

Believe me, my dear Count, with great esteem,

Your very faithful and obedient

EDWD. CODRINGTON.

*From Sir E. C. to H.E. Count Capodistrias, President of
Greece, &c., &c., &c.*

'Talbot,' at Malta : March 3, 1828.

MONSIEUR LE COMTE,—I sincerely congratulate your Excellency, I congratulate Greece, and I congratulate the allied
friends of peace and commerce, on the enthusiasm with
which you have been received and the facilities which you
will derive therefrom for benefiting a whole people, whose
future prosperity depends upon their obedience to the laws
and regulations which you are about to promulgate. Without pretending to have any personal attachment to a people
to whom, until lately, I was a perfect stranger, it is natural
that I, as an Englishman, should feel interested in the
struggle of another nation for the attainment of that liberal
form of government, and those wise institutions, which
create the happiness with which my own country is blessed.
But your Excellency and the Greek people have a much
stronger security that I shall assist you to the utmost of my
power, in the Treaty of July 6, 1827, and the orders and
instructions emanating from it, for the regulation of my own
conduct. For by this Treaty it becomes my duty to my own
country to endeavour, as far as in me lies, to establish that
regular government in Greece, and those peaceful and in-
dustrious habits in the Greek people, by which all surrounding nations will benefit in common with themselves. I most
fully agree with your Excellency in the necessity of your
having at your disposal an army and a fleet regularly paid
and provided for service. Under this impression I sent off
immediately to England, by way of Marseilles, copies of your

letters and other documents, accompanied by a despatch from myself to H.R.H. the Lord High Admiral, pointing out as forcibly as I was able the advantage of acceding to your request, as being, in my firm opinion, not only the most efficacious but the most economical way of obtaining the object of the three Allied Powers.   It is right I should inform your Excellency that my office of Commander-in-Chief of His Majesty's naval forces gives me no authority for the employment of pecuniary assistance under any circumstances whatever.

I have, &c.,
EDWD. CODRINGTON.

From Sir E. C. to H.R.H. the Duke of Clarence.

Malta: March 6, 1828.

SIR,—The packet yesterday brought me your Royal Highness's letter of February 5.   I have not only to thank Your Royal Highness for the King's Speech, which it contained, but for the kind observations which you have been pleased to add as to the effect of the Duke of Wellington's and other speeches to which it gave rise.   As Lords Goderich and Lansdowne were in office when I executed those measures which have lately been so much scrutinised, their manly avowal of my having done my duty is particularly agreeable to me, and in my humble opinion no less creditable to them. I would fain hope that the Duke of Wellington, as well as some others still in office which they held before the late changes, are equally sincere in their praises.   But it must be admitted that their speeches, when compared with those of the above two noble lords, appear to have been extracted from them by other considerations than mere justice to me. I am free to make these observations to you, Sir, because you yourself have taught me the value of well-timed approbation arising from just and generous feelings, and because your kindness has taught me to write to you without reserve upon matters in which you are pleased to take an interest, and on which I have not, indeed I cannot have, anything whatever to conceal.   The Duke of Wellington says that the chance of the battle leading to war made it 'untoward.'   Now, Mr. S. Canning says that it produced a marked attention of the Reis Effendi to his observations which he had not before met with ; and, also, that it did not at all hasten his demanding his passports on his coming away.   By this it would appear to be a fortunate rather than an untoward event.   But when His Grace takes the converse position, of the battle not having led to war, he slips away from the evident conclusion that the event would no longer prove *untoward*, by substituting ' an impediment to the final amicable settlement of the question! ' I have adverted to the above speech, Sir, because it comes from the present Prime Minister, and because that Minister is the Duke of Wellington.

I beg pardon for having so far extended this subject, to your Royal Highness, who has acted so differently, in my wish to justify opinions which I had no choice in embracing. The words attributed to His Grace by the newspapers have forced this opinion upon me, in spite of my wish to think differently.

I have documents which show that the Porte had always expected and was fully prepared for a battle : and that under those preparations, aided by an endeavour to catch us off our guard, they were confident of success. The words of the Kiahya Bey, one of the oldest and highest esteemed members of the Divan, in conversation with a person whom he termed his friend, were : ' Nous aurons la guerre, vous le croyez, et je le crois de même. *A l'heure qu'il est elle est peut-être déjà commencée !* '

This conversation took place on October 20, at the time the battle was actually raging. But the rest of his observations were so interesting, as showing that predetermination on the part of the Turks which has been unjustly attributed to me, in defiance of my assertion, that I will trouble your Royal Highness with a little more of it. The Bey continued : ' Mais, sachez en toute vérité, que depuis près de deux ans nous avons prévu cet événement, et nous l'attendrons sans aucune inquiétude. Le mal tombera sur ses auteurs. Nous sommes décidés à courir toutes les chances. Jamais, au grand jamais, nous n'admettrons la moindre ingérance étrangère dans nos affaires internes, etc.'

The whole of the confidential communication was in the same strain, and confirms the substance of that Hati Sherif (manifesto) which I sent your Royal Highness some time ago. Force, and force only, according to all appearances, can bring this matter to such a decision as the Treaty contemplates. Little of such means would have been required when the Sultan first learned of the destruction of that fleet which he had calculated on for defeating the object of the Allies.

The longer we continue without adopting strong measures, the greater will be our difficulty and our expense. I am persuaded that a little firmness and decision would settle the matter at once : in delay, I see dangers innumerable.

I have, &c.,

EDWD. CODRINGTON.

From Sir E. C. to H.E. Count Capodistrias, President of Greece.

'Talbot,' at Malta : March 3, 1828.

SIR,—I have the honour of enclosing for your Excellency's information a list of the force which was at Alexandria on February 10, and also of the detachment which left that port ostensibly for Candia. Although the Viceroy declared it to be destined for that island only, your Excellency will see the probability of the supplies which it carries reaching the Morea in smaller and foreign vessels, unless intercepted. Such cargoes would all be good prizes to Greek vessels of war, and their capture would have the doubly good effect of relieving the Greeks and distressing their opponents at the same time. I call your attention to this because I am in some difficulty as to the propriety of English ships of war stopping Ionian boats from going to places not blockaded by a belligerent in regular form. There were about fifty of these boats at Navarin and Modon, whilst Sir Frederick Adam was communicating with Ibrahim Pacha. But, however strong his desire to check such proceedings, he does not feel himself authorised to do so without instructions from England.

I have, &c.,

EDWD. CODRINGTON.

From Sir E. C. to the Admiralty.

'Talbot,' at Malta : March 10, 1828.

SIR,—Although the services of the 'Cambrian' are well known to his Royal Highness the Lord High Admiral, the unfortunate termination of those services has made it imperative on me to request his Royal Highness's consideration of the enclosed documents.

At a time when the agents of other Powers seemed to be doing their utmost to facilitate the reduction of the Greeks to their former state of degradation, Captain Hamilton, by a wise, an able, and enduring devotion to the strict neutrality avowed by Great Britain, established that superior respect for the Government and the nation which will not lose its impression under any fortunate change of circumstances, and which will be felt in all our future arrangements with the Greek people. Strict and impartial in his decisions as to right and wrong in all cases of doubtful conduct on the part of either of the belligerents, he has acquired the esteem and regard of both by his unbounded attention to humanity, whenever the sufferings of either in their inhuman warfare gave him an opening for such interference.

I have, &c.

EDWD. CODRINGTON.

From Sir E. C. to H.R.H. the Duke of Clarence.

Malta : March 9, 1828.

Sir,—I have put two private letters from Sir T. Staines into my last letter to your Royal Highness, which show the importance of the seizure of Grabusa, and the difficulties attending the operation.   Count Capod*istrias* (as he now writes his name), is labouring extremely to effect the desire of the Allies, and I cannot help regretting my inability to give him that pecuniary assistance which he wants and which he deserves ; and by means of which he might carry the rising spirit for regular government to its desired perfection.   One of the Russian ships has killed thirty pirates of a vessel which fired on her boats and wounded two men.   This is much better than bringing them to Malta.   The Count is . anxious to punish these fellows by a Greek tribunal, and I therefore intend placing such as we catch at his disposal. By his making every place responsible for the piracy of its own people, and having those pirates which are caught also punished by their magistrates, much more good will be done than by giving them the benefit of our legal flaws.   The Count seems to be very cleverly turning to account even the assumed patriotism of Colocotroni, and all that gang of plunderers who have hitherto been above control; whilst he collects for offices of trust Tricoupis and others like him, of high character for honesty and patriotism.   The departure of Lord Cochrane under these circumstances is a very fortunate event. Captain Parker's services, and the presence of the 'Warspite,' have been extremely useful to the measures of the President; and I shall direct him to continue them instead of going to Corfu, where they are much less wanted.

I beg to mention to your Royal Highness that I had ordered the painting of the yards and masts *white*, instead of blacking them in the usual way, merely to save the spars from destruction, and not at all to please the eyes of the officers. If the direction of the Board not to allow of this arise from the value of the paint being above that of the blacking, I imagine the deterioration of the spars makes more than a balance in favour of the paint.   It was years before Lord Nelson effected a similar reformation in the painting of the sides, which is now established as a system of economy even in the Ordinary.   I have this day assured the 'Cambrian's' crew that their good conduct throughout, and more particularly during the late trying occasion of her being wrecked, will ensure them the favorable opinion of your Royal Highness.   One-half of them have lost all their clothes ; and I have therefore directed that they may be paid one pound each, as advance on their wages, that they may be able to buy as much as will keep them in health during their passage home, and I propose sending them home by the ' Ariadne ' and the ' Galatea,' whenever those ships return to Malta.

March 11.

I have enclosed with this some additional information from Sir T. Staines about Grabusa, which will show how fully piracy was organised at that place, and that we have not been inattentive to that part of our duty, as alleged by some of the mercantile community at different times. As they are so ready to make complaints, they might as well represent the unfitness of the ' Lady Mary Pelham ' for a packet. A merchant vessel beat her in coming from Gibraltar by three days. The ' Pelham ' left England on January 4, reached Gibraltar on February 8, and did not arrive at Malta till the 21st. She is a noted bad sailer.

Your Royal Highness will be aware of my not having nominated anybody for the promotion to lieutenant with which you were graciously pleased to favour me personally. I therefore humbly request your Royal Highness will so far extend your goodness as to let that nomination stand over until my own son has served his time, and passed his examination, which will be June 1, 1829.

I have, &c.,

EDWD. CODRINGTON.

From Sir E. C. to Rear-Admiral De Rigny.

Malta : March 11, 1828.

MY DEAR ADMIRAL,— . . . . The discussions in our Parliament are very satisfactory to me upon the whole. If the Ministers had not put their *untoward* word into the King's Speech I should never have obtained the public commendations with which I have been honored. I think that word will prove more injurious to the authors of it themselves than it is to me. I conclude their object was to avoid irritating the Sultan by praising my conduct. I think they went the wrong way to manage him, and that they would have done better by complaining of his aggression. In this case they might have made it a *fortunate* instead of an untoward event. You will be pleased to see that the Duke of Wellington has declared that the Treaty will be executed in all respects. We shall do a great deal this summer if there is as much energy in the councils of our Governments as I trust we shall show them there is in their admirals.

Yours, with great esteem,
EDWD. CODRINGTON.

From Sir E. C. to the Navy Board.

'Talbot,' at Malta: March 11, 1828.

GENTLEMEN,—In reply to your letter of December 28, 1827, I have the honour to state, that from all the experience which I had in the battle of Navarin, as well as at sea previously, I am of opinion that giving ships the circular sterns is an improvement, the advantages of which are incalculably great. With respect to the masts made upon the new principle, I am strongly impressed with the justice of a similar opinion. Although I cannot take upon me to say that a mast on the former principle might not have equally withstood the injury to which the 'Asia's' mainmast was exposed, I must express my great astonishment that a mast which had been wounded in twenty-eight different places, some of the wounds embracing one-third of its whole strength, should not have been carried away in spite of the best fishing we could give it, when the ship was pitching in a very alarming manner as she crossed the Malta Channel after a gale of wind. I am not aware of the mizenmast having been more injured, although it went by the board in the battle.

I have, &c.,
EDWD. CODRINGTON.

From Sir E. C. to His Excellency Count Capodistrias,
President of Greece, &c., &c.

Malta: March 15, 1828.

M. LE COMTE,—I beg leave to congratulate your Excellency upon the successful termination of the affair of Carabusa, and the breaking-up of that horde of pirates who would have impeded the progress of your Excellency's measures for establishing order and regularity in Greece, more than all her open enemies. The cause of the Greeks has lost many friends by the piratical conduct of vessels under the Greek flag, although I am persuaded that buccaneers of some other nations have committed robberies under this mask; and I trust the destruction of that system will give your Excellency's Government great popularity throughout Europe. As your Excellency, no doubt truly, observes, the immediate success of the wise regulations which you have promulgated, depends upon your obtaining pecuniary assistance from the Allied Powers. But I must add that the permanence of that success depends upon the destruction of piracy, which has brought such a stigma upon the Greek name, and which, by the interruption of commerce, has deprived those Allied Powers in great part of the means, if not of the inclination, to grant that very assistance. I am sure your Excellency will feel, as I do, the importance of inflicting condign punishment upon the principals in this horrid system, who have been taken at Carabusa. I am equally confident you will agree with me in the advantage of having that punishment inflicted on them contiguous to the Greek Islands, by a tribunal of their own countrymen; and under this impression I have directed Sir Thomas Staines to place them at your disposal, with such proofs of their delinquency as he may have collected.

I have, &c.,
EDWD. CODRINGTON.

From Sir F. Adam to Sir E. C.
(*Extract.*)

March 14, 1828.

As to difficulties, I hold that few men in command ever were placed in a situation of more extreme difficulty than yours—difficulties of every kind, and many of them quite out of the line of professional, occurrence. The difficulties cannot be appreciated by the public, who are only half informed.

Sir E. C. to Captain Sir Thomas Staines.

Malta: March 18, 1828.

DEAR SIR,—The Tunisian papers certainly assist to confirm the conviction of a design on the part of the Turks to resist hostilely any interruption of their movements on our part. But they relate mostly to the operations of the Tunisian squadron. Even the last trial which took place here, when seven fellows were pronounced guilty, affords so little example to deter others, that I am persuaded it is best to make over those seized by you to the President of Greece. He promises me to award the punishment which may be their due; and he knows that a failure in this promise would damp our ardour in his future support, as well as his authority over the piratically disposed themselves. We shall, however, watch closely how he comports himself in this matter, and act accordingly thereafter. I sent your letters about Carabusa off to the Lord High Admiral. . . . As the

Count Capodistrias is now in full authority, and the Capitani and Primate are yielding to his directions, you will have the goodness to consult his wishes in any of your movements and operations which immediately concern the Greeks. As to the four vessels which you sent here with the 'Cambrian's' people, I have preferred making them over to the President, upon condition of his using them for the public good, and not allowing them to fall again into the hands of any claimants as owners. You are aware that although we could destroy them, we could not condemn them to the captors.

Very sincerely yours,

EDWD. CODRINGTON.

From Sir George Cockburn to Sir E. C.

(Extract.)

Admiralty: February 15, 1828.

I hope to be able to send the 'Asia' back to you in about six weeks, if not sooner, when we shall desire you to send back 'Warspite.' Let me also know if we can with safety reduce the Mediterranean force any lower. Our information respecting the naval force at Constantinople varies a good deal, but we consider them to have about seven sail of the line if they put the whole into commission, &c.

Sir E. C. to Sir George Cockburn, Admiralty.

Malta: March 20, 1828.

Sir Thomas Fellowes, in the 'Ariadne,' did not arrive here till yesterday, and to my astonishment did not bring me one official letter of any sort. Thus I still remain without instructions as to my future proceedings, at a time of no ordinary importance, and when delay must largely increase whatever difficulties we may have to contend against. Under these circumstances you desire me to let you know if you can reduce the force on this station. Now, I must first know what we shall have to do before I can form an opinion as to the force requisite for carrying it into execution; and even when that information shall be obtained, I must say, from the experience I have lately had, I do not feel much encouragement to risk an opinion voluntarily on such a matter. Nor indeed could I undertake to state what force the Turks may have at Constantinople—information which may with much more precision be obtained from Mr. Stratford Canning.

I am glad to hear, for many reasons, that the order for the 'Asia' to be paid off was rescinded. I cannot understand upon what principle the intention could have been founded; if that of *economy*, surely it would have cost more to have fitted another ship for the flag than to have repaired the 'Asia,' which must have equally been repaired for ordinary. However, I have yet much to learn in respect to our late political proceedings, which, whilst they appear to me from their tendency, to invite war, are, as I am told, expected to preserve peace.

As to the result of the late debates in which my name was mentioned, I am more than satisfied with the commendations so liberally bestowed upon me from all quarters. Although I cannot but be alive to the 'animus,' by the term applied to the battle, yet I may well feel proud of the encomiums which it gave rise to from men of high intelligence with some of whom I am not personally acquainted, as they indicate the feeling of the country generally.

Very sincerely yours,
EDWD. CODRINGTON.

From the Duke of Portland to Sir E. C.

Nice : March 4, 1828.

DEAR SIR EDWARD,—As I am no longer a member of the Government, and am therefore at liberty to speak my own individual sentiments, I hope our long acquaintance, which began in the Mediterranean, may serve as an apology for troubling you with this letter to express the great gratification with which I learned the events of Navarin as far as they concerned yourself. As a mere naval achievement, it is not too much to say of it that it has been surpassed in brilliancy by none (even of those in the glory of which you have shared) which have preceded it. But it has always appeared to me that there belongs to it a praise, if I may be allowed to say so to an Admiral, of a higher kind. It is impossible for a moment to have doubted, that perhaps no Commander ever was placed in a more difficult or delicate situation; and that the decision to which you came was beset with dangers and a responsibility, to which few persons would have had the resolution and nerve to expose themselves. It would have been so easy to have found good, and very good, reasons rather to have taken the chance of being blown off the coast than of being blamed for the possible consequences of the bolder and more decisive step which you adopted. I should do great injustice to my late colleagues if, in paying this just tribute to the transcendent merit of this victory, I allowed it to be supposed that I did not concur with them in

regretting it not only on account of those calamities from
which victory is inseparable, but on account of the possible
effect of it in exasperating the Turks and making an accommodation more difficult. For this reason, if I had still been in
the Cabinet, I should have been obliged to impose upon myself the cruel restraint of withholding those public expressions
of congratulation and thanks which so brilliant an achievement deserved, in order to avoid anything which in appearance could tend to make the preservation of peace more difficult. I am persuaded, however, the time will come when no
reasons of State will exist to prevent the performance of
that public act of justice, and when everybody will be as
anxious as I am to pay their tribute of respect and gratitude
for the most eminent service performed, because under the
most difficult circumstances.

I was happy to hear the other day, by persons returned
from Malta, that your son has recovered from his wound.
Without knowing that, I should hardly have dared to write
you this letter. I have only to beg that you will not give
yourself the trouble of answering it, and that you will believe me,

Dear Sir Edward, ever yours sincerely,
Scott Portland.

Sir E. C. to Lord Viscount Granville at Paris.

Malta : March 21, 1828.

My dear Lord,—Your letter of February 21, by Sir
Thomas Fellowes, is very gratifying to me. It seems
strange to me that our Ministry should have been so backward in seeing the true state of our affairs with the Porte,
compared with that of France or Russia. It cannot well be
attributed to deficient communication from me, for I will
venture to say that no Admiral ever detailed at greater
length his proceedings and his sentiments, than I have done.
For, after writing all that I thought justifiable in my public
letters, I have largely added to the subject in private letters
both to the Lord High Admiral and Lord Dudley. I had
falsely imagined that I was to be judged by the spirit which
animated the maker of the Treaty. He would have known
at once how to have profited by the battle of Navarin. To
him it would have been a *fortunate* instead of an *untoward*
event. If we had profited by the insult and aggression by
at once declaring a blockade of all the Turkish ports and
those whence Ibrahim receives his supplies, the affairs of
the East would now have been under our entire control.
But it appears to me that the public measures which we

have adopted of securing peace have invited war. Accordingly, the Porte is now proposing to execute the pardon and the amnesty, the inefficiency of which was declared by the Allied Ambassadors long ago.

I have not had any instructions for my future proceedings since the battle, I look to those emanating from the Treaty for my conduct respecting these proposals; and I have little doubt of Count Capodistrias refusing to entertain them, upon the same principle of their not being in the spirit of the Treaty, and on the conviction of that Treaty being to be carried into full execution. I am very glad to hear of the continued cordiality of the several Governments of the Allied Sovereigns; because any failure in that respect might be fatal to the Treaty, which, however roughly it may be handled for political purposes, in my humble opinion is well calculated to prevent a general disturbance of the tranquillity of Europe, so essential to the welfare of all. Count Capodistrias is working very hard and very well; but I fear the want of money may impede his measures sadly, unless he obtains some speedily from the Allied Governments. Your Lordship is aware that I have no power to furnish aid of this sort. Indeed, I am not informed of the intention of our Government as to any of my future proceedings, not having had a line of instructions since the battle of Navarin. And as I have no longer any authority to refer to in these parts, my difficulties are much increased. I trust we have effectually broken up the nest of piracy at Grabusa, although it has cost us the 'Cambrian' frigate. The fortress is garrisoned with French and English, to the exclusion of all others, until Count Capodistrias can find a suitable garrison for their relief. Colonel Urquhart, whom he had sent there, was accidentally killed by a gust of wind blowing down a shed which fell upon him.

Sir E. C. to Vice-Admiral De Rigny.

'Talbot,' at Malta: March 22, 1828.

SIR,—I have had the honor of receiving yesterday, by Her Majesty's sloop 'Ganet,' your Excellency's despatch of March 8, exclosing a copy of a letter from Baron d'Ottenfels, of another from Baron Millitz,* and your Excellency's reply to them. In reply to these documents I have to observe that I do not consider myself authorised to assist in any proposal whatever of this sort, unless made in the full spirit

---

* Containing proposals from Turkey for an armistice for the Greeks, if they submitted.

of the Treaty of London of July 6, 1827, and the instructions emanating from it. The communication from the Porte through the Austrian and Prussian Plenipotentiaries does not appear to me to be made in that spirit, but on the contrary to be an attempt to carry into execution, under our sanction, the measures which the Allied Ambassadors considered as inefficient and therefore objectionable. All I propose to do respecting these documents, is, not to interfere with the consideration of them on the part of the Greeks, but merely to submit them to the English Government. Without further instructions from our Governments, I think we cannot relax in the meantime from the duties prescribed to us by the Treaty, even if the Greeks should assent to the Turkish proposals—an assent which, under the circumstances, I cannot contemplate as within the bounds of probability.

I have, &c.,
EDWD. CODRINGTON.

*From Sir E. C. to the Admiralty.**

'Talbot,' at Malta: March 24, 1828.

SIR,—I have the honor of sending for the information of his Royal Highness the Lord High Admiral, several documents, embracing a proposition† from the Porte to effect an object which appears to have been already rejected by the Allied Ambassadors as quite inefficient for its professed purpose of pacifying Greece.

The Greeks may well suspect both the medium through which the proposition is made and the agent through whom the amnesty would have to be executed : and I think Count Capodistrias is too wise to assent to a measure which would render null the Treaty, on the execution of which alone will depend the salvation of that country from horrors heretofore unknown, and her people from becoming a nation of pirates and freebooters.

I have, &c.,
EDWD. CODRINGTON.

From Sir Thomas Staines to Sir E. C.

'Isis,' Grabusa: March 12, 1828.

I am sorry to have to acquaint you with the demise of the late newly-appointed Governor of Grabusa, Colonel Urquhart.

---

* Received April 9.

† This was an indirect overture made by the Porte, through the medium of the Austrian and Prussian Ambassadors and the Greek Patriarch of Con-

His death was perfectly accidental—caused by a heavy mass of timber and plank forming a shed being hurled by a sudden squall or gust of wind over upon him on his coming down from the fortress into the lower town, which completely doubled him together, and by which he was so seriously injured internally that he expired in two hours after. His remains were deposited on Friday last in one of the bastions of the fortress with military honors, the Greek corvette firing minute guns, and the Greek troops under his command firing over his remains. This unfortunate event had nearly caused a general insurrection among the Grabusa Greeks, who were seeking an opportunity, and who lamented having allowed even the Greek troops to enter the citadel, but were furious at our having got in our Marines, almost without their knowing it. On Wednesday last, when the body of the deceased was taken up to the garrison, it seems it was the expectation that I should have ordered a large detachment of both English and French Marines from the garrison to accompany the body, in which case a general revolt was intended by the Greek population, to have overpowered and expelled the remainder of the British and French garrison, and to have possessed themselves of the fortress again at any expense of blood. This I received positive information of in the course of that afternoon; at the same time, men were found clandestinely making ball cartridges. A house was found with 13 barrels of powder, and quantities of ball cartridge therein, whence many hundreds had been contributed on that day, when Captain Strangways of the Marines (commanding officer of the fortress) had been most positively assured by the Greek local authorities that there was no powder within the garrison not deposited in the magazines, of which he (Captain Strangways) possessed the keys. By all this I found that prompt and coercive measures were absolutely necessary. Our friend Antoniades, so tenacious of his character, was arrested and sent on board the ' Isis,' the powder and ball cartridges being found in his domicile, although he had declared that the barrels contained nothing but flour. It being late in the afternoon, and not having time to put my plans in execution before dark, I merely despatched a strong detachment of about 70 more British and French Marines to reinforce our party, with directions to remain under arms the whole night, with constant patrolling parties and a vigilant observance of every movement of the turbulent Greeks;

stantinople, as well as through Ibrahim Pacha, for a general pardon to the Greeks as the price of their submission, giving them three months' time to submit.

at the same time issuing a proclamation, which was made known and stuck up in the garrison, prohibiting any Greek being out of his house from 8 P.M. until daylight in the morning, on pain of being instantly shot. Thus, being secure and tranquil for that night, I, the following morning, proceeded to put my further plan into execution, by forwarding a detachment of blue jackets from the squadron with muskets, bayonets fixed, &c., under the orders of Commander Prowse; and, after making all the necessary preparations, expelled the whole of the Greeks from the fortress, to their utter discomfiture—their houses being, almost without an exception, receptacles for plundered property. On the two following days, the women, children, household and other effects, also quitted, and were allowed to be taken from the garrison. The sick were conveyed with care and kindness to the lower town, where we have fitted up a hospital which they occupy, attended by our medical men. Having had great cause of dissatisfaction from the irregular, insubordinate, and almost mutinous conduct of the Greek troops, subsequent to the death of their Governor, Colonel Urquhart, I found it necessary also to reduce their numbers in the garrison, and this morning to expel the whole of them, at least until our general search has terminated, and the property secured; for they are absolutely greater robbers than the pirates themselves—'every finger a fish-hook.'

4 P.M.

At this moment not a Greek of any description is remaining in the fortress; it is wholly occupied by the English and French Marines. And I am positively certain, my dear Sir, that unless we keep possession of this said Grabusa, or at least keep a commanding force in the fortress, it will most indubitably dwindle into the same horrible, depraved residence of iniquity and enormity which it has so long given cause to all European and maritime nations to be disgusted with and irritated at. Why might it not be taken into our hands as one of the Ionian Islands? Cerigotta, one of them, is within three or four gunshots of it; at all events, it is my intention to keep possession until I receive your further orders respecting it. And, in fact, it is absolutely necessary that we should do so, at least until after we have embarked the whole of the plundered property for Malta, as well as having recovered all that can be so done of the 'Cambrian's' effects, &c.

From Sir E. C. to Commodore Sir Thomas Staines.

'Talbot,' at Malta : March 26, 1828.

SIR,—Your letter of the 12th inst. reached me by the
'Gannet' on the 21st.   I very sincerely regret the unfortunate death of Colonel Urquhart,* on his own account and
on account of the difficulty the President will have in finding a successor on whom so much reliance can be placed.
I regret it, also, as it affects the important service in which
your are engaged.   I am very sensible of the difficulties you
have met with in destroying that nest of pirates at Carabusa,
which have so long infested the seas of the Levant with comparative impunity, and it gives me satisfaction to say that
you appear to me to have shown great zeal and sound judgment in your mode of overcoming them.   It is necessary
that we should guard against any such future injury from
this fortress, and you will, therefore, retain it in the possession of the Allied forces until Count Capodistrias can put
it into the charge of a garrison upon which he can fully
rely.   I send the 'Ann and Amelia' transport with provisions and stores, and you will let her return to this place as
soon as she is loaded with the stores of the late 'Cambrian'
and plundered property accompanying the latter, with any
information you can obtain as to the vessels from which it
was plundered.

I am, &c.,

EDWD. CODRINGTON.

From Admiral De Rigny to Sir E. C.

'Trident,' à Milo, 1er avril 1828.

MONSIEUR L'AMIRAL,—J'ai reçu la copie confidentielle
que vous avez bien voulu me transmettre, de votre dépêche
du 10 décembre à S. A. R. le Lord Haut-Amiral.

Si les explications claires et positives que vous donnez
sur les démarches des escadres alliées avaient besoin d'être
renforcées de mon propre témoignage, je n'hésite pas à dire,
Monsieur l'Amiral, qu'ayant participé à ces démarches
depuis le 21 septembre, que je vous rejoignis devant Navarin,
jusqu'au 25 octobre, que nous nous sommes séparés en
quittant ce port, j'adhère complètement aux éclaircissemens

---

* Killed at Grabusa by the accidental fall of a house during a gale of
wind.   He was in the service of Greece, and had been sent by Count Capodistrias to be commandant of the fort and island after Sir T. Staines had
taken possession of it.

que vous donnez sur les points en question. Nous avons été conduits, par le traité même, à adopter la mesure d'entrer à Navarin comme la plus propre au but de réduire à l'inaction la flotte et les troupes d'Ibrahim ; car pendant que par un blocus qui devait être souvent interrompu, nous laissions l'une en liberté, les autres pouvaient à leur aise, sans aucune contrainte, ravager le Péloponnèse.

Je déclare hautement que tous les rapports que j'ai faits à mon propre gouvernement sont entièrement conformes aux explications que vous avez rédigées ; et que je suis préparé à lui adresser tous les détails dont la conformité et la concordance démontreraient, si cela était nécessaire, que la mesure d'entrer à Navarin était plus propre qu'aucune autre à atteindre le but du traité, quoi qu'il ait pu en résulter un conflit qui deviendrait inévitable dans la rencontre des flottes en dehors.

En vous adressant cette lettre je n'ai pas la présomption d'ajouter plus de poids aux vérités que vous avez exprimées ; mais j'ai pensé qu'ayant délibéré avec vous,—ayant agi avec vous,—je devais à mon propre caractère de me lier à toutes les conséquences qui peuvent résulter des actes publics auxquels je m'honore d'avoir pris part de concert avec Votre Excellence.

Je suis avec la plus haute considération,
Monsieur l'Amiral,
Votre très-humble et obéissant serviteur,
Le Vice-Amiral H. DE RIGNY.

From H.R.H. the Duke of Clarence to Sir E. C.

Admiralty: April 20, 1828.

DEAR SIR,—A few days ago I received yours of February 20, and yesterday your letter of March 23. Anything that can prove the unanimity of the flag officers must be to me satisfactory, and of course the enclosure from Admiral De Rigny is conclusive. Sir Thomas Staines has actively done his duty ; and I trust piracy is, if not entirely, nearly extinguished by the fall of Grabusa. Having myself named Captain Parker to the 'Warspite,' I must feel pleasure in the energy shown by that officer in the various duties in which he has been engaged. Not being myself in the Cabinet, I do not enter into the political part, or those leanings that Austria may take in consequence of the Treaty of London, or of the line Russia may pursue on the frontier of Turkey. The case is as novel as it is interesting and singular. Firmness and great discretion, and acting without passion is your great object. Things in Greece have taken too quiet and too regular shape for Lord Cochrane.

Ever, believe me, dear Sir, yours truly,
WILLIAM.

Sir E. C. to Captain Parker.

H.M.S. ' Warspite,' Malta : March 24, 1828.

. . . We must do what we can to check the supplies going to Ibrahim; but till Adam has answers from England the Ionian boats will keep up his stock. A Greek blockade would make them good prize to Greek vessels; and we can support them in blockade against a superior force, although not being belligerents we cannot originate a blockade, unless, indeed, to cause an agreement such as Ibrahim made with us to be fulfilled. I have sent the Count's list of the ships at Alexandria and of the expedition which went from thence on February 12 ostensibly for Candia, but not the less intended to find its way to the Morea because the Viceroy says it is for Candia. If it is still in Candia it should be watched. Cradock is to wait an answer from Constantinople to the Viceroy's letter, which is quite useless; he has, however, notified this to England. Ask the Count if I am to write his name Capo d'Istria, or Capodistrias.

Very sincerely yours,
EDWD. CODRINGTON.

Sir E. C. to Lieut.-Col. Sir Thomas Reade, Kt. and C.B., H.B.M. Agent and Consul General, Tunis.

' Talbot,' at Malta : March 25, 1828.

SIR,—In reply to your letter of February 3, I said I would accede to the wish of his Highness the Bey of Tunis. You will please to inform him that the Austrian vessel ' Procaccio ' sailed, under the charge of his Majesty's sloop ' Brisk,' on the 12th of this month, the commander of which was directed by me to convey her first to Navarin and then to Smyrna. And I will beg you to explain to his Highness that I have done this with the knowledge, by means of intercepted despatches, of his having directed his admiral, Kiutchuk Muhamed, ' to employ all his means and his utmost efforts to obtain victory and conquest over all Infidels;' of his terming us ' the enemies of his religion;' of his hoping to learn that the ships of the three Allied Powers have suffered much in the battle, and that they have even

been destroyed;' and of his having given orders to his admiral 'to act in accord with his colleagues and to obey the
will of the Sublime Porte in everything,' even after he knew
of the battle of Navarin.

I have, &c.,
EDWD. CODRINGTON.

Sir E. C. to H.R.H. the Duke of Clarence.

'Talbot,' at Malta: March 28, 1828.

SIR,—I cannot part with Captain Lewis Davies, who will
sail this evening for Plymouth in the 'Ariadne,' with part
of the 'Cambrian's' crew, without giving Your Royal Highness my opinion that he is one of the best officers I ever had
under my command. His conduct in the battle of Navarin
has been already placed before Your Royal Highness, and he
deserves the honors and the promotions which it gained
him at Your Royal Highness' hands; in every respect, in his
ship and in his boat, his gallantry and his ability were
equally conspicuous. He went personally to board the fire-
vessel which had repulsed the boats of the 'Dartmouth;' and,
notwithstanding the dexterous occupation of the 'Rose' described by Captain Hugon, of 'l'Armide,' by sending his
boats to tow a fire-vessel off from the bows of the 'Scipion'
he probably saved that ship also from total destruction. But
his conduct is equally praiseworthy on all occasions. He
never makes a difficulty; his ship is always ready for any
service required; and he bears with cheerfulness that endurance of privation which has no alluring hopes of reward
to make it palatable. I believe he is desirous of temporary
rest and retirement; but I am confident that if circumstances
should require increased naval exertions, Your Royal Highness will find Captain Davies at all times ready to obey the
call, with zeal and ability suited to the occasion.

I have, &c.,
EDWD. CODRINGTON.

At this time reports prevailed that Russia had declared war with the Porte independently of her two
Allies in the Treaty of July. The report, however,
was not true then, though the intention was carried
out some months later.

Sir E. C. to Admiral De Rigny.

Malta: March 29, 1828.

MY DEAR ADMIRAL,— . . . But the most important bit of
news that has reached us is, that Russia is about to declare,

or has already declared, war with the Porte. I have no doubt of her having taken some very strong measures of this sort; because we hear that Abbas Mirza has been serving her as Ibrahim served us, and that by instigation of the Porte the Persians are renewing the war instead of signing the treaty of peace. The irritation of Russia has occasioned various ridiculous reports—of her making war against England, and again against France, and also against Austria, &c. &c. I have no doubt but that the Emperor Nicholas is impatient at the delay in our Ministers, as he well may be; and I hope his despatch, whatever it may be, will hasten their decision. I am still the object of attack by one of our newspapers, the ———; and the arrival of the vessels at Alexandria from Navarin has led it to say the Turkish fleet being destroyed is unfounded; and that if the report of their superiority of force were true, I should have enumerated it in my letter. You will therefore oblige me by giving me Bompard's account of it, in readiness for any occasion of sending it home. Hamilton is gone to Marseilles on his way to England. It bespeaks very good feeling on your part, your writing about his services : a consideration which they well merit.

You will see that although I thought it safest for me (subject as I am to such a scrutiny of every word I write) to write separately and in form, in answer to the Turkish proposal, both De Heiden and myself view the measure in the same light as you do. I think you will have him up in the Levant with you very shortly, as his Emperor has been anxious for his being again at sea. I imagine it was expected that I should already have been there, and that he feared Heiden's not being with us. But even yet I have not a single line of instruction as to my future proceedings, and I cannot leave Malta until I have it. You will therefore see, my good friend, that I have my 'embarras' as well as you. Lord Granville tells me that both your new Ministry and ours are quite agreed as to pursuing the object of the Treaty.

Your very sincere and faithful,

EDWD. CODRINGTON.

From Sir E. C. to the Admiralty.

'Talbot,' at Malta: April 4, 1828.*

SIR,—In the newspaper reports of the proceedings in Parliament on the 5th of last month, one of the Members, referring to a statement of from two to three thousand Greeks having been seized by Ibrahim Pacha and sent to Alexandria, is said to have observed, that 'such a trans-

* Acknowledged May 7, 1828.

Q 2

action could not well have taken place without the consent of the Allied forces,' &c.; and Mr. Huskisson is stated, in reply, to have attributed the successful removal of the Greeks to 'the injury done to the allied squadrons having interrupted the blockade.' Mr. Huskisson is reported to have added, 'that Government was most anxious to put an end to this traffic, and had sent orders into the Mediterranean to intercept all vessels' found engaged in it. As the error contained in this statement, besides compromising in some measure my conduct in the command with which I am honored, may be otherwise injurious to his Majesty's service, I beg his Royal Highness the Lord High Admiral's permission to explain: that I do not consider myself empowered by my present instructions to institute blockades of any sort; that I do not consider myself authorised to examine into the composition of any part of the Ottoman forces which may return to Africa or Turkey in general; and that I have as yet no orders to intercept vessels found engaged in the traffic in question. In the execution of so complicated a measure as the Treaty of July 6, 1827, I may well be diffident of my having clearly understood the whole purport of the instructions, in which it is observed, that it is impossible to foresee all the cases which may arise. I beg therefore to request that his Royal Highness the Lord High Admiral will be pleased to inform me if I am hereafter to intercept vessels carrying on this traffic, and to institute a blockade, or to take any means for putting an end to it. The harem of Ibrahim Pacha himself formed part of the detachment referred to; and his Royal Highness will be aware that no measure would be more likely to produce hostility with Mahometans than an attempt to examine their harems;— and several previous communications from me will show the liability of getting into disputes with the Austrian marine, by the interruption of their communication with the Ottoman forces. But I have no hesitation in saying, that in my opinion the adoption of these two measures would greatly forward the object of the Allied Powers described in the Treaty, and would eminently promote the cause of humanity. Commander Richards, of the 'Pelorus,' informed me that some six hundred Greek children were publicly sold in the slave market at Alexandria; and le Capitaine Pujol, in his report to Vice-Admiral de Rigny, makes the number of Greek captives sent over amount to 1,200. The return of these and other Greeks might be stipulated for in exchange for the troops who would be placed at our mercy by the measures contemplated. I should observe, that the only blockade which I have hitherto considered myself authorised to adopt, was that of the force in Navarin under Ibrahim Pacha, and that solely because he had broken an armistice solemnly agreed upon; that I had ample experience of the extreme difficulty of supporting it against the querulous interruption of the Austrian marine forces; and that after having deprived the Ottoman commander of the means of executing the hostile measures he had contemplated, I have not found myself justified in continuing it in the absence of further instructions from his Majesty's Government.

I have, &c.,

EDWD. CODRINGTON.

Sir Edward Codrington being at this time placed in direct communication with the Secretary of State, some of his official letters were thenceforward addressed to Earl Dudley, to Mr. Huskisson, and subsequently to the Earl of Aberdeen.

From Sir E. C. to H.R.H. the Duke of Clarence.

Malta : April 6, 1828.

SIR,—I received, yesterday, by the 'Wellesley,' from Corfû, Your Royal Highness's despatch of 19th March, with that of Lord Dudley of the 18th.

As the latter does not appear to contain anything more than an enquiry into my proceedings, I lament that it should not have gone in the usual course through Your Royal Highness, to whom all those proceedings are minutely known. I am uncertain whether I ought to place before Your Royal Highness a copy of my explanations, which is my very anxious desire; and I therefore, in the first place, thus ask permission so to do, if not immediately, at least at some future period. For as I owe it to the kindness with which Your Royal Highness has honored me, to do nothing which shall not be worthy of that kindness, I would wish that my whole conduct in my present command should be submitted to Your Royal Highness's inspection. In the meantime, I will beg leave to assure Your Royal Highness that I have not swerved from the line pointed out in my instructions either from Mr. S. Canning or my Lord Dudley, as his Lordship seems to have imagined (as it appears to me) for want of thorough examination of those instructions. I cannot but esteem myself fortunate in having anticipated this subject by my official letter to Your Royal Highness of the 4th. I have just received despatches from Count Capodistria of his having collected eight armed vessels under Satoris, to form a blockade of the Turkish possessions from Dragomestre along the Morea, and as far as Grabusa, of which I have signified the joint approval of Count de Heiden and myself. For although we cannot ourselves institute blockades, as not being belligerents, we are instructed to support such as the Greeks may themselves establish. I assure Your Royal Highness, I watch these matters as closely as I can, and am as much upon my guard in every respect as circumstances justify, whilst preserving that confidence upon which the successful execution of my complicated duties seems mainly to depend. I refer now to the caution in Your Royal Highness's letter of 17th February, which, as also that of the 2nd March, reached me by the packet of the 7th of this month. Of the vessels which some time ago went from Navarin to Alexandria, several were seen to go into the former port by Captain B. Hamilton, which he thinks came from the Dardanelles, Mytilene, &c., and others were collected from Prevesa, Patras, &c. The transports were, I conclude, Austrians, whether under their own or Turkish colours. But Your Royal Highness will hardly believe with what alacrity the Egyptians now manage their maritime matters, compared with former times. In a gale of wind in which I thought it necessary to put the 'Asia' before it without a stitch of sail, in order to prevent accidents, I did not see one of all the ships of war then off Patras which had undergone any injury.

I have, &c.,
EDWD. CODRINGTON.

From Earl Dudley to Sir E. C.

Foreign Office : March 18, 1828.[*]

SIR,—By the reports from Captain Richards of the 'Pelorus' and Mr. Consul Barker to yourself, forwarded to Mr. Croker in your letter of the 21st January, it appears that on the 27th and 28th December, 45 Egyptian or Turkish vessels, of which 30 were ships of war (including 17 which in a return transmitted by you, are said to have arrived at Navarin on the 7th December), returned to Alexandria from Navarin 'with invalid and wounded soldiers of the army of Ibrahim Pacha, and having also on board a considerable number of unfortunate Greek children who have been disposed of in the slave markets at Alexandria.' Similar statements have reached his Majesty's Government from other quarters. A

[*] Received April 6, at Malta.

letter from Mr. Consul Barker at Alexandria to Mr. Stratford Canning, after stating that Ibrahim Pacha had sent away in this expedition all whose maintenance had become burdensome, all such of the crews of the destroyed ships as could not be converted into soldiers, the sick and wounded, and otherwise disabled of the fleet, and all superannuated invalids and useless followers of the army, adds, that 'the number of Greek slaves, chiefly young women and children, amounted to 5,500, and described them as having arrived in the most wretched state of suffering from hunger and grief.' This latter intelligence has caused the deepest concern to his Majesty, and is calculated to excite the most painful feelings throughout the country. From the circumstances of the first intimation of this expedition from Navarin having been transmitted to you from Alexandria, after it had arrived at that port, as well as from the statements received from Corfù of there having been no naval force before the ports of Navarin, Modon, and Coron since the battle, it would appear that these ports had not only been free from blockade, but that the movements of Ibrahim Pacha, and of the remains of the Turkish and Egyptian naval forces in the Morea, had not even been watched. Adverting to the paragraph in your instructions of the 16th October (of which you acknowledge the receipt on the 8th of November), which directs you 'to concert with the Commanders of the Allied Powers the most effectual mode of preventing any movements by sea on the part of the Turkish or Egyptian forces,' and more particularly 'within the line described in the protocol of the Ambassadors at Constantinople for the operation of the Greek blockade,' I have to desire that you will forthwith furnish me with a detailed statement of the orders given and the steps taken by you in pursuance of that part of these instructions.

This information is the more requisite, after the events to which I have already called your attention, as, in an enclosure transmitted in your letter of the 8th of November, already referred to, his Majesty's Government were given to understand, in your own words and those of the Allied Admirals, that an 'armistice de mer existe de fait du côté des Turcs ; leur flotte n'existe plus.'

I have the honour to be, &c., &c.,

DUDLEY.

From Sir Edward Codrington to Earl Dudley.

Malta: April 7, 1828.*

My Lord,—I had the honour of receiving yesterday, by way of Corfù, Your Lordship's despatch of March 18, 1828, accompanied by an order from his Royal Highness the Lord High Admiral, ' to follow such orders and instructions as I may from time to time receive from his Majesty through one of his principal Secretaries of State ; in addition to all other orders which I may have received or may from time to time receive from his Royal Highness.' In this despatch Your Lordship refers to some Egyptian or Turkish vessels having conveyed from Navarin to Alexandria a considerable number of Greeks, several hundred of whom were sold in the slave market at Alexandria. As I myself announced this fact, it will not be necessary for me to repeat the extracts which your Lordship quotes in confirmation of it. I feel called upon, however, to observe, that by the manner in which those quotations are made, as well as the expressions by which they are accompanied, Your Lordship appears to think I have either not understood or not guided myself according to the instructions which I have had for my proceedings. Your Lordship implies that it was my duty to have blockaded the ports of the Morea, and to have prevented the transmission of Greeks to Egypt ; whereas it is my impression, guided by the same documents, that I was bound to encourage the return of all Turkish and Egyptian forces from Greece, and that I had no right whatever to question the composition of any such returning force. In other words, that although I feel myself justified in supporting the Greeks in blockades established by them, I am not authorised to institute blockades myself; and that I have no order or instruction whatever to prevent the transmission of Greeks to Alexandria. I will endeavour to establish this point to Your Lordship's satisfaction. I beg leave, in the first place, to say, that I consider the letter from Your Lordship of October 15,† from which you quote, not to apply in any way to the change of affairs occasioned by the battle of Navarin, and the retirement and dispersion of the ambassadors, but to refer solely to the Treaty and the instructions emanating from it. It is true it directs me ' to concert with the commanders,' &c., as Your Lordship quotes; but Your Lordship omits the important addition, that we are to decide in conjunction with the ambassadors, which ambassadors left Constantinople on

* Acknowledged in England May 6, 1828.
† The Instructions are in Appendix of Vol. I.

December 8, one month after my receipt of it. But the fact of its application merely to the instructions emanating from the Treaty, is evinced by its commencing words, whilst the third paragraph and what immediately follows shows that it was framed to remove doubts which were expressed by Vice-Admiral De Rigny and myself as to the interference with Austrians carrying supplies, and as to the movements of any Ottoman force from one Turkish possession in *Greece* to another.

The Protocol itself referred to by Your Lordship further elucidates this matter.

After speaking of the inutility of any demonstration at the Dardanelles and Smyrna, and of the possible utility of a movement towards Alexandria, 'dans le but d'accélérer la retraite de la flotte égyptienne;' it adds under the head No. 7, 'Les amiraux agiront dans le sens du Traité, en protégeant, selon le besoin, toute portion des forces navales, grecques ou mussulmanes, qui s'engageroit à ne pas prendre part aux hostilités, et en favorisant d'après ce principe le retour, soit à Alexandrie soit à Constantinople, de tout bâtiment de guerre turc et égyptien, de même que tout transport de l'une ou de l'autre nation ayant à bord des troupes retirées;' and the letter from Mr. Stratford Canning, dated September 8, 1827, accompanying that Protocol for my guidance, concludes with ' You will probably agree with me that every practicable facility should be afforded for the complete evacuation of the Morea by the Mussulman forces.'

All my communications from first to last have shown I was under this impression; and that I deemed it my duty, even at the risk of hostilities, to effect, if possible, the return of all or any part of the forces under Ibrahim Pacha to Alexandria or the Dardanelles. And if I have been in error it is one in which I have been suffered to continue by the Government; since it does not appear that any doubts of it entered Your Lordship's mind until March 18, 1828, although it must have been brought forcibly under Your Lordship's consideration when Sir John Gore reached London with my answer to Your Lordship's Queries; for when asked by the 10th Query what the propositions were which we meditated making to Ibrahim Pacha, my reply is, 'that he should retire with his forces to Alexandria or the Dardanelles.' It is hardly necessary for me to remind Your Lordship that notwithstanding this, and that the last instruction which I have received for my guidance in this complicated service is dated October 15, 1827, Your Lordship has not given me any further instructions for my future guidance even in this last despatch of March 18, 1828, which attributes to me an erroneous view of the orders under which I have heretofore acted.

With respect to the quotation which Your Lordship has made from the joint letters of my colleagues and myself, in French, I really am not aware how it is made applicable to the case in question. I can only, therefore, explain that it was written with a view of urging the Greek Government to recall their cruisers from the pretended employment of intercepting Turkish vessels in order that they might concentrate their forces on the coast of Greece. It was intended to point out to them that there was no longer a Turkish force of sufficient magnitude to prevent their blockading the ports of the Morea.

In answer to Your Lordship's desire that I will forthwith furnish you with a detailed statement of the orders given and the steps taken by me in pursuance of my instructions, I beg to refer Your Lordship to the regular and voluminous communications which have been made by me to his Royal Highness the Lord High Admiral of the stationing and the proceedings of the ships under my command; repeating that the whole of my arrangements have been made with a view of suppressing piracy and preventing the arrival of supplies of men, arms, &c., destined against Greece, and coming from Turkey or Africa in general, and of encouraging at the same time the retirement of the Egyptian expeditionary force from the Morea, altogether or in part (which I considered as the particular object of my instructions), without investigating the materials of which it was composed, whether of Greeks or Turks, slaves or free people, for which I do not find myself possessed of any authority whatever. A reference to those communications will show that though the ports of the Morea have not been blockaded they have been watched, and that the force under my command has been both actively and arduously employed during the utmost violence of a Levant winter season.

To show how far I was guided by my instructions in making my arrangements for intercepting the arrival of supplies coming to Greece, I request Your Lordship's attention to my circular instructions—to my letter to the Hon. Lieut.-Colonel Cradock—and to a letter of the 4th of this month, to the secretary of his Royal Highness the Lord High Admiral, only two days previous to the receipt of Your Lordship's last despatch, of all of which I now enclose copies.

It is necessary for me to apprise Your Lordship that if I were myself to fall in with another such detachment as that referred to, proceeding from Navarin to Alexandria, I should not find myself authorised by any instruction which I have even to this day received, to scrutinise its composition or to interrupt its movements; and, therefore, that I may no longer be liable to misunderstand the line of my duty in this important point, I request Your Lordship will be pleased to inform me :

If I am henceforth to consider myself empowered to establish blockades.

If I am to prevent the return of any Turkish or Egyptian forces from Greece ; and in case the return of such force should be permitted,

If I am to examine the ships containing it, and to release any Greek captives which may be found on board them.

As to the right of blockading, my opinion is corroborated by Your Lordship's statement of November 28, 1827, to His Highness Prince Esterhazy, that ' it is perfectly clear that His Majesty, not being at war with the Porte, cannot claim the exercise of belligerent rights. It is equally clear that blockade is one of those rights, that even in case of war could not be exercised without notification.' In this Your Lordship lays down the principle ; and you add, ' this is a principle that has been strictly attended to in the instructions which have been furnished by His Majesty's commands to his Admiral.' And Your Lordship will remark that this letter to Prince Esterhazy is dated forty-four days subsequent to the instruction, which appears to Your Lordship to bear an opposite construction. The only blockade which I have attempted was that of the force under Ibrahim, in consequence of his breaking an armistice solemnly agreed upon. And I may remind Your Lordship that the propriety of my entering the port of Navarin under those circumstances for the purpose of preventing his devastating the country and making slaves of the inhabitants, those very people perhaps whose suffering, as Your Lordship truly observes, is calculated to excite the most painful feelings throughout the country, has been questioned by the Government itself.

I will conclude by assuring Your Lordship that a power to liberate such Greeks as may hereafter be seized in slavery, or to redeem those who have already been taken to Alexandria, will be a very gratifying part of my duty.

I have, &c.,

EDWD. CODRINGTON.

Extrait d'un Rapport du Capitaine Lieut. Kadian, commandant le brick de la Marine impériale russe 'l'Ousferdie,' en date de Rhodes le $\frac{28\ février}{12\ mars}$ 1828.

'Dans le second port se trouvait une frégate turque venue de Navarin. Ce fut le hasard ou plutôt la Providence qui l'avait portée ici, car elle avait été quelque tems à la merci des vents et des flots—sans une once de pain à bord, et le corps du bâtiment dans un état pitoyable ainsi que le gréement. Elle avait déjà perdu la moitié de son équipage, et le restant était composé de blessés et de malades : personne nosait s'en approcher, de peur d'être infecté. Cette frégate est pour Rhodes une triste trophée de Navarin.'

From Admiral De Rigny.[*]

Milo, 1er avril, 1828.

MON CHER AMIRAL,—Je suis, comme vous, sans aucune nouvelle instruction de mon gouvernement; mais je suis d'opinion qu'on a pu s'exagérer l'effet du Hati Scheriff, car il ne fait aucune sensation chez les Turcs. Je pense qu'il en fera davantage *en Russie.*

Vous savez que les bâtimens égyptiens sont repartis pour Alexandrie. Capitaine Latreyte, qui est devant Navarin avec l' 'Iphigénie' et un brick, me dit, qu'il passe de tems à autre de petits bateaux, mais que ce qu'ils portent n'est pas de grande conséquence. Je lui ai recommandé d'éviter toute hostilité, mais d'empêcher les transports de vivres ou munitions d'entrer, et de les renvoyer en Candie.

.   .   .   .   .   .

Je suis pressé de repasser à Égine ; de là j'irai à Smyrne pour suivre les communications, s'il y en a, et vous les transmettre. Il n'y a rien de mieux à faire jusqu'à ce qu'on sache ce qu'on veut ; car enfin, aujourd'hui, si la Porte ne cède pas un peu, il faut la guerre, qu'on veut éviter. Guerre *directe,* ou *indirecte ;* directe en la poussant nous-mêmes et les Russes ; *indirecte* en la bornant à la Morée et à fournir des secours à Capodistrias. C'est en ce sens que j'en ai écrit à nos ministres, qui sont bien embarrassés d'autre chose.

Vous devez penser que j'ai vivement ressenti la peine que vous avez dû éprouver en lisant le discours du Roi d'Angleterre. Il a pour effet de faire tourner la tête aux Turcs, et à nos marchands, et s'il y a guerre, peut-être le *mot* (untoward)

[*] Received April 12.

en sera-t-il cause.   Quoique vous n'ayez pas reçu les remer-
cimens du Parlement en cette occasion, vous n'en êtes peut-
être que placé plus haut dans l'estime publique.   .   .   .   .
   Je crois fermement, qu'il était (Canning) le seul ministre
en état de profiter de la circonstance actuelle, et de conduire à fin cette affaire difficile de l'Orient.   Je crains que
ses successeurs n'en aient ni le goût ni la capacité.
   Je suis et serai toujours, mon cher Amiral,
Votre très-dévoué,
H. DE RIGNY.

From Sir E. C. to H.R.H. the Lord High Admiral.

Malta: April 12, 1828.

SIR,—I have been so occupied by the arrival of various
communications from all parts of the Levant, and by replying to the late despatch of Lord Dudley, which obliged me
to review almost all my correspondence as well as the Treaty
and my instructions emanating from it, that I fear I cannot
enter into as much detail as I wish respecting what is going
on, without delaying my reply to his lordship.   I most
anxiously hope that reply will be placed before Your Royal
Highness immediately, as it is in no way of a secret nature,
but merely concerning my conduct; there is no additional
instruction contained in his lordship's letter, but merely such
observations as tend to complicate the former ones.   Every
day's delay in deciding on the line we are to take adds to
the difficulty, and will most grievously protract the final
arrangement of affairs.   The letter or address from the Greek
Bishops at Constantinople to the Greeks, expresses the grounds
of the insidious interference of the Austrian and Prussian
Ambassadors without communicating with the Dutch Ambassador, to whom our affairs are entrusted.   This document
I shall put into an official letter, as it belongs to the other I
have before sent.   As, in obedience to my original instructions, an entire confidence of communication has been
established between my colleagues and myself, I submitted
to their inspection my answers to the Queries, to which they
signified their perfect sanction.   The answer of Admiral De
Rigny in writing reached me a few days ago, and I enclose
a copy of it, which I think will be satisfactory to Your Royal
Highness.   The letters of Captain Parker will show how
erroneous is Lord Dudley's supposition, that the ports of
Navarin, &c., have not even been watched.   He little knows
how difficult it is to watch any port during the gales of a
winter in those seas; nor does he appear sensible of any

other difficulties than in managing the affairs of his own office; for I may say to Your Royal Highness that he has largely increased mine by leaving me so long uninformed of what policy is to be adopted. I will enclose an extract of a letter from Admiral De Rigny upon our present relations with the Porte. I am sure Your Royal Highness will not suspect me of want of respect to my Sovereign, who has so lately honored me with a special mark of his approbation, by introducing any remarks upon the word which has excited so much sensation; nor should I have now sent this extract if I had not known by Your Royal Highness to Sir Thomas Fellowes, as well as through Sir Charles Paget from His Majesty himself, his disapprobation of the use which was made of it. The facts will abundantly show that His Majesty took a correct view of this matter at once.

Count de Heiden, having orders from His Imperial Majesty to put to sea, will get away in a few days. He is directed to be guided by me; and he is embarrassed by my inability to instruct him how to proceed. I am persuaded that the Emperor gave his orders, in fear of my being already enforcing without him certain measures which he expected I should long ago have been instructed to adopt.

I have, &c.,
EDWD. CODRINGTON.

As early as February 24, 1828, a memorandum from the Duke of Wellington to his Cabinet proposed—

(Extract.)*

1. That the three squadrons should blockade the Morea.

2. That a detachment of the fleet should cruise off Alexandria to prevent communication between Mehemet Ali and Ibrahim Pacha; and that a Greek ship might attend for preventing provisions being sent in neutral ships.

3. That the Greek Government must name their vessels of war, giving each a commission; and to be employed in aid of the blockade by the combined fleet for preventing supplies by neutral ships.

Other ships to be employed in the active pursuit and destruction of Greek pirates, &c.

* See ' Wellington Papers,' vol. iv.

On page 278 in the same volume is the following letter from

The Duke of Wellington to Earl Dudley.

February 29, 1828.

'MY DEAR LORD DUDLEY,—I think it advisable that your proposition at the Conference should, in addition to what I proposed in my Memorandum sent in circulation on Wednesday with the letters received from the Admiralty, contain orders to the Admirals to intercept the communication between Mehemet Ali and Ibrahim Pacha,' &c.

And again—

*From the Duke of Wellington to Mr. Huskisson.**

April 5, 1828.

'But I think we might in the same sense in which we wrote heretofore to the Lord Commissioner and to the Admiral, write again to both, and inform the first that this supposed armistice must not produce a relaxation of the measures ordered to prevent the supply of Ibrahim's army with provisions from the Ionian islands, Zante, in particular; and to the second, that as it is hoped he will have resumed his operations to carry into execution his instructions of October 15, it is likewise hoped he will not discontinue them in consequence of hearing of this suspension of hostilities until he shall have further orders from the Conference in London. In respect to the Austrian commerce we must speak to Esterhazy.'

Sir E. C. had enforced these arrangements as far as possible, and beyond the instructions then in his possession; but these memoranda show that fresh instructions were contemplated, and were considered necessary. They were, however, 'hung up,' according to the term used in the following letter:—

From Mr. Huskisson to the Duke of Wellington.

April 6, 1828.

'From your letter I infer that you are under the misapprehension that the instructions which I prepared some two or three weeks ago for Sir F. Adam have been sent. *They as*

* Vol. iv. page 337.

*well as those which had been settled for Codrington were hung
up by the last note from Lieven,* as they embraced several
points—such as the Greeks withdrawing from Scio, Candia,
and Western Greece, their co-operation with us in the Morea,
and the supplies to be furnished to them if so co-operating,
—which could not properly be proceeded in except as a joint
instruction.   The interruption of the supplies furnished from
the Ionian Islands made one part of that despatch, and reference was also made to the supply by Austrian neutrals,
&c.

A curious comment on the debate of March 5, 1828,
is afforded by the above letter, giving distinct evidence
that fresh instructions were considered necessary, but
were not furnished to Sir E. Codrington.

From Admiral De Rigny to Sir E. C.

'Trident,' Milo, 4 avril 1828.*

Mon cher Amiral,—Je sens tout l'embarras de votre
position par suite du silence de vos ministres.   Vous et moi
n'avons pas l'avantage, vu l'inconvénient, que nos démarches
ne soient pas discutées par le public ; Heiden peut faire tout
ce qu'il voudra, *la presse moscovite* ne l'inquiètera pas.   J'ai
envoyé, comme je vous l'ai dit, à Corfou, croyant que les trois
ministres y seraient réunis.   J'ai des nouvelles du 31 du Cte
Guilleminot ; il était encore seul, et n'avait pas reçu un mot,
pas plus que moi, de nos ministres : d'où j'en conclus qu'on
est assez d'accord, à Londres et à Paris ; mais qu'on ne sait
pas encore ce qu'on veut faire.   Il y a, il me semble, de la
franchise dans la note du Cte Nesselrode ; il propose même
d'assez bonnes mesures, mais ! ! !

Si la déclaration de guerre de la Russie est réelle, on
l'aura sans doute fondée sur les griefs particuliers qu'elle a
pu élever, d'après les expressions même du manifeste ; il faut
convenir que les Turcs ont fourni par là des armes à la
Russie, et qu'ils ont évidemment calculé que la France et
l'Angleterre se tiendraient à part, pour le moins.   Il faut
bien que tout ceci finisse par quelque chose.

Le 'Warspite' était encore il y a deux jours, avec
l''Iphigénie' devant Navarin.   J'y ai envoyé deux bricks.
Il faut bien espérer que nous recevrons quelque chose après
la mission de Lord Stuart.

Je suis votre très-dévoué,

H. De Rigny.

* Received April 12.

From Admiral De Rigny to Sir E. C.

'Conquérant :' ce 13 avril 1828.

MON CHER AMIRAL,—Je ne doute pas que vous n'ayiez eu communication de la dépêche du Cte Nesselrode au Prince de Lieven du 14 février. Je viens de la recevoir de Corfou. Le Cabinet de la Russie presse Londres et Paris d'agréer les propositions du 29 décembre en ce qui concerne le Traité; et il fera alors marcher de front ses griefs particuliers contre la Porte, et sa co-opération dans le but du Traité.

Capo d'Istrias demande instamment des secours. Je n'ai encore rien reçu de Paris à ce sujet. Cependant je lui ai fait donner quelques barils de poudre pour Napoli, vu qu'il n'y avait pas une seule cartouche. Il paraît que Heiden a reçu des authorisations à ce sujet. Le géneral Guilleminot me mande que la Conférence de Londres s'était décidée pour la limite de l'isthme de Corinthe; mais cela avait eu lieu avant le manifeste de la Russie. Certainement ce manifeste est très-habilement rédigé; la stupidité des Turcs y a donné beau jeu. Cependant il ne faut pas oublier que les griefs particuliers dont se plaint le Cabinet Russe sont le résulat du Traité du 6 juillet, et non de celui d'Akerman; qu'ainsi nous ne pouvons être absolument indifférents aux complications nouvelles et aux exigences que la Russie en tire.

. . . . . Le Trident et l'Iphigénie et le Palineure sont devant Coron et Navarin. J'ai établi aussi une communication de l'Archipel à Corfou.

Je suis toujours votre très-dévoué,

H. DE RIGNY.

From Sir E. C. to Count Capodistrias.

Malta : April 12, 1828.

MONSIEUR LE COMTE,—I am so pressed with business that I can only tell you by this opportunity of the 'Mastiff' returning to survey your coast (which is a work more beneficial to Greece herself than to England) that I will do my best to support your blockade. Captain Parker will readily receive and act upon your wishes in that respect, and Count de Heiden will send a ship of the line to assist in the same service. I am as yet without further instructions for my proceedings. I cannot say how much I regret the difficulties which have arisen at Grabusa. I shall instruct Sir Thomas Staines to place the fortress at your disposal when you can put into it a garrison which will satisfy yourself of its not permitting future acts of piracy.

You are aware of the position being so adapted to the interruption of commerce, that I should not be justified in leaving it undestroyed if I had not full confidence in all your proceedings.

Yours, &c.,
EDWD. CODRINGTON.

Sir E. C. to Vice-Admiral Count de Heiden.

Malta: April 13, 1828.

MY DEAR COLLEAGUE AND COMPANION IN ARMS,—I will not let you quit Malta without expressing the pleasure that I have had in your society, and in the cordial regard which mutual esteem, founded on mutual exertion in obeying the orders of our Allied Sovereigns, has cemented between us. I had great satisfaction in accepting your friendly offering of the star, appropriate to the very distinguished order of St. George, with which your august Emperor has honored me. Prompted by the same feeling, I was prepared by the first private information of both you and our colleague, De Rigny, being named Commanders of the Bath, to make you an offer of the star which I have often worn. I am confident you will not value it the less for having decorated the breast which a time of severe trial has warmed with a sincere regard for you. I have delayed my offering thus long, in daily expectation of the official notification of the honor intended you, and which, I trust, I shall have very shortly to send after you. I hope it will not be long before I receive orders from England which will enable us to rejoin our squadron, that we may again serve together, and again support each other cordially and successfully through whatever difficulties we may be destined to encounter.

Believe me, my dear Admiral,

Your sincere and faithful friend,
EDWARD CODRINGTON.

From Admiral Heiden to Sir E. C.

'Azoff:' le $\frac{3}{15}$ avril 1828.

MON CHER ET DIGNE AMIRAL,—Votre aimable billet d'hier, et le précieux don que vous y avez joint, me pénètrent d'une reconnaissance qu'aucune expression ne saurait bien rendre. Heureux de votre amitié, fier de votre estime, j'en recueille toutes les preuves et les conserve dans mon coeur. Vous m'associez, mon cher Amiral, d'une manière généreuse et cordiale à votre gloire militaire en m'offrant cette même étoile devant laquelle le Croissant a pâli.

J'en décorerai ma poitrine avec orgueil le jour où il plaira à votre auguste Souverain de m'accorder une distinction si flatteuse. Je me dispense d'exprimer ici à Votre Excellence tous les regrets que j'éprouve en quittant Malte, sans savoir au juste l'époque où nos escadres se trouveront encore réunis. Mais vous me permettrez, j'espère, avant de partir, de demander vos directions et vos conseils sur les mesures qu'il serait opportun de prendre dès mon arrivée dans l'Archipel.

Veuillez agréer, mon cher Amiral, l'hommage des sentimens que vous portera toute sa vie

Votre plus dévoué ami et serviteur,
Le comte L. de Heiden.

Sir E. C. to Vice-Admiral Count De Rigny.

Malta: April 14, 1828.

My dear Colleague and Companion in Arms,—There cannot be any doubt of the intention of my Sovereign to confer on you and our colleague, De Heiden, the Commandership of the Bath, although some delay in the forms of the herald's office has hitherto prevented the insignia reaching my hands. Be the cause, however, what it may, I will no longer withhold my request that you will do me the kindness of accepting from me the accompanying Star of the Order. There are no bounds to my satisfaction in reflecting that I have been the fortunate medium of a cordiality between our professions, which we may hope, according to the wish of our august Sovereigns, by whose example we have been guided, will extend and become permanent throughout our two nations. Nothing of the character of my little offering is necessary to remind you of this great national blessing which the Treaty of London has originated. But I trust it will be received by you as a small token of the respect and regard with which I am inspired by the counsel and support which I have received from you during the most trying period of my professional life.

Believe me, my dear Admiral,
Your sincere and faithful friend,
Edward Codrington.

From Admiral De Rigny to Sir E. C.

'Conquérant:' ce, 1er juin 1828.

MON CHER ET DIGNE ADMIRAL,—Après l'honneur d'être admis dans l'Ordre du Bain, ce que je pourrais désirer de mieux c'est de porter l'étoile donnée par votre main. Je l'accepte et la reçois comme un gage durable de votre estime. J'ai l'espoir que vous dans votre pays, comme moi dans le mien, nous serons élevés à quelque considération pour avoir été les premiers et les heureux instrumens d'une alliance que je désire voir durer autant que dureront mon respect et mon amitié pour vous.

Votre très-dévoué,
H. DE RIGNY.

Candia was not ordered to be included in the operations of the Allies, but the liability of its being used for the supply of Ibrahim by boats, &c., induced Sir E. Codrington to put restrictive measures in force against it. The 'Dartmouth' was sent there with preventive orders; and similar instructions were given for the 'Glasgow' frigate at Alexandria to assist in such prevention as far as possible, by orders dated April 10, 1828.

Sir E. C. to H.R.H. the Duke of Clarence.

Malta: April 19, 1828.

SIR,—   .   .   .   .   .   .
We have various reports of the intentions of Russia, of which your Royal Highness is better informed than I can be. I must say, however, that I believe Count Heiden has apprised me of all the instructions and information which he has received; and, as he is evidently one of the most open and guileless persons I ever met with, I feel confident he was quite sincere in desiring to be guided by me in his present movements; and I think his arrangements of his squadron will prove it. It is, however, impossible, I think, that Russia should continue passive under a delay, by which she is suffering so much more than either of her Allies, however ready she may have been to confine herself to the terms of the Treaty, so long as she had hopes of its being carried into full execution. The Russian squadron got out on the 17th, leaving here one of the ships of the line and a frigate, which

* Received at Corfu June 25, 1828.

are to return to Russia when made equal to the voyage. I look with great anxiety for the arrival of the 'Asia,' and the receipt of your Royal Highness' further orders.

Having the honour to be, &c.,

EDWARD CODRINGTON.

Upon May 3, 1828, the Duke of Wellington quoted, in a memorandum to his Cabinet, the circumstance mentioned in the following letter from Captain Parker of 'a Turkish fleet being seen to enter Navarin,' as the ground for recalling Sir E. Codrington from his command; and the despatch of the Cabinet thus recalling him is dated May 18 and June 4, 1828.

Yet on *May 7th* there was at the Admiralty (the receipt of it acknowledged) another letter from Captain Parker correcting this, his own erroneous information, and stating that the supposed Turkish fleet was 'a French convoy from Alexandria accidentally carried in this direction by contrary winds.' If this correction had been sent to the Duke of Wellington the commonest sense of justice would have prevented use being made of the original error when the correction of it was known. But, nevertheless, the erroneous information was used—from some unjust or discreditable omission—as the ground for the recall of Sir Edward Codrington. —W. J. C.

From the Wellington Papers, Vol. IV., Page 423.

Memorandum: The time has come for the Cabinet to deliberate whether Sir Edward Codrington shall or shall not be recalled.

May 3, 1828.

I have just read despatches from Sir Edward Codrington, in which he reports that an Egyptian fleet had found its way into Navarino. He sends the report on the subject from Captain Parker, of the 'Warspite,' who received the information from certain Greeks who saw the fleet enter the port from the hills.

WELLINGTON.

From Captain Parker of H.M.S. 'Warspite,' to Sir E. C.*

Napoli di Romania : March 3, 1828.

SIR,—The Governor of Napoli last night brought intelligence, from a person on whom dependence could be placed,
that fifteen large vessels were on Saturday morning, 1st
instant, observed from the heights of Arcadia, standing into
Navarin Bay.† As this account corresponds with a report
that had previously reached us of a fleet from Alexandria
having been seen at Candia; we come to the conclusion that
the vessels at Navarin are either out for the purpose of
removing Ibrahim's forces from the Morea, or bringing
reinforcements; and I feel very anxious to proceed with
the 'Warspite' to ascertain the fact. As our departure
would, however, defeat every hope that the President entertains of getting possession of the Palamidi, which becomes
of more importance in the event of Ibrahim receiving any
accession of force, I have consented to remain until Wednesday evening, by which time we trust the chiefs Grivas and
Strato will be induced to retire, and we may at least expect
further information from Navarin, by the return of a messenger despatched yesterday with a letter to Ibrahim,
proposing an exchange of prisoners, a copy of which I have
the honor to transmit. In the meantime I have directed
Captain Martin, who joined me on the 25th ult. at Poros
with despatches from Sir Frederick Adam for Count Capodistrias, to proceed off Navarin *for correct intelligence.* I
hope this will be obtained from the 'Iphigénie' French
frigate which is cruising on that rendezvous. But should
Captain Martin find it necessary to land, I have charged him
with the delivery of a duplicate of my letter to Ibrahim
Pacha, as the ostensible reason for communication. And
having forwarded from Zante some despatches from Mr.
Baynes for Sir Frederick Adam, together with this letter,
and every intelligence that may be obtained for your information, the 'Musquito' will either rejoin me at this
anchorage or on our passage to Navarin, accompanied by
the French and Russian ships, which I hope will meet your
approbation.

I have, &c., &c.,

W. PARKER.

* This letter was sent to the Admiralty by Sir E. C. on March 24, and
acknowledged April 19, 1828.

† Subsequently found to be erroneous.

The report was ascertained to be erroneous, and the fifteen large vessels
proved to be a French convoy, communicating with the French frigate off
Navarin.

From Captain Parker, H.M.S. 'Warspite,' to Commander Martin, H.M.S. ' Musquito.'

Napoli di Romania : March 3, 1828.

* Having received intelligence that fifteen large vessels were seen to enter the Port of Navarin on the morning of Saturday the 1st inst., it is my direction that you proceed with all possible despatch for the purpose of reconnoitring that port and Modon, and ascertaining correctly both the force and object of those vessels.   You will probably obtain every necessary information from the captain of the French frigate 'Iphigénie,' who is stationed on that rendezvous, and for whom you will herewith receive a letter on the subject; but if you find it desirable to communicate with Ibrahim Pacha (to learn his movements, as well as the object of the vessels seen going into Navarin), you are at liberty to land, and deliver the accompanying letter in duplicate to him, proposing an exchange of Turkish and Greek prisoners.

From Captain Parker, H.M.S. 'Warspite,' to Sir E. C.

Napoli di Romania : March 7, 1828.

The messenger who was despatched to Ibrahim Pacha on the 2nd inst. is not returned; but reports from various quarters all tend to confirm our belief that a fleet of thirty or forty sail, including two frigates and several small vessels of war, had sailed from Alexandria. Fifteen of the merchant vessels, with provisions for Ibrahim's troops, it appears, have been left at Suda in Candia; the rest *we imagine* to be the vessels seen from the heights of Arcadia OFF Navarin on the 1st inst.†

From Capt. Martin, H.M.S. ' Musquito,' to Sir E. C.

Zante : March 8, 1828.

SIR,—I have the honor to inform you that in pursuance of the accompanying order from Captain Parker, of H.M.S. 'Warspite,' I proceeded to Navarin, and having yesterday morning fallen in with the French frigate ' Iphigénie,' I send the captain's report for your information. He states that he has been cruising off that port for the last seven days; that he had reconnoitred the port on the afternoon of the 8th and

---

* See Captain Martin's letter of March 8, 1828, which showed this report to be erroneous.

† Copy to Admiralty March 24, 1828 ; acknowledged April 19, 1828.

three days prior; that in Navarin there was only *one* line-of-battle ship (dismasted and entirely unfit for sea) and a brig; that in Modon there were only two vessels having the appearance of men of war, and the rest small craft, most probably coasters. That the 'Émulation,' French corvette, had arrived from Alexandria with a convoy of fourteen vessels, and in passing Navarin had informed him that a squadron of Turkish ships, amounting to forty ships, sailed from Alexandria on February 15; that in the squadron there were *two large frigates, ten other men of war, corvettes, and brigs,* the rest transports or merchantmen; that the *French representative* at Alexandria had received the most *positive assurances from Mehemet Ali* that the squadron was destined *for Candia* (as was publicly made known at Alexandria) and that there was *no intention whatever of sending it to the Morea.* It may not be unlikely that the intelligence Captain Parker received of fifteen vessels having been seen to enter Navarin, arose from the circumstance of the French convoy amounting to *exactly that number,* being *off the port.*

At Spezzia, on the afternoon of the 4th, I received information that forty vessels had sailed from Alexandria, twelve men of war, and the rest armed transports, no troops on board, only supplies and provisions. The Greeks stated that fifteen of the transports remained at Suda, and that the rest had proceeded to Navarin or Modon.

The latter part of this information must be incorrect; as the Captain of the French frigate has not seen any vessels in Modon or Navarin, nor have I in my way from Napoli in Roumania. I was close off yesterday evening, and could not discover any in either port. Having obtained what I conceive to be every requisite information from 'Iphigénie,' I did not find it necessary to make use of the duplicate letter; and not finding any vessels and the wind blowing strong from the southward, I arrived here this morning at 10 A.M. I shall lose no time in joining the Commodore in completion of my orders.

I have, &c.,

G. BYAM MARTIN.

*From Captain Parker, H. M. S. 'Warspite,' to Sir E. C.**

Off Navarin: March 17, 1828.

SIR,—The 'Warspite' arrrived off Navarin on the 12th inst., when I learnt from the Captain of the French frigate

* Sent to Admiralty April 11, 1828; receipt acknowledged May 7, 1828.

'Iphigénie,' cruising here, that the vessels reported at Napoli to have been seen off this Port on the 1st inst., were a *French convoy from Alexandria accidentally carried in this direction by contrary winds.*

I cannot believe that the Egyptian fleet will attempt to enter either Navarin or Modon collectively, but they may attempt to send the supplies from Candia, by single vessels or in neutral bottoms; Sir F. Adam is of this opinion. General Guilleminot seems very anxious that the port should be closely watched, and as I am desirous of manifesting a cordial co-operation, and cannot reconcile the idea of leaving an insufficient force here, I have determined to remain with the 'Warspite' on this rendezvous in company with the 'Iphigénie,' until I ascertain positively that the provisions, &c., have been *landed* at Candia,* and the ships of war gone to Alexandria.

I have, &c.,

W. PARKER.

From Captain Parker, H. M. S. ' Warspite,' to Sir E. C.

Off Modon : March 30, 1828.

SIR,—If my letters of the 10th and 17th have reached you, they will have apprised you that I had proceeded with the 'Warspite' off Navarin and Modon for the purpose of intercepting the Egyptian convoy from Alexandria, should they attempt to enter with supplies for Ibrahim Pacha. The 'Armide' French frigate returned yesterday from Milo, and I have positive information from Captain Hugon that after landing provisions at Candia, the whole convoy and ships of war had returned to Alexandria.†

From Captain Parker, H. M. S. ' Warspite,' to Sir E. C.
(*Extract.*)

Off Sapienza : April 4, 1828.

Captain Mitchell, whom I had despatched to Carabusa and Suda for intelligence of the Egyptian convoy, rejoined on the 2nd inst., confirming the intelligence that I had received from Capitaine Hugon of the ' Armide,' of their return to Alexandria.‡

* Candia was excluded from the operations of the Allies.
† Sent to Admiralty April 11, 1828 ; receipt acknowledged May 7, 1828.
‡ This extract was sent to Mr. Huskisson, April 30, 1828 ; receipt acknowledged in London May 23, 1828.

From Captain Parker, H. M. S. ' Warspite,' to Sir E. C.

Off Venetico : April 5, 1828.

Sir,—On examining the Egyptian corvette brig 'Crocodile' this morning, we find, contrary to the statement we understood her Captain to have made last night, and to which my letter of that date alludes, that her hold and decks are full of provisions and canvas, and about 250,000 dollars on board. I have, therefore, felt it my duty to prohibit her proceeding and have warned her off in writing. The Captain has requested me to allow Ibrahim's secretary to be landed at Modon with his despatches, and I have directed Captain Smith of the ' Brisk ' to put him on shore, and having received Ibrahim's answer, the Captain of the brig consents to return to Alexandria.*

From Sir E. C. to Captain Parker H. M. S. ' Warspite.'

' Ocean,' at Malta: April 23, 1828.*

Sir,—You appear to me to have done precisely as I should myself have done as to the Turkish vessels which arrived off Navarin. The Greek blockade since established will cut off Ibrahim's communications more effectually, and I hope the meditated plan of getting over in Ionian boats those supplies which the Viceroy of Egypt has sent to an agent at Zante, will be frustrated. Since the Viceroy has been false to his assertion, that none of the supplies which went to Candia were intended for the Morea, we may justly be more rigid in turning back vessels actually charged with despatches only, by which means we shall also prevent a collision betwixt the two belligerents. But all this will now be rendered more simple by the Russians being at war with Turkey; for they will, of course, seize every ship they can; and I imagine the Viceroy will take some less ostensible means of keeping up his intercourse with Ibrahim.   By the observations made by our Ministers in Parliament on the transfer of Greeks to Egypt, although not at all in accordance with any orders or instructions which I have yet received, I am disposed to impede as much as possible any such transfer. If, therefore, Ibrahim should propose or assent to his return to Alexandria, we must stipulate for the exchange of all those Greeks already sent over, as well as others he may have in possession.

I have, &c.,

EDWD. CODRINGTON.

* Sent to Admiralty April 18, 1828; sent to Mr. Huskisson April 30, 1828; receipt acknowledged by Admiralty May 28, 1828.

CHAPTER VI.

From Sir E. C. to the Admiralty.

'Ocean,' at Malta: April 20, 1828.*

SIR,—Although I have already troubled His Royal Highness the Lord High Admiral upon the subject of certain observations made in the House of Commons, a repetition of similar observations by Mr. Peel and Mr. Huskisson, stated to have taken place on April 3, interpreting the instructions which I have received differently from the view I have taken of them, induces me to recur to it. Mr. Peel is said to have stated, 'that Instructions issued before the battle of Navarin, and which still remained in full force, directed the Admirals in command of the combined fleet to prevent any deportation of the sort.' I have again examined the Instructions sent with the Treaty in Mr. Stratford Canning's despatch of August 31, 1827, as well as those of October 15 last, and I do not find one word which would justify my interference with the deportation of Greeks who may accompany any of the Ottoman forces returning to Egypt. Mr. Peel is said also to have stated that 'within forty-eight hours after intelligence of the fact reached this country, communications were sent to the British Admiral and full inquiry was directed to be instituted,' &c. And yet although the receipt of my letter of January 21 (No. 11) reporting this fact, and thus giving an opening for such instructions, is acknowledged by a letter from Mr. Barrow of February 18, the despatch of Earl Dudley consequent on it bears date March 18, and still gives me no further or precise instruction for the conduct of the ships under my orders in case of such deportations being repeated. Mr. Peel is further said to have stated, that 'undoubtedly if the instructions of Government had been strictly complied with, the transportation of those persons would have been prevented.'

Certainly I could not have blockaded Navarin effectually

* Acknowledged May 26, 1828.

if I would; His Royal Highness knows that I had not the means at my disposal of making such an attempt, and that the vessels under my orders have been arduously employed in the suppression of piracy.

As to the assertion of this fleet, ' containing sixteen thousand Greek captives, and having worked its way through the superior combined force of the Allies unnoticed, unobserved, and unknown,' I trust it does not require any further notice from me.

I beg to assure His Royal Highness that I would act upon any wish of His Majesty's Government, if I were fully aware of it, as readily as I would upon a regular order; but as this wish, respecting the deportation of Greeks, is only thus implied in statements in the newspapers, and seems to be contradicted by the doubts thrown on the propriety of my entering the port of Navarin for the purpose of preventing the devastating expedition of Ibrahim Pacha, one of the objects of which appears to have been the collection of the Greek slaves in question; and as no such wish as to the future is defined in the above despatch of Earl Dudley, it does not appear to me that I am sufficiently justified in acting upon it. I cannot but lament the necessity of troubling His Royal Highness upon a subject which at first sight may appear to be merely personal: could I have viewed it in that light, I would gladly have avoided the harass of mind which it occasions at a time when I find that the service I have to perform requires all the uninterrupted consideration I can give it. I feel that my character as Commander of His Majesty's naval forces on this station is, in some measure, implicated by such statements coming from such high authority; and I am confident His Royal Highness will agree with me, that whilst I am ready at all times to place my life at the disposal of my country, it is not the less my duty so to preserve my character from reflection, that I may the more perfectly execute the duty confided to me.

I have the honour, &c.,

EDWD. CODRINGTON, Vice-Admiral.

Sir E. C. to Rear-Admiral Count de Heiden.

Malta: April 27, 1828.

MY DEAR ADMIRAL,— . . . You will have received the Russian declaration addressed to Prince Lieven, and your own orders how to act upon it. You will have a more serious part to perform; but the battle of Navarin will have much lessened all your difficulties, and I hope the Porte will soon be brought to reason. I conclude we and the French shall continue to execute the Treaty as before; and our joint object, as well as the separate object of Russia, will be promoted by the operations of each. Mr. Miège received a copy of the Russian declaration from Count Guilleminot. I must say that I think it one of the best, the cleverest, the most just, and what you and I understand by one of the most *straightforward* state papers I ever read. I give you this opinion freely and in confidence, without knowing what view may be taken of it by my own Government. Indeed as you are well acquainted with my sentiments, you would have felt confident in my thus judging this important document if I had not mentioned it. De Rigny had another communication with Ibrahim, who still holds the same language of devotion to the Sultan's orders, but who would be very glad of a fair opportunity for retiring. His father has sent provisions to an agent at Zante, who is directed to pass them over to Modon or Navarin in open boats; but I hope the Greeks will take care and prevent his being supplied in this way any longer. All my family desire to be kindly remembered to you.

Yours with great regard,
EDWD. CODRINGTON.

From Mr. Huskisson to Sir E. Codrington.

Downing Street, London: April 6, 1828.*

SIR,—Intelligence has been received that orders have been sent to the Commanders-in-Chief, by sea and land, of the Ottoman forces in Greece and the Levant, to suspend all hostilities for three months.

The Greeks will of course exercise their own discretion in respect to the Armistice.

The Allied Powers are no parties to these proceedings of the Ottoman Porte. Their object must still remain the same—to carry into effect the Treaty of London; and their measures for this purpose cannot be suspended in consequence of any steps resorted to by the Ottoman Porte without their intervention or concurrence.

I think it right to lose no time in sending you this explanation, as I have reason to believe that a communication has been made to you from the Ministers of Austria and Prussia residing at Constantinople, respecting these proposals from the Turks to the Greeks.

* Received April 29, 1828.

Should an armistice take place between them, it will afford His Majesty much satisfaction, not only on the score of humanity, but possibly as paving the way by negociations between the Allies and the Porte, to such arrangements as may give a practical execution to the Treaty of London.

The first step towards this desirable event must be the evacuation of the Morea by the Turkish and Egyptian forces. The blockade and other measures ordered by the Instructions of October 16 (to which you have been recently more than once referred), were directed to this object. Those Instructions you were still to consider as the guide for your conduct; and you will appropriate all the naval means at your disposal, not wanted for other indispensable services, to strictly watching and blockading according to the tenor of those Instructions, the ports of Greece occupied by the Turks or Egyptians, from the Gulf of Volo to the western side of the Isthmus of Corinth; and to a like blockade of the port of Alexandria.

If any information should reach you from which you may be led to infer a disposition upon the part of the Pacha of Egypt to profit by the armistice in withdrawing his forces from the Morea, you will renew to him the assurance and offer of affording every facility and assistance in your power for that purpose. But you will intimate, at the same time, both to Mohammed Pacha and to his son Ibrahim, that in return for the aid afforded by His Majesty and his Allies to extricate Ibrahim Pacha from the difficulties in which he is placed, His Majesty anxiously hopes, from the friendly disposition which the Pacha has always professed towards this country, that any Greek women and children who, contrary to all the laws of civilised war, have been unfortunately sent from the Morea to Egypt since the affair at Navarin, should be restored to freedom and placed at the disposal of His Majesty's Consul jointly with the Consuls of His Majesty's Allies at Alexandria, for the purpose of being sent back to their native country.

Instructions have already been given to our Consul at Alexandria to make application to Mohammed Pacha for the liberation of these slaves, and to urge it, to the utmost, upon His Highness, as a point which His Majesty's Government have greatly at heart.

I have the honour to be, &c.,
W. HUSKISSON.

From Sir Edward Codrington to Mr. Huskisson.

'Ocean,' at Malta: April 30, 1828.

SIR,—I had the honour of receiving your despatch of April 6, last night. I cannot but regret that it does not define explicitly the plan of operations which his Majesty's Government wish me to pursue, instead of referring me to the Instructions of October 16, 1827, which have never appeared to me to bear the construction that has been given them by Earl Dudley's letter of March 18.

Zealously anxious to perform the duties of my station, not only according to the letter and to the spirit of my orders, but also, according even to the wish of his Majesty's Government, I have, by my letter of April 7 to Earl Dudley, asked for such explanations as appear to me absolutely necessary to prevent my falling into errors of primary importance in the execution of this difficult service.

I reckon that my letter will arrive in London about April 28, and that an answer may reach me about May 14. In the meantime I do not propose to assume any other blockade than such as I understand by the Instruction of October 16, 1827, jointly with the Protocol No. 5 of the Ambassadors, which is, a support of blockade established by the Greeks themselves, and a confinement of their cruisers within prescribed limits, accompanied by an interception on our part of all ships bringing troops, arms, &c. (with the exceptions mentioned in the secret letter of the same date), and also a prevention of any movements by sea of the Ottoman forces within those prescribed. I trust that no injury will arise from the short delay which may take place before all doubts will be removed by the explanations I shall receive from His Majesty's Government, particularly as the disposition which I had already made of the ships under my command, and the Greek blockade established from Dragomestre to Carabusa, will, in the meantime, prevent the efficacy of any movement of the Ottoman naval forces.

In addition to this, looking to the tenor of your instructions, I have taken advantage of circumstances to issue the accompanying Order,* and I trust that this measure will be an additional means of accelerating the evacuation of the Morea.

In my letter No. 49, of March 24, 1828, to the Secretary of the Lord High Admiral, which enclosed copies of those of the Austrian and Prussian ministers at Constantinople, and

* An order to intercept vessels with supplies coming from Candia to Ibrahim.

more fully in my letter to Vice Admiral De Rigny, I observed that the proposal therein mentioned appeared to me to embrace merely that measure which the Ambassadors of the Allies had rejected as inadmissible. I have since sent to the Secretary of the Lord High Admiral, the letter of the Greek Patriarch substantiating this fact; and I have now the honour of adding a letter from Monsieur de Canitz, correcting the erroneous impression which his predecessor's letter was calculated to give. These documents would appear to dispel all hopes of the proposed suspension of hostilities leading to any eventual good; at all events, I at once declined, as you will see by my communications, becoming a party to any such propositions; thus anticipating the substance of the 3rd paragraph of your despatch of April 6.

Should an armistice, nevertheless, take place, I shall, of course, guide myself by the tenor of your Instructions and forward the pacific purpose of the Treaty to the utmost of my power.

You will see by the accompanying extract of a letter to Captain Parker, of the 'Warspite,' that I have also, in some measure, anticipated the latter part of your Instructions, relative to the redemption of the Greeks conveyed to Alexandria.

In reference to the term of 'a like blockade,' it is right for me to observe that the extension to Alexandria of a similar blockade to that prescribed for the coast of Greece, 'preventing the movement of any Ottoman naval forces from one port to another,' would cut off all communication with the most contiguous Ottoman dependencies. In this case the Viceroy would either offer an open hostile resistance, for which he is making active preparations, or he would resort to the aid of Austrians and other neutrals, the interruption of which would seem to be an assumption of belligerent rights, contrary to the doctrine laid down in Earl Dudley's letter to Prince Esterhazy of November 20, 1827.

When I adopted a partial blockade of the port of Navarin, I was accused by the Austrian officers of having usurped the rights of a belligerent without having given due notification; a blockade of Alexandria, even if limited, would, no doubt, meet with the same objections from neutrals, whilst it would militate greatly, at this particular period, against both French and English interests. The trade with Alexandria is almost the only trade now left to Marseilles, and, as this has been the particular object of France, it would probably be very sensibly felt by the French Government.

It is hardly necessary for me to remind you that its effects on Malta would be still more fatal. Now that the usual supplies are cut off from Odessa, and that France herself as well as Leghorn is importing, Egypt is become a source of the greatest importance towards the subsistence of the numerous population of this island. I may also add that ships on Government account for this island are now loading with corn at Alexandria under the protection of our vessels of war.

It is perhaps necessary for me to explain that, in the objections to the blockade of the port of Alexandria singly, which I have now submitted, I consider it as a measure very different from a general and rigid blockade of all the Ottoman ports at once, which, as I have before suggested, would probably have forced the Porte to accede to the Treaty; a measure which, even now that the Sultan is so much more prepared for resistance, I still think, besides expediting the pacification of Greece, might be the means of restoring his amicable relations with Russia, and by diminishing the period of his resistance, diminish proportionably the injury which will unavoidably attend it.

In the observations which I have here introduced I have been actuated by a desire to inform His Majesty's Government of what is my own impression, as being more contiguous to the scene of action, and to enable them to define their wishes, so as to prevent my falling into error which may lead to consequences not in their contemplation.

I have not, I cannot have, a partiality for any one line of policy in preference to another. My object is to ascertain clearly the intentions of my Government; the principle of my conduct to pursue their fulfilment to the utmost of my abilities.

I have, &c.,
EDWARD CODRINGTON.

Sir E. C. to H.R.H. the Duke of Clarence.

Malta: May 4, 1828.

SIR,—I cannot any longer withhold my pen from the expression of my anxiety for Your Royal Highness's perfect recovery, and your being again able to superintend the important concerns which have already benefited so much by your directions. I may safely say for myself that but for the protection I have had under Your Royal Highness's command, I should not have been able to execute fully and satisfactorily the multiplied and harassing duties which have fallen to my share. The Council find fault with my not sending more frequent dispositions of the squadron. I am persuaded that no Admiral ever wrote more fully upon this and all other passing events than I have done. But in such service as this in which we are engaged, it is quite impossible to say at all times where the ships actually are. Even the senior officers in the Levant at times report vessels at particular spots in those seas, when they are actually at Malta : and I in return lead them to expect the aid of vessels which never get within their reach. I am aware, by reference to Lord Dudley's letter, that search has been made at the Admiralty for this information at a time when his Lordship mistakenly says the coast of the Morea was not even watched, since he quotes a mere acknowledgment by me of the instructions of October 6, which contains no other information. Admiral De Rigny and Captain Hamilton both took opportunities of informing themselves as to what was passing then, even before Captain Parker had the superintendence of that service, which he has performed so ably. If Ibrahim had told me he was going to send away those ships in that state, and so filled with Greeks as well as others, I could not, consistently with my instructions, have interfered. If, indeed, they had returned with supplies and reinforcements, I might be open to comment. But Your Royal Highness will see that whilst Sir T. Staines has executed my orders so fully in destroying piracy, Captain Parker has been equally successful in preventing supplies going from Alexandria to the Morea.

In fact, but for Ionian boats over which Sir F. Adam himself had no control until we effected a blockade by the Greeks, Ibrahim would by this time have been at our mercy. I will only further assure Your Royal Highness that I shall most gladly find myself in those seas again, under instructions by which I can guide myself without falling into errors which might lead to serious consequences : for the being at sea will be to me a great relief from the sedentary pen-and-ink employment under anxiety to avoid censure, which my health would not much longer support.

I am, &c.,

EDWD. CODRINGTON.

Sir E. C. to Captain Parker, H.M.S. ' Warspite.'

Malta : May 5, 1828.

MY DEAR SIR,—I have an instruction from Mr. Huskisson to establish a like blockade at Alexandria to that on the coast of Greece directed by an instruction of October 15, which was merely to confine the Greeks to their own coast from Volo to the Aspropotamo.   I have replied that a like blockade is impracticable, and that therefore I shall only, until I have further order, include Candia in our partial blockade according to the accompanying order.   This order will confirm you in what you heretofore did as to the vessels going to Ibrahim, and thus increase his difficulty.   And as Adam has now formally warned Ionians not to break the blockade, I think the said Pacha will shortly propose returning to Egypt. I wish the proposal to come from him and not from us as De Rigny's letters indicate; because he would then the more readily agree to restore the Greek slaves.

Although it is signified in a sort of way by both Lord Dudley and Mr. Huskisson that I ought to have prevented the taking the Greeks to Alexandria, neither of them ventures to give clearly that interpretation to the instruction of October 15, to which they refer, because they know it will not bear it; and under such circumstances, and seeing such disposition to put me in the wrong, I dare not act otherwise than as my instructions shall justify.   You have acted quite in the spirit of my orders, and will see that I now take advantage of the deception offered to be passed on you* to draw the line tighter.

Sincerely yours,
EDWD. CODRINGTON.

I do not like to show myself in the Levant until I can take decisive measures of some sort.   Explain this to Count Capodistrias.

From Sir E. C. to H.R.H. the Duke of Clarence.

Malta: May 8, 1828.

SIR,—Although the errors which are imputed to me in letters from Your Royal Highness's secretary are probably without Your Royal Highness's knowledge, as being of trivial import compared with the many matters of most serious consideration upon which my mind is necessarily fixed at this moment, I must say it hurts me that there should be upon record any appearance of my having acted inconsistently with any wish of Your Royal Highness's.   I can safely say that the labour and anxiety of searching through all the documents which I have to consider, for justification of myself against the errors which have been imputed to me, has more than once disabled not only myself but all the people in my secretary's office.   No doubt it is our duty to make

* By the Greeks.

this sacrifice, and we shall always be ready to do it.　But it will be evident to Your Royal Highness that a protracted failure of this sort would subject the more important branches of this important service to injury; and it is therefore that I now take the liberty of mentioning it.　The want of that disposition of the squadron which is now complained of, has perhaps been the cause of Lord Dudley imagining I was sitting down quietly with my family and leaving the affairs of the Levant to take their chance.　It would have been much more agreeable to me, that a search of the Admiralty records should have explained to his Lordship or any other of his Majesty's Ministers, the real occupation of my time; a matter, however, which has been, I trust, clearly made known to Your Royal Highness by the addition of my private letters.　Information of this sort would have saved his Lordship the pain of attributing to me errors which I have had the pain of throwing back upon him by a reference to his own directions.　Enquiry of me in the first instance would also have prevented statements attributed to Mr. Huskisson and Mr. Peel in the House of Commons, which facts will sooner or later contradict.　And they would have been also saved the pain of attributing to me misconduct, which such enquiry would have enabled me to place to the account of circumstances which we could none of us control.　I know my situation too well to discuss the right or wrong of what is disapproved of in the name of Your Royal Highness; and shall feel well contented with the happiness I have in finding expressions of satisfaction in the confidential letters with which Your Royal Highness honors me.　I therefore refer to these matters only to prevent any ill impression being given to Your Royal Highness, and to prevent at the same time any deterioration of the multiplied and important duties by which my mind should be almost entirely engrossed.　I write in some apprehension of my thus expressing myself having the air of complaint; yet I think I can rely upon Your Royal Highness's usual kindness for attributing it to its true motive.

Complaint indeed I am obliged to make of the enclosed letter* or note, coming to me as if in answer to my official letter asking his Majesty's permission to wear the Insignia therein referred to, increasing the confusion detailed in my said letter and unaccompanied by the decorations themselves. The delay respecting these honors has been sensibly felt by Count Heiden; and I must confess it is somewhat painful to

---

* A note without a signature, beginning with 'Mr. Croker's compliments.'

me, the not being yet empowered to fulfil my own Sovereign's intentions of a similar nature towards the Count himself and the Chevalier De Rigny. I should inform Your Royal Highness that I had a similar note in Mr. Croker's name, my answer to which, from its irregularity, I particularly requested might be acknowledged; but which has not procured me such an acknowledgment, although I have received it of the letters by which it was accompanied. When Your Royal Highness considers the subject of the documents demanded *in the name of Mr. Croker*, you will understand the grounds of my uneasiness.

I have, &c.,
EDWD. CODRINGTON.

From Sir E. C. to Mr. Huskisson, Secretary of State for the Colonies.

'Ocean,' at Malta: May 12, 1828.*

SIR,—I have the honor of enclosing the copy of a letter which I yesterday received from Vice-Admiral Chevalier De Rigny, respecting the Island of Samos. This island being, as it were, detached from the Treaty, and under peculiar circumstances, makes me desirous of having the particular instructions of my Government respecting it.

I have received, also, from Count de Heiden a private letter, as well as official reports from officers under my command, which give an unpleasant picture of the proceedings off the ports of Coron, Modon, and Navarin. The commodore of the 'Trident' (le Commodore Arnous) appears to have permitted a Turkish vessel to go into Modon, which, under similar circumstances, had previously been turned back by Captain Parker, of the 'Warspite.' Concluding that communications respecting this affair have been already sent to you by Sir Frederick Adam, I will not enter into the details on the present occasion. It has produced much ill-blood between the French and Count de Heiden, who attributes the return to order of the revolted Albanians at Coron, to their having been paid money claimed by them, which was carried in by the Turkish vessel before mentioned. Count de Heiden does not appear to have received any new instructions up to the $\frac{12}{24}$ April, although despatches which came from Naples to Malta must have reached him very shortly afterwards. Although my flag-ship is not yet arrived, I think my presence may be more beneficial to the service at this moment off Navarin than here; and I therefore shall profit

* Received June 14.

by Commodore Campbell's offer, and proceed to sea to-morrow morning in the 'Ocean,' for the purpose of adjusting these differences as far as I am able. Having so done, it is my intention to return here to meet such despatches as may be collected for me, to remove my flag into the 'Asia,' and then again proceed to the Levant. It is very difficult to judge of what turn affairs may take in that quarter; but as I am desirous of giving Government every information in my power, I will trouble you on the present occasion with my opinion of what is likely to take place. I think that, notwithstanding the unpleasant occurrences before alluded to, the measures which I had previously taken, and which are now in more full execution, will reduce Ibrahim Pacha to the necessity of making proposals to us for his return to Egypt. I consider the invitation lately made to him by Vice-Admiral De Rigny, so immediately following the missions of Sir Frederick Adam and Colonel Cradock, as unfortunate although certainly well intended.

I consider the present object of the Government to be not only the retirement of the Egyptian forces, but the restoration of the Greeks whom those forces have made slaves. If the first measure be obtained by Ibrahim's assenting to proposals originating with us, he might claim a right to exact conditions; if, on the contrary, we reduce him to the necessity of making proposals to us—and nothing but necessity will produce his consent, with whomsoever they may originate— we shall be able to claim conditions from him. The conditions which I should then claim would be the restoration of the Greeks in question, and as many others as can be obtained in exchange, as it were, for his army. Even his consent to this arrangement would leave great difficulties to be overcome as regards the harems of himself and his officers, which require the instructions of his Majesty's Government thereon. There will still be many difficulties left to be overcome as to the means of conveying them to their destination, although it is a subject about which my mind has been much occupied. The whole of the fleet forming the last Egyptian expedition was not competent to convey more than half the people, which, according to report, would now have to be carried back; and you are aware that all the vessels which the Viceroy of Egypt could now collect would be insufficient for the purpose, except by the hire of transports. In the case of my being called upon to procure the assistance of transports for facilitating the return of the Egyptian forces, I wish to be informed if I am to stipulate with Ibrahim Pacha that the freight of these hired transports shall be paid by the Pacha of Egypt, or if I am permitted, under any circumstances, to assent to a different arrangement.

I am, &c.,

EDWD. CODRINGTON.

Sir E. C. to Sir Frederick Adam at Corfù.

Malta: May 12, 1828.

MY DEAR ADAM,—The 'Rifleman' brought me yesterday evening her budget from other quarters as well as your letter of the 5th. Complication seems to succeed complication; and I fear the half-measure system which we seem to have decided on pursuing will eventually fulfil the prophecies of those who have foretold a war either with Russia or the Porte before the affairs of the Levant are settled. I still feel confident that if I had received such orders as I expected, and as appeared to me to belong to the Treaty, we should have prevented a Russian war with Turkey, and by this time have settled the whole affair. As it is, I may wear out my time here, and leave quite enough work for any ambitious successor, before things arrive at that state. I have been long expecting the 'Asia,' the delay in the return of which is unaccountable and rather mysterious. I am, however, obliged to hamper my friend Campbell with my flag, in consequence of the proceedings of the French off Navarin and Modon, in letting vessels into those ports which Parker had turned away. It will be quite impossible to bring them and the Russians to act together again with any cordiality. Indeed, De Heiden thinks them playing the game of Ibrahim against us. The conduct of the Albanians seems to have depended upon the money which the French allowed to enter Modon. If the 'Asia' were here I should enter at once upon my quarantine campaign. But, as it is, I must either turn Campbell into a mere flag captain, or consent to live upon him for an indefinite period as a friend, without either my own officers about me or the other means of making my ship my professional home. Under these circumstances, I intend to avoid, if possible, getting into quarantine on the present occasion, and, therefore, shall probably return without seeing you, to meet the 'Asia' here. I should find it awkward to receive from Count Guilleminot singly any ambassadorial instruction, more particularly now that the two corps with whom I am allied seem at such variance. I believe De Heiden has reported his complaint to him as well as to De Rigny, by whose orders in what he did the captain of the 'Trident' says he was acting.

I could wish Mr. Huskisson were aware of the situation of affairs here, that he might feel the effects of the milk-and-water way in which Mr. Canning's plans are now being carried on. You were surprised at my expectation, some time ago, that the affairs of the Levant would be settled this summer. I shall, perhaps, now get into the other extreme. But I had then seen a despatch of Count Nesselrode's accompanying the substance of the proposal of Russia of December 25, which gave me reason to expect orders to act up to that proposal. And I still think that if on the 13th of last month the Sultan had been told, that unless in eight days he accepted our mediation war would be declared by the Allies and his ports blockaded, the business would have so ended. However, here we are, and now we must try and make the best of it. I cannot believe that De Rigny will justify the commander of ' le Trident;' but at all events I cannot. I shall send a short letter upon this subject, I think, to Mr. Huskisson by way of Naples, and another through you ; but I hardly know which of my several masters I ought to write to on this occasion. De Rigny's letter to Ibrahim, I am sure, is well meant; but I must say I think it ill-judged. He was not likely to succeed when your mission had just failed. But he asserted that Russia *had declared war,* which De Heiden might well consider hasty, and as opening hopes to the Turks of the Treaty being annulled. But each party has gone too far ; and you will see in it a spirit which, I assure you, required in me more caution from the first than will now restore harmony. However, my present object is to put this object to rights as well as I can, and to reduce Ibrahim to make proposals to us; in which case I can stipulate for the return of the Greeks from Alexandria in the first instance. Having put this in train without getting into quarantine, I propose returning here to put myself into the ' Asia,' and then see you, and pursue the object of our Government as far as I can ascertain it by their orders and instructions.

As to Capodistrias, I hope it is not quite as decided as you suppose. We must recollect that it is Russian money only that enables him to go on. He, like the others, claims my presence as a remedy for difficulties, thinking I have a power, the absence of which disinclines me from quitting Malta. It was my wish, and, I trust, entirely divested of selfish feelings, not again to appear personally in the Levant until I could carry with me a decision, which now I look for only in despair.

Yours with great regard,
EDWD. CODRINGTON.

P.S.—Samos is a new difficulty which will keep De Rigny in that quarter.   Let me hear from you off Navarin.   I have found the instruction of 1826 about Greeks which you reason upon, and which, Mr. Peel said, fell to the ground upon its appearing Ibrahim had not the intention reported.   It is endorsed as executed, which prevented my examining it.   I see it gives me no power whatever to conclude that under our present circumstances I could have interrupted the ships in question.   In fact I knew nothing whatever of the movement, not being able to blockade Navarin if I would.

This correspondence will show clearly one of the great difficulties of Sir Edward Codrington's position, —the having to keep up harmony (where harmonious action was indispensable) between two coadjutors so unsympathetic—so antagonistic to each other in national feelings and interests.

That he did succeed in it was most fortunate for the service in which they were jointly engaged; and it was owing to the power he acquired over them both, by the influence of his own character, and the warm regard towards himself with which that character had inspired them.

As time and intercourse changed the tone of correspondence from the expression of esteem into that of friendship and intimacy, the private letters of Admiral Heiden became more and more informal, until they reached that familiar style of freshness and originality which gave them so much zest—passing (as in his conversation) from one language to the other, according as he found in each the words best suited to express his thought.   The following is a specimen of these hearty and amusing letters.

From Admiral Heiden to Sir E. C.

'Azoff,' at Sea before Modon: April $\frac{15}{31}$ 1828.*

DEAR ADMIRAL,—We arrived before Navarin three days ago, and found here coming the French squadron, the 'Trident,' 'Iphigénie,' with two bricks, some Greek bricks, and the 'Rifleman.'   Captain Mitchell was so kind as to join me as soon as he saw me.   By that occasion we saw the superior sailing of that vessel, and as I suppose the 'Pelican' her

* Received May 11; answered May 14.

equal, no trial is necessary to be convinced that she sails better than any of our squadron; et donc, point de pari,—je baisse pavillon. Avant d'aller plus loin je vous prierai, Mons. l'Amiral, de faire savoir à tous vos bâtimens qui pourraient me rencontrer, que si je hisse *le Jack on the main-top* I wish to speak that vessel; de cette manière j'aurai occasion de vous écrire plus souvent. C'est dommage que nous n'avons pas vos signaux,—on ne peut rien se dire que de vive voix. Je désirerais beaucoup que vous eussiez une croisière dans ces parages. Le 'Warspite' y a fait beaucoup de bien, tandis que mes chers Frenchmen they seem to be the allies of Ibrahim against us; they have every day parlementaire with him, as they say pour le persuader d'évacuer la Morée. L'amiral de Rigny lui a fait dire que la Russie avait déclaré la guerre à la Turquie, et, chose incroyable, a donné des instructions au capitaine du 'Trident' de faire entrer des bâtimens de guerre à Modon, pourvu que, s'ils viennent avec des provisions ou de l'argent, ils doivent jeter cela à la mer, et ensuite ils peuvent y entrer. Unfortunately, I caught them en flagrant délit, car à mon arrivée devant Modon, je vis l'escadre française au vent de moi, ayant avec elle une corvette turque; j'envoyai sur-le-champ ma frégate pour savoir ce que c'était et me l'amener, ce qui ne plaisait pas à monsieur le commandant, qui l'avait depuis dix jours près de soi. Cette corvette avait été ici du tems du 'Warspite,' qui la renvoya jusqu'en Candie. Je priai le commandant français de la renvoyer de suite, d'après nos instructions communes, que je lui lus moi-même. C'est alors qu'il me communiqua ses ordres, en me priant d'envoyer la corvette à Modon, après l'avoir strictement visitée, ayant donné sa parole d'honneur à Ibrahim de la faire entrer. Réponse: 'Monsieur, si vous avez donné votre parole d'honneur en opposition directe des instructions du protocole que nous connaissons, vous devez avoir vos raisons, et donc je laisse cette corvette à votre responsabilité. Mais comme maintenant je suis ici le plus ancien, je vous prie de vouloir bien ne pas permettre à quelque bâtiment que ce soit d'entrer à Modon ou Navarin;' ce qu'il m'a promis. J'y ai ajouté que dès que je verrais M. de Rigny je me faisais fort de lui faire avoir ce même ordre. Il m'assure qu'il est en pourparler avec Ibrahim pour l'évacuation de la Morée; but it is all stuff. Je lui ai dit, 'N'en croyez rien, il vous trompe, c'est un homme sans foi ni loi, et vous devez le savoir, monsieur, par ce qui est arrivé l'année passée.' Another brig of war, Turkish, came in yesterday morning under their nose, and they speak with the captain, who had a little fight with two Greek brigs. So the commandant told

me. Unfortunately we were on the west side of Modon, and
the brig came from the east. Of course I turned myself to
the eastward, and am with a fresh breeze from the S.-E. at
this hour, on the east side of Modon, and don't care much
about them. Nous prendrons soin de prévenir Mr., I don't
know his name. He is gone again to Ibrahim, as I suppose,
to tell him all the news he heard from me; and to console
him, for by their former news, I believe, Ibrahim was expecting me to attack him. Two days ago he left Old Navarin,
and concentrated all his forces in Modon and Navarin. In
Coron the Albanians, who are the strongest, are in rebellion
for not having received their pay. But I suppose the French
Commodore will send the money from the corvette, if she has
any, to him. It is a pity the 'Warspite' is gone! As soon
as the weather will permit, I will go to Coron to know myself
what they are about. My intention is to leave the 'Ezekiel'
and the 'Castor' (when she joins) here, mais n'ayant rien de
commun avec les Français, puisque ses instructions sont
diamétralement opposées aux nôtres, c'est-à-dire des trois
amiraux. Nous aurons une petite guerre avec le cher Rigny;
mais je vous avoue que maintenant je suis surpris, car nous
avons les faits et les documens en main. Je voudrais vous
voir arriver.

Votre très-dévoué serviteur et ami,

HEIDEN.

Sir E. C. to Count de Heiden.

'Ocean,' at Sea: May 14, 1828.

MY DEAR ADMIRAL,—I received your letter of April $\frac{12}{24}$, by
the 'Rifleman' before I left Malta. I will begin by referring
to the part of it that is the most important, that is the conduct of the French Commodore and the orders of your
colleague. The line of proceeding adopted by them is certainly one of which I cannot approve, although I think it
admits of some palliation. The French having lost the trade
of Smyrna, which was very extensive, have been doing their
utmost to secure that of Alexandria. Their intercourse with the
Viceroy, and the greater confidence he had in them, arose out
of this; and although De Rigny is as much alive to Ibrahim's
deceptions as we are, he finds it right, on account of the
people of Marseilles, to keep up as well as he can that friendly
communication which will facilitate a renewal of mutual
confidence. This, I have no doubt, led to his late letter
to Ibrahim; and was also the occasion of his strengthening his advice by statements which have given you offence,
and which exceed the bounds of prudence. *I* most certainly

would not have so written, or have so acted; but I will not undertake to say I might not have done so if I had been in his peculiar situation. That he has been guided by the best motives, I have no doubt. He, like us, is anxious to induce Ibrahim to retire to Egypt; and he probably thinks that if *he* could effect it after our failure, he would eventually receive a return from the benefit which Egypt would derive from it. Besides being led by this feeling to strengthen his reasoning with Ibrahim, I have no doubt but the same consideration induced him to permit that partial supply which *we* cannot but disapprove. I hope the view which I have thus taken of this affair, will diminish your discontent with our colleague and those of his nation; and that instead of suffering it to interfere with the harmony which is so necessary to the final success of our mutual object, you will only join with me to counteract by a more sharp look-out any little ill effect of this narrow policy. Henceforward 1 shall most likely have some older officer off the Morea, with orders to enforce the blockade more strictly; and I expect that Ibrahim will by this means be soon brought to make proposals to us. This is my policy, instead of making proposals to him. Nothing but necessity will induce him to retire in opposition to the orders of the Sultan, however much he may wish himself at home again. Aided by the Greek blockade, we can soon put him to that necessity. If then we induce him to make proposals to us, we who are *not strong* can exact from him the condition of his restoring not only all the Greeks lately carried to Alexandria, but others who have been seized by him and made slaves since the war, as the price of our assistance. If he agree to this, which I think he must whether he like it or not, I should propose that the ships which we should then permit to come from Alexandria for the purpose, should bring back the Greeks, to be exchanged for some of his troops. We might readily allow a larger number of his people to be taken back; but we should certainly keep his principal officers as well as himself, as a sort of 'bonne bouche,' to ensure the restoration of any Greeks who might be purposely concealed and kept back in Egypt. My object in now coming from Malta, where the 'Asia' is daily expected to arrive, and encumbering my friend Commodore Campbell with my flag, is to make arrangements to the above effect. I wish to be able to return to Malta without being in quarantine, and I therefore propose having no personal communication but according to the rigid rules which are now laid down by the Health Office at that island. Whenever I return to these seas in the 'Asia,' I must communicate freely with all parties, as usual. The attack on Samos, which I find by a letter from Admiral de Rigny, the Turks are preparing to make, must decide us on including it under our protection as much as Hydra or any other island near the Greek coast. I shall write to De Rigny to this effect, and I hope you will take the same view of it. Indeed, you have now a much more straightforward game to play than we have; you can take a lead in any suit, and can play out trumps with impunity; whilst I require the eyes of an Argus, and could not with impunity go half the length which our colleague has latterly done.

Towards the middle of May, 1828, when the measures adopted by the allied Admirals were leading to decisive results, Sir Edward Codrington left Malta in H.M.S. 'Ocean,' as his own flag-ship, the 'Asia,' had not arrived. He was off Navarin on the 19th May,—in the Gulf of Coron on the 21st and 23rd May, where he communicated by letter with Ibrahim Pacha;* again off Navarin on the 24th May, returning to Malta on the 30th May to meet his flag-ship the 'Asia,' the arrival of which he heard of on the 29th May, when at sea in the 'Ocean.' He had thus been deprived of any proper ship in which to go to sea with his flag, for a period of seven months.

The imminence of war being declared between Turkey and Russia—the latter Power being a party to the Treaty—now became an additional element of difficulty. Count Heiden received the Declaration of War on the 29th May; but he had orders to keep his character as a belligerent in abeyance when acting in concert with the Allied squadrons.

Sir E. C. left Malta in the 'Asia' on the 13th June, in order to meet his brother admirals and Mr. Stratford Canning at Corfù, and concert measures with them; it was there, on the 21st June, that he received Lord Aberdeen's letters of recall.

Sir E. C. to Lady C.

On board H.M.S. 'Ocean': May 17, 1828.

I could not have made a better hit, if trespass I must upon any captain of twenty-eight years' standing; for my friend

* See Appendix.

Campbell* goes on steadily in his own quiet way, without seeming to be in the least put out by me. His ship is a more roomy 'Asia'; and as I have a large slice of the after-cabin allotted to me (as you may have observed it when you were on board), I have more swinging room than I have in the 'Asia.' We are still above 100 miles from Navarin.

Sunday, 18.

Sapienza in sight, some forty miles off. The more I look back into the duty I have had to perform, and the more I scrutinise the manner in which I have executed it, the more I am satisfied with myself and dissatisfied with the proceedings and the policy of men in power upon whom the further execution of the Treaty depends. There are two erroneous impressions that possessed my mind at an early period certainly. But even now that I have had reason to dispel them, I cannot find fault with myself for having entertained them. The first is the insincerity of De Rigny, and the second the disposition of the Viceroy of Egypt to obey the wish of the Allies. Now, as you know, aye and even in spite of H.'s late letter, I am confident of De Rigny meaning to act honestly and correctly according to the Treaty; and not less so of the Viceroy intending to retain his allegiance to the Sultan, because he thinks it will better suit his ambitious views so to do. He has certainly been cajoling us, and I suspect the Sultan has all along been cajoling him, without the least intention of giving him either Syria or Damascus, which he so much covets. God bless you all, says

Your ever affectionate,

EDWARD CODRINGTON.

Sir E. C. to Captain Parker.

'Ocean,' off Navarin: May 19, 1828.

MY DEAR SIR,—From what has taken place betwixt Count de Heiden and le Commodore Arnous, as to the latter permitting the 'Crocodile' to enter Modon after your having turned her back, and indeed other vessels, in a manner which has given great offence to the Russians—I am induced to say I wish you were here. Under these circumstances, and in the view of reducing Ibrahim to solicit our aid in returning with his forces to Egypt, the support of the Greek blockade in these parts is of the utmost importance; and the prevention of communication betwixt the suspected infections of Hydra and those on the mainland appears to be of minor importance, and one which may be left to others.

* Commodore Patrick Campbell.

I have written to the President a proposal that the 'Perseverance,' with some other vessels as a flotilla, should occupy the Gulf of Lepanto and prevent supplies getting across to Patras, where I hear Ibrahim has sent a division of his army.   Another division is said to be at Calamata, each in search of food, which is beginning to be scarce.   I have not yet been into the neighbourhood of Coron to communicate with Commodore Arnous, as I intend to do, my opinions as to the mode of blockading; nor indeed have we yet been able to look into Navarin.   I think Count Guilleminot will probably instruct the commodore to adopt a different mode of proceeding ; and I think De Rigny will do the same when he hears from De Heiden.   I have no doubt of De R. intending to do what he thought the best for inducing Ibrahim to retire ; and that the commodore has exceeded his orders ; and I think the prejudice of those about De H. has led him to go beyond what the case requires.   No one can better soften these little asperities than yourself.   There is another disagreeable subject to which I must call your attention.   I hear of the President making exertions to get a Russian party around him exclusively.   Pray watch this closely as opportunity offers.   Mavrocordato, who is, or was, English, may instruct you on this head, or perhaps Tricoupi.

From Sir E. C. to Mr. Huskisson.

'Ocean,' in the Gulf of Coron : May 21, 1828.*

SIR,—In obedience to the direction contained in your letter of March 23, I have the honour of enclosing a copy of the orders which the Emperor of Russia has directed to be sent to Count de Heiden through Count Nesselrode, which I received to-day from Malta.

From the friendly intercourse which has been established between us, the Count has used the medium of a private letter to express his opinions and feelings on the occasion. I may, however, venture to inform you, judging both from my knowledge of his general sentiments and the tone in which he expresses himself on this occasion, that in my opinion he will not only avoid as much as possible taking any measures which may appear to militate against the object for which the three Powers are allied, but that he will most readily do all he possibly can, in concert with us, for the fulfilment of the Treaty of London.   I have merely written a hurried acknowledgment of his letter, assuring him that I cannot imagine it possible that anything should arise,

* Received June 14.

from whatever different line of conduct he may be directed to pursue, which can prevent a continuance of the friendly communications which have heretofore obtained between us. The Count tells me, that desirous of continuing to act with me in straitening Ibrahim, he will leave the ship of the line and frigate now here to continue on this service. Guided by your letter of March 23, I certainly shall not suggest to him any particular line of conduct. But you, Sir, will be well aware how much his being a belligerent might be made to facilitate the blockade of the Morea and to remove the difficulties which we are under in some particulars. In explanation of this, I beg to refer you to the position of Navarin and Modon on the map of La Pie, which is upon a larger scale than the Admiralty chart. You will see that there is a passage within the islands of Cabrera and Sapienza, through which vessels going to Modon and Navarin would pass in preference, with either an easterly or southerly wind, having their port under their lee; whilst there being no anchorage for blockading vessels, they would be in great danger, if caught there in bad weather, from the heavy sea which sets in. It was by means of this passage that Austrian vessels of war, with Ibrahim's despatches, evaded us last year; and the Ottoman vessels have adopted the same practice. Fast-sailing vessels, such as those now employed by the Viceroy of Egypt, will probably take a station, in the first instance, either off Cape Matapan, in order to profit by a strong wind from the southward or eastward, or off the Strophades Islands, ready to take advantage of a wind from the northward or westward: and if suffered to cruise there under any other pretence, it will be impossible to ensure their not getting into one or other of the two ports. I propose stationing ships to watch those two positions. But I wish to call your attention to the difficulty in which I shall be placed upon our ships there meeting with them. If they should refuse to go away under a declaration that they are not going to the blockaded ports, am I to use coercion?* and am I still to prevent a collision betwixt them and the Greeks under such circumstances, if the latter should have a force competent to attack them?†

It is evident that, under these circumstances, the Allied object would be facilitated by the Russians assuming that belligerent character that seems to be given them by the accompanying document. An instance of the difficulty of preventing success in a case of this sort occurred yesterday, and, at the same time, the opinion which I gave in my reply

* Question never answered.   † Question never answered.

to the Queries of the impossibility of effectually blockading
these ports by keeping the sea, was practically confirmed.
A heavy swell, with light wind towards the coast, not only
prevented our reconnoitring Navarin for two days together,
but, by setting us down upon the island of Sapienza, placed
us in a very uncomfortable situation. Failing in this, and
learning that the French squadron was off Coron, I was proceeding to communicate with them as to the measures to be
pursued, when the 'Jasper' brig joined me, with information
that she had sailed in company with two corvettes from
Alexandria, which were suspected to be coming to the
Morea, although avowedly going to Trieste. The 'Talbot'
being considerably to the northward, under signal to recon-
noitre Navarin in company with the Russian 74 'Ezekiel,'
I sent the 'Philomel' to warn the Honorable Captain
Spencer of the movement of these corvettes, and to assist in
stopping them. It seems that they had already at that time
attracted the notice of Captain Spencer; but that they were
enabled to push into Navarin in defiance of his utmost efforts
to cut them off. I consider, however, that supplies obtained
by such means are too partial to have any material effect in
feeding a force which is said still to amount to from 25
to 30,000 people, and not to militate against the opinion
which I gave in my letter to you of the 12th of this month.
If indeed, the Commander of 'Le Trident' had continued to
act under that mistaken view of his duty of which Count De
Heiden complained, the case would have been different; for,
besides the concealed money, as well as other things, which
are supposed to have been received by the Pacha under his
admission of despatches, a vessel returning with some 500
invalids, which he did not feel empowered to stop, is reported
to me from Alexandria to have carried also twenty women
and several Greek children; and I have strong reason to
believe the story, although the French Commander tells me
the vessel was searched by his Greek pilot.

I trust these errors will not be repeated; for, upon my informing the said French captain of the 'Trident' that, in
consequence of the deceptions practised, I had directed that,
for the future, no vessels whatever should be permitted either
to enter or to leave the blockaded ports, he informed me that
he had received similar orders from Vice-Admiral De Rigny.
The difficulties of the President of Greece, as well as of ourselves, have been increased by the contagious fever which
prevails at Hydra and at Spezzia, and which will probably
reach the Continent notwithstanding the exertions of Captain
Parker for preventing communication. I now expect the

'Warspite' here hourly, when Captain Parker will devote himself more particularly to this difficult service. In the meantime I have sent the 'Pelorus' to assume the service off Alexandria and Candia, assisted by other sloops of war, and have directed the 'Dartmouth' and 'Glasgow' to join the 'Warspite' here. I am aware that I have entered into particulars that may appear to be merely professional, which may possibly be considered as beyond the line prescribed for me by your letter of March 23. It is therefore due to myself to assure you that, in giving this detail, and submitting opinions which are not officially called for, I have no other motive than a desire to submit to the Government all the information which local knowledge affords to a person in my situation. I do not assume that my opinions have any superior value; and I confidently refer to all my professional conduct for my disposition to obey zealously and cheerfully whatever instructions I may receive, whether accordant with, or opposed to those opinions. I ask only, with submission, that they may be such as will not admit of any misconception.

I have, &c.,
EDWARD CODRINGTON.

From Admiral Heiden to Sir E. C.

Milo : ce $\frac{21 \text{ avril}}{3 \text{ mai}}$ 1828.

MON CHER AMIRAL,—Je vous envoie officiellement la copie des instructions que je viens de recevoir; vous y verrez que la guerre n'est pas encore déclarée, mais que j'en attends la nouvelle à chaque instant—et cela tout seul. Cela me chagrine beaucoup; ma position et la vôtre deviennent très-délicates; mais j'espère que nous nous entendrons de manière à remplir nos devoirs sans nous montrer les dents ou causer plus de refroidissement entre nos deux Gouvernemens; et en même tems contribuer au grand ouvrage, quoique je ne vois pas comment il pourra s'accomplir, car il paraît que le Gouvernement anglais ne se soucie plus du tout de la Grèce. Pour la France, il paraît qu'elle ne sait pas trop ce qu'elle veut, et se réglera d'après le vent qui souffle. En attendant ma position est très-désagréable et me dégoûte : j'en suis vraiment tout-à-fait chagrin et abattu. Je continuerai cependant à agir avec vous avec toute la franchise que mes devoirs me permettront, et j'espère que nous pourrons rester en harmonie comme par le passé, d'autant plus que je n'aurai pas à bloquer les ports que vos bâtimens fréquentent, excepté les points dans la Morée : mais il me semble que d'après le

Traité ce blocus sera résumé par vous, de sorte que j'espère
encore que nous n'aurons pas de sujets de refroidissement.
J'ai vu notre ami l'amiral Rigny.   Je lui ai fait part de ce
que j'ai vu à Navarin : il m'a montré ses instructions au
capitaine de l' ' Iphigénie,' qui sont diamétralement opposées à
ce que m'a dit le capitaine : il a convenu avec moi que ce
dernier a été mis dedans par Ibrahim. Ma foi! je n'ai jamais
vu des étourdis pareils, et ne sais qu'en penser.   En attendant
je laisserai une frégate et un brick pour serrer de plus près
Ibrahim, et verrai ce que je pourrai faire.   Monsr le capitaine
Mitchel vous aura mis au fait de tout ce qu'il a vu : je ne
puis que me louer de ce dernier, qui me paraît un officier de
beaucoup de mérite et d'activité.   C'est bien malheureux que
nos rapports avec tous ces excellens officiers doivent devenir
plus resserrés et moins sincères ; car, malheureusement, à la
moindre chose entre les Cabinets, commence le refroidissement, ensuite méfiance, puis bouderie, et finit souvent par
brouillerie ouverte.   Vous connaissez mes sentimens, Monsr
l'Amiral,—j'irai toujours le chemin droit, et agirai franche-
ment.   Après cela, ma conscience tranquille, arrive que
pourra.

Dans le moment Rigni m'a montré une lettre qu'il a écrite
à Ibrahim, et que D'Arnous lui a remis la veille de notre
arrivée, dans laquelle il l'engage d'évacuer la Morée en lui
disant que la Russie venait de déclarer la guerre.   Je ne
conçois pas pourquoi il lui a fait dire une chose qu'il ne savait
pas être vraie : il pouvait la supposer, mais il ne pouvait la
savoir, puisque moi je ne la sais pas, et je viens de recevoir
un courrier en droiture de Pétersbourg.   I confess I don't
understand that politick, but it explains to me the poor
Captain Arnous thought I was going to take the corvette,
and therefore wished to save her from the hands of the barbarians ; but I proposed to convey her to Milo to Admiral
De Rigny, and to leave it to his decision what to do with
her ; but then he told me of his engaging his word of honor,
&c.   I dined to-day with Admiral De Rigny, and it is all
well again ; but c'est un brouillon, the good man ; and it
shows again, my dear Admiral, that a Frenchman, sans y
entendre malice, cannot live without a little intrigue, pour
passer le tems.   Ayant reçu le courrier aujourd'hui, je m'empresse de vous envoyer le brick 'Oural.'   Monsr de Rigny
voulant vous envoyer la copie d'une lettre du Comte
Nesselrode au prince Lièven, je m'abstiens de vous la faire
copier.   C'est une pièce très-importante et intéressante.
La paix avec la Perse est faite, ratifiée, et l'argent pour le
dédommagement reçu et encaissé : voilà pour nous une grande

nouvelle. Le général Paskewitz à été nommé Comte d'Erwan, et Sa Majesté lui a fait don d'un million pour soutenir son titre. Je pars demain pour Naples de Roumanie pour voir le pauvre Comte Capodistrias, et je resterai près de lui je ne sais jusqu'à quand, mais en tout cas pour attendre Rigny, qui va à Vourla pour huit jours, to repair his capstan, which was rotten, and broke after he had lost his iron chain cable. From there I suppose and intend to go to have a look at our friend Ibrahim; and it is possible, after a time, I may go to Malta for provisions, or some other reason, if you will not shut your ports for us poor fellows, who have no other pied à terre in the whole Mediterranean.

Croyez-moi pour la vie, your most devoted
HEIDEN.

Sir E. C. to Count Heiden.

H.B.M. Ship 'Ocean,' off Coron : May 21, 1828.

Fear not, my dear Admiral, that anything which can arise out of the present state of affairs will diminish my regard for you. Although our duties under the altered circumstances you announce to me may differ, I do not see any grounds for the 'méfiance' and following consequences which you forebode. Nor, even if we were not still bound together by the Treaty, need any diminution take place in the friendship which our previous intercourse has cemented. I hope shortly to assure you in person of these sentiments being engrafted into my system. My present object is to return to Malta as expeditiously as possible, to relieve my friend Commodore Campbell of my flag, and to return here in the 'Asia,' which is by this time, I imagine, arrived there. Let me induce you to continue to rely upon our colleague doing all that is right, in spite of any little difference in the manner of setting about it. He has given orders that nothing whatever shall be permitted to enter these ports, nor anything go out which has got in. I have done the same; and I shall inform Ibrahim of this, and warn him against ravaging the country, and sending away any of the Greeks as slaves. Two corvettes got into Navarin yesterday in spite of all the 'Talbot' could do. The 'Ezekiel' did not seem to observe them. Their plan will be to wait off Matapan and Grosso for a southerly or westerly wind, or off the Strophades islands for a northerly or easterly wind; and thence push through the blockading force, when the same strength of wind and bad weather may oblige us to keep further off. Even if we find them in those positions, we cannot use force to drive them away, and the Greeks are not strong enough. I will conclude with assuring you of the unalterable regard of my family, as well as of your sincere friend,

EDWD. CODRINGTON.

From Admiral Heiden to Sir E. C.

Égine : ce $\frac{5}{17}$ mai 1828.

MON CHER MONS. L'AMIRAL,—Church demande de l'argent, car ses troupes en demandent à grands cris, et mécontens. En Morée les Albanais sont mal avec Ibrahim, mais avec tout cela on n'entend rien d'évacuation. Je ne sais pas ce que les Français y font—tripoter, voilà tout ; ils laissent sortir qui veut : les miens ont attrapé une corvette, la même que D'Arnous a fait entrer ; elle retournait à Alexandrie avec 600 hommes, mais comme je me doutais qu'il y avait des Grecs, j'ai fait mettre à terre 540 personnes, et puis examiner bien le bâtiment, et, Dieu merci, nous avons sauvé onze pauvres enfants mâles et femelles, qui allaient être vendus à l'encan à Alexandrie. Je les ai ici, et nous les aiderons autant que possible en les remettant au comte. La corvette est ici ; et je désire votre opinion et avis qu'en faire.

Grâce à mes croisans, la corvette autrichienne la ' Caroline ' n'a pas pu entrer à Navarin, Modon, ou Coron ; elle a essayé des deux côtés, mais trouva partout des bâtimens russes ; et cependant elle prétendait croiser seulement et aller à Zante. Ici nous avons eu un brick et un schooner, mais ils sont partis pour Smyrne. Ils sont bien intrigués de savoir ce que nous faisons ici.

À Alexandrie il paraît qu'on veut envoyer tout ce qu'on a en bâtimens de guerre à Constantinople : j'espère que vous les empêcherez, puisqu'on m'assure que vous avez des ordres pour bloquer ce port.

L'excellent capi^{ne} Parker va bientôt nous quitter ; j'en suis bien fâché, mais surtout pour le comte : mais il pourra être beaucoup plus utile dans la station de Corfou. Je compte aller à Poros, et de là, après avoir vu Rigny, peut-être une course à Samos pour du moins en imposer. Dieu veuille, mon cher Amiral, que nos relations ne se refroidissent pas. J'espère que le noble lord mettra un peu d'eau dans son vin du Rhin de Metternich.

Voilà $\frac{6}{18}$ mai, dix jours qu'il n'y a point de morts ni de malades à Hydra, de sorte que bientôt cette maladie cessera : les médecins assurent que ce n'est pas la peste, et je le crois aussi. À Modon, d'où le typhus vient, on pense de même. Nous venons de recevoir de là la nouvelle qu'Ibrahim n'a

plus que très-peu de provisions, et donc ou il devra partir
par mer ou se faire jour pour aller en Roumélie pour faire
des incursions et enlever les récoltes dans l'intérieur : c'est
ce que je crois, et dans ce cas on tâchera de brûler les
récoltes à son approche. If we had the riflemen of Malta
and four guns, our friend Ibrahim would very soon have the
honor of drinking a sorbet in Colonel Brown's tent.   Mr.
Proschek is gone to Smyrna, I suppose to warn the Turks of
me, for they certainly believe we are going to Smyrna or the
Dardanelles.   The situation of the poor Count* is very unpleasant ; without resources, without army, and, I believe,
very few friends amongst the notables ; for by the nation and
common Greeks he is adored.   To look at all we see here is
very much like a comedy—people of all nations, all sort of
dresses are to be found here. J'ai vu ——, qui me paraît un
brave grenadier, mais une espèce de roi de théâtre.   Quand
on examine tout cela un peu philosophiquement, on se dit, que
sont les hommes ? et on a plus de pitié que de courroux pour
eux !   Nous voilà à Égine, quatre bâtimens de guerre russes,
trois français, un turc, une frégate américaine, et un vaisseau
anglais.   Il n'y manque que des autrichiens.   Adieu, mon
cher Amiral. Votre bien dévoué serviteur et ami,

HEIDEN.

From Admiral Heiden to Sir E. C.

'Azoff,' à Égine : le ⁶⁄₁₈ mai 1828.

MONSIEUR L'AMIRAL,— . . . L'approche de la récolte
des grains en Morée, et les projets d'incursion qu'Ibrahim
paraît former, donnent les plus justes craintes aux habitans
de la Péninsule.   J'attends avec impatience l'arrivée de M^r
de Rigny dans cette rade pour me concerter avec lui, ainsi
qu'avec Mr Parker, sur les moyens de prévenir cette nouvelle
dévastation ; je proposerai une nouvelle et forte intimation
par écrit à Ibrahim, quoique je doute de son effet.   Des
lettres récentes de Syra annoncent que Samos est de nouveau
menacé ; il faudra donc nécessairement porter aussi quelque
surveillance sur ce point. Permettez-moi, Monsr l'Amiral,
de vous dire encore, avec ma franchise ordinaire, que votre
absence de ces contrées dans un si critique moment est une
véritable calamité.

J'ai l'honneur d'être, etc.,

HEIDEN.

* Capodistrias.

From Admiral De Rigny to Sir E. C.

(*Extract.*)

'Conquérant': ce 5 mai 1828.*

Suivant les nouvelles que j'ai de Paris, Mr de Metternich travaille beaucoup en Angleterre vos Ministres pour faire rompre le Traité. Les Cabinets de Londres et de Paris paraissent n'être pas du même avis. Sur le point de savoir si la Russie l'a rompu de son côté, en élevant des griefs particuliers contre la Turquie, chez vous on est disposé pour l'affirmative; chez nous on dit que jusqu'à ce que la Russie ait manqué à un des engagemens du Traité on ne peut l'en accuser d'avance. Je crois moi que le duc de Wellington est bien aise de saisir cette occasion de se débarrasser de ce legs de Monsr Canning. Je n'ai pas d'autres instructions que celle de me conformer aux anciennes; c'est-à-dire, je crois, de continuer d'empêcher, *sans hostilités*, les Turcs d'envoyer des renforts en Morée. On croit cependant toujours à Paris que nos Ministres se décideront à maintenir le Traité.

Sir E. C. to Admiral De Rigny.

H.B.M.S. 'Ocean,' in the Gulf of Coron: May 21, 1828.

MY DEAR ADMIRAL,—I have only a moment to acknowledge the receipt of several documents from you, which went to Malta by the 'Mosquito,' and to tell you that after making my arrangements here I shall return to Malta to meet the 'Asia,' and relieve my friend, Commodore Campbell, of me and my flag, that he may sail under his own broad pendant. Captain Arnous certainly appears to have misunderstood your instructions; but, as he now tells me he has now got your orders to suffer no vessel whatever either to go in or come out of these ports, which is exactly similar to what I have given to the English ships, I dare say we shall bring Ibrahim to his senses. I propose letting the said Pacha know of this decision, and cautioning him at the same time against ravaging the country and carrying away the Greeks as slaves. I hope the affairs of the Turks with Russia will prevent their attempting anything against Samos before we have instructions how to consider that island. I do not like to detain the 'Pelorus' any longer, as I wish Capt. Richards to proceed off Alexandria and Candia, that the 'Dartmouth' and 'Glasgow' may come to assist here. Two corvettes got into Navarin yesterday in spite of the 'Talbot,' whilst

* Received 21st May.

all the French ships were in the Bay of Coron. But such partial supplies cannot do much for such a force as there is to feed. Their plan is to wait either off the Strophades or off Matapan, and run in when a strong wind favors them.

Yours, with great regard,

EDWD. CODRINGTON.

From Sir E. Codrington to his Highness Ibrahim Pacha.

H.B.M.S. 'Ocean,' in the Gulf of Coron : May 23, 1828.

HIGHNESS,—It becomes my unpleasant duty to inform Your Highness that henceforth no vessel whatever will be permitted to enter any port of the Morea in the possession of the Ottoman forces, nor any vessel to come out of those ports which may have entered them.

Reports have reached me of Your Highness having declared that in case of our establishing a rigid blockade you would pursue the system of devastation which you had adopted last year. I trust a recollection of the consequences which arose from that cruel exercise of power, will induce Your Highness to prefer a line of conduct more suitable to the practice of civilised nations.

But if you should unfortunately attempt to carry this threat into execution, Your Highness must remember that whenever your own fate and that of your army comes to be decided by the Allied Powers, as it soon must be, you will have strong reason to dread the consequences of such conduct.

The earnest desire of my Sovereign to fulfil the Treaty of London of July 6, 1827, has been strongly marked by his having renewed the same terms, since the battle of Navarin, which had been refused by the Viceroy of Egypt before that memorable event—an event which I will not enter into the merits of more minutely, because it must be painful to Your Highness to recollect the return which was at that time made to the conciliatory proposals of the Allied admirals. Even since the late missions to the Viceroy and Your Highness, deceptions have been put upon the Allies which would justify harsher measures than they are yet willing to employ. Supplies which were permitted to leave Alexandria, ostensibly for the use only of the army in Candia, have been clandestinely conveyed to the Morea in vessels which were allowed to pass the blockading force with your despatches; and vessels returning with invalids under the same indulgence, have carried to Egypt in slavery unoffending Greek women and children, although notice

was given to Your Highness in the year 1826 that His
Britannic Majesty would not permit so inhuman a proceeding. So great is the indignation which this conduct
has excited throughout Europe, that both Your Highness and
those who now serve under your orders, will be brought to
feel effectually the heavy responsibility which attaches to it.
My wish to make due allowance for the difficulties of Your
Highness's situation, and to diminish as much as I can the
greater difficulties to which the protracted resistance of the
Sultan will expose you, has induced me to offer you these
concluding observations.

I have, &c.,
EDWARD CODRINGTON.

To the respective Captains and Commanders.
(General Order.)*

'Ocean,' off Navarin : May 24, 1828.

It is highly important at this particular juncture to deprive the Ottoman forces in the Morea of all sorts of supplies
and reinforcements, and of all resources whatever, in order
to effect a desire in Ibrahim Pacha to return to Egypt. It
becomes, therefore, the business of all the ships and vessels
assisting in the blockade of the ports of the Morea to prevent, if possible, the entrance of every description of vessels
of whatever nation, down even to boats; and to be equally
rigid in not permitting anything to come out which may
have got in, with the sole exception of a flag of truce coming
to communicate with the senior officer. Now, in order to
evade the blockading ships, it is probable that fast-sailing
vessels coming from Egypt or any of the Ottoman dominions
will, in the first place, take a station either off Cape Matapan
with the intention of pushing in betwixt the islands and the
main with a strong easterly or southerly wind, or off the
Strophades islands, ready to profit by a strong westerly or
northerly wind.

It is, therefore, requisite that a ship of sufficient force to
ensure obedience should be placed in each of those positions
to drive away any Ottoman vessels which may come there.
And upon falling in with any such vessels, their presence
should be made known to the rest of the blockading squadron
by showing Ottoman colours at the main-topgallant mast
head, and firing guns until the signal is observed.

If Russia should be at war with Turkey, we are not to

---

* Copies sent to Admiral De Rigny, to Admiral Sachturis in Greek, to
Captain Arnous—'Trident,' to Captain Swinkin, 'Ezekiel.'

take part or interfere with the ships of either of them.   And although the ships of H.B.M. are to prevent a collision generally betwixt the Greek and Ottoman forces by sea, they are not required to do so in cases where the Greek vessels are strong enough to act successfully.

EDWD. CODRINGTON.

Extract of a Letter from Count Capodistrias.

June 22.

Je ne saurois assez exprimer à V.E. la gratitude qu'inspirent à la nation grecque les nouveaux témoignages d'intérêt que vous vous plaisez, Monsieur l'Amiral, à lui donner par les mesures que vous venez de prendre.   Elles semblent déjà avoir produit une impression salutaire sur l'esprit d'Ibrahim Pacha.   Il paroît avoir modifié son système de conduite, attendu que l'expédition qu'il avoit adressée à Pyrgos, pour acheter du bétail et autres vivres, n'a commis aucun acte hostile, et que les chefs de cette expédition ont acheté argent comptant les vivres qu'ils ont pu se procurer.

Sir E. C. to Admiral De Rigny.

Off Navarin : May 24, 1828

MY DEAR ADMIRAL,—Your letters of April 6 and May 5 from Milo reached here from Malta with the official enclosures about Hamilton on the 21st inst.   I feel very sensibly, my good friend, the kind desire which your letters show to support me through all the unnecessary difficulties which are thrown in my way.   I will not deny that the illiberal and unjust attacks which have been made on me for mere party purposes have been very teasing to me; because, besides the trouble I have had in writing home the facts, in order to prevent their injurious effects, they have called my attention from the public service by which alone it should be occupied.   But I am, nevertheless, convinced that if those attacks had not been made upon me I should never have received such commendations as I have from the most distinguished persons which my country boasts.   I value such eulogies as these above all which Ministers could possibly have done for me, if they had had discernment enough to have found their true interest in considering the aggression of the Turks at Navarin a most fortunate instead of an untoward event.   Had they taken that just view of it, the whole affair would by this time have been settled, and without a Russian war.   I am now tormented by the Ministers imputing to me power and authority which they seem afraid to give me.   But I have put to them the direct questions— Am I henceforth empowered to blockade? am I to allow any invalids to return to Egypt? and am I, in such a case, to search the vessels containing them for Greeks, and to take them out?   In the meantime, I have taken upon myself to issue an order to let nothing go in or come out of the blockaded ports; and I find you have done the same.   I hope your communication with De Heiden, personally, has removed the impression which was made on him by the commander of 'Le Trident.'   Poor fellow, he is very unpleasantly situated, and is over anxious about the consequences of any separate operations he may be called upon to undertake.   We must make great allowances for the susceptibility which arises from his more responsible situation.   If he sends some of his ships to assist you in protecting Samos, it will be made more easy by the rupture between Russia and Turkey.

Your letter to Ibrahim gave him another friendly opening; and now we must make him feel the necessity of making the next advances to us, and which we must not seem too eager to attend to, in order that we may get back all the Greeks whom he has sent to Alexandria.   I have suspended the blockade of Alexandria until I have a further order, after the observations I have made as to its effects on Marseilles and on Malta.   I have mentioned the latter to strengthen my remarks; but as the Viceroy will sell no more corn, it matters little to that island now.   The order I received was to perform a 'like blockade' to that mentioned in the despatch of October 16, which I have told the Colonial Minister referred only to a blockade by the Greek cruisers within certain limits of their own coasts, or the support of them in any blockade which they might establish.   In fact, the Ministers appear to want me to do that which they would not venture to order me to do on their own responsibility.   Indeed, my good friend, I cannot wish to see your Ministers so treat you, either in the Chambers or by their instructions.   If they had acted more fairly by me, I could easily have removed from them all censure on account of the deportation of these Greeks; but by imputing misconduct to me, I was obliged to show that, if misconduct it was, they were to blame and not I.   I am in hopes that the candour of the Russian orders to De Heiden will facilitate restoration of peaceful intercourse.   I think the Duke of Wellington knows Metternich too well to be cajoled by him in anything, more particularly into war, which it is his policy to avoid. I believe the Seraskier is in danger of his Albanians doing as Ibrahim's did; but he may not get money to quiet them as Ibrahim did, for the Porte has none to give him. I have accounts from Alexandria of twenty women and several children having been concealed in the Turkish vessel with invalids, which was searched by the Greek pilot of the 'Trident,' and then allowed to pass. It is very kind and considerate of you to have expressed yourself as you have about our friend Hamilton. Lord Ingestrie happened to be in Paris when he (Hamilton) passed through there, and he was then well again.

There is a more peaceable appearance in London than there was; and I am in hopes the very movement of the Russian army, which led people to think the contrary, will prove, by its effect on the Sultan, to have brought him to reason.

I shall proceed to Malta as soon as any wind will enable me, in order to return here in the 'Asia,' by which time Mr. Canning will probably have joined Count Guilleminot at Corfù.

Yours, &c.,
EDWD. CODRINGTON.

From Sir John Gore to Sir E. C.*

April 23, 1828.

MY DEAR CODRINGTON,—I have for some time been very desirous of an opportunity to send you a letter free from the chance of being opened and read, which I suspect all those are that go by post through France; and this supposition is strengthened by my having read in an extract from a French paper verbatim what I had written to you a few days after Wellesley left London : I was anxious to communicate the subject to you, and sent it by the post. Nothing can be more irregular than the receipt of letters from you. While I was at the Admiralty yesterday, your despatches of the 25th arrived, but the official had not transpired, for, as you are now under the Secretary of State, Mr. C. takes them all to Lord Dudley as soon as read to the Lord High Admiral. I was, and still am, exceedingly vexed that I did not know when the messengers were sent with certain queries to you. It took place during Spencer's extreme illness, when he could not write or see any person; and I feel well aware that no friendly hand was ready to give you a useful timely hint, and it might now be useless to repeat it. The anger created by

---

* Received at Malta, May 29th, 1828.

the carrying away the Greeks to Egypt as slaves was great
here, and heightened by the feelings on that subject in
France.   I was asked why you allowed it.   I, in return,
asked, 'Has he any orders to bear him out in searching
the Egyptian fleet going from Greece to Egypt? Would
not such an act be a direct violation of his orders and your
wishes to suffer, nay, to urge, Ibrahim Pacha to evacuate
the Morea, in effecting which you offer every facility? If
a search had been attempted, resistance would have been
made; hence would have arisen the collision, and hostility
must have ensued.'   'But his orders were to blockade all
these ports, instead of which he continues at Malta doing
nothing.   Why is he not in the Archipelago?'   'Has he
such orders?   For he writes to me that he is anxiously
awaiting for orders to act.'   'Yes, he has those orders, acknowledged to have been received on November 11.'   'But
they must have been written here before the Battle of
Navarin was known.'   'What has that to do with his obeying them?'   'Is it not natural he should suppose that
such a battle might change the aspect of affairs, and that
some new orders and instructions would be given to him?
Had I been in his situation I should have expected such.'   I
was much delighted yesterday in a long interview with Lord
Exmouth (who charged me to make his regards to you), to
hear him express precisely the same sentiments upon both
the above points, and that the anger which is expressed
towards you upon them, emanates entirely from their own
neglect.   For until I told them you had no orders to act
upon, they never thought of sending you any; and then
raked up those which you received on November 11, to
place you in the wrong instead of themselves.

Lord Dudley retaining the office he held during the late
most weak administration, preserves leaven of that feebleness;
but you have a most steady supporter in the present head; and
if your replies to all those questions are as full and as incon-
trovertible as I feel confident they will be given long before
this can reach you, that head will do you justice; and I am
under error if he does not, so soon as the squall is quite
blown over, do ample justice to your merits and great exertions in fulfilling your most arduous duty.   Therefore, my
good friend, do not be displeased with me for offering one
piece of advice,—i.e., in all your replies to these various
interrogatories, do not let any anger or vexation escape you.
Give your replies full and dignified, but in mild terms,
for they will be read by many who are too ready to lay a
stress upon any strong expression, and thereby convey a

meaning you never intended. I write this from conviction. 'A mild answer turneth away wrath;' and you want a friendly advocate to explain and to prevent words and meanings being twisted. This was attempted when your replies which I brought over were read in council; and had I not been present, would have had the full effect. But my explanation called forth, 'Gore is right.' This hint may serve for some future occasion. Be cautious in your private letters, and to whom you express your sentiments; for it is impossible for me to convey to you the ingenuity with which sentiments are perverted, any more than it is for me to imagine how they get into circulation. But the fact is, that much of what you write, and your conversation at your own table, is repeated in this town, to the very great annoyance of your brother and friends, not from the facts, but that you should have such Paul Prys about you. I will relate one fact to elucidate this :—About a month ago a messenger met me at the door, (going to Datchet), desiring me to attend the Lord High Admiral directly. On entering his audience room,—'Oh, Gore, I am very anxious to see you, for I am told your friend Sir Edward Codrington has written in such strong terms of objection to the conduct of the Government, that I wish you to write to him on the subject.' I was so much startled by this address, that I was obliged to consider a few seconds before I replied; when I said : 'I am very much obliged to your Royal Highness for this opportunity to explain, and will take upon myself to be a pledge that you have been misinformed. The last letters from Sir E. C. are to Mr. Bethell and myself, of February 11, at which time he could not, and did not know of the existence of the present administration; and if he did so, I will further be his pledge that he will be more likely to rejoice at than to lament the Duke of Wellington being Premier. At the late Administration Sir E. Codrington was displeased, for he did feel that they had not acted kindly towards him.' 'I think so too, Sir; they did not act as they should have done towards him.' 'But I think the Duke of Wellington and the present Ministers have done all they could under present circumstances to heal that wound.' 'Right, Sir, you are quite right.' 'I can therefore repeat to your R.H. my pledge that he has not said or written one word against the Duke of Wellington and his Administration.' 'I am very glad to hear you say all this, and shall take care to contradict what I have heard upon such good authority. Now, good day, come here whenever you are at leisure, and more particularly when you have letters from Sir Edward Codrington.' About a week after I received a letter from

you of a later date, when I went and renewed my pledge.
'Oh, I was perfectly satisfied by what you said before; but
your friend has so many repeaters of all that he writes
and says, that he cannot be too much on his guard. We
have put him under the Secretary of State, and Lord Dudley
desires to know why he stays at Malta. Can you tell me?'
'Sir Edward Codrington tells me, Sir, that he anxiously
awaits orders, and expresses his surprise that none have
been sent.' 'Is that the case?' 'Yes, Sir.'

This is a specimen of how much you are the subject of
conversation here: and as the public mind is entirely occupied by Turkey and Russia, and the best mode to avoid being
drawn into a war (which I consider inevitable in the course
of the next two years), everything relating thereto puts even
the 'Test Act' into shadow; and you, your sayings and
doings, are the Test of the Times. Last club-day at the
Thatched House—Lord Melville there as a guest—Yorke,
in the chair, after a neat speech, proposed your health in
a bumper, which was adopted with cheers by all. The whole
was very well done, and gratified your friends extremely.

I am much interrogated about you and Navarin, and
where I see and know that *Paul Pryism* is not the foundation, I not only explain, but give my copy of all the papers;
and have thereby gratified many zealous brother officers whose
approbation would please you. *A propos*, respecting Lord
Dudley's question and my reply (though the thing is gone
by), he asked, 'Why you did not anchor further from;' I gave
the reasons why: had he asked, 'Why you anchored so
near,' I should have replied *as you have written*. In the
conversation which ensued I did fully state all and much
more to that effect—even to a joke—that we never consider
ourselves near enough until we can discover the colour of
our opponents' eyes. My object was to do away or to
weaken the universal impression that you '*premeditated the
battle*' and 'went into Navarin overlooking your instructions
for your own aggrandisement.' In point of fact Lord
Dudley's question so much surprised me and appeared so
absurd, that my first impulse was to laugh; as the Duke of
Wellington actually did when I repeated it to him, and he
said, 'Is it possible he could have asked such a question?
if he had asked you why he went into Navarin at all, there
might have been some sense in it, but that was folly: now
Gore, explain to me why Codrington went into Navarin.' I
did so *fully* : ' I see,—I see,—he could not have avoided it :
but I am sorry Cradock brought back the letter, for it may
give rise to a question.' But all this treats of a subject gone

by and almost forgotten. Peace, peace,—and how to avoid
hostilities, is now the cry: and the only apprehension is,
according to Arthur Legge (who desires his kindest regards
to you and Lady C.) that 'you knocked down the wrong man
at Navarin.'

From Sir John Gore to Lady C.*

April 25, 1828.

You know how easy it is to find fault where ill will prompts
it ; and as fault was to attach somewhere, it has from the
first arrival of the battle of Navarin been the desire to attach
it to C. His replies by me averted it. The complaints
respecting the Greek slaves being taken to Egypt opened a
fresh door, but I am in error if C. cannot with equal
success throw that off his shoulders. The point I have laid
great stress upon to Lord Dudley, Cockburn, and Croker, is,
that as to 'collision,' it took place at or near Patras : and
there also the overt act of hostility took effect by Ibrahim
Pacha being forced by cannon shot to relinquish his purpose.
This act was highly approved ! then why not the equally bold
measure of going into Navarin to effect the same purpose ?
But this subject is at rest; and that to be quieted is, why
C. has continued at Malta ? and why the Greeks are allowed
to be carried to Egypt in slavery ? Would the advocates of
'non-collision' and 'non-hostility' and the 'evacuation of
the Morea by mild persuasion,' have had C. search the
Turco-Egyptian fleet quitting Navarin on their way to
Alexandria ? Would *their* Admiral have permitted it ? And
had C. desired it, must not he have enforced that desire by
'*cannon shot*'? Is not the evacuation of the Morea a
primary object? and have you not offered aid and convoy to
effect it? How then could C., had he been off the harbour
with his whole force, have risked the interruption of so
'*desirable*' an object? Such are the subjects of discussion ;
and so are words and meanings twisted to answer the feelings of unwilling minds. I will name no name ; my wishes
are at all times to preserve peace and amity, and not open a
breach which I may not be able to refill. But it is most
painful to me to see and to hear, that while a man of high
mind and principle is doing all that mind and body can
effect to fulfil a most arduous and unprecedented duty as
becomes a British Admiral, *vile diplomacy* endeavours to cast
a shadow over him, and obscure his conduct by directing it
into the crooked ways of *that art*. I only hope and trust

* Received May 29th, 1828.

that C. will, in all his replies to his new master the Secretary
of State, give the most ample detail of facts and information
with all the caution he can observe; for he must now be
aware, that his *words and meanings are twisted.* I state facts;
it is for him to attend to or pass them by: all that I press
and most earnestly desire is, that he will preserve his high-
minded spirit, and at the same time not suffer any strong
expressions to escape him in word or writing; for I cannot
tell you (and I repeat it) how quickly his words are put into
circulation here!

From Admiral Heiden to Sir E. C.

Ce $\frac{17}{29}$ mai.

MON CHER AMIRAL,—Dans ce moment Mr Godefroy m'arrive avec la nouvelle de la déclaration de la guerre, et des
instructions que j'ai l'honneur de vous envoyer, M^r l'Amiral.
Assurément vous y verrez que notre Souverain agit avec toute
la modération possible, et que nos relations quant au blocus
existeront tout comme auparavant; et je tâcherai de ne
donner aucun sujet de jalousie ou de mécontentement aux
bâtiments des nations alliées qui bloquent les ports de la
Morée conjointement avec nous. J'ai ordonné à Monsieur
Swinkin de se concerter sur tout avec le capitaine Parker, qui,
je suppose, commandera le blocus de votre part, et de suivre
en tout ses désirs et ses ordres. J'espère, Monsieur l'Amiral,
que vous m'approuverez. . . . . Il paraît qu'Ibrahim
se prépare à se faire jour vers la Roumélie dès qu'il sera
réduit au dernier moment: ainsi nous pouvons espérer d'être
en possession des débris de Modon, Navarin et Coron avant
la fin de l'été, à moins qu'il n'y entre encore quelque bâtiment. J'attends Monsr de Rigny à chaque moment: ensuite
je ferai une tournée vers Samos, pour voir ce qui s'y fait, et
de là je viendrai à Navarin dans l'espérance de vous y trouver.
Les nouvelles de Modon disent que la peste y fait des
ravages, et qu'Ibrahim, pour se mettre hors du danger, s'est
embarqué sur un bâtiment de guerre à Navarin. Peut-être
cette circonstance favoriserait une dernière sommation par
les trois amiraux réunis. J'attends Monsr de Rigny à chaque
moment; peut-être viendrons-nous ensemble vous chercher
à Navarin, Monsr l'Amiral : les Français attendent à chaque
moment un débarquement de troupes en Morée venant de
Toulon. Comme ils ne s'en cachent pas, et qu'il y a un
commissaire chargé de faire des achats de provisions, il faut
supposer que c'est d'accord avec les autres Puissances. Cepen-

dant le comte (Capodistria) n'en sait rien, ce qui naturelle-
ment le met dans l'embarras et dans une position désagréable.

From Sir E. C. to Consul Barker, at Alexandria.

Malta : June 1, 1828.

SIR,—It is right that you should be aware of the great
probability there is of the port of Alexandria being put under
rigid blockade, on account both of the Viceroy's refusal of
the proposals twice made to him by the English Government,
and of the deceptions put upon us as to supplies clandestinely
sent to the Morea, and Greeks carried away in slavery. You
had better therefore communicate with Captain Richards, of
the 'Pelorus,' as to your plans and wishes in such a contingency. You will, I conclude, have heard from Government
upon the subject of the deported Greeks. I doubt not but
we shall before long have to enforce restitution by making
Ibrahim himself and other chiefs hostages. I wish, therefore, you would endeavour quietly to obtain the names and
disposal of those already taken to Alexandria since the signature of the Treaty of London ; and, at all events, to have a
satisfactory report of their numbers in readiness. Mr. S.
Canning is expected at Corfù, when probably more decisive
measures will be taken for the fulfilment of the Treaty.

I have, &c.,

EDWARD CODRINGTON.

Sir E. C. to Captain Parker, 'Warspite.'

'Asia,' at Malta: June 1, 1828.

I quite agree with Admiral Heiden in the propriety of
taking some decisive step for saving to the Greeks the harvest in the Morea, but I cannot say that I think the mode
of effecting it proposed in your letter likely to be successful.

The time is probably already arrived for cutting the
corn, and no doubt Ibrahim will use the superiority of
his force for the purpose of obtaining it; and it is quite
clear to my conviction that no negotiation would prevent
his success. By my letter of 23rd of last month I have
already warned Ibrahim of the consequences of devastating
the country ; and repetition would only weaken the effects of
that warning. You observe that unless the Greeks can obtain the corn for their own use, they must starve. In this
respect, then, it makes no difference whether the Turks get
the corn or it is destroyed; my opinion, therefore, is that,
rather than let it fall into the hands of the enemy, it should

be burned; and I can contemplate no other measures in the present state of affairs as likely to be effective. If the Turks get the food, their stay in the country will be prolonged, possibly to the next harvest, when they would repeat the same process; whereas, if they are deprived of this supply under present circumstances, they must either starve or evacuate the Morea altogether. It is painful to propose such an expedient to people undergoing such privations as those which the Greeks are at present enduring; but under the inability to improve their own condition, it is at all events desirable to reduce their enemy to the same extremity. If I had authority from the Allied Powers to use pecuniary means for effecting the purpose of the Treaty, I would gladly purchase a right to this destructive operation by procuring the inhabitants an equal quantity of corn from other places. Having no knowledge of the locality, or of the troops which the President may have at his disposal, I suggest with deference my ideas as to the best mode of executing this measure. My plan would be to send forward such corps, however small, as could watch and be in some degree a check upon the movements of the Ottoman forces. Upon their attempting to advance, the corps retiring should set fire to the corn as they pass through it. This measure would check the movement of cavalry upon the practicable part of the country, give the retiring corps an opportunity of gaining rocky impassable positions, and warn the inhabitants more distant from the scene of action to exert themselves in saving as much as they may be able to collect. Were the plan proposed in your letter to be adopted, I should fear that instead of outwitting so wily a chieftain as Ibrahim, he would not only obtain his object respecting the harvest itself, but benefit by the additional supply proposed to be afforded him, until the arrival of answers from the Viceroy. Although I have thought it advisable thus to state my opinion on this important point, I cannot leave the decision in better hands than yours; and I shall be very happy to support whatever arrangement is made by my colleagues, yourself, and Count Capodistrias, whose presence on the spot better enables them to form a correct judgment. I need not say how much I approve of your having remained where you are instead of proceeding to the western coast; and I will endeavour to communicate to Sir Thomas Staines my wish that he should assist in that service. Sir Frederick Adam was not aware when he wrote of an ambiguity in the instructions about the blockade of Alexandria. It is not my intention to do more than watch that port until I get answers from England to the letters I have written on that subject. I would gladly meet my colleagues at Egina to consult with them on this important question, but for the expectation of further instructions from England, and the attention which is required of me at so many other different points.*

From Admiral De Rigny to Sir E. C.
(*Extract.*)
'Conquérant,' Vourla: le 19 mai 1828.†

Il paraît qu'il y a eu quelque malentendu devant Modon au sujet d'une corvette turque que le 'Trident' avait arrêtée, au moment où l'escadre russe parut. Le capitaine du 'Trident' crut qu'en faisant jeter les provisions à la mer, il pouvait laisser entrer la corvette, qu'il supposait devoir être capturée par les Russes; c'est la même que le 'Warspite' avait déjà détournée: elle était retournée à la Sude, et là elle avait remis 40 mille talaris, qu'elle avait à bord, à une goëlette de guerre autrichienne, qui les a remis à Ibrahim. Vous voyez que Messieurs les Autrichiens continuent. Je vais écrire à Monsr Dandolo. Heiden m'a dit qu'il s'opposerait à ce que les bâtimens de guerre autrichiens entrent à Modon. Je n'ai pas d'ordre à ce sujet; donc je n'ai pu en donner aux capitaines du 'Trident' et de l' 'Iphigénie.' Je crois aussi que la présence des Russes a empêché les Albanais de Coron de suivre le projet qu'ils avaient, et cela est assez naturel. Ainsi de tems à autre il peut arriver des malentendus, qui élèvent quelque méfiance.

From Admiral De Rigny to Sir E. C.
'Conquérant' : 1er juin.‡

Mon cher Amiral,—Quoique depuis quatre mois je sois sans une seule lettre du Ministre de la Marine, je crois cependant être plus à l'aise vis-à-vis de nos Ministres, que vous ne l'êtes peut-être vis-à-vis des vôtres. Je crains que les tergiversations de votre Cabinet n'éloignent le but. Au reste, les Russes vont plus vite que la diplomatie.

Poros · le 3 juin.

Je suis arrivé hier ici: le Cte Heiden m'a communiqué les ordres qu'il a reçus de sa Cour. Il en résulterait que le Cabinet de Paris ne regarde pas comme incompatibles l'exercice des droits de belligérans et l'accomplissement du Traité; en tant toutefois que les conséquences de l'attitude

---

* Note by Sir E. C. in letter-book.—'This letter shows my reason for staying at Malta, and my expectation of some fresh instructions.'
† Answered June 2nd.
‡ Received at Corfù, June 25, 1828.

qu'a pris la Russie n'iront pas au-delà des termes du Traité et du redressement des griefs dont se plaint le Cabinet de St.-Pétersbourg.   Il est toutefois évident que de nouvelles instructions doivent nous parvenir, soit de la conférence de Londres, si l'accord subsiste, soit de chacun de nos Gouvernemens, s'il y a quelque divergence dans leur manière de voir une question à la vérité fort embrouillée.   Je n'ai encore rien reçu du mien, si ce n'est de suivre les anciennes instructions jusqu'à ce qu'on se soit accordé à Londres sur ce qu'il y aurait à faire. . . . .   Vous remarquerez dans les papiers que vous communique le Cte Heiden une déclaration du Cabinet russe aux Puissances maritimes pour le blocus et les bâtimens neutres, fondée sur son traité avec vous de 1801.   Il résulte de là que nous qui ne sommes pas en guerre nous n'avons pas le droit d'arrêter les neutres ; nous ne sommes pas belligérans ; nous n'avons pas fait la déclaration d'usage.   Mon opinion à cet égard n'est pas détruite par les instructions du 16 octobre : elles ne constituent pas le droit, et je n'ai pu, d'après nos propres principes, donner des ordres positifs pour l'arrestation de quelque bâtiment neutre que ce soit.   Des avertissemens, à la bonne heure ; mais si un bâtiment de guerre, autrichien ou autre, demandait de quel droit, je serais embarrassé d'y répondre.

Vos officiers vous rendent compte de ce qui se passe, et de l'état des choses ici.   Je crains bien qu'il nous faille créer cette Grèce, car je ne sais où la trouver : et c'est un assez curieux ordre de choses que d'être obligé de payer ces gens-ci pour les faire se battre dans leur propre cause, et de les payer encore pour qu'ils ne soient pas pirates.   Voilà pourtant un coup-d'œil vrai du tableau, et peut-être le plus vrai.

Votre bien dévoué,

H. DE RIGNY.

From Sir E. C. to Vice-Admiral De Rigny.

Malta, June 2, 1828.

MY DEAR ADMIRAL,—I fear the mistake of Count Guilleminot as to the *blockade* of Alexandria, as well as the same mistake being made by Sir Frederick Adam, will have induced you to take measures respecting that port which you would rather have postponed.   I wrote to England immediately, to say that the order to which I was referred did not so empower me to blockade, and that I should wait further instructions. I believe I have told you this before.   It appears to me that Heiden's being a belligerent will enable us to enforce more strictly the terms of the Treaty, if we are permitted to profit by that circumstance.   I do not know how to answer his question to me of what he shall do with the Turkish brig. He was not at war when he asked it, but I suppose he will now make her a prize. If I had caught her coming out of Navarin or Modon, I should have taken out the Greeks and forced her in again; and if she came out again, I would take away her rudder and perhaps cut her rigging or otherwise disabled her. I see your orders are qualified as to Austrians: mine are not. I have directed that not even a boat shall have permission to go in or come out. The Turks fired upon two of the 'Etna's' boats which went to warn back some boats from Navarin. Our lieutenants fired a blank cartridge up into the air, which I suppose they did not understand. But it was a hostile proceeding on their part, which I shall not forget. I have not been anywhere but on the coast of the Morea, and returned here to meet the 'Asia' and my despatches. I hope shortly to find myself again at sea with some decisive instructions to guide me, that we may bring matters to a crisis.

I wish you joy of your correspondence with ———, if the tone of his letters should be similar to that which he used in writing to me. I considered that tone so ungentlemanlike, that I have not answered him, and I only sent copies of his letters with my remarks on them to my Government. Nor do I mean to admit any personal communication with a man who has so conducted himself towards me. The Greeks, our *Allies*, having established a regular blockade which we are bound to support, I should use no ceremony with ——— himself if he attempt to break such blockade. I hear a Turkish brig with a flag of truce is gone to Corfù with a brig of yours. I do not expect any good from any of these communications: I rely upon necessity only for bringing Ibrahim to terms. I have given my opinion that the corn in the fields should be burned if he attempt to take it: I would press this point more strongly if I could advance money to buy the Greeks an equal quantity. Adam tells me he expects Mr. S. Canning, and he is anxious that I should meet him. I am equally anxious for such an interview, as I shall then have a *master* who must answer my direct questions as to what I am to do; and I think my first movement must be to Corfù for this purpose. I trust Heiden's presence as a belligerent will prevent any movement of the Turks against Samos, which I hear is again threatened. He presses my meeting him; but besides the above-mentioned reason for going to Corfù, I do not wish to meet him until I know clearly how I am to act with him. This makes me more desirous of meeting you at Corfù, if circumstances will admit of your coming away from the Archipelago,

Sir E. C. to Admiral Heiden.*

'Asia,' at Malta: June 3, 1828.

MONSIEUR L'AMIRAL,—I am much obliged to you for the interesting document † which accompanied Your Excellency's letter (of May $\frac{6}{18}$, 1828) relative to the different situation as regards Turkey in which Russia is now placed. England being no party to that difference, I have received no orders from my Government which authorise me to take or concur in any measures of direct hostility against the forces of the Ottoman Porte, or to proceed one step further forward in the way of coercive interposition either as respects the naval forces of Turkey and Egypt or as regards the commerce of neutrals, than is pointed out in the joint instructions of the Plenipotentiaries in London; and, consequently, that the distributions and exertions of the British ships of war under my immediate command, must be limited by the tenor and directed to the execution of those instructions, until I receive further instructions either jointly from the Plenipotentiaries of the Allies in London, or separate from my own Government. So soon as I can arrange the business which has occasioned my return to Malta, I propose meeting Mr. Stratford Canning at Corfù, where he is expected, in order to concert further measures for enforcing the return of the Ottoman army to Egypt, and the restoration of the Greek captives—the most important of the many objects of interest to which we owe our attention.

I have, &c.,

EDWD. CODRINGTON.

Sir E. C. to Mr. Huskisson, Secretary of State for the Colonies.

'Asia,' Malta : June 3, 1828.‡

SIR,— . . . (After stating that the typhus fever had diminished). . . .   I have before stated my opinion to His Royal Highness the Lord High Admiral that pecuniary aid to the President of Greece would be the most efficacious as well as economical mode of fulfilling the Treaty of London. I cannot but lament the consequences which are liable to attend his deficiencies in that respect at this very critical

* Enclosing orders and letters relating to the blockade of the Morea; and the harvest.

† The declaration of war by Russia against Turkey.

‡ Enclosing 13 documents of correspondence, between Sir E. C., Count Capodistrias, Admirals De Rigny and Heiden, and Captain Parker; all relating to measures adopted in furtherance of the Treaty of London.

period. I have sanctioned the calls which have been made
on Captain Parker's humanity as to giving food to those who
would have absolutely starved without it.   Calls of this sort
we shall still be subject to both on account of the fever now
prevailing and the intention of Ibrahim to collect the harvest: for whether he be successful in this object or fail from
its being destroyed, the natives in those districts will be
equally subject to the severest privation, owing to the pecuniary inability of the President to obtain for them a supply
from other ports.

I am, &c.,

EDWARD CODRINGTON.

Sir E. C. to Count Heiden.

Malta : June 3, 1828.

MY DEAR ADMIRAL,—I found such a mass of documents
upon my arrival here to occupy my attention, that I am tired
to death of pens and ink.   Since the date of your letter, I
imagine you are become a regular belligerent, and therefore
no longer require my opinion as to what you should do with
the Turkish brig.   Had I met with her I should have taken
out the Greeks, as you have done, at the risk of being
accused of establishing a harem ; and I should have made
the brig go back into Modon with the invalids, and there
wait the fate of the army.   I cannot tell you how much I
lament the not having power to give pecuniary aid to the
President at this critical period.   I feel it the more since I
find that 500,000 francs are actually on their way to De
Rigny for that purpose.   Arnous certainly misunderstood
De Rigny's orders to him ; but I hope we shall now do better.
Ibrahim will certainly collect the corn, if the Greeks themselves don't burn it as soon as his people approach it.
Money could not be employed more effectually than in buying
and procuring from other parts as much corn as is so
destroyed.   Time will not admit of the process of sending to
Mehemet Ali, and negotiating about it; and Ibrahim is too
wily and too devoted to his object to be led away by such
means.   I have not such orders for blockading Alexandria
as Sir F. Adam and the French suppose.   The term is a
' like blockade ' to that of the Morea, which is a confinement
of the Greeks (according to the instruction it refers to) to
their own coast, and a prevention of the movements of any
Turkish force from one port *in Greece* to another.   A blockade
of the Morea is to encourage the Turks going back to Egypt
and to prevent others going to Greece.   A blockade of Alex-

andria *similar* to this would be exactly contrary in its effect. I have therefore asked for an explanation, and decided to wait until I get it. Again let me say, that whatever different line our Governments may adopt, no difference need take place in the intercourse between us individually. The General* will always admit your ships; but if any prize comes here, she must be under Russian colours only, and not Russian colours over the Turkish.† For God's sake, I hope De Rigny and yourself will prevent the Turks attacking Samos, as I would certainly do if I were in that part. I would gladly be with you if it were possible; but I must make the blockade and my communications with England and with Mr. S. Canning, who is expected at Corfù, my principal object for the present. All my family unite in kind regards to you. As to myself, my good friend, I am not to be changed by any change of policy in our Governments.

EDWD. CODRINGTON.

Sir E. C. to H.R.H. the Duke of Clarence.

Malta: June 3, 1828.

SIR,—I have not yet been on board the 'Asia,' having since my arrival been entirely engrossed by the mass of despatches which had been collected here during my absence. I hope the alarm about Tunis will prove to have arisen from some drunken riot, and that I shall learn by the return of the 'Wasp,' which was despatched there, that the Bey has exerted himself to prevent a repetition of it: but these different Turkish dependencies require constant attention to prevent ebullition of the barbarians who form their population. The visit of the 'Erebus' by the orders of Your Royal Highness did much good, and I have employed the 'Zebra' in the same manner in the Levant. I have not met the 'Parthian' lately: but I suspect from the weakness she showed in the winter, that I shall find it requisite to send her home in exchange for the 'Wasp,' in preference to the 'Zebra.' I had but just finished the above sentence when the 'Glasgow' arrived with information of the 'Parthian' having been wrecked near Alexandria, and with Captain Hotham and the whole of the crew on board in safety. The vessel herself is no great loss, and I hope we shall save the greater part of her stores. I shall direct Captain Thompson to proceed with the 'Revenge,' which is now ready, off the Morea in company with the 'Glasgow,' and there hold the

---

* General Ponsonby, Governor of Malta.

† Prizes cannot be sold here, save under Russian colours only.

court-martial. I trust some inquiry will be made respecting the outfit of the 'Blonde,' for I can assure Your Royal Highness that the defectiveness of stores and the demands made upon this arsenal by ships on their first arrival from England, added to the quarantine, reduces by one-half the effective strength of the force allotted to this station: I cannot but think that the best economy will be found in keeping all His Majesty's ships fully efficient to their purpose.

The reports of the means which Ibrahim has of subsisting his army are very various and contradictory. I think he has relied upon supplies from the Ionian Islands which he will no longer be able to command. He will certainly do his utmost to collect the harvest, and the Greeks may not be in sufficient force to save it for themselves. I have advised its being burned in preference to its falling into his hands; a measure which I could press more satisfactorily if I were enabled to furnish them with an equivalent means of subsistence. I have had the honour of receiving by the 'Asia' Your Royal Highness's letters of April 7 and 24. I cannot conclude without assuring Your Royal Highness that I am very sensible how entirely I owe it to the decision of Your Royal Highness that the 'Asia' has again become the bearer of my flag.

I have, &c.,
EDWD. CODRINGTON.

From Sir E. C. to Viscount Granville.

(*Extract.*)

Malta: June 4, 1828.

MY DEAR LORD,— . . . . . .
No man is more anxious to get this business settled without war than I am; but I have thought the best way of obtaining such a conclusion would have been prompt as well as vigorous measures before the Turks were prepared for resistance. I should have relied upon such means averting a Russian war with the Porte.

Yours, &c.,
EDWD. CODRINGTON.

From Sir E. C. to Lord Cowley at Vienna.

'Asia,' at Malta: June 7, 1828.

MY LORD,—I had yesterday the honour of receiving Your Lordship's letter of May 4 last, stating that the Emperor of Austria had given orders that his subjects should be prevented from introducing provisions into the blockaded ports of the Morea, &c. If these orders should be complied with both in their spirit and letter, no doubt the retirement of the Egyptian forces will be considerably expedited. But looking to the experience I have had of the conduct of the Austrian marine acting in these seas, I must confess that I have no reliance upon the intentions of His Imperial Majesty being strictly complied with, in respect to the conveyance of despatches and of money in the Austrian vessels of war, when there is a hope of their being able to do so undiscovered. The evasions employed by the Austrian officers, not even excepting ———, in pursuit of the traffic, show that they take personally a strong and peculiar interest in it. I have lately been informed that some 40,000 dollars, with which a Turkish corvette had returned to Canea in Candia after being turned back by the blockading ships, were immediately transferred to an Austrian schooner of war, and by her conveyed to Ibrahim. And I am also informed that the commander of the Austrian corvette 'Caroline,' of whom I have heretofore had to complain as being so conspicuous in this traffic whilst he was so loud in his complaint of our interruptions, so late as last month made several attempts to run into Navarin or Modon, and was only defeated in his purpose by the Russian squadron closely watching her.

I am, &c.,
EDWD. CODRINGTON.

From Sir E. C. to Captain Parker, H.M.S. ' Warspite.'

' Asia,' at Malta : June 12, 1828.

SIR,—In the present critical circumstances of the army of Ibrahim Pacha, it appears to me that our consultations upon the subject of his retirement would be more conveniently held off Navarin than at Egina or at any other place distant from the Pacha's head-quarters. I therefore wish you to proceed yourself to communicate my opinion to my colleagues, or the senior officers whom they may have left to represent them. If, however, they should think it necessary to remain where they are in present communication with the President, you will be pleased to continue with them as the representative of my sentiments on the measures to be pursued. You are already apprised of my opinion that a prospect of indulgence would incline the Pacha to protract giving his assent to evacuate the Morea; and that decisive proofs of our determination to prevent his receiving any supplies whatever, and to make him pay the penalty of any ravages which may be committed by his troops, would produce an immediate consent to such terms as we might dictate, in return to the proposals which his difficulties would induce him to offer. After fully stating my sentiments on this delicate subject, you will understand that if my colleagues should still be of a different opinion, I shall readily acquiesce ; and you will, in that case, assist in carrying the measures decided upon into execution with the same zeal for their success as if they had originated with me.

I have, &c.,
EDWD. CODRINGTON.

Sir E. C. to the French and Russian Admirals.

Malta · June 12, 1828.

MY DEAR COLLEAGUES,—I have directed that Captain Parker, of the 'Warspite,' who is so fully informed of all that has passed, and who is the depository of my sentiments on the delicate subject which has lately occupied your deliberations, should again join you as my representative. He will state to you my opinion that the fittest way to negotiate with Ibrahim is to let him understand that no supplies whatever will be granted to him ; and that if he attempt to ravage the country in order to prolong his power to hold his present position, he will suffer that starvation himself in common with his army, which he inflicts upon the Greek unoffending inhabitants. He has always said that he could yield to nothing but necessity. Be assured it is that alone which has now induced him to open the communication, and that if we stand firm to our purpose, he will give way at once. In this case, we can stipulate for the return of all the Greeks whom he has sent over since the Treaty ; and if those under his command, who have claimed them as prize of war, find that they are made the price of their own ransom, they will all, or nearly all, be produced. These being my sentiments, *I* would not make any terms with him respecting the harvest, but would warn him of the peril of such a measure. If he ask what we would have him do to feed his army so blockaded, the answer is obvious. 'Return with it to Egypt.' If ever he should make his threatened attempt to collect the harvest, I am persuaded that the burning of one field of corn, as an earnest of what is intended, will deter him from proceeding. Now, having given you my opinion, I beg to assure you, that if you should still think the plan of sending to the Viceroy, mentioned in your letter as proposed by the President, the preferable mode of proceeding, Captain Parker will assist you to the utmost of his power in making your plan successful. I would gladly communicate with you, preferably personally, if I did not feel·it so much more important to the object we have in view, to meet Mr. Stratford Canning and his colleagues at Corfù. I think we should all meet off Navarin, in readiness to carry into more speedy execution whatever arrangements may be agreed upon with Ibrahim Pacha. I shall go there, at all events, as soon as I have had the requisite communications with the Allied Ambassadors.

Believe me, &c.,
EDWD. CODRINGTON.

From Sir Frederick Adam to Sir E. C.

Corfù : June 1, 1828.

MY DEAR CODRINGTON,—A Turkish brig-of-war with a flag of truce came in yesterday, having on board Baki Effendi, a confidential officer of Ibrahim, bearing a letter to Count Guilleminot and one for me; the letters contained only that this officer was charged to communicate with us. This communication is to ask that supplies should be allowed to go to Ibrahim, and that the Pacha should be permitted to send vessels to communicate with his father and with Constantinople. To this in substance we replied that it was impossible to comply with his demand for supplies—that the Admirals were authorised under the orders of their Governments, and that we could in no way interfere with these their orders—that, with regard to his sending vessels, that was equally out of the question ; that any correspondence he wished to send either to Constantinople or to Mehemet Ali the Admirals would take care should be forwarded without delay and with perfect safety. Even if a person was required to go (a point he pressed much) for verbal communication, if the Admirals could with safety (by stripping, changing clothes, &c.) receive such person on board, they would forward him to his destination.

Such is the substance of our communication to this officer ; but we both of us write also to Ibrahim ; and you shall have copies of the letters, as also of Count Guilleminot's to De Rigny.

It appears that this brig received your letter for Ibrahim and carried it to him into Navarin, remained some time there, and therefore probably the instructions of Ibrahim to his delegate now are, in consequence of your communication,

modified from what they were originally. We took care to
make Ibrahim's messenger understand that violence to the
Greeks, or ravages, would recoil on his master, who would
be less favorably treated if such measures were resorted to.
In the meantime, you will have received from Capodistrias the
Memoir addressed to yourself and your colleagues, as well
as his letters and Parker's on the subject; and you will perceive that the President fears that maintaining the strict
blockade of the ports will cause Ibrahim, who is already
prepared for it, to make himself master of the whole crops of
the Morea, and thus reduce the population to a state of starvation and misery. It is very difficult, under these circumstances, to say what should be done, for the object of the
whole operations is to save the population from destruction.
To press on Ibrahim so as to cause his exhausting the country certainly militates against this object; to allow him to
receive supplies, except under express stipulations, will, or
may, postpone his departure; and it is the conciliating of
these opposite difficulties which is the point to be attained.
I shall write to-morrow fully on this point after having seen
Guilleminot, and fully considered the whole question; in the
meantime, I think it right to send this by the transport.   It
is very clear that Ibrahim is *hard up* before he would come
to this measure of sending to us, and I look upon it only as
the precursor of a demand for terms and an arrangement
for evacuation; and doubt not we shall hear to this effect
very soon after the Effendi reaches the Egyptian head-
quarters. I hear from Stovin, on what he considers good
authority at Modon, that the Pacha prepares and sends
away a regiment of foot 2,500, 1,000 horse, and about 800
irregular horse to Patras, with a sum of money to purchase
grain, cattle, &c., from the Greeks; this information from
Modon is dated the 20th, and all accounts coincide in stating
that he is not now inclined to commit ravage or violence on
persons.

Ever yours,
F. ADAM.

The amount of business that devolved upon Sir E.
Codrington at this time may be estimated by my stating
that what is here published is only a very small portion selected from the mass of official despatches and
semi-official correspondence relating to this period.
Most of this correspondence is of great interest; but
the labour entailed by it was a severe addition to the

weight of the anxious service which had thus to be carried out.

Sir E. Codrington returned to Malta in H.M.S. 'Ocean,' and hoisting his flag in the 'Asia,' sailed for Navarin and Corfù on June 13, 1828.

Sir E. C. to Lady C.

June 14, 1828, at Sea.

Relaxation of some sort is absolutely necessary, to enable one to stand the intense anxiety which I sometimes feel for a good result to my labours. It is not, in truth, that I have any doubts about it, other than those arising from the want of firmness and decision which my masters evince in their communications to me, 'letting I dare not wait upon I would;' but this desired result does not advance in pace with my wishes, for I am by nature very impatient; and the endurance which I have had to undergo, and must still be subject to, before my whole conduct is placed before the public, absolutely wears me. You have certainly lightened this burden, and at the same time have given me increased strength to support the weight remaining; but I fear it has been to the severe cost of your own shoulders, in even greater proportion than in the relief which you have afforded mine. However, if you will but sacrifice to the preservation of your health, as I mean to do for the security of mine, be assured we shall have the sweet reward of the unqualified approbation of all those whom we hold dear, to the discomfiture of the envious, the jealous, and the malignant. When I ask myself why there should be any of the latter, I can hardly account for the fact, since even political ambition scarcely deserves to be charged with such a feeling. To be sure, the worst passions of the human heart are liable to be engendered in the exposed failure of an unworthy purpose.

The excellent breeze with which we started, after having disposed by signal of the Navarin detachment, carried us some eighty miles before 8 P.M., when, like the rest of us, it died away into sleep, until about 4 A.M. this day, when it again gave us a handsome lift, and brought once more into view the 'Pelican' and little 'Hind,' which we had left far astern.

Corfù: June 19.

We came to an anchor here Tuesday 17th, at 3 in the morning; the lights in the channel and at this place being excellent guides, under the directions given by our poor

Smith* for avoiding the dangers. Our excellent friend Adam came off, breakfasted with me, and arranged for my being on shore at half-past 10. There I was met by Woodford and all the heads of departments, in their Bath as well as other Orders; guards of honor and a large concourse of people 'making a lane' for me to the palace, where I had to make my bow to the Senate before I went upstairs to Lady Adam. Then came a visit to Count Guilleminot, his return to me, and so forth. Nobody performs all this better than Adam; and therefore, under his guidance, these ceremonies, which I admit to be proper however disagreeable, lose much of their tiresomeness. The reception I have met with, wherever the task I have had to perform is known and the difficulties justly estimated, is flattering to a degree which might turn the head of a younger subject. I trust, however, I shall not be thrown off my guard by it; and that it will not in the smallest degree diminish my ardour in the performance of what is left to be done. The feeling which at present prevails in me is to be, if possible, more alert: first, that I may show I am not unworthy the confidence and the kindness which I have met with; and, secondly, that my detractors may be put to shame; in the prospect of which I own I have a somewhat malicious pleasure. I was glad to find here my friend De Rigny, although, poor fellow, in long quarantine. He will probably return off Navarin to wear out his time, and then come here in pratique.

Ibrahim is in a quondary. He tells me his Albanians are in revolt, but adds that, in making their progress towards Roumelia and their own country, they will commit excesses in spite of him. But as he has threatened to do the same himself, if forced to retire and join the Seraskier, I consider all this unworthy attention. If he finds that devastation will best suit his purpose; he will not be restrained by any considerations of humanity; and therefore I am for distressing him all I can, and obliging him to resort to his final course as speedily as possible, be it what it may. He boasted to us last September of his *humanity* to the poor wretches of Tornese Castle, whom he permitted to live in Modon and Coron, but he forbade their moving out; and as the fathers or husbands disobeyed this order, the women and children were sold immediately to the highest bidder! My friend Parker cut up an Egyptian brig the other day which tried to force the blockade, so close to Navarin that it must have annoyed the Pacha extremely. Her masts and yards were

---

* Smith was Master of H.M.S. 'Asia'; killed at Navarin.

much wounded, and four men were killed. Parker put her
to rights for the voyage, and sent 'Rattlesnake' to take
her back to Alexandria. The captain said he knew what
he had to expect, but that his orders were positive to do
his best to get in. Parker has since sent Ibrahim's despatches to the Viceroy in the 'Rifleman.' We have no
further news of Mr. S. Canning, who is probably detained
by the changes which *Galignani* of the 28th reports to be
taking place in our Ministry. I need not dwell on this,
as you will probably have later papers; nor need I say that
I am pleased with the prospect of the retirement of *my
particular friends*, Lord Dudley and Mr. Huskisson;—and
if there be honor amongst the less noble part of mankind,
I could name another who ought to go with them, for he
has certainly helped them into their errors.

Guilleminot, with whom we dine to-day—as he says, *à la
militaire*—is quite the right sort of fellow. Adam has had
full experience of him; and his straightforward manner, and
his undiplomatic and easy ways, are agreeable earnest of his
conduct. He enjoys my letter to Lord D. very much, and
confirms the soundness of my reasoning on my instructions.

Our drives in the evening in this beautiful country, on
most excellent roads, give me a good sleep for my five hours;
and I expect to continue in good health. I find the Emperor
of Russia has sent me a very brilliant sword : but more of
this when we have received it.

Spencer is gone to Sta. Maura and Dragomestre, to see if
Church has means of getting out of his difficulties. Poor
Hastings died of his wound very suddenly, and is a very great
loss. And now, God bless you and yours.

E. C.

June 20.

This morning Adam received his *Galignanis* up to June 2,
in which the Ministerial changes are described as being
partly settled. I can have no objection to see Sir G. Murray
Secretary for the Colonies, and even Lord Aberdeen, or anybody else, in the place of Earl Dudley ; but I do not think such
a merely military Ministry can stand. However, the most important information for me personally is, perhaps, the account
Woodford has in a letter from his brother, of P. Malcolm
having been *actually* at one time *named* to supersede me. I
cannot believe it to have reached that length ; because it
could not have been done but by the Cabinet, and therefore
could not have been again undone. Gore's conversation with

the Premier, where he admitted that I could not have done
my duty otherwise than by entering Navarin, would lead to
his seeing my defence, which, by the expressions he then
used, he had not then seen. That would lead to his examining my subsequent communications; and thence he would
be led to see that I had done my duty since. .   .   .
This is my reading of the changes which Will just now tells
me are, by the paper of June 2, confirmed by kissing hands.
I imagine this to have detained Mr. S. Canning, and that
we must shortly have either him or a messenger.

From Sir E. C. to Commodore Campbell.

(*Extract.*)

Corfù: June 19, 1828.

If Parker is still off Navarin, pray let him know that
although I have only seen his letter to Sir F. Adam, he may
rely upon my approval of the thrashing he gave the Egyptian
brig, as well as of his sending Ibrahim's despatches to the
Viceroy. This letter will probably go by Admiral De Rigny,
with whom I have talked the matter of the Albanians over,
and who will authorise by his presence the measures which
may be deemed advisable. In the meantime, all that is said
upon this subject in Parker's letter to Adam seems to me to
give a correct view of it. *I* should prefer their being kept
with Ibrahim's army until its fate is decided on, if it can be
done; because I am confident he is desirous of getting rid of
them; and I fear their being more injurious to the Greeks
anywhere else, short of the north of Albania. But I shall
sanction whatever else may be decided on by those nearer at
hand, and nobody is more likely to take a correct view of it,
as it may affect Ibrahim, than Admiral De Rigny. We know
nothing more of Mr. Canning, and I suspect he stays for the
new arrangement of Ministers mentioned in *Galignani.*

I cannot well quit this until I hear of or from Mr. S.
Canning, since Count Guilleminot is as uninstructed as I am
as to our future proceedings. I am happy to find that he,
as well as Adam, agrees with me as to all that I have done,
and also as to what measures would now best serve the
cause.

Last night Parker's letter to Adam of the 12th arrived.
He judges every thing very satisfactorily. If the sending
Ibrahim's messenger and the conferences with the Albanians
should enable the Greeks to secure any considerable part of
their harvest, I shall be as well pleased as surprised. If we
should be thus successful, it will be owing, I think, to Ibra-

him's fears; for humanity is out of the question. It will show, too, that he never meditated going into Roumelia, from whence he would never, I think, have returned to Egypt. If any communication take place with you, it will be well to hint that you collect from what I have said, that his devastating the Morea would probably occasion a landing of the army here upon Tornese, and the passage of our ships into the gulf of Lepanto. In fact, this is what we *ought* to do at once; only our Governors don't think so. The non-hostility of not blockading by land whilst we do so by sea, is somewhat unintelligible policy in my mind.

The whole vacillation and delay seems to be owing to our Ministers. The French see the necessity of settling the matter at once, to stop the proceedings of the Russians, who will, of course, go on until it is settled. But they, the French, cannot act on their own account without our joining in it. Thus time wears away, and thus we are in the state of protracted war which a proper execution of the Treaty would have prevented. I fancy if the smaller vessels should find themselves within Sapienza, it will not be amiss for somebody to ascend the height on the island nearest to Modon, and take the distance by a sextant. Besides the information we should thus gain, Ibrahim would begin to calculate on the possibility of our taking military possession of it. As our force now off Navarin is numerous, it is good to send a vessel now and then to see what is doing near Patras and Misolunghi. Spencer is thereabout just now, finding out the condition of Church and his army, which we may find it requisite to take out of their difficulties. We must not let them starve or be cut to pieces.

Yours, &c.,
EDWD. CODRINGTON.

From Admiral De Rigny.*

' Conquérant,' devant Modon: 10 juin 1828.

MON CHER AMIRAL,—

À Paris, je vois qu'on est disposé à attendre que la Russie aille au-delà de ce qu'elle a promis, avant de la blâmer; il me semble que votre Ministère est un peu plus inquiet; mais entre nous, il y a un peu de sa faute. Le mot *untoward* peut avoir de graves conséquences. D'Égypte, j'apprends que Mehemet Ali, qui s'était d'abord emporté sur des menaces de blocus, a mis de l'eau dans son vin; il laisse comprendre qu'il espère revoir bientôt son fils et qu'il rendra les Grecs.

J'ai rencontré hier la ' Diligente ' venant de Toulon en 14

---

* Received June 25, at Corfù.

jours ; elle porte d'Égine un agent français, qui doit déployer
son caractère officiel quand le vôtre sera arrivé ; mais qui
porte aux Grecs quelque chose de mieux pour eux qu'un
agent,—c'est de l'argent. Il paraît que votre Ministère trouve
quelque difficulté à en faire autant, et en cela je le comprends
bien ; car, en définitive, je vois que tout cet argent pourra
bien tourner en subside pour les Russes. Quant à celui
qu'ils donnent, ils sauront bien dans leur Traité se le faire
rendre par les Turcs ; mais la philanthropie est si à la mode
en France que nos Ministres ont été obligés de donner
500,000 francs pour qu'on ne les force pas de donner dix
millions.

Votre bien dévoué,
H. DE RIGNY.

CHAPTER VII.

WHILST Sir E. Codrington was taking the energetic measures described in these letters, a blow was being struck against him in England, the real origin of which may have had many sources—either political, as against the Treaty, or personal, as shown in Mr. Huskisson's private letters (published in the 'Wellington Papers,' 1871), or professional, as shown in ample information against Sir E. C. being sent from the Admiralty to the Cabinet, but that which was in his favor being withheld by that Board,—for, the correction of the supposed fact quoted by the Duke of Wellington in his memorandum to the Cabinet as a ground for his recall, was acknowledged to have been received by the Admiralty sixteen days before that recall left England. Not only was the Cabinet allowed then to remain under error, but on a subsequent occasion (in 'Wellington Despatches,' page 36), Lord Aberdeen refers, on 19th August, 1828, to 'some papers from Codrington which have been at the Admiralty these ten days, but which we only received yesterday;' and he adds, 'up to this moment I have never seen any account of the conference of Ibrahim with the Admirals which has given rise to the expectation of the Morea being evacuated.'

Yet this conference with Ibrahim, sent home by Sir E. C., is acknowledged by the Admiralty on August 9, 1828. These dates tend to justify the opinion above given as to the hostile feeling against Sir E. C.

W. J. C.

*From the Earl of Aberdeen to Sir Edward Codrington.**

Foreign Office: May, 1828.

SIR,—After carefully examining the orders conveyed to you by His Royal Highness the Lord High Admiral, and comparing them with the explanations now received from you, I regret to be under the necessity of stating that His Majesty's Government, however they may lament the circumstance, cannot reconcile your proceedings with the Instructions conveyed to you, more especially those of October 16 last.

The Instructions contained in Mr. Croker's letter to Vice-Admiral Sir Harry Neale of February 8, 1826, which were handed over to you on March 3, 1827, and of which you acknowledge the receipt as 'Instructions executed, but transferred to you, in the event of a possible recurrence to the subject of them,' have put you in possession of the intentions of His Majesty's Government that the transportation of the Greeks of the Morea to Egypt should not be permitted.

You were directed by the Protocol signed at Constantinople on September 4, 1827, to favour the return either to Constantinople or to Alexandria of all Turkish and Egyptian vessels of war and transports having on board troops ; and, by the Instructions sent to you on October 16, you were directed to hold out every inducement to the Pacha of Egypt, and to his son, to withdraw the Egyptian ships and land forces altogether from Greece, and to assure them that every facility and protection would be given for their safe return to Alexandria, but on no account to enter into any stipulation for allowing the ships to return without the troops to Alexandria.

When you were directed to favour the return of the Egyptian troops, and on no account to enter into any stipulation for allowing the ships to return without the troops, you were necessarily authorized to ascertain what the ships about to return contained. But your fleet does not appear to have been so disposed as to have been able to prevent the movements of the Turkish and Egyptian ships, whatever they might have contained, or whatever might have been their destination. By the only returns received from you by His Royal Highness the Lord High Admiral since the battle of Navarin, of the disposition of His Majesty's ships under your command, which returns bear date respectively November 21, 1827, and February 26, 1828, it does not appear

* Received June 21, at Corfù; answered June 22, 1828.

that any ships were specifically directed to watch the ports of the Morea.

The first information received by you of the sailing of the Turkish and Egyptian fleet from Navarin appears to have been obtained when you learnt its arrival at Alexandria. That fleet appears to have been unwatched at Navarin, to have been considerably reinforced there by ships of war collected* from other ports of Greece in the possession of the Turks, and it might have conveyed the effective force of Ibrahim Pacha to any other point of the Morea, or to any of the islands, with the same facility with which it conveyed all the useless persons of the army to Alexandria.

- Neither do any measures appear to have been taken to prevent the return of that fleet from Egypt. It was unobserved during its passage, and would not have been adequately, if at all, opposed, had it directed its course again to Navarin instead of to Candia.

Captain Parker of the 'Warspite,' who did not arrive at Navarin till March 12, determined to remain there in company with the French frigate 'Iphigénie,' not, as far as it appears, in consequence of any particular instructions from you, but because General Guilleminot seemed very desirous that the port should be closely watched.

Thus, from December to March, the movements of a large fleet between Egypt and the Morea seem to have been free from interruption, and not even exposed to observation.

By your Instructions of October 16, 1827, you were directed, 'to intercept all ships, whether of war or merchants, having on board troops, arms, ammunition, stores or provisions for the use of the Turkish force employed† against the Greeks, either on the continent or in the islands;' and you were further directed by the same Instructions 'to concert with the commanders of the Allied Powers, the most effectual means of preventing any movements by sea on the part of the Turkish or Egyptian forces.'‡

The Instructions on this point were absolute. It was undoubtedly 'left to the judgment and discretion of the admirals to decide, in conjunction with the Ambassadors, whether any portion of their force should be employed either off Constantinople or Alexandria, and to vary according to circumstances the line described in the Protocol of September 4, 1827, for the operation of the Greek blockade;' but you were posi-

---

* The word *collected* is inserted in the duplicate.

† 'Or intended to be employed' is here omitted, although in the Instruction thus quoted.

‡ Meaning from one port in Greece to another port in Greece.

tively directed by your Instructions above cited 'to intercept all vessels of war, or merchants, and to prevent any movements by sea on the part of the Turkish and Egyptian fleets.'* It was for you alone, and the commanders of the Allied Powers to concert the measures best calculated to effect these objects.

The Instructions of October 16, which confirmed, explained, and extended those previously sent to you, were received by you after the battle of Navarin, and, in acknowledging the receipt of them at Malta on November 8, you add 'that you will pay the strictest attention to them.' It was not deemed necessary to send you other Instructions after the battle of Navarin was known in this country, as that event occasioned no variation in the principle upon which the Allies had acted for the attainment of the objects of the Treaty of London.

The Instructions of October 16 were thought sufficient for your guidance, minute directions being contained therein for your conduct with regard to [neutrals, and the nature of the measures you were to adopt with regard to]† Turkish and Egyptian vessels being therein clearly defined.

In the general order issued by you on March 2, 1828, you have used the words of your Instructions of July 12, 1827, but you have omitted to give the officers under your command the additional authority given to you by your Instructions of October 16 to intercept provisions destined for the use of the Turkish force.

By the same Instructions you are directed ' not to restrain the Greek naval forces from exercising, in respect to neutrals attempting to break the blockade, all the rights of a belligerent.'

But by a letter from Captain Parker of the 'Warspite' of March 30, 1828, it appears that at that period he had received no positive instructions, which enabled him to decide ' whether the ships of the Greek navy might attack and seize Turkish and neutral vessels near the ships of the Allies.'

Upon a consideration, therefore, of all the circumstances connected with this unfortunate misconception of the views and intentions of Her Majesty's Government, they have found themselves under the necessity of writing to His Royal Highness the Lord High Admiral requesting His

* Meaning from one port in Greece to another port in Greece.

† The words between brackets are inserted in the duplicate, although omitted in the original despatch.

Royal Highness to relieve you in the command of the squadron in the Mediterranean.

I have the honor to be, &c.,

ABERDEEN.

June 4, 1828.

P.S.—The above answer to your letter to Lord Dudley of April 7, was approved by His Majesty's Government on the 19th ultimo, but circumstances intervened which delayed its transmission to you till after the receipt of your despatches of April 30, addressed to the Right Honorable William Huskisson.

Those despatches have since been taken into the consideration of His Majesty's Government.

The objections therein stated by you to the establishment of a blockade of Alexandria, apply only to a blockade enforced by the exercise of all the rights of a belligerent [and are wholly inapplicable to the blockade]* you were directed to establish, according to the tenor of your Instructions of October 16. By those Instructions you were directed 'to take care to abstain from giving any interruption of the regular commerce of neutrals with any of the ports of Turkey or of Greece, though occupied by the Turks;' and you were informed, 'that it was to be taken as a general rule, not only that the regular commerce of neutrals—that is, such as is not carried on in order to aid the belligerents—should proceed uninterrupted, but that the interruption should be confined to neutrals sailing under the convoy of Turkish ships of war.' Whenever the term 'blockade' has been used you appear to have understood it in its most extended sense, and not to have adverted to your Instructions, to which you were constantly referred, for the precise definition of the limited measure of blockade you were authorised to adopt.

I must observe that it appears by your despatches last received, that it was not till April 19 that you stationed three of His Majesty's ships between Egypt and Candia, with orders to watch and intercept the movements of any Ottoman ships carrying supplies from Alexandria to the Morea.

I regret to be under the necessity of informing you, that notwithstanding the receipt of your despatches, dated April 30, His Majesty's Government do not see reason to depart from the measure they had before found themselves con-

* The words within the brackets are omitted in the duplicate.

strained to adopt—of representing to His Royal Highness the Lord High Admiral, the expediency of appointing a flag-officer to relieve you in your command.

ABERDEEN.

Sir E. Codrington to the Earl of Aberdeen.*

' Asia,' at Corfù : June 22, 1828.

MY LORD,—I have had the honor of receiving your Lordship's despatch, the first part of which bears the date of May 1828, and the second part that of June 4, 1828.

As I am supposed to have misinterpreted the Instructions sent to me from the office over which your Lordship now presides, and as my ambition to promote the good of my country has failed (according to Your Lordship's despatch), by my not having rightly comprehended the tenor of those Instructions, I cannot lament that His Majesty's Government should have chosen some other officer for the arduous and important duties of this station, more competent to understand the language in which they are couched. There cannot be a period when it would be more essential to the success of whatever measures may be in contemplation, than at this moment when Ibrahim Pacha is pondering on his return to Egypt, that the wishes of His Majesty's Government should be clearly understood. I think it, therefore, the more unfortunate that Your Lordship's despatch now before me should contain no reply to the direct questions contained in my despatch of April 7 last, and that it should still leave me at such a crisis in the same doubt (or error as Your Lordship considers it) which appears to His Majesty's Government to have produced effects which have excited the most painful feelings throughout the country.

No doubt my successor will be better informed by Your Lordship previous to his leaving England than it has fallen to my lot to be ; and I therefore most earnestly hope that there will be as little delay as possible in his arrival. In the meantime, I beg your Lordship will rely upon my doing the best I can under these complicated circumstances ; leaving my defence against the manifold charges which Your Lordship's, and some preceding despatches have arrayed against me, for another and more suitable occasion, and begging to assure Your Lordship that this determination on the part of His Majesty's Government excites in me no uneasiness whatever, and that I look forward with unbounded satis-

* Acknowledged July 8, 1828.

faction to the opportunity of having subjected to the severest scrutiny of my country the whole of my conduct and the principles by which it was guided in the execution of my Instructions emanating from the Treaty of London.

I have, &c.,

EDWD. CODRINGTON.

From Commander Peter Richards to Adm. Sir E. Codrington.

'Pelorus,' Alexandria: August 11, 1828.

DEAR SIR,—Whatever you may have heard as to the condition in which the shattered remnant of the Turco-Egyptian fleet arrived here from Navarin in December last, I can scarcely believe it equal to their wretched and truly pitiable plight. With those who witnessed it the matter of astonishment was how ships in such a state could have been kept afloat even under the circumstances which attended their passage. It appears the wind was fair during their voyage, and yet on their arrival here they had no longer even a morsel of provisions left—the truth of which is placed beyond a doubt by supplies being instantly despatched to those who could only gain Aboukir, and of whose starving condition no secret was made.

But whatever risk they ran of suffering the extremity of want had the wind been less favorable, it could only be exceeded by that of destruction by sinking, by the greater part of five frigates and four corvettes, which appeared to have taken part in the battle of Navarin. Their shot holes, sufficiently numerous, were principally stopped with patches of tarred canvas, and some even without the canvas being tarred. This novel mode of stopping shot holes for a winter voyage is still visible in those ships in the harbour, which it is found impossible to repair. One corvette arrived off the reef after dark so nearly foundering, that it was thought preferable by those on board to risk the passage of the reef, in a windy night, than to attempt the more hopeless task of endeavouring to keep her afloat till daylight. She succeeded in passing the reef, and the crew were saved by running her on shore in the harbour, when she had so far settled in the water that her scuppers were below the surface of it. The hazard of entering the harbour of Alexandria in the night is so great, that it is never attempted by the pilots even in the finest weather. The jury masts of these ships also were of the most miserable kind, and their capability of doing anything, had they met with contrary winds, may in some measure be estimated by the fact, that one of the frigates was nearly lost on the reef here from the extreme difficulty of getting her head off shore. Not fetching sufficiently to windward for the passage, she attempted to tack, and five trials at tacking and wearing were successively made ere they were enabled to get her head from the land.   In short, not to be tedious with the details of their wretchedness, nothing but a total ignorance of the hazards to which they exposed themselves, during even so short a run, could ever have allowed any people to have put to sea in the disabled part of the fleet, which, had the circumstances of their passage been less favorable, must inevitably have perished. The line-of-battle ship which reached Candia was, if possible, in a state even worse than the ship that arrived here.

I have read with astonishment in the English newspapers most exaggerated accounts of the Greek slaves and captives brought over in this squadron. No attempt was made at concealing these unfortunates, and from my own observations and enquiries at the time of their arrival as well as since, I can by no means think the number of children, as stated at 600 in my letter of January 20 last, in any way underrated, and supposing the men and women to amount to as many more will, I am convinced, place the total number sufficiently high.

Very truly your obedient humble servant,

PETER RICHARDS, Commander.

The following extracts from speeches in the House of Lords, although of a later date, refer to this question of Greek slaves—Lord Goderich having been Colonial Minister when these orders were issued in February, 1826.

In a debate in the House of Lords on the subject of Greek slaves (February 18, 1830), Viscount Goderich said :—

It is undoubtedly true, that in consequence of information which reached this country, that there was an intention on the part of Ibrahim Pacha to remove the Greek population from the Morea, and to substitute a Mahometan population in its stead, instructions were sent to our admiral in the Mediterranean, directing him to obtain a categorical answer from Ibrahim Pacha on the one hand, and from the Sultan on the other, as to the reality of such intention, in order to intimate to each of them, in case they avowed such intention, that the British Government would not allow a measure of that nature to be carried into effect.

All he had to do was to communicate the fact to the Government at home, in order that he might receive further instructions. In point of fact, Ibrahim Pacha disavowed the proclamation, though he wished to throw the responsibility of all he did upon the Porte. If I recollect rightly, the Porte disavowed the proclamation too. If so, there could be no doubt that those orders, having been founded on a conditional state of things, which in point of fact never existed, must be a dead letter; and therefore any authority which our admiral might have, to intercept Turkish vessels with Greek slaves on board, must be quite distinct from the orders given to Sir H. Neale.*

After several other peers had spoken, Lord Ellenborough said :—

It is impossible for me to say whether or not there were Candiotes amongst the number of those released;† but it should be observed that there is a great difference between the transportation of a number of prisoners of war, and the transportation of a whole population. A number of such prisoners were no doubt conveyed to Alexandria; but to show that there has been exaggeration and misrepresentation abroad upon this subject, I need only state a simple fact. It is well known that there were many Greek slaves attached to the Turkish army in the Morea; and when that army was about to evacuate the Morea, and they were left to their choice, either to go with their masters or to remain with their relations; they preferred going to Egypt to remaining in Greece.

Viscount Goderich :—

Therefore there was no blame attributable to any one for not preventing them from going there.

The following is the opinion of Mr. Sconce (who had been Secretary to Sir Harry Neale during his command) relating to the despatch of February 8, 1826:

The order was to send an officer to remonstrate with Ibrahim, as ministers *had heard that he* intended to make a deportation of Greeks to Egypt, and replace them with

* Lord Bathurst, on being asked by Sir E. C., entirely agreed in this interpretation given to their order by Lord Goderich.
† By the Treaty of Alexandria.

Egyptians, that he should on no account be allowed to do so, &c., &c.   This mission was performed by Captain R. Spencer.   Ibrahim said it appeared to him a *political question*—that he being a *soldier* could have nothing to do with it; but there were there 'two persons, servants of the Porte, lately come, who can give you the Sultan my master's opinion better than I can.'   They came in, and *prohibited Ibrahim* from saying a word; nor would *they* give any answer themselves; *nor was* any answer *ever* given.   The report of the interview was sent home, and no further notice was ever taken of the subject, either by Sir Harry Neale or the Government; and Ibrahim may have sent, or may not have sent, slaves to Egypt for aught Sir H. Neale ever knew.   At all events, had his cruisers met with vessels so freighted, they could not have interfered with them, Sir H. N. having no orders so to do.   *No subsequent* communication ever took place from Government on that subject—the order was acted upon more than a twelvemonth before Sir E. C. took the command—and the paper was docketed and put by as ' *executed.*'

Extrait d'une Dépêche du Comte la Cerronaye à M. l'Amiral de Rigny.*

Paris: 14 juin 1828.

Je regrette, Monsieur l'Amiral, d'avoir à ajouter à ces nouvelles celle du rappel de Monsieur l'Amiral Codrington, que l'on m'annonce avoir été arrêté dans le cabinet anglais. Nous pensons que cette disposition a pour but d'éloigner des principaux emplois les personnes regardées comme plus particulièrement attachées aux opinions de Monsieur Canning; mais nous ne pouvons nous défendre d'exprimer les plus vifs regrets, en voyant écarter un homme aussi loyal, et dont nous avons eu tant à nous louer.

&c., &c.

Sir E. C. to H.R.H. the Duke of Clarence.

Corfù: June 22, 1828.

The despatch of Lord Aberdeen announcing my being to be superseded, reached me yesterday.   The decision having been taken, it is not necessary that I should enter on my defence against the accusations on which it has been grounded, until a more leisure moment.   But I will not lose the earliest opportunity of assuring your Royal Highness that I shall be able to repel all the charges which are con-

* Minister for Foreign Affairs in France.

tained in this remarkable document.   Your Royal Highness will see at once that my original sin was the battle of Navarin; and that this predetermined mode of throwing upon me the natural, the inevitable consequences of the Treaty, though prevented heretofore by the kind protection of his Majesty and your Royal Highness, has been persevered in till a better opportunity has offered.   So situated with respect to the Ministers under whose instructions I have to act; harassed by my anxiety to perform the service required of me; harassed still more by the impediments thrown in my way by instructions to which the compilers of them give a construction so different from the executors; your Royal Highness will readily believe that my supersession will not cause me much regret personally: and that I may well consider the power which it will afford me of explaining my whole conduct in the face of my accusers, a very satisfactory equivalent to a command so encumbered.   Had not observations been made in Parliament, the subject of the Greek slaves which I announced by letter of January 21 which was received on February 18 and which is so observed upon on March 15, would probably have still remained unnoticed as it had done theretofore, although this very transmission of Greeks in slavery had continued from the first of the revolutionary war according to the practice amongst the Greeks themselves from the earliest ages.

Yet it is made a fault in me the having *permitted* (as it is said) this practice in one instance, and that upon the authority of a paper which was left to me by my predecessor, marked on the outside as *Secret* with a note that the service here directed has been executed; and Mr. Sconce has given me his opinion that the language of this very paper ought itself to have prevented my interfering in any similar manner to that directed therein, without express orders for the purpose.   But a reference to the document itself which is in the Admiralty Office, will at once show your Royal Highness the spirit of injustice in which it has now been brought forward.   It professes to pass by these mere customary excesses, and only to interpose against a systematic extirpation of a whole community; and it then proposes only to send an officer to demand Ibrahim's disavowal, or to inform him that effectual means will be taken to prevent, by the intervention of his Majesty's naval forces, the accomplishment of so unwarrantable a project.   The said officer is then instructed to give the Pacha a week to consider of it, and not then giving an answer the refusal is to be forthwith reported to His Majesty.

Now your Royal Highness knows, that however little this document can be made to refer to me, I did so report even this partial deportation as soon as it came to my knowledge; that no notice was taken of my letter for 29 days after it was received; that no instruction was then given me to prevent its being repeated; and that even in this last despatch from Lord Aberdeen, which makes my mis-construction of my orders the ground of my supersession, no answer is given to a direct question put by me on April 7, to prevent future mistakes on the subject. I have troubled your Royal Highness with this as a specimen of the other charges which are arrayed against me: and I trust that when other considerations will allow me to give my attention to this despatch, I shall be able to show that they are equally untenable.

June 25.

The Government having decided, although principally upon assumed grounds, and your Royal Highness being the true judge of what my conduct ought to be, I have profited by even this short delay in the departure of Sir F. Adam's despatches to trouble your Royal Highness with a pretty full though hurried explanation which I anxiously hope will be satisfactory. It is evident to me that I have been taken as it were from under your Royal Highness's immediate instructions for the purpose of gaining this object: and I feel myself very fortunate in not having given reasons more plausible for so extraordinary a proceeding. I am persuaded it will be agreeable to your Royal Highness to hear, that not only my colleagues but the French Ambassador, Sir Frederick Adam, &c., have interpreted the instructions exactly as I have done. With respect to Greek slavery which has been lately so much discussed, I may inform your Royal Highness that it has continued from the first moment of the revolt in the same degree as it has done since I assumed the command, and it will appear evident to your Royal Highness that if an order were given to take out Greeks from ships returning to Egypt, it could not be executed. The Turkish army is partly composed of Greeks, and it is presumed that part of Greece will still remain in Turkish possession. In fact, the Greeks made slaves of each other.

I have the honor, &c.,
EDWD. CODRINGTON.

Sir E. C. to Lady C.

Corfù : Sunday, June 22, 1828.

It is probable that duplicates of Lord Aberdeen's despatch have been received by Ponsonby and communicated by him to you. But lest they should not I send a copy. If I know myself, my dear Jane, the only, or at all events the principal, cause of my regretting this event, is that you will feel it strongly. Now, it is evident that this point has been determined on ever since the battle ; and as they have done it on grounds to which I can reply satisfactorily, and with the support of my colleagues, we should be satisfied that it did not take effect at some future and more unguarded (' untoward ') moment.

It is some fun to me that the authors of this determination are themselves superseded.* I have not another line from anybody.

I conclude they did not give the Duke of Clarence an opportunity of writing. It will be some occupation for you to prepare for old England. Can we not resume our Brighton house by six months' notice ?

I shall not leave this at present, in hopes of meeting Mr. S. Canning, of whom, however, we know nothing more. And it is possible we may settle about Ibrahim's return to Egypt before my successor (who is said to be Malcolm) arrive. The Ministers themselves seem to be in a pretty mess.

We are very hot, and reducing in flesh, but all well. I hope you will soon contemplate, as I do, the pleasure of again finding myself freed from such anxiety as I have lately endured.

God bless you !

E. C.

From Captain R. Spencer to Sir E. C.

(*Extract.*)

Admiralty : June 8, 1828.

MY DEAR ADMIRAL,—The first I heard positively of your being relieved in the command was twenty-four hours after the messenger set off; and I mention this to account for your not hearing from me on that occasion as early as possible my regret at the circumstance. My letters of June 2

---

* This refers to Lord Dudley and Mr. Huskisson. Sir E. C. was never aware that it was by the direction of the Duke of Wellington to his Cabinet, on May 3rd, that he was superseded ; as shown in vol. iv. page 423, of the Duke's papers published in 1871.

and 3 will have shown you how ignorant I have been, and still am, of all relating to you, even to the wording of your recall, except the letter from this office.

Yours truly,

R. C. SPENCER.*

Sir E. C. to Admirals Heiden and De Rigny on his Supersession.

'Asia,' at Corfù : June 23, 1828.

MONSIEUR L'AMIRAL,—I have the honor of informing you that I have received a letter from the Earl of Aberdeen (who has succeeded Earl Dudley as Secretary of State for Foreign Affairs), stating that His Majesty's Government have decided on sending another admiral to supersede me in the Mediterranean command.

Having served together as we have served—having agreed together as we have agreed in the execution of the services in which we are allied—those services and that concord having united us in an intimacy and a confidence hardly before witnessed amongst officers of different nations—I feel it incumbent on me not merely to announce to you the simple fact, but the causes which appear to have led my Government to this decision.

It is stated that I have not acted according to my instructions, and particularly to that of October 16, 1827. It is alleged that I ought to have prevented the transmission of Greek slaves to Egypt; and I am referred to an order given to my predecessor of February 8, 1826, of which he left me a copy, with a note on it, that the secret service therein mentioned had been executed, and which does not seem to me at all applicable.

That I ought to have blockaded the port of Navarin after the battle, and examined the contents of the Egyptian ships which returned to Alexandria, in order to have prevented such transmission of Greeks.

That I did not so dispose of my fleet as to prevent the movement of the forces of Ibrahim Pacha wherever he might desire to transport them, with the same *facility* (I use the word of the despatch) with which the remainder of his fleet returned to Alexandria.

That from December to March any movements of a large fleet between Egypt and the Morea were not only free from interruption, but were not even exposed to observation, &c.

* This letter gives curious evidence of the ignorance in which Sir E. C 's 'friends were kept (and as it would seem, the Lord High Admiral himself also) of the fact of his recall.

A reference to the instructions which I have received, and the orders I have given, is made, in justification of these accusations; and there are some minor charges added, which it is not necessary to notice on this occasion.

As we are supposed to be acting under the same orders and instructions, and as I am not aware of our having ever differed in opinion as to their meaning or the best mode of carrying them into execution, I have thought it necessary to inform you of the view taken of my conduct by my Government, in order that if I should have fallen into error you may be guarded against a similar misfortune.

It is, however, a duty to my own character, not less than to the unbounded confidence with which you have honored me in the execution of our joint services, that I should assure you I feel no doubt whatever of being able to refute all these charges and allegations, and of proving to my country that I am not unworthy of that confidence which you have placed in me, nor of the unqualified commendation and the distinguished honors which your Sovereign has so liberally bestowed upon me.   I have, &c.,

                    EDWD. CODRINGTON.*

From Admiral De Rigny to Sir E. Codrington.

(Translation.)

'Conquérant': June 29, 1828.

MONSIEUR L'AMIRAL,—I have just received the letter of June 23, which you have done me the honor of addressing to me.

It is no less my duty, than, in accordance with my own feelings, that I should not lose a moment in testifying my strong and sincere regret at the cessation of that official intercourse which a common service had established between us.

But when I consider under what circumstances this separation takes place; when I consider the cause that has produced it; when I recall to my mind all the difficulties which we have only been able to surmount by our mutual confidence and the frankness of our proceedings; and when I re-examine with the most scrupulous attention the instructions given under the approbation of our respective Governments, I only feel a stronger disposition to regard the imputations thrown upon you as attaching equally to myself, and to share with you before the world that moral responsi-

---

* A similar letter to the above, dated the same day, was addressed to Vice-Admiral Le Chevalier de Rigny.

bility, which, among men of honor, is considered the most effective pledge that can be given.

In this view, and although I have hitherto received no mark of disapprobation from my own Government, it becomes no less my duty to join you in the position in which you are placed, to enter into explanations which are now become necessary, and to strengthen, if possible, by my own evidence, the observations which you may have to submit either to the Government or to the public of your country.

The instructions which are common to us bear two dates; the first are of July, and the others of October 6.*

It appears from what you do me the honor of communicating to me, that no reference is made to the first, which followed immediately upon the signature of the Treaty of July 6, although it was in the execution of those that an event, variously qualified, took place on October 20, and to which I should not now have referred had I not remarked that in every publication to which it has given rise one important circumstance has always been omitted—that of part of Ibrahim's fleet having left Navarin, going towards Patras, and your meeting with him three or four days after he had made an engagement to remain inactive until he should receive an answer from the Porte on the subject of the Provisional Armistice. Now this answer, calculating the shortest time, could not arrive before October 15 or 18, and it was on the 1st of that month that, taking advantage of the momentary absence of the squadron, he violated his word.

This important circumstance was one of the motives which decided the entrance of the fleets into Navarin on October 20; and it has been sufficiently well ascertained that it was on the 16th or 17th of that month that Ibrahim received such positive orders from the Porte, that an action outside of the harbour was rendered inevitable, whilst there was some chance of warding it off by entering with a force then become more imposing, since the three squadrons were at that time united.

It was only by these means that that part of the instruction of October 6 could be carried into execution, which refers to the necessity of entering into no transaction which should not have for its object the departure of the fleet with the troops.

It is true that the instructions directed that hostilities should be avoided; but what had the squadrons been doing for two months but treating and temporising without any

---

* Those to Sir E. Codrington bear date the 16th.

result? What was passing under the eyes of these same fleets but scenes of horror and devastation? And if they had patiently suffered the continuance of such scenes, if they had not found means of putting a stop to them, can it be supposed that voices would not have been raised to even a higher pitch than has since taken place in the exaggerated transportation of slaves; and perhaps have called forth, without more justice, the same severity towards the commanders of a powerless and inefficient blockade?

But in these explanations, which might, if requisite, be more detailed and more demonstrative, I forget that in the charge of non-execution of instructions reference is only made to those of October 6.

The foundation and spirit of those instructions must therefore be examined. Now they were only a confused explanation and answers to the questions naturally referring to foreign flags.

These questions were the necessary result of the situation in which the Powers signing the Treaty of London were placed towards the Porte—a situation which I cannot find a term to designate.

Neither of the Powers had declared itself belligerent; with what justice, therefore, could the restrictions of a blockade be applied to neutral flags, when they had not yet been established towards the Turks? These questions were submitted to the Ambassadors of the Allied Courts, and to the Conference of London; and in a Protocol held on September 4, at Constantinople, the Ambassadors gave it as their opinion that in order to crush the growth of piracy, which was increasing under the pretence of forming blockades, and to reconcile, on the other hand, the acknowledged right of the Greeks to the character of belligerents, their blockades, and the expeditions which their lawful Government should be able to undertake, should be restricted to a limit of twelve miles following the outline of the shore from the Gulf of Volo to Lepanto; this boundary was adopted on the same principle by the Conference of London. This is not the place to examine what effect this might have in fixing the limits by land.

But then, it must be recollected, that the Greek Government and navy was in such anarchy that at that time no good effect was to be derived from that measure. A blockade by the Greeks, if regularly established, was certainly to be supported by the Allied squadrons; but still it was necessary to wait until they were in a fit state for such a measure; for it would have been absurd and manifestly contrary to the

Instructions of October 6, that the ships of the Allies employed on the coast of the Morea should have countenanced by their presence the system of cruising and pillage which the Greeks had adopted until that time, and which would evidently have committed the flag of the Allies towards Neutrals.

But as soon as some order was introduced into the Greek navy by the arrival of Count Capodistrias, and that a blockade declared in the name of the Greek Government was regularly established, that blockade was immediately supported by the ships of the Allies; regular and permanent cruisers were left before Modon and Navarin, and that part of the instructions was as completely executed as possible.

It is necessary also to remark, now that more than eight months have already passed, that the instructions of October 6th, to which reference is made, had preceded the battle of Navarin, and that after that event the Admirals were allowed to suppose that they might require new ones. This was done without suspending, as far as was possible, the execution of those which they had.

It must also not be forgotten that the Ambassadors of the Allies were at Constantinople; that there, at Smyrna, and in other places, the subjects of the Allied Powers might be exposed to some risk; and that one of the first duties of the Admirals was to provide for them, to establish more frequent and rapid communications with the Ambassadors at Constantinople.

Now, the strength of the fleets was very much diminished. On leaving Navarin on October 26, the squadrons required refitting : one went to Toulon, the others to Malta. It was agreed that I should remain in the Archipelago with the 'Trident.'

I ought therefore to be considered as the admiral to whom the task of watching the Port of Navarin was allotted (terms of the Annex A), and it is upon me that ought to be thrown the blame of not having prevented the deportation of Greek slaves to Egypt, a circumstance which seems to be the basis of all the accusation.

But, to such an accusation, were I the object of it on the part of my Government, I should answer in this manner; and I am confident that there is no person of any experience in our profession who will not admit a part of what I shall now state.

It is with difficulty under any circumstances, and particularly in winter, that the entrance into and egress from such a port as Navarin can be prevented. Now, it was on the 19th of December that by means of a gale of wind from the north-east, Ibrahim sent away the remains of his fleet, having on board, besides the crews, some thousands of wounded, and six or seven thousand men belonging to his army.

At liberty to send them when he chose, it was evident that he awaited favorable circumstances, and these circumstances, according to the report of Captain Pigol, of H.M. brig 'la Flêche,' then lying at Modon with three anchors ahead, were such as to make it impossible for any vessel of that fleet to be visited.

As to preventing its return to Egypt, in the state in which it was, with the great quantity of wounded on board, I declare that had I been in a situation by which I should have been enabled to do so, I should have considered the act by which any obstacle was thrown in its way, as equally barbarous and cruel; and that I could not have found, either in the wording or the spirit of the instructions, one single word which, under circumstances so unforeseen, could refer to such a prohibition.

On the contrary, I should have considered the departure of a number of men from Ibrahim's camp proportioned to his means of transport, as a partial fulfilment of the Instruction B. It would be an extraordinary error to believe that, with the same means and the same facility, he would have been both able and willing to transport all his army to any other point.

The first basis of every instruction was to prevent every reinforcement sent to the Turks from being introduced into the ports of the Morea and the Islands, according to the line described in the protocol of September 4.

Now it was rather difficult to consider, as a reinforcement, the return to Egypt of the remains of the fleet and a part of the troops.

But it is also alleged that from December to March the movements of large fleets between Egypt and the Morea were not even exposed to observation. This is incorrect; the sailing of the fleet from Egypt in February which arrived in Candia, was made known at Malta and in the Archipelago, by English and French vessels which were stationed at Alexandria. Mehemet Ali had declared that that fleet was only going to Candia; could we, or ought we to have prevented it, when the blockade of Egypt had not been ordered, and when Candia was out of the fixed limits?

It is true that single vessels of that fleet attempted to pass over from Suda to Modon; one or two were enabled to succeed; but it is no less true that the English ship-of-the-line the 'Warspite,' the· French frigate 'l'Iphigénie,' and others of the Allied vessels turned back several neutral vessels as well as Turkish and Egyptian. According to the information I have obtained, two Austrian, one Russian—three vessels in all—entered Modon. I do not speak of the Ionian and Greek boats; but it cannot possibly be supposed that a peace blockade, during which the vessels exposing themselves run no other risk but that of being turned back, can be completely efficient, when so many blockades in a state of the most general and determined war have been so often violated with impunity either by entrance or egress. Such circumstances must be still in the recollection of those who took part in the late wars.

As to the blockade of the Dardanelles and of Egypt, the instructions declare that it was left to the judgment and discretion of the Ambassadors and Admirals to establish them. Now, the Ambassadors consulted upon this point, answered that they should not take place; is it then fair, in such a case, to say that the instructions have not been obeyed when the points to which reference is made were by those same instructions left to the judgment and discretion of the Admirals?

I think it superfluous to enter into more details, though it might be done without difficulty.

In addressing them to you in this manner, Monsieur l'Amiral, I have wished to offer you a pledge which cannot be effaced, of the mutual responsibility which ought to exist in all the acts of the common service in which we have been engaged; and I trust that all the generous and enlightened men of our respective countries will think that we have done as much as possible towards its fulfilment.

Believe the sincere assurance of my constant esteem,

H. De Rigny.

From Admiral Heiden to Sir E. C.
(Translation.)

'Azoff, in the Gulf of Coron: $\frac{20 \text{ Jun.}}{\text{juillet,}}$ 1828 *

MONSIEUR L'AMIRAL,—I have received with as much surprise as sorrow the letter with which Your Excellency has honored me to inform me of your recall to England.

My astonishment has been still greater in learning the motive upon which this determination is founded.

Our instructions having been similar, and all our operations planned by mutual agreement, your colleagues, who have as well as yourself, Monsieur l'Amiral, the conviction of having faithfully and strictly fulfilled their duties, take pleasure in

* Received August 4

considering themselves as involved in every responsibility which may result from an examination into their conduct.

Fortunately, the events are so well known, the facts so patent, the localities and even the dates so easy to make out, that every investigation of the possibility which Ibrahim may have found to get Christian captives conveyed to Egypt, would, in my view, have no other result but to prove to our respective Courts the inefficacy of a marine blockade in putting a stop to all the varied horrors that are committed in those countries. This inefficacy, which the Ministry of the Emperor my master has more than once pointed out to the Cabinets of his august Allies, becomes daily more evident.   Even at this moment, when the season and the assembling of our squadrons enable us to blockade and to observe closely the fortresses occupied by the Egyptian army, we all know that thousands of Greek slaves, mostly women and children, are confined in the casemates of Modon.   It is true that Ibrahim can no longer send them to the slave market of Alexandria, but they remain to perish of plague and famine.   If any responsibility results from the prolongation of this state of things, assuredly it cannot weigh upon us.

I cannot close my letter without repeating to you, Monsieur l'Amiral, the deep regret caused to me by your departure from these countries; and my ardent wish that the justice and the respect which are due to your eminent merits may be rendered to you everywhere and for ever.

I have to add my request that you will continue to me that cordial friendship with which you have honored me, and to offer to you, Monsieur l'Amiral, the expression of my high esteem and inviolable attachment.

I have the honor to be, Monsieur l'Amiral,
Your humble and obedient servant,
LE COMTE L. DE HEIDEN.

It will be seen, by the letters quoted at page 239 from the Duke of Wellington and Mr. Huskisson, that fresh instructions were contemplated* and were considered necessary, though they were not sent.   They were not framed for delivery till July, 1828, when they were received by Sir E. Codrington's successor in the command, but never by Sir E. C. himself; and they are described by the French Minister for Foreign Affairs as 'being the same which were prepared in the month of March last, and this date had been retained upon them.'

---

* February and April, 1828.

Yet in the despatch of Lord Aberdeen recalling Sir E. Codrington from his command, it is written, ' It was not deemed necessary to send you other instructions after the battle of Navarin was known in this country, as that event occasioned no variation in the principle upon which the Allies had acted for the attainment of the objects of the Treaty of July.'—W.J.C.

From Count Capodistrias to Sir E. C.
(Translation—Extracts.)

On board H.M.S. ' Warspite ' · June 25, 1828.
July 7,

Your Excellency leaves us ; but wherever you may be, Mons. l'Admiral, you will not refuse to take an interest in that Greece which you have saved. .   .   .   .

Rest assured, Mons. l'Admiral, of the sincere 'gratitude of the nation which has confided to me its interests. That nation accompanies you with its benediction and its good wishes : your name occupies its place in the hearts of the Greeks, and it will also occupy that which they reserve to it in the port of Navarin, when this port shall belong to Greece.

From Sir E. C. to the Admiralty.

' Asia,' at Corfù : June 24, 1828.*

SIR,—I have the honor of informing His Royal Highness the Lord High Admiral that on the 21st instant I received a despatch signed Aberdeen (by which I am led to conclude that Lord Aberdeen has succeeded to the office of Lord Dudley), informing me that His Majesty's Government had requested His Royal Highness to relieve me in the command of the squadron in the Mediterranean, on account of what his Lordship is pleased to term an unfortunate misconception of the views and intentions of His Majesty's Government. I greatly lament that I should have so misconceived those views and intentions, however expressed. But since the same understanding of the terms in which they are couched has obtained in the minds, not only of my colleagues, but of Count Guilleminot the only one of the Allied Ambassadors with whom I can immediately communicate, and other high authorities who have necessarily been privy to them; I am induced to believe that His Royal Highness will not only think that the offence was insufficient to the production of so unusual a result, but that it was more justly attributable to those who did not indicate the intentions of

* Acknowledged July 8, 1828.

the Government in language by which they could be more clearly understood. I never had a conception of any such misapprehension on my part until I read in the newspaper reports of what passed in Parliament, assertions attributed to members of His Majesty's Government respecting my orders and my conduct which appeared to me to be unfounded. I felt that it became me, for the sake of my own reputation, for the good of the service entrusted to my execution, and, I may add, for the credit of the persons themselves to whom those expressions were attributed, to communicate to His Royal Highness, through whom my instructions were transmitted, my uneasiness upon the occasion. I could not imagine what could have induced Mr. Peel and Mr. Huskisson to attribute to me orders and instructions of which their language on that occasion gave me the first notice, and to have induced the former to describe a certain event as being comprised within a space of only forty-eight hours, when the very dates of the official letters extended it to an entire month.[*] His Royal Highness knows that immediately upon reading these statements I wrote to point out the error,[†] and that the receipt of my letter was acknowledged on May 7th last, and even to the date of Lord Aberdeen's despatch of June 4, the error as to a fact important to truth, to my reputation, and more particularly so to the cordiality of opinion and complete understanding between the Allied Admirals, still remains unaccounted for.

I will now proceed to the charges themselves, as nearly as I can collect them from the despatch before me.

It is alleged that I ought to have prevented the transmission of Greek slaves to Egypt; and I am referred to an order to my predecessor of February 8, 1826, which is marked with 'the service here directed has been executed,' and it was transferred to me, in the event of a possible recurrence to the subject of it. I consider this as a document which could not be acted upon in the sense mentioned in Lord Aberdeen's despatch without further instructions from His Majesty's Government; and this view of it is clearly confirmed by the words of the document itself.[‡] For it passes

---

[*] The despatch from Sir E. Codrington to the Admiralty, dated 21st of *January*, 1828, giving the account of the deportation of these slaves, is officially acknowledged to have been received on the 18th *February* 1828. No communication whatever was sent to Sir E. C. until the despatch from Lord Dudley, dated 18th March, 1828 ; that is, *one month after* the receipt of Sir E. C.'s despatch.

[†] See letters from Sir E. C. to the Admiralty of 4th and 20th April, 1828, page 227.

[‡] See Lord Bathurst's letter 8th February, 1828.

by partial barbarities of the description of the one referred
to, as excesses of which His Majesty deplores the continuance, but in which he has not thought fit to interfere, except
in cases in which the rights of his subjects, &c., have been
clearly compromised ; and it is only when designs are avowed
to extirpate a whole community, &c., that His Majesty cannot
hear of such an attempt without demanding an explicit disavowal or a formal renunciation of it. And, even if Ibrahim
Pacha should refuse to attend to the remonstrance of the
officer to be selected to make the communication, the instruction only says that the Pacha is to be informed that
'effectual means will be taken to prevent, by the intervention of His Majesty's naval forces, the accomplishment of so
unwarrantable a project,' and—not that the Admiral should
take any measures whatever in consequence ; but—that 'this
refusal will be forthwith reported to His Majesty.' The declaration referred to in this despatch was made to Ibrahim
Pacha, the report was made to England, and this instruction
does not appear to have authorised the Admiral then in command to take any measures whatever had Ibrahim carried
into execution even 'the systematic extirpation of a whole
community, and the transportation to Egypt of the women
and children of the Morea.'[*]   Denying then positively that
this order is applicable to me, and only seeing in it an indication of the disposition of Government at a former period,
I did, upon receiving the intelligence of the late deportation
of slaves to Alexandria, transmit it immediately by land to
His Royal Highness the Lord High Admiral, thus reporting
to His Majesty. And seeing by Lord Dudley's despatch of
March 18, although it still withheld from me the authority
to prevent such transmissions in future, that it would be
consistent with the views of His Majesty's Government, I
not only gave instructions for their prevention hereafter,
but warned Ibrahim Pacha that he would have to dread the
consequences of even partial and concealed transmissions of
this sort.

I am next accused of not acting according to the instruction of October 16, and a construction is given to it quite
inconsistent with the object in which it originated. The
original instructions, not appearing to contemplate movements of Ottoman forces from one port in Greece to another,
each in their own possession, or of the transmission of supplies in neutral vessels, Vice-Admiral De Rigny and myself
wrote to the Ambassadors at Constantinople ; and we, at the

---

[*] Confirmed by both Lord Bathurst and Lord Goderich, in Parliament,
(parties concerned) being then in the Cabinet   (See p. 181.)

same time, observed upon the conduct of the Greeks cruising at a distance from their own coast. This gave rise to their Protocol, and this Protocol and their observations gave rise to the instruction of October 16. In the second paragraph of this instruction it is said: 'His Majesty's Government observes with satisfaction that the construction which the Ambassadors and Admirals are disposed to put on these passages, is agreeable to the spirit of the Instructions themselves, and to the intention of those by whom they were framed.' And the third paragraph evidently shows that it was intended to relieve us from a responsibility which we had assumed ; and, but for my present experience of the fact, I should not have conceived it possible that to instructions so framed ' to exempt the commanders of the fleets entrusted with the execution of an arduous and delicate task, from the possibility of doubt or hesitation as to the precise line of their duty ' should be given a construction which, was not contemplated by the Ambassadors at Constantinople, or either of my colleagues, any more than myself. With respect to my being ' on no account to enter into any stipulation for allowing the ships to return without the troops to Alexandria,' I have to observe that I did not enter into any such stipulation : but, without dwelling merely on the words, I will refer to the spirit in which that Protocol was formed. The Protocol directs that I am to favor the return to Egypt or Constantinople of all Turkish or Egyptian ships of war or transports having on board troops ; the paragraph in the instruction of October 16 ' not to stipulate for the return of the ships without the troops,' to which Lord Aberdeen's despatch attributes so very different a meaning, was only inserted in order that the Admirals might know that they were not called upon to give protection to any ships so returning without troops ; but it was never intended that they should enforce the right of search, which would certainly have ' degenerated into hostilities.' I have thus replied to the charge of not searching this fleet, by showing that, if there was an error, that error was not mine. I have done so as a defence against the charge of having misunderstood my orders; but His Royal Highness well knows that I had no immediate means of resisting any of the movements of that fleet without having withdrawn all the undisabled ships under my orders from other important services to which they were destined. The 'Cambrian,' for instance, was gone to the seat of the Greek Government to excite them to exertion on their own coast, to watch the very port of Navarin, and to effect the establishment of a blockade by their cruisers.

The 'Dryad,' 'Zebra,' 'Gannet,' 'Rifleman,' 'Raleigh,' 'Weazle,' 'Camelion,' and 'Alacrity,' were spread over the whole Archipelago including stations off the Dardanelles and at Smyrna, attending upon the Ambassadors, securing the Consulates and British inhabitants against any violence which might have arisen for want of their presence, and protecting the trade against piracy. The 'Glasgow' and 'Jasper,' and subsequently the 'Pelican,' were sent to cruise from Carabusa to Cape Matapan, for the prevention of piracy and the interruption of supplies. The 'Isis,' after a visit to Tripoli for the safety of British subjects and the security of the Consulate, which were represented to me to be in danger, was ordered, in the first instance, to Smyrna to communicate with Admiral De Rigny, and then to destroy the pirates at Carabusa. With respect to the port of Navarin having been unwatched, and the first intelligence of the sailing of the Ottoman fleet having been received by me after its arrival at Alexandria, I have to remark in opposition to that statement, that the 'Pelican' was watching that port as closely as weather would permit, from November 27 until December 22, 1827, and on the 27th of the same month the 'Pelican' arrived at Malta with the intelligence that the Ottoman fleet had sailed five days previous, taking advantage of a north-east wind for that purpose. Again, as to the 'facility' with which that fleet returned to Alexandria, I have only to refer His Royal Highness to letters from Commanders Richards* and the Honorable William Keith, enclosed in my letter (No. 11) of January 21, 1828, to show with what difficulty, and in what state, it succeeded in reaching the coasts of Candia and Egypt; and how totally inadequate it was to the conveyance of an expedition which would have subjected them to any opposition; and it will also show the little justice there is in using that term which has been brought forward in accusation against me.

It is said in the despatch, ' neither do any measures appear to have been taken to prevent that fleet returning from Egypt; it was unobserved during its passage, and would not have been adequately, if at all, opposed had it directed its course again to Navarin instead of to Candia.' In answer to this, I have to inform His Royal Highness that the fleet which went from Egypt to Candia, such as it was, sailed under a promise of the Pacha, given to both French and English officers, that it was only going to Candia and not to the Morea. I may add, that the force at that time in Alexandria consisted of the ' Glasgow,' ' Galatea,' ' Philomel,'

* See page 315.

'la Vestale' (a double-banked French frigate), a French corvette, and two French brigs; and the 'Warspite,' and the 'Iphigénie,' with some smaller vessels, were then off Navarin. As a further proof of the incorrectness of the assertion that the movements of Ottoman ships might have taken place to and from the ports of the Morea from December to March unobserved, I may further remark, that it was during this period that Sir Frederick Adam's mission to Ibrahim Pacha took place. He was conveyed in the 'Wolf' to Modon, accompanied by the 'Galatea,' with Colonel Cradock, the 'Weazle,' and a Russian brig of war. . . . If the assertion of the port of Navarin not having been watched, arose from the absence of returns from me, I request the consideration of His Royal Highness to the impossibility of collecting dispositions to be relied on at such a moment, to the appeals made to me for protection from the British subjects in all parts of the Ottoman dominions, of the mercantile clamours on account of piracy, and the attention required to the disposal and refittal of the ships disabled in the action, &c. But although returns may not have been sent home, it does not justify the assumption that no measures were taken by me in the execution of these multifarious duties. In answering these charges, I have referred only to the disposition of the English ships; but having sent home more than one report made by French vessels on that part of the coast, their presence also still further negatives the assertion in Lord Aberdeen's despatch. Moreover, the 'Warspite' was to have been sent on this very service, and would have been so employed had not I received the order of the Lord High Admiral to employ a ship of war in the conveyance of Count Capodistrias to Greece; but I again say, that had the 'Warspite,' or any force under my command, met that fleet, they could not have otherwise interfered than by merely watching their progress so as to ensure their not entering upon any hostile operation on their way to Alexandria. In addressing His Royal Highness the Lord High Admiral, it is hardly necessary for me to comment upon Lord Aberdeen's observation, that an officer like Captain Parker should have acted on the suggestion of the French Ambassador, instead of that of his own commander-in-chief. It might be equally said that I have been acting under the suggestion of Sir Frederick Adam in preference to the orders of His Royal Highness himself, because I have been at all times ready to give due attention to his able advice and opinions. Having made Captain Parker fully acquainted with the tenor of my instructions, and explained to him minutely every point con-

nected with them, on his first arrival under my orders, he
was guided in his answer to Admiral Sachtouris by these
instructions; and he was enabled to decide correctly in consequence of that explanation. I am next referred to my
instructions of October 16, for preventing any 'movements
by sea on the part of the Turkish or Egyptian forces;' and
Lord Aberdeen observes, that the instructions on this point
were absolute. I admit them to have been absolute with
respect to forces going to act against the Greeks, but I
deny its applicabilty in any way to the ships in question, by
preventing the movement of which I should have acted in
direct defiance of those very instructions, which order me
positively to afford every facility and protection to Egyptian
ships and forces withdrawing from Greece.

It has been said both by Lord Dudley and Lord Aberdeen
that there is no difference in my position since the battle of
Navarin, and that therefore no additional instructions were
necessary. Having from the first been directed to look to
the Ambassadors for information, the loss of such a reference
alone undoubtedly made a great difference in my situation,
independent of the battle; and this circumstance, added to
the scrutiny of my conduct by means of the 'Queries' I still
think, with due submission, fully justified me in looking to
the Government for some further instruction as to whether I
had or had not rightly conceived the line of my duty. The
very despatch now before me is a proof of this. For I am
herein accused of having been ever since under a misconception of the intentions of the Government; and it further
declares, that it is on account of that very misconception,
which such further instructions would at once have prevented,
that His Majesty's Government is now induced to request His
Royal Highness to supersede me in this command. As to the
charge of having omitted to insert the word 'Provisions' in
my order of March 2, instead of including it under the
general head of Supplies, I trust I can offer some excuse
even for this additional complaint upon which His Majesty's
Government has requested my supersession. On September
8 I gave an order in the terms which I had selected from the
Treaty and original Instructions, which I deemed it proper
to make secret and to limit to the captains of post ships.
But when a similar service fell to be performed by commanders of sloops, and circumstances no longer required
secrecy, I drew out the order from that which I had previously given. Nor is it surprising that I should not have
thought such an insertion of importance, when I had so
frequently called the attention of my superiors to those Sup-

plies being preferably received through neutrals, and when fifty Ionian boats at a time were thus trafficking in the ports of Navarin and Modon without my being empowered to interfere with them, as observed in Captain Parker's letter.

With respect to the question of 'a like blockade' of the port of Alexandria, originally mentioned in the letter of Mr. Huskisson, and now referred to in that of Lord Aberdeen, I am still at a loss to understand what was intended by it. I cannot comprehend how it was possible to establish a 'like blockade of the port of Alexandria' to that limited blockade established on the coast of the Morea for preventing the arrival of supplies. That I have not 'understood the term blockade in its most extended sense whenever it has been used,' must be apparent from the limited blockade which has been carried on under the orders of the Allied Admirals on the coast of the Morea from the commencement of the execution of the Treaty of London up to the present time. And as to its not having been until the 19th of April that three of His Majesty's ships were stationed off Candia for preventing supplies being introduced into the Morea, I have to state that the force under my orders, not occupied in indispensable services, has been constantly employed in the interception of supplies on that coast. Although His Majesty's Government having decided on my conduct, renders any further explanation towards them useless, I have considered it important to my professional character, that his Royal Highness the Lord High Admiral should be made fully acquainted with the whole of my proceedings and the motives by which they have been guided: with this view I enclose copies of the letters I have before written in explanation.*

His Royal Highness well knows that the English squadron has been always arduously employed in bringing about the objects of the Treaty; but it seems that the Government has considered me responsible for executing all those measures of which the fulfilment was entrusted to the squadrons of France and Russia, as well as to that of England. In proof that the port of Navarin was unwatched, the English ships only are referred to, and the aid given by our Allies is unnoticed; whilst on other occasions, with the same purpose of throwing blame on my conduct, I am supposed to have command of a fleet sufficient to watch the whole of the Ottoman ports and control the whole of the Ottoman forces. Far be it from me to assume that I may not have erred in the performance of these complicated operations. I well

* Copy of a letter of April 7, 1828, to the Earl of Dudley. Copy of a letter of April 30, 1828, to Mr. Huskisson: both in this volume.

know that it is not given to me to be free from error, and I should tremble for myself if I were led by vanity into any such persuasion; but I can safely and solemnly declare, that I have not voluntarily swerved from the orders and instructions which I have had for my guidance; that during the time I have held this command I have used the utmost exertions of mind and body in the performance of the very arduous, the intricate and important, duties, with which I have been entrusted; and that however I may have failed in ability, I have not failed in the ardent devotion of all the energy I possess to the service of my sovereign and my country.

I am, &c., &c.,
EDWD. CODRINGTON.

The two following letters, although of a later date, especially refer to the erroneous statement in Lord Aberdeen's despatch relating to Captain Parker's motive in remaining off Navarin :— .

From Sir E. C. to Captain Parker, 'Warspite.'

'Wellesley,' at Malta : September 5, 1828.

SIR,—In a despatch to me from the Earl of Aberdeen, one of his Majesty's principal Secretaries of State, it is observed that I omitted to give the officers under my command authority to intercept 'provisions' destined for the use of the Turkish force in the Morea. I therefore request you to inform me whether or not you had understood by my previous communications with you that provisions were to be stopped; and if you did actually, in consequence of those communications, so intercept provisions destined for the use of the Turkish force. It is also observed in the despatch from the Earl of Aberdeen, that you appear to have determined on remaining off Navarin, not in consequence of any instructions from me, but because General Guilleminot seemed very desirous that the port should be closely watched. I therefore request you will inform me of the motive by which you were guided on that occasion.

I have, &c.
EDWD. CODRINGTON.

From Captain Parker to Sir E. C.

'Warspite,' at Malta : September 5, 1828.

SIR,—In reply to your letter of this day's date, I have no hesitation in saying, that before the 'Warspite' sailed from

Malta in December last, I understood from the different communications I had been personally honored with by you, that provisions destined for the use of the Turkish force in the Morea, and coming from Egypt or Africa, were to be stopped; and influenced by this understanding, together with your instructions in the circular letter of September 8, I not only did intercept provisions so destined on my arrival off Navarin with the 'Warspite,' but I had determined to proceed from Egina to the west side of the Morea (to ascertain whether the respective vessels of the Ionian squadron were acting in the spirit of such instructions) *before* my attention was more particularly directed to the interception of the Egyptian convoy, which I was informed had sailed from Alexandria about February 15, and to which I especially referred in my letters to you of the 3rd and 7th March. I have further to state that my determination to remain with the 'Warspite' off Navarin, was made *before* I was acquainted with General Guilleminot's desire that the ports should be closely watched, and solely from my own conviction that it was my duty to do so in compliance with your wishes, and in execution of the Treaty of July 6; and it was not until I had positive intelligence of the return of the Egyptian ships of war and convoy to Alexandria, that I consigned the duty of watching Navarin to the zeal of Captain Mitchell of the 'Rifleman,' supported by the French ships then stationed there, in order that I might proceed to meet the transport which you had despatched with supplies for the 'Warspite' and the ships at Carabusa, as well as to attend to the important duties entrusted to me near the seat of the Greek Government.

I have, &c.

WILLIAM PARKER, Captain.

Sir E. C. to Lady C.

Corfù: June 29, 1828.

I hear no more of Mr. S. Canning's coming, of which we may reasonably doubt in consequence of the changes, and therefore, to-morrow, I shall leave this for Navarin. Count Guilleminot and his secretary agree with Adam in taking the same view as I have done of my instructions, and my conduct in consequence. The instructions of October 16 were verbatim from a Protocol of the Allied Plenipotentiaries in London, and therefore De Rigny's orders are exactly the same.

Count G. has stated his sentiments upon this and upon the

z 2

whole despatch of Lord Aberdeen, to Paris. There must be some secret motive in all this treatment of me, beyond any reference to me personally.

It is impossible that any Ministers can be so weak or so base as to commit injustice and folly such as this, which must shortly be subjected to public criticism, without having some strong motive which they consider a justification. Perhaps the harmony, the deference to me, which in the eyes of others redounds to my credit, may interfere with the policy of the present Administration.

Huskisson, in his speech where he addresses Peel, points out plainly what he would have the world believe to be the policy of the present set of men. If what he says be true now, it was equally true when the Duke of Wellington first took the office of Premier. I shall not be surprised if an alliance be concocted between us and Austria against Russia. In such a case I should not be a fit admiral for the occasion. In fact I shall, I think, be well out of a difficulty by being superseded; for under any circumstances I could not serve with any confidence, nor would the Ministers put any confidence in me after having instilled into me doubts of our each having the same understanding of common English phrases.

Wednesday, July 2.

Now, that I see by your letter of the 10th of last month, by the 'Racer,' that you take my supersession as you ought, philosophically, I am quite easy, my dearest Jane, as to all the rest.

The poor wife put on, for her husband's sake, a 'philosophy' that was not natural to her anxious mind. I was with her at the time at Malta, and well remember the distress occasioned to her by the news of my father's recall. She was, in truth, deeply wounded at what she felt to be the undeserved treatment of him of whom she was so justly proud.

(Letter continued.)

I shall be an instance, no doubt, of that sort of honor-seeking persons who are said to have honors forced upon them. For I shall be dragged into publicity eventually which I should have gladly avoided, and that publicity will gain me an extent of approbation which would not have fallen to my lot under just treatment by men in power. The approval of my countrymen comprises the honors I covet, and next to that the approval of others; and if the stars and ribbons which have been so bountifully given me are not evidence of that feeling, they become the mere gew-gaws which might ornament any Court sycophant of any monarchy. Shortly after your letter came away you will have received mine, and, I trust, have been satisfied with my reply to Lord Aberdeen. As the steamer did not go till a couple of days after I had weighed matters, it was agreed that I had better explain to the Duke of Clarence this part of my proceeding, with which the placing me under the Secretaries of State had left him unacquainted. We were hurried so as to draw upon our time of rest of both night and early morning. But both Adam and Count Guilleminot are contented with it, and if it contain nothing objectionable, I shall consider it of minor importance there being any omission which I shall have probably too much opportunity of correcting.

Corfù : July 3.

Several letters arrived here with the news of my supersession, even before the courier with the despatch of which I now enclose you a copy. In this you will see that blame *is* thrown upon me as thick as power can supply it, by the reasons therein given for my recall. I will trust none of the politicians with my character whilst I have myself the power to preserve it unsullied. For my country I am ready to make any sacrifice, because my character can never be required to be included; but for a party, and such a party, no. Preserve the serenity, my dearest Jane, which you justly desire to see in me, and be assured all will go right and well. As to my talking about it, why, all France is talking about it, to better purpose than I could do myself; and all here echo the sentiment, because they see that mischief must arise from it. As to court-martial, it is out of the question. Again, my dear Jane, let me entreat you, as you love my peace, to diminish that excess of anxiety which diminishes your power of judging correctly; for it is material to me that you should feel as I do in all this matter. I see my way clearly, and am confident of a good result by pursuing my own line firmly; and I rely upon your agreeing with me in this when we meet and can talk the matter over coolly. What is one to think of Ministers who can give one reason to the Lord High Admiral and others to me. As to their verbal explanations which came through our anxious friend G., it is not worth a moment's deliberation.

As to Ibrahim, he is now either feigning, or about to punish exemplarily the 5,000 Albanians who, according to a letter *to us from him*, have marched to Patras. Will has so much to do he can scarcely write now, or Harry either. They are both well, and I trust will keep so. Poor Smith's death and that of little Horatio Paget, may diminish your regret at leaving this climate. I cannot say my feelings amount to regret under the circumstances, and I think they will soon become rejoicings. And now, once more, God bless you.

E. C.

Sir E. C. to Vice-Admiral Count Heiden.

'Asia,' at Sea · July 4, 1828.

MONSIEUR L'AMIRAL,—I have had the honor of receiving your Excellency's letter of May 23 and June 4.

I feel it incumbent on me to declare, that in all the information which I have had through your Excellency of the intentions of your august Sovereign, as well as in all the intercourse which I have had with your Excellency personally and the officers of the Russian navy, I have experienced the most open and candid communication; and that I have ever been impressed with a full conviction of his Imperial Majesty's determination to fulfil the engagements to which he was bound by the Treaty of London. I am further impelled by the cordiality which our joint services have so happily established, to declare my full persuasion, that if it had pleased my Government to continue me in this command, the same cordiality would have remained undisturbed and undiminished until the object of that important Treaty should have been effectually accomplished.

I have, &c.,

EDWD. CODRINGTON.

Sir E. C. to Count de Heiden.

Off Corfù . July 4, 1828.

I fear, my good friend, that owing to your being subject to long quarantine, in consequence of having had communications with the main land, I shall not be able to have that personal intercourse with you which would be consistent with our mutual regard. I therefore have taken up my pen to tell you some of my present feelings on the subject of my supersession. It is evident that our men in office have sought means for disgusting me ever since the battle of Navarin, in order to make me resign my command; and that the approbation of the King and the Lord High Admiral prevented their recalling me immediately. But finding that I was determined not to resign, and having some object which they do not think me a fit medium for accomplishing, they at length made their determination. What that object may be it is not for me to anticipate; but no doubt it will be very soon seen by their conduct. However, I know it will be satisfactory to you, my good friend, and I would fain hope that your good and august Emperor will also feel pleased with it,—to be assured that I can repel all the imputations and surmises which any man may venture to give utterance to, as to my not having clearly understood and fully executed my orders.   .   .   .   .   .   .

I should not, however, have entered so much into this subject, but for the intimate friendship which has arisen out of our late intercourse, and the anxiety which I know you will feel about it. For myself, personally, I have nothing to regret, except the not finishing jointly with my colleagues the great work in which we have been so cordially engaged. Now that I find the dear companion of my retirement takes the same philosophical view of the treatment I have experienced from the party that now governs England as I do myself, I look forward with cheerfulness to my return to that domestic life which you, my good friend, know is competent to afford happiness to one of my turn of mind. In that retirement we shall not forget you.   .   .

I will not quit this subject without begging you to rely upon the upright intentions of our colleague De Rigny, and not allow the little mistakes which your very different nations are liable to in so very complicated a service, to interfere in any way with the success of that service, and with the satisfaction of carrying it harmoniously into execution. I am told privately that Sir Pulteney Malcolm is to be my successor; that he was to leave England on June 23 in the 'Wellesley;' and that I am to go home in the 'Warspite.' As I hope in a day or two to have such personal communications with you as the quarantine regulations will admit of, I will only add that, wherever I may be, I shall always feel towards you that warm and friendly regard which has been happily cemented by mutual approbation in fulfilling our joint services on a very interesting as well as important occasion.

Your sincere and faithful friend,
EDWARD CODRINGTON.

From Sir John Gore to Sir E. C.*

June 4, 1828.

MY DEAR CODRINGTON,—You both know how highly we are interested, and how deeply we feel all that concerns you; and

---

* Received beginning of July, 1828.

more particularly at this moment when we consider that you are not fairly dealt with, and that amidst the pressure of executing a most important and unprecedented duty, you are not aided by the kindly countenance of an approving Government, but are perplexed by questions, when it would have been more to their dignity and your satisfaction had they said, do so—and do so—than to ask why—. The questions asked and the answers given are kept close; the Duke of Clarence does not know them.

We are kept in a state of feverish anxiety by an *on dit* that you are to be superseded; this feverish anxiety has prevented me writing to you since 'Asia' sailed; for as reports prevailed and nothing certain could be learnt, I could not sit down to write what was as distressing for me to hear as it must be for you to read. But as *Galignani* must have conveyed to you these reports before this letter can reach you, I will not let to-morrow's mail be made up without a few lines. The reports still exist, and Malcolm is in readiness for a start in the ' Wellesley '; yet at half-past four yesterday evening, the Lord-High Admiral told me 'the Duke of Wellington has been here to communicate that the Cabinet object to my going to Ireland in the present crisis of affairs, but he did not name Sir Edward Codrington to me.' The report and subject of general conversation is (and it emanated from Holland House) that the Cabinet have determined on recalling you for non-obedience of an instruction dated October 15, the receipt of which is acknowledged by you at Malta on November 11; that by such non-obedience the Turks had been permitted to traverse the Archipelago from the Dardanelles under Tahir Pacha, and take Greek slaves from the Morea. I think it fair thus to give you the substance of the complaint against you, in order that you may be prepared to meet and combat it, as I have no doubt you can do triumphantly. I will at the same time state to you the opinion I have given from the first moment the subject was named to me, without having seen any such instructions, or knowing their bearings on the Treaty of London. I can understand that Sir Edward Codrington may consider that the battle of Navarin, which took place subsequent to the above instructions, commenced a new era, and materially changed the aspect of affairs; consequently demanded new instructions. The Duke of C. and Sir G. C. both said, 'I wish he had asked for such; he would have been fully justified in doing so, and it would have saved him from the idea of disobedience.' I further stated my understanding that De Rigny had pledged himself to you to take care of the Dardanelles and Archipelago, and that consequently the rendezvous of his whole squadron was Smyrna; and that, in my opinion, had you been off Navarin with your whole force when the Egyptian force came out to return to Alexandria, that you could not have risked 'collision and hostility' by searching them for Greek slaves. How far I may have been correct in my view of these two points, I know not; but you know how difficult it is to found an opinion without facts as data. The general opinion is that you will be relieved, but the Cabinet have not yet come to a decision. Since Lord Dudley's resignation, all the papers are put into the hands of Lord Ellenborough to form a digest of them upon which the Cabinet will meet and discuss before they decide; this fact I know from authority. In a visit to Huskisson yesterday (June 3), he asked me 'if I knew what was decided on in your case?' 'No; I should ask you that.' 'Nothing was when I left office, and there are many serious points to be considered before so strong a measure is resorted to.' You will see that all the papers, Ministerial, opposition, and neutral, send either Malcolm or me to supersede you. Of myself I can say, nothing tending to an offer or a hint has been held out to me; and after I left the Duke of C. yesterday, I asked Malcolm what grounds he had to 'expect to be ordered' (as he does, having his secretary and flag-lieutenant and all his clothes, &c., ready for a start). 'None whatever except the Duke of W.'s good will that I shall have the first vacant command, and that he was very angry that Codrington got it instead of me; he urged it for me, but Cockburn carried his point for Codrington.' 'Then why, on such vague supposition, have you ordered Mr. Edie up from Plymouth to be your secretary?' 'Oh, I like to be ready, and whoever goes will be ordered off in 24 hours, as the "Wellesley" is detained purposely.' I replied, 'I am very glad you have not more substantial foundation, and I still think and hope that the Duke of W. will not recall Codrington.' And here the case rests. But you will know too soon if the decision is inimical, and may be left in painful suspense if otherwise. At all events you will have abundance of time to prepare for either, and to make up your mind accordingly.

*From Sir John Gore to Sir E. C.**

Saturday, June 7, 1828.

MY DEAR CODRINGTON,—I wrote to you by the packet on Wednesday last, and stated the substance of *reports* and conversations which prevailed in this strange metropolis;

* Received beginning of July, 1828.

and I wrote to you on the following day, by the post to Marseilles, to state to you in how much those reports were falsified, and verified, by the fact of Malcolm's appointment and order to proceed and relieve you in your command (in the 'Wellesley') on the 23rd. 'You are to hoist your flag in "Warspite," and return to Spithead,' so soon as Malcolm arrives. I had yesterday (by command) a long interview with the Lord High Admiral and Spencer on this subject; the latter will write to you fully by the 'Wellesley,' as he did by the packet on Wednesday. His Royal Highness desired me to write to you so soon as I could, and to tell you from him 'that he is very desirous that you remain as quiet as your feelings will admit; and not to write or to speak on the subject until you arrive in England—that blame is not attached to you*—that your recall is on political expediency emanating entirely from the Cabinet, from existing circumstances, and that he had nothing to do in it whatever but to obey the King's mandate through the Secretary of State.' †
I can only add to the above my earnest hope that you will adopt it in letter and in spirit; and though you will, of course, arrange all requisite documents in case any more questions should be asked; yet pray do not volunteer any defence until blame is attached to you. At present, I understand, none is or is intended to be. Your relief in the command of the Allied fleet is called for upon 'political expediency' of which the responsible advisers of the Crown can alone judge, and are not bound to give any reason for. I do not mean to dispute that this is a very strong measure, and a very distressing one towards you or any other individual similarly circumstanced. But you will recollect that I predicted the probability of such a measure as a preliminary to any amicable negotiation with the Porte. Our Government have disowned the battle of Navarin, *you* are represented as the offender : 'then show your sincerity by removing the offender from this command in order that he may not offend again, and we will treat with you in confidence.' Such, I conclude, is the language held to our Government, whose anxious object is to preserve peace by every sacrifice short of national honor and independence; and I earnestly hope and trust that in being obliged to hurt your feelings individually for the general good, that they will, as soon as possible, make every reparation. In the meantime you have the consolation

* Sir J. Gore had been misinformed.
' † This and preceding letters show how completely the Duke of Clarence and other friends of Sir E. C were purposely kept in the dark as to the charges which had already been made the ground of his recall.

to know that your honor and character remain unshaken
on the high ground you have placed them; nor can you
imagine that the Government collectively or individually can
entertain any opinion or wish to injure you.   Their minds
are too much engrossed to admit of such sentiment, even if
their wishes had such bias.   I therefore earnestly hope and
entreat of you not to volunteer a defence until your conduct
is arraigned; and if it is, I feel assured that you possess
ample means to place your conduct before the world in such
light that no censure can attach to it.   If I were to attempt
to write all our feelings on this most anxious subject, I should
tire out all your patience.   I will, therefore, only add our
united sincere and affectionate good wishes to yourself, Lady
C., and family.   Pray believe me, at all times,

Your faithfully attached friend,

JOHN GORE.

From Sir E. C. to H.R.H. the Duke of Clarence.

'Asia,' off St. Maura : July 5, 1828.

SIR,—I did not receive Sir John Gore's letter of the 7th
of last month until after I had replied to Lord Aberdeen's
despatch, and had also addressed Your Royal Highness upon
the subject of my supersession, by my letter of the 24th.   I
judge, by what Sir J. Gore tells me, that Your Royal Highness was not then aware of the blame which the above despatch contains, and of the very different grounds therein
mentioned as having brought the Government to such a decision, from those which I understand to have been given
to Your Royal Highness.   As to secrecy, private letters
which reached Corfù even before Lord Aberdeen's despatch
arrived, mentioned the fact; and it was known throughout
France, and the purpose of it freely discussed, before any
hint of it reached me.   I therefore trust Your Royal Highness will approve of my having noticed it by my explanation through Mr. Croker, as well as by my reply to Lord
Aberdeen, of which I have herewith sent a copy.   The time
allowed for my writing those replies was shorter than such
a subject demanded, but it seemed to me very necessary
that Your Royal Highness should be informed without loss
of time, that the conduct of an officer who had received such
substantial marks of your good opinion had not fallen off
during an interval in which it had been withdrawn, as it
were, from your inspection in a somewhat mysterious manner.
To that explanation I shall have to make additions which
will elucidate the treatment which I have met with, and will

show at the same time in how much the ' good of His Majesty's service ' has been considered.   I will not go a step
further without assuring Your Royal Highness that I am
well aware of the necessity of such a desire on the part of the
Government being complied with, let their motives be what
they may; and that this very unusual proceeding cannot in
the smallest degree diminish my grateful sense of the kindness of His Majesty or of Your Royal Highness towards me.
Indeed, it is under this feeling that I find myself at liberty
to defy all the charges that can be arrayed against me, in
a full conviction of my being able to repel them by a plain
exposure of all my proceedings.   I only ask for publicity
and truth ; and under such circumstances no one can refuse
my claim.   Let me further assure Your Royal Highness, in
allusion to an expression of my friend Gore's letter, that
' irritated feelings ' I have none.   I feel that I stand upon
too high and too solid ground to subject me to such excitement.   That I have possessed the ambition to be distinguished
even among the distinguished men of which our profession
may well be proud, I am ready to acknowledge.   But I have
never felt the mean desire to receive unmerited applause ;
and I therefore trust I may with the greater propriety defend
myself against unmerited censure.   Gore seems to consider
the public good as requiring a sacrifice of me individually.
It is not requisite for me to discuss this matter politically ;
but I think events will again show that this very attempt is
the very worst way of bringing about the object proposed.
There are none near the scene of action who do not attribute the present unsettled, complicated, and unfortunate
state of affairs in the Levant to this very erroneous principle ;
and with such a conviction before me, I am confident it is
not less my duty to my country than to myself personally,
that I should defend myself against all the imputations of
my accusers.   The copy of Mr. Consul Barker's letter to
Lord Dudley will show that the deportation of Greeks has
been a continued practice ; and if the Government did not
take measures to prevent it, I cannot see what good is to
arise from my being loaded with the opprobrium of this barbarous practice, which I am sure Your Royal Highness will
believe I would gladly have put a stop to.   Ever since the
receipt of my letter, in which I put the simple question ' if
I was henceforth to stop the deportation for which blame
was imputed to me, and to take Greek slaves out of any
Turkish vessels going from Greece,' I have had no answer ;
but instead of their preventing a repetition of this offence,
to which the Allied fleet was liable, I am informed of my

meditated supersession for not having already done it without order or justification, and, in fact, in defiance of the instruction for my guidance.

I have, &c.,
EDWD. CODRINGTON.

Sir E. C. to Sir F. Adam.
(Extract.)

Sta Maura : July 5, 1828.

I hear that orders are gone after Count Guilleminot to join Mr. S. C. at Corfù. If so, M. de Ribeaupierre will be sent there likewise. Here I must stay, at all events until I know what line Ministers that are, or are to be, are decided on taking. I cannot act according to my own opinion, because it is evidently too strong for such feeble men as have had to do the work of Mr. Canning, and by Mr. S. C. not telling me what line he took with the Porte after the battle, I conclude he also has not ventured to use that decision which, in my humble opinion, would by this time have removed the Sultan's obstinacy. Half measures will only produce half effects ; and the present injurious state of affairs will produce increasing discontent, and oblige us in the end to proceed to still greater extremities.

Sir E. C. to Lady C.

Zante : July 9, 1828.

Well ! things become more and more complicated every day. It is quite impossible to guess even how Ibrahim will act. It would be a pretty moment for Malcolm to begin his command, and I wish he could have been present at a three hours' communication which I have just had with Capodistrias, de Heiden, and Parker.*

10 P.M.

We are again at sea, working up to Corfù to have a consultation with such of the principals as I may find there. At the conference with Ibrahim lately, he mentioned his knowing of my recall; upon which Heiden said, ' Yes, but do you know what it is for? not for the battle of Navarin, but for not having prevented you sending over the Greek slaves !' When Campbell told him my proposals for the redemption of those now in Egypt, he was quite furious ; and it is said† that De Rigny was much annoyed at its being mentioned. His ' inconséquence,' of which Heiden com-

---

* Captain Parker, of H.M.S. 'Warspite,' afterwards Admiral Sir William Parker.

† Which turned out to be without foundation.

plains so much, has led to a persuasion that he has entered
into some secret negotiation of his own for Ibrahim's retirement, and one which would not satisfy any of the other
parties. Lord Yarborough did not meet with the 'Dartmouth' (where he hoped to see his son), and is now going
back to Corfù with me. He and his party dined with me
yesterday. His 'Falcon' seems really a flyer, of which I
am very glad, as he deserves to have a good vessel under
him.

July 11.

We have not yet passed Cephalonia, but are working hard
for it against a foul wind, the quantity of which makes the
air very agreeable, although the thermometer stands at 81.
Adam has gone through my public and private letter books,
which increases his interest in my concerns. Will and I
have been working on with such fresh materials as have
reached me; and I verily believe I have as strong a case as
was ever exhibited. I really begin already to rejoice in my
supersession; from a conviction that whilst it relieves me
from a load which I could hardly hope to bear much longer
with impunity, it will at the same time occasion me more
credit in the end than if I had continued in the command
under such masters. Nothing can be more satisfactory to me
personally than the sensation made by my recall, and the
evident sorrow of those under my command; and this
notwithstanding that my successor is a popular commander.

I fear you are beginning to suffer from the heat, and I
must say that I wish we were on our way to England, as I
have lost the prospect of getting Ibrahim away as I expected,
unless the ambassadors bring an order to land troops and
proceed with more energy. Dyer* has been very ill, and is
still confined to his cabin; and Will does his duty, and does
it more usefully to me just now; he and Hal are quite well,
and as to me, I have ridden all over Corfù, and since at
Zante, with impunity. The commodore of the Royal Yacht
Club, Lord Yarborough, is quite pleased with my making
use of his 'Falcon.' I have put him in orders as directed
to wear a blue ensign, in order that the Allied ships during
the time he is with us may not take him for a Turk; and
we have therefore put his R.Y.C. into blue broad pendant,
that his letters may not be mistaken for crescents. I have
signalled him off to Corfù to announce my approach, and
prevent despatch vessels coming away in search of me.

On the 15th I received an order directed to the command-

* His Secretary.

ing officer who might be here, to send a ship to Ancona for
Mr. S. Canning, and accordingly the 'Talbot' is gone;
Spencer hoping that this will just wear out his time, and
that his relief may come so as to enable him to go home at
the same time with us. It is curious, that whilst De Rigny's
little inconsistencies lead not only the Russians, but all our
people to suspect him of playing a double game, he is actually
as much bent upon getting Ibrahim out for the sake of me
personally as for the good of the cause; and I believe
Guilleminot partakes warmly of his feeling. All this adds
to the singularity of my situation; that I should be so
approved of by not only all the English in these parts who
know what is passing, but by all the foreigners not only here,
but in their own countries; and that a line adopted in
common by my colleagues under the sanction of their Instructors, which is fully approved of in them, is to be the
occasion of my being superseded. What better could I have
under the circumstances? My case is now as strong as possible, and my right to make it public cannot be disputed, as
it might if I had not been officially censured. I hope we
shall have settled all the arrangements for Ibrahim's retirement before Malcolm reaches Malta; and I have no business
to quit the important service in execution here until I know
of his being actually arrived. The worst that can happen
will be his putting me into the 'Warspite' at once to make
room for him in the 'Asia'; but in that case 1 cannot give
him information on papers which are left at Malta, which 1
have to make over to him.

July 18.

The first part of this letter about De Rigny is, as you will
see, directly contrary to this latter part; and you will also
see that it is his own fault that these different impressions
are received. I do not believe those under him fully comprehend what they have to do, because whilst some of them
excite suspicion, others appear to act in harmony with our
plans of operation. I had to undergo the same suspicion of
him myself until we came to the time of trial, after which I
told him he need never thenceforward make himself uneasy
on account of any reports of difference betwixt him and me.
Will will write out for Ponsonby my last secret order to
Campbell, and I need not therefore go at length into the
prospect we now have of Ibrahim's retreat, so much in contradiction to the first part of this letter, which gives you the
impression on the minds of all the parties there mentioned.
If Heiden arrive here as we hope in a day or two, we shall
form a conference with Guilleminot and Adam, draw out a

Protocol, and proceed at once in execution of the project in regular form. If he fix the rendezvous at Zante, we shall draw up our Protocol here without him, and join him there. In the meantime, I have ordered the thing to be done, as you will see, and De Rigny has given the same orders to his ships off Alexandria, that no time may be lost. It is a long time since you heard of me, and you will be anxious, although you will have relied upon my working to good effect. I assure you that although we may be said to live in gaiety as far as our evenings are concerned, we are not idle; and you will again have reason to complain of Will's not giving more time to his sketch book. If I felt sure that you did not suffer from the heat I should be contented. I have no doubt of showing you that our time has not been lost. 'Racer' is in sight at a great distance, and little wind to help her. Mr. S. C. writes to his attaché here, that he does not expect to remain here many days. I conclude they are all going on to Constantinople again, and to tell the Sultan that the offending admiral is disgraced; and if they should have to add to my charge the retirement of Ibrahim against his sovereign's orders, they will have a nice message of it.

There was truth in this supposition, though not on the grounds which Sir E. Codrington imagined. The Government of England thought it worth while to employ a foreign ambassador for this their 'commission,' which was estimated at its full value by the amusing incredulity of the Reis Effendi!

Lord Aberdeen, writing to the Duke of Wellington on August 26, 1828, says, 'Monsieur de Zuylen appears to have *executed our commission* perfectly well in informing the Reis Effendi of the cause of Sir E. Codrington's recall,' and—

'The Reis Effendi had the utmost difficulty to comprehend the business at all ; and the notion that the Admiral had been remiss in the execution of measures of severity, seemed to him incredible. On the whole it made a very unfavourable impression at the time.'*

W. J. C.

---

* See Wellington Papers, vol. iv.

Sir E. C. to Lady C. (letter continued).

July 19.

Yesterday evening I got the letters by the 'Racer,' and late at night those by the 'Alexander Newsky.' I cannot describe the pain which it gives me to find you taking so much to heart an event which I am persuaded will eventually be beneficial to me, and consequently to us all. Nothing but a bad cause could justify your admitting such feelings as your letters betray. I well know the sense of justice and the warm affection, my dear Jane, in which those feelings originate; and I well know that I have much to endure before I can fully overcome such a power as that to which I am unwillingly opposed. But as truth and publicity are the only supporters I require; and as the choice of time, if left to my own judgment or the chance of a favorable opportunity over which I have no immediate control, are all the contingencies necessary to consider, I feel as fully confident of victory, if life be left to me or mine, as if I had again to deal with the Turks at Navarin. In the meantime, there is no great suffering or merit in this *endurance* as I have termed it; for, whilst I contemplate the exposure of false friends and accusers, I not only prove real friends who do honor to that title, but am making more and more friends every day. In short, my dear, over-anxious Jane, I am gaining 'golden opinions from all sorts of men;' and what would you wish for more?

Why, the interest which this business has excited in such people as the Ponsonbys and Bathurst at Malta, and Adam here, is a balance for any loss that falls upon me in quitting my command; and yet we have a catalogue to add which may well excite the envy of the most fortunate. Again, then, my dearest Jane, let me urge you to resume your natural firmness, and to show by your usual serenity and cheerfulness your reliance on a good cause. For myself, my only fear is that I shall become as proud as Lucifer, and look down upon other Secretaries of State as I do upon —— and —— and ——. As to your coming here, it is now too late, certainly, much as it would have gratified me and my ever dear friend Adam. I have kept my mind to the one point—my duty— and it is no fault of mine that it unexpectedly led me back to this place, instead of going to Navarin from Patras.

Ponsonby, or you, will have my secret order to Campbell, which will let you know what we are at, and by what my movements have been guided. Upon being joined by Malcolm, &c., I am to shift my flag into the 'Warspite;' and I propose sending the 'Warspite' to Malta to clear off

her quarantine, continuing out myself in execution of the
measures arranged. Malcolm will either send or come to
me. The worst he can do will be turning me out of the
'Asia' at sea,* which will be a harsh proceeding that will
hurt him more than me.

I look back to your letters before me, that I may leave
nothing material unanswered Be assured that if my letters
to Lord Dudley and his coadjutor Mr. Huskisson did not
prevent my supersession, nothing would have done so; and
therefore I repeat my content with things being as they are.
I must, however, declare my conviction that my supersession
is on account of the battle and the battle only. As to anything altering the decision of the Ministers, I not only don't
wish it, but I am persuaded I should lament it at first, and
have reason to regret it afterwards. Will will write to
Ponsonby an amusing *exposé* of our conference at Zante,
and of the Austrian consul's view of it.

2 P.M.

I hear Heiden is gone on to Kalamata, and I expect we
shall follow to-morrow.

Sir E. C. to Admiral de Rigny.

'Asia,' at Sea: July 10, 1828.

MONSIEUR L'AMIRAL,—It has always appeared to me that
Ibrahim Pacha would in no case proceed to Roumelia, and
that after the failure of the missions to him and to the
Viceroy, necessity, and necessity alone, would induce him to
consent to retire to Egypt. I was very sanguine in my hopes
to have reduced him to that necessity before this time, relying not only on a strict blockade by sea, but that some
effectual measures of a similar description would have been
carried into execution by land. In the event of his being
actuated by the pressure of such necessity, I am confident we
could prevent the deportation of any more Greek slaves; and
I also believe that we might reclaim a considerable number
of those already deported, and it certainly would be our
duty to press that point with all the force that the occasion
would justify. I am the more confident of the justness of
this opinion, by finding that it concurs with that now expressed by Your Excellency. The instructions given to me
by my Government respecting the blockade of Alexandria,
did not appear to me to contemplate the local peculiarities
which militated against it. In announcing this to my Government I requested further instructions; in the meantime

---

* This was done at Zante.

I have endeavoured to comply with the intentions therein indicated* by the order of which I have now the honor of enclosing a copy.

I have, &c.

EDWD. CODRINGTON.

From Sir E. Codrington to the Admiralty, enclosing a letter from Mr. Consul Barker, of May 24, 1828.

'Asia,' at Sea: July 11, 1828.

SIR,—I enclose, for the information of His Royal Highness the Lord High Admiral, the copy of a communication from Mr. Consul Barker on the subject of Greek slaves conveyed from the Morea. Mr. Barker's letter establishes the fact that the transmission of the Greeks in the vessels that quitted Navarin after the battle was one of those excesses which have been continually practised since the commencement of the war in the Morea, but with which His Majesty's Government has not thought fit to interfere. It is perfectly clear, however, that, even if the case referred to had been the general deportation described in that order, and, even if that order had been still open for me to act upon, instead of the service therein mentioned having been executed by my predecessor, I could not have interposed, and could only have reported the fact as I did. The practice of these excesses was well known to all our consuls and others resident in the Ottoman dominions, and also by the Government itself, as evinced by this very order. In reporting the fact alluded to, I courted instructions on this head; I subsequently asked the question in direct terms; and although my not having already done it is made one of the principal causes of my supersession, up to this moment I am not furnished with any authority to justify the officers on this station in preventing a repetition of these excesses. I have said in a former letter that, even if I had had a disposable force for the purpose—which I had not—and that if I had made an attempt to search the ships in question, which I must have enforced in case of refusal, it would necessarily have led to those hostilities which I am directed by all possible means to avoid. I think so still; and I am still of opinion, that my so doing would also have been in direct defiance of my instruction to encourage the return of the whole or part of the Turco-Egyptian forces to Greece. On the other hand it was laid down by His Majesty's Government for the guidance of my

* Order of July 9, 1828, directing that supplies be not permitted to leave Alexandria, for Candia or Greece.

A A 2

conduct, that England, not being a belligerent, could not claim the exercise of belligerent rights ; and it appears to me that the search of Ottoman ships of war, and the necessity of using force for carrying that search into effect, must be considered as the exercise of those rights.   If it should still be said that, by the allowing the return to Alexandria of so many useless mouths, I enabled Ibrahim to remain so much longer in the Morea, I might reply that the removal of his ships disabled him from performing any operations whatever in any other part, and exposed him at once to the consequences of a blockade which the Greeks could not have established in the presence of that fleet.   I very seriously lament being called upon to trouble His Royal Highness so much at length upon this subject.

He will, however, see how important it is to me to take the earliest opportunity of removing an imputation which the proceeding of His Majesty's Government in requiring my supersession might otherwise attach to me.   His Royal Highness will sanction my feeling that my character as an English Admiral should be above all blame, and I am doubly called upon to protect it on the present occasion in consequence of those distinguished honors which I have lately received,

I am, Sir, &c.,
EDWARD CODRINGTON.

Sir E. C. to Count Capodistrias, President of Greece.

'Asia,' at Sea . July 11, 1828.

MONSIEUR LE COMTE,—I feel it right, in regularity, that I should acknowledge the receipt of Your Excellency's letter of $\frac{May 23}{June 4}$, notwithstanding that I yesterday had the honor of discussing the subjects therein mentioned in a personal interview.   I am free to confess that I have never been able to form a satisfactory opinion upon the question of admitting certain supplies conditionally to Ibrahim Pacha, owing to the view which I was disposed to take of it being opposed to the sounder judgment of Your Excellency.   But, however ready to give up my own opinion on this point, I should not find myself at liberty to act on that of Your Excellency without the sanction either of the Ambassadors of the Allied Powers or of my own Government, seeing that it is in direct opposition to those orders to which I am already supposed not to have been sufficiently attentive.   All I can now do is to communicate the views and the wish of Your Excellency to the Ambassadors, whom I hope to find at Corfù.   I fully agree with Your Excellency as to the impossibility of opposing regular forces with the Roumeliotes or such other troops as you have at present at your disposal, however useful they may be in guarding defiles and cutting off communications.   Should the Allied Powers decide on a blockade by land in addition to the blockade by sea, the fate of Ibrahim's army must be decided immediately.

From Sir E. C. to Commodore Sir Thomas Staines, ' Isis.'

' Asia,' off Paxo : July 13, 1828.

MY DEAR SIR,—As the reason given by Lord Aberdeen for my supersession is a misconception on my part of the intentions of His Majesty's Government, I have sent you the best explanation I can of those intentions; and I have only to lament that I cannot so collect them myself from the documents which I have had to guide me, as to ensure your not falling into the same error, little as you may be likely to meet with similar consequences. I presume my successor (who I hear by private letters is Sir P. Malcolm) will not come out without more intelligible instructions, by which those under his command may benefit as well as himself.   I am returning to Corfù in the hope of meeting Mr. S. Canning, according to the wish of my colleagues and Count Capodistrias, all of whom have taken the same view of the instructions as I have.   In this view also I am joined by the Count Guilleminot, Sir F. Adam, and General Ponsonby ; so that it is presumable that the political expediency upon which my recall is grounded, means some concession to the Turks.   Be it what it may, I have no regret in being no longer exposed to the treatment which I have met with from the men in office, ever since the battle of Navarin.   No doubt I should have been glad under other circumstances to have seen this business well finished. Ibrahim was lately very much disposed to retire, but I think his knowledge of my recall will induce him to persevere, in expectation of some concession from our Government. I have written thus much now, because I doubt my having leisure to do so after the receipt of all the despatches which I understand are waiting for me at Corfù.   With an anxious desire that your future operations may be as successful as those at Carabusa,

Believe me, my dear Sir,
Your very sincere and faithful,
EDWD. CODRINGTON.

The increasing difficulties of Ibrahim's position in

the Morea led him to open a communication with the
Allied squadrons, which resulted in the following

*Conference at Modon, 6th July, 1828, between Ibrahim Pacha
and the French and Russian Admirals, and Commodore Campbell, on the part of Sir E. Codrington.*[*]

Les Amiraux français et russe et le Commodore Campbell
s'étant trouvés réunis devant Modon au moment où le brick
le 'Rifleman' arrivait d'Alexandrie et rapportait les réponses
aux dépêches pressées qu'Ibrahim Pacha avait demandé le
12 juin à faire passer à son père, convinrent de demander
une entrevue à S. Altesse pour l'interpeller au sujet de cette
réponse. Cette entrevue a eu lieu le 6 juillet à 11 heures du
matin, et voici autant que possible la substance de ce qui
fut dit :
On demanda d'abord à S. A. si la réponse qu'il avait reçue
était satisfaisante et d'une nature décisive.
Après quelques phrases évasives, suivant l'usage, Ibrahim
Pacha convint que la réponse était telle que si les moyens de
transport arrivaient, il s'embarquerait à l'instant avec ses
troupes et retournerait en Égypte. Sur la prière de répéter
cette assertion il la confirma. Tels étaient les ordres de son
père, a-t-il dit.
On lui représenta alors qu'une telle détermination demandait qu'on s'accordât d'avance sur certains points, dans
le détail desquels il convenait d'entrer.
Il répondit que ces détails s'arrangeraient facilement au
moment de l'exécution de la mesure principale ; que quant à
la quantité de troupes et aux moyens de transport nécessaires,
son père connaissait la situation exacte, et proportionnerait
l'une à l'autre.
On lui demanda alors si, supposé la flotte arrivée aujour-
d'hui, il était prêt à s'embarquer. 'À l'instant,' a-t-il
répondu.
Dans ce moment un des colonels (le col. Sève) de son armée
(il y en avait cinq présens [†]) prit la parole et dit : 'Messieurs,
il ne peut y avoir de doute là-dessus, et quand il ne le voudrait,
nous le forcerions. Nous avons résolu de quitter ; nous avons
écrit à Méhémet Ali pour lui faire savoir la résolution des
régimens : elle est unanime. Que la flotte vienne ; nous
l'embarquerons de force s'il le faut ; nous sommes venus ici
pour faire la guerre et non pour mourir de faim.'
On raisonna alors dans la supposition de l'arrivée de la

---

[*] This was received by Sir E C. at Corfù, July 14.
[†] Ils l'avaient exigé.

flotte d'Égypte accompagnée de bâtimens alliés, et de la nécessité où se trouveraient ceux-ci d'entrer dans Navarin pour que l'évacuation se fît avec ordre. Ibrahim ne fit à cela d'autre objection que celle que les Russes étant en guerre déclarée, cela pourrait inquiéter les troupes, mais qu'après tout cela ne ferait pas une difficulté. Le comte Heiden offrit, s'il s'en élevait à ce sujet, de ne pas faire entrer ses bâtimens dans l'intérieur.

Ibrahim prit une occasion favorable pour demander si les amiraux alliés n'avaient pas connaissance que depuis huit mois qu'il savait les désirs et les déclarations des cours alliées au sujet des ravages de la guerre, il s'était abstenu de toute hostilité et toute attaque de quelque genre que ce fût contre les Grecs. On reconnut que telle était la vérité.

Il demanda encore si les amiraux ignoraient que depuis peu de jours il avait fait remettre en pleine liberté 800 à 900 Grecs prisonniers, dont il s'était fait donner reçu.

Rentrant alors dans les conditions préliminaires de l'évacuation, on lui déclara qu'il lui restait interdit d'emmener aucun esclave grec en Égypte. Il répondit qu'il s'engageait à n'en emmener aucun.

Le commodore Campbell, ainsi que les autres officiers anglais, firent à Ibrahim la proposition de rendre non-seulement les esclaves actuellement en Morée, mais encore ceux portés en Égypte depuis la bataille de Navarin.

Ibrahim se récria à cet égard, en disant qu'il offrait tout ce qui était en son pouvoir, et qu'une telle condition excédait son pouvoir et sa situation.

Sur cela le commodore répliqua qu'il faisait cette proposition d'après les instructions de son amiral, et afin que si au moment de l'arrangement définitif elle venait à lui être répétée, S. A. ne pût pas alléguer qu'on lui faisait des propositions nouvelles. Qu'au reste le commodore ne peut pas dire que c'était une condition *sine quâ non* de son Gouvernement.

Enfin, après quelques interruptions, la conférence fut résumée, et terminée à peu près en ces termes :

Si les moyens de transport (Ibrahim avait déclaré qu'il ne voulait quitter que sur un bâtiment turc) lui arrivent, il devra évacuer en emmenant aucun Grec esclave.

La flotte et les bâtimens de guerre alliés entreraient dans Navarin.

(Nulle mention n'a été faite dans cette discussion de ce que deviendraient les places qu'il occupe.)

On ne prétend pas avoir ici le tracé, tous les détails, et les incidens de cette conférence, qui a duré près de trois heures, et dans laquelle le nombre des assistants et des interlocuteurs était assez considérable.   On s'est attaché à en présenter la substance et le résultat.

La question ne roule aujourd'hui que sur deux difficultés. Car il est évident que, soit par le manque de vivres, soit par la volonté des chefs et des troupes dont il n'est plus maître, il faut qu'Ibrahim quitte ou qu'il dévaste le pays.

Ces deux difficultés, les moyens de transport à lui laisser venir d'Égypte, dans la crainte que ces transports ne servent par ruse à lui apporter des vivres ; mais il est évident qu'en les escortant, et qu'en entrant dans Navarin avec eux, il n'y a rien à craindre à cet égard.

La seconde tient aux esclaves disséminés dans toutes les parties de l'Égypte depuis le commencement de la guerre, et dont personne ne connaît ni le nombre ni le catalogue.

Mais c'est une convention *sine quâ non* à faire si l'on veut avec Mohammed Ali, qui doit donner des garanties pour la libération de ces esclaves.

J'ai été présent à la conférence dont le résumé se trouve ci-dessus indiqué.

LE COMTE DE HEIDEN,

Vice-Amiral au service de Sa Majesté l'Empereur de toutes les Russies.

PATK. CAMPBELL,

Commodore, His Britannic Majesty's Service.

H. DE RIGNY, Vice-Amiral
Com^t· l'Escadre de S.M.T.C.

Notes made by Captain Gregory of the Conference at Modon with Ibrahim Pacha, July 6, 1828.

After the usual compliments, Monsieur De Rigny said, the interview had been requested in order to know what answer had been brought by the messenger who arrived in the 'Rifleman.' The Pacha replied, he had written for supplies, and Mehemet had referred him to the Allied Admirals. He was told the Allied squadrons were here to prevent supplies arriving, and that the blockade would be continued with the greatest rigour. Count Heiden added that the period was probably not very distant when troops would be landed in addition to the naval forces. The following is the substance of Ibrahim's answers to various questions and remarks by Count Heiden and Admiral De Rigny. If troops are landed they should know how to defend themselves—that they could die but once. He was fully aware of the kind intention of the Allies towards him, and had given proofs of it in remaining quiet without making any movement for eight months, and in giving their liberty to 800 Greek slaves without any ransom, which he contrasted with the conduct of the Greeks towards him. The time was not yet arrived for his giving up the possession of the Morea, and he would convince the Allied officers of it by showing them his magazines. He was not in the situation of European generals, who might capitulate with honor, as in their country there were laws and customs that enabled them to do so, none of which existed in the country and under the government he served. Whatever his own wishes might be, he must consult the prejudices of those about him. The Pachas who had capitulated did not do so until they were reduced to eat human flesh and leaves of trees; but that he was not yet reduced to that, nor ever intended to be. He said it was true he had told the Allied officers at their last conference that he was very much straitened for provisions, and that his colonels and troops wished to return to Egypt. He objected to or adjourned the exchange of four Greeks who were named by Count Heiden, and made some allusions to the corvette that had been detained by him. He entered into explanations relating to the late affair with Albanians. The conversation then became general, and Monsieur De Rigny was talking very earnestly with the dragoman and the Pacha, when he suddenly called everyone's attention to what he said was an important fact, and might be of service, and begged the dragoman to repeat what he had just been saying. The following is the verbatim of what was said by Ibrahim in answer to different questions and propositions:—He was quite ready and willing to embark and evacuate the Morea the moment a fleet arrived to bring him away; he came in a Turkish ship, and would return in no other. The conditions could be made, and guarantees given, when the fleet should arrive, when it would be time enough to enter into details; but he was quite ready to go. On Captain Mitchell observing (in answer to an observation of Admiral De Rigny that he had private intelligence that the Pacha of Egypt intended to send vessels in thirty days to bring away Ibrahim's army), that the Pacha had held language to him, Captain Mitchell, which did not tend to confirm such a report,—Ibrahim was again asked to declare frankly what answer he had received. He said it was that he should receive an answer in twenty-five days. Monsieur De Rigny again said, that he understood Mehemet had consented to send ships to bring him away in thirty days. To which Ibrahim replied, turning to Monsieur de Rigny: 'If

you have such intelligence, why press me any further?'
Suleiman Bey then said, that he spoke in the name of the
colonels and chiefs of the army, who were all tired with the
service upon which they were employed, and would embark on
board a fleet the moment one came to fetch them; and if
Ibrahim made any opposition they would bind him hand and
foot and take him on board. That the answer received yesterday merely desired them to have patience, and care should
be taken of them. This having caused some interruption,
during the time that everyone was standing, Commodore
Campbell told Admiral De Rigny that Ibrahim must be informed, in order to be aware of the conditions upon which
Mehemet's fleet would be allowed to enter Navarin, and of
which nothing had been said, that such a step would not be
allowed until sufficient guarantees had been given, both by
himself and Mehemet, for the restitution of the Greek slaves,
both those in the Morea as well as those already conveyed
to Egypt; as the instructions of the British commander did
not authorise him to close any negotiation without this being
agreed upon. It was explained, that although it was not
positive that such a condition would be required, yet it
still was one on which the Government might insist before
coming to any decisive arrangement; and that he, Commodore Campbell, thought it right not to quit his Highness
without making him acquainted with it; that, in case the
negotiations were renewed, the Pacha might not say that
fresh conditions had been brought forward since this present
conference. The Pacha protested loudly against this; he
said he was perfectly willing to give up all the slaves he
had with him in the Morea, but to make such a request
for those already conveyed to Egypt, was a blow at their
religion and their customs, and would be looked upon as
the greatest of exactions and the grossest injustice; that
it would come in contact with their most inveterate prejudices, and would infallibly create confusion and revolution
from one end of the country to the other; and however
willing to give up their own slaves here, they would all
rather die than consent to a proposition they deemed so
monstrous; that it ought not to be proposed, and was an
act of injustice as regarded the time of making it; that
it should have been done immediately after the battle of
Navarin, and before those slaves had been sent over.

From Admiral Heiden to Sir E. C. *
(*Private.*)

Navarin · ce 7 juillet 1828.

MON CHER AMIRAL,—Je profite du 'Rifleman' pour vous dire deux mots. Nous avons eu une conférence avec Ibrahim sur le désir de M. de Rigny. Nous sommes tout aussi loin que nous étions, avec la seule différence que les troupes d'Ibrahim veulent partir; mais, au reste, le père ment, le fils ment et tout le monde trompe. Aussi longtems qu'on n'enverra pas 3 à 4 mille hommes et une batterie de canons on ne fera rien, mais du moment que ceux-là débarquent la capitulation est faite dans une semaine. M. de Rigny veut que nous écrivions à Méhémet; je crois que c'est seulement nous compromettre et nous rendre ridicules.   .   .   .

Adieu, mon cher Amiral. Je me recommande à votre souvenir et amitié.

HEIDEN.

From Admiral De Rigny. †
(*Private.*)

'Conquérant,' sous Céphalonie: 8 juillet.

MON CHER AMIRAL,—Je rencontre le 'Loiret,' qui m'annonce que vous êtes parti de Corfou, venant à Navarin, que j'ai quitté avant hier à minuit. Je suis désespéré de ne point vous trouver dans un évènement décisif, et qu'il ne fallait pas que vous laissiez à votre successeur.

Il m'est impossible de vous donner des détails circonstanciés sur ce qui vient de se passer à Modon. Nous avons eu une entrevue avec Ibrahim; je joins ici à tout hasard le protocol.

From Admiral De Rigny to Sir E. C.

'Conquérant,' près Paxo: 11 juillet 1828.

MONSIEUR L'AMIRAL,—Les mesures que V. E. a si judicieusement prescrites dans l'ordre général du 24 mai ont eu le résultat que nous pouvions espérer, et peut-être même ont-elles dépassé nos espérances.

Ibrahim Pacha, réduit par la sévérité du blocus, se voit contraint, sois par le manque absolu de vivres, soit par la révolte établie dans son propre camp, de déclarer qu'il est prêt à retourner en Égypte aussitôt que les moyens de transport lui seront fournis par son père.

Nous pouvons donc croire que, sans ajouter l'emploi de troupes de terre, l'évacuation de la Morée est sur le point

* Received at Corfù, July 14.   † Received July 14.

d'être accompli. Cet évènement, qui ne peut manquer d'être vivement désiré par nos gouvernemens respectifs, ne me paraît plus tenir qu'aux conditions que nous y mettrons. Je me hâte, après avoir pris connaissance de l'état des choses dans l'entrevue que le comte Heiden, le commodore Campbell (en votre nom) et moi avons eue avec Ibrahim le 6 juillet, de venir vous rejoindre pour combiner les moyens d'exécution qui doivent amener ce dénouement.

Je dois désirer en mon particulier qu'avant de quitter le commandement de l'escadre de S. M. B. vous assistiez à l'accomplissement d'une telle mesure—d'une mesure aussi décisive—et qui terminera avec un succès incontestable la série des devoirs difficiles que nous avons été appelés à remplir en commun.

Agréez la nouvelle assurance de ma haute considération.

Le Vice-Amiral

H. DE RIGNY.

Sir E. C. to Count Heiden.

Corfù: Monday night, July 14, 1828.

MY DEAR ADMIRAL,—Mr. S. Canning is not arrived nor is Monsieur Ribeaupierre. But after a consultation with our colleague, Count Guilleminot, and Sir F. Adam, I am most decidedly of opinion that we should forward Ibrahim's retirement in the manner proposed, with all the haste which the circumstances admit of. In order to arrange our plans, I propose that you should come here directly, and if our Ambassadors should arrive in the meantime we should be ready to meet them. If you should be got past Zante before you receive this, and should prefer our meeting at Zante by way of saving time, write word so by Captain Mitchell, and De Rigny and I will meet you there. I wish you could have heard De Rigny explain to us all his sentiments as well as all that has passed betwixt him and Ibrahim, his Dragoman, the Viceroy, Drovetti, &c. I am quite sure in such case you would agree with us in his zeal and honest anxiety to perform the service in the manner most satisfactory to us all. I will undertake whenever I meet you to convince you of the rectitude of his intentions throughout in spite of those little 'inconséquences' which give rise to that 'méfiance' which I know it is disagreeable to you to entertain towards anybody. I shall not have time to write to Count Capodistrias now: I will therefore beg you to explain that upon weighing well his objections to the fortresses being put into the hands of the Turks, in whose possession they were before Ibrahim arrived in the Morea, I do not think it a consideration that should interfere with the great object of getting rid of the Egyptian forces. If Ibrahim gave those places up to the Greeks, he might be accused of treason, and therefore would refuse to go away upon those terms : and the Allies would be more inclined to land a few troops to finish the remainder of the work, than to land a large force to attack the whole Egyptian army. Indeed after getting rid of the principal force, there are various means of obtaining possession of the fortified places which would be left in the hands of a few unwilling Turks. A little money might do the thing at once. The preparation of the ships at Alexandria, whatever may be the pretended purpose, depend upon it, is with the view of bringing Ibrahim over. The Viceroy himself consents to their coming under the protection of our ships; and if we once have them at sea, surely we can do as we wish with them. We need not let them enter Navarin without our fleet going in with them by a previous agreement with Ibrahim, which he is very desirous of making. However, I have said enough for the present, and am very confident in the good results of the proposed plan : and not less so of the uprightness and sincerity of our colleague.

Your sincere friend,
EDWD. CODRINGTON.

From Admiral Heiden to Sir E. C.*

Zante : ce $\frac{4}{15}$ juillet 1828.

MON CHER AMIRAL,—   .   .   .   .   .
Il n'y a pas de doute qu'il faut laisser partir Ibrahim avec toutes les facilités possibles, et le plus vite le mieux; mais je n'y crois rien encore ; ils nous ont tant de fois trompés que je crains que ce n'est pas la dernière fois. Pour ce qui regarde la reddition aux Turcs, c'est une idée qu'on leur a mis en tête ; je ne sais trop pourquoi : il pourrait y avoir une arrière-pensée. Mais il est vrai que nous n'avons pas les moyens de le forcer, et c'est pourquoi nous serions trop heureux d'être quittes de lui, sauf à nous arranger avec les Turcs après. Le comte† dit qu'il n'a jamais fait d'objections à cela; mais seulement il dit que si Ibrahim s'en va, qu'alors le 'Pélopon-nèse' ne sera pas encore libre pour cela. Je suis aussi d'accord que nous devons entrer ensemble à Navarin, et (quoique je n'entrerai pas moi-même si cela ferait des difficultés, comme notre ami Rigny l'a insinué à Ibrahim en ma présence, quoique je ne l'ai pas entendu moi-même,) je voudrais cependant que quelques bâtimens y fussent présents, et nous

---

* Received at Corfù, July 19.   † Capodistrias.

devrons choisir celui qui aura le commandement sur tous. Je voudrais que ce fût vous, Monsr l'Amiral, en personne. Au reste j'étais d'accord sur tous ces points avec Monsr de Rigny; mais pour envoyer à Méhémet Ali je crois que, puisque la négociation a commencé par les Francais, et sans que les Anglais s'en doutaient, puisque Mr. Mitchel n'a pas été mis du secret, qu'il vaut mieux que Monsr de Rigny fasse cette démarche seul : il peut dire que nous, ou du moins j'y accède de bonne foi, et protégerai tout bâtiment qui aura une destination pour emmener Ibrahim en Égypte; mais encore une fois, Monsr l'Amiral, je crains que ce diable de Méhémet Ali ne nous trompe. Je serai toujours bien avec notre collègue, mais je n'aime pas ces intrigues françaises, dont au reste je n'ai pas peur, car nous avons des yeux et du *common sense* tout comme un autre ; par conséquent je ne serai pas dupe, mais loyauté et franchise sont ma devise. Adieu, mon cher Amiral.

Votre très-dévoué ami,

HEIDEN.

P.S.—Le comte Capodistrias se hâte pour retourner chez lui; cela me lie plus ou moins les mains pour le moment, puisque je l'ai pris à bord de mon vaisseau dans l'absence de son escadrille, et je ne voudrais pas le faire retourner sur son brick grec sans personne pour l'accompagner.

Sir E. C. to J. Barker, Esq., H.M. Consul at Alexandria.

'Asia,' at Corfù : July 16, 1828.

SIR,—I think it right to apprise you of the result which we expect will arise from the conference which took place with Ibrahim Pacha, upon the return of His Majesty's sloop 'Rifleman.' The Pacha is certainly very willing to retire from the Morea, if he can find such a justification as will secure him against the anger of the Sultan, and no doubt the Viceroy will be very glad to have him back upon those terms. His fleet is now preparing *ostensibly* to convey provisions, which he well knows it could not effect without our sanction. This fleet *can be permitted* to come out unperceived, and after being out, can be conveyed under protection of our squadrons to Navarin. When off Navarin, an agreement can be made with Ibrahim for his fleet and the blockading fleet to enter together, for the purpose of securing the embarkation of his army, and conveying it to Alexandria. I think you will find the Viceroy ready to sanction all this, and as fully prepared for it as Ibrahim is ; but you and Monsieur Drovetti can communicate privately with his confidant without loss of time

upon this matter, and let me know the result. We have sent
for Admiral de Heiden to arrange the business more fully, and
you will then hear further. He will give up entirely his
belligerent character for the occasion, and we shall be responsible for the honorable execution of the plan. Our object
is so to execute it that neither the Viceroy nor the Pacha
may be compromised by it with the Porte. Ibrahim is ready
to give up all the Greeks he can, and you know the Viceroy
is the same; and in restoring all the Turks we can collect,
including those of the corvette, we shall require the Viceroy
to recover as many of the Greeks already sent over as he *may
have it in his power to do*, upon the footing of a general exchange of prisoners. The Viceroy must be made to understand clearly that it is only upon these terms the blockade
which has been ordered off Alexandria, can be, for the time,
suspended; and that any attempt to deceive us will be made
by us fatal to Ibrahim and his army; for from that moment
we could rely upon nothing but their entire destruction. As
this plan of operations has been already arranged principally
by Monsieur Drovetti, with whom the Pacha of Egypt has
been so long in confidence, I could wish you to allow him
rather to take a lead in it. I did not like that such an important arrangement should take place, without you, as our
representative, being equally a principal in it; and in thus
giving you my confidence, I am sure I can rely upon your
discretion in the mode of effecting it.

I have, &c.,

EDWD. CODRINGTON.

From Sir E. C. to Commodore Campbell.
(*Secret.*)

'Asia,' at Corfù : July 16, 1828.

SIR,—I have the honor of enclosing the copy of a letter
which I have written to Mr. Consul Barker, which will
sufficiently explain to you the line of conduct which it will
be requisite for you to observe when the operation therein
referred to will be to be carried into effect.* If therefore at
any time the Viceroy's fleet should be observed coming out of
Alexandria, the blockading force must be drawn away to
such a distance as will prevent in the first instance any
apparent understanding with us, leaving small vessels to
watch and give notice of its movements. When once caught
(as it might seem) at sea, we can insist upon its coming to

---

* This plan arose from a suggestion of Mons. Drovetti, Consul-General of
France in Egypt.

Navarin to embark the army. Ibrahim has pledged himself to embark in any Ottoman fleet which may come to Navarin; and in order to ensure his doing so, the Ottoman fleet is not to be suffered to go into the port, until Ibrahim's consent is given to the Allied fleet accompanying it. These preliminaries once arranged, the execution then devolves on ourselves; and as in fact the whole plan has been made in concert, our business is to carry it into execution in such a manner as that neither the Viceroy nor Ibrahim may be compromised by the Sultan. Admiral De Rigny will give particular orders to the French officer commanding the detachment of French ships employed on the same service, to communicate openly and confidentially with you on this occasion. Under the present circumstances, this service becomes much more important than the blockade of the Morea; and I therefore wish you to proceed in the execution of it yourself.

I have, &c.,
EDWD. CODRINGTON.

Sir E. C. to H.R.H. the Duke of Clarence.

'Asia,' at Corfù: July 20, 1827.

SIR,—I have considered it right to make *secret* and to address to Your Royal Highness personally, some part of the information which leads me to rely upon the success of the measures which I am now, jointly with my colleagues, about to carry into execution. There has been an understanding between Vice-Admiral De Rigny and the Viceroy of Egypt, which has given rise to suspicions amongst both the English and the Russian officers, which the Admiral could not well explain to any other than myself, without danger both of compromising the Viceroy and his son, and of frustrating the plan proposed. This will account for many seeming inconsistencies and contradictions, which are much dwelt upon in confidential letters to me, but which I have not thought it advisable to place before Your Royal Highness. These representations have at times caused me much anxiety, until personal communications with the Vice-Admiral have removed it; and yet it has not been in my power by similar disclosure to produce the same effect on others, because the whole success depended upon secrecy. In these circumstances I have all along wished my colleague to act the principal part, under a persuasion that both the Viceroy and Ibrahim would be more confidential with him than with me, and that however necessity, and necessity alone, might pro-

duce the wish to retire, it would be brought about sooner
and on better terms through his mediation. The public
avowal of the revolt of the Albanians, and the reported
discontent of other portions of Ibrahim's army; the mission
of Baki Effendi to Corfù; the report of the extreme want of
provisions, and the petition of the colonels of Ibrahim's
army, both publicly sent to Alexandria; and the violent
conduct of Suleiman Bey (le Colonel Sève) at the late conference at Modon, have all been put forth to reconcile the
Porte to the necessity of the evacuation; and in order to
make still more plausible to the Sultan that retirement
which is considered as the first step towards the practical
execution of the Treaty of London, I propose waiving the
question of the fortified places being left in the hands of the
Turks, from whom Ibrahim received them. He has strongly
expressed his determination not to deliver the fortresses into
other hands than those of the Turks; and by yielding to
this objection we shall be enabled to press more strongly
that point which His Majesty's Government has so greatly
at heart, viz., the restoration of the deported Greeks. Your
Royal Highness will observe that no mention was made of
the fortified places in the conference at Modon on July 6.
This is a very difficult subject in the eyes of the Viceroy,
and it is mentioned only in Mons. Drovetti's letters to
Comte Guilleminot and Admiral De Rigny; but 1 may
inform your Royal Highness of my conviction that Count
Capodistrias would find it in the end a better measure to
leave them for the present in the hands of the Turks, than
be obliged to give the command of them to chiefs whom we
cannot trust. Ibrahim Pacha's objections are so strong, on
the ground that his delivering them to the Greeks would
seem a compromise with subjects, rebels to the Porte, that
the making it an indispensable condition might produce the
failure of the whole plan; but, nevertheless, we shall insist
as far as possible, without endangering the success of the
measure, on the complete evacuation of the Morea. I think
it will be evident to your Royal Highness that I cannot
possibly expect that any agreement we can make with Ibrahim should be reduced to writing. Had the business been
of a less delicate nature, I should have demanded it on this
occasion, notwithstanding its having been in vain attempted
by me at a former period. It is my intention to proceed to
sea this evening, in company with Vice-Admiral De Rigny,
to join our colleague, in order to carry into execution this
measure, which has been decided on in conference with Count
Guilleminot, Vice-Admiral De Rigny, and Sir Frederick

Adam: the látter has seen these letters to your Royal
Highness on the occasion.

I have, &c.,

EDWD. CODRINGTON.

From Admiral De Rigny to Sir E. C.

'Conquérant,' devant Navarin: 30 juillet 1828.

MONSIEUR L'AMIRAL,—Je pense que vous désirerez apprendre ce qui se passe à Modon.   Voici les détails que j'ai reçus
du Consul d'Autriche, qui s'est sauvé avant hier dans un
bateau, et m'est venu demander la permission de se retirer à
Zante.   Ibrahim est parti le 23 pour aller chercher des
vivres.   Il a pris 2,000 hommes avec lui; les Albanais, qui
s'étaient d'abord dirigés par l'Isthme de Corinthe, sont en
quelque méfiance des Grecs, et sont revenus vers Patras.
Achmet Pacha, qui commande là pour Ibrahim, a voulu les
faire rentrer dans l'ordre, ils l'ont tué; de manière qu'il y a
une grande confusion.   Si Ibrahim revient à Modon sans
vivres, le Consul dit qu'il y aura un grand tumulte; on ne
donne que deux onces de farine à chaque homme; tous les
chameaux sont mangés; il croit qu'il n'y a plus que pour dix
à quinze jours.

Hier j'ai envoyé un drogman au camp pour demander à
parler à Ibrahim.   Le Kiaja Bey a répondu (ce que je savais)
que son maître est allé vers Patras, et qu'il ne pourrait être
de retour avant six jours; et qu'il avait ordre de l'envoyer
chercher si nous le faisions demander.

Dans la conversation, tous les Turcs et Arabes qui ont
parlé ont répété qu'ils étaient prêts à s'en aller, mais qu'ils
mourraient plutôt de faim que d'évacuer sur d'autres bâtimens que les leurs.   Ils disent qu'ils seront 20,000 en tout.
Turcs et Arabes, et y compris ceux de Patras.   Je crois que
cela est exagéré; ils ont demandé si le vaisseau pourrait
sortir dans l'état où il est, et qu'on comptait y mettre les malades, qui sont 1,000 à 1,200.   Tout cela se disait en conversation sans caractère officiel.   Hier un bateau appartenant à un des bricks de Navarin, et qui allait faire de l'eau,
s'est sauvé par la petite passe de Sphactérie, et s'est dirigé
sur 'le Conquérant.'   Il y avait onze Grecs de la mer Noire:
ils ont fait les mêmes dépositions sur la quantité de vivres
qu'on donnait, et ont ajouté que des huit bâtimens qui sont
dans Navarin, deux seulement ont encore quelques jours de

* Received August 3, 1828.

provisions; les autres reçoivent leur pitance chaque jour de terre. Startouris dit la même chose.

Agréez l'assurance de ma haute considération.

H. DE RIGNY, Vice-Amiral.

From W. J. C. to General Ponsonby.

Corfù . July 19, 1828

DEAR SIR,—On *the* subject, it is quite useless for me to express how strongly I must feel in common with many, I am sure very many, others; besides, it wastes both time and temper when I may be telling you of as important things. I do sincerely trust that, after so much work of both mind and body, the time is not far off when Ibrahim will be forced to yield, and show those who have superseded my father, as well as England itself, that the ' unfortunate misconception ' of the instructions has nevertheless brought about the first main practical effect of the Treaty. It would, indeed I hope *will*, be a triumphant way of hauling down the flag, and carry conviction to everyone, except the authors of the injustice, that he has acted up to even more than the spirit of his instructions.

The ' not restraining the Greek naval forces,' &c., and the not having inserted the word ' provisions,' are the only charges that have a shadow of truth or common sense in them. My father has certainly no positive written order to show that the conduct of the fleet was guided by that spirit. But the complaint is not that ' collision took place between the Greeks and Turks,' or that the Turks in the Morea received any supplies by means of neutrals, or that ' provisions ' were introduced; it is only, ' it might have so happened.' Parker decided correctly, and so decided in consequence of that full explanation and insight into everything that my father gave him, and generally gives instead of written orders to those who have the superintendence of any particular service. The other charges are iniquitous, and really, to me, betray a want of common sense in bringing charges which are refuted with so much ' facility.'

As to the ' facility ' with which that fleet got back, my father sends home a report of De Rigny's of where the line-of-battle ship and frigates were obliged to stop on their passage; and that at the time of their starting the ' La Flêche ' was anchored at Modon with three anchors ahead, blowing a gale from N.E. De Rigny has written a very strong and handsome letter, that he was responsible for Navarin being watched, that he could not have searched that fleet or stopped it by any order whatever in his possession; on the contrary, it was a partial fulfilment of his instructions —that it would have been both impolitic and inhuman to have prevented so many wounded people from returning. When we were at Zante lately we met Heiden, Capodistrias, and Parker, with whom my father had a long conversation at Stovin's Mole. Heiden being in quarantine as well as the other, my father was constantly doubling his fist at him to keep him off, and once was apparently drawing his sword, &c. It seems that all this, with certainly an eagerness of conversation on all sides, has produced an account of the Admirals having had a serious difference almost amounting to personality; Capodistrias, not feeling so hot as the rest, kept his hat on, while the others had theirs off. The Austrian Consul, we hear, has *written this all officially*, which account will be very amusing to you perhaps if you hear it. Heiden, Capodistrias, and Parker were all brimful of De Rigny's apparent doubledealing. I send you the report of the conference at Modon on the memorable *July* 6. Mons. Dovretti has been using his influence apparently well; De Rigny knew what the others at that conference did not know —that Mehemet Ali had tacitly agreed to withdraw his troops from the Morea. Mitchell's interview with the Pacha of Egypt was productive of this answer only—that he could not answer before twenty-five days; so that, when Mitchell came to Navarin, De Rigny having also received despatches from Dovretti, the latter went much further, and felt so certain of the evacuation as to write an official letter to Capodistrias, saying it was agreed on, with one or two conditions. This further information of De Rigny's made all the others suspect there was underhand work for a different object. Of course the Pacha did not wish to commit himself to more than he could possibly help, and Dovretti is an old acquaintance of his, so that he naturally would not open to Mitchell or to Parker, or to anybody else in the same way. There was also a tremendous complaint against De Rigny, for having been overheard saying to Abro, 'Tell the Pacha to object to the Russians coming into Navarin when the fleet comes.' To their indignation, I may almost say, there were no bounds at this; but it came out very quietly from De Rigny to my father the other day: ' Oh, Ibrahim will make no objection to the Russians coming in, for the suggestion came from me, and I did it only out of a delicacy to Heiden on account of his belligerent character.' De Rigny is honest in this point of evacuation; he is so sure of it, that my father has sent for Heiden from wherever he is to come here,

or rendezvous at Zante, and then it is proposed that a protocol should be formed. A letter from Capodistrias attributes
the change for milder measures in Ibrahim to my father's
last intimation to him, and the strict measures of blockade;
and another from De Rigny attributes perhaps a greater
effect to the same causes. These will be sent home by the next
opportunity, and I hope will be used by the Duke of Clarence
to show the Ministry the justice of their cause. Barker en-
closes to my father his despatch in answer to Lord Dudley's
enquiring about slaves, which shows (to Lord Dudley most
provokingly) that ever since the beginning of the war in the
Morea, and subsequent even to 1826, prisoners and slaves
have been sent to Egypt, and no means taken to prevent it
by Government. The order to blockade Alexandria lately
given, is, to stop all vessels whatever under Ottoman flag, and
all neutrals under Ottoman convoy, from leaving the port.
The Pacha is to be given to understand fully, that the temporary suspension of this blockade will take place only on his
agreeing to the measure of evacuation; and a strong hint
that, should he attempt to deceive the Allies, their only means
of ensuring the effect of the Treaty would be in the entire
destruction of his army. The said blockade seemed to come
rather inopportunely, but it is thus made to help the cause.

Yours very truly,
W. J. CODRINGTON.

Sir E. C. to Lady C.

Off Corfù : July 21, 1828.

We came away from Corfù last night, as I may call it, for
it was nearly dark, after dining with Adam and meeting
·Guilleminot and De Rigny. We have the 'Falcon' and two
cutters with us, and the 'Syrène' is with 'Le Conquérant'
to leeward. I propose now, my dearest Jane, noticing the
contents of your lately-received letters. I do not agree with
you that there can be 'no recompense for my supersession,'
even in any sense of the word. In that which is of most
value in my eyes I feel that it depends mainly on myself to
produce, to the full extent, that approval of what is right of
which I have already had such strong evidence. I certainly
cannot prevent the worldly injustice of men in present power;
but, as we have experienced fully of late, they may not continue long in that power; and, in the meantime, I have such
practical evidence of the heart-felt approbation of those whose
good opinion is truly valuable, that I ought, on this account

alone, to rejoice rather than lament the persecution of such men as have been arrayed against me.

I will keep myself fully prepared for my defence against all assailants, and having justice on my side, I shall find myself, according to Shakespeare, three times as well armed as my opponent. De Rigny's view of this affair is perfectly just, and his feelings not less generous. As La Fayette has said, 'France has not the reproach of treating him ill,' and therefore he should not forsake her interests at an important moment. He is anxious, to a degree, to get Ibrahim's army away before I go; and I think he will find, in the completion of that great object of the Treaty, a good opportunity for his own retirement. It is most gratifying to witness the interest which both Guilleminot and De Rigny jointly take in my cause, and they have each expressed their sentiments to the French Government.

Rely upon it I am fully sensible of what I owe to the Duke of Clarence, and I will take care that he shall not find in me the least diminution of the feeling due to him in consequence of his not being able to protect me as much as I am sure he wishes. How sorry I should have been if his resignation had been produced by this act of injustice towards me; and yet how difficult it is to describe to him a feeling thus founded on esteem, lest it should hurt his consequence. I shall be able to bring it out one of these days. Next comes your letter of the 5th and 6th. But, my dear Jane, this very supersession is but a secondary point. Had I deserved such treatment, then indeed there would have been cause for lamentation; so, indeed, would there have been cause, if I had not the opportunity of making public the injustice of that treatment. Do not let me exceed you in that female virtue, 'patience'! Supported as I am, not only by conscious rectitude, but by the generous commendation of so many high-minded rivals in the pursuit of fame, I could endure an age of suspense with such a prospect as I have before me of eventual exposure. As Lord Essex writes, 'Justice, though slow, is sure to come sooner or later;' and her arrival will certainly be much expedited by my return to England.

My conviction is that the whole arises from the mistaken 'political expediency' of sacrificing me, if not to the Turks, to the Austrians. I trust a different policy will ere long give rise to a different expediency.

According to what you have experienced in your daughters, and I in my sons, their conduct alone repays our annoyance. What baseness it is in Huskisson to say that this matter was not decided on when he left office, unless Lord Aberdeen has falsely stated that it was settled on May 19! But they appear to me all alike in this sort of thing, and to stick at nothing that answers their temporary purpose. I shall throw no impediment in the way of M. putting to sea in the 'Asia' after we meet at Malta, if he settle on so meeting; because it will relieve me from more extensive explanations—explanations, moreover, upon some things, such as my instructions, I cannot be required to offer, since I am accused of not having understood them.

I cannot agree with you that this '*untoward* circumstance' could have been obviated; for I have no doubt of its having been always intended as a prelude to renewing negotiations with the Turks; and when could reasons have been given for it which are so easily refuted?

Recollect the load of falsehood and inconsistency by which this recall is now accompanied. The Duke of C. is told that it is in order to have the Treaty fulfilled, whilst I am myself told it is on account of my misconceiving the intention of Ministers. Then comes an assertion by Mr. H., the ex-Secretary, which is contradicted by Lord A., the in-Secretary. But it is needless to say further in how many instances I can expose the justice of my cause and the conduct of my accusers. My last letter will explain the grounds of my movements, and I hope will show you also some consoling probabilities.

Zante: July 24.

We are this moment arrived, and De Rigny in sight astern. I fear Heiden may have passed outside for Corfù; but I have sent to stop him, and, at all events, we have his assent, and shall proceed without him. My present purpose is to proceed myself towards Alexandria, by way of forwarding the object. This heat reduces our clothing to shirts and trousers, and I think we shall all benefit by *native climate air*. And now, my dearest Jane, let me entreat that, instead of being worried, you will take my view of my situation, and let my pleasure in the prospect before me be doubled by your being a sharer in it. E. C.

*Sir E. C. to Honorable Captain Spencer, Admiralty.**

Off Ithaca: July 22, 1828.

I had hardly time to read your two letters, my dear Spencer, of June 2 and 4, as you will see by my hurried acknowledgments of them, before Guilleminot's courier went away. In looking back to them I observe you have received

* Then Private Secretary to the Lord High Admiral.

that erroneous impression which others have purposely given
to the instruction of October 16.   Several points which did
not appear to be explained by the first instructions led both
De Rigny and myself to write upon them to the Ambassadors.   They in consequence had a conference, and sent home
a protocol with their opinions.   This produced a conference
and protocol in London, and the instructions of October 16
arose out of it.   We pointed out the effect of Turkish supplies going in neutrals ; of the Greek vessels quitting their
own coast, cruising at a distance and plundering our merchant ships ; and *I* specially dwelt upon the want of information as to preventing the movement of Ottoman vessels from
one port in Greece to another port in Greece both in their
own possession.   I also wrote to Lord Dudley in a private
letter about this ; and his private answer is his own condemnation, as it confirms most clearly that it was never
intended to bear the construction now put upon it.   This
answer is dated F.O., October 16, 1827,* the very date of the
Admiralty letter enclosing his order of the 15th.   He says,
' The instructions which go out to you along with this letter
are calculated to save you from what is most painful in the
discharge of an important public duty—any doubts as to the
limit of it.'   There are other things in this letter of his,
which begins by acknowledging the receipt of mine upon
this subject, which are valuable to me, as showing not only
that the true meaning of the instruction of October 16 is
entirely different to that which —— has applied to it for the
purpose of censuring me, but as marking the character of
the writer ; who, having given it to relieve me from ' what
is most painful,' now employs it by a most constrained reasoning for my condemnation.   But, my good friend, I must beg
you will look at the document itself, and the former instruction to which it refers, and which it is meant to elucidate.
You will then see that I could not possibly act upon it in
this new sense, without disobeying the principal injunction
so strongly enforced.   Lord Aberdeen (another great scholar)
says the instructions of October 16, for ' preventing *any*
movements by sea on the part of the Turkish or Egyptian
forces, were absolute.'   How then am I to effect the return
of all or part of those forces to Alexandria ?   Now, here am
I, who in the course of nine years during which I was a
midshipman, was never directed or advised to write or read,
or cultivate my mind in any way, pitted against two very
learned lords, with nothing but plain common sense to guide
me.   And if it were not for my conviction that common

* Vol. I., page 460.

sense and truth are more than a match for learning and
misrepresentation, I might well partake of those fears and
doubts which I see you and some other of my anxious
friends entertain as to my defence.   As it is, I fear not.

Thrice is he armed who hath his quarrel just, &c.

No doubt it is very disappointing to my family and friends, as
well as myself, to be so recalled, and at such a moment; and
undoubtedly it is very inconvenient, pecuniarily, after so
costly a battle, and an extra outfit in consequence; and I
should gladly have finished the arduous work in which I am
occupied, and completed my tour of duty with what credit my
conduct might have fairly earned me.   But in my proceedings
under my instructions I have not anything to lament whatever; and I am confident that the more those proceedings
are scrutinised the more credit I shall gain with all the unbiassed part of my countrymen.   Why, I am now on my
way, in company with De Rigny, as my last despatches show,
to effect the retreat of Ibrahim's army, in direct defiance of
this 'absolute' dictum of Lord Aberdeen, according to the
understanding of Adam, Guilleminot, De Rigny, De Heiden,
and myself of those same instructions.   Will Malcolm prevent this if he arrive in time with Lord Aberdeen's new
reading, and pacify Greece by forcing Ibrahim to ravage the
Morea for food ?   or will he adopt that construction for which
he is sent to supersede me?   In the one case, he will be at
issue with his colleagues and his instructions; in the other,
he is at variance with the Secretary for Foreign Affairs.
Now, my good fellow, once for all I shall never attribute
anything you may say or do in this all-engrossing concern
of mine to any but a kind feeling towards me; and the more
facts you can give me, and the more doubts you enable me
to clear away from your mind and that of other just persons,
the better.

.   .   .   .   .   .

You think these men in office are not personally hostile to
me; now, if *they* are not, their conduct is; and I have no
reason to believe the public good at all enters into their consideration.   In fact, the accusations are so weak that I am
induced to think that the blow given me was aimed at the
Lord High Admiral through me, whom he so nobly protected; and as my supersession is in such a case a very
secondary consideration, I entreat you, and all persons about
him, to prevent as much as possible his coming into collision
with Ministers upon my subject, and to leave my defence to
myself.   You must see that the Premier wishes to get rid

of him ; and you will know how important it is to the country in general, and to our service in particular, that he should hold his present situation. As to my speaking against the Government, you have here a specimen of the extent of it. Defend myself I will; and if in so doing, and showing my own rectitude, I prove their injustice, it is they who abuse themselves.

In fact they save me the trouble of abusing them by their own letters. Mr. Peel publicly asserts that a certain fact was comprised in forty-eight hours, which I show by dates, which he must have seen, extended to a whole month. Surely no one can offer a milder contradiction; and if my right honorable friend leaves his assertion unexplained, it is Mr. Peel who censures him and not I.

As to Mr. Huskisson and his closeted assistants,* I must remark that his declaration to John Gore that 'nothing was decided on as to my supersession when he left office, and that there were many serious points to be considered before so strong a measure should be resorted to,' is in direct contradiction to Lord Aberdeen's despatch, which says that the answer to my letter to Lord Dudley, mentioning my supersession, 'was approved by His Majesty's Government on May 19.'

Which of these two abuses the other, I don't pretend to say; but if they lived in the country of the Houyhnhnms, one of them would be supposed to have said 'the thing which is not.' Now pray, my dear Spencer, let our friend Wollaston indulge himself in accusing the Government of injustice; it is only what he thinks just, and he gratifies me by it extremely; for I consider the warm regard of such a friend as he is, ample balance against the hostility of a Secretary of State.

It seems that His Royal Highness partook of the surprise which his head councillor· loudly expressed at my staying at Malta. First, I naturally expected new instructions, if not on account of the battle, certainly on account of the Ambassadors leaving Constantinople without giving me any information of our then situation with the Porte. To Mr. S. C. I was told to look for instructions, and he retired without giving me any. I did not even know what passed betwixt him and the Porte relative to the battle or the cause of his coming away, although I know that he had directed the consuls to strike their flags. He had then attending on him, the

---

* This refers to the known hostility of certain individuals officially connected with his own profession.

'Dryad,' besides having had the 'Rifleman' a long time at the Dardanelles; the 'Raleigh' was conveying Mr. Elliot under his directions, and others carrying his despatches; whilst the 'Warspite,' the only ship in which I could have gone to sea, was, by Admiralty order, conveying Capodistrias to his presidency.   The 'Talbot,' which ship had my flag after the 'Asia' went away, was the first ship in which I could have proceeded to the Levant; and even if I had not known that I was doing much better service by being at Malta, I do not think it was to be expected that I should attempt to blockade the Ottoman ships in such a flagship.   And even if I had had an 'Asia' for the purpose of keeping the sea in winter, where was I to receive the loads of despatches which came to me much more fitly to Malta, and to carry on that correspondence with all the Ottoman dependencies, my colleagues, &c., or to meet such orders as I had a right to expect from Government?   Could I, by being at sea, have arranged the general service with my colleagues, and have put down piracy?   Why, the complaints of the Malta trade against the treatment they met with at Constantinople, which I sent home in a letter specially to say that, under my ignorance of the intentions of Government I did not propose to take any measure for the redress of the grievance, justified me in expecting further orders.   I have to add, that De Heiden showed me, by desire of his Emperor, instructions dated December 25, accompanied by information that I might expect similar orders from England.   And I am free to say that if such orders had been given to me, the Porte *must* have accepted our mediation, there would have been no Russian war, and we should have been arranging the affairs of Greece according to the Treaty.   Thus, whilst one of my colleagues had had orders which he was told were similar to what I might expect—and I was the more confirmed in this expectation by knowing how well those orders were suited to the occasion, and by his being directed to act entirely under me in the execution of them—my other colleague was, like myself, daily expecting fresh instructions, which his Government could not give on account of the indecision of ours; and under these circumstances, —— not only says 'What is the reason he is not at sea?'—but adds, 'Why does he stay at Malta, *doing nothing?*'   I think, my dear Spencer, you have now got a pretty full statement of my case; and whenever you hear me talked over in society, pray say that I am myself quite confident of being able to satisfy the public that I have done my duty, and that I court publicity that others may be enabled to judge for themselves.   As to any over zeal of my friends doing me harm, I am not of that opinion, and am delighted with such an expression of feeling.   I can never look for justice from people who have so treated me.

We are now panting for breath in a light air, betwixt Ithaca and Ataco, after having entered this channel in a breeze which made us go 10½ under skysails and royal studding-sails. I know not what chance there may arise for sending this, but here it is, ready, if any such should offer.   And thus endeth

Yours, with great regard,

EDWD. CODRINGTON.

CHAPTER VIII.

The result of the measures detailed in the last chapter, and the meeting of the three Admirals at Zante, was recorded in a Protocol* July 25, 1828, in consequence of which Sir E. Codrington sailed for Alexandria to communicate with Mehemet Ali himself.

Sir E. C. to Lady C.

Off Zante : July 25, 1828, 8 P.M.

De Heiden having joined us this forenoon, we had our conference at Stovin's parlatorio, which ended in the Protocol of which Datchkoff made the copy, which was smoked and given to me properly signed, and which was then copied twice by my *Foreign Secretary* (Will), signed by me, and given to my colleagues. This being settled I got on board after four o'clock, weighed, and came away for Navarin, where we shall be in the course of the night. If I escape to-morrow being called to Malta, I shall push on towards Alexandria, as required by the Protocol, in order to contribute personally as much as I can to the fulfilment of this primary object of the Treaty.

I can but make an apology for thus acting in opposition to Lord Aberdeen's ' absolute ' reading of my instructions !

De Rigny will come on to-night, and will have another interview with Ibrahim, and De Heiden will follow in a couple of days to continue the blockade (except getting his provisions somewhere among the islands), in readiness for the final operation if we succeed in our plan. I think by Ibrahim's not having committed himself to any objectionable proceeding since the receipt of my last *friendly epistle*— having paid the Greeks for all the provisions he has got in his expeditions for the purpose—having liberated eight hundred Greeks, and having promised to send no more away—is sufficient encouragement to us to believe in his decision to embark whenever the Alexandrian fleet appears, as he declares. And if the whole fails, we are but where we were,

* See Appendix.

with additional reason for using less ceremony with him.
Our boats at Prodano have been offered goats and fowls at a
moderate price, and have therefore concluded that there was
no scarcity in the camp; but I suspect this to be a plan of
my wily friend to deceive us; although he may not have
eaten all his camels and some of his horses, as Mr. Barker
at Alexandria reports, and as Ibrahim's colonels have notified to Mehemet Ali. In fact he gets up one trick for us
and another for the Sultan, in order to obtain from each
the better terms   But as he yields as far as he can to all
the terms my letter imposes in the first instance, and which
were renewed at the conference with him, I have endeavoured
to qualify the conditions of his retirement as much as I can,
to save him and the Viceroy from being compromised with
the Sultan; whilst we thus avoid any cause of interruption
to the execution of the measure. We may probably claim the
complete evacuation of the Morea in order to secure some
other doubtful point—perhaps about slaves—by giving it up.

For in fact, as I believe I have convinced Capodistrias
himself, the fortresses are more secure in the hands of the
Morean Turks than in those of any Greeks to whom he could
entrust them. At the same time he is right in using this
argument for the Allies still landing an army, because that
army would secure him against his villanous Capitani, who,
for want of such means of putting them down, are already
intriguing against him.

July 26.

Katakasi told us that the Emperor Nicholas showed a
trait of his character in his mode of doing what has never
before been done by a sovereign of Russia. A certain tribe
of Cossacks, persecuted by Catherine on account of religion,
settled under the dominion of Turkey; and one of them had
even become an Aga, and then a Pacha of two tails. These
Cossacks offered submission to Nicholas upon his reaching
the Danube; and he chose to show his confidence in them, by
actually crossing the river in the boat which had conveyed
the Pacha over, the said Pacha steering the boat.

1 P.M.

We have just had a fair view of the larboard broadside of
our Ottoman friend (the 'Asia's' opponent in the battle).
The division between the two midship ports of the main
deck, and also of the lower deck, is gone, and there remains
the great open space on each deck. The bow seems a mass
of patchwork. I cannot add more than

Your ever affec.

E. C.

Sir E. C. to Lady C.

Off Candia : July 30, 1828.

I know not when I have been so long at sea without addressing a line to you. I am now doing so actually for relief; I have been working again and again at this notable despatch from my Lord Aberdeen until I am quite sick of the whole mess of them. The more I look into my case, the stronger I find it, and the greater is the disgust it excites in me at such conduct from such men.

My friend Campbell must have pushed forward at once for Alexandria, as we are now doing after him, for we have not seen a single vessel of any sort the whole length of Candia. If I can once see the Viceroy's fleet outside under our control, I shall send you word of it; for then I shall have carried my point, let me be superseded whenever I may; although I should prefer seeing them again fairly out of Navarin also, with their cargo. My principal anxiety just now, however, is about you, and the heat which I fear you must find oppressive. I assure you for myself, I doubt if I could stand a third summer of such relaxation of body with such worry of mind, without permanent injury. The determination of the Government in itself gives me no uneasiness, although it causes me much trouble; since, besides suiting all of us on the score of health, it gives me the opportunity, the want of which made me uneasy, of making known the baseness of my traducers and the true character of my own conduct. I do not believe there is upon record a more flagrant instance of injustice—gratuitous injustice; for if they wish my removal as a compliment to the Porte, I would at such a suggestion have asked to be superseded at once. As it is, I can show proof of all their accusations and imputations being unfounded. Were I to stay here after Ibrahim's return I should have to be principally about Greece, where, from our narrow policy, things are likely to get worse; I cannot decide in my own mind what line will be taken respecting me by these people, and therefore can only prepare for every bad mode of proceeding, and I feel confident in being able to repel any attack which can be possibly made upon me.

Off Alexandria : at anchor, August 1, 9 P.M.

We anchored here, where we found ' Ocean ' and 'Pelorus,' about an hour ago. Campbell, who has just parlatorio'd with me under the quarter, with Richards, has read me a note from the Consuls to Boghos. The note says more than I think it ought; but they know their men better than I do. It seems the Viceroy is supposed to have had positive orders from the Sultan for Ibrahim's going to Roumelia. If he continue in this wavering state, or if he refuse to let the fleet, which is ready according to their fashion, come out, I shall not stay here; but if I do not hear of my successor I may perhaps return towards Corfù to explain to the Ambassadors the present state of things. In the meantime the advance of the Russians may verify Katakasi's opinion, that their successes will regulate the affairs of the Morea. We are all well, and all full of affection for you and yours.

E. C.

Sir E. C. to Mr. Consul Barker, Alexandria.

'Asia,' off Alexandria: August 2, 1828.

DEAR SIR,—As I find there has been a communication about carrying a messenger back to Navarin, I think it is as well to say that I do not feel at all disposed to accede to any more measures of this sort; if the fleet is to go for the troops, now is the time, or never. They (the troops) once moved towards Roumelia, will never again see Egypt: they will either be destroyed by the way, or taken permanent possession of by the Sultan. I fear the Viceroy is trying to deceive us; he had better pursue an open line of communication, as he will eventually find. His sending his vessels upon this experimental cruise just now is not consistent with his desire to send out the fleet for Ibrahim, and he must understand that, although I pledge myself to the safety of his ships from the Russians during this operation, I will not be responsible for them on experimental or other such cruises.

Very truly yours,

. EDWD. CODRINGTON.

Sir E. C. to Mr. Consul Barker, Alexandria.*

'Asia,' at anchor off Alexandria: August 4, 1828

SIR,—In consequence of the information contained in your letter of yesterday of His Highness the Viceroy of Egypt having decided on coming to Alexandria in order to confer with me personally on the arrangements for bringing Ibrahim Pacha and his army from the Morea, I propose entering the harbour in His Majesty's sloop 'Pelorus' this morning in order to meet His Highness' wishes. But before I commit myself to a long quarantine which will subject the other duties of my station to interruption, I must request that you will

---

* The arrival of the 'Asia' off Alexandria was telegraphed to Cairo; when the Pacha immediately came from thence to Alexandria

procure, on the part of His Highness, a distinct understanding, that the basis of our conference is to be a positive decision on his part, that his army shall be conveyed to Egypt from the Morea.

I have, &c.,
EDWD. CODRINGTON.

Mr. Consul Barker replied on the 4th that he had had an audience of an hour and a half with Mehemet Ali, and had conveyed to him all the purport of Sir E. C.'s message, and, in conjunction with Monsieur Drovetti, had discussed the matter with him, with the proposal of Sir E. C. to wait upon him, in order to carry out the negotiation.

His Highness replied, that there must be no precipitancy, that nothing must be done which could compromise, or commit him with the Porte; and seemed to think he had reason to complain that we were acting with too little regard to the extremely delicate situation in which he was placed. Having paused, Monsieur Drovetti and myself, in turn, seized the opportunity to assure him that His Highness had only to point out by what means the object he had in view could be best secured; and he would find Your Excellency most ready to co-operate with him in so desirable an end; and that the very steps now taken afforded abundant proofs of the friendship and regard which our respective Governments profess to entertain towards His Highness. ' Well, well,' lifting his hand to his forehead, ' my head is confused, I have not yet recovered from the fatigue of last night—to-morrow you shall have an answer.' . . . .

I have, &c.,
JOHN BARKER, Consul.

Sir E. C. to Mr. Consul Barker, Alexandria.

H.M.S. ' Asia': August 5, 1828.

SIR,—I cannot but regret the delay in the Viceroy's decision. It does not evince that good faith which my readiness to diminish his responsibility has entitled me to meet with from him. It puts me personally to great inconvenience; but that is trifling to what the Viceroy's own army is now undergoing. It has given me great pain to be the involuntary cause of their privations; and His Highness, upon reflection, will feel ten times more deeply the loss of his troops, if he should voluntarily occasion by unnecessary delays the prolongation of that misery which is now daily diminishing their numbers. However, this is his affair personally. My business is to let him understand that orders have been given to me by my Government even since the 6th of last April, to establish off Alexandria a like blockade to that on the coast of Greece, and His Highness well knows what have been the effects of that measure; a measure of which I have postponed the execution in order to prevent consequences which he would not cease to feel the effects of during the remainder of his life. I request that this letter may be immediately placed before Monsieur Boghos, that he may make known to the Viceroy the sentiments it contains.

I have, &c.,

EDWD. CODRINGTON.

On the 5th Mr. Barker had an interview with the Pacha, and wrote to Sir E. C. :—

His Highness said that no doubt could be entertained of the sincerity and ardour of his desire to treat for the object in question, since it was by his own order that Ibrahim Pacha had declared he was ready to embark, he and his army, whenever his father's ships should arrive to afford him the means of doing so. By which declaration he was in no danger of contracting any engagement inconsistent with his own honor, or that of the Vice Bey, because he well knew that if the ships did arrive, his father would have secured that point by stipulating that the fortresses should not be given up. Viewing, therefore, the case in his light, and considering that the offer to evacuate made by his son was, *bonâ fide* his own act, he had rather questions to ask than one to answer. 'Upon which conditions,' said he, 'is it proposed that the evacuation shall be effected?' Perceiving that the question was unexpected, and even unintelligible, he proceeded to ask another. How was the regard due to his honor to be provided for? which were at length both sunk in the simple declaration that he would send his vessels for his son, and his army, provided that you should not require the evacuation of the fortresses. That *that* condition was a *sine qua non*, for he would rather his son and all should perish than that his honor should be tarnished by his consenting to deliver up strongholds that had been mostly in the possession of the Sultan before he sent an army into the Morea. Neither myself nor Captain Richards being authorised to say that the question of the fortresses should not be considered as forming any part of the Treaty for the cuation of the Morea, it was agreed that the substance of this conference should be submitted to Your Excellency's consideration, and that you would let His Highness know whether you consented to come on shore to settle the minor points in the arrangements on the above-mentioned basis.

I have, &c.,

JOHN BARKER, Consul.

The English squadron was at anchor outside the reef which forms the port of Alexandria; but upon Mehemet Ali agreeing to the evacuation of the Morea as the basis for a Treaty, Sir Edward Codrington entered the harbour of Alexandria in one of the smaller vessels of war, anchoring near the Viceroy's palace, in which he had a conference with Mehemet Ali.

Minute of the Conference between Mehemet Ali Pacha and Vice-Admiral Sir E. Codrington.

Alexandria : August 6, 1828.

The Admiral, being at anchor off Alexandria, ordered Captain Richards, of H.M.S. 'Pelorus,' to obtain an interview with Mehemet Ali, and to state to him that, before he subjected the public service to any inconvenience by putting himself in quarantine, he must be assured by the Pacha, that the fixed basis of any conference between them should be the evacuation of the Morea.

In the interview which Captain Richards, with Monsieur Drovetti and Mr. Consul Barker had with the Pacha, he expressed himself ready to agree to this basis, but that his honor must not be compromised ; and after some time he declared that the delivering up the fortresses would be such a breach of good faith that he would rather allow Ibrahim and his whole army to perish, than that his honor should be tarnished by such an act. This interview here terminated, and the result being reported to the Admiral, it was considered a sufficient guarantee for him to treat upon the subject.

The Admiral accordingly went on shore about nine o'clock on August 6 to the Pacha's palace in the harbour of Alexandria.* He was met at the landing-place by Mons. Drovetti and Mr. Barker, with whom he had some conversation as to

---

* The Pacha with a crowd of his officers, was at his window looking on : the Capitana Bey and Moharem Bey were there, but retired as soon as the Admiral entered the Palace.

forms, &c., and, passing through the crowd of both Franks
and Turks assembled on the outside and within the palace,
we were conducted through an outer hall into the Pacha's
divan. He was standing up when we entered,* and his ad-
vancing some way into the room to meet the Admiral was
considered an additional mark of distinction. The Admiral
then presented the several officers who accompanied him,
after which we took our seats on the divan. The Pacha
having ordered coffee,† and after the usual questions about
health were asked according to custom, with some other
usual compliments, the Pacha· desired all his attendants,
except Mr. Boghos, his confidential interpreter, to withdraw;
and the Admiral also requested the greater part of those who
accompanied him to retire, leaving Commodore Campbell,
Captain Curzon, Captain Richards, Monsieur Drovetti, Mr.
Barker, and Captain Codrington.

The Admiral then enquired of Mr. Boghos if there would
be any objection on the part of the Pacha to the agreement
being made in writing, when the Pacha, understanding that
he referred to notes being taken of the conversation, made
objections to it. The Admiral then said that it was not the
conversation, but only the result that he referred to; that
his not having had a written agreement on a former occasion ‡
had led to some misunderstanding, and he therefore wished
that the final Treaty should be in writing and signed by both
parties. To this the Pacha acceded.

The Admiral then said that, as he was come to further the
arrangement for the evacuation, he would be glad to know if
His Highness had any particular proposals to make on the
subject; when the Pacha, bowing at the same time, answered
that it was for the Admiral to make any proposal he should
think fit.

The Admiral observed that His Highness must, of course,
be well aware of the state of the army under Ibrahim Pacha,
of the extreme misery to which it had been reduced, and
that those privations had given rise to revolts among the
troops, whose murmurs would certainly increase as their
distress became more pressing.

---

* With a scrupulous attention to his dignity, he adopts this mode, in order
that he may not be forced to rise from his seat, when the rank of the person
would call for such an attention.

† When Colonel Cradock went on his mission to him, he refused to give
him the pipe, saying that his so doing would be giving him the rank of *Ambassador*, that as dependent on the Porte, he could not receive him in that
light; and not being an ambassador, his rank was not equal to his own

‡ The interview of the Admirals with Ibrahim Pacha at Navarin, September 25, 1827.

His Highness allowed that the army was in a bad state, and remarked that misery would produce discontent in any troops, and he could not blame them for it; that the Admiral must also consider the extreme difficulty and delicacy of the situation in which he was placed, and that measures must not be hastily adopted, or without a regard to his honor.

The Admiral answered that he could well understand those difficulties, for *his* having been relieved in his command for not having carried his instructions into effect with what was considered sufficient strength, would show the Pacha that he also had his difficulties to contend with; that His Highness knew to what sufferings his army in the Morea was exposed, as well as how faithful that army had been to him under such privations; in return for this, he could not do less than afford them relief as quickly as possible; that, knowing the situation in which His Highness was thus placed, he had come, on the part of his colleagues and himself, to do what lay in his power towards removing the obstacles to the accomplishment of an object desired by the Allied Governments, and which could not be of less importance to His Highness.

The Pacha said he had heard of the Admiral's recall; he made but few remarks on the rest.

The Admiral continued, that the Allies were positively determined to carry the Treaty into effect; and that the anxiety to do so by pacific measures, and the consideration in which the Pacha was held by the British Government, had been shown by the several missions of Colonel Cradock and Sir F. Adam.

The Pacha answered, 'Ah! but there are now only two Allied Powers.'

The Admiral immediately said, that there could not be a plainer proof of the unanimity of the three Powers, than this measure having been adopted by their three Admirals in concert; and that the voluntary restriction of those belligerent rights which the Russians could exercise towards his fleet, was a sufficient earnest of the cordiality of the Allied Courts in carrying into effect the measures for the execution of the Treaty of July 6.

This passed without much remark from the Pacha.

The Admiral observed that his having come without express orders to Alexandria, must convince His Highness of his wish to terminate the business satisfactorily, without having recourse to other measures which had been for some time ordered. That the state of Ibrahim's army now, bad as it might be, would soon be worse; and His Highness must know that the terms under which his son would at length be forced to capitulate, would not be rendered easier on that account.

The Pacha answered, that whatever might have taken place, the subject must not be treated with precipitation, and observed that the difficulties of the Admiral's situation were light compared to his, for he had more to lose by having more at stake.

The Admiral said that *his* responsibility was great in treating on this subject under present circumstances, without a knowledge of the terms on which the Allies might now insist from the Pacha; that the Ambassadors might, for all that he knew, have received different instructions; and that whilst he was certain that any treaty entered into with His Highness would be ratified by them and their Governments, still his conduct might be disapproved of, and he himself hanged for it on his return to England.

At this the Pacha laughed heartily, and said there was no fear of that; but again repeated that a due regard must be paid to the difficulties of his situation, which were great.

The Admiral then dwelt on the necessity, for the sake of his own interest as well as his honor, and even his son's existence, that His Highness should employ without delay all the means he possibly could obtain in withdrawing his troops from the Morea, where their numbers were daily diminishing by hunger and disease.

The Viceroy replied, that when once the articles were settled, it would evidently be to his advantage that the evacuation should take place as quickly as possible.

The Admiral then brought the Pacha's attention to the fortresses, to the cession of which the Pacha had previously stated he could never consent; the allowing these fortresses to remain in Ottoman possession was a measure which, although he did not see any difficulty in acceding to, yet he might not be justified in the event; when the Pacha said that it was impossible that he could so sacrifice his honor as to give up those places which had been delivered into his charge; that he would rather that his army should be destroyed than that the Sultan should have reason to charge him with such a breach of faith.

The Admiral then mentioned that Navarin not having been at that time in possession of his troops, was, of course, not included, when the Pacha answered directly that this would be even a greater compromise of his honor than any other; for having been at the expense of conquering them for the Porte, the giving them up would be held as a wilful sacrifice to his own convenience, and a betrayal of the trust reposed in him by the Sultan.

The Admiral answered, that however he might take upon himself to allow the other fortresses to be retained, this was a much greater difficulty than any that had occurred in the whole negotiation; and willing as he was to make all allowance for His Highness's situation, this was a point which he had no authority for conceding.

The Pacha again repeated, that his honor was concerned in this more than any other part of the negotiation, and which, therefore, he dare not and could not concede; that the Admiral must know that in the last note presented by the Ambassadors, they agreed that the fortresses should remain in Ottoman possession.*

The Admiral said immediately that he had no knowledge of such an offer having been made, and would be glad could His Highness show him any written document in which that could be distinctly shown him.

The Pacha again said that it was the case, when Monsieur Drovetti confirmed what was said by the Viceroy.

The Admiral stated that he heard it then for the first time, and had no official intimation of it at all. His Highness, however, must see that what was agreed to in December might not now be conceded.

The Pacha again referred to this offer of the Ambassadors as a proof of their acquiescence, and repeated his former determination.

This point was very much discussed in all its bearings,† when finding that the Pacha was resolved, whatever consequences might ensue, not to agree to it,

The Admiral said that the only circumstance which might perhaps remove any objections on the part of his Government would be an engagement on the part of His Highness to do everything in his power towards obtaining the liberty of as many Greek slaves as possible; that His Highness was aware how loud the cry had been, both in England and France, on this subject, and more particularly by the deportation which took place subsequent to the battle of Navarin.

His Highness stated positively that not one slave had been made subsequent to the battle of Navarin; that the numbers had been absurdly exaggerated by the newspapers, both in

---

* Mr. S. Canning says that no such proposal was agreed to by the Ambassadors

† The Admiral always intended to yield this point, but pressed it hard in order to gain as much concession as possible with regard to the Greek slaves.

France and England, for there were not more than 1,900
Greeks brought over in all, of which nearly 1,200 were
Candiotes; that the greatest part of them were wives of the
officers and soldiers of his army in the Morea, who had been
married two or three years, and who took that opportunity
of sending them, as well as their children, to their own
country.*

The Admiral observed, that the not having prevented this
return of the ships containing slaves, was a great cause of
complaint against him, so that he must require everything
which could be done to obtain their release.

The Pacha insisted much on the very erroneous idea which
prevailed in Europe of the condition and treatment of slaves
in Egypt;† and among other remarks, brought the Mamelukes
forward to show this to be the case; for there were frequent
instances of Turks having called themselves Mamelukes in
order to become slaves.

The Admiral reminded His Highness how important it
was, for the sake of his own character, as well as that of his
son, that the truth should be known; when the Pacha said
that he would cause enquiry to be made and give the Admiral
a note on this subject. He promised, on the subject of the
galley slaves being mentioned by the Admiral, that as a
beginning he would place at his disposal those slaves in his
possession at the arsenal,‡ and that he would do all in his
power to obtain, as far as he could, the liberation of others.
He desired that it should be conducted on the footing of an
exchange of prisoners, and that the Admiral should obtain
the release of those in possession of the Greeks.

To this the Admiral consented.

The principal points having thus been settled, it was
pressed upon His Highness that preparation should commence instantly, and that it would be of advantage if even a
small number of vessels could be sent at once as an earnest
both to the Allies and Ibrahim that the evacuation was

* By the intercepted despatches from the Porte to Ibrahim Pacha, it is
proved that he had seriously intended to leave the Morea subsequent to the
battle of Navarin, but he was positively ordered to remain there by Mehemet Ali. It was in preparation for this departure that he and his officers
sent away their harems, &c, and it was in consequence of this reported intention on his part that the missions of Sir F. Adam and Col. Cradock took
place

† The women and boys are certainly not so unhappy as the name of
'slavery' implies. The two boys sent as presents by Tahir Pacha to Sir
E. C after the battle of Navarin cried bitterly on leaving him (Tahir Pacha)

‡ Notwithstanding all the Pacha's assurances, there is no doubt that the
slaves in the arsenal are miserably treated

begun; this the Pacha agreed to, and Mr. Boghos was ordered to hurry everything forward as much as possible. The Pacha requested that he might send some things for Ibrahim personally; to which the Admiral thought no objection would be made when once the evacuation had really commenced. His Highness also wished that he might have a safe conduct for a new frigate which was at Trieste, quite ready, and could assist in the embarkation; the Admiral replied that he did not anticipate any objection to this on the part of his colleagues.

The Pacha also wished, as it was on account of the communication between the Morea and Candia that the blockade of that island had been established, that he might now be permitted to send supplies from Egypt to that island.

The Admiral said that as Ottoman troops would still remain in the Morea the cause was not removed; that he had made his Government acquainted with that measure, and that their sanction must be obtained before he could allow anything to proceed to that island. Should the Ambassadors be at Corfù he would represent the matter to them, and it was possible that the point might be conceded, but that he could not take upon himself to decide that question.

The Admiral then rose to retire, when the Pacha hoped that he would come to see him again before he sailed, &c.*

Sir E. C. to Sir Frederick Adam.

Off Alexandria, 10 P M. · August 6, 1828.

A good story, my dear Adam, is seldom a very long one. I should not have sent off a vessel, perhaps, till one division (however small) as an earnest was actually out of the port. But as De Rigny's anxiety requires that his 'Diligente' should start with the first bit of intelligence, I take this means of telling you that the Viceroy, upon my assenting, after a hard wordy fight, to let Navarin be given up with the other fortresses to the Turks, has agreed to release not only all the Greeks he has here, and Ibrahim has in the Morea, but to recover all he can of those gone into the interior. He has acceded to our having this on paper, a point I pressed hard, and we are to sign to-morrow. In the meantime exertion is used, under a conviction that it concerns him more than me, to get some of his vessels off; that the army

---

* The Admiral told Mr. Boghos after the interview, that he would come to the Pacha again when his ships were outside the harbour; but he would not do so before. For formal Treaty see Appendix.

may know that they are to be brought over, and that no
more of them may die of starvation. I have agreed to permit one of his vessels to go from Navarin with a crew to
bring his new frigate from Trieste, to be loaded with troops
at Navarin with the rest; and I wish you would sanction
her taking from Zante the corn which he has there to feed
them on their passage, as it will facilitate the operation.
I shall send the Greeks now here to the President, to be
exchanged for the corvette's Turks and any others that
he has. By the way, you might now sanction the vessel at
Prevesa going to Navarin to assist. After a first division is
fairly away, I think I shall proceed to Navarin myself, *unless*
interrupted by my successor. . . . When the operation
is fairly in execution, I shall notify it officially either to you
or through you. In the meantime, I am yours with warmth
and sincere regard,

Edward Codrington.

Sir E. C. to Vice-Admiral De Rigny.

'Asia,' off Alexandria: Wednesday, August 6, 1828 —8 P.M.

I shall only write you a few lines, my dear Admiral, because M. Drovetti will tell you more at length what has
passed to-day with the Viceroy. I think, however, I may
say the affair is settled, and settled upon terms which will
be satisfactory to you and our colleague, as well as our
friends at Corfù. I dwelt a long time upon the difficulty of
including Navarin in the list of fortresses to be left in the
hands of the Turks—a point upon which the Viceroy insisted
strongly. At length, I observed that I might, perhaps, find
my justification in it if His Highness would not only give up
the slaves which he now had here, but would endeavour to
recover as many others as possible of those which were gone
into the interior, &c. In all this he expressed and showed
as much readiness and goodwill as we can expect; and I think
the information I shall collect through the Viceroy himself,
M. Drovetti, and Mr. Barker, will put some people in England to shame. The Viceroy is convinced that it is of the
greatest importance to him, as well as Ibrahim, that the
operation should begin as soon as possible; and I have settled
that the very first vessels which can be got out shall go to
you immediately, without waiting for the others, so that
there may be a practical proof of the sincerity of both
parties.

I shall send the Greeks which he has here at once to
Egina, or Poros, to be exchanged for the Turks of the cor-

vette, and any others Capodistrias may have; and perhaps the vessel which will take them may be hired to bring back some of Ibrahim's army. The Viceroy asked me to let one of his vessels take a crew from Navarin to the place where his Trieste frigate now is, to bring her to Navarin to convey part of the army here. To this I consented: and I think she might be permitted to perform another of his wishes in her way: that is, to load at Zante with the provisions which he has there for the supply of the troops to be brought over. Harmony being the order of the day, all this may be granted readily, with the approbation of our colleague. We may also show our goodwill by permitting additional food to be supplied to the troops which remain, *after we have embarked a first division*. He wished to send money to the troops in Candia. I told him I could not answer this at present, but I thought it might be done when the other operation was once in satisfactory progress. This, however, ought to be made known to Capodistrias, that he may make his arrangements about the war in that island; and I think some instructions should be obtained from the Ambassadors, whether we are to consider Candia as within the limits of our protection under the circumstances. I am not sure that we shall get the agreement signed before 'La Diligente' sails, but you will know this either from Drovetti or M. Duval d'Ailly (captain of the frigate).

I will not conclude, my good friend, without expressing my satisfaction that this important effect should have been so much owing to your able management.

I received your letters by the yacht, and also by the 'Zebra,' and have only time to thank you for them.

Yours, &c.,
EDWD. CODRINGTON.

Sir E. C. to Vice-Admiral Count Heiden.

'Asia,' off Alexandria: Wednesday, August 6, 1828.

I think, my good friend, all your doubts will soon be removed by seeing a first division of the Viceroy's vessels arrive at Navarin to bring away the troops. I pressed very much the not letting Navarin be given to the Turks with the other fortresses, not with any particular desire to succeed, because I know it would have put Count Capodistrias to great difficulty now to garrison it; and if he gets the assistance of troops, without which he will not be able to keep down the Capitani, he will have no difficulty then in getting all those places from the Turks. But by resisting this point, without which he positively declared that he could not make the agreement, I was enabled to insist more strongly upon the liberation not only of the slaves who are in misery here, but of all others which can possibly be procured.   He said he would do his utmost to recover all those who have not embraced their religion, and become with their own consent a part, as it were, of themselves.   He is to get out a division of such vessels as can be ready most quickly, that we may show that the operation is actually in operation, and the ' Blonde ' will accompany them.

I shall send, probably, in a hired merchant vessel, the Greeks now here, to be exchanged for your Turks of the corvette and any orders the President has ; and perhaps the same vessel may go afterwards to Navarin for some of the troops.   I have also said that one of his vessels will be permitted to take a crew from Navarin to bring his new frigate from Trieste to load at Zante with his corn now there, and then bring troops from Navarin here.   Therefore, my good friend, give this your sanction, *and send your belligerent character up to the Black Sea* until the Morea is evacuated. As to the poor devils of sick being put into the ship of the line now in Navarin, we must not suffer such a cruel experiment.   My intention is, *if no orders from home interrupt me,* to proceed towards Navarin whenever I have seen a division of these ships fairly off.   Whatever others he can send will follow as speedily as they can be got ready, we may be sure, for, as he says, he is much more interested in the success of the operation than I am.   I have reason to think that this arrangement would have been greatly retarded, if performed at all, but for my arrival.   He came from Cairo immediately, and he was yesterday under great anxiety, from fearing that I would not grant the point of the fortresses, in which case I doubt if he ever would have consented, owing to the danger he is in as to the Sultan's anger at the army not going into Roumelia.   I cannot write more now, but I dare say De Rigny will have much more detail of what passed from Drovetti, whom I have requested to inform him of everything.

Yours, &c.,
EDWD. CODRINGTON.

I have received your kind letter about my recall, and your private and truly friendly letter also, which I cannot answer now, except by assuring you that the regard which my family and myself bear you, will not be diminished by any distance at which we may be separated.

From Admiral Heiden to Lady Codrington, at Malta.

Poros: $\frac{26 \text{ juillet}}{7 \text{ août}}$ 1828.

MADAME,—Monsieur l'Amiral m'ayant prié de lui faire copier deux papiers, et de vous les envoyer à Malte, je profite de cette occasion, non pour vous dire la part que je prends à la perte que nous allons faire, car vous connaissez assez mes sentimens pour l'Amiral, mais pour vous prier, Madame, de ne pas le moins du monde vous chagriner pour cela; certainement c'est très-désagréable pour lui, pour vous, et pour vos chers et bons enfans, mais votre mari se retire avec tant de gloire, et tellement aimé et estimé de tous ceux qui ont eu l'honneur de le connaître, que pour un héros philosophe, ou, pour mieux m'exprimer, pour l'homme sensible, c'est une des plus belles récompenses, dans le service surtout, que d'emporter l'estime et l'amour des braves Anglais qu'il a commandés et conduits à la gloire, des Russes et des Français qui en ont acquis aussi sous ses auspices et qui rivalisent avec ses compatriotes pour lui témoigner leur attachement, de tous ceux qui ont été en relation avec lui, et enfin l'amour chevaleresque que lui porte un jeune souverain qui est aujourd'hui (pour ses qualités du moins) le premier de l'Europe, et qui peut-être est innocemment la seule cause pourquoi l'Amiral est changé; parce que le Ministère *diplomate* ne peut concevoir, ni chez eux ni chez les autres, une admiration et un attachement purs, et non mêlés d'égoïsme ou de vues politiques. Vos bons amis viendront vous voir, vous porter leur marque d'attachement pour l'Amiral; nous, Russes et Français, nous vous *bombarderons* de tems à autre d'une lettre pour savoir comment vous vous portez, ce que vous faites, et puis encore je me flatte aussi que je serai un jour votre conducteur à St.-Pétersbourg, où vous devez, Madame, venir jouir quelques moments des grandes qualités de notre famille impériale, et de l'estime que porte à l'Amiral toute la Russie.

Adieu, my dear Lady Codrington; dans ce moment j'apprends que l'Amiral Malcolm est arrivé, je n'ose donc plus me flatter de vous voir encore. Dieu vous conserve et vous donne un heureux voyage. Je vous prie d'être assurée que mon estime et mon amitié pour vous et pour votre chère famille ne finira qu'avec ma vie.

HEIDEN.

Admiral Heiden and his Russian ships went to Malta after the battle of Navarin, to undergo their repairs in the English dockyard. This detained them there throughout the winter, during which time we had frequent intercourse with the Admiral, whose spirited character, and frank, open, hearty manners were so winning that we all became cordially attached to him. Admiral de Rigny shifted his flag into a fresh ship, and remained in the Archipelago carrying on the service there, while the disabled French ships of course went to their own French ports for their repairs after the battle, and did not go to Malta at all; so that we had no opportunity of becoming acquainted with the French Admiral, as we were with his colleague. In fact, we saw him for the first time at Paris in 1831.

After this agreement to the terms of a treaty on August 6, 1828, a Tatar arrived from Constantinople, and was supposed to bring orders from the Porte for Mehemet Ali not to sanction Ibrahim's quitting the Morea. Mehemet Ali now proposed inadmissible conditions, and in presence of the Consuls of France and England, declared he would not sign the Treaty. The negotiations appeared to be at an end, and the following letter was written for communication to the Pacha.

From Sir Edward Codrington to Consul Barker.

H.M.S. 'Asia,' off Alexandria: August 8, 1828.

SIR,—It appears by the contents of your letter of yesterday that His Highness the Pacha is not disposed to fulfil the engagement into which he had solemnly entered. If this should be his determination he will have to answer for all the consequences. In such case it will become my duty in the first instance to proclaim it to the Allied Powers, whose good opinion he will have forfeited when he may find himself most in need of it; and it will also be due to myself and my colleagues to make known to Ibrahim Pacha and his army, that whilst the Allies had offered to make considerable sacrifices to save them from destruction, Mehemet Ali himself, by the breach of an agreement in which I assented to all he required, consigned them to their miserable fate. Since the Pacha has not thought proper to assign any reason for this change, I am left to conclude that it originates in his own free will; and it is therefore needless to enter upon the subject of Monsieur Drovetti's discussion with him.

Should His Highness have taken fresh alarm at the effect which this measure might have upon the Porte, he should recollect that he has virtually given that offence already, and that by breaking the engagement made in the presence of competent witnesses, he will thereby sacrifice that honor upon which he values himself, and lose all claim whatever on the support of the Allied Powers, whenever their differences with the Sultan may come to be arranged.

I have now only to beg you will demand a categorical answer as to whether His Highness has decided on this line of conduct or not. And you will be pleased to guide yourself accordingly in giving the consuls and merchants the information which may enable them to act as they think best under the circumstances.

I shall not attempt to prescribe any line of conduct to you personally in case of a termination of all amicable intercourse with the Pacha. But I shall direct the officer who may be left in command off this port, and whatever may be the exigencies to which the Pacha may be driven, to receive from him none but written communications.

I beg you will take the proper means of making the contents of this letter known to the Pacha without the least delay.

I have, &c.,

EDWD. CODRINGTON.

Sir E. C. to Lady C.

Off Alexandria : August 5.

I have received within this last half-hour copies of De Rigny's new instructions, which are similar to those given to Malcolm; and they alone bear me out by being in substance, to do all that I have done without them; and the main object described in them is that which I am now probably about to perform in defiance, as it were, of Lord Aberdeen's despatch; for he, by an incorrect quotation, makes the instruction of October 16, *absolute* in directing me ' to concert with the Commanders of the Allied Powers, the most effectual means of preventing any movements by sea on the parts of the Turkish or Egyptian forces; ' denying what is clear as day, that that passage meant ' proceeding from one port in Greece to another, each in their own hands, for the purpose of hostility.' But it would clear me of all his feeble attack, if I were merely to place the true against his incorrect quotations. I dare say Sir —— —— expects me to ask for a court-martial. Shallow Buckingham! He would select my charge, and —— ——

would have the pleasure of wording it so as to shut out all my defence. No, no; I shall not be caught that way, nor, as I trust, by such people at any time.

August 7.

Yesterday I had my conference with Mehemet Ali, and I thought the whole affair was settled. But in the evening he advanced a condition to the consuls who had to draw up the Protocol, to which I have refused my assent, and there the matter rests until I hear again. This is very harassing to one who is as anxious as I am, and who sat up late to say how smoothly all was settled, both to Heiden and De Rigny, as well as to Adam and Spencer.

10. P.M.

I have no answer to the negative I gave this morning, but the Pacha is hastening his ships as much as possible, and this looks very like knocking under. It would, however, have better suited me to have the certainty to lie down with, for it is a very anxious moment, although by my having got De Rigny's new instructions, '*which are the same as those to his two colleagues,*' I know that Malcolm must pursue the operation. Those instructions themselves sanction all my measures, and therefore help to strengthen my case. In case of Malcolm's not being come, it might still be worth your while to come out if the (General's) yacht could still be spared. But it is impossible for me to give you more ' precise orders; ' and I can only promise not to supersede you for mis-conceiving your instructions! Good night.

A letter from Mr. Consul Barker, of Aug. 8, 1828, describes an interview with the Pacha on presenting the translation of the letter from Sir E. C.; and after discussion, the Pacha agreed to propose a limit of 1,200 men being left to garrison the five fortresses in the Morea, saying at the last, 'Were you to see the letters I receive from the Porte you would pity me.'

From Sir E. C. to Mr. Consul Barker, Alexandria.

'Asia,' off Alexandria: August 9, 1828.

In consideration of the delicate situation which His Highness the Pacha is placed in with the Porte, I shall consent to the additional article in your letter. But as I am now making further sacrifice to the honor of the Pacha, I must claim his directions that he will order a detachment of his vessels now ready, to come out of the port immediately; that I may be enabled to give to my colleagues that proof of his good faith in the transaction.

I have, &c.,
EDWD. CODRINGTON.

From Mr. Consul Barker to Sir E. C.

Alexandria: August 9, 1828.—7 A.M.

SIR,—I think it right to lose no time in informing Your Excellency that Monsieur Drovetti has this instant called upon me to communicate to me a letter, which he received this morning from Mr. Boghos, saying that before forwarding my report to Your Excellency it was proper to remind him to insert, *as agreed upon last night*, in the article relating to the Greek slaves in the Morea that *none should be prevented from coming here who had embraced the Mahomedan faith.* Not a word to such purpose having been promised last night, nor at any former period of the negotiations, Monsieur Drovetti replied that if this were brought forward to put an end to them, or in order to gain time, such a proceeding was disgraceful to him, or his master.

I have, &c.,
JOHN BARKER, Consul.

Sir E. C. to Mr. Consul Barker, Alexandria.

H.M.S. 'Asia,' off Alexandria: August 9, 1828.—10.30 A.M.

SIR,—I have this instant received your letter, dated seven o'clock this morning. My answer is, that I will admit of no alteration whatever to the terms which I agreed to an hour ago and sent by Captain Richards. That agreement declares, that no Greeks desiring to come away shall be prevented; and I consider the Pacha as bound in honour to ratify that agreement without loss of time. I need not remind him of the consequences of offering insults to the Allied Powers, of whom I am the representative in this transaction.

I have, &c.,
EDWD. CODRINGTON.

From Sir E. C. to Sir Frederick Adam.
(Extract.)

August 9, 1828.

The Pacha desired to have the additional article separate, that he might humbug the Sultan with the other. In fact,

I doubt any Egyptians being left at all, and Tornese being included is, as you know, mere deception. Capodistrias cannot do better than keep the fortresses in the hands of such a number of Turks as he can just confine within them, allowing them to buy a limited proportion of provisions to keep them going until he can provide means to keep them going himself. This Pacha has said nothing about provisions, with the view, as I can see, of stocking the places to any extent he likes; but my colleagues and myself talked that matter over beforehand, and he will be met on that ground at once.

Sir E.C. wrote from Alexandria an official account of the terms of the Treaty for the information of his successor, Sir Pulteney Malcolm, adding, 'As my presence is considered to be material to the execution, I propose remaining here to see it fulfilled, after which I shall join your flag as speedily as possible.'

Sir E. C. to Vice-Admiral Sir Pulteney Malcolm.

'Asia,' off Alexandria : August 8, 1828.

MY DEAR MALCOLM,—My public letter will explain my present position. This man is no more to be trusted than his adopted son, and a trifle would turn the scale whether he is to let his army starve to death or put his own neck in jeopardy for bringing them away. As I expect it to be decided to-morrow morning, I feel disposed to keep the 'Mosquito' until then. The business in which I am engaged here is not a very agreeable one, I assure you, and I shall be very glad to have it over and to join you as soon as possible. Many thanks for your kind offer to meet my wishes. As they centre in an ardent desire to find myself in England, I shall be glad to deliver up my charge to you as soon as it can be effected. Had I had any preparatory hint of the intentions of the Ministers before I quitted Malta in the expectation of being absent all the summer and autumn, I could have had this ship ready for you.

Believe me, &c.,

EDWD. CODRINGTON.

August 9, half-past 10, A.M.

I gave my assent this morning to the additional stipulations required by the Pacha, from a conviction that they would not affect the cause and that they were put forth merely to pacify the Sultan. I have this minute received a fresh demand, to which I have given a direct negative, and shall keep the 'Mosquito' for the result. If it be that the agreement of this morning remains unaltered and to be carried into effect, I shall send the public letters I have written to you and to Sir F. Adam as they are at present.

Sunday, August 10.

I have now got the Pacha's signet in return. He wishes to see me again. I answer, whenever a large detachment of his fleet is outside—which I am assured will be to-morrow; and you may rely upon my turning my back upon this place as soon as I can.

Sir E. C. to Lady C.

'Asia,' August 9, 1828.

Yesterday the 'Mosquito' brought me Malcolm's announcement of his being on his way to Navarin. I shall not, however, quit this place until the negotiation may be quite broken off, or the ships to form the first detachment are outside the harbour. I think being subjected to a week more of this Pacha's tergiversations would destroy five years of a strong man's life. This morning, an hour after I had agreed to his last somewhat reduced proposals, out comes something now to which I have put a direct negative, and have declared I will hear nothing more than the fulfilment of the above agreement.

9, P.M.

I signed my part this evening, and the Pacha's counterpart signed by him is to come off to-morrow morning early, followed by some of the vessels, which are to anchor alongside us. Robb will be able to tell you what he sees, and I shall send a duplicate of my letter to the Admiralty and of the agreement, through Ponsonby officially, by which means you will know more than I can write. I have now got Curzon, Will, Hal, Captain Airey, besides Dyer and his clerks, all at work. I fear my more full defence, after a closer examination of all the papers, which Will and I have been concocting, will not be ready. I am satisfied that I have disproved every insinuation contained in Lord Aberdeen's despatch on my supersession. Whenever I have a considerable number of these fellows outside and under our control, I shall push for Navarin to join Malcolm. I know not if he mean to bundle me out at sea or not; but I know that it will be a very awkward quantity of things to turn out at sea into a strange ship not prepared to receive them.

Sunday night, August 10.—10, P.M.

I feel lighter than I have done lately.

I have finished my defence—I have got the Pacha's signet —and I have seen two of his vessels outside.

Monday, 11.

There seems to be a general movement amongst my friends in the harbour, and I may, therefore, say there is now no doubt of the execution of the measure for which you have been so anxious. This might of itself be considered as a sufficient answer to the alleged inattention to my orders. Lord Aberdeen's quotation in the extract I put up for Ponsonby, is the basest thing possible. Out of a paragraph composed of two sentences, the one being the condition of the other, he not only leaves out the condition which an inaccurate examiner might by possibility overlook, but he excludes three words beginning the very sentence he quotes, by which and by which alone its meaning can be perverted.* We have endeavoured to avoid using offensive language, but the facts are so strong, so directly opposite to His Lordship's imputations, that there will unavoidably be an appearance of rudeness in the contradictions.

August 11.—4, P.M.

I am just returned from a take leave of the Pacha; fourteen of his vessels are outside, and I therefore send Robb off.

God bless you.

E. C.

Sir E. C. to Mr. Consul Barker, Alexandria.

' Asia,' off Alexandria : August 10, 1828.

SIR,—I have to signify to you my authority for having a vessel to convey to Greece such slaves as His Highness the Pacha of Egypt may order to be delivered over to you, in virtue of the Treaty which has been entered into. And, as it appears that these slaves are in a very destitute condition,

---

* This refers to the paragraph in Lord Aberdeen's letter of recall.

The Instructions of 16th October, 1827, say :—' He will concert with the Greek authorities, that the whole of their naval force shall be exclusively appropriated to the blockade of the ports of Greece, now occupied by the Turkish or Egyptian forces.

' *In that case*, he will not restrain the Greek naval forces from exercising, in respect to neutrals attempting to break the blockade, all the rights of a belligerent.'

The three words ' In that case ' are omitted by Lord Aberdeen : thus giving the impression that the Greeks were not to be restrained at all in their belligerent rights, whereas this right was to depend upon the whole of their naval force being occupied in blockading the ports of Greece.—W.J.C.

you will furnish them with such clothing as they may immediately stand in need of, and provide for their subsistence on the passage.

I have, &c.,

EDWD. CODRINGTON.

From Sir E. C. to the Admiralty.

' Asia,' off Alexandria : August 9, 1828.

SIR,—The enclosed copy of a conference which took place between my colleagues and myself at Zante,* will inform His Royal Highness the Lord High Admiral of the reason of my coming here. The Pacha of Egypt was at Cairo when I arrived, but upon my arrival being announced by the telegraph he immediately came to Alexandria. I declined waiting upon His Highness until he agreed that the basis of any conference between us should be the evacuation of the Morea by his army, and I entrusted to the able management of Commander Richards of the ' Pelorus,' the arrangement of this preliminary. An audience being obtained by Commander Richards, Monsieur Drovetti, the French Consul-General, and Mr. Consul Barker, at which His Highness consented to this basis, I waited upon him on the 6th inst. After the usual formalities, and the retirement of those whose presence was not required, a long discussion ensued. It became evident to all the party that the Pacha neither would nor could come to terms without a stipulation that the fortresses should be left in the hands of the Ottomans. The unavoidable delays in drawing up and translating the outline of the agreement then made, gave opportunity for the arrival of a tatar, in ten days, from Constantinople. The communications which he brought irritated and affected the mind of the Pacha to such a degree, that all negotiation seemed at one time to have been put an end to. At length by a little management he was induced again to open the communication, and I have this day consented to sign an* agreement upon terms of which the following are the heads. The Pacha of Egypt engages to restore the Greek slaves taken from the Morea after the battle of Navarin ; he will begin by placing at my disposal those whom he can liberate at once, and will use his utmost endeavours to procure the recovery of others ; in return for which I am to obtain the release of the Turkish prisoners taken in the corvette and such others as may be in the hands of the President of Greece. The Pacha promises to send without delay all the

* See page 358.

ships of war and transports of which he can dispose, to
embark the Egyptian troops, which shall evacuate the Morea
immediately. These ships of war and transports shall be
escorted by English or French men-of-war, which shall enter
the port of Navarin with them.*   The same ships on leaving
Navarin shall in like manner be escorted in sight of the port
of Alexandria.   Neither Ibrahim Pacha, nor any one of his
suite, or army, shall be permitted to bring away any Greeks
without their own consent.   Ibrahim Pacha, in evacuating
the Morea, may leave a sufficient garrison in the fortresses
of Castel Tornese, Coron, Modon, Patras, and Navarin. And,
by an additional article, the number of Egyptian troops
(in the absence of the Turks) is to be limited to 1,200
men.   There is so much vacillation and tergiversation in the
Pacha's conduct that it is impossible to place any confidence
in him whatever.   And therefore, as it is thought that without my presence no arrangement of the sort would have been
made at all, I propose remaining here until a division of the
Turkish ships shall be fairly out of the harbour, under our
immediate control, and then making the best of my way to
join Admiral Sir Pulteney Malcolm, at his rendezvous off
Navarin.

Sunday, August 10.

I have this day received the agreement with the Pacha's
signet attached, in return for the one I sent with my signature yesterday.   Some of the Turkish vessels are now moving
towards the harbour's mouth, and I am assured that
several will be outside to-morrow.   Whenever I may have
this practical proof of there being no further difficulties in
the way, I shall hasten to join Sir Pulteney Malcolm's flag
and deliver the command into his hands, in obedience to
His Royal Highness's order of June 5 last.

I am, &c.,
EDWD. CODRINGTON.

P.S.—I feel it incumbent upon me to inform His Royal
Highness the Lord High Admiral that I had directed Commander Richards to take upon him the arduous duties of
this particular station on account of a well-founded reliance
I had upon his judgment, his zeal, and his ability; that I
am greatly indebted to him for the manner in which he has
contributed to bring about this most important object, and
that I consider it my duty to call his services on this occasion to His Royal Highness's particular attention.

EDWD. CODRINGTON.

---

* Together with the Russians who may be off the port.

Memorandum.

On August 11, 1828, came on board Mr. Sloane, having received these messages from the mouth of Mr. Boghos, and the answers were given the same day to him.

S. Altesse désirerait que l'Amiral donnât une lettre à *Mahomet Capitan* pour aller à Trieste prendre la frégate construite à Venise. Elle est toute prête et viendrait tout de suite à Navarin prendre Ibrahim Pacha; les deux corvettes auraient à bord l'équipage nécessaire. S'il y a des difficultés dans ce moment, S. A. désire qu'on permette à ces corvettes de suivre l'Amiral à Navarin ou à Corfou, où elles attendraient la décision de ses collègues, dans la vue de ne pas perdre du tems en attendant une réponse à Alexandrie.

S. A. est plus que persuadée que d'après la promesse de S. E. l'Amiral, que l'île de Candie resterait libre du blocus après l'évacuation de la Morée,* et qu'après avoir parlé à ses collègues il devait faire connaître à S. A., mais qu'en attendant il priait l'Amiral, s'il était possible, d'être permis le chargement de trois bâtimens d'approvisionnement pour son armée dans cette île. S. A. désire avoir ci-dessus une réponse précise.

The Admiral will write to Admiral De Rigny to permit Ibrahim to send a person, or persons, to Zante or Corfù to procure provisions, and to Cephalonia to procure vessels. The Admiral promised that he would refer the situation of Candia to the consideration of his colleagues and the Ambassadors. He did not promise that it should be free from blockade, because he had no power whatever to do so. Consequently it is not in his power to allow the vessels loaded with supplies to proceed to that island, until it has the above sanction. The Admiral has already proposed to his colleagues that a vessel should proceed to Trieste with a sufficient crew to bring the frigate to Navarin, calling at Zante if it can be permitted, to take in the provisions belonging to the Pacha there, and then proceeding to Navarin to assist in the evacuation. The two corvettes had better accompany the first division which sails for Navarin, but the Pacha should be cautious not to send so large a number of people as may excite suspicion that the frigate is not intended to bring away her proportion of troops.

---

* NOTE BY SIR E. C.—No such promise was made. On the contrary, I said I could do nothing in it without orders from my Superiors, whom I had informed of the restriction I had placed on it. But that I would mention it to my colleagues.

As the Allies are desirous that the Morea should be evacuated, the Admiral apprehends no difficulty in means being afforded for having additional vessels for that purpose from Corfù, Zante, Cephalonia, or any other place.

Official letters conveying the information of the Treaty of Alexandria, were also forwarded to Admirals De Rigny and Heiden, General Ponsonby, Sir F. Adam ; and Count Capodistrias, President of Greece, was also fully informed by Sir E. Codrington of this great success for his country.

Order to Commodore Campbell, C.B.

Alexandria: August 11, 1828.

Having ratified a convention with His Highness the Pacha of Egypt for his fleet going over to Navarin to bring away his army from the Morea, the concealment mentioned in my secret letter* to you of July 16 last is no longer necessary. I leave it to you to make such arrangements as you may think proper as to which ships shall accompany the Turkish fleet, according to the strength of the several detachments of which it may be composed, taking care to avoid as much as possible any unnecessary delay in their arrival at Navarin. As I observe an Admiral's flag in one of the frigates which I presume will come out to-morrow morning, it appears advisable to consult him in regulating the movements.

Alexandria should be watched, and the island of Candia should be considered under the same restrictions as heretofore, until some further decision respecting it shall be made either by the Allied Ambassadors or the Allied Admirals. I propose proceeding myself at once off Navarin to make known the present state of affairs in this quarter.

EDWD. CODRINGTON.

Sir E. C. to Commodore Campbell, H.M.S ' Ocean.'

Monday, August 11, half-past 4 o'clock.

I think I may now congratulate you, my dear Commodore, upon having a very nice little fleet to manage, under the assistance of their own Capitana Bey, as I find he is dubbed. I saw him standing up on the hammock boards in a flowing pair of purple breeches, looking out very sharp for a clear channel amongst the other ships in a very officer-like style.

---

* See p. 367, letter, July 16, to Commodore Campbell.

In my official letter to you I say Alexandria must be still watched as heretofore; the vessel, or vessels, which you direct for that service will be as well, if not better, inside than out.   I promised Richards, who had so much of the disagreeable part, to ask you to let him go with the fleet to Navarin; he deserves all that can be done for him.   Candia must continue under the same restrictions until the higher powers arrange what is to be done in its peculiar circumstances. .The wily Pacha is trying hard to send supplies there; but I have told him that no permission can be granted until the Allied Ambassadors so permit.   I cannot say I see any occasion for your staying here, if you like to go with the fleet to Navarin : because blockade of this place is now out of the question, at least for the present, and any vessel can do what is required of us. If we should not meet again until we talk over these matters in England, I may now say how much I wish you a successful return to that little spot which, in my view, take it for all in all, is worth the whole of the rest of the world.

Your very sincere and faithful,
EDWD. CODRINGTON.

Sir E. C. to Lady C.

'Asia,' at Sea : August 18, 1828.

You will have anticipated the event, my dear Jane, which, I trust, the 'Hind' will shortly confirm to you. I sent her off as soon as the determination of Mehemet Ali *evinced* by his *signet* was *confirmed* by several of his vessels loaded with provisions being out and anchored amongst our ships; fourteen brigs of war, or at least armed, were so anchored before I came away on the evening of the 11th, and three frigates, one bearing an admiral's flag, at the entrance of the port ready to come out and join them. I conclude all this batch would come away on the morning of the 12th. I would have staid to see them actually on their way; but, although this would have been more satisfactory in one respect, I deemed it prudent to be able to say I had done my part completely, in case of any *tatar* arriving with news of negotiations being begun, or any other event which might still induce the Pacha to withhold the execution.

The new instructions, of which De Rigny has sent me a copy, are dated July 9, and, according to Prince Polignac, are the same as *were prepared in March*, and are ' basées sur les annexes A.B.C. aux deux Protocoles du 15 octobre 1827.' Guilleminot told Adam that France is to send a corps to the

Morea with our consent, if Ibrahim does not withdraw. As he and Adam suggested, I kept this intelligence from Mehemet Ali, lest he should wait that measure for his justification. If he should hear it now and break his treaty with me, it is not my fault. I have done my part, and that part is so desired by the Government that they would have a French army landed in the Morea to enforce it! I think I have now put His Grace's Ministry as much in the wrong towards me as I did the said Ibrahim towards the Allies, if our Government had known how to profit by it.

I sent the 'Mosquito' off with my despatches for Malcolm and *his* colleagues, and also for Adam, and thence to the Lord High Admiral the day before we started, but yesterday evening we passed her. I have felt the heat much more this year than I did the last. I must own I feel very uneasy at times about you and the Malta Scirocco. An English frosty winter will do us all good. I am writing to you, evidently with the prospect of conveying my letter myself. But it is relaxation, and of the sort which I feel I want. I know not how I should have got on without Will's head and pen to assist me through my examination of papers, and composing my reply to the misrepresentations of Lord Aberdeen's despatch. I, as you know, considered it very material to do away as early as possible any ill-impression which might really be made on the mind of the Duke of Clarence or my real friends, who, without knowing what reason was given for my supersession and what means I had of meeting it, might have felt it impossible to think me right. No doubt but the more time one takes to examine papers and reflect on circumstances the stronger one's defence may be made; but I doubt if we could have added anything with advantage.

CHAPTER IX.

THE comparative leisure of the time spent on board
the 'Asia' on the passage from Corfù to and from Alexandria, enabled Sir E. Codrington to look into papers,
and to write, under the date of August 10, 1828, a more
detailed defence of his conduct for record at the Admiralty.   A copy of it was sent by the Admiralty to the
Foreign Office.   It will be of interest to professional
readers, and will be found in the Appendix.

From Sir John Gore to Lady C.
(Extract.)

June 18, 1828.

If C. bows patiently to the imperious necessity of 'political expediency' I have no doubt his feelings and wishes
will be fully gratified; at present, 'no blame,' 'nothing personal attaches to him,' of this I am assured, and all his real
friends are most intensely anxious that he shall not make
this political expedient a measure of personality by entering
on a defence of his conduct when it is not arraigned in any
manner.   He should arrange documents, he should be prepared in every way to answer questions and rebut charges;
but he must be silent and quiet until those charges and
questions are exhibited.   Codrington would commit an act
of injustice to himself in supposing himself in the wrong,
if the Government do not place him so.   Why should he
imagine it from paragraphs in newspapers and the vile
whispers of London clubs?   Since I wrote last, by command
of the Lord High Admiral, His Royal Highness sent for me
again.   He expressed himself very anxious about Codrington
and about you; regretted the circumstance very much, and
concluded by saying, 'I hope you have written to him as I
desired, to be *quiet*: if he is so, all may go well; but if he is
not, I will not answer for the consequences; and if he
breathes the terms court-martial, he is a ruined man ! ! !'

I think it my duty, as a friend, to state this to you both,

and I anxiously hope that during the quiet of your passage home you will all coolly and dispassionately weigh the case in all its bearings and exercise your excellent judgment and discretion under such circumstances.

Codrington's reputation stands unimpeached; he has placed it above the reach of anyone—nothing attaches to sully its lustre—there is no desire anywhere or in any person to do so. He is the only person who can shake the foundation upon which his high professional character is raised; then why should he be the first man to raise a hand or a voice against himself?

Government are responsible for the measures they adopt, and they have a right to appoint those to carry them into effect whom they think most likely to fulfil them. I understand they have gone out of the usual course and have given a reason for recalling Codrington,* i.e. 'in order the better to carry all the provisions of the Treaty of July 6 into full effect it is thought expedient to appoint another officer to command the Allied fleets in the Mediterranean.'

The Turks have proposed to treat for an armistice if C. is recalled. Mr. S. C. is ordered to proceed to renew the negotiation, and Codrington is to make way for him—not you, Edward Codrington, but the commander of the Allied fleets; and, as a public man, you are bound to submit, and I do hope and entreat you will do so as patiently as you possibly can. I am aware how much more easy it is to give than to take advice, and how difficult it will be for you to adopt these views; but, as I see them and feel them all, I dare to offer you the dictates in honest sincerity of heart and mind.

'Be quiet: say not, write not, a word on the subject of your recall until you have had an audience with the Lord High Admiral.' These were his words; and here I shall quit the subject, hoping soon to see you all in health and all the comfort that an upright mind and clear conscience can afford under such very distressing circumstances.

As it is not improbable that C. may be absent when Wellesley arrives, I send this letter to you.

J. GORE.

From Sir E. C. to H.R.H. the Duke of Clarence.

'Asia,' at Sea: August 21, 1828.

SIR,—In my letter of July 22 I expressed my satisfaction that Your Royal Highness had not been mixed up with my defence against the accusations brought forward as the cause

---

* This error of 'no blame being attached to Sir E. Codrington' seems to have been, for some purpose, instilled into the mind of Sir John Gore.

of my supersessiòn. I rejoice more and more every day in this circumstance, and that my being taken so entirely from Your Royal Highness's protection has made the act itself merely that of the Ministers, because it will enable me to put forth my defence with less embarrassment, in the full confidence that the more complete it is the more it will meet the wishes of Your Royal Highness. This feeling has induced me to revise what I have already written, and to look further into the immense heap of documents which relate to my proceedings; and I confidently trust that Your Royal Highness will not think it too much trouble to give your attention to the result, for I cannot but think mine is not merely the cause of an individual, but that of all officers who may henceforth be appointed Commanders-in-Chief. I propose placing before Your Royal Highness copies of all the communications by which the arrangement for evacuating the Morea by Ibrahim has been brought about, according to the principle which has all along guided me of concealing nothing. I am nothing deterred in this plan by the advantage my accusers have taken of it. The consolation of having sent home all the information I could, without considering whether it would tell in my favour or not, has more than balanced the trouble it may have brought me into. I have always relied upon my own conscientious feeling of having devoted myself entirely to the execution of a very difficult as well as important duty, for my justification against the censures to which I might become liable from politicians according to their party purposes; and I have, therefore, courted investigation into all my conduct. I certainly did not expect such an attack from the Ministers whose wishes, as far as I could judge by their orders and instructions, I consulted to the fullest extent. But since such have been my assailants, I have the stronger reason for claiming that publicity to which every officer so situated has an inherent right, for the purpose of eliciting the truth on which every officer has a right to depend for the support of his professional character. I cannot but fear that those who have so acted towards me will do what they can to keep my defence from the public eye; and it is for this reason that I now mention it to Your Royal Highness, who will not be deceived by any supposed injury which such exposure could be to the public service. I ask the disclosure of no secret; I ask only the opportunity of publicly refuting accusations publicly made. It would be no State secret which prevented Mr. —— from correcting an assertion, which, if made in ignorance, could not be persevered in with innocence, after being contradicted by facts brought to his attention. No State secret could have required that those who imputed to me two important errors should decline to set me right when asked two plain questions to prevent my erring in future. As no State secret has withheld the grounds upon which my supersession has taken place, no State secret will be disclosed by my showing the fallaciousness of the accusations arrayed against me.

August 22.

Yesterday, upon my joining the 'Wellesley' with Sir Pulteney Malcolm's flag, I received a letter from Sir John Gore of June 18, in which he quotes from Your Royal Highness that I should remain quiet until I have the honor of an interview with Your Royal Highness, since there is no accusation made against me. Besides that this information did not reach me in time, Your Royal Highness is now informed that there are several accusations put forth against me which appear to have been purposely concealed. Had they remained unrepelled, I have no doubt but similar industry would have been shown in giving them circulation which was exhibited about the battle; and I therefore rely upon Your Royal Highness's approval of my not allowing such unjust imputations to obtain in any but the minds of their inventors. I think Your Royal Highness would not approve of any officer, as one fit for a post of high trust and confidence, who could feel indifferent about his professional character. I have lived long enough in public to know that prudence has taught another lesson in our service. But those who have so obeyed her dictates for their worldly advantage, have lost in that which I value much higher—their own honor and the esteem of their brethren; and when I look back to the sentiments which I have had the high gratification of hearing Your Royal Highness express upon that subject, I feel a strong conviction that the line I adopted will ensure me that approbation which is now the principal, I might almost say the only, professional object I have. I have now learnt that a French army of 9,000 men was destined to enforce the measure which I have been the medium of bringing about without so expensive a process. As I thought it an object of great moment, I sent a duplicate of my despatch to General Ponsonby for him to forward by Marseilles and Paris; and I therefore earnestly hope it will be in time to prevent their embarkation.

Zante: August 24.

As Sir Pulteney Malcolm has no vessel to send, I shall send this, with the triplicate of my despatches, by a Russian brig to Corfù. The French troops will probably arrive at the same time as the Turkish ships, thirty of which were ready when the ' Diligente ' left Alexandria the day after we did.

I have, &c.,
EDWD. CODRINGTON.

From General Sir Henry Bunbury * *to Lady Codrington.*

Genoa : August 25, 1828.

I shall be delighted to hear that Codrington brings back the Egyptian fleet, and has the satisfaction of seeing this difficult affair accomplished *by himself*; and then he may proudly present to this ungrateful Ministry the battle of Navarin, and the consequent evacuation of Greece, as the glorious fruits of his short service. They dare not attack him; and they cannot escape condemnation if they remain silent after the act of which they have been guilty. They are now putting about a report in London that Codrington *voluntarily resigned* his command. One of the black parts of the case is, their having left him so long a time without instructions. Did they hope to disgust him? or to catch him in some act of indiscretion while obliged to decide for himself under circumstances of singular delicacy and difficulty?

Sir E. C. to Lady C.

August 21, 1828.

. We are now (1 P.M.) approaching Sapienza, and I expect to join my successor before dark. The more I ponder on my whole proceedings the more I am satisfied; and I feel that as strongly regarding my late convention with the Vizier of Egypt as any of the former ones. I shall now prepare copies of the whole communications by which this matter was arranged, and I think they will show that I did the best that could be done under the circumstances, and according to the object of the instructions given me. Surely even you must admit that it is better for me that I should be superseded than continue exposed to the bad designs of such governors, now that I have the power not only of showing that their imputations are unfounded upon which they have superseded me, but also that I have fulfilled all the objects contemplated by those instructions, to which they say I have not paid due attention. I do not see how they can prevent the

---

* Formerly Under-Secretary of State for War and Colonies.

publicity of my case, or how they can stand the exposure it
will make of their folly as well as their injustice.

August 22, 10 P.M.

This morning we joined the 'Wellesley' off Navarin, and
are now both working up together to Zante to meet the
Ambassadors; and there I am to turn out of the 'Asia' into
the 'Wellesley.' This turn out is a very disagreeable thing,
and one on which Malcolm was most decided, and for which
he had made his preparations. He has copies of the letters
to me and my answers, as far as they had reached when he
came away; and, upon the whole, I think sufficient papers
to bother him if he had not the Ambassadors to apply to.

It is ridiculous my writing this to you, as I shall most
likely take it myself; although it is very possible that I
may just peep at Navarin to see if the Turks are em-
barking.

From Sir E. C. to Sir Pulteney Malcolm.

'Asia,' at Sea: August 22, 1828.

SIR,—In delivering into your hands, according to the
orders of the Lord High Admiral, the command of His
Majesty's ships and vessels on this station, I think it right
to apprise you that I have frequently found myself called
upon to adopt measures, for the better execution of the object
of the Government, not directed by the instructions for my
guidance. It is true, that in almost all these instances it
has been my good fortune to have anticipated the intentions
of my superiors. But still, since I am told that I am superseded on account of a misconception of the views and intentions of His Majesty's Government, it is right that I
should guard you against continuing my supposed errors;
and that, at the same time, I should be relieved from all responsibility for measures which may not be suitable to
another period or under other circumstances, and which I
am not myself to see carried into execution.

In revising the orders given out by me, and comparing
them with the instructions you may find yourself under, no
doubt the measures referred to will at once strike you. But
I beg to mention the orders I have given respecting Candia,
as a particular instance requiring consideration. Mehemet
Ali having made Sude an entrepôt for supplies intended for
the Morea, I gave the order of April 30, 1828, for their interception. On the other hand, the Greeks having used
the fortress of Carabusa for the purposes of piracy, I directed
Commodore Sir Thomas Staines to reduce it. Thus the

means of each party engaged in the war which they are carrying on in Candia, have been checked by measures on my part not in the purview of His Majesty's Government. But as the two great objects of my instructions are now happily gained—the putting down piracy and the evacuation of the Morea—it becomes a question for your consideration, whether or not the Pacha of Egypt is to be permitted to use the means which this latter measure will place at his disposal, for the destruction of the Greeks who seem at present to be in possession of all that part of Candia not commanded by the fortified places. The accompanying copy of a message which I received on August 11, will show the Pacha's anxiety on this subject and the desire he has to take advantage of any opportunity that may offer of carrying his wishes into execution. It is as well also to draw your attention to the orders which I gave respecting Alexandria, that you may consider how far it may be necessary to discontinue or alter those orders, under the change of circumstances which has now taken place. I enclose for your information copies of the protocol of a conference held at Zante between the Allied Admirals, and of the convention entered into with the Pacha of Egypt for the evacuation of the Morea.

I have, &c.,
EDWD. CODRINGTON.

After the successful arrangement of the Treaty of Alexandria, and when a detachment of the Egyptian fleet and convoy were outside the harbour, Sir E. Codrington sailed on August 11, 1828, for Navarin, for the purpose of meeting Sir Pulteney Malcolm, his successor, should he have arrived, or for carrying out the Treaty himself with Ibrahim, should he not have arrived.

The 'Wellesley,' with Sir P. M.'s flag, was met by Sir E. C. off Navarin on August 21, 1828; and he there gave up to him the Mediterranean command, and with it the Treaty of Alexandria for execution by the Allied Admirals.

He was not permitted to take his own flag-ship, the 'Asia,' to Malta, but had to shift his flag to the 'Wellesley' at Zante; and on re-appearing after that change before Navarin, he saw the 'Asia' bearing Sir Pulteney Malcolm's flag, in the harbour with ships of the Allied squadrons under their respective admirals.

On a wish being expressed by Sir E. C. to go into the harbour, he received a note from the new Commander-in-Chief, saying, 'If you are desirous to see your Bay, perhaps it will be as well if you come in by boat without your flag.' This proposal was declined by Sir E. C., with the remark, 'I have no desire to boat it into Navarin;' and he sailed at once for Malta and England.

It was thus that the victor of Navarin parted from . the scene of his unremitting, anxious labours, and their successful and glorious results.

From Sir E. C. to Sir Pulteney Malcolm.

Off Navarin : Friday, August 29, 1828.

MY DEAR MALCOLM,—From what I hear of the position of the Turkish ships when the brig now in Navarin left them, they may yet be some days before the embarkation begins ; and as General Maison's presence will ensure its taking place at all events, it appears to me that no good can arise from my staying here. If, therefore, you have no objection, I wish to be off at once. I had a very satisfactory five-hours' conversation with Mr. S. Canning yesterday. I pressed the point respecting Candia on his consideration, and told him that after giving you all the same information I had just given him, I advised your immediately applying to him for instructions on it, and I apprehend he will have written about it to Government by the steamer to-day. I entered also into other matters which I hope may lessen your difficulties at a future period.

I have no desire to boat it into Navarin. I hope —— will not find fault with your entering that harbour prepared for battle, and supported by your allies in the same readiness, and attribute to you a hostile spirit. But, as the proverb says, 'One man may steal a horse, whilst another must not look over the hedge.'

Very truly yours,
EDWD. CODRINGTON.

Memorandum by Sir E. C.

Off Navarin · August 29, 1828.

Admiral De Rigny having signified his wish to retire from this command, was answered by M. de la Ferroneys that there were great objections to his being superseded just now ;

not only because, having done his duty so well hitherto, they were anxious that he should continue here until the service now contemplated was executed, but because their accepting his resignation at this time would induce people to think the French Government had coincided with the English Government in their supersession of me.   E. C.

Memorandum by Sir E. C.

Mr. Stratford Canning said that upon hearing of my being likely to be superseded, he wrote a private letter to Mr. Huskisson expressing his opinion that it would be a very injurious measure, regarding its effect on the Porte; that Mr. H. told him that, although he admitted that he still thought the intention should be carried into execution, he considered it his duty to take the letter to the Duke of Wellington, who, nevertheless, saw no reason to alter the decision.   Mr. H. must at this time have been still in office, or he would not have gone to the Duke of Wellington.

The following letters were written and received after the official position of Sir E. Codrington in the Mediterranean had terminated.

From Admiral De Rigny to Sir E. C.

Devant Navarin : ce 23 août 1828.

MON CHER AMIRAL,—J'ai reçu hier votre billet du 22. Le 'Mosquito' arrive dans l'instant.

Pendant que nous travaillions pour faire évacuer Ibrahim, on ne croyait pas dans nos pays à la réussite, et on décidait l'envoi des troupes. Le Général Maison est parti le 15 de ce mois de Toulon.   S'il trouve Ibrahim parti, il n'aura plus rien à faire qu'avec les forteresses. Il me prie de le rencontrer ici, de sorte que je ne puis m'écarter d'ici.   Avant de nous quitter officiellement, permettez-moi de vous renouveler encore, mon cher Amiral, l'assurance de tout le prix que j'attache à conserver votre amitié. J'espère vous voir encore, quand vous partirez pour Malte ; vous y ferez quarantaine plus longue que vous ne croyez.   Je vous y écrirai.

From Admiral Heiden to Sir E. C.

Zante : ce 26 août 1828.

MON CHER AMIRAL,—J'avais le projet de venir vous faire mes adieux ce matin, mais je ne suis pas bien.

Je ne prends cependant pas encore congé de vous, espérant vous voir devant Navarin avant votre départ définitif pour

Malte. En tout cas, mon cher Amiral, nous ne nous oublierons jamais, et c'est au nom de tous mes capitaines et officiers que je puis vous dire cela : tous jusqu'au dernier, sentent vivement votre départ ; mais aussi tous espèrent en retournant en Russie pouvoir de bouche vous témoigner l'estime et le respect qu'ils vous portent. Je vous prie de me rappeler à votre digne épouse et à vos chères filles, que j'espère un jour revoir sinon à Pétersbourg, du moins en Angleterre ; car je trouverai leur demeure.

Croyez-moi pour la vie

Votre plus dévoué serviteur et ami,

HEIDEN.

From Count Capodistrias to Sir E. C.

Égine : le $\frac{14}{26}$ août 1828

MONSIEUR L'AMIRAL,—Je ne mets aucun retard à répondre à la lettre que V. E. m'a fait l'honneur de m'écrire en date du 14 courant.

J'éprouve un besoin trop vif de vous exprimer, Monsieur l'Amiral, la reconnaissance que vous doit la Grèce pour le service que vous venez de lui rendre encore à la veille de quitter le commandement que S. M. B. vous avait confié dans la Méditerranée.

Il eut été sans doute à désirer que l'évacuation du Péloponnèse fût absolue, au moins de la part des Égyptiens. Cependant le résultat obtenu par la persévérante sollicitude de V. Excellence et de ses collègues est d'une haute importance. De nombreuses victimes de la barbarie égyptienne vont être rendues à leur sol natal, et la délivrance finale des places de la Messénie semble ne devoir plus rencontrer de grands obstacles.

Vous avez donc, Monsieur l'Amiral, achevé ce que vous avez glorieusement commencé dans la mémorable journée du 20 octobre.

V. Excellence laisse en Grèce des souvenirs qui ne s'effaceront jamais.

Si, à l'aide de Dieu, la restauration de ce pays repose enfin sur une base solide et immuable, il y restera de ces souvenirs des preuves qui les feront apprécier par la postérité. Dans mon particulier je me félicite, Monsieur l'Amiral, d'avoir fait votre connaissance personnelle, et je ne saurais assez vous témoigner ma gratitude des sentimens dont vous avez bien voulu m'honorer. Je remercie V. E. des vœux qu'elle forme pour le succès de la cause à laquelle je donne peut-être le peu de jours qui me restent à vivre.

Veuillez protéger toujours cette cause. Elle est digne des nobles affections de votre belle âme.

Sir E. C. to Lady C.

'Wellesley': September 1.

A foul wind and little of it, and no prospect of improvement. At Zante, on the 28th, I had an interview with Mr. S. Canning. He is certainly a cautious, measured man, and also a clever one. I imagine he must have unbent to me more than usual, by what passed, and by its being preluded by the observation that 'he saw the turn of my disposition, and therefore that it was best to be perfectly candid with me in all that he had to say.' In this feeling he let out, that believing that he had used the expression in a *private* letter, he was not satisfied with my quoting the term 'cannon shot.' I replied that I thought he must be wrong; for having every reason to be contented with the communications I had received from him, I was not likely to act unjustly or injuriously towards him in any way; and that if I had not thought it creditable to him to have used terms so clear and appropriate, I should not have quoted them, but have given the substance: that I could confide in my not having done any ill-turn to him whom I had reason to esteem, because I had withheld so using a private letter of Lord Dudley, who had behaved so unworthily. He said he had nothing to regret as to the substance, but that the expression was not so diplomatic as it should be, and in a public letter he should have given the same sense in other language. By this time, however, he has got my letter explaining that he uses the expression in two letters, each *confidential*, as he calls them, beginning, 'Sir,' and speaking the opinion of his colleagues and himself, in answer to my asking for instructions. They are, in fact, official letters, and only distinguished from protocol joint instructions by his '*confidential.*'

Friday, September 5, 7 A.M.

I think we shall be very unlucky if we are again stopped by calm, now that our prospect of getting in is so fair, and I shall finish this to be smoked for you at once. Schembri tells me the Duke of Clarence has resigned his situation. I am rather glad of it upon the whole, as he must otherwise have lowered his support of the navy; and as to me, he can now be on my side entirely. (Going into Malta, in quarantine.) I have had the pleasure of hearing of your being all well, and seeing you at the window. We are quite well. God bless you.

E. C.

From Sir E. C. to Mr. S. Canning.

'Wellesley,' at Sea: September 3, 1828.

MY DEAR SIR,—Although I sent you a hurried assurance from off Navarin of your letter from which I quoted the words 'cannon shot' not being a private one, I am so desirous of setting myself right with you in this matter, that, for the chance of your not having your correspondence by you to refer to, I have now enclosed full copies of the two letters in which the term is used. They are both 'confidential,' but not private, and the whole tenor of them will show that they were instructive replies to my observations on August 12, 1827, speaking of Admiral De Rigny and myself. 'Neither of us can make out how we are to prevent the Turks, if obstinate, from pursuing any line of conduct which we are directed to oppose, without committing hostility,' &c. Those who have scrutinised all my proceedings with the view of fastening upon me undeserved censure, may well find fault with the expressions in question; but, judging by those who have seen the letters, I am persuaded they will make an impression upon all honorable and candid men with which you will have reason to be satisfied. Surely, in instructing an officer situated as I was, there ought to be no doubt or obscurity; and the intention of his Government should certainly be signified in terms which he can clearly understand. The second instruction says, 'And it is of importance that you should have a perfect knowledge of the object proposed by the Powers, and of the means on which they reckon to effect it.' And yet in defiance of this comes a reproof for not blockading and not taking out Greeks for which I had no authority, and an order to establish a 'like blockade' of Alexandria to that of the Morea, which is impossible; and in answer to my plain, simple questions to prevent future errors, I am told I am to be superseded for misconception of the intentions of His Majesty's Government! Which it is of the several Governments whose intentions are referred to, is a question I cannot solve; but I confidently appeal to the Treaty and other documents, to show that *I* have not only understood, but acted up to them in every respect. However, I will not tire you with any more of this now, although I shall have pleasure in talking over with you our joint services on this occasion, when we may hereafter meet in England. In the meantime, I again beg you to be assured, that I would not have quoted any expression of yours, even if it had been more material to my defence than it was, if I had imagined that it would have been disagreeable to you. If it is now cavilled at by others, I imagine that it arises from the defeat of the hostility to me, and that the substance in other words would have produced the same effect on them. Lord Dudley, in a letter of *October* 16, says, 'The instructions which go out to you along with this letter, are calculated to save you from what is most painful in the discharge of an important public duty—any doubts as to the limits of it,' &c.

Again, 'The conduct of neutrals, especially the Austrians, has been provoking enough. But whatever we may be driven to by and by, we are as yet in no condition to exercise belligerent rights,' &c. And in another letter of November 5, after the receipt of my narrative of all that passed in the Gulf of Patras, he writes, ' an Ionian messenger goes to-day. Though it is not my business to communicate with you officially, yet I may be allowed to tell you as a friend how much I am gratified by the spirit and ability you have shown in the late transactions with the Turks,' &c. These letters were written by His Lordship whilst he was still under the influence of Mr. Canning's principles, and are the last which I have received from him. You have a copy, of course, of his official despatch of March 18, and, I believe, of my reply; and can judge of the uprightness and the consistency of his conduct subsequently to the death of Mr. Canning and to his very patriotic retention of the same office under the Duke of Wellington. You can also judge of his conduct to me personally, in trying to convert to my injury in his later capacity, that order which in his earlier and more respectable position he had penned for my support under difficulty. And what was it in me which His Lordship so admired off Patras? *There* I did actually commence hostilities against Ibrahim at once, without further parley, when I had merely a tenth part of the force which the Allies had allotted for the purpose of preventing them : and on that occasion many who might not think it necessary to make allowance for the feelings of a professional man whose conduct would undergo professional scrutiny, might reasonably have questioned the propriety of the proceeding. You will see, my dear Sir, that whilst these letters would have well served my purpose in replying to the queries, I denied myself the use of them on that public occasion because they were private communications : and you will therefore, I trust, be convinced, that possessing my esteem instead of that feeling which I cannot avoid bearing my Lord Dudley, I would not have quoted from you anything which in my view could have been injurious to you. I find I have left at Malta or mislaid, the Turkish protocol of your last conference and also the conversation which I mentioned as having taken place with the Kiaja Bey, and the intercepted Turkish despatches. In my letter to the Duke of Clarence I quote the words of the said Bey, as, ' Nous aurons la guerre. Vous le croyez, et je le crois de même. *A l'heure qu'il est,* elle est peut-être déjà commencée. Mais sachez en toute vérité que depuis près de deux ans nous avons prévu cet évènement, et nous l'attendons sans aucune inquiétude. Le mal tombera sur ses auteurs. Nous sommes décidés de courir toutes les chances. Jamais, au grand jamais, nous n'admettrons la moindre ingérence dans nos affaires internes,' &c. It is curious that this conversation took place on October 20 whilst the battle was actually raging. I have found Chabert's translation of the Tunisian letters which were in a false head of a cask at Grabusa; but they are not worth being copied, although they show that a battle was expected, and that if it should take place the Tunisian Admiral was to employ ' tous les moyens et efforts·pour la victoire et conquête des infidèles.'

The letters to Ibrahim from Constantinople intercepted by Church, were sent to me by Count Capodistrias with a French translation, which I sent to the Duke of Clarence; and you can get another copy from Capodistrias himself. I conclude the translation into French was made by Mavrocordato, who must know the meaning of the Turkish expression which the Count considers as confirming the intention of the fleet to resist us. But the accompanying letters from Captain Richards are very convincing of this matter. The prospect of what I shall have to do after my arrival at Malta, and the short time I shall have for removing my family, in my anxiety to get to England, has induced me to finish this before my arrival. But if I can find any of the papers you require, or any which are likely in my view to be useful to you, I will add them. For I not only wish anxiously for your success, but for the full execution of the Treaty which, however it may be abused by some, in my humble opinion does high honor to the minister under whose auspices it was signed : and I am persuaded that if his life had been spared to his country, all those voices which have been raised by self-interest or other such feelings against it, would have been·loud in its favor and support. I have given to Sir P. Malcolm all the information and assistance which the circumstances of my hurried turn-out admitted of, nothing deterred by the ill-treatment I have met with, from doing whatever I can for the good of the service. The same principle will actuate me after my return to England, and if you should require any information as to what may have passed during your absence from the Levant which it may be in my power to give, I shall be at all times ready to attend to your wishes. It amused me to find my friend Malcolm had gone into Navarin without consent, prepared for battle, and supported until he had passed the batteries by his two colleagues in the same preparation.

Believe me, my dear Sir,

Yours with great esteem,

EDWD. CODRINGTON.

Memorandum by ————.

On September 2, 1828, the Egyptian fleet and transports, escorted by Commodore Campbell, arrived at Navarin* and found the ' Asia ' and ' Conquérant ' (French Admiral) with several other ships of war, anchored in the bay, with springs on their cables, and quite prepared for hostile operations. Ibrahim Pacha was absent, and it was signified to the Kiaja Bey that Vice-Admiral Count de Heiden, then outside, wished to enter to confer with his brother chiefs. The Bey replied that, Ibrahim being absent, he could not allow the ' Azoff ' to enter the port, but that the Count might come in person in a boat. On the 3rd the ' Azoff ' entered the bay; her tompions were out, and her guns double shotted, and the *silk* St. George's ensign flying, bearing, however, a flag of truce. Would not this collision have degenerated into hostilities had the Turks possessed what they did on October 20 ? In what did this forcible entry, sanctioned by the British admiral, differ from the entry of Sir Edward Codrington ? If his were imprudent, could this be thought otherwise ? As far as opportunity offered, there was the same disposition in the new admiral to violate the peace between ourselves and our ' ancient allies ' which Ministers have affected to censure in his predecessor. Why was the British admiral's flag-captain sent with a British flag to be present at the mock storm of Navarin—why was that flag left flying several days, with the French and Russian flags, on the walls at Navarin ? Why was Captain Maitland, of the ' Wellesley,' sent to force the gates of Modon, and his ship placed to batter Coron ? Why were the ' Blonde ' and ' Etna ' sent to bombard the castle of the Morea ?   Where is the difference, *in principle*, between the events of the autumn of 1828 and those of 1827? Had there been a fleet to have supported the Turkish com-

* In execution of the Treaty of Alexandria

manders of the castles and land forces, could battle have
been avoided ?   What, then, is the conclusion to which all
unprejudiced minds must come ?   Simply this—that the late
Commander-in-Chief adopted the only means by which the
Treaty of July 6, 1827, could be carried into effect, and which
his instructions prescribed ; since his successor, though aware
that his predecessor had incurred the displeasure of Ministers
as not having understood or obeyed his orders, has found
himself obliged to follow precisely the same line of conduct.
Can he have the same instructions which his brother officer
is said to have misconceived ?

From Sir John Gore to Sir E. C.*

Stowell . August 11, 1828.

MY DEAR CODRINGTON,—Your highly interesting letter of
July 5 from Zante, and ended 26th, going to Navarin, has
· reached me, and I need scarcely add, has excited all our
feelings for you under the situation in which you are placed.   I
can safely say that no day has passed in which my good wife,
her excellent father,† and self have not fully and deeply
talked you over under all the circumstances of your unprecedented case, the great difficulties you have had to overcome, and the cruel manner in which you have been treated,
all of which you so clearly define in your above-named letter,
and those I received about a month ago with the copy of
your correspondence with the Secretary of State ; and
although I do not expect you in England before the 1st, or
between that and September 7, yet I will send this to Stopford to await your arrival, that you may have time to peruse
·it while under the yellow.   So soon as I received your letter
with the copies of your said letters, I went to London, and
then took them to Spencer and left them with him to read
at leisure.   He did so, and returned them with the enclosed,
which I think it of importance that you should see.   I have
subsequently made Mr. Bethell take a copy for the perusal
of all who can enter on the subject; and I have promulgated
them as much as possible, for I consider them as facts that
bear you out.   But as you say that Lord Aberdeen's letter
is composed of faults and charges against you, you know
much more than I do.‡   When I wrote my two letters early

---

* Received at Portsmouth on his arrival, October 7, 1828.

† Admiral Sir George Montague

‡ It is again made evident by this letter from Sir John Gore, how completely the blame actually thrown upon Sir E. C. as the reason for his recall,
was kept from the knowledge of those friends most anxiously interested in
his behalf.

in June, of which you acknowledged the receipt, it was under very different impressions, for not only was I informed that no blame attached to your conduct, but the Duke of W. answered my interrogatory—'Has my friend Codrington got into any scrape with you?' 'No, none at all!' 'I ask Your Grace because you may have just heard the Duke of Gloucester tell me that he is superseded;' to which the Duke made no reply, but took hold of Lord Dudley's arm and went into the next room (at Lady Kerrison's ball), and after half-an-hour of close conversation they left the house together. This occurred a few days before Malcolm's appointment. I relate these facts, which, combined with others, show the ground for my belief, that no fault was found or blame attached to you. You appear to have construed my letters into my own opinions on all the subjects which they treat of; I assure you, my good and ill-used friend, they are not so. I have endeavoured to give you as many facts as I was possessed of, in order that you might avail yourself of them, and had I even known that blame was attached to you, I should have advised, as the Duke of C. desired me, that you should be silent in words and on paper until you had seen him; but to prepare for your defence and justification. As an officer, it is natural that a Court Martial should occur to you as the tribunal of justice before which to defend your conduct; but this will require deep consideration before it is adopted. In the first place, you are acting under the Secretary of State—if they do not furnish the Lord High Admiral with subject of charges against you, the Lord High Admiral cannot order you to be tried on a *blank*—if you claim a Court Martial, and it is granted, but no charge exhibited, you can make no defence; and even if charges are exhibited, and the trial goes on, as we do not admit solicitors to take notes or to speak, or shorthand writers into our courts, a publication of the proceeding may *be absolutely forbid*. And lastly, if the Cabinet do state blame to you, it is political, not professional blame. A Court Martial cannot take cognizance of political opinions; and the Cabinet can, and in the present juncture will, refuse the promulgation of political documents and opinions, as they lately have done to the Houses of Parliament. And yet I see, and *I feel*, that it is of vital importance to you that your conduct should be justified to the public, who will judge impartially; and if you can throw every shadow of blame off your shoulders, they will find no difficulty in attaching it to where it belongs. My cool advice therefore is, that you wait as temperately as you can under your injuries, until you have seen the Duke of C., Lord Aberdeen, and the Duke of W., and

heard what they have to say, and then with dignity and forbearance justify yourself. I am aware, and can most sensibly
feel, how much more easy it is to offer this advice, than to
follow it under the wounds which have been inflicted on you;
but as a sincerely anxious friend, and a cool bystander,' I
could not excuse myself if I withheld this advice, and earnestly entreat you to attend to it as much as possible under
all the circumstances in which you are placed.   You are
now removed from amidst all the exciting events of the
theatre of action, and from amongst men whose national
prejudices and individual interests may have induced them
to view circumstances and interpret words very differently
from what they are seen and understood in this country;
and thereby left to the full exercise of your own judgment,
aided by sound counsellors and real friends.

May God bless you all, my dear ill-used people.

Your truly attached friend,

JOHN GORE.

The following letter from a sincere and earnest
friend, and the grateful answer which it called forth,
are inserted as a specimen of true friendship, and as
doing equal honor to the heart and character of both
the individuals.

From General Ponsonby to Sir E. C.

Malta   September 8, 1828.

MY DEAR ADMIRAL,—I have something to say that will
require your patience, but I have such confidence in your
head and your heart, that I feel assured you will receive it
as the advice of a most attached friend.   Your case is, in my
opinion, unanswerable : all violence and anger must injure it.
In speaking of it with everyone you make use of no measured terms; it would be more dignified not to discuss it at
all if you cannot command your feelings more.   You may
say 'Why should I spare them ? they have done their worst
to me.'   This I deny; they may make the case a party
question, and then you will be defeated, for your recall only
becomes then collateral to whether the King may appoint
and recall at pleasure.   I well know the person upon whose
shoulders everyone throws the odium of your recall.   I never
knew a man who was more willing to listen to reason when
calmly urged, but he is the last man in England to give way
to anything urged with violence or anger. . . . .

Recollect that your honor and character have not been in the most remote degree attacked; and recollect what I say, that you are the first admiral whom this very man would select for command if anything like hostilities take place. Consult some friends upon whose judgment you rely (not people who are afraid to give an honest opinion in opposition to your own), follow their advice, and avoid men who will wish for party purposes to encourage your animosity to those in power. Endeavour to suppress and, at all events, to conceal, your prejudices against those you consider your enemies. Act with dignity, prudence, and great moderation, and the business will end to the satisfaction of yourself and your real friends. Believe me, there is no one that feels a greater interest in all that concerns you, and I look forward to the time when you will add another laurel to those already gained; for you have that within which few possess—extraordinary energy and decision of character. This is great and excellent in war, but sometimes in private life it is a fault. Do not let it upon the present occasion be so, but follow the advice of those whom you can really trust.

Ever sincerely yours,
F. PONSONBY.

From Sir E. C. to General Ponsonby.

September 9, 1828.

I am, my dear Ponsonby, very sincerely thankful for the interest you have taken in my defence. I value it highly on account of your sound judgment and your clear discrimination, and not less than either for your cordial regard. But I must say you do not appear to me to take a correct view of my position, and of the line which the different light in which I see it becomes me to take. In reasoning this point with you, I am confident you will not think I undervalue your opinion in the smallest degree ; and I think you will be confirmed in this conviction by my telling you that your sentiments accord with those of her whose judgment I consider second to none, and whose heart contains as much real virtue as that of any human being on earth. Undoubtedly, if you two agree in thinking my language violent, it must be so, although I am not aware of it. I do not feel anger or irritation on account of my treatment, and it is therefore a misfortune if I express them unconsciously. As far as I can judge, my feelings are those, certainly, of contempt for the deficient capacity of men who have so mismanaged our affairs as to have occasioned the evils they profess to desire to have prevented, and indignation at their unjust treatment of me for having strenuously tried to fulfil the Treaty according to my instructions. But I am not sensible of giving expression to those feelings, as I am said to do, however little I wish to conceal them from such friends as sympathise in them. But to the point. You think my honor and character have not been in the most remote degree attacked. I, on the contrary, think that great art has been used for the purpose of injuring both, and that currency has been industriously given to false reports for that purpose. . . . It is true that Ministers in their official letters cautiously term the result of their various accusations an unfortunate misconception; and you truly observe that they may persevere in considering themselves as the best judges of this. But it is on this account that I wish to make the public also judges of this matter, in a full conviction that my opponents will never relax in the hostility which squares with their political expediency, unless forced to do so by public opinion. Nothing but that public opinion has hitherto shielded me; and independent of my seeing no other means of support, unless I deceive myself, I value the approbation of my countrymen in general more than all the favors which the Crown or the Government could possibly bestow upon me.

Recollect, my good friend, that in the first instance I was accused of disobeying my instructions for my own aggrandisement, and be assured that that idea is still kept up; that I am accused of 'staying at Malta doing nothing,' instead of obeying my orders; and that, in the meantime, in defiance of my instructions, I have suffered a mass of Greek women and children to be carried away and sold in open market for the most bestial purpose; that the dexterity of Mr. Huskisson has been employed in aiding, and the reputation for truth and honesty of Mr. Peel in confirming, this impression on the minds of those whose support has hitherto been my safeguard; and that whilst Gore was led by the apparent candour of the Duke of Wellington to recommend me to communicate directly with him as the person I might rely upon for supporting me, he had already decided on my supersession. In spite of the reliance which you and many others have on His Grace's openness to reason and conviction, I am not singular in observing in his conduct, as a politician, strongly opposing qualities. If he has deemed me a necessary sacrifice either to the Turk or the Metternich, or to an inward desire to bring the Treaty of Mr. Canning into disrepute, I do not contemplate any love of justice inducing him to suspend my doom. In this conviction, I consider it necessary to repel at once every imputation put forth which may tend to compromise the favorable opinion of my countrymen; and if exposure of injustice by open denial of false reports be abuse, I know not how I can avoid it. Now as to ——, I think that having the character of friend has enabled him to do me more mischief than any other could have done. My own brother (Bethell) went to him unknown, as thinking mutual regard for me sufficient introduction, whilst he, in the double character of professional friend and counsel of the Duke of Clarence informed of all particulars, was putting forth the severest censure. I have therefore thought it necessary to tell all my real friends to be guarded against him, a measure on which I still find reason to congratulate myself; for although I have nothing whatever to conceal, a man so disposed may temporarily pervert both words and actions to one's disadvantage. You will admit that the sooner false reports meet their contradiction the better. When ——, for instance, stated that part of De Rigny's conduct was disapproved of by his Government, I removed all excuse for his repeating it, by my having documents to show the contrary.

What I may do, or what line I may adopt, I know no more than how I should attack a hostile fleet, or resist an attack from it, until I had observed their movements. I may well mistrust my own judgment as to the mode in which I express myself, after attending to your dispassionate and friendly observations on that head. But be assured, my dear Ponsonby, I go away with a full determination to show neither anger nor violence towards anyone in discussing my subject; that notwithstanding I do not agree in your opinion of my position, I shall pay due attention to all the observations with which you have favored me; and your having so confided them to me will always be considered by me as a proof of your sincere regard. As far as I can decide at present, I do not propose communicating with any *individual* in office. I shall present myself in the first instance in due form to the Board of Admiralty, and then to the Duke of Clarence. I have no reason, that I am aware of, for waiting upon any of those who have personally taken part against me. As to my having a command in case of war, I have neither wish nor expectation to hoist my flag again without some better prospect of justice being done me. I would not willingly trust myself to people who have so treated me. Once more, my good friend, believe me very thankful for your candid and kind advice, and very strongly impressed with sincere regard for you and your dear Lady Emily.

EDWD. CODRINGTON.

From Sir John Gore to Sir E. C.

Stowell Lodge : September 1, 1828.

MY DEAR CODRINGTON,—The change that is about to take place at the Admiralty * will, I fear, deprive you of a supporter; His Royal Highness is virtually out, though until a new commission is signed, that of the Lord High Admiral must be in force, or the naval department would be totally paralysed. Therefore he occasionally attends, and all orders are given in the name of the Lord High Admiral, and will continue so until the Duke of Buckingham's answer arrives. Of all the mighty tricks, magic spells, and witchcraft that have been used to unship the Duke you will hear much ; but I am taught to believe that the fact lies in a nutshell, as follows :—Mr. Canning, when in the zenith of his joy he proposed the appointment, overlooked the high powers of the office, and on reflection, introduced into the commission 'the Lord High Admiral *and his Council.*' This the Duke overlooked ; and when from Portsmouth he sent an order, it was met by a 'No' from his Council; and on remonstrance, he was told ' you have no responsibility, it all lies on our shoulders.' He met this with, ' Either my Council or I must go out.' This was interpreted as a resignation, and so acted upon ! Do you recollect what I told you the Duke of Sussex said to me three days after the Duke of Clarence's appointment ? How fully it is verified. As Lord High Admiral and his Council he had much less authority than a First Lord, for the First, as a Cabinet Minister, could send a minute to the Board, who must obey or walk out ; the Duke stood alone— was opposed at every corner, and always out-voted ! The service has lost a sincere friend in His Royal Highness, and I, for one individual, grieve at it most truly.

Your attached friend,

JOHN GORE.

* The retirement of H.R.H. the Duke of Clarence from the office of Lord High Admiral.

CHAPTER X.

SIR EDWARD CODRINGTON left Malta on September 11, to return to England with his family in the 'Warspite'; and many were the expressions of hearty regret which were called forth on the departure of the superseded Commander-in-Chief. The feeling seemed to be universal, both at Malta and among the officers of his fleet. On leaving the 'Wellesley,' and the blue flag being hauled down, the ship was manned, and the crew cheered; and on approaching the 'Warspite,' where his flag was hoisted, he was received with the same demonstration—the value of which consisted in its being not an official matter, but a spontaneous expression of respect and sympathy. At the entrance of the harbour the salute of the batteries merged into the much more gratifying one of a long and loud cheer of hearty farewell from the Rifle Regiment, the whole of which was assembled there on purpose to pay him this unexpected compliment; and many were the little boats full of friends that accompanied the ship beyond the harbour, to speed the 'homeward-bound' with a parting cheer.

The 'Warspite' reached England on October 7, 1828. On the Admiral's flag being hauled down, he went to the Admiralty, according to official custom, to wait upon the Board. He was asked if he wished to see Sir George Cockburn, or either of the other Lords of the Admiralty. He replied, 'No; I am come to wait upon the Board of Admiralty.' He was again asked if he wished to see any one of the Board in particular, and he again answered in exactly the same words. After a short time Sir George Cockburn and one of the other Lords came in; and then Sir Edward said,

'He was come to wait upon the Board of Admiralty.'
The conversation which ensued was short and unim-
portant, the Board confining themselves to ordinary
topics. Sir E. C. rose and said, 'If the Admiralty have
no further commands for me, I beg to take leave, as I
wish to go out of town.' Sir George Cockburn then said,
'I don't know, but I dare say the Duke of Wellington
would see you.' Sir E. C. replied, 'If the Board of
Admiralty order me to wait upon the Duke of Wellington, I will do so.' Sir G. Cockburn said, 'Oh, the Board
of Admiralty won't order you to go.' 'Then,' said Sir
E. C., 'I certainly shall not go;' and he bowed and retired.

On arriving in England Sir E. C. sent to the Duke
of Clarence (October 17, 1828) some papers, which he
said,

will, I trust, have the effect of removing whatever doubts may
have obtained in the mind of Your Royal Highness, owing to
reports which appear to have been industriously circulated to
my disadvantage, before I had an opportunity of repelling
them. It is hardly possible to believe that the authors of my
supersession had not some other motives for adopting so
unusual a proceeding; and I cannot but lament that a more
just and generous feeling did not lead them to a different
mode of effecting the end they had in view.

If it had been signified to me that it was politically desirable that I should retire from my command, not an hour should
have elapsed before I would have expressed my wish to be
superseded. I trust I am free from any disposition to place
myself in collision with those under whose authority I seek
to obtain credit with my sovereign and my country; and
there is no sacrifice of personal convenience which would not
have been amply repaid to me by the friendly disposition of
those whom I now find arrayed against me, &c. &c.

It is a true saying, that a man may be judged by
knowing who are his friends and associates: it is
scarcely less true that he may be judged as well by
the letters he receives as by those he himself writes;
and in this way I have ample means of showing the
character of my father, through the medium of his
friends.

Besides those on general subjects, letters of congratulation on his victory, of indignation at his recall, and reprobation of the injustice with which he was treated, came from friends and from comparative strangers—from civilians as well as from admirals and generals. I could multiply them to any extent, did I not fear to weary unprofessional readers; for *they* cannot perhaps fully estimate the value of these communications to an officer ill used and sacrificed as he was. Great, however, was the consolation and support derived under such ill-usage from the frankly expressed opinions of officers of high standing in both services, best qualified by their professional experience and liabilities to judge rightly the professional acts of a brother officer.

Lord *Spencer** to *Sir E. C.*

Althorp: October 10, 1828.

DEAR SIR,—I cannot resist writing a line to congratulate you on your safe return from a station where, notwithstanding all the *untoward* reflections which have been circulated in various quarters, in a manner, according to my poor opinion, so unjustifiable, I continue to be one of those who look upon your proceedings with sincere admiration, and as being entitled to the gratitude, instead of the censure, of your countrymen.

Your very faithful, &c.,
SPENCER.

From *Sir John Gore to Sir E. C.*

Datchet: October 16, 1828.

At the last interview I had with ——, after explaining that you did not intend to apply for a court-martial, he said, 'I am very glad to hear you say so; for then all will go on quietly.' I said, 'But, surely, ——, something will be said or done to soothe his wounded feelings?' 'Why, he is not the first admiral that has been superseded at the King's pleasure, without a reason being assigned. Look at your friend Lord Rodney, who was superseded in the arms of victory.' 'That is all very true; but in all former instances the officers commanded a British fleet. Codrington commanded an allied fleet; his name stood embodied in the Treaty of July 6 as such; he was acknowledged by the King of France and Emperor of Russia, whose admirals were

* Earl Spencer, formerly First Lord of the Admiralty.

ordered to obey him; and in superseding him he stands
blamed in the eyes of those sovereigns as by his own!' He
replied, 'That certainly places it in a point of view I had not
before contemplated it.' Your not going to Lord Aberdeen
uncalled for is consistent with the high bearing your conduct
entitles you to exhibit. You have amply fulfilled your duty
in all its relations, and I would not have you descend one
inch from the station in which you have placed yourself. The
Secretary of State may direct your flag to be lowered, but he
cannot reach your professional reputation; and as the Admiralty do not attach any blame to you, and so far as they are
concerned you have completely done your duty, the Cabinet
may hide themselves in the labyrinth of their political expediency. Is it not curious that Malcolm should have been
obliged to adopt in the first instance the line of conduct that
he most loudly condemned in you?

Faithfully yours,
John Gore.

When Sir E. C. returned to England from the Mediterranean in the autumn of 1828, he met an acquaintance
in the street, a country gentleman of that sort to whom
foreign events or public interests are a blank, who,
seeming only to associate the thought of him with turnip
fields and pointers, greeted him with 'How are you,
Codrington? I have not met you for some time; have
you had any good shooting lately?' He merely answered, 'Why, yes, I *have* had some rather remarkable
shooting;' and passed on.

The following letter from Admiral De Rigny is a
curious commentary upon the philanthropic outcry on
the matter of Greek slaves.

From Admiral De Rigny to Sir E. C.

'Conquérant,' Navarin · le 4 octobre 1828.*

Mon cher Amiral,—Ibrahim nous a quittés ce matin, et
20,000 hommes à lui étaient partis d'avance en trois convois.
La convention a été exécutée; mais sans le Général Maison
cela eut éprouvé des difficultés, car il était venu des bâtimens
chargés de vivres, et nous avons bien fait d'entrer ici, avec
ou sans *springs*. Après-demain on sommera les places. Le
'Breslau' est où étaient la 'Sirène' et le 'Dartmouth.' Si
le fort tire, nous tirerons. Nous sommes devant Coron, et

* Received in England November 1828.

Patras. Presque tous les habitans ont demandé de s'en aller en Égypte—cela a un peu augmenté les provisions des places; mais il aurait toujours fallu les renvoyer. D'autres embarras vont commencer. Je vous félicite donc, mon cher Amiral, d'en être quitte, et en datant cette lettre de Navarin, je me plais à croire que vous y trouverez le sentiment qui guide ma plume aujourd'hui. Je vous renouvelle l'assurance de mon sincère et inviolable attachement.

H. DE RIGNY.

Presque toutes les femmes grecques ont voulu suivre les Turcs en Égypte: il a fallu employer la force, même envers les enfans, pour les faire rester *libres* en Grèce. Croira-t-on cela chez vous et chez nous?

From Sir E. C. to Lady C., at Merley, in Dorsetshire.

52 Baker Street · Monday, November 24, 1828.

Fifteen hours after we parted I got to this house, where I scrambled into a bed and got a couple of hours' sleep. Wollaston's * appearance is very afflicting, and the disease seems to pervade the whole body more or less. His head is nevertheless quite clear, and he continues dictating to different people on scientific subjects about which his mind has been employed. A paper of his on making platina malleable, was read on Thursday last at the Royal Society, partly written by himself, and partly under his dictation. His articulation is very faulty; but I have fortunately caught all he said thus far. My visits have been so received that I am amply repaid for my journey. He shows at least as much anxiety about my case as about his scientific objects. He gave Ralfe † to his old servant, saying, 'John, take that book, and you will read something that will be as agreeable to you as anything you ever read in your life.' This friendly feeling is not confined to me, but is one instance of that warmth of heart which is more brought out just now by the reflection that the time for its exertion is limited. He is very anxious to ascertain that Lyttelton is become Lord L. by his brother's death, and that he gets the estate. Be assured that, devoted as he is at this trying time to the exertion of the finest qualities of head and heart, he will die the truly great man that his intimate friends have thought him. Die, however, of his present attack, I sadly fear he must, although some little oscillations between better and worse have occasionally

---

* His valued friend, Doctor Wollaston, was gradually dying of paralysis.
† Ralfe's pamphlet on the Battle of Navarin.

excited hopes. I say *fear* when one might rather be expected to say *hope*, considering the physical dependence of one who has ever been the most physically as well as mentally independent of any man I ever knew. But his mind is still competent to do much for science, and the world may still benefit largely by the prolongation of such an existence. I caught a passing wish to see you in his enquiries, which may yet be gratified.*

E. C.

From Admiral Sir George Montagu to Sir E. C.

Stowell Lodge : January 9, 1829.

MY DEAR CODRINGTON,—I wish, to the best that my head and eyes will permit, to express my fullest approbation of your correspondence with the Admiralty. The Ministry cannot face your question, and therefore have returned an answer that reflects on themselves, and is therefore useful to you. The Secretary of State's reply is a downright shuffle, and I believe the charges and your recall went out at the same time. All of this, however, does not appear likely to obtain for you that justice which the injuries you have received in your professional calling so loudly call for.

I observe that which I had anticipated—the use of the King's authority. I think it reflects on Ministers to have drawn up instructions of the highest national import, upon which there could be two opinions. It may be supposed that the French and Russian admirals had counterparts of the same instructions, and their construction of them must have coincided with yours. Ministers will quash the question in both Houses, but they cannot prevent your laying your hard case before the public; and as you will do so with the guarded moderation that you have wisely observed in your correspondence with them, I cannot doubt of its good effect. Silence on your part would be considered as self-condemnation. Nothing can be more clear than that the Admiralty have no blame to impute to you, and they would have done *themselves* credit by acknowledging it. With every good wish for the success of your just but arduous undertaking, I am, my dear friend,

Most sincerely yours,
GEORGE MONTAGU.

---

* It was not destined to be gratified; Dr. Wollaston passed away on December 23, before Lady Codrington was within reach of seeing him.

From General Sir Henry Bunbury* to Sir E. C.

January 26, 1829.

Your letter of August 16 and 22 was extremely interesting to me. I have always felt the fullest confidence that you have a victorious case throughout, and that when it came to be brought before the public, the innumerable persons of all parties and conditions who still think for themselves (and, thank God, they are still innumerable) will feel what your services and what your treatment have been. I conclude that the present blessed Ministry (or rather Minister) has rendered you no justice, and that you are now busy and impatient to claim your vindication from Parliament and from public opinion. I am not one of those who consider Canning's interference in the affairs of Greece to have been politically wise; and as I lean to the Turks in my political affections rather than to the Russians, or to that mongrel breed which enthusiasts fancy to be the representatives of Pericles, Leonidas, and Epaminondas, I have been the less likely to be unfairly biassed in forming my humble judgment upon the transactions in the East during your command. I do not see that under the circumstances in which you were placed you could have done less than *enforce* your instructions; and, considering the great variety of difficulties, the contradiction of real intentions, and the unfair silence and coldness of the Ministry, it is quite astonishing that you should have been able at last to effect so much—to effect, indeed, *all* the maritime objects, the attainment of which was the sole acknowledged motive that led England and France to embroil themselves in the affairs of Turkey. I cannot conceive a situation more difficult or more anomalous than that in which you were placed! Expected to work out results which were attainable only by the use of powder and shot, yet liable to be made the scapegoat if your employing those means should tend to produce a war. That you have been offered up as a propitiatory offering in the vain hope of reconciling Mahmoud to the new Cabinet, I entertain no doubt; and therefore view the trick of Ministers in catching at the pretext about Greek slaves as a very mean and dirty manœuvre.

Poor Wollaston! I have grieved for the loss of such a man, and I have lamented his death the more because I know how much you valued his friendship and delighted in his society. .

---

* Long Under-Secretary of State.

Sir E. C. then devoted himself to clearing up the misrepresentations of his official conduct, and the errors of the despatches from the Home Government on which the Admiralty had been ordered to recall him. Having reason to believe, from communications with the public Offices, that he was viewed with personal hostility by the Government of the day, he wrote the following note to the Prime Minister:—

From Sir E. C. to the Duke of Wellington.

48 Upper Grosvenor Street: January 28, 1829

MY LORD DUKE,—Although I am not aware that a verbal explanation can place my conduct in my late command in a clearer point of view than I have already done by my official letters, the hostility shown me by the Government is so very painful to me, that I am induced to ask for an interview. Knowing that I devoted myself to my duty, and feeling confident that I was successful in executing it, I am quite at a loss to comprehend the grounds of this hostility; and I ask this personal interview with Your Grace in the sanguine hope of being able thereby to remove it.

I remain, my Lord Duke,
Your Grace's very obedient servant,
EDWD. CODRINGTON.

To His Grace the Duke of Wellington.

The Duke of Wellington to Sir E. C.

London: January 28, 1829.

MY DEAR SIR,—I have received your letter, and I assure you that neither I nor any individual in the Government, nor the whole Government, feel any hostility towards you; and that I shall be very happy to see you whenever you will call.

Believe me, my dear Sir,
Your obedient, faithful servant,
WELLINGTON.

To Vice-Admiral Sir Edwd. Codrington.

The Duke received him with every appearance of cordiality.

Sir E. C. said that, from the communications he had had with the Government Offices, he had reason to believe that the Government had a strong feeling of hostility to him:—

DIALOGUE.*

Duke. Hostility! I give you my word that neither I myself nor any one member of the Government, nor the Government as a whole, have the most distant feelings of hostility towards you. I know no officer for whose services or whose conduct I have a higher esteem.

Sir E. C. Then will Your Grace let me ask you why I was so superseded?

Duke. Because you seemed to understand your orders differently from myself and my colleagues, and I felt that we could not go on.

Sir E. C. I only understood my orders in what appeared their very obvious sense to *my* colleagues as well as myself, to Adam and Ponsonby, whose sense and whose judgment you well know, and also to Count Guilleminot, the only remaining Ambassador to whom we could refer for instruction; and I therefore could only act upon that understanding of them. But if Your Grace, or any one member of either of the three Governments with which I had to act, had instructed me to take a different reading of them, I should readily have guided myself by it.

Duke. Well! I still understand them as I did at first.

Sir E. C. And *I* understand them as I did at first. But let me ask Your Grace which is the part in which we differ?

Duke (after a pause). You must excuse me!!!

Sir E. C. (a low bow; taking up his hat and turning to depart).

Duke. If at any time, while in town, you should wish to say anything further to me, I should be very happy to see you.

Sir E. C. Pardon me, Your Grace; but if you feel you cannot answer that simple question, I have nothing further to say, and it will be quite unnecessary for me to trouble Your Grace again (and he retired).

From Sir E. C. in London to Lady C. at Windsor.

Wednesday, January 28, 1829.

I had a very satisfactory conversation with Lord Bathurst this morning, although he could not say more than his own full conviction of my desire to do my duty in all respects;

* In Sir E. C.'s handwriting—written down at the time.

that he had vouched for it, and my not being guided by any
political feeling whatever.   In short, as he said, his situation
was a delicate one, and I replied that I did not expect him
to speak, but merely to hear what I had to say in my own
defence.   I then asked an interview with the Duke of Wellington, and had it after waiting a long time.   He received
me equally in kindness.   He assured me that there was not
any hostile feeling whatever in him, in the Government
generally, or in any one individual composing it; that there
was no man whom he esteemed more for my professional
conduct and all my services; that the long and short
of the matter was, that I had an understanding of my instructions different from theirs, and that they felt it impossible to go on under those circumstances.   I could not get
him to point out the part to which he alluded, but he said
that Lord Lyndhurst, who had been in the three Cabinets, had
always taken the same view of them that he (the Duke) did.
I told him that Adam and Ponsonby, besides my colleagues
and Guilleminot, read them as I did, and so did every man
to whom I had shown them; that if I had been told of any
other construction which they put upon them, I should have
been guided by it as readily as my own, &c.   In short, he
cannot be wrong, and therefore only is not wrong.   But it is
clear to me that they know that I am right.   He, like Lord M.,
observed that the Treaty of Alexandria was a very important
measure.   I have lost the day's shooting, as you will agree
with me, to some good purpose.

From Sir E. C. to Lady C. at Windsor

Thursday, January 29.

I have never ceased conning over my interviews of yesterday, and the result is a conviction on my part that the
Premier is very sensible of the injustice done me, and hardly
less of his own error in superseding me; but that nothing
except 'political expediency' will lead him to do me justice.
I mean, that if I am brought fully and fairly before the
public, in Parliament, the tone and temper of the members
may induce him to go with the current.   His complimentary
style, and indeed apparent friendliness, I cannot but think
was intended to throw me off my guard, into a reliance on
him, which might defeat me.

I had a caution on this head before I saw him.   He would
not name the point of difference in the instructions, or come
to anything which would admit of explanation; although he

dwelt much and readily upon his colleagues agreeing with him in his view of them.

But, instead of being put down in my own reading, I said I thought them quite clear in my understanding of them, and so did every man to whom I had shown them; and that, although I should willingly have acted upon any interpretation of them which the Government would have pointed out, in the absence of such explanation I could only act upon that interpretation in which my colleagues, and all others whom I had the opportunity of consulting, agreed with me.

I hear he was very short and contradictory of S. Canning's opinions as to the best policy, and I am, therefore, the more suspicious of his conciliatory manner to me.

I began this by candlelight, but a dim sort of sun is now shining through the fog.

Not being able to publish official documents, Sir Edward Codrington, by the advice of a friend, drew up a narrative* of his proceedings during his command, and had it printed with several other documents, for private circulation amongst his many professional and other friends.

The letters called forth by the perusal might show the judgment passed upon his conduct by those to whom the truth was thus made known. Nothing could be stronger than the expressions used by such men as Sir Benjamin Hallowell, his old messmate Admiral Bowen, Lord Spencer, Sir George Montagu, Sir Robert Stopford, Lord Northesk, Lord Goderich, Sir Sidney Smith, General Ponsonby, Sir Hussey Vivian, Sir James Gordon, Mr. A. Baring (Lord Ashburton), Sir James Graham, Mr. Poulet Thompson, Sir Richard King, and many others.

Many letters of interest from friends in the Mediterranean followed Sir Edward Codrington to England, especially from his former colleagues, who did not cease to regret his loss, or to express their continued regret.

From Admiral Heiden to Sir E. C.

Navarin : le 10 octobre 1828

MY DEAR ADMIRAL,—Encore dix jours et nous boirons doublement à votre santé, car j'espère que vous êtes bien

* See Appendix

convaincu que nous le faisons souvent, et que votre nom est journellement à la bouche de chacun.

'Ah, si l'Amiral C. était ici, cela irait comme cela'—pour ne pas dire cela irait *tout autrement.* Oui, my dear sir, we want you every day and every hour. Vous étiez notre point central ; aujourd'hui nous sommes trois étoiles errantes ; cependant cela va, mais il faut bien autrement agir pour parvenir au même but qu'avec vous.

L'arrivée du Général Maison nous a été d'un grand secours ; car sans lui je crois que nous ne l'aurions (Ibrahim) pas chassé sans en venir à des coups de canon. Mais il paraît avoir beaucoup de respect pour 1,200 Français ; il est devenu doux comme un agneau.

Le $\frac{26 \text{ septembre.}}{6 \text{ octobre.}}$

Ibrahim est parti avec tout son monde, environ 18,000 hommes, y compris une quantité des habitans turcs de la Morée. Il a laissé par 400 Arabes dans chacune des trois forteresses, et environ 160 Turcs à Navarin, 500 à Modon, et autant à Coron. Le lendemain du départ d'Ibrahim nous avons pris Navarin par assaut. Les Turcs et Arabes nous laissaient faire, et fumaient leurs pipes. Modon a été pris de même ; on a forcé la porte, et est entré avec une centaine d'hommes. Les Turcs n'ont rien dit ; ils ont un peu protesté, mais la chose est faite, et nous avons Modon avec 56 pièces en batterie, beaucoup de poudre et des ammunitions de toute espèce en abondance, et huit mois de vivres. Ibrahim sera furieux, mais la chose est faite ; et voilà donc la Morée délivrée des Turcs, à Patras près. Le Général français Schneider est allé pour le prendre ainsi que le château. Peut-être que les Turcs feront quelque défense là. Cela doit avoir commencé aujourd'hui.

Maintenant je pars pour Malte pour faire mes provisions, et de là j'irai à Poros, pour savoir ce que nous avons à faire. Dans ce moment nous recevons la nouvelle que Patras et son château se rendent aussi sans tirer un coup de canon. Dieu merci, tout est donc fini ici ; le Général Maison va en Attique prendre Athènes et Négrepont ; et alors notre affaire sera finie, à moins qu'on ne veuille avoir Candie ; et si l'on enverra les mêmes médecins et médecines, nous aurons Candie comme nous avons le reste. Voilà la manière d'agir avec nos amis les Turcs, si on agit collectivement et que les trois Grandes Puissances veuillent une chose unanimement et sincèrement. Adieu, mon cher Amiral. Mille choses à madame et à vos chers enfans, que Dieu bénisse. Mille et mille choses de Lazareff, Katakasi, et Daschkoff, enfin de tout le monde, sans oublier mon fils.

Votre bien-dévoué ami,

HEIDEN.

From Admiral Heiden.

Poros : le $\frac{8}{20}$ janvier 1829.

MY DEAR ADMIRAL,—A happy new year to you and your dear family is the hearty wish of your humble servant. I had this day the great satisfaction to receive your very kind letter of October 13 last. Vous voyez que nous sommes aux jadis. Voilà deux mois que je n'ai pas un mot de chez nous. Quelle désagréable situation est la mienne—continuellement des conférences, des protocoles, des expéditions, et tout cela en alliés, tandis que d'un autre côté je dois être plus prudent que jamais pour ne pas mettre le feu à la maison—c'est cruel et désagréable. Je vous avoue que j'y perds mon Latin. On *vous* accuse pour avoir donné la bataille de Navarin; c'est-à-dire, de vous être défendu; tandis que sans guerre, sans convention, on attaque Patras sans façon, y jette 200 bombes, met des canons à terre, et agit le plus hostilement possible—et tout cela est parfait ! ! ! Je suis entièrement de votre opinion sur la Grèce, et j'ai toujours dit la même chose; mais il paraît qu'on ne veut pas cela, ou qu'on ne sait pas ce qu'on veut, et cela fait le malheur de ce pauvre pays, qui devra pour subsister être mis sous la protection de quelqu'un, si on ne veut pas employer de l'ensemble et de l'énergie. Le pauvre Comte Capodistrias se tue à force de travailler, et ne trouve que peu de soutien dans les soi-disants grands de sa nation.

From Admiral De Rigny to Sir E. C.

Paris : le 25 mai 1829.

MON CHER AMIRAL,—J'ai été à la vérité fort bien reçu par le Roi, et je puis le dire aussi par mes compatriotes. Je dois une si grande part de cet accueil aux circonstances que nous avons partagées ensemble, vous et moi, que je ne puis le séparer de votre souvenir et de votre amitié. Je serai bien malheureux si vous venez à Paris et que je n'y sois pas. Je désire comme vous que des explications parlementaires vous donnent occasion de faire comprendre à vos *countrymen* (s'il leur restait quelque doute à ce sujet) que votre conduite et vos actions ont été telles que, placé dans les mêmes circonstances, vous feriez encore ce que vous avez fait. . . .

J'ai laissé Heiden fort embarrassé à Égine; Capodistrias aussi fort embarrassé avec les Grecs. Je pense que dans la situation où s'est mise la Russie nous aurions dû nous en tenir à la déclaration du 16 novembre dernier; agir d'après un fait accompli, qui était la libération complète de la Morée, et renvoyer nos ambassadeurs à Constantinople, en déclarant que ce qui était fait l'était irrévocablement. Mais les renvoyer, pour *négocier* une limite plus étendue, lorsque les Turcs ont persisté à ne pas négocier—c'est dire aux Turcs, *Ne nous cédez pas*; et c'est ce qu'ils feront, sans qu'après cela nous puissions rien répliquer. Quant à la paix, je désire que nos ambassadeurs puissent l'accélérer; mais j'en doute, avant que la campagne des Russes n'ait amené quelque changement; il est certain que les Russes ne feront la paix qu'après un succès, et que le succès les rendra peut-être assez exigeants. J'ai vu Cradock, et beaucoup de vos compatriotes; je puis dire avec orgueil et reconnaissance qu'ils m'ont traité comme un ami et compagnon de Sir Edward. Ce sont deux titres que je tiens à cœur de conserver. Adieu, mon cher Amiral.

Votre très-dévoué et sincère ami,
H. DE RIGNY.

On May 25, 1829, about a year after the signature of the despatch by which Sir Edward Codrington was recalled from his command, he was at a party at Prince Leopold's, and was somewhat surprised at the following offer being made to him personally on that occasion by the Duke of Wellington, who drew him aside, and said to him—

'I have made arrangements by which I am enabled to offer you a pension of 800*l.* for your life.' The Admiral's answer was ready and immediate. 'I am obliged to Your Grace, but I do not feel myself in a position to accept it.' 'Not accept it? But why not? The King has offered it to you, and I don't see how you can well refuse it.' 'Your Grace must excuse me; I cannot receive such a thing myself while my poor fellows who fought under me at Navarin have had no head money, and have not even been repaid for their clothes which were destroyed in the battle.' 'But you have no precedent for head money.' 'Yes,' said Sir E. C., 'there is Algiers.' 'But there war was declared.' Sir E. C. replied, 'Lord Exmouth was sent on a mission, with a proposition failing which he was to declare war. I was sent to execute a treaty, and was told, if peaceable means failed, to use cannon-shot. In both cases a battle was brought on by the guns of the enemy, and in both cases he was defeated.' 'Well, but I don't see very well how you can refuse a pension when it is offered you.' 'I must beg to repeat to Your Grace, that while my men are denied what is due to them, I cannot accept anything for myself.' Shortly afterwards, one of the Duke's political friends asked him, 'What are you going to do with Codrington?' To which the Duke answered, 'What *can* you do with a man that won't take a pension?'

This incident, remarkable enough in the life of any man, however disinterested, is the more worthy of note when the two personages in question were the Duke of Wellington, Prime Minister of England, and the (by him) superseded Commander-in-Chief of the combined fleets of three nations.

From Sir John Gore to Sir E. C.

May 27, 1829.

If 'money is the criterion by which to judge a man,' your sentence is recorded indeed. We are all prouder than ever, and glory more in our friend than even at Patras or Navarin. Surely this fact is not to be hid under a bushel; surely the nation at large is to enjoy the delight of knowing that they have one noble-minded man whose spirit is above temptation and lucre. The nation have a right to know the fact and our profession (particularly those whose cause you advocate, and who nobly did their duty under your banner) to feel that that man is one of *us.* I hope you had on your three distinguished orders and medal to shine in the Duke's eye: he of all men on earth should understand and feel the force of such index, and should acknowledge, ' Palmam qui meruit ferat.'

From Captain George Martin to Colonel Codrington.

June, 1829.

MY DEAR CODRINGTON,—Thanks for your letter and the news contained in it—the *offer* of the pension is truly, as you say, worth anything as a practical confession of your father's correctness; and also as a *practical expression* of the *iniquity* of *Ministers.* But what shall I say to you of the *refusal,* and the *manner of it?* Not that I ever doubted your father's conduct on such an occasion; but there was a nobleness in the manner it was done which ought and must be remembered by every one of the profession with feelings of gratitude and admiration. You and I feel alike as to our surprise that your father could be supposed to compromise

his character for anything; but some, and even in the
Navy, have done so. What their feelings were afterwards, I
know not, and care not.

From Captain Peter Richards to Colonel Codrington.

Stonehouse: June 4, 1829.

DEAR CODRINGTON,—Few things could have delighted me
more truly than the confirmation of Sir Edward's triumph in
the offer and refusal of the pension. This I have just learnt,
and I cannot deny myself the pleasure of congratulating you
all, and I do so from my heart, on so great a triumph over
tyranny and injustice.

It is the first great step which must lead to full and ample
justice to the Admiral in reparation of wrong, as well as in
honours and rewards due to his services, and which have
been long decreed him in the hearts of all who *know* the
events of 1827-8. From the moment of the Admiral's return it was clear the Ministers felt their position with
respect to him untenable; and now their chief has acknowledged it—the day of final and complete success cannot be
far off.

From Admiral De Rigny to Sir E. C.

'Conquérant,' à Toulon: 8 septembre 1829.

Au moment de partir pour le Levant, mon cher Amiral,
je reçois votre lettre et je m'empresse d'y répondre. J'aurais
quelque difficulté de vous expliquer les motifs qui ne m'ont
pas permis d'accepter un poste dans le ministère. . . . .

Je n'oublie pas que la faveur que je trouve dans mon
propre pays je la dois à la chance heureuse d'avoir été
associé avec vous; et je n'en serais pas digne si je ne
ressentais l'injustice qui vous a été faite dans le vôtre.
J'ai appris que le Duc de Wellington vous a offert une
pension, et que vous l'avez refusée. Ou vous avez eu tort,
ou vous avez eu raison. Si vous avez eu tort, on ne vous
doit pas de pension; si vous avez eu raison, on vous doit
autre chose qu'une pension—on vous doit une *réparation.*
Telle est mon opinion. Je vais retrouver à Malte et au
Levant quelques-uns de vos officiers. Ce sont ceux qui vous
conservent attachement et respect, que je recherche le plus
volontiers, et je suis sûr d'en rencontrer bon nombre.

Adieu, mon cher Amiral. Je serai bien contrarié de n'être
pas à Paris si vous y venez. Ma sœur et ma famille seront
très-empressées de vous y rechercher. Je vous renouvelle
toujours mon inviolable attachement.

H. DE RIGNY.

The following letter relates to a previous conversation with the Duke of Sussex.

From Sir E. C. to H.R.H. the Duke of Sussex.

Eaton Square: February 9, 1830.

SIR,—I do not think that I gave Your Royal Highness a correct view, in answer to the question put to me yesterday, of the relative position of Candia on the map. This arose in all probability from the impression made on my mind of its being separated from the proposed arrangements for Greece by the other causes which I mentioned to Your Royal Highness as influencing its future destination. If the Treaty of July 6 is to be the guide, I think it must belong to the Ottoman States. But if the conditions of that treaty are abrogated by the persevering resistance of the Porte, by the insult offered to the flag of the Allies in enforcing the measure they deemed necessary for the repose of Europe, and by the assent of the Porte to the article respecting Greece in the Treaty of Adrianople, I think there is ample reason for attaching that important island to regenerated Greece. Though more contiguous to another part of the Ottoman dominions, it is more distant from the Government of Egypt, in which it has been and is still included: and although the fortresses being in the hands of the Viceroy give him military possession of the island, the country generally is in the hands of the Greeks. Now, referring to the opinion which I gave of equivalencing between the parties at issue, the property of the people of Scio and Ipsara, as well as those of Samos, all which islands must be attached to Turkey from their locality, may justly be taken into consideration; and if the individual claims on the part of Turkish subjects on the Morea, Negropont, and Candia should not be balanced by that of the Greeks in question, the improved condition of regenerated Greece and the revenue consequent on it would facilitate the execution of that part of the treaty which promises an adequate remuneration for such losses. In all my opinions or observations I speak merely as an Englishman, keeping constantly before me what appears to me best for my own country, without being led away by Philhellenism, philanthropy, or by any particular political bias. And in this character I am decidedly of opinion that the more the meditated limits of Greece can be extended the better. The conduct of Austria respecting this treaty, which she expressed by public document so much desire to see fulfilled, should exclude her from all consideration in its final arrangements. But as it is more than probable that the influence of her present Government may bar the extension of the new State in the direction of her Italian provinces, it appears to me so much the more desirable to have Candia included in it. Moreover, the benefit arising from that island as a part of the Ottoman States was possessed by Mehemet Ali, who, in conjunction with his adopted son Ibrahim, has been the author of her principal sufferings, and therefore may be justly made to pay the price in this respect of his breach of faith and his cruelties. I trust I need make no apology to Your Royal Highness for having troubled you with this lengthened explanation.

I remain, Sir, with great respect,
Your Royal Highness's faithful and obedient servant,
EDWD. CODRINGTON.

Neither of the two maps which I send with this include Candia and Alexandria, so that, to judge of the relative situation of the former, some more general map must be referred to. The map of Greece is marked so as to show nine different boundaries suggested by Sir Frederick Adam. The ninth includes Prevesa, although on the Turkish side of the proposed boundary of Arta, because it commands the entrance of that gulf, whilst it is separated from the mainland by a long sand like the neutral ground at Gibraltar. The little pamphlet by Ralfe, I think, makes our claim very clear; I only lament that he has not excluded me personally in his enumeration of the precedents. To the above, and the set of my papers, I take the liberty of adding, and of requesting Your Royal Highness will do me the honor of accepting a set of the prints intended to elucidate the affair at Patras; an event which, I humbly conceive, it would have done the country more credit to have made public than to have kept entirely out of sight. My postscript has become so long as to require a further apology from

Your Royal Highness's obliged and obedient servant,
EDWD. CODRINGTON.

From Sir E. C. to Viscount Melville.

Eaton Square : June, 1830.

MY LORD,—It is very painful to me to feel called upon again to address Your Lordship on the following subject; and I can assure you that I would gladly spare Your Lordship and myself this trouble, if the welfare of the public service and my own professional duty were not each deeply involved in it. In a letter of November 15th, 1827, I represented to His Royal Highness the Lord High Admiral the great destruction in clothes which had been sustained by many of the seamen and marines under my command in the battle of Navarin, and that some of them had lost every article belonging to them, including their beds. In reply to my request that those sufferers might be remunerated, I was informed by His Royal Highness that there was no instance of any such allowance having been made; and His Royal Highness was pleased to observe that as, by memorial from Lord Exmouth to the Admiralty, head money was granted in the case of Algiers, I ought to send him a similar memorial in favor of those who fought at Navarin, and which he would place before the Treasury. Such a memorial was therefore entrusted to the care of Sir John Gore, and was by him delivered at the Admiralty on January 3, 1828. The substance of these communications being generally known in the fleet, with the high approbation which His Royal Highness the Lord High Admiral and His Majesty's Government had been pleased to bestow on their conduct in the battle, they incurred with cheerfulness, under the prospect this held out to them, that charge against their wages which their losses had rendered indispensable. When Your Lordship looks back to the time that has elapsed since this memorial was presented, and when your Lordship reflects on the circumstances which gave rise to it, you will understand how distressing it is to me to be unable to give any satisfactory answer to the frequent applications of unfortunate claimants invalided from the service and in a state of destitution; people who naturally seek from their Admiral those rewards for valour and good conduct in successful battle which have been awarded to others on similar occasions.

Indebted as I personally feel to them for such conduct in a time of severe trial, I am sure Your Lordship will admit that it becomes my imperative duty to persevere to the utmost in strenuously, but respectfully, advocating their cause. In conclusion, I venture to submit to Your Lordship's reflection that a contrary course to that which I now solicit may endanger the adoption of a system of deliberation, where no other feeling should obtain than implicit obedience to the commands of superiors.

I have the honor to be, &c., &c.,

EDWD. CODRINGTON.

In September 1830 Lady Codrington having gone
to spend some time in France for the health of one of
her daughters (taking the other two with her), Sir E.
C. occupied that time in going with his eldest son to
St. Petersburg, to pay his respects to the Emperor
Nicholas, from whom he had, in 1827 and 1828, received
such gracious marks of favor.   The scenes they went
through, and the gratifying reception met with at St.
Petersburg, are, as usual, minutely described by Sir
E. C. in his letters to his wife, from which a few
extracts are inserted.

From Sir E. C. to Lady C.

Hamburg: Monday, September 6, 1830 (Half-past 8).

We embarked on the Friday, as we had intended, were
under way at two A.M. on the Saturday, and betwixt two and
three o'clock to-day were here ; making good 500 miles in
sixty hours. So much for speed, and almost certainty, in
making a passage.

The coming up the latter part of this river is extremely
agreeable, for the vessel keeps close to the Danish (Altona)
side, which is very thickly studded with villa-like residences
upon the top of the bank, and with neatly-kept gardens
down to the creek. Altona and Hamburg are, in fact, one
continuous town, very odd and Dutch-like, very large, very
populous, paved with round pebbles, and with a broad
planked walk, neat and well kept, railed off from a large
basin of water in the middle of the town. Amongst our
fellow-passengers was Mr. de Pedersen, the Danish Minister
to the United States, with his family, on their return to
Copenhagen. He told me the sentiment in America was
unanimously favorable to me.   I heard the same from a
very intelligent, rough, real English shipowner of Newcastle,
and other English and Germans, and Professor Struve, the
highly-famed Russian astronomer, on parting to-day said he
should ever esteem it a fortunate circumstance in his life to
have passed three days in my society, and to have made the
acquaintance of a person 'de qui le nom appartient à l'histoire.' This was a very prettily turned compliment, and one
which, from such a man, I have a right to value. To Lübeck
to-morrow. I embark in the steamer for Cronstadt and
St. Petersburg on the 9th ; and so, God bless you and yours !

E. C.

St. Petersburg September 22, 1830.

We arrived here on the 18th. The Emperor went away that same morning for a week, which has thrown us out very much. From Hamburg to Lubeck is the most abominable road ever travelled ; the jolting of the *pavé* annoyed me so much I was obliged to turn out and walk, whilst other parts were so boggy and sandy that we walked to lighten the carriage ; and we were extricated from a complete stick-fast by the leaders of another carriage behind us. Our journey, therefore, of about 32 English miles cost us 13 hours, and loaded me with an increased disability from pain in the shoulder. At half-past 8 the next morning we were in a minor steamboat, which put us into the larger one at Travemunde at noon (on the 9th). When we weighed, a foul wind saluted our weighing, and continued to check our passage the whole way ; and thus our passage was eight days instead of four or five. It was so strong at times that we could not advance ; and after sheltering once under Dago Island, we at another time put into Revel. There we passed one whole day with the agreeable and most hospitable family of the Governor, Budberg ; and I think the marked distinction there shown me in my *habit de voyage* by all parties would have contented even you. Here, indeed, I have every reason for saying the same ; and were I not bound by other ties, I might well accede to the proposal put to me by all whom I meet, to fix myself here for the winter. Heiden has been heard of in the Cattegat, and has been daily expected to reach Cronstadt ; so that I feel quite sure of our meeting. His wife is a very nice-looking and pretty elderly woman, and was delighted at seeing me. The younger son is a very handsome, agreeably mannered young fellow, whom we have taken possession of as our cicerone.

With Krusenstiern, who served as midshipman with Sir A. Cochrane, I feel quite at home.

After mentioning his hospitable reception at many houses in Petersburg, Sir E. C. continues :—

I found myself much of a lion before I mounted the star of St. George ; and I am now such an object that I shall wonder probably at passing unnoticed as I do at home. I am somewhat too old, however, to feed on such an aliment to vanity, and shall be glad to find myself once more in my little home circle, where the gratification of having been so distinguished here may excite more pleasure in the recollection of it. My shoulder—my confounded shoulder—still checks my pleasure, owing perhaps to the roughness of the *pavé*, and the carriages in which speed is the order of the day.

Sontag gave us four songs two nights ago for 25 roubles each (say francs), and gets about £800 or £900 sterling whenever she plays at the Court, and she is all over Imperially-given diamonds! Better be a foreign singer than a British admiral.

St. Petersburg: Friday, September 24.

The Emperor arrived at Tscarscoe Selo (Czarial village), and on the same day Prince Lieven wrote a note by his desire inviting W. and me to dine and sleep on Sunday, 26th. Well, we got there at 2 P.M., and at 3, in our full dress, after waiting some little time in expectation of being taken in hand by Prince Volkonski, the Lord Chamberlain, an attendant opened an adjoining door and pointed us to go in. At the very door, before I could take a look, my hand was seized as if by an old friend, and I met the most cordial welcome I ever had from anybody. As all I meet pay me the same high compliments which accompanied this warm reception, I answered my unknown friend as usual, asked him if it was customary to wear gloves here, as I was told, so contrary to our custom, and was told in the most easy terms to do whichever way I liked best. The question then succeeded of 'Comment trouvez-vous *mes* cadets sous Krusenstiern?' This question told me whose hand had been shaking mine and Will's in such welcome cordiality. But hoping he had not seen my mistake, and not being embarrassed, I brought in 'Your Majesty' directly, and thence slid into a little more deference in my manner. After some twenty minutes of such cordiality—he said, 'Mais attendez un moment. Je désire vous présenter ma vieille femme'— 'my old wife'—and away he went. She came forth directly, dressed for dinner very nicely, and ornamented with large aquamarines and very fine diamonds. Her *àbord* was suitably cordial, but evincing something of shyness. As to the compliments she paid me, in a very pleasing manner, I cannot undertake to repeat them, and shall leave you to imagine what you would have felt and said had you been in her place. They then went away, and a somebody came and conducted us into a large rotunda, where I was presented to princes and princesses, and so forth, till all the vanity I could muster was glutted with their compliments, their pleasure at seeing me, their hope I was come to stay, the gratification they assured me my arrival afforded their Emperor and Empress, &c., &c., &c. Shortly after their Majesties came into the saloon and did their court in an easy, pleasing manner, and thence proceeded to the dining-table, where they sat side by side. Their attendants of the first rank sat next to them, and I was conducted opposite, and seated betwixt two big-wigs. Will was some little distance on my right, with an excellent cicerone, who was with us in the steamer 'General Frederichi.' Both their Majesties addressed me frequently throughout the dinner, having placed me, I imagine, for that purpose, and their manner was so easy and so kind I felt quite at home. He speaks a little English, and she much the same, but understanding it, I think, better. I took Heiden's method of using either English or French as best suited me, and got on, as Ponsonby says, 'somehow or other' without difficulty. As to the dinner itself, it was, I presume, much as usual—the appearance elegant, the viands good, and the music noisy. Our number was betwixt seventy and eighty. After sitting a moderate time we returned to the saloon, gradually separated into detachments, and were told to be ready for *dancing* at eight. I was not sorry to be relieved of my harness, and that heavy sword particularly. We had had a short walk with Prince Lieven before dinner, and we took a long walk *en bourgeois* with our friend Frede-richi after it, and had tea in our own rooms before we again dressed. Their Majesties tried to pass in as quietly as any others, and at all events showed a desire to put everybody at their ease. The Empress danced, I believe, every dance —a pastime in which she takes much pleasure. She favored me with frequent conversations, and he did the same in the most easy, agreeable manner, and presented as their son one of the nicest boys of twelve years old I ever saw. The Em-peror in manliness and manly beauty shone most conspi-cuously, as did his 'old wife' for agreeable lady-like elegance in appearance and movement. It would hardly be fair to discuss her as a beauty, although there is a highbred *pleas-ingness* in her person, which is in my eyes more valuable. In dancing the 'Mazourka,' as they call it, but which is no more than our cotillon, she danced with everybody, as others do, and she did the same in walking the Polonaise, to which she invited me, in one instance, and in which I subsequently joined two or three times, as did the Emperor.

Are you shocked at this Sunday dancing? You are not a Catholic, and may think that they had better choose some other day for such amusement. However, you will agree with me that such sovereigns, who strive to dispense happi-ness to those around them whose welfare is at their mercy, cannot lose favor with the Creator of the Universe for not being quite of our way in thinking in all matters.

Wednesday, September 30, 1830.

I start afresh with my trip to Cronstadt yesterday. The Emperor desired Lieven to convey me to Peterhof, where we were to meet him and embark in his steamer for Cronstadt. We drove at once to the boat, which was waiting in a canal fronting the palace, and shortly after our arrival came the Emperor. After shaking me cordially by the hand and an easy 'Good morning' to Prince Lieven, Count Tolstoi, Admiral Greig, and the two or three others, all of us being in caps and without swords, by way of undress uniform, the Emperor stepped actively into the coxswain's berth and took the tiller. He desired me to sit amidships, directly before him. I shyed. 'Ici,' said he. I still shyed, approaching a little nearer. He repeated his 'Ici' in the same good-humoured way, until I was quite in the Admiral's berth, when I told him I did not feel comfortable thus sitting with my back to him. We first used paddles, and when the canal widened we took the oars, he giving the word as a coxswain would. He continued performing this *duty* throughout the day; but, upon my sitting down the next time we took to the boat in a sort of determined way, so as to see and be able to talk to him, he smilingly consented. I mention these trifles because they show the tone of his manner towards one. From the steamer, upon entering which he took me down to see the cabin, and showed me his cups and saucers, glass, &c., purposely made for her, he pointed out the berth for his 'old wife;' his own, where the bed, as he observed, was necessarily a foot longer, and all the minutiæ, in which I took great pleasure. We were very soon in the roads of Cronstadt, where we first visited a ship just returned from round the world; and then in succession six of the line and a frigate, one of the former being named after the Empress, and which he therefore called 'my wife.' We then landed, that he might show me Cronstadt. But I have omitted a visit to a very perfect battery in progress, which he took me to before we visited the ships. I there observed to him that His Majesty was treating me as an enemy, showing me what I might expect if ever I should come in that character. He laughed and shook me by the hand, and said, 'I hope it will not be you that will be ever sent in that character.' I replied, 'Your Majesty may depend upon it; for I should decline it, both by inclination and the certainty of failure in attempting it.' At Cronstadt britchkas were ready for us, and he desired I should accompany him in his. I went round to the left side; he did the same, and, stepping actively in, down he sat on the *left* side, and I was necessarily obliged to go round and take his right. He then showed me and explained in the most agreeable manner all the works, the town, ' my old friends,' as he termed them, the 'Azoff,' 'Ezekiel,' 'A. Newski,' 'Ganggout,' &c. After this we returned to the steamer to an excellent dinner. He went below himself at first, leaving us on deck, and shortly after called out to us to come to dinner. I found him on the left of the head of the table, and he made me take the place of distinction on his right. Looks, on my part objecting, and on his insisting, were interchanged. But down I sat, with the same interchange of looks as preparative. By the time dinner was over we had reached Peterhoff, where, with a cordial shake by the hand with me, and some little kind expressions to the others, he set out for Tzcarkoe Selo with his aide-de-camp, young Prince Suwaroff, and we for our lodgings, both Lieven and myself sleeping most of the way. You will see in this visit to Cronstadt the manner in which the Emperor had received me, and you will not wonder at the reception I meet with from all classes.

St. Petersburg : October 4, 1830.

Notwithstanding my having explained in my letter of yesterday that W. would not be invited to the dinner for to-day, I had a message this morning from Prince Volkonski that the Emperor had ordered him to be invited; he consequently attended as my aide-de-camp this morning (being also mounted on one of the Emperor's horses), at one of the most brilliant and imposing spectacles I ever saw. We were scarcely in our stirrups when the Emperor cantered past, wishing us 'good morning' with his good-humoured smile. We then followed into the centre of the palace parade, where the 3rd Regiment of infantry guards and a regiment of cavalry guards formed a square. We cantered briskly along their fronts, the Emperor bidding 'good morning' and the troops answering their 'God bless you;' the Emperor afterwards manœuvred them, the Empress being over the palace entrance, the Grand Duke Michael and the Emperor's son keeping close to him on horseback. After these manœuvres the whole marched into the square within the palace, where we all dismounted except the Emperor, the son, and Grand Duke. After regulating the troops, they also dismounted, and we all approached the centre of the square, where the priests and the choristers were prepared with their ceremonies previous to blessing the new colours. This was very imposing, and the singing beautifully simple : it was altogether, however, too long, as it included a prayer for each individually; and I found the part where we rested one knee on the gravel and pavement much too long for my angular marrow-bones. After this ceremony was over, we took to our horses, and after the troops were manœuvred out of the palace yard, we again dismounted, entered our carriages and came home. The windows of the palace were filled, and the crowd of heads filled the intervening space betwixt the troops and the wall, and when the whole troops cheered by signal beat of drum it was very fine. The Empress occupied the top of some gateway or other all the time, having a bird's-eye view of the whole ceremony, and must have been delighted.

6 P.M.

We have not been a whit disappointed in the dinner. W. and I first went to the large *manège*. I saw the tables laid ready for 5,000 men, with an excellent repast and a bottle of wine for each, all in one room. We then went to the lesser *manège* close by, where 500 covers were laid for the officers. Shortly Prince Volkonski sent for me, and we went back to the large one, to meet the Emperor, and there saw the soldiers all assembled in their places, with the Grand Duke Michael and all the attendants of high rank in waiting. The Emperor came in, attended by his very dignified ' old wife ' and her ladies. They walked up each of the avenues, left open in a cross-like form, and took a mouthful and a sip at two places to the health of the soldiers, which act received their simultaneous thanks, the Emperor occasionally noticing an old friend amongst them.

The Grand Duke Michael called my attention to a party of retired grenadiers who, he told me, now held places in the Douane ; and he observed, after telling me the amount of their present pay and advantages, ' Voilà à mon avis *le vrai libéralisme* ; n'est-ce pas, monsieur l'amiral ? ' to which I said, ' Monseigneur, je suis entièrement d'accord.' But I might have added that, as custom-house officers they were somewhat too minute in examining commercial travellers. The soldiers were now, by word of command of the Emperor himself, directed to begin their dinners, and we passed over to ours in the other *manège*, which, by the way, I must tell you is a very beautiful building, prettily ornamented on the roof, and attached to the stables, where the horses are more neatly bedded than in any of our stables, the floors being of wood, and there being stoves for warming them. Two or three general toasts were drank, appropriate, I presume, to the occasion, but without any speeches from the Emperor, and with a band that drowned all that could be said. So ended this magnificent spectacle, of which I never before have seen the equal.

Having met the Emperor and Empress at the Academy, and been very kindly received by them, Sir Edward Codrington says, October 6, 1830 :—

If all their little kind expressions were to be repeated, it would make me appear vain and foolish as overvaluing trifles. But it is the custom of this very exemplary couple thus to express their feeling of kindness to those around them, and there is no dissentient of any nation here to their just praises. They certainly afford an example which many other Courts require, and which the most morally disposed may take as their guide.

When I first joined the Emperor in the gallery he called me a 'paresseux' for not being at the parade. He repeated this to the Empress when we first joined with her; to which I replied, that I was 'confident Her Majesty would approve of my excuse, for it was writing to my wife.' 'And what were you writing about?' said he. 'Sire, I was describing the fête of yesterday.' 'Very well, very well.' These little anecdotes will enable you to understand precisely the character of the reception I meet with from those who give the tone to others; not that I have any reason to doubt the unbiassed disposition of all I meet with to show me the marked kindness I have experienced, of which I shall have so much to say to you hereafter.

October 6, 1830.

One week more will terminate our career in this round of gratifying attention, when we shall be again in the steamer for Lubeck. That I am still rheumatic I attribute to the place and the way of life; and to that rheumatic disposition I attribute the stiffness which my ride with the party on the parade has given me. I told you of the singing on blessing the new colours being beautiful. To-day we were favored by the head of that establishment calling nearly sixty of these singers together, and giving us some of the most beautiful and faultless vocal music I ever heard. The strains of the Sontag, who is so much run after, are as nothing in comparison. The General-Governor was delighted with our admiration, and is to repeat the treat on Saturday. The correctness and perfection of the little urchins who composed two-thirds of the number, is accounted for by the selection of any children whatever who exhibit at an early period an aptness for the purpose.

October 7, 1829.

As the Emperor had called me lazy for not being at the parade the day before, we went to that of yesterday. He

himself acted as inspecting general, his brother and a great
number of other generals—probably all here—assisting.

After the infantry had marched off we had an exhibition
of the Circassian cavalry, which was very curious.   A piece
of paper was placed on the ground, and was shot at on full
gallop.   The pistol man did not quite hit it, but one of two
of 'Les Amours du Nord,' who had also a musket, hit it very
fully.   Their facility of turning their little Barb or Arab
horses is very striking, as is their costume ; but I cannot
approve of either mode of doing things for adoption by
others.   They are very picturesque objects, and their dress
seems a very agreeable one.

October 7.

A note from Count Nesselrode, to tell me that the party
at Tzarscoe Selo is put off.   I believe this arises from the
sensation produced in the country by the deaths arising from
the cholera morbus, which has reached Moscow, and will
probably come here eventually.   I begin to feel very anxious
for our reunion, notwithstanding the gratifying, the warm-
hearted reception I have met with here from all sorts and
conditions of persons.

Sir E. C. to his Brother, Mr. Bethell.

Petersburg: October 5, 1830.

MY DEAR BETHELL,—   .   .   .   .
In the magnificence of the buildings no accounts have said
too much of this city ; and I am quite sure that none have
said enough of the merits of the Emperor as an absolute
monarch.   Absolute he is certainly, but with an inclination
to do everything which is just and right, and with a mind
competent to direct it.   I might well be suspected of being
biassed by his conduct to me personally, were not my feelings
and principles fully known, and become a habit which at my
period of life is not easily changed.   Absolute as he is, I
have never seen the man who, in my opinion, is more fit to
govern a *free* people.   There is no quality which excites
popularity in England which he does not possess in a superior degree.

Sir E. C. to Lady C.

St. Petersburg: October 12, 1830.

This morning we are going to take leave of the Empress
at Tzarscoe Selo, and to-morrow we embark for Cronstadt;
from whence we are to start in the night or early morning
of the 14th for Lübeck.   We were to have had a fête at

_Tzarscoe, but the Emperor receiving bad accounts from Moscow of the disease and the want of proper management, set out on Saturday morning to arrange matters himself. He will put everything into proper train, expose himself to diminish others' fears, and submit to 21 days' quarantine before he returns to the bosom of that family in which he finds real domestic happiness. If ever mortal man was worthy of being entrusted with absolute power, this is the man; and God speed him in his virtuous course, say I.

Half-past 10 p.m.—12

We are just returned from Tzarscoe, and a very gratifying take-leave we have had. The Empress has evidently been suffering under that anxiety about the Emperor's visit to Moscow which she has so frequently endured on his account. She received me in her own room in the company of all her children and one pretty maid of honor (Princess Ourusoff). After calling my attention to my own portrait already hung up, and expressing her regret that I felt obliged to go, and that the Emperor had not had the opportunity of seeing me last Sunday, I said I felt sensibly the loss I had had, but that I was repaid by the contemplation of the noble conduct of a sovereign so devoted to the good of his country, and that I did not believe there was any other like him. I then said I had a sort of conscientious desire to mention to her a mistake I made at my first interview with the Emperor.

Sir Edward Codrington described the scene to the Empress, at which she laughed heartily and enjoyed it very much.

She then called my attention to the children, who form a group that any mother might envy possession of, talked over their likenesses, &c., leading me on to the reception I had met with at Petersburg, and her hope that I was satisfied with it, which produced from me the expression of what you know I really feel for such kindness. She then desired W. might come in, and kept up conversation with him for some time. After this she desired to know what she was to say to the Emperor for me. 'That I have a very grateful sense of all the kindness he has shown me, and shall never forget it, and that I shall quit Petersburg with the highest admiration of his personal conduct and character.' She showed her satisfaction at this, expressed a wish that I should come again, took off her glove, and said she must shake hands with me 'à l'anglaise.' This she did heartily, but I did not let that hand go without kissing it with the sincerest admiration of the person to whom it belonged. We dined with the Prince Volkonski; I sat next to his very intelligent *instruite* and agreeable daughter. I found it a very pleasant dinner. In the evening we were presented to the Grand Duchess, whom we found not only very handsome, but particularly conversible and agreeable. I was only this evening informed that I ought to have asked to be presented. This opportunity arose from my expressing my regret to one of his attendants that I was going away without having seen her. If your old husband has not been led away from his judgment, these are two of the most delightful women he ever met with.

Hamburg: November 1, 1830.

We reached this place only this morning at 10 A.M., having left Petersburg on the Navarin day, but not, as I had feared, without seeing our friend Heiden. He arrived at Cronstadt on the 18th, in the evening, and Prince Menzikoff, a sort of Lord High Admiral, went down to him on the 19th. On the 20th he had leave to go up to Petersburg, and Prince Menzikoff sent the Emperor's steamer for him. I sent him word of my movements, and he therefore had a boat to take me from the Petersburg steamer on our arrival and convey me to his flagship. It is singular that he should arrive at Petersburg, and I go away, on *the* anniversary. He had prepared a sort of dinner, and had his Navarin officers to meet me. We drank the day in champagne, the Emperor, and each of us three Navarin Admirals, and each was accompanied by a salute; and we wound up, but not with a salute, with you and your family. Upon our quitting the 'Vladimir' in his boat, she saluted me with 15 guns; after which I joined my steamer to come this way, and he to rejoin his Countess, after an absence of three years and four months. That our meeting was more hurried than we could have wished is true; but it was a cordial one, and will not be forgotten by either of us, as you well know. He has been hard-worked, and under much anxiety, but is nevertheless looking well. He will learn more from his friends Greig and Krusenstiern of my endeavour to impress his Emperor with a full knowledge of his merits than it became me to tell him myself; and I shall have unbounded satisfaction in hearing that he has been well received. So much for this subject until we meet.

We started on that evening from Cronstadt with favorable appearances, but on the 22nd were again forced to shelter in Revel. I had no hesitation in putting on my St.

George, and asking the excellent Governor to let W. and myself share his family dinner. The Baroness Budberg being in mourning for a brother prevented their having any company, and we had therefore the pleasure of dining with them and their two daughters only, that day and the 23rd, during which we were still detained in Revel by a westerly gale of wind; and as they are an excellent and most agreeable family, and as they received and treated us as if we were old friends, our stay with them was a very good break into the disagreeable time we had to undergo in the steamer.

On Saturday 23rd we again put to sea, with the wind though not quite so strong, still against us, and, after a hard fight against wind and a head sea, we got sheltered under the island of Bornholm, which, having anchorage all round it, is made this use of by vessels of all sorts going and coming. We had no encouragement to move until the 30th, and I more than once wished we had kept snug, fearing our coals which we had no means of replenishing, would not hold out: however, the vessel and her master both managed well, and we accomplished our object. My next will be from England. And now I must say may God bless you and yours on the part of W. and myself.

E. C.

Sir E. C. arrived in England with his son, on the 9th November, having been detained at Lübeck by the illness of his servant, an old friend, who had then lived with him for twenty-one years, and continued to do so for twelve years more.

From Sir E. C. to Lady C.

Eaton Square: November 11, 1830.

When off Gravesend in the steamer on the 9th I wrote you a few lines, merely to let you know of our arrival after our gale-of-contrary-wind passage. Upon our reaching London we heard of the King's *not* going to dine with the Lord Mayor.

I trust you will have received my letter from Hamburg telling you of my meeting Heiden at Cronstadt on October 20, and his toasting you and yours, but, as I desired, without the salute which accompanied the other toasts. My letter to him about De Rigny appears to have mainly contributed to their finishing on the best terms possible.

From Sir E. C. to Lady C.

December 6, 1830.

.   .   .   .   .   Kempt is Master-General of the Ordnance. Lord Hill told me this, and that he is not required to be in Parliament at all.   Sir W. F. Gordon would have had it, but that Lord Hill opposed his having with it one of the sinecure Governments which are reserved for those who have distinguished themselves on service.   Well done, both Lord Hill and also Lord Grey, for relying upon good conduct gaining them just support.

5 P.M., 7th.

I went with Lord Essex to hear Chancellor Brougham give a decree on an intricate Scotch appeal, whence I went to Lord Goderich, whom I found full of kindly interest in my concerns.   I judge by him that the memorial will receive the serious consideration recommended by the King to the great Dictator, who would *not* have given it.

The memorial is the first point I aim at; and until that is accorded I could not take anything satisfactorily to myself, feeling sure that the denial would produce mutiny in case of war.   You will see that the agitation of this question, which must come before Parliament, will lead to a discussion by which the sentiments of the Ministers and others will be known; and till then I must keep quiet as to other matters. If I asked anything else now they might thus *pay me off*, whereas all the public avow that I *ought to have* what I *will not ask*.   .   .   .   The new Government are acting with right energy, and the country will settle down in quiet soon.

London : December 12, 1830.

Parliament is adjourned, and when my engagement to dine with Lord Goderich is over, I shall have nothing to prevent my meeting you at Paris whenever you fix.   Although it may be as well to keep out of Paris when sentence is passed on the Ministers.   As to the affairs of Belgium and the North, my friend, the Emperor, and the others will now have enough to do in Poland, without being brought into contact with France.   Indeed, the revolutionary spirit must now be excited in all countries where there are grievances demanding remedy.   But we seem to be as much disturbed in England as anywhere; the misfortune is that there are some grounds for such men as Cobbett to work upon, and many of the farmers are parties to the mischief.

Lord Minto, whose family is at Paris, and who is going

back there, says the whole scene is changed, the streets dull, much want of employment, and scarcely any English to be seen.

From Sir E. C. to Lady C.

December 27.

My mind is carried back 28 years by the contemplation of this date, and I dare say you are dwelling on the same subject at this moment. Well! we have had our share of ups and downs; but I think upon the whole, we have no reason to be discontented with the condition in which we now find ourselves. The storm at Paris seems to have been allayed by the firmness and able management of the King and the authorities; and therefore there is not anything of that sort to prevent our meeting there.

From Sir E. C. to Sir James Graham.

92, Eaton Square : January 5, 1831.

DEAR GRAHAM,—I wish you to consider me as a candidate for the Mediterranean command. You are probably aware, from what has passed between us before you were in office, of my considering myself precluded not only from asking, but even from accepting any command under the late Government, so long as they denied the just claims of the crews engaged in the battle of Navarin. The change of Government, and the candid explanation of your sentiments, and those of many other of my friends now in office, has placed me upon a different footing; and in spite of a desire to pass the rest of my life quietly with my family, I now court the opportunity of showing I am not unfit for the situation from which I was withdrawn in a manner so harsh and so unusual.

Yours, with great esteem,
EDWD. CODRINGTON.

The Mediterranean command was also asked for at the end of Sir Pulteney Malcolm's time by Sir John Gore, who, however, expressly stated that he put forward his request as only second to that of Sir Edward Codrington, whose claim for that command ought to be considered as paramount to that of all others, and before whom he himself would gladly give way. It was, however, given to neither of these two admirals,

but to an officer (Sir Henry Hotham) who had *not*
asked for it, and who so little wished for the appointment, that he took some days to consider whether he
should accept it.

In January 1831 Sir E. C. went to Paris and
spent a portion of the winter there. Nothing could
exceed the distinguished reception he met with from
King Louis Philippe, and the gracious kindness extended to him and his family by His Majesty, by the
Queen, and by Madame Adelaide. The Royal family
were then all young, the only one grown up being
the handsome and princely Duke of Orleans; and
both Sir E. C. and Lady C. learned to feel personally
interested in them all, from being then admitted to the
unformal evening réunions, in which they found the family
party sitting round a table with work and similar occu-
pations, and the younger children coming up to them
with simple friendliness, trying to talk to them in their
then imperfect English.

The King's familiarity with English, and their long
conversations being held in that language, was of
course a great relief to Sir E. C. ; for, though he
understood French well, he never was able, from not
having learnt it early, to master the pronunciation of
it: and it was the constant amusement of his daughters
to watch his conversations with the marshals, generals,
and distinguished men he met with, these courteous
persons listening with imperturbable gravity to his la-
borious and strangely-pronounced words, in deference
to the worthy thoughts and opinions conveyed in them;
while their own replies and arguments (and their high
compliments, too!) were given with a rapid fluency
which he could follow and admire without ever approaching to it. The courteous attentions paid to him
were unbounded, and so was also the genial and frank
kindness, which was evidently much deeper than the
matter-of-course French *politesse;* and which was received and appreciated by him and his family with
heartfelt gratitude as well as gratification. He found
himself an honored guest among the most distin-

guished, and the welcome he met with everywhere was
as flattering as it was cordial. Among many names I
can mention only a few:—such as Marshal Macdonald,
Marshal Duke de Trévise, Prince de la Mosqua, Duc
and Duchesse de Massa, Princesse de Wagram, Duc de
Dalmatie (Marshal Soult), General Lafayette, and his
gallant companion in arms and zealous supporter in
trial, Admiral De Rigny, now at the head of his profession as Ministre de la Marine.

Soon after his arrival in Paris, the King asked him
what French Order he had; and finding it was that
of St. Louis, given him by Charles X., His Majesty said,
'Then I must now give you the Legion of Honour.'
And with that Order he was consequently invested
by Louis Philippe at a special interview.

From Sir E. C. to Captain W. Codrington.

Hôtel Brighton, Rue de Rivoli   January 13, 1831

I took possession here yesterday, and went last night to a
concert at the Palais Royal.   I had an invitation direct from
the Queen, who received me very graciously.   Passing over
introductions to I don't know whom, we came up to our friend
the young Orleans.   His hand was put forth in the same
warm manner as when in England, and observing 'how delighted his father would be to see me,' he led Lord Granville
and myself to where he had placed himself (as His Majesty
himself observed) a little à l'abri in the passage entrance to
another room.   His reception of me was exactly what I
might have expected; and his subsequent conversation, of
which I had a large share in the course of the evening, in
which he described the difficulties he had had to overcome and
the conduct of the people, and especially the National Guard
in such extraordinary circumstances, was extremely interesting in every point of view, and particularly agreeable to me
from the candour and confidential tone in which it was described.   The ladies all had seats, and the men stood on the
outside of the circle they formed round the music.   We had
Malibran, with the arrival of her husband depicted on her
countenance; Lalande, David, a fine singer of great compass;
two other men whose names I don't know, and Lablache.   I
stood by the King during the first course of the concert, and

Lord Granville on the other side, and we divided the conversation between us.   He led us away to see the illuminated garden from a window in a further room, and there, besides being introduced to Duperré, and I think the Duc de Damas, and another or two, by the King, I at length fell in with De Rigny, and none of us had anything of the second course of the music.   I talked to De Rigny about the crest, and he spoke to the King, who touched on the tricolour, in which he delights.* But I said: ' Sire, the battle being fought under the white flag we cannot transfer it to the new colours, and as the object is to mark the union of the nations, not the flag merely, the effect is the same.'   I told him I thought De Rigny should wear the same distinction.   He was very easy and good-natured throughout the whole of this conversation, and we talked over his observation to me in London about the effect of the word ' untoward,' and our joint hopes that present circumstances would reproduce the concord between the two nations which that mischievous word had destroyed.

From Sir E. C. to Sir James Graham, First Lord of the Admiralty.

Paris . January 18, 1831.

My dear Graham,—We dined to day at the Palace, and after dinner the King took me into a separate room, and there entered into a conversation with me which I think it may be important to our Government to be made acquainted with; and there are obvious reasons on my part for preferring you as the medium of this communication. An apparent wish to sound me as to the feelings of our Government and the people generally, led me to warn him at once that no member of it had communicated to me any intention or desire to employ me in the execution of any of their plans, and that therefore I could only speak my individual opinions, and the sentiments which I might have heard in general conversation. He nevertheless entered at large upon the present situation of European affairs, and of his own conduct and speculations as to the future.   Of all that part which is of course already well known to your colleagues and yourself I need not say anything.   His views as to Belgium, however, whether known or not, appear to me of too much interest to be withheld

* Sir E. C. was seeking permission to wear the French flag in union with the Engl sh and the Russian, which he wished, and ultimately did adopt as his crest, the three flags united by a ribbon, on which was inscribed the word *Navarin.*

under any apprehension of detailing a previously-told tale. He considers Belgium in a state which cannot be prolonged without danger to the peace of Europe. He professes not to feel any strong bias in favor of one or other of the modes of disposing of it now in agitation; but to be bent on a speedy decision, in order to put down the agitation to which it at present gives rise. For, whilst the present uncertainty prevails, the Belgians on the one part will continue to clamour for union with France, and a large party of French to urge their incorporation with what they call their natural protectors. He himself has enough to do with France as it is, without the addition of his turbulent neighbours, of whose disposition he a long time ago cautioned the King of Holland. He would willingly see them settled quietly under any king of their own, so as to form some security for the maintenance of peace, which is the object he has most sincerely at heart; but that it will not be in his power to leave them in a situation to produce an interference of the Northern Powers, and thus oblige him to act in defence. I observed that the prevailing desire in France—annexation of Belgium—was the only thing which, under the present similarity of free governments, I could contemplate as a source of interruption to the concord which the people of both countries seemed so desirous to establish. To which he replied, that it was on that account he was so anxious for its being otherwise disposed of at once. We then discussed the possibility of the desire prevalent in France and Belgium becoming irresistible. I mentioned that in such case I was forcibly impressed with an opinion of the Duke of Sussex, that the objection of England might be palliated, if not entirely removed, by putting Antwerp upon the footing of Hamburg, Lübeck, and Bremen. He had previously suggested England being put into possession of Flushing. But it appeared to me that objections might be made, both on the score of expense and the unhealthiness of the place; and that I therefore thought the opening of Antwerp and the Scheldt to the free trade of all nations a much preferable arrangement. He questioned me as to a reported difficulty, in case such a measure should be agreed upon by our two Governments, of enforcing the opening of the Scheldt by the union of the French and English squadrons, according to the agreement assented to, but not fulfilled, by the King of Holland. I told him in reply, that looking back to what we had done with the Walcheren Expedition, I did not contemplate any difficulty in the execution of such a measure if deemed requisite. I believe the above is all the most material part of the conversation with which His Majesty honored me, although it lasted about an hour. It is, however, as well to add that he frequently repeated that the object he had most at heart was the intimate and amicable union of the two countries, as the most certain means of preserving peace throughout Europe; and he terminated his observations on this head by using the expression which Admiral De Rigny employed, at a fête given to us when together at Corfù, in describing the effects of that harmony which we had jointly made it our greatest glory to be the means of establishing between our two nations—that with the friendly union of England with France, and a correct view of their mutual interests, they might prevent hostility being raised by any other nation in Europe. Our occasional conversations upon political subjects, my dear Graham, will probably bring to your recollection how much I have regretted the revulsion produced in France by the use of the word 'untoward.' I cannot describe to you how much this feeling has prevailed amongst all classes here; and how ardently they count on the change of Ministry restoring that better disposition in which they see our mutual interest, and a prospect of permanent peace and tranquillity. It is not in my power to judge how far what I have thus detailed may be useful; but I rely upon your giving me credit, my dear Graham, for having no desire to obtrude myself by submitting it to your perusal.

Sir E. C. to Captain W. O.

January 19, 1831.

Yesterday we all dined at the Palace. Our number was about thirty-four. Marshal Macdonald, Duke, I think, of Tarentum; Admiral Truguet, who commanded a ship before I was born, and who, though 84 years old, looks younger than I do; another old Admiral, De Rigny, La Bretonnière, &c., &c., being of the party, and also Duperré, whom I had nearly forgotten. I was desired by Madame Dolomieu, the head lady of the Court, to take out the Queen, and the King handed out your mother. The Orleans not being ready, Janey was handed out by the little Nemours. I found my neighbour the Queen very agreeable, and my left-hand neighbour, the eldest daughter, very well for a young one and a stranger. I was surprised at Her Majesty helping the soup, fish, &c., as did the King opposite, in the middle part of the table. His Majesty desired me to drink wine with him, and I got a glass of better sherry than I ever tasted, which he got at Cadiz when I was there in the 'Blake.' The

dinner was excellent, and very agreeable for a royal performance. After dinner we returned to the salon, from whence
the King led me into a billiard-room adjoining, and kept me
in intimate conversation upon public matters for an hour, in
the course of which he spoke of his own proceedings and intentions in as open a manner as any intimate friend could
do. It was to me a very interesting conversation, and I have
detailed a part of it to Graham for the information of Government, which may be of some importance, if they should not
have been already apprised of his sentiments. The object
nearest his heart is a close alliance with England; and it is
curious that he should, as I observed to him, have used the
very expression used by De Rigny at Corfù. Everyone of
the influential men I have conversed with, whether in office
or out, has followed the compliments in which they have all,
without exception, addressed me, with the expression of their
anxious desire for the amicable intercourse betwixt the two
nations, of which we had set the example in our squadrons.
I might put you *au fait* as to my reception here, by telling
you it is the counterpart of that of Petersburg; and after
being treated in so distinguished a manner by those who live
under the most despotic governments in Europe, as well as
those under perhaps the most free, I cannot help being the
more strongly impressed with the contrast in England. I
know scarcely anyone, except Lord Goderich, who has shown
me any extra attention since my striking my flag. And
even after such of them as I was taught to rely upon came
into power, not one word of good intention towards me
escaped any of them; which, let them say what they will,
has appeared very extraordinary to all others who have mentioned the subject to me.

January 20, Midnight.

I have just written a letter to Lord Granville requesting
he will apply for leave for me to accept the Grand Cross of
the Legion of Honour which the King is desirous to give me.
I have engagements to dine with Sebastiani, De Case, and
D'Argout, the Minister of Marine, the parties being made
for me; and also with Marshal Macdonald, Duke of Tarentum.

Everything seems to be settling down quietly in Paris.
The National Guard is composed of shopkeepers, who have
more reason than any other class to prevent the plunder desired by the rabble; and the latter are being enlisted by
thousands for the general army and for the corps in Algiers.
I judge by what the King said to me that the formation of
an effective army is considered as the means of averting war,

and that the absence of such defensive power in France might probably induce the Northern Powers to risk the attempt to restore despotism throughout Europe. I trust there is little chance of such an attempt being henceforth successful.

January 24, 1831.

. . . It is most curious that whilst my society is avoided by all party politicians in my own country, here every Minister in turn, and all the influential people, are courting it. The National Ball was a very beautiful sight. We were two hours and a quarter in the line going; had the carriage broken; were too late to see the King, &c., received, but saw them go away enthusiastically cheered. We got com-fortably placed in the Ambassador's box next to Royalty, where the Duke of Orleans came and talked to us; and we got away very well. We go to a grand ball at the Palace to-night, and there are others forthcoming. At Sebastiani's dinner 1 sat between Soult and Decase, the latter of whom has been particularly kind, and I know has made his dinner purposely for me, as he first asked me, and then postponed, because all the Ministers, &c., who wished to meet me were engaged on that day. Yesterday I went with Cradock to Lafayette, who wanted to know me, and was even stronger than others in the expression of his approbation. These are great repayments for the littlenesses of my 'friends quotha' in England. We had forty people at Sebastiani's, and I never had such a large succession of dishes put under my nose.

Paris: January 28, 1831.

I think I see clearly the predetermination to keep me down, and to make any excuse for it which ingenuity can discover. I drew up the narrative, that by this means my papers might be the more fully and clearly understood. Graham was not then one of *the* party; and after studying my papers in the hope of being able to bring the whole question before Parliament, of Navarin and all, he frankly told me that it was quite impossible to do so successfully, because there was no word which he and others could say in favor of my side of the Greek question, which would not hit equally with the then Ministers, both Huskisson and his friends, without whose assistance the Duke of W's party would be too much for them. I wish to know if Hobhouse will take up the Memorial, in case of nothing being done by Ministers; for, 'to this complexion it must come at last.' Nothing can be more decisive of the disposition of those in power, than being uneasy at my receiving kindness here and at Petersburg. . . . Perhaps they will protest against a panorama of Navarin, which will be opened to the public to-day or to-morrow, which gives an excellent notion of the latter period of the battle, and which delights all Paris. It gives the position of the English ships exactly as I should have described them myself, or rather as I have always described them; and the view is from the 'Scipion,' as seen by her officers, most aptly situated for the purpose. The subject is not worn out here, I assure you. But the French take a more sensible view of the good effects which have arisen, and those which may further be made to arise from it, than our mere party politicians.

Paris : February 6, 1831.

I went by order to meet the King and the Royal family yesterday at the panorama of Navarin, and the Queen took my arm and received the explanation of everything from me; and she joined with the King and all the rest in delight at the representation, and the difficulties I had to contend with, and my success in overcoming them.

·. . . I dined at the Palais Royal the preceding day; and, as before, handed out the Queen, and was shown very marked attention.

I told Mons. D. Argout, the Minister of Marine, that my receiving kindness here was said to be an offence in me toward the English Ministers. 'Then,' said he, 'I hope we shall be the means of offending them much more before you leave Paris, for we cannot do too much to prove the estimation in which we hold you.' I told the King the same, and he laughed heartily at the folly of it. To-morrow Soult has *marshalled* a dinner, as De Rigny says, purposely for me.

Paris : February 16, 1831.

The scenes in the town yesterday were curious. The 'Bœuf Gras' and all the masquerade fun going on, on the Boulevards, and afterwards in the play-houses, which were full; whilst in the Fauxbourg St. Germain the people were dilapidating and sacking the Archbishop's Palace, in spite of the National Guard being all out to prevent riot.* Janey and I in the meantime went first to a ball in the above Fauxbourg, and passed quietly and uninterruptedly from

---

* We saw these two lines written on one of the walls:—

'Quel est ce tumulte ? quel est ce cri d'effroi ?
C'est le Souverain qui veut parler au Roi.'

thence to another at Rothschild's, which was quite full.
Many of the National Guard went from the dance to join
their regiments under arms. The row began with the Carl-
ists, whose effort was soon put down by the people, and they
were then excited by the Republican party. But the majority
are for the King and Ministers, and above all, for union
with England. The King told me 'that if the Duke of
Leuchtenstadt had been proposed from without, he would
not have objected; that his opposition arose from his being put
forward by the war party here;' and the name of Nemours
being permitted to go to the vote was in fact to prevent the
election of the other, which would probably have occasioned
breaking peace with England. Be assured he is honest and
trustworthy.

Sir E. C. to Mr. Bethell.

Paris March 18, 1831.

Casimir Perrier has just given out his plans of Government, and the Chamber and all the auditors seemed satisfied
with and likely to support him. Upon this depends peace,
which he and his colleagues are anxious to preserve. Sebastiani, in reply to La Fayette's interceptions, which, he
thought, implicated Russia with France, said that those
papers referred to an application from the King of Holland
for assistance, and the Emperor's readiness and preparation
to grant it until he found Prussia and Austria would not
admit his army through their territories. C. Perrier said the
Ministers were determined to put down all riots and enforce
the peace against all ' émeutes : ' and a law was proposed
to-day by them similar to our Riot Act. In short the Ministers will be supported and the peace of France, desired by
them, by the King, and by all thinking people, will be preserved. For they will not interfere for either Poland or
Italy. Salverte's speech was very good; Sebastiani's was
very hot and angry, and that diminished its good effect. I
got into the box allotted to the King's family, and sat betwixt the Duke of Orleans and the Duke of Nemours. We
were at the Palace concert on Wednesday, and heard Paganini, who is a sort of fiddling Quixote, and, as far as I go,
in spite of some beautiful tones, more worth, or rather more
extraordinary, to see than to hear.*
    The King told me that he had heard from Talleyrand that
our King expressed his desire to signify his consent to my

* This refers to Paganini's famous *tour de force* of playing very difficult
music upon *one string only* of his violin.

having the Legion of Honour in the way most agreeable to King Louis Philippe, and that he would send the written document in a few days.

Sir E. C. to Colonel W. C.

Paris: February 20, 1831.

These last three days I have attended the Chamber of Deputies, where, as you will see by our own newspapers, the debates have been very stormy but very interesting. I have now heard almost all the best speakers, and some of them, such as Dupin (senior), Odillon Barrot, Guizot, are very eloquent. They have more gesticulation perhaps than one might wish, but it is generally appropriate, and not in that hammering style which has obtained amongst our senators; and indeed they are more attentive to their tone of voice than our speakers in general, who rant about nothing. Lafayette to-day described what he and his friends considered as republicanism in his plain, quiet, appropriate manner, which pleased me much. Read it in the French papers, and you will perhaps learn to admire this kind-hearted, benevolent, and consistent old man as much as we do.

There is a deal of trickery, I think, amongst the ins here, as well perhaps as elsewhere amongst those who profess so much straightforwardness. The Chamber will be dissolved as soon as certain money bills and a new election law are passed, because it is probable that most of the present deputies will be re-elected now; but after the electors become numerous it might be otherwise. This is the explanation of the general wish expressed by them to-day, and therefore I conclude the law will not take effect until the elections for this time are over. Lafitte is not considered as equal to his post, and it is said Montalivet will not remain with him as the head, and he insists upon Odillon Barrot being removed from the Prefecture of the Seine. Decase is looked to as likely eventually to replace Lafitte. These discussions have arisen out of the late riots, which have certainly shown some want of management, but there has not, in fact, been any *question* before the Chamber all the time.

How much I lament the death of Bolivar! He and Washington are those whom I reverence, and not such men as our English politicians, who make no sacrifices.

From Sir E. C. to Captain W. C.

Paris: March 21, 1831.

I find many people more than doubting if the present Ministers can continue in place. *I* think they will. I have had conversations with Perrier before he took office, by which I see consistency in his avowal of the same principles since he accepted, and I am persuaded that France cannot become stable in her institutions unless under such management as he proclaimed in the Chamber. The violent invectives of the war party are so similar to our anti-reformers, and to the professed anticipations of the ci-devant anti-Catholics, that I expect the same results as to the continuance of the Ministers in power, the perseverance in their plans of establishing quiet, and the success of their exertions. If the King continue firm, as I am persuaded Casimir Perrier will, the anarchists will be put down, and trade, &c., will consequently revive. If once they give way, however, France will go to war with the despotic Powers, and become a prey, as before to adventurers. Nothing would be more likely to preserve her from falling into such a state than an evident sympathy in England for her difficulties, and a support of those in authority bent upon the preservation of peace abroad and quiet at home. On the contrary, evidence on our part of a disposition to encourage despotic interference in her liberty would be a truly untoward event.

Paris: March 24, 1831.

The official permission having been duly received yesterday, by Sebastiani, the King this day conferred upon me the Grand Cross of the Legion of Honour. After himself putting the ribbon over my shoulder, he kissed both my cheeks, observing that it was a French, although not an English, custom, and a mark of regard which he was glad of such an occasion for showing me; that his desire to invest me with this honorable distinction arose from the high estimation in which he held my conduct for the manner in which I led the French squadron to victory in the battle of Navarin, and for the esteem in which I was held not only by that squadron but all France. Nothing could be more gracious than his manner of doing it, or more cordially friendly than the shake of the hand which accompanied it. Sebastiani was there in uniform as Foreign Minister, and Marshal Macdonald, Duke of Tarentum, as Chancellor of the Order. The King regretted having detained me so long for this, and in order to ensure seeing me again before my departure, desired

I would dine with him to-morrow, and ask your mother and sister to come also. Thus, here is another *slap in the face* to my soi-disant friends. I trust those said friends will compare the treatment *I* have met with, with that of De Rigny under my orders. He has been made a Vice-Admiral, a Count, and Lord High Admiral; I have been falsely accused, judged, condemned, and punished without being heard in my defence, by one party; and censured by another in order to excuse a pre-determination to withhold justice from me, because I am not content under such circumstances to rely upon their supposed good intentions!

In the summer of 1831 Sir E. Codrington was appointed to the command of the Channel Fleet, for the purpose of exercise in evolutions, &c. The proceedings of this fleet are given somewhat in detail, on account of the interest attaching to one of the latest of our *sailing* fleets. Sir E. C. hoisted his flag (white at the fore) on board His Majesty's Ship 'Caledonia,' at Spithead, on June 7, 1831.

In offering the command of the squadron, Sir James Graham wrote:—

In the selection of an admiral to take the command of this squadron it has been my duty to choose an officer of tried experience and approved merit; and I have, therefore, the greatest satisfaction in offering this command to you, as a mark of respect for your past services, and under the conviction that whether in peace or war His Majesty's fleet cannot be entrusted to a more zealous or meritorious officer.

Squadron under the command of Sir Edward Codrington, August 1831 :—

	Guns.	
'Caledonia '	120	Captain Curzon (flag of Admiral Codrington).
' Prince Regent '	120	Captain Dundas (flag of Admiral Parker).
'Britannia '	120	Captain Hope Johnstone.
' Asia '	84	,, Hyde Parker.
' Donegal '	76	,, Dick.
' Talavera '	74	,, Colby.
' Wellesley '	74	,, Rowley.
' Revenge '	76	,, Hillar.
' Barham '	50	,, Pigot.
' Alfred '	50	,, Maunsell.
' Stag '	46	,, Sir Thomas Troubridge.
' Galatea '	42	,, Napier.
' Curaçoa '	26	,, Dunn.
' Victor '	18	Commander Ellice.
' Charybdis '	10	Lieutenant Crawford.
' Recruit '	10	,, Hodges.
' Royalist '	10	,, Williams.

From Sir E. C. to Captain W. C.

Portsmouth : June 10, 1831

I find much zeal and desire for information in the squadron, and I think my appointment has given general satisfaction. The ship ('Caledonia') is magnificent, and, I think, will prove the propriety of having altered her, although I would not have risked any change in so good a ship.

From Sir E. C. to Lady C.

South of Bill of Portland : Sunday, July 10, 1831.

You will have learnt by the 'Alban' of our having anchored for a few hours in a calm to prevent being driven upon the Princessa shoal.   We have ever since had lovely weather, but generally too little wind for exercising.   To-day there is a nice little breeze, which, besides enabling us to manœuvre a little before muster and church-time, will facilitate our doing so again when the people have dined.   We are very merry in the cabin, and ditto amongst the amateurs, who criticise and argue professional matters with great eagerness.

Continued by Captain W. C.

We have had a very nice time of it altogether, but, except to-day, not much of a breeze for working, and accordingly, to-day, we are tacking in succession and together in famous style.   Yesterday, Captain Parker of the ' Asia,' dined with us, bringing his guests.   The 'Asia' was signalised up close to us, and passed quite within hail, looking beautiful.   The ' Donegal ' is the one astern of us, looking also very beautiful.   The next in our line is ' Wellesley.'   The ' Talavera ' and ' Wellesley' are the worst sailers, I think : the ' Regent,' I think, we shall beat.   We have to-day got into much closer order than we were.   The first morning after our departure we were here, there, and everywhere, but to-day we have had two most capital lines.   We have as yet been only sailing close to the wind, thus :—

' Caledonia.'	
' Donegal.'	' Regent.'
' Wellesley '	' Talavera '
' Barham.'	' Revenge '
' Alfred.'	' Asia.'

Sir E. C. to Lady C.

Off Plymouth : July 13.

I cannot say how much I, or rather we, regretted yesterday that you could not share with us the pleasure of seeing the squadron manœuvre in Exmouth bay, in sight of the inhabitants contained in the sweep from Berry Head to beyond Sidmouth. The weather was perfect, as is also the scenery : red rocky points, and tracts of agricultural ground, contrasting with the verdure.

The bay was well supplied with parties coming to see the ships, a sight no one remembers seeing in that bay, often as we went to Torbay in 1793 and 1794; and the ships were full of visitors. The first day we had a calm, and I furled all sails ; and as Yarborough, even when sitting beside me at dinner, thought we were at anchor, I doubt not that all our visitors went away under the same impression. We have plenty of work, but I assure you we are all very merry, and only want you and yours to make us quite contented.

From Sir E. C. to Lady C.

Off Plymouth . July 16, 1831.

We have been off here these three days, two of which have been calm, and during one of which the Plymouth world thought us at anchor, because all the sails were furled. This morning we had a stiff top-gallant breeze, and I have worked my friends well before breakfast at tacking, and shall repeat the work presently when Jemmy Gordon * goes away again, from the visit he is now making us. I think all the squadron is pleased with the cruise, and I am sure the spectators all along the coast are delighted with the sight of us. The evening being calm, we all visited the Eddystone lighthouse. The ships are improving fast, now that they begin to comprehend, and we are improving in signals now. Mirth seems the order of the day amongst the amateur and cabin passengers.

July 19.—9 P.M.

I get so tired by this time that I can hardly do anything but turn in ; and I find so much occupation during the day that I cannot take my pen in hand. The Duke of Portland's new brig 'Pantaloon'† has been all day trying sailing with

* Admiral Sir James Gordon.

† The 'Pantaloon' brig was built for the Duke of Portland by Captain Symonds R.N., and was to be brought into the Government Service if she beat those vessels of her own class. She carried weight representing the guns and stores of the Government vessel. She was bought by Government after these trials

the 'Barham,' which she beat as completely as she has
done everything else.   I thought yesterday the squadron
had got into very good trim, for the evolutions in close order
were beautiful; but to-day there was a sleepiness in some
which annoyed me and spoilt our operations.

July 25 —9 P.M.

We have not been able to get the length of Scilly, as I
have taken every opportunity of exercising the squadron,
instead of pushing onward for no particular purpose.   I
cannot say but that some of my scholars are very unapt at
their lessons ; and it shows the more how necessary it was to
recover by such practice the information which the long war
had taught us, and which has been sacrificed to patronage
and jobbing.

By the way, as to my (reported) defective seamanship in
keeping near the land, such an observation can only originate
in ignorance ; for instance, danger arises from not knowing
one's situation, and with such good light-houses as we have,
it is become as safe to make the land by night as by day
when coming from abroad ; and surely by keeping sight of
such marks for information, one retains the best facilities for
running into port for safety, if requisite.

By going from light to light I beat the ships which sailed
before me in two instances when ordered to Plymouth, and
they were thrown out by keeping out at night and having to
make the land at a guess in the morning, and with the chance
of being embayed to leeward of their port.

Five bells—tell me to give you up for my cot.

E. C.

From Sir E. C. to H.R.H. the Duke of Sussex.
Off the Lizard : July 28, 1831.

SIR,—   .   .   .   .
The want of information which I find in the different officers
under my command as to all matters relating to the higher
branch of the naval service, the language of signals and the
evolutionary movements of a fleet, amply proves the wisdom
of reverting to the ancient custom of sending our guardships
to sea during the summer months.   Your Royal Highness
will be aware that the many years which have elapsed during
which this object has been sacrificed to false economy and
political patronage, has made the recovery of that knowledge which was acquired during the war rather up-hill
work.   I trust, however, that as great an advance has been
made in this squadron as the time and circumstances have
admitted of ; and that I may venture confidently to submit

its improvement to the professional eye of His present Majesty. I feel extremely ambitious of so doing; and I am persuaded that his presence would have a very beneficial effect upon the future exertions and the future well-doing of the naval service at large.

I have the honor to be, &c.,

EDWARD CODRINGTON.

From Sir E. C. to Lady C.

Off the Lizard : July 28.

On Tuesday, 26th, we had an exercise of great guns and small arms, in fine calm weather, which had quite the effect of a battle ; and the slow rising of the successive volumes of smoke, each fresh explosion being more white than its more diffused predecessor, had a very beautiful appearance. Yesterday we had another trial of sailing : first, the 'Pantaloon,' with 'Asia' and 'Revenge,' which she ran round very speedily; and then with the 'Barham,' 'Curaçoa,' and 'Stag,' which I started on a separate trial by themselves about four miles to windward of the others, and all of which the 'Pantaloon' passed round in the same style as she had done the 'Asia.' In five hours and a half she had beaten everything opposed to her, at the rate of one mile to windward per hour, or three miles an hour in one line. She is certainly a most extraordinary sailer, and I am glad to learn from Hardy that Symonds is to build a brig of the size of our 18-gun brigs, but to carry only 16.

We had a dinner yesterday, which included the 'Falcon' party, Yarborough and Captain Forbes; and to-day we have the 'Asia' and 'Revenge' parties, having been with all sails furled in a hot sun without 'a zephyr playing upon the bosom of Oceanus,'* although there were 'clouds impinging the cærulean arch.' I never saw a more perfect calm than has continued during the whole day, and the surface of the sea was quite like a mirror.

The ships improve, and I trust the officers who have charge of the watches will begin to find out what they have to do ; for the ignorance in all these matters which they exhibit is quite surprising.

I long to hear more of the affairs of Portugal. We have merely heard that the French had entered the Tagus, without learning whether there was any fighting or not. God bless you !

EDWD. CODRINGTON.

* Quotation from the *log of a midshipman.*

Extract of a letter from Sir E. C. to the Admiralty.

'Caledonia,' off the Lizard : August 6, 1831.

Considering the evolutionary movements as first in importance, I have lost no opportunity of putting them in practice;
the practice of signals having been simultaneous with these
operations. And I trust that the officers of the different
ships of the squadron are now as well informed in these two
branches of the profession as the time and circumstances
have permitted; and further, I have given them an opportunity of observing the lighthouses and the marks relating to
all the shoals and dangers on the coast, from the Isle of
Wight to the Land's End and Scilly Islands inclusive.
Although I consider the use of the great guns as more
effectually learned by the exercise of a few guns every day
on board each individual ship, I have embraced such opportunities as have offered for ordering a general exercise,
when the wind or weather was unfavorable for evolutionary
movements.

From Captain W. J. C. to Lady C.

The Downs: August 9.

Here we are at our immediate destination, which was kept
a secret by order from the Admiralty. This looks like being in
the neighbourhood of Holland if that Power means to attack
Leopold, as the papers tell us he has done already, and
that the French, per contra, have advanced 50,000 men into
Belgium. However, my Father thinks that our readiness
with the fleet, and within so short a distance of the Scheldt,
with the promptness of the French, will frighten the King of
Holland, if he is acting by himself, and not pushed on by
others, such as Prussia and Russia. It was two days ago
that we received the order for the eastward ; and here we
are : for promptness is everything in a case like this.   We
were off Brighton last night, having taken the turn in there
with the faster sailing ships, whilst the 'Regent' kept on her
course to Beachy Head.

August 10.

We are now anchored in a regular North Sea day, thick
and mizzly, in three lines; and have had some of the idle
folks of Deal off, to all of whom permission is given to
enter and look about the cabin; and we had a fellow that
looked very sick to-day, who was hailing his boat from the
Commander-in-Chief's stern walk !

In a letter to Sir James Graham written from the Downs, August 11, 1831, Sir E. C. says :—

If we should have to enter the Scheldt it is material that I should know what places are in possession of one or other of the contending parties. If wanted, I trust you will find us well on the alert. I tell the captains I will grant every indulgence and give all the notice that circumstances admit of; but that when I call upon them I expect increased exertions. I am glad you are getting to rights again. It will not do to be ill in these times. I hope you will find an opportunity of visiting this squadron, whether the King does so or not; for, in spite of the inaptitude of some of my scholars, by which I am worried, I think I can show you that we have gained ground.

From Sir E. C. to Lady C.

August 11, 1831.

My pen has been hard at work to-day, and I have scarcely been out of the cabin, and this minute I have received your letter (quarter before three), when Parker and sundry others up to eighteen dine with me. I think you will learn through friends at the Admiralty more about our destination than from us; but you shall hear all we can tell you. The details of this squadron just now are occupation for more than one, I assure you.

August 12.

As the Dutch have a three-decker now there (the Scheldt), in addition to their frigates, this ship may go also; and I cannot imagine that their squadron will, under any circumstances, be rash enough to risk their fortune against this. If matters should go to such an extremity, it will certainly be the policy of our Governmemt to effect their purpose through such a force as will make it more becoming to yield than to resist.

The Admiralty sanction the adoption of all my proposals about the signals.—E. C.

The expectation of hostilities with Holland passed away, and the fleet were ordered to return to the westward ; and on their way went through trials of sailing and much evolutionary practice.

From Sir E. C. to Lady C.

August 14, 1831.

You know as much as I do of our movements, since you have the same means of judging. An immense number of visitors have almost tired us out of our civility. .   .   .   . Among others came old Sir Gilbert Blane,* aged eighty-four, and so feeble he required more help than any of the party. But as wishing to see me, and to compare ' Caledonia' as she is, with the ' Sandwich ' as she was when he was surgeon of her with Lord Rodney, and as being really attached to the service and his branch of it in particular, I devoted myself to him.

From Sir William Parker to Sir E. C.

' Prince Regent,' off Portland   September 11, 1831.

My dear Sir Edward,—We were so suddenly and unexpectedly despatched yesterday from Portsmouth that I could only regret it was not in my power to do more than leave a parting message for you.

I am anxious, however, to profit by the first opportunity that may occur in our way down Channel to convey my farewell in writing, with the assurance how much I have felt gratified by my late service under your command, and my conviction that much general benefit must result from the evolutionary exercise of the squadron under your able direction; but I will not transgress by expressing *commendation,* which may in a junior savour of presumptuous conceit, feeling satisfied that you will give me credit for sincerity when I repeat that I shall be at all times happy to find myself under your flag.

I am, my dear Sir Edward,

Ever faithfully yours,

WILLIAM PARKER.

* Sir Gilbert Blane is remarkable for having instituted a medal to be given yearly as a prize for the best medical report from a Naval Surgeon. It is called by his name, and much prized in the service.

Sir E. C. to Lady C.

'Caledonia': September 21.—3.30 P M.

I have just now received orders to go to Cork and stay there about four days, merely to please Paddy, and our cruise is extended to October 10, when I am to anchor at Plymouth, but to strike my flag at Spithead in the 'Caledonia.'

Cove of Cork, September 24.

After getting the order on the 21st, we came across the St. George's Channel in admirable order. As to my staying here four days—unless the wind come well to the north we cannot get the ships out again, and therefore it may not depend on me.

25

The time of the year, the moisture of the weather overhead, and of ould Ireland herself under foot, dispose me to confine my four days' time for staying at this anchorage to the neighbourhood of Cork. It is a nice and a pretty harbour, studded round on the points as well as in the coves, on the hills and in the valleys, with houses which indicate fortunes made in business; and the scenery deserves even the name of 'riant.' And yet we know that dulness, poverty, and discontent prevail around it; and therefore it is impossible to contemplate all its evident powers of production without feeling that it has been borne down by misgovernment. The discontent at reducing the naval establishment here, I believe, is confined to a few individuals who much benefited by it; and therefore our coming here will probably not content them, although it may do something for the poorer sort of retail articles. I saw two Cork newspapers last night, and learned of the destructive capture of Warsaw, and the fearful ferment which it has occasioned in Paris—both very sorrowful events in their immediate effects, and in the consequences which may arise from them. I grieve most sincerely for both. How far they may affect England depends so much upon the opinions, or rather conduct, of those in power, that I can hardly form any judgment. But I calculate on Lord Grey and a reformed Parliament preventing our again entering on a crusade against France, even if her Lamarques and Maugins should force out the present Perier Government and grasp the power they are so incompetent to wield for their country's good. A more firm, unbending conduct in the King Louis Philippe—taking the high ground of having accepted the crown for the general welfare under great sacrifices and upon certain conditions—might have established him in almost absolute power to *govern well*, as I am quite sure he is disposed to do. And now a truce to this subject. And I have only further to add, may God bless you all!

EDWD. CODRINGTON.

From Sir E. C. to Lady C.

Cork: September 29, 1831.

We are this minute returned from Killarney, the lovely Killarney, which far exceeds the Scotch or the Cumberland lakes. No trip ever paid better, and, in spite of wet weather, we saw everything to great advantage, and are all delighted with our excursion.

I cannot enter on this subject, however, until a more leisure and suitable moment, for I have enough to do to prepare for the Corporation dinner to-day, at which all the captains and amateurs are invited to attend.

October 1, 1831.

Here we are again on board, after having undergone an extreme of gaiety, from which I am glad to return to my floating home. Our dinner with the Mayor and Corporation went off remarkably well, and I may say I never attended on such an occasion where mirth and good humour prevailed so conspicuously throughout, even to the period of it when the wine had driven away the wits of many of the party. We sat down at about half-past seven, and did not get away until two o'clock, and some remained until four. The Cork papers which I have sent to you will give you most part of our movements, and I am not sorry that they do not include *all* that was said, for, although it was very well there, it would not be quite well to detail in print. The Mayor himself did his part well, for although he blundered most ludicrously into scrapes, he most good-humouredly blundered himself out again. My health was drunk in more than one shape, and as I had to propose toasts in return, I was often on my legs. I have certainly been received here with most unbounded kindness; and the object of sending us here, as far as pleasing the people, has been eminently successful. The steamer which brought us down to-day (gratis)! and is to take us up again on Monday if still here, has brought 5,000 persons to visit the squadron; and you may imagine the boats of Cove have been well employed in bringing off those who came down by land, in addition to the numbers which came by water from Cork in sailing and other vessels.

Whilst the gaieties have been going on, a hard gale from the S.S.E. has been blowing into the harbour, and torrents of rain have fallen, so that we have had an escape from rough treatment. God bless you all!

E. C.

I was *ordered* to stay four days, but not told not to stay more.

Cove of Cork, October 5, 1831.

Considering the strong political hostility of the persons who subscribed, to the number of some two hundred, to give me this last dinner,* and the almost irresistible disposition to enter upon the subject, the meeting went off remarkably well. Under these circumstances, as I had sat till past two o'clock at the Corporation dinner, I considered it right to do the same on this occasion; and appearances and words are very deceitful if I have not given great satisfaction to all parties of whatever way of thinking. The various speakers were ever and anon upon the brink of hostile ground, and it was amusing to watch the progress of their sentiments under the avowal with which they all commenced of a determination to avoid the expression of any opinon which could possibly interfere with the great object they had throughout, of marking their ' unbounded admiration of the illustrious individual who had honored them with his presence.' At length, the list of toasts agreed upon by both parties being gone through, one man proposed a toast to which he 'thought the most fastidious of the opposite party could not object— "The People, from whom all power emanated." ' A more sensible one immediately, in a very well-judged and well-delivered speech, entreated his friend to withdraw his toast. This produced a counter-speech from another friend and a negative reply from the original, who was convinced that ' The gallant Admiral himself would find no difficulty in showing his approbation of a sentiment which was the foundation of our glorious Constitution.' The chairman had observed to me in answer to my fear for the result, that I alone could smoothen matters into harmony again; and this appeal to me gave me the opportunity I had been watching for. I should tell you that one of them, who avowed himself a radical reformer, had congratulated the meeting upon their having banished all discordant feelings in their desire to welcome my arrival amongst them, and to do honor, &c. &c. (I need not repeat the complimentary language in which I was

---

* The mercantile body of Cork.

always referred to.) And I had, in reply to this, dwelt upon the particular compliment thus paid to me, and expressed my hope that it would prove a prelude to their burying in oblivion that political hostility which was so injurious to the common weal of their common country, which so well merited the attachment they all had for her.   In rising, therefore, to ask this Mr. Burke to withdraw his toast, I disavowed any objection to the sentiment itself, considered abstractedly, but that my wish for its withdrawal on the present occasion arose from its being often used as a watchword of more objectionable meaning, and therefore liable to excite unpleasant feelings in persons of different sentiments amongst the present company. That, as I had before said, whenever I put on my uniform, I banished from my mind all political bias, and confined myself to a strict and rigid execution of the instructions of those in authority over me; that under less liberal governments the merely sitting in a society where such a toast was drunk would become a ground of reproach; and therefore, under these different considerations, I trusted the gentleman would consent to withdraw the toast.   He really did so, in compliment to me; but in the blundering way in which they do most things, he talked away his willingness into other appearances.   I took the first opportunity after this of beating my retreat, and this person, as well as all the others, pressed forward to ' have the honor of shaking hands with me,' and he again assured me that the furthest thing from his mind was to do anything unpleasant to me. Will is writing, and will probably touch upon other points of this mirthful and ludicrous, but highly complimentary and gratifying fête.   The avowed radical started by calling me Lord Codrington, and when corrected, he said I ought to be so, and therefore he should continue so to address me, as, in fact, he did, showing that it was not a mistake in the first instance.   The whole scene, although I sat in fear of an ebullition, was ludicrous in the extreme, and I wish you could have a full account of it.   E. C.

On the Land's End · 'October 16, 1831

At length we have got off thus far on our way home, and probably shall be in Plymouth Sound to-morrow; there is not wind enough to carry us there to-day.   We got out yesterday at the earliest possible moment, and the wind came more fair after we made an offing.   Our confinement in Cove has been very tedious; because the necessity of being ready to start suddenly, prevented our going out of sight of the ships, and the badness of the weather deprived us of the little enjoyment within the harbour which we might otherwise have had. Cork will much regret us; for according to what we hear, we have caused the circulation of some 40,000*l.* in that neighbourhood, and we have gratified the sight of nearly that number of spectators; for some came even from Dublin to see us. The Mayor told me I might come in for Cork if I would stand; but I am not so disposed.

Sir Edward Codrington's flag was hauled down on October 24, 1831, and he returned to his home in London.

CHAPTER XI.

In 1831 Sir E. Codrington canvassed the borough of Devonport. The 'sailor's friend' was popular; the borough was newly enfranchised, and enjoying its first election, and he was returned with ease. Of course there were many who opposed his election, one of whom becoming excited beyond measure by his political feelings, actually sent him a challenge, accompanied by a threat that if unnoticed he should be posted as a coward. It did remain unnoticed; and shortly after, a friend meeting him in London greeted him with—' I congratulate you, Codrington, on being in a position to laugh at a challenge.' His great object in going into Parliament was to advocate the cause of the Navy, which he felt to be little understood by the generality of the people ; and especially to plead the cause of his own ill-used sailors in the battle of Navarin. He had felt it as a heavy injustice towards himself and his fleet, to be, from mere expediency of party politics, denied the thanks of Parliament, which are the customary acknowledgment of such services; and also the gratuity which had been so justly deserved by them. To this latter object he determined to devote his untiring exertions, and never to rest until he had obtained for his men the reward which was their due, and which previously had been given for other similar services. When in the House of Commons he confined himself to naval subjects, and frequently brought forward cases of special ill-usage in the service. He said, that on first rising to speak in that assembly, he felt it a more trying ordeal than going into action.

In December 1831, notwithstanding the former refusals of the Government, Sir E. C. again attacked the question of the gratuity to the fleet of Navarin, by sending an official letter to the Admiralty, with a private letter to Sir James Graham, the First Lord.

From Sir E. C. to Sir James Graham.
(Private.)

Brighton: December 28, 1831.

MY DEAR SIR JAMES,—Although I trust my official letter will satisfactorily account for the irregularity in my mode of presenting the Memorial, I take this mode of calling your attention to me in the first instance of acting precisely as the King pointed out. Because, hitherto the whole has been his act, not mine: and in whatever public manner I may feel obliged, in support of my professional character, to explain my proceedings in it, it is important for me to show that I was his agent. I shall, however, be quite ready to adopt my own line, if any such alternative should unfortunately become necessary.

From Sir James Graham to Sir E. C.
(Extract.)

Admiralty · February 21, 1832.

Your Memorial has been referred by the King in Council to this Board, and we have felt ourselves bound to adhere to the previous decision of the Board of Treasury on a strict · review of the merits of the case. I fear this decision will be rejected by you as unsatisfactory: but the Board were unanimous in their opinion.

From Sir E. C. to Captain W. C.

February 23, 1832.

The negative to the Memorial announced to me in Graham's note upon another subject, has disgusted me so much that I feel indifferent as to whether this Admiralty or the former hold dominion over us.

I have in reply expressed my surprise at the Board being unanimous as at present constituted in rejecting such a claim: as it will be as unsatisfactory to the King and to the profession generally as it is to me; that my regret is not merely personal; but that I lament it on account of the Navy in general and the Admiralty Board in particular.

In 1832 Lady C. again went abroad with her two youngest daughters for their health, and Sir E. C.

made a tour of visits with their eldest daughter. This tour was extended to North Wales and the Menai Bridge (the most beautiful wonder of that time). They went from Liverpool to Manchester by railway, the first yet opened in England; and that short transit was an exciting and delightful novelty to Sir E. C. He wrote of it ·

The sensation of passing with such rapidity accompanied by such a load of coaches and passengers, was as agreeable as extraordinary; and when we met another train of carriages, or waggons with coals, &c., coming towards Liverpool, the sight was quite astounding.

Such was the impression then produced on the mind of a man who had seen many extraordinary things, of that which has now become a familiar object to almost every child in England.

After his election at Devonport Sir E. C. and his daughter went to Paris, in December, 1832, where they were joined by Lady C., and spent a part of the winter, as on the former occasion, receiving most marked and gratifying attention and kindness from King Louis Philippe and his family.

Sir E. C. to Lady C.

February 17, 1833

I dined yesterday with the Duke of Sussex, and was specially placed betwixt him and Monsieur Clode, Bey of Egypt. I don't know the name exactly; but he is a clever French doctor, at the head of 300 medical pupils at Cairo, on a salary of about 1,200l. a year.

Amongst other interesting anecdotes of the superior intellect and enlightened mind of Mehemet Ali, he mentioned his having requested the priesthood of every different sect in his dominions to join the usual ceremony of the Ulemas of Egypt in offering up thanks upon the island of Rhoda for the rising of the Nile: and he described in animated colours the whole of these very opposite religionists offering prayers and thanksgivings at one moment for the common blessing.

Reminding us of the rule against any but those of their own faith wearing *white* turbans, he said some of the Pacha's Ulemas observed upon his permitting an Armenian Secretary to exhibit the white turban in his presence. 'Come hither,

Antoine,' said the Pacha; 'lift up your robe; now open your trousers and show your shirt;' and after the secretary had so done, with great reserve, he gently dismissed him to his former occupation; and then addressing the Ulema, 'Is it not more respectful to the colour that he should wear it on his head than on his thighs?' Thus by these quick-sighted remarks he is overcoming the prejudices which impede the civilisation of his people. This Bey, who by the way is a good courtier, says he speaks his mind and puts forth his sentiments very fully although with due respect: that one day having got on perhaps a little faster than was prudent, the Pacha interrupted him with, 'Now, you are a "médecin." I ask you if you do not think that instead of pouring all your different prescriptions down one's throat at once, it is better to administer them " peu-à-peu "?' He explained the difficulty he had in getting pupils of any education fit to study under him: that he explained to the young Ulemas that their influence over the minds of the people was fast wearing out, whilst the study and consequent knowledge of the medical and surgical profession would enable then to retain their influence upon a more solid foundation; and that thus he brought them to his purpose: that he had great difficulty in overcoming the prejudice against dissection, partly owing to a belief that bodies are in a state of suffering some time after death; that he told them to consider, that even if such were the case, it is better that they should undergo the little pain they could feel under such circumstances for the good of the living; and that now, Mehemet Ali himself, Ibrahim, and all others attend the anatomical lectures. He is the only Christian, for he avowedly has not changed his faith, who was ever made a Bey. We talked over the battle of Navarin (to which he attributes lasting good effects even to Egypt and Turkey), and the reports and feelings to which it gave rise. The daughter of the Viceroy first told him of it, as a secret, before he heard it from her husband the Defterdar, at Cairo. The latter attributed their failure to our burning the Ottoman fleet with fire-vessels, &c., upon which this Bey preserved silence. Upon the others leaving the Divan the Defterdar remarked upon this, and asked if he doubted the report. He replied he did, because that neither the French nor English practised such means: and upon being asked how then the destruction could have been caused, he said by our ships going close alongside and blowing their opponents out of the water. The Defterdar was violently angry, but was pacified by the Bey reminding him that he did not obtrude until asked by him. Whether true or not, all this was very entertaining to me, as it perhaps will be in some measure to you; and you *may* agree with me and the Bey, that his Viceroy has much of the character of Peter the Great in his persevering in his plans and objects, and sacrificing his feelings when necessary for the purpose of carrying them into execution.

On March 25 and 26, 1833, a discussion in Parliament, principally between Sir Edward Codrington and Sir Robert Peel, took place, relating to a statement supposed to have been made by Sir R. Peel in 1829, 'that on hearing of Greek slaves being sent to Egypt from the Morea by Ibrahim, forty-eight hours did not elapse before instructions were sent to the Admiral.' Sir E. C. having charged this as a mis-statement by Sir R. P. at the time to his prejudice, Sir R. P. brought the subject before the House of Commons the following day, when he stated that reports of his speech at the time made use of the words immediately on the receipt of the news 'instructions were sent out to the British Admiral;' but that he had since ascertained that within sixty hours a communication was made, not to the Admiral, but to Mr. Barker, our Consul at Alexandria. Sir R. Peel took the greatest pains to show he had not intentionally stated that which was unfair or prejudicial to Sir E. C., whose principal statement towards the end of the debate was as follows :—

*House of Commons.**
Tuesday, March 26, 1833.

SIR EDWARD CODRINGTON: My complaint was this—that where everything depended on character, if any expressions had been used by any individual which could possibly induce the supposition that I had acted contrary to orders—and this, too, on a circumstance which produced a great sensation in the country—I was bound to consider them in the light of a serious and injurious charge; and thinking it was of great importance to my character that I should not be supposed to have disobeyed orders, or to have possessed a power which I did not possess—of preventing the transmission of those slaves—I wrote immediately to the Admiralty, and stated that I had seen such a report, adding, that, if

* Extracted from the 'Mirror of Parliament.'

it were the intention of Government that I should stop such
transmission, I should be glad to receive orders to that
effect, which it would be a pleasing part of my duty to
carry into execution. I shall doubtless surprise the House,
when I mention that I never received from the Government
power directly to stop the transmission of any such slaves
to the last day on which I held the command. With respect
to the communications stated to have been sent out to Mr.
Barker, the Right Honorable Baronet may be correct in what
he says. Whether he is so, I know not; but this I do
know—that without any authority from any Administration,
when Colonel Cradock, sent by the Government, had failed
owing to want of proper powers, in effecting it, and even
under orders for my supersession—I succeeded in gaining
the liberation of all the slaves then remaining in the possession of the Viceroy, although I have never yet received
thanks for that or for the treaty which I made on that
occasion for the Ottoman army evacuating the Morea. I
will not continue to attribute to the Right Honorable Baronet
words which he has once denied. I would not tie any man
down to words, even if he had uttered them, when he asserted
that he did not intend to utter them; but when I saw observations attributed to the Right Honorable Gentleman which
were made to the people of England in this House, on a question which excited their feelings so strongly, and which were
derogatory to my character, I felt it my duty to notice them.
It was a duty I owed to my own character to notice them, considering the situation which I then filled; for I had to retain
the esteem and respect of the two squadrons which were combined with my own. I had to keep up a moral influence
over the Greeks, and had also to exercise a moral power
over the Turks—that power which at last enabled me to
make with them a treaty which all the power of Government had failed in persuading them to make. If the Right
Honorable Gentleman had said that he did not mean to impute to me any disobedience of orders, the admission was all
I should have required. I was only desirous that it should
be made here in the same manner as that in which the supposed derogatory expressions were thought by me to have
been used. I have, throughout, courted public investigation
as much as any man could. The Right Honorable Gentleman may think me sore; but I hope that he will consider
the treatment which I met with—that I was superseded
without any one positive fault which could be brought before
a court-martial having been alleged against me—at a time,
too, and under circumstances, when that supersession was a

greater reflection than anything else which the Government could inflict on me.   I am well aware that a change in politics was greatly the cause of it.   I stated, however, at the time, that if orders had been sent out to me, I should have executed them; that it was my duty to obey, not to choose.   I can fearlessly look to my whole conduct and defy anyone to prove that I have disobeyed any orders, either in letter or in spirit, since I have been in the service. It is a bold assertion, but one which I make with the utmost confidence.   My conduct has been investigated by many of my friends, not with the partiality that might be supposed to arise from intimacy, but in the same strict manner that it might be expected to be dealt with by a court-martial. They have discovered no blot or stain upon it, and I therefore boldly throw out the challenge to the whole world.   I am sorry to have thus troubled the House.   I can only repeat in conclusion, that had the Right Honorable Baronet said at any previous time what he has now stated, the matter would have gone no further.

Sir E. C. to Captain W. C.

Wednesday, March 27, 1833.

The newspapers will have given you the pretty full account of what I said upon the navy estimates.   Last night Peel took the opportunity of ' *explaining.*' . . .   However I refer you to the speeches in the papers (the ' Times') where his is exact, and an excuse is made for my reply not being so.   But this event gave me unexpectedly an opportunity of giving the House an outline of my proceedings, of which I was glad to avail myself, and which was very gratifying to my well-wishers, as also was the termination of the affair. For, in consequence of his professions of esteem, and of his taking such laboured pains to show that he had not and could not have any wish to do me injustice, I stated that even if I had heard him speak the words which until now I had believed him to have uttered, his present denial at once put an end to the feeling which I had imbibed.   Although my reply is not given as I could wish, there is quite enough for you to understand all that passed and the good effects to arise from it.

Sir E. C. to Lady C.

At Brighton: April 7, 1833.

The Admiralty go on reducing in the dockyards, and thereby exciting great discontent, proportioned to the severity of the distress it occasions, and to the people thus thrown, with their families, upon the parishes. The pensions to the navy are equally illiberal, of which I have a practical instance just now brought to my notice. George Carlow, the man in question, received six wounds in his right thigh (at Navarin), one very severe, and five slighter ones, a musket ball in his left groin, one wound on his forehead, and one on his lower lip, besides the wound in his head, which occasioned the loss of one of his eyes; a large shot passed through his bedding, and all the clothes he had on were rendered useless, and he is now invalided, owing to defect in the other eye, probably due to the injury done by his wound to the optic nerve. Upon my first coming home, and asking if no consideration was to be shown for wounds, and being told by Sir George Cockburn, 'No, unless totally disabled,' I mentioned this man as one of the signalmen of the ' Asia,' in particular. The only prospect held out was, that whenever invalided his wounds would be considered. And now what have they given him, think you? You will scarcely believe me when I tell you sixpence per day! Pretty economy this !

Sir E. C. to Captain W. C.

Brighton: April 12, 1833.

(After speaking of Lady C.'s health)—The time is arrived with us when home and quiet is the best and most natural resource, instead of longings after Rome and so forth.   I think the Mediterranean affairs will pass over by Mehemet Ali getting a good slice, and more decided independence ; and some good may arise from Russia having shown her disposition.

The Order of the Bath.—House of Commons.

Friday, April 18, 1834.

Sir Edward Codrington.—I hold in my hand a bill of fees which was presented to me in consequence of my having had the honour of being made a Knight Grand Cross of the Order of the Bath. I was quite shocked at seeing this bill—not on my own account, because I was determined never to pay one farthing of the money ; but I was shocked to find that any officer having received such an honour from his Sovereign should be called upon, under such circumstances, to pay for it. This honour was conferred upon me gratuitously. I never asked for it, nor would I have had it if I could only have obtained it by asking for it. Whether asked for, or paid for, if obtained by either means, it would have been equally valueless in my estimation. Indeed, the Order itself

was lessened in my estimation from the moment I received
this bill, for I did not receive it till some three years after the
honour had been conferred upon me.   Upon receiving it, I
showed the bill to the First Lord of the Admiralty, who observed that it was very hard upon me to have such a sum to
pay.   'Not the least,' I replied, 'for I don't mean to pay a
farthing.'   I was told there was an Order in Council that
everybody must pay the customary fees; but my reply was
that I had nothing to do with the Order in Council; and
that as I had neither contributed to the Order in Council,
nor asked for this or any other such distinction, I would not
pay one single farthing for it; and I wish, Sir, all the officers
on whom the honour was conferred had done the same thing.
It would have upheld the distinction very much.   Among
the items which struck me most forcibly is the charge of
122l. to the King's household.   What patent right can they
have to entitle them to this sum?   The bill which I hold in
my hand——

Several Honourable Members.—Read! read!

Sir Edward Codrington.—It is short, and I will read it.

MEMORANDUM OF FEES.

	£	s.	d.
The Secretary of State's Office	16	17	6
The seven Officers of the Order . . .	164	17	2
The King's Household . . .	122	2	0
The Lord Chamberlain's Office . . .	26	14	6
The College at Arms, for Supporters . .	55	16	0
Total	386	7	2

After a certain time I was sent for by the First Lord of the
Admiralty, who told me that I should hear no more of this
claim.   I said: 'If this distinction is conferred only upon
the condition of paying for it, you may take it back again
from me, for I would not have it on such terms;' and I do
think, Sir, that in acting as I did, I only performed my duty
as well to the Order as to the service; and I repeat that it is
my conviction, that if every officer had acted as I did, the
Order would have been held in higher estimation than it is.

Note written down by J. B. C.

May 17, 1834.

Sir E. C. was stopped to-day, in coming out of the House
of Commons, by Mr. ——, who asked him for his advice under
particular circumstances.   A member had thrown very dis-

graceful reflections upon him in a most pointed manner, but yet without actually naming him; and turning away from him so as to render indistinct a portion of what he said, and partly to remove the appearance of its being directed at him. The strong and full report in the papers, however, left no doubt on the subject, and he was on the point of sending his friend Colonel —— with a *message* to Mr. ——.

Sir E. C. said, that though averse to *offering* his advice on such a subject, he would not hesitate to give it when asked for; professionally, he was always desirous of making his experience or his opinion available to younger officers, which he considered as one of the duties of an officer of his standing; and he would not refuse his opinion in this instance.

The principle he had laid down for himself through life was to avoid duels, for he considered duelling an odious and unjustifiable practice; and his own conduct had been guided by this principle; he did not mean to state that he would never fight a duel—there might be cases where a man of honourable feeling had no other alternative left him—but having made it his rule to avoid fighting, he considered himself especially bound to avoid also the giving offence to any man—that sort of offence which should make him consider himself wounded in honour. And he also considered himself especially bound, should he *so* have offended any man and afterwards find himself to be in the wrong, to make ample excuse and reparation to that man; and if the offence had been given in the presence of ten, he would wish the excuse to be in the presence of twenty.

It was a part of the principle he had thus laid down to himself, that when a man said anything of him which he deemed injurious to him, he desired to leave him an opportunity of removing that impression, or of explaining the circumstances that had given rise to it; and of this there had been an instance in his own case.

Under all these considerations, therefore, his opinion was, that instead of sending a hostile message by his friend Colonel ——, Mr. —— should write a letter to Mr. —— in the most conciliating spirit of which the case admitted—taking the ground of his having (unconsciously perhaps) said that which cast severe reflections upon him, and requesting that if, as he did not doubt, this had been done unintentionally on his part, he would have the goodness to state it publicly in the House of Commons. And this letter, he added, should be sent by his servant.

The letter was *so* written, and *so* sent; all intention of blame or reflection was disclaimed by Mr. —— as publicly

as the supposed insult had been offered; and Sir E. C. was
thus the means of preventing a duel between a man of middle age, the father of a large family, and a young man whose
life was valuable as being that of a man of high talent and
promise.

At this time came at last to Sir Edward Codrington
the opportunity he had so long yearned after, to which
he had sacrificed his own interests, and for which he
had himself gone into Parliament—of bringing before
the country the still unrequited services of his men,
and publicly urging their claims to that justice which
was still denied to them by the Government.

On June 17, 1834, the debate took place in the House
of Commons on Sir Edward Codrington moving for a
Committee to enquire into the claims of those engaged
in the Battle of Navarin.

Though opposed officially by the Government, represented by Mr. Labouchere and Lord Althorp, yet the
feeling and support of the House was so strongly in
favour of the motion, that the consent of the Government was given, and the object of Sir E. Codrington
secured.

House of Commons.

BATTLE OF NAVARIN.

Tuesday, June 17, 1834.

Sir E. Codrington brought forward the following motion,
and commenced by reading it:—'That this House resolve
itself into a committee to examine into the propriety of presenting an address to His Majesty, humbly requesting him
to be graciously pleased to take into consideration the claims
of the officers, seamen, and royal marines, engaged in the
battle of Navarin, on October 20, 1827.' He was sorry, he
said, to be under the necessity of troubling the House at all
on the subject, and could not conceive what difficulty Government could feel in doing justice to the men who had fought
under him. He had moved for papers, showing that head-money was given every day—that it was allowed for the capture of negro slaves; and why should it not be allowed for
the capture of Greek slaves? It was bestowed largely in
cases of piracy: and one gallant officer had received something like 800l. as his share for a battle with pirates. He

(Sir E. Codrington) had been engaged with those who were to be looked upon in the nature of pirates, for the fleet he had destroyed was meant to do more than ever pirates did or could do—to exterminate a whole people.   His own merits and claims, whatever they might be, he put entirely out of the question; but he hoped the noble lord would do him justice on the matter which preceded the battle, and by which it would be amply justified.   Most unfair and shameful misrepresentation had gone forth upon that point, which the noble lord would be able to contradict.   If credit were due to him for the battle of Navarin, much more was, in fact, due for what preceded it.   The honourable and gallant member then referred rather hastily and indistinctly to the enter-- prise in which Commodore Staines had been engaged, and to the loss of (we think) the ' Cambrian ' frigate, when the crew lost everything they possessed in the world.   He complained also that what ought to have been given to the men for the capture of one of the forts, had been unjustly seized as Droits of the Admiralty; thus, those who deserved most, in reality had got nothing.   He could not understand on what ground remuneration was now to be refused; when, as far as his knowledge went, head-money had been given in many cases before a declaration of war had been issued.   It had been granted to Admiral Boscawen, to Admiral Byng, to Sir G. Warren, to Admiral Gambier, and to several others who had been engaged with the enemy before the issue of any de- claration of war.   He had looked with great attention into those cases which were similar to the battle of Navarin, and he had found that the head or gratuity money had been given in them.   At the time that Murat was about to be deposed, Lord Exmouth blockaded the Bay of Naples, and sent to de- mand possession of the fleet.   Although he had only nominal possession of the fleet, yet a sum of one hundred thousand pounds was awarded to him for that action.   There was another case which bore a strong resemblance to his, and in which the same gallant admiral, Lord Exmouth, was the actor.   He alluded to the expedition to Algiers.   Lord Ex- mouth was sent by the Government, in the first instance, to negotiate with the states of Barbary relative to the barbarous practice of Christian slavery, and he was next commissioned to proceed to hostilities, and to use force if his demands were not complied with.   Now he really could perceive no distinction between the two cases.   It had, indeed, been pre- tended that the reward had been given to Lord Exmouth because he redeemed a certain sum for Sicily.   But surely when a reward was given to a British officer for redeeming a

trifling sum for another power, it was not too much to expect
that the same course should be pursued in a case where a
whole people were redeemed [hear, hear].   If such a distinction was to be allowed, it certainly would be an astounding anomaly.   He assured the House that the exertions
which he made in regard to this subject were not dictated
by any personal consideration ; the worry and the anxiety
which he had suffered, the misrepresentation to which he
had been subjected on account of this business, were such,
that there was no benefit which he could derive from it—
that he would have given double out of his own pocket in
order that he might have escaped the annoyance and the
distress of mind to which he had adverted.   When he stated
to the illustrious personage under whose commands he acted
that he would give up his own share, the answer was, that
he would on no account be allowed to do that.   ' You,' said
the illustrious individual to whom he had referred, ' You may
be in a situation to do without that share to which you are
entitled, but recollect that this question does not alone concern you.   Remember that you are the advocate of the other
officers and men, who may not be able to afford such a sacrifice ; and therefore on no account must you relinquish your
due.'   He (Sir E. C.) had thought it necessary to say this
much, in order to show to the House that, in making the
present motion he was actuated by no pecuniary—no personal
considerations [hear, hear].   There were some cases in
which this head-money was differently denominated.   In the
case of Algiers, for instance, the money was styled a Royal
grant, and he had seen it also described as gratuitous remuneration in lieu of head-money.   In the case of a Turkish ship
which was taken by the ' Seahorse,' head-money was refused, because the vessel had been taken before the war, and the reward
given was then called compensation money.   In the case of Admiral Byng, although a declaration of war was subsequent, and
some time subsequent, to the capture of the enemy's vessels,
yet the value of these vessels taken was awarded to him as a
prize.   Now, had he (Sir E. C.) made war, instead of taking
prompt measures for insuring peace, he would perhaps have
had a claim to head-money which could not have been resisted.
It was well known that he took the utmost pains to prevent
bloodshed, and to make a peace ; and now what was the
course pursued towards him for his attention to the interests
of the country ?   See what an example the treatment which
he had received held out to officers.   After he had done what
he thought was due to the British flag, he took such measures,
that it was seen by the enemy that he did not contemplate

further hostilities, and the consequence was as successful as he had already stated. He saved a war taking place, and a reward was refused. If a war had taken place, their prize-money would have been awarded to his squadron. Another consequence of refusing all rewards under these circumstances, under circumstances which they had always considered to entitle them to a reward, was the effect which such treatment would have upon seamen hereafter [hear, hear]. On two occasions the men had been in such a state that the captain and officers, who had great difficulty in quelling the disturbance, had declared that it would be necessary hereafter to make a specific bargain with them before they could be called upon to enter into an engagement. Let them weigh well the consequences of that. He called upon Ministers to dismiss from their minds all that political feeling, which he did not mean to say pervaded the present Government, but which alone had influenced the former Government in their decision upon this question. He called upon them to consent to award that remuneration to which both officers and men were in justice entitled, and which he was of opinion they would have received had the present Government been in office at the time the event occurred. The honourable member concluded by moving the appointment of a committee in the terms stated.

Mr. Buckingham seconded the motion.

Mr. Labouchere said that he not only spoke for himself, but on the part of the Government, when he said that it was impossible that the honourable and gallant member could have been engaged more gracefully and honourably than in endeavouring to obtain for the gallant officers and seamen with whom he had served, rights to which they considered themselves entitled. Mr. Labouchere then opposed the motion on the ground that hostile proceedings were not contemplated in the instructions, and that it was a general rule not to grant head-money or gratuities for actions, unless they were preceded by a declaration of War.

Sir F. Burdett said he could assure the House that he had felt pained that the motion was opposed, for he must confess that in whatever light he looked at the case, it appeared to him clearly made out, being founded on justice, policy, and the best interests of the country [hear, hear], and therefore deserving the consideration of Parliament. It was a question which did the honourable and gallant member great credit in whatever way it was regarded, and the manner in which he had brought it forward was highly honourable to him. If it were true, unbendingly true, that let the most

gallant action be performed which it was in the power of
man to perform, placed in the most trying and delicate
situation, yet he should, on account of some punctilio, be
refused that.reward to which he was entitled, he begged them
to remember the consequences that must flow from such a
doctrine. He could not but call to mind the unparalleled
situation in which the honourable and gallant member was
placed. If he had acted with a little less spirit [hear, hear],
if he had acted with a little less decision, he would have cast
the worst of all discredits that it was possible to cast upon
any country or any cause upon them; he would have thrown
a stain upon the arms of England, and degraded the character
of the British officer. Yes, if he had sailed back from Navarin—if he had not had the honour of the country so
deeply at heart, he would have been reproached for not having
accomplished the views entertained by Government, and on
him would have been imposed the full blame of all the disastrous consequences which might have ensued [hear, hear].
The gallant admiral had met with praise from all quarters—
from the officers in the same service as himself, from the
nation, and from a member of that Government who refused
his claim—the Secretary of the Admiralty, who was not a
stranger to the brilliant achievements of his country—he
meant Mr. Croker—who was not ill-calculated to form an
opinion of such an action, who was secretary at the most un-
rivalled, at the most memorable period of our naval history,
and who could not but allow the highest praise to the daring
achievement of the honourable and gallant officer. He well
recollected the period when Sir J. Hobhouse brought his
motion before the House, and he then denied that the honourable and gallant member had committed any fault. It
then appeared to him that the gallant admiral deserved all
the praise which was so liberally bestowed, that his conduct
merited the highest commendations, and that his decision in
action, his skill, his good taste, his tact—he knew not how
to describe his various qualities—were equal to that of all his
predecessors who lived in the memory of his country. When
he remembered how he obtained the command of the fleet,
how he put a stop to the jealousies of the commanders of the
Allied fleets, and how he contrived to combine their strength,
to direct their movements and unite their efforts, he could
not but say, that if any action ever redounded to the honour
of a commander, this brilliant achievement redounded to the
honourable and gallant Admiral, and covered him with laurels.
But suppose that the honourable and gallant officer had
committed a fault. The question did not there terminate.

It was of a two-fold nature. The case of the officers, of the seamen, and marines, still remained. They had nothing to do with the instructions sent out to the gallant Admiral. They were not responsible for his disagreement with the Government. They nobly performed their duty, and on the common principles of justice they were entitled to their reward. What would be the consequences if they mixed up the case of these brave men with a quibble as to the circumstances under which they had entered into the agreement? Might they not expect, in some future critical time, the officers and men to say to their commanders, 'Pray are we justified in obeying your orders?' What would then become of the service? If, as it was alleged, there was no precedent for rewarding the men under such circumstances of credit to them, then let a precedent be made; it was, indeed, time to make one. He repeated that it was impossible to have a stronger case, founded on policy and the best interests of the nation, to be brought forward. This claim could not be disputed; there was no doubt of it, and there was no doubt of the slander which would occur, if after performing services that all men praised—if after hazarding their lives and fortunes, they were not only to be denied their reward, but even denied remuneration for the sacrifice of their property, and the injuries they had sustained. Now, when they brought forward their claim, they were met with some distinction about head-money. He could not understand the distinction; all that he could understand was, that those unfortunate men had been kept out of their property since 1827, and that they ought, on this appeal to the House, to be both rewarded for their conduct and compensated for their losses. There was no doubt about the merit of the men, and he was sure that the performance of this act of justice to these men would be hailed throughout the country with the greatest satisfaction. He saw no difference between the cases of Algiers and Navarin. The gallant Admiral was sent out upon a most difficult mission, and he used those means which he found himself bound to adopt. They had performed that very action. The honourable and gallant Admiral was in a difficult and singular situation at Navarin; but his position in that House was still more singular. He should give his cordial support to the motion. It was the first time in the annals of history that a distinguished officer, after having achieved an action which reflected the highest honour upon his country, was compelled in that House to defend himself; to hear himself censured for having said he hoped that the

House would consent to relieve these ill-treated seamen, and do them that tardy justice which has been so long delayed.

Lord Althorp said that he conceived himself called upon to make a few observations, in consequence of the reference which had been made by the honourable and gallant member to what took place about a year after the battle of Navarin was fought, between the Lords of the Admiralty and himself, in respect to that subject. The question that he (Lord Althorp) then asked was, *Why the action was not gazetted?* * for he then felt, and he had always felt, that that action was one of the most brilliant [cheers] which had occurred. The answer which he then received gave him a certain degree of doubt as to the origin of the action, and it was observed that no shots were fired from the Turkish party; but he had since ascertained that many shots were fired [hear, hear]. With regard to the daring nature of that engagement, if that was not to be called most brilliant—if that was not to be admitted as inferior to no other, if not superior—an action in which one line-of-battle ship, one sloop-of-war, and one frigate, engaged fifty sail of vessels, some of them of no mean size, and well armed and manned, and although opposed to their full fire, compelled the whole fleet to return to their original position—if that was not a brilliant action, then, indeed, he did not know what other engagement could be dignified by that appellation. He was perfectly ready to give his opinion, and his honourable and gallant friend knew that he was very accurately aware of what took place on that occasion as to the commencement of the action, and to acquit his honourable and gallant friend of any unfounded censure or misrepresentation to which he might have been subjected on that point. With respect to the question before the House, and with regard to the conduct of the gallant Admiral before the battle of Navarin, he wished not to throw out any insinuations against him, or, in the observations which he should make, to give him any unpleasantness. His course, under the circumstances and difficulties by which he was encompassed, was a very arduous one to pursue, and no man could throw the slightest blame upon him for going into the port of Navarin, considering that it was the best proceeding he could adopt under the circumstances of the case [hear, hear]. The question, when he and his colleagues came into office, stood thus—an application had been made by the honourable and gallant Admiral to the Government which preceded the present Administra-

* Alluding to the encounter at Patras.

tion, and who were of opinion that the gratuity ought not to be awarded. The application was then made to the present Government, who had not employed his honourable and gallant friend, and who had not even succeeded to the Government that employed him. They were then called upon to consider the propriety of reversing the decision which had been given by those former Governments upon this question. He appealed to his honourable friend, although perhaps it was not right to revert to those decisions, whether those appeals were different from the present statement. The action commenced accidentally, as his honourable friend had already stated, and it was not intended by the Government which employed him that any engagement should take place. As the action, therefore, was quite accidental, and as the claim was quite unprecedented, the question was, whether they ought to reverse the decision of the Government under whom the action took place?

Sir E. Codrington was understood to remark that Mr. Canning had died.

Lord Althorp said it was true that Mr. Canning was no longer at the head of the Government of that time. The Government was not the same as that which had given the honourable and gallant member his instructions; but then the Government had not reversed those instructions. His gallant friend acted under those instructions; and, as far as he was aware, there had been no change in the instructions given by Mr. Canning. That Government, therefore, ought to have been the best judge of the propriety of awarding head-money. It had been urged that night that the sailors ought to be remunerated for the losses they had sustained. Now his honourable friend might have been informed that all claims for such losses, though those which had been made were very small, both in number and amount, had been attended to; and he was ready to pledge himself that any future claim should be attended to. The question before the House was one in which the action arose by accident, arose on the part of the opponent party certainly, and the point was, whether they should exceed the usual rule and give a gratuity to this fleet. He, however, must observe, that a very serious example would be afforded, and he besought the House to remember to what consequences might the rashness of any person in a fleet lead under circumstances similar, or, at all events, slightly differing from the present. He had looked at the action with every feeling of partiality, and no one would be more inclined than himself to give a gratuity or reward; but when he considered the facts to which he had referred, he was of opinion that it would not be proper

to make any such gratuity as that required. With regard to
the action itself, he must again repeat that it was a most
talented achievement, that it had shed a splendid lustre upon
the name of the honourable and gallant member, and that
he, of all men, ought not to be blamed for what he did, or
made the subject of misrepresentation. The grounds on
which the Government had acted had been stated by his
honourable friend, and in stating his concurrence in those
grounds, he must still express his regret that he felt it necessary to oppose the motion.

Mr. Warburton would ask if any one had pointed out what
course the gallant Admiral could have pursued other than
he had pursued, namely, to enter the bay of Navarin [hear,
hear]? Why, then, should the seamen employed in that
expedition be treated differently from those engaged in other
expeditions of a similar nature? The proper course would
be, if an error was committed, or if the gallant Admiral who
commanded exceeded his orders, to call him to a court-
martial [hear, hear]. If he had erred, let him be punished;
but why refuse to the seamen the reward which they had so
well earned [hear, hear]?

Mr. O'Connell said that his principle always was not to pay
those who did not deserve payment, but to pay those well
who deserved it. Acting on this principle, he would vote
that those seamen who fought so well at Navarin should be
rewarded. The men, in his opinion, ought not to be refused
the customary reward on account of any error committed by
the commanding officer. In such a case the proper course
would be to call the gallant Admiral to answer any charge
which might be brought against him before a court-martial.
But in this case the Government, by the mere fact of not
calling on the gallant Admiral to answer any charge, had
tacitly, though not expressly, approved of his conduct [hear,
hear]. Whatever the opinions of different parties might be,
all would acknowledge that the gallant Admiral had achieved
a brilliant victory in the cause of humanity and liberty
[hear, hear]. It would be quite unintelligible to the seamen
themselves by what species of special pleading they were
deprived of the customary reward [hear, hear]. There was
no special pleading when called on to do their duty [hear,
hear]. No! they did what English sailors would always do
—they annihilated the fleet they were ordered to fight, and
they could not do more [cheers]. It was time that the
Government of this country should at last accord to those
brave men the praise which was freely admitted to them by
the whole world [hear, hear]. It was time for the House of
Commons to tell the people of England that those seamen

might be recompensed, and he would therefore cordially support the motion [cheers].

Mr. H. L. Bulwer supported the motion.

Sir J. Sebright said he recollected his father having mentioned a speech made by a gallant admiral in that House, on an occasion similar to the present. It was made at a time when speakers were not so numerous as at present [a laugh], and when none spoke who had not something to say [a laugh]. That such was not now always the case, he was afraid he would be one of the living proofs [a laugh]. At that time, officers in the navy had not the eloquence of the honourable and gallant Admiral who had brought forward the present motion; but an old admiral, who had never been known to address the House before, got up with his mouth full of tobacco [a laugh], and, much to the surprise of all present, addressed the Speaker as follows:—'Mr. Speaker, I am not an orator, and I don't know how I could be, seeing that I have been forty years at sea; but this I know, that if you don't pay well those who serve you well, you'll not be served at all [laughter].'

Sir Robert Price hoped his noble friend would withdraw his opposition to a motion, in favour of which there appeared to be an almost unanimous feeling in the House [hear, hear]. He would earnestly entreat of the noble lord not to persist in his opposition.

Admiral Adam supported the motion, and said that the gallant Admiral had done himself great honour by his disinterestedness throughout the transaction.

Lord Althorp rose and said that he had formerly stated his reason for opposing this motion; but no one seemed to concur with him in his opposition but the honourable member for Middlesex [hear, hear]. In such circumstances he could not think of dividing the House on the question, and would therefore not persist in his opposition [cheers]; and he hoped his honourable and gallant friend would allow him to congratulate him on the result of his motion. He was sure that his gallant friend well knew that any opposition which he gave to it was merely from a sense of duty [hear, hear]. He would only add, that this result was a reward which the honourable and gallant Admiral well deserved for his distinguished conduct throughout the transaction [cheers].

The motion was then carried without a division; and it was ordered that the House should resolve itself into a committee to-morrow (this day) se'nnight.

Sir Edward Codrington then said that he was deeply sensible of the kind conduct of the noble lord on this occasion [hear, hear]. He knew that the noble lord's personal feeling could not be opposed to the motion; especially when he recollected that his brother, Captain Spencer, was one of the officers engaged. He would only add, that he could assure the House that he could not have done otherwise at Navarin than he did [hear, hear].

That was a day of *such* relief and gratification to him, that he said to us in the evening: '*Now* I can go to bed without that subject weighing on my mind as it has done hitherto. For years past it has been my last thought at night, and my first in the morning.' When he came home from the House of Commons he gave us an account of what had passed in the debate,—the closing speech of Lord Althorp in withdrawing the ministerial motion opposing the grant, and his own final reply and motion; and then added playfully, 'The gallant Admiral would have said more to the Noble Lord, had but his voice answered the helm.'

It was in order to keep himself free and unfettered in the struggle against the Government for obtaining this act of justice to his officers and men, that he had refused to accept from Government the offered pension to himself of £800 a year. And so it ever was with him; the spirit of duty was the constant guide of his life—it was warmed by the spirit of chivalry which glowed within him unchilled throughout his long life of active devotion to the duty of the hour, whatever the duty that the hour might bring.

From Captain Frederick Spencer to Sir E. C.

Althorp: June 19, 1834.

The result of your motion and the manner in which it was received by the House of Commons, must be very gratifying to you as well as all your friends; as to us who had the honour and good fortune of serving under you on that memorable occasion, what can we say? I have never attempted to express to you the admiration I felt for your conduct during those difficult and eventful times, nor shall I try now, for I hope you know it.

From Admiral Sir Richard King.

July 9, 1234.

I received yesterday the debate. . . . . I congratulate you sincerely on its success, and I think the service in general must be thankful for your perseverance. I trust now such justice is established to the service; and I do think the point ought *not* to have been disputed.

From General Sir Henry Bunbury.

August 3, 1834.

Before I left Florence I had very great pleasure in gathering the fact, from the English newspaper, that you had carried your motion for compensation to the Navarin fleet in the most triumphant and gratifying manner. . . . The act of justice has been tardy, but the unanimity of the House of Commons, when you had at length the power of stating your case, must have made amends to you individually for your long and vexatious ill-treatment.

Still, in all such cases of delay there must remain the painful fact that many brave and deserving men—perhaps, too, disabled from gaining a livelihood—must have died between 1827 and 1834, without any benefit from this vote, or even the gratification of knowing this tardy acknowledgment of their services obtained for them by the untiring efforts of their chief.

In January 1835, upon the dissolution of Parliament, Sir George Grey and Sir Edward Codrington were re-elected for Devonport.

In April 1836, Sir E. Codrington received a very gratifying testimonial from his Navarin officers through their representative, Captain Curzon. It was a very beautiful silver vase, ornamented with representations of the bow of the 'Asia' (an actual likeness), and naval emblems of various descriptions; with the following record engraved on one of its sides:—

Presented to Vice-Admiral Sir Edward Codrington, G.C.B. by the Officers who served under his command at the Battle of Navarin, in testimony of their admiration of his able and persevering advocacy of their claims in Parliament. June 1834. 'Forti et fideli nihil difficile.'

From Sir E. C. to Captain Curzon.

Eaton Square : April 24, 1836.

MY DEAR CURZON,—You will readily believe me, that I prize above all price the beautiful and magnificent memorial presented to me by you and my other brave companions in arms who so nobly supported my flag and the honour of our country during that day of severe trial, of which it will descend through my family as a lasting record. That my zealous advocacy of your just claims was crowned with success would alone have been felt by me as a sufficient reward for my exertions; but the addition of such a splendid proof of your esteem and regard has made an impression on my heart which will continue to the end of my existence. I will beg you to communicate these sentiments to those who have united with you in this testimony of their attachment to their old Commander-in-Chief.

Your sincere friend,

EDWD. CODRINGTON.

In January 1837 Admiral Codrington lost the dear wife who had been the treasure of his heart for thirty-six years; and deeply did he feel this misfortune. In our home retirement after that great loss, he and I used to walk up and down the room together for hours (following out his old professional habit), while he talked to me of her. I had long been his most habitual companion, as well as hers, amongst their children; a habit that had grown up insensibly out of the two circumstances of my brothers being older and withdrawn from home by their schools and their professions, and my sisters being considerably younger.

Having always taken great interest in what I considered his *live anecdotes*, I got him, in this time of leisure, into the habit of letting me write them down from his dictation. He used to 'walk the quarter-deck,' as he called it, while I wrote, taking the drawing-room from corner to corner, because he said the side of the room was too short—'like a fisherman's quarter-deck, two steps and overboard;' and I was always astonished at the command of language he showed in this occupation, considering what I had heard him say of his want

of educational training, and his never having learnt a
rule of grammar; for he never hesitated for an expression, and never changed a word in the sentences which
he dictated so distinctly and deliberately.   The inci-
dents related as having taken place at and after the battle
of the ' First of June ' and before and after the battle of
Navarin, &c., were caught and recorded in this manner.

The influence of this dear wife and mother ever
remained, and pervaded the home of which she was
the guiding spirit: it survived as a power of blessing.
On one occasion, many years after her death, I ventured
to call it in as a help in the time of need.   My Father
was very much irritated at a circumstance that had
happened, and in the excitement of the moment seemed
bent upon taking a course which, however spirited,
we all felt to be very imprudent ; but our remon-
strances were powerless.   In the evening, while walking
up and down the room, still talking the matter over, I
said quietly, ' I cannot help thinking very much of what
she would have felt about it ; I think she would have
been very sorry.'   He made no answer, and we parted
for the night: but the thought of *her*, the peace-maker,
acted like a charm to soothe the irritation; and when
he joined us next morning a calmer judgment had taken
the place of it.   I felt, however, that so sacred a spring
of influence was not lightly to be touched, but to be
cherished with reverence; and rejoice that no other occasion ever arose to make me have recourse to it again.

CHAPTER XII.

DEVOTEDLY faithful to the duty he had undertaken
of advocating the cause of the Navy, Sir Edward
Codrington, undeterred by the difficulty of gaining
the attention of the House of Commons to the subject, brought before the House on July 25, 1838, the
grievances of naval officers. He spoke with heartfelt
earnestness, with knowledge of his subject, and with
careful exactness, giving details gathered out of official
documents and regulations.

He began with the admirals, and went through the
other ranks of the service, with details as to pay and
pensions, and comparing the half-pay retirement of naval
officers with that of civilians. 'Sir, the position I have
laid down is, that there is no office under Government
from which persons of secondary rank and importance
are not allowed to retire after less than the time of servitude, and with more than double the remuneration that
is given to the most distinguished officers of the Navy.
I will refer as an example to Sir Thomas Foley, an
officer with two medals, and who has earned high distinction through a long period of servitude; to Sir R.
Keats, Sir Benjamin Hallowell, Sir Samuel Hood, and
many others.' . . . 'A gentleman whose name I do
not wish to mention, because it might look invidious,
served fourteen years as Collector of Customs in Barba-
does, and then retired with a pension of £1,000; whilst
an admiral who had served from fifty-five to sixty-five
years would have received only £766 10s., that is,
£243 less reward, for four times the period of servitude.
Another gentleman, who served as Commissioner of the
Navy for thirty-three years, has now a retirement of
£750 a-year, after having had a government house and
an official salary of £1,000 a-year; whilst a Rear-

Admiral who had served from forty-five to fifty-five years would only get £456 5s. . . . .

Now, let the House compare this state of things with the retirement given to Secretaries or Under-Secretaries of the Admiralty; or let it be compared with the treatment of Commissaries of the Army.'

Sir E. Codrington, in the course of a long speech, went much into detail, and moved the following resolution: 'That the attention of this House be called to the injustice that is done to officers in Her Majesty's Navy, and that a Committee be appointed to enquire into the subject.'

In February 1839 Sir E. Codrington received a beautiful piece of plate, presented to him by many naval officers, through his old friend, Admiral Thomas.

The piece of plate was a large and massive salver, embellished with naval devices, with the following inscription in the centre of it:—

Presented on the 27th February, 1839, to Admiral Sir Edward Codrington, G.C B., G.C.M.G., G.C. of St. Louis and of the Legion of Honour of France; G.C. of the Redeemer of Greece; Knight of the Second Class of St. George of Russia; and M.P. for the borough of Devonport (by a limited subscription) from 500 naval officers, as a mark of their esteem, respect, and regard, and in testimony of the deep and grateful sense they entertain, not only of his unwearied, independent, and able advocacy of the rights and privileges of their profession in the Commons' House of Parliament, but also for his generous support and defence of the forlorn and friendless officer, the distressed widow, and the destitute orphan, whether suffering under injustice and oppression, or sustaining injury and wrong.

Sir E. C.'s answer to the above:—

Eaton Square : February 29, 1839.

MY DEAR THOMAS,—When I first became a candidate for a seat in Parliament, I avowed my object to be the attainment of a more just consideration for the interests of our profession, and of those connected with it. In pursuance of that object I have laboured assiduously, and I trust I may now feel I have not laboured in vain. That I have not been as successful as I wished, may be owing to my want of that

Parliamentary knowledge, and of that oratorical power for which our early life so little fits us. But I can confidently say, that it has not been owing to any deficiency of zeal or exertion for the cause I had undertaken. I own I have sometimes felt disheartened by my want of support, both in and out of the House of Commons; but this feeling has now given place to one of the highest gratification, at receiving so splendid a testimonial of the approbation of my brother-officers. And in the proud satisfaction of exhibiting it amongst my naval friends as an heir-loom in my family, I trust I may lead others to feel, as I do, that their best exertions are due to the welfare of our naval strength; and that the most gratifying reward they can have, for the zealous use of their exertions, is the spontaneous approbation of their professional brethren. If anything could add to the satisfaction I feel on receiving this highly valued memorial, it is that you, my dear Thomas, with whom I have been associated in much arduous and interesting service, should be made the medium of its presentation.

Yours with warm and sincere regard,

EDWARD CODRINGTON.

In November 1839 Sir E. Codrington was appointed Commander-in-Chief at Portsmouth. He consequently gave up his seat in Parliament, and removed with his three daughters to the Admiralty House in the Dock-yard. His eldest son was at that time with the Guards in Canada, and his youngest in command of H.M.S. 'Talbot' in the Mediterranean. Captain John Montagu was his flag Captain. The three years at Portsmouth were spent in the regular routine of official duties, varied by constant open-house hospitalities. The Admiral's hours were early and punctual: his officers were sure of finding him in his office at ten. He was never seen out of uniform while in commission: even in the rare evenings of being alone at home, or in his afternoon rides, or yacht-sailing excursions, he invariably wore his undress uniform, and he enjoined as far as possible on others under his command a similar practice. Nor did he in any ship he commanded, permit any one to smoke in any part of the ship except the galley.

In 1840 Sir E. C. received from the Prime Minister

(Lord Melbourne), the offer of the Government of Greenwich Hospital. He declined it with expressions of gratitude ; adding, 'It is not that I am at all insensible to the value of the boon; but that I feel still equal to serve my sovereign and my country usefully and with credit to myself, if unfortunately a war should take place ; and I would not willingly for any pecuniary advantage put myself out of the opportunity to which such an event might give rise, of undertaking whatever services I may be deemed competent to perform.'

From Sir E. C. to Lord John Russell.

Portsmouth . November 15, 1840.

DEAR LORD JOHN,—I cannot help thinking that you have had something to do with Lord Melbourne's kindness in offering me the Government of Greenwich Hospital, and I therefore assure you that my refusal of it does not arise from either a want of sense of the kindness of the offer, or of the value of the boon itself. As I have told Lord Melbourne in my answer, I feel that I have still something left in me in case of war, and I am not willing at any price to put myself aside under such circumstances. To you I may add, that it being my opinion that so distinguished a retirement should fall to the lot of each distinguished officer from the top of the list, I should not feel comfortable in possessing a professional situation to which, in the opinion of the profession at large, there were others who had a better right.

Yours with sincere regard,

EDWD. CODRINGTON.

While writing these words Sir E. C. had a strong wish and hope that this highly-prized situation might be offered to his old friend Sir Robert Stopford, and was much gratified in seeing his hope fulfilled.

One great pleasure Sir E. C. enjoyed at Portsmouth was the circumstance of his son Henry having been present in Sir Robert Stopford's fleet at the siege of Acre, November 3, 1840. In command of the 'Talbot' 28 guns, he was engaged with an earthwork battery on the south front. The Companionship of the Bath was given to him for this service, and he shortly afterwards returned to England to be Flag Captain to Sir E. C. at Portsmouth.

From Sir E. C. to his Son Captain Henry C.

Portsmouth: November 30, 1840.

This morning your account of Acre came by the Cross Post from Devonport. I cannot describe my present feelings, nor need I attempt it; suffice it that our joy is equal to that felt by yourself when you took up your pen to announce these glad tidings. You have now had your fair share of fighting, my dear Harry, and I shall certainly be very glad to find you once again of our home party. It ought to have fallen to my lot to have commanded on this memorable occasion. But so far from any jealous begrudging feeling, it gives me unbounded satisfaction that my old friend Stopford, who openly avowed a most just and liberal opinion of all my conduct on the occasion of Navarin, should wind up his professional career so honourably. Besides your very interesting account, including also your own proceedings, in which we are so personally concerned, we have seen an excellent detail with a plan by Mr. Saunderson to Admiral Bouverie, and we consider ourselves quite *au fait* as to the whole affair. You seem to have had a very considerable share in the preliminary proceedings considering your standing and the inferior craft you command. I must say I think the plan of attack you had formed in your own mind strikes me as being an extremely good one and very easy of execution. I rather hope you may be sent to resume your station at Constantinople, and that the Turks will see that you have not been more backward in support of their cause than you were on the other side when you were equally performing your allotted duty. However, as my present object is to express merely my joy at the good fortune you have had in being in such a battle and escaping unhurt, and also my high gratification relative to your whole proceedings, I shall make over this to one of your sisters to be finished. We shall most likely have Stopford's official account to-morrow. In the meantime, my dear Harry, accept the hearty blessing of your greatly admiring and warmly affectionate father,

EDWD. CODRINGTON.

Continued by Maria C.

November 30.

Your own clear and full account of your gallant proceedings at Acre, my dear Harry, has doubled even the joy we felt the other day on the mere hearing you were there, had fought well, and were safe out of it. Your plain and natural but most vivid description brought the whole thing before us. If you had seen how our dear father's eyes ran over, when he read your letter at breakfast, with tears of pride and pleasure, you would have thought yourself sufficiently rewarded by these alone. There is an affection in your tone of referring to him that only makes your own independent merits shine out the more. Yes, you do *indeed* owe much to him—but you owe us much, my dear Harry, to your own activity and energy of mind, which, whether in peace or war, prompts you to carry on your duty with so much vigour and zeal as to secure the good opinion of those professionally connected with you.

*From Sir E. C. to Captain Henry Codrington, H.M.S.
'Talbot.'*

Portsmouth: January 10, 1841.

. . . .

And now for a subject of a different sort. I long ago took up an idea that England would derive great benefit by encouraging our trade with Turkey. That country could grow raw silk to the greatest extent so as to supply our silk manufactories, and take our goods in return, to the great benefit of both: and this would improve the intercourse and attachment for which all our late proceedings in Syria offer so good an opening. If you have the direct means through your and my friend Tahir, or any other Turk of influence, entertain the subject with him. I put forth my opinion on this matter in the House of Commons as a groundwork of an alliance which should supersede the influence Russia has gained by the Treaty of Unkiar Skelessi: all of which influence arose from the squadron under my orders being sent to the Downs, instead of to support the Sultan against Mehemet Ali. If we had been sent to Turkey at that time the English influence would have been unbounded.

I hear Stopford is offered Greenwich, and his son has no doubt of his accepting it. It is a highly honourable retirement and I think will suit him very well; and under other circumstances I should have willingly accepted it. I conclude I told you (in confidence) of Lord Melbourne having offered it to me, and of my declining it on the score of my ability to serve if a war should ensue. I do not wish S. to know this lest it might make the boon less welcome to him.

E. C.

From Sir E. C. to Mr. Sidney Herbert, Admiralty.

Portsmouth : October 3, 1841.

. . . .

And when that new order may come I fear it will not be

found easy to carry it into execution, on account of the dissatisfaction, I may say disgust, that has been created by the forcibly turning over the crew of ships coming home from Foreign stations, when they had calculated upon the usual custom of being paid off. I gave my private opinion on the consequences of this measure, upon the first proposal to try it on the crew of the 'Donegal.' It was unheeded, and fifty-four men at once deserted, leaving their pay and sacrificing their claims arising from previous servitude, whilst others who professed to volunteer for other ships in order to get their pay, took the first opportunity of following the example. From that time, the Navy, which ought to be so popular, became so much the contrary that all the means which I have since been permitted to use for removing the impression of a want of good faith in the Board of Admiralty, have not enabled us to recover our lost ground. Out of the number of men lately paid off at this port, it is lamentable to contemplate the paucity of prime seamen who have come forward to complete the ships since commissioned, and now wanting men to fill the vacancies of petty officers. This is what makes me fear we shall find great difficulty in manning the 'Queen,' even with the more limited complement mentioned in your letter; and I have been induced to enter thus much into the subject with you from concluding that it is quite new to you, and that you will feel an interest in it as material to the execution of your present office. I need not say how fully I agree in the propriety of having our ships completed to the war complement when sent on Foreign service, having recorded my opinion to that effect by motion in the House of Commons; and my subsequent experience since I assumed this command has strengthened that opinion.

I will only add that, however desirable it may be to economise, and however right it may be to counteract unjust claims of all sorts, my conviction is, that it will not be an easy matter to undo the ill effect of those principles having been carried to excess in the fleet and in the dockyards also.

From Sir E. C. to Mr. Sidney Herbert, Admiralty.

Portsmouth: October 6, 1841.

DEAR SIR,—I have been tempted by the tenor of your letter of the 4th, and the reliance of the public good being your object as it is mine, to open to your consideration a matter which I think of the highest importance. I assume that we must before long establish steam engines on the orlop decks of our ships of the line, upon the screw principle.

Until we adopt this expedient, I cannot deny that we may be subject to destruction by steam vessels: but possessed of the power of pivoting (if I may adopt the verb), no steamer can work round us on the larger circle so as to rake us, but in attempting to do so will always be exposed to our broadsides. You will readily see the importance to this country of the great superiority we have in ships being preserved, notwithstanding modern inventions, instead of becoming, according to the predictions of Sir John Ross, 'mere colliers to the steam vessels;' and in my opinion this is a ready and facile way of effecting it. But besides the benefit arising from this use of steam, there are others of considerable importance which will naturally arise from its adoption; one of which I will at once advert to. It is procuring fresh water from the sea, in quantity as one portion of fuel to twenty of water. The patent for this application of steam was purchased by Captain Sir James Stirling and his late friend, Mr. Middleton, with a view to its introduction into the Navy; and we have often entertained the subject together during the fittal of the 'Indus' at this port, contemplating the extensive advantages to which it would give rise. Although I shall be ready to discuss this subject further whenever it may be wished, with a prospect of its adoption, I will only at present refer you to an inspection of the first imperfect engine which was made experimentally, and which is now at Mr. Bramah's manufactory, Lower Belgrave Street, Pimlico. I suggested to Lord Minto in conversation, that a combined experiment should be made in one of our inferior steam vessels employed as a tug, of the rotatory engine of Lord Dundonald, and the distilling process above mentioned; and I am persuaded that it is an experiment well worth making. I am well aware of the impossibility of the Government trying all the plans which projectors are almost daily suggesting. But according to my view of these matters, the readiness to put them to trial should not be dependent merely on the probability of success, but also upon the importance of the results. It may be well worth while to try an experiment even at great expense and with doubt of its success, if great results are involved in it, when in cases of minor consequence it may be inexpedient to risk alterations. This principle I consider applicable to the experiment I have recommended, for if Lord Dundonald's rotatory engine becomes established, as I think it will, it will do away with all the engines we now have in use. I am writing with difficulty owing to a rheumatic wrist; but I trust I have said enough to show the importance of the subject.

Sir E. C. to Vice-Admiral Sir W. Gage, Admiralty.

Portsmouth : November 25, 1841.

MY DEAR ADMIRAL,—Binstead being made a Commander, and Edwards the Second Lieutenant of the 'St. Vincent' also; and there being still much of that arduous duty to be done which Binstead has performed with so much advantage to the service; I feel it incumbent on me to request that he may be allowed to continue in his present office, and that the rule of not appointing a Commander to the flagship here may be relaxed to this extent. It is my opinion that the flagship here should not be so limited in her complement, and that her being so is mere false economy. The inefficiency of the 'Britannia,' when as a demonstration ship her services for the Mediterranean were required, is a strong example of this; and the deficiency of able seamen for the ships fitting out further shows it. I have always from my first coming permitted the captains to volunteer any of the crew from my flag-ship, of which they have taken advantage, most beneficially for the service. Rising men, who have come to us as A.B.'s, and have shown themselves fit for it, have gone into the smaller vessels as petty officers; and some of those already having had such rating, have carried it into larger ships on their being first commissioned, by which their outfit, as well as the entry of other men, has been advanced; and if the ship had more means, of course the advantage referred to would have been the greater to the service. In all this Binstead has acted fairly up to my intentions, instead of following the common practice of preferring the immediate advantage of his own ship; and it is on this account that I think the service will be benefited by his remaining where he is, whether the complement may be increased or not. From the limited system referred to, the 'Caledonia' could not have gone to sea with my flag in 1831 but for the additional marines (which the division could then furnish); and from the ship having been considered as a mere guardship, the captain reported to me that there was only one of the lieutenants who could work the ship, and hardly one of the quartermasters who could conn her! My opinion is that the guardships should be so efficient as to be ready for service whenever wanted : for it is the exhibition of that readiness, whenever a force is wanted, which is our best security against insult or aggression. The condition of the 'Howe' and 'Britannia,' on their arrival at Spithead, *demonstrated* our weakness rather than our strength; and it was the want of a

few sail-of-the line to send to the Mediterranean at the time
I was sent to the eastward to threaten the Dutch, that
brought to a climax the troubles in the Levant, which originated by the impolitic word 'untoward.' You will say,—
'Enough of this!' So says,

Yours sincerely,
EDWD. CODRINGTON.

In February 1842 Her Majesty the Queen came,
accompanied by Prince Albert, to spend a day at
Portsmouth, and slept at the Admiralty House. The
next morning Her Majesty went off to Spithead in
the yacht to visit the 'Queen,' new three-decker, accompanied by Admirals and Generals, Lords of the
Admiralty, and the Duke of Wellington. The latter
was at that time far from strong; more infirm indeed
than at a later period of his life; and he caused great
uneasiness to the sailors around him, by unsteadily
mounting and descending the companion ladders with
his hands encumbered with his large cocked hat and his
umbrella, and pertinaciously refusing any help whatever.
Many a hand was offered to relieve him of the umbrella,
and none could imagine why the offer seemed to vex
him so much, until we afterwards learnt that this offer
of holding his umbrella for him had often been used as
a trick by his admirers to obtain and carry it off as a
memorial of him: he had lost so many umbrellas by this
means, that he was now resolved to hold it for himself.

This visit of Her Majesty was a real pleasure to the
Admiral; for his seventy winters had in no degree
chilled the chivalrous loyalty of his nature, which had
been especially called forth towards her when he had seen
her ascend the throne as a young princess of eighteen;
and he was gratified, too, by the special kindness and
consideration shown to him both by her and Prince
Albert in many little ways.

From Sir E. C. to Sir Isambard Brunel.

Portsmouth March 2, 1842.

Thanks! many thanks! my good friend, for bringing my
mind, even in the winding up of the hurly-burly in which I

have been for the last week, to the interesting work* which is now so near its completion; and which will add high honour to those splendid abilities, the useful exertion of which for the benefit of the country of your adoption has already placed you in so eminent a position. In the hurried view which Prince Albert and the Archdukes could only afford to give on this occasion to the block manufactory, I was glad to take the opportunity of expressing my sentiments on the merits of the inventor. Remember, my good friend, that whenever you can find spare time to come and see how this astonishing work is going on, you will be sure of meeting a hearty welcome from all the inhabitants of the Admiralty House. The railroad to Gosport is now satisfactorily established, and the journey performed in about three hours and a half.

My daughters desire to add their kind regards to those of your sincere friend, E. C.

In the summer of that same year Sir E. C. had the pleasure of a visit from this old friend, and of course he went to inspect his own block machinery. We walked with him about the dockyard, and it was very interesting to observe the simple pleasure he took in re-visiting the remarkable work that had brought him great distinction. We found there one grey-headed workman who instantly recognised him and never took his eyes off him while within reach. This man accosted him reverentially, saying he was one of the men placed by him at that machinery when he first set it up so many years ago.† As we returned to the house, he said, in answer to an observation of mine, ' Yes, it is very good; I do not see anything in it that I could wish now to change;' and the words were spoken with unaffected gratification, quite free from any tone of self-vaunting.

From Sir E. C. to Mr. Sidney Herbert, Admiralty.

Portsmouth: October 28, 1842.

. . . .

I conclude that the object of the ' Excellent's' establishment is to make the practical knowledge of gunnery general throughout the service, and not merely to establish a limited number in the higher and more abstruse branches of science;

* The Thames Tunnel.   † Thirty-four years.

Edwᵈ Codrington,
1843.

and with this feeling I have marked my approbation of the instruction in those ships in which the orders were given by each of the officers at their own quarters. In my opinion every inducement should be offered to all classes to profit by the instruction in the 'Excellent,' so as to make this branch of the duty as general and as much a matter of course as seamanship or any other. I am not sure that we have not lost ground in the latter in consequence of the greater encouragement given to gunnery; and we may eventually be obliged to have an establishment for teaching seamanship, as we have done gunnery.

Very sincerely yours,
EDWD. CODRINGTON.

My Father's three years' term of command at Portsmouth being finished, his flag was hauled down on the 10th December, 1842, and he returned with his family to settle himself once more at home, and enter again into London society. But with all his eager enjoyment of society, it was his home, after all, that was his 'natural element.' His bright and original remarks, and the professional stories collected throughout so · active a life, seemed to be most naturally called forth in that atmosphere; and when some racy anecdote came out quite fresh and new, and I asked him, 'Where can that come from *now*?' he would answer, 'Oh, it is out of my old bag of shakings' (an expression which will be readily understood by sailors). The bag of shakings seemed indeed to contain an endless store, and went on supplying the home fireside with many a bright gleam, even until near the close of life.

His eldest son, who had long been married, continued, after marriage as before, to have his home with his wife and children in his father's house; and the younger son also, when not at sea, always shared the home of his father and sisters.

In 1843 Sir E. C.'s eldest daughter was married to Captain Sir Thomas Bourchier, who was already a valued friend of his; he wrote of him as his 'adopted son,' and the intercourse was always of that character. They settled near him in London, and very rarely did a day pass without the welcome sound of his knock at the door of the little home (that peculiar knock—one, *two*, THREE—so well known to his friends, and always so gladly heard at their door). Nothing ever was like his welcome to those he loved; his old-world courtesy—his graceful high bearing—were not disturbed by, but simply merged in the heartfelt cordiality of the welcome which was such a pleasure to himself as well as to them.

From Sir E. C. to Admiral Sir Robert Stopford.

Bishopsgate, Chertsey: October 20, 1844.

MY DEAR STOPFORD,—In my to-day's newspaper I read, 'that the Acre prize-money of 60,000*l.* is ordered for distribution.' From my first hearing of the *same sum* being asked for which was granted for Navarin, I stormed against the injustice of it in all quarters, as having made an inroad into the precedent of Algiers, which I made the foundation of my claim when I carried the grant in the House of Commons against the decision of the Government. I claimed, not the same sum as a whole, but the same sum per head for officers and men, and carried it upon the principle of equal claim; and I considered it as establishing the principle for future similar occasions. Had I been in the House of Commons, I would have urged this principle for Acre, and feel sure I should have carried it; nor do I think it too late even now, if pressed with spirit. If I were you, I would present a petition to the Admiralty in the first instance; and if refused by that Board, I would get some member to move 'for a copy of that petition,' as ground for 'a motion for a Committee of the whole House, to examine into the propriety of presenting an address to Her Majesty, humbly requesting her to be graciously pleased to take into consideration the claims of the officers, seamen, and marines engaged in the successful attack of the fortress of Acre on &c., &c., &c., to a similar amount of gratuity to each individual employed on that service, which was granted to those engaged in the battle of Algiers, and also in the battle of Navarin.' I do not think that the sum at present allotted to you need in any way militate against this proceeding, any more than the neglect of those naval men in the House of Commons who ought to have urged the claim in the first instance; and if I were still an M.P. I would bring the question forward, whether I had the sanction of the Government for it or not, or even were it against your consent. For I consider it a matter of importance to our service to keep this precedent established, as is the payment for clothes, for which I fought so hard, and which is now established by a printed circular.

Your sincere and faithful,
Edwd. Codrington.

In July 1846 Sir E. C. received a letter from Lord John Russell, saying, ' I have the Queen's permission to offer you the situation in Her Majesty's Household of Groom in Waiting. Her Majesty is desirous of having a naval officer of distinction in her household.'

Sir E. C. held this situation for a few years; increasing age induced him to resign it.

Sir E. C. to Jane Bourchier.

July 1, 1246.

I have read Peel's speech, and also ' The Times'' comment on it, with great pleasure, and, I must add, with great admiration; nor do I consider his encomium of Cobden as the part of it the least to be admired. I think it not less just than generous his giving so much credit to a man who has so well avoided disturbing the peace of the country by his manner of carrying out so popular and so excitable a purpose. Thinking him most able and understanding on the question of trade, I hope Cobden will become a party in the Ministry, in which he would be very useful, and to which his name would attract great general confidence.

Sir E. C. to Jane Bourchier.

Malvern : July 22, 1846.

. . . (After recurring to the subject of the water-cure, Sir E. C. continues) . . As to those who tell me I am so well that I need nothing of the sort, they know nothing of what sensations I am annoyed by, because I have not indulged in that which has so much bored me in others— the detail of all my physical grievances. I do not believe even *you* have ever been fully aware of the extent of the bodily torments by which I am occasionally assailed. You think I am unnecessarily venturing a life of precious importance to you all. Now, relying upon those feelings in you, I may ask if it is not becoming in me to do the best I can for the preservation of that life, and to prevent its becoming irksome to those whose more or less comfort may depend upon my more or less fitness for social intercourse during my remaining years? Whatever may be in inconveniences ' incidental to my advanced age,' I would rather diminish them than have my mind for ever occupied by them; and with my conviction that I am taking the most rational means of obtaining this desired relief, I cannot think it would be wise in me to abstain from pursuing it.

Bishopsgate: Friday, October 16, 1846.

Got up a little before 7, and was on horseback a little after 7; rode pretty fast down the Park towards Lachestergate, where the park-keepers were to rendezvous, in order to drive the red deer into a corner near Cranbourn Tower, and net a few of them for hunting. Rainy, thick fog; could see nothing; pressed on towards Cranbourn; saw the whole herd come past the corner paling of the Flemish farm at full speed, led by the master stag, the two keepers on their left keeping pace with them towards Cranbourn Tower. Tried to keep pace on their left, but could not do it; lost sight of them all; was thrown out by their having doubled back in the thick woody part where I had last seen them; and after wandering about the Western walk, and coming to the part near what we call the 'main-top,' learnt that they were gone towards the Horse or 'Commendatore,' as we call him. Saw a considerable herd of red deer on the plain, and one of the keepers driving a single hind at a little distance from them. Tried to be of use, but could not go the pace, and after wandering about went home to breakfast. It was now about 11 o'clock, and I had not felt any uneasiness of hunger, although I had had nothing but one tumbler of water on getting out of bed, but I had so good an appetite as to eat a hearty breakfast. After this I took a sweating bath and wet sheet rubbing, shaved, dressed, and was again on horseback with Maria at about 2 o'clock. Rode to where the nets were placed, and found three had been driven in but were out again; went to look if the herd of red deer had collected together again. Saw the old master stag and ten hinds; and in the neighbourhood found the two park keepers looking after a hind they had nearly run down, when their own horses, from three hours and a half hard galloping, could do no more. They were now on fresh horses; and shortly afterwards seeing their object, away they went at their former pace, too fast for us, and we did not recover them until we found them at a pond in which the deer had taken refuge, and was swimming about. After much delay in procuring ropes and cart, the hind was got out, and with much resistance was at length carted away. We then galloped home, where we arrived at 5 o'clock. And thanks to the 'water cure,' I am not more tired than after my usual daily ride.

E. C.

Bishopsgate : October 23, 1846.

MY DEAR JANE,—Congratulations are always agreeable.
Our servants' dance (on Navarin day) went off admirably.
The room was beautifully dressed up with flowers, by the
help of their guest Mitchell, the gardener, NAVARIN in
dahlias surmounting the end window; and they had a
regular supper in the entrance ante-room. I started with
Dame Hills,* and went through *five country dances*, without
being any the worse for it then or on the next morning.†

Yours, E. C.

Sir E. C. to J. B.

December 25, 1846.

Thanks, my dear Jane, for your letter and the affectionate
expressions of both yourself and your husband, on which I
set a just value. I assure you you cannot miss me more than
I miss you. It is well to be without absolute suffering at my
period of life, and I am probably as free from it as most of
my compeers approximating my 77th anniversary, after many
trials of severe excitement. But the aches, pains, and inconveniences, and the deterioration of memory accompanying
age, under the most favourable circumstances, greatly diminish the desire for protracted existence; and such is my
present feeling.

God bless you and yours!

E. C.

At the latter part of 1846 Captain Henry Codrington
commissioned the 'Thetis,' and his father being anxious
to see his ship before sailing, actually set off from Eaton
Square in the morning, with his eldest son, travelled to
Portsmouth, went out to Spithead, examined the ship,
and returned the same evening to London. In his letter
to J. B. he says:—

We got home at about nine o'clock, very chilly with the
last part of our journey. The 'Thetis' is a fine bold-looking
ship, but not quite entitled to be called handsome. I did
not think much of the crew, but I was well pleased to see
such a show of comfort in the berths of the people as to
crockery, glass, &c., on the nice uniformly fitted shelves in
the side, as would have done credit to the return from a station, including mess-kids. We got on shore from our visit

* The housekeeper, who had come into the family as nurse in 1814.
† Sir E. C.'s age was then 76½.

to the ship in sufficient time to call on Ogle and see a little
of the dockyard doings. I was not the worse for my trip the
next day.

Up to this time Sir E. Codrington had never been
offered the naval good service pension, although services
which had begun in 1783 had carried him through four
general actions, besides the war service at Walcheren,
on the Coast of Spain, and New Orleans. The offer now
came to him from Lord Auckland, as detailed in the
following letter to his daughter:—

From Sir E. C. to Jane B.

February 25, 1847.

I was in the Admiralty yesterday, when I received a message that Lord Auckland wanted me. He said that a good
service pension having fallen in by Lake's death, he considered me as the most entitled to it, if I chose to accept it;
that he did not think any just claims should be passed over
without giving the choice, upon the ground of the claimant
being wealthy, although in some instances, poverty, accompanied by other circumstances, might justify a preference.
I said that I had considered myself unfairly treated by being
passed over in favour of Rowley and Lake, the former of
whom I believed had received more money than had fallen
to my lot, that my income was principally annuity, and that
I should gladly accept the boon, and was gratified by being
restored to the condition of distinguished and meritorious
services.

Nothing could be more kind and gentlemanlike than his
whole way of talking the business over, and I consider myself booked for this very convenient addition to my pecuniary
means. But thus the matter stands until I hear it officially.

Sir E. C. to Jane B.

June 21, 1847.

We who are deputed to seek an extension of the order
of June 1 met to-day, but must meet again to sign our
representation which we for the present are to keep to
ourselves. Byam Martin and his committee are over-
whelmed with letters and claims. It is in reality a very
difficult question, take it which way we will. The *Gazette* is
not a criterion of general merit, nor are the medals heretofore given, and, as being given for some single actions, open

a fair claim for many others ; nor is success a just criterion of merit.   Woodruffe's action with the Rochfort squadron, by which he saved his convoy, is a noble achievement, although he was necessarily made a prisoner.   The 'Mars,' and the 'Alexander' are of the same sort.   And the 'Queen Charlotte's' on June 23, 1795, was one of the finest operations ever done.

It was very gratifying to Sir Edward Codrington to have offered to him for the second time the proudest and pleasantest retirement that could be given to an old and distinguished officer.   But as, when first placed at his disposal in 1840, he found it too early to reconcile himself to final retirement; so now, in 1847, he felt it too late, at seventy-seven years old, to enter upon a new home and the duties of a new situation.

Sir E. C. to Jane B.

(*Confidential.*)

June 27, 1847

Lord Auckland wrote yesterday to see me, and offered me the much coveted Greenwich.   He said the appointment was in the Premier, but would go by his recommendation.   We talked the matter over fully and freely, and I cannot say I feel at all desirous of accepting it.   The whole hospital wants reformation, and the Governor in that respect is a mere cypher.   I should go away from all my present pursuits and habits of society, and the power of saving two or three thousand pounds, without a prospect of doing any real good, does not appear to me sufficient temptation.   Thus the balance of my present feeling is against my acceptance of it. The comfort of this home and the London intercourse during last severe winter, with the gratification of every real want at my age, ought to content me.   E. C.

June 29.

I have pretty well made up my mind not to take Greenwich, although I am advised not to decide in a hurry.   As to that, I have been conning the matter over long enough, and I cling to my own present mode of occupation and the comfort of this my home, and I cannot contemplate a change with any satisfaction.

This offer was made in very gratifying terms by

M M 2

Lord John Russell, to whom Sir E. C. sent the following answer:—

Eaton Square: July 3, 1847.

DEAR LORD JOHN RUSSELL,—I need not say how much I am gratified by the offer contained in your letter. I consider the government of Greenwich Hospital as the most honourable and most distinguished retirement which a naval officer can receive. And the offer of that appointment coming to me with the approbation of the Head of the Admiralty, in addition to your own as the head of the Government, and, moreover, crowned with the gracious approbation of Her Majesty, is prized by me above all price. With these feelings, if I could believe myself capable of being useful to the country and my profession by undertaking the duties of the office, I would not hesitate. Circumstances, however, of private feelings and considerations, which I need not detail, induce me to ask Her Majesty's permission to decline the offer, which I do with great regret.

In thanking you most sincerely for your own personal kindness, and the terms you have made use of towards me, I will beg you to place my request before the Queen with the expression of my high feelings of gratitude for Her Majesty's gracious consideration.

From Sir Thomas Bourchier to Sir E. Codrington.

Chatham: October 3, 1847.

MY DEAR SIR EDWARD,—I wish to know your opinion as to doubling upon the enemy's line; my own is that it would be better to do so by placing two ships on the bow and quarter of the enemy on the same side; as, if placed on opposite sides of the enemy's ship, they might injure each other by their own shot, whereas handy ships, skilfully managed on the bow and quarter, would be very overpowering. I am strengthened in my own opinion by having read in Captain Miller's charming account of the operations of the 'Theseus' at the Nile, that he had ceased to fire at his opponent, because the 'Vanguard' had anchored abreast of her on the opposite side.

Answer to the preceding.

October 5, 1847.

I fully agree with you about doubling the opponent line in battle. Even at Navarin the shot from the frigate line of the horse-shoe came to our line, as no doubt ours did to theirs; moreover, a ship having two opponents in different directions to train her guns for is under greater disadvantage than if on the broadsides in which direction the guns, as I may say, point themselves naturally. Is Miller's account included in the Nelson correspondence of the battle of the Nile? The bow and quarter plan is particularly applicable to that battle at anchor, where, with springs *on the anchors,* a choice can be made how to direct the fire, so as that the shot of the two ships might meet in destruction.

E. C.

To Jane B., in answer to an inquiry about the new 'War Medal.'

March 26, 1848.

The clasps on my new medal are June 1, 1794, June 23, 1795, Trafalgar and Navarin. The committee seem to exclude Flushing, where the 'Blake' was close under the batteries and set on fire three times by red-hot shot, and where she fired above thirty rounds in aid of the bombardment; and also all the different affairs on the east coast of Spain.

To Jane B.

May 27, 1848.

You may judge of the relief we have derived from your letter just arrived, after the sad account received last night; for the regard and esteem in which we hold Bourchier makes suspense painful.

E. C.

Sir Thomas Bourchier recovered from his illness at that time; but the climate of China had done its work upon him. In April 1849 he died, while Superintendent of Chatham Dockyard, and Sir E. Codrington felt this sorrow very much. Owing to the position he had filled, the funeral was a public and military one; and he who took the part of chief mourner, walking all the way in the slow and solemn procession, was the sadhearted 'adopted father' of seventy-nine years old, who mourned him with such true affection.

From Sir Henry Ward* to Sir E. C.

Steam Vessel 'Ionia,' Bay of Navarin: July 1, 1849.

MY DEAR SIR EDWARD,—I did not see you before I left England to say good-bye, so I will write a line from the scene of your triumph twenty-two years ago, which I have taken the opportunity of visiting on my way from Zante to Cerigo, to the great astonishment of the garrison in the forts who are evidently much puzzled with our manœuvres, and cannot conceive what we are about. Never was there such a place, certainly, to catch an enemy's fleet in, but it must have been murderous work—something like 'blunderbusses for two in a sawpit'—where nothing but English pluck and English discipline could have gained so complete a victory. I was fortunate in having on board an Englishman named Forrest (now commanding the 'Ionia'), who served under you, and gave me all the particulars of the battle, from the spot where the 'Asia' took up her position. Few things have gratified me more than this sight of the scene of so memorable an action; and having seen it, my next impulse was to tell you so, which I hope you will excuse.

Pray remember me to Lady Bourchier, whose loss I heard of with much regret, for Sir Thomas was a fine officer; but I saw too clearly when I was at Chatham that his days were numbered, and that nothing but the energy of his mind sustained the man.

Hoping that you bear your years and honours as well as when I last saw you, believe me, my dear Sir Edward,

Yours most truly,

H. G. WARD.

Memorandum in Sir E. C.'s handwriting when he was within three months of eighty years old.

January 1850.

The first professional book of which I acquired possession on entering the navy in 1783, was 'Hutchinson on Practical Seamanship'; and it taught me a lesson which I have never known to be promulgated in any other work, or to have been adopted. I am strongly impressed by the N. E. gales at present prevailing, and the disasters which they occasion, with one of the lessons inculcated in the above work; and which is superior, in my mind, to Manby's, or any other plan ever recommended, for effecting a communication with the shore from

* Newly appointed Governor of the Ionian Islands.

a vessel wrecked.   It is by the employment of a kite.   Kites for this purpose may be made of strong paper even, according to the force of the wind; of light linen, or strong canvas. The kite should be so slung as not to rise high above the ground; it might have a tripping-line to the end of the stick to force it down when it has reached over the required spot; or this may be effected by slacking the rope suddenly. I take shame to myself that I never exhibited this when I had the opportunity.

From Sir George Pechell to Sir E. C.

July 27, 1850

MY DEAR SIR EDWARD,— I brought forward the case of the Vice and Rear-Admiral of Great Britain last night (in House of Commons).   Sir F. Baring said there was a general rule as to these appointments being given to those at the top of the list, and that Sir George Martin, on being appointed Admiral of the fleet, did not resign the Vice-Admiral's Commission, and that his successor has also held it, without however, receiving the salary.   I enforced your claims to the Rear-Admiral of Great Britain, as by the present arrangement you were deprived of those honours which were due to you; and the Board of Admiralty, seeing what had occurred in Sir G. Martin's case, might have withheld the appointment of Admiral of the fleet until the person entitled to it had resigned the other.   Sir F. Baring admitted this, and said that in the event of a vacancy, he had no doubt that the First Lord of the Treasury would give it to *Sir Edward Codrington*; and Lord John intimated that such would be the case, and the House joined in the cheers as a tribute of justice to the claim which you have established, and the respect to which you are entitled for the independent manner in which you acted for so long a time in Parliament; and it was highly gratifying to me to have had such an opportunity of witnessing the unanimous feeling of the House of Commons on the occasion.

I am, my dear Sir Edward,
Most truly yours,
GEORGE BROOKE PECHELL.

When I first proposed to publish this record, a friend wrote to me, ' How *will* you be able to describe him— represent him—make this generation understand him? There are none such now : all at once so frank, free, spirited, dignified, kind, and warm !   His presence and manner can no more be written than his beautiful head could ever be painted. How *wooden* I used to think all his pictures were when I was a child, and wonder painters should see him *like that.*'

I do *not* attempt to describe him; the few left who can remember him will themselves be able to fill in the outline indicated by the natural expression of his thoughts and feelings in his own letters to his home.

J. B.

In the summer of 1850 Sir E. Codrington's wonderfully healthy constitution began to give way. The action of the heart was weakened, and dropsy began to show itself. Still, the natural vigour of so fine a constitution, uninjured by either hard living or bad climates, gave full play to the doctor's remedies, and he rallied again for a time. He was staying at Roehampton for the summer, and he took advantage of his first day of improved strength to drive to his lawyer in London, to settle a doubt in his mind as to whether he had in his will done as much as he wished for his servants. He soon after returned home to Eaton Square, and having quite given up society, he received but few of his friends after that time.

His favourite solace had habitually been, and was to the end of life, his home music, which he would listen to for whole evenings with pleasure. At first his choir had comprised five united voices: latterly there were only the two youngest daughters left in the home; but theirs was the choicest of amateur singing, and he dearly loved it. He had always been extremely fond of music; and without any knowledge of it himself, he had a refined and discriminating taste. With a perfectly true ear and pleasing though untrained voice, he formerly used to sing some of Dibdin's and other sailors' songs with excellent spirit and expression; but though every kind of music was welcome to him *if* it was *good*, sacred music was that upon which he always set the highest value.

About the month of March, 1851, the disease re-asserted itself, and did not again give way: its progress was very slow, for he had a wonderful reserve of strength; but it gradually subsided into lethargy.

By degrees the lethargy deepened into those longer and ever-lengthening intervals of silence and apparent insensibility, or at any rate freedom from suffering— that mysterious condition in which doctors and meta-physicians conceive that spirit and soul are set free to roam backward and forward over past and future in their high converse, untrammelled and unimpeded by the quiescent body.

We cannot know, but we may believe it.

On April 27, 1851, he completed his 81st year ; and on the following day he closed his long, and happy, and useful, and honorable career.

He was buried in St. Peter's Church, Eaton Square. A memorial tablet was placed there, and another in the church at Dodington in Gloucestershire.

Extract from Sir E. C.'s Will.

March 10, 1816.

It is my desire that whenever or wherever I may die, my corpse shall be buried in one of the nearest churches or burying-places, without any ostentation, and with as little cost as possible. If the distance will admit of it, I should wish to be carried to the grave by a suitable number of the poorer persons of the parish, or by old sailors, and that each of them should have a guinea for his trouble. I further wish that a simple tablet should record the place of my burial, and that a similar record should be put up in the family church at Dodington.

The wish thus expressed, and confirmed by a codicil in 1830, was carried out, to the disappointment of many friends who, like the writer of the following note, would have wished to collect around his grave, in token of the esteem they had borne to him in life.

His two sons and his eldest daughter were present.

From Admiral Baynes to Colonel C.

You say the last sad offices are to be attended only by yourselves I had hoped to have been allowed to have paid the last tribute of respect to the remains of one who has been in truth my most kind and constant friend in boyhood and manhood for upwards of forty years, and whose memory I must always cherish with the warmest affection. I will not, however, press further on this subject than expressing the wish.

Inscription on the Tablet at Dodington—

IN MEMORY OF

ADMIRAL SIR EDWARD CODRINGTON, G.C.B.,

THIRD SON OF EDWARD, THE YOUNGEST SON OF SIR WILLIAM CODRINGTON

OF DODINGTON, FIRST BARONET.

BORN, 27TH APRIL 1770.   DIED, 28TH APRIL 1851.

BURIED IN THE VAULTS OF ST. PETER'S CHURCH, EATON SQUARE, LONDON.

HE ENTERED THE NAVY 1783, AND SERVED AS
LIEUTENANT OF H.M.S. QUEEN CHARLOTTE, IN THE BATTLE OF THE 1ST JUNE 1794.
COMMANDER OF H.M.S. BABET, IN THE ACTION OF THE 23RD JUNE 1795.
CAPTAIN OF H.M.S. ORION, IN THE BATTLE OF TRAFALGAR 1805.
CAPTAIN OF H.M.S. BLAKE, IN THE SCHELDT, AND ON THE EAST COAST OF SPAIN 1809-13.
COMMODORE AND CAPTAIN OF THE FLEET ON THE COAST OF NORTH AMERICA, 1814.
COMMANDER IN CHIEF
OF THE ALLIED FLEETS OF ENGLAND, FRANCE AND RUSSIA,
IN THE BATTLE OF NAVARIN, 20TH OCTOBER 1827.

At the time of his death Sir Edward Codrington was a Knight-Grand Cross of the Order of the Bath.

,,   ,,   of St. Louis, and of the Légion d'Honneur of France.

,,   Second Class of St. George, of Russia.

,,   Grand Cross of St. Michael and St. George.

,,   Grand Cross of the Saviour, of Greece.*

He held the Naval Gold Medal as commanding a ship-of-the-line at the battle of Trafalgar; and the War Medal with four clasps for

Lord Howe's action, June 1, 1794.
Lord Bridport's action, May 23, 1795.
The battle of Trafalgar, October 21, 1805; and
The battle of Navarin, October 20, 1827.

On seven different occasions† he received letters of commendation from his official superiors, besides letters

* This order was sent to Sir E. Codrington in February 1834, by King Otho, of Greece, ' pour vous donner un témoignage ostensible de la reconnaissance de la nation grecque.'

† As stated by Admiralty order calling for record of Services in 1846—for which see Appendix.

of thanks from the Admiralty for the services therein referred to.

Also letters of commendation and thanks from the Ministers of Spain in 1813, and of Greece in 1827.

An autograph letter of commendation from the Emperor of Russia in 1827.

He was included in the vote of thanks of Parliament four times, viz.

For Lord Howe's battles in 1794.
Lord Bridport's action in 1795.
Battle of Trafalgar in 1805; and
The Capture of Washington; and operations on the Coast of America in 1815.

The thanks of Parliament were withheld from the fleet that gained the battle of Navarin, by the Ministry of the Duke of Wellington.

From Colonel Codrington to Admiral Count Heiden.

110, Eaton Square, London : May 1, 1851.

MY DEAR ADMIRAL,—Your old friend, my father,—your old commander-in-chief on a glorious day—breathed his last in this house on the 28th of April—the 27th having been his 81st birthday. To no one did he give a more cordial share of his regard and affection than to yourself, both on public and on private grounds ; and I need scarcely tell you that those feelings, formed and cemented as they were by the most trying and glorious circumstances of professional service, were not changed towards you during the last days of his life. Up to his 78th year, he was in full enjoyment of personal and mental activity, constantly on horseback, and in society, and participating in every thing that could give him interest or pleasure.

But this could not last to the end, and for the latter two years of his life he had been infirm though well, until about a year ago he was attacked by dropsy. The skill of his medical attendants kept this off, till a more serious break-up this spring. He was confined to his house only for about three weeks before his death. We were all with him—myself, who am still in the army—my naval brother, whom you remember—my eldest sister, whom you called ' Varinka,' whose husband, Sir T. Bourchier, died two years ago—and my twin sisters.

All of our most kind remembrances to you, my good Admiral; I know no one will feel and share our sorrow more than yourself.

Your very sincere,
W. J. CODRINGTON.

Kind and gracious messages of enquiry were repeatedly sent by Her Majesty the Queen during the illness of Sir Edward Codrington; and also by Her Royal Highness the Duchess of Gloucester, whose kind and steady friendship for him had been kept up until the close of his life: and many, very many, were the letters received by his family bearing witness to the love and esteem in which he was so generally held. A very few specimens of these are added to close this memoir.

Lord John Russell, after expressing his 'deep and sincere sympathy,' adds :

'The loss of so distinguished a man is national, but his kindness of heart could be felt only by his family and friends.'

Sir James Stirling says :

'In that loss, you may rest assured, the world and the naval profession will sincerely participate, for a brighter or nobler example of what an English gentleman and an English Admiral should be, never existed. I can most truly say, that ever since I have had the honour to know him, it has raised me in my own esteem to feel that I could estimate the value of his character, and do justice in my own mind to his rare and valuable qualities of truth, candour, frankness, and benevolence.

'It must be a most consolatory thought to you that the part he was allotted to perform in the world was so well executed.'

From Lord J. H. :

'If ever there was a man who combined the qualities of a high-minded gentleman, with all the requirements of a first-rate officer, that man was Sir Edward Codrington. It will be a satisfaction to those who had the honour to rank amongst his friends, to know that his last moments were tranquil and free from suffering.'

From W. B. H.

'It may indeed be wished by any of us that knew him as I did, that when we shall be called away we may be found to have worked as ardently and faithfully for our country and our fellowmen, as he has done.'

From Admiral Sir William Parker:

'You have reason, my dear Codrington, to be proud of the name you bear. Your father's services will be handed down to posterity in our naval annals, and there can be but one feeling of regret amongst his surviving friends. Peter Richards has described to me the closing scene, which marks the unostentatious character of the lamented and single-minded individual who directed.

From the 'Journal des Débats' of July 9, 1851:

On lit dans le 'Courrier d'Athènes' du 28 juin:

Dans la séance du 17 juin, M. Zanos, député de Santorin, après avoir rappelé à la Chambre tout ce que le pays doit à l'amiral Codrington, dont la mort vient de porter le deuil dans le cœur de tous les Grecs, a demandé—

Que la Chambre exprimât sa douleur pour la mort de l'amiral Codrington. . . .

La Chambre, fidèle interprète des sentimens de la nation, adopte par acclamation ces propositions:

1° La Chambre des Députés exprime sa profonde douleur pour la mort de l'illustre philhellène Sir Edward Codrington.

2° Afin de témoigner la reconnaissance éternelle de la nation envers l'amiral Codrington et les amiraux De Rigny et De Heiden, la Chambre décide que leurs noms illustres, surmontés d'une couronne de lauriers, seront gravés sur des tableaux qui seront placés dans la salle des séances.

3° Le président aura soin d'envoyer copie du procès-verbal à chacune des familles des illustres défunts.

Le sénat, sur la proposition de M. Psylla, a exprimé également, par une mention spéciale consignée dans le procès-verbal, les sentimens douleureux que lui a causés la mort de l'amiral Codrington.

APPENDIX.

Extrait du journal de Monsieur Bompar, Ex-Lieutenant de la Marine française, Capitaine de la frégate de Méhémet Ali, 'l'Égyptienne.'

[See p. 71.]

L'armée égyptienne est partie d'Alexandrie.*

Elle a mouillé à Marmorice pour remplacer l'eau.

Elle en est partie, et le 29 elle a relevé le Cap^ne Raxatin, ainsi que la côte de Barbarie, où elle a passé plusieurs jours retenue par les vents contraires et le calme.

Elle a mouillé dans Navarin.

Elle a eu en présence une division anglaise, composée de trois vaisseaux, deux frégates, et deux corvettes, en croisière devant la rade.

Les bâtimens de l'armée ont embarqué des troupes.

On a fait appareiller 15 corvettes.

Deux vaisseaux (le troisième a manqué son appareillage), 11 frégates, 8 corvettes et 6 brûlots, ont mis sous voiles.

A 4 h^res après-midi une frégate anglaise a envoyé un canot à terre pour porter un pli au Pacha.

Le brig la 'Satalie' est partie pour Alexandrie. A 8 h^res du matin la même frégate anglaise est venue se mettre en panne dans la passe, a envoyé un canot au Pacha, et aussitôt après son retour elle a fait servir. 4 vaisseaux et une frégate (français) ont rejoint l'escadre anglaise.

La même frégate anglaise a mouillé en tête de rade et a communiqué avec le dragoman du Pacha.

La frégate française la 'Sirène,' portant le pavillon de M^r l'amiral de Rigny, a mouillé à 3 h^res et ¼; l'amiral eut une conférence avec Ibrahim Pacha.

La frégate anglaise a appareillé. Au jour toute la division turque qui était sous voiles est rentrée au mouillage. A 11 h^res du matin M^r l'Amiral De Rigny a mis sous voiles et fit dire au Pacha qu'il

---

Année
1827,
Août,
du 5 au 6

17 au 18

21 au 22

Septembre
du 7 au 8
le 10

le 18

19

20

21

21 au 2

22 au 23

23 au 24

allait rentrer avec l'amiral anglais—et effectivement il rentra à 5 h^{res} avec un vaisseau anglais portant pavillon carré au mât de mizaine.

24 au 25.　A 8 h^{res} du matin les deux amiraux eurent une conférence avec le Pacha, et à la nuit du 25 tous les bâtimens anglais et français appareillèrent.

Octobre, du 1 au 2　14 bâtimens légers (frégates et corvettes), après avoir débarqué leurs troupes, appareillèrent; sous le prétexte d'aller évoluer, ils furent sur Zante.

2 au 3　Ils furent en vue du convoi et de la division qui était partie la veille pour Patras, au nombre de 41 voiles, sous les ordres de Patrona Bey.

3 au 4　Les 14 bâtimens, sous les ordres d'Ibrahim Pacha, rallient le convoi, et voulant tromper la vigilance de l'amiral anglais, font tous route dans la nuit pour le golfe de Patras.

4 au 5　Les meilleurs voiliers, au nombre de 26, dont 9 frégates, mouillent de relâche forcée sous le Cap Papas, et les traînards sont chassés et forcés de laisser arriver par le canon de l'amiral anglais. Les autres appareillent nuitamment de Papas et prennent fuite par la passe de l'ouest.

5 au 6　Toute la division de 26 voiles tient la mer bâbord amure, grand frais de S.E. et gagne le large.

6 au 7　La division fait route pour Navarin; au jour elle en était en vue, à 11 h^{res} du matin, étant à 3 lieues de terre. Quelques bâtimens rentrent à la nuit; les autres, pris par le calme, restent à la mer.

7 au 8　Le reste de la flotte entre; il reste 29 bâtimens dont on n'a aucune nouvelle, et dont majeure partie sont rentrés peu de jours après, chassés par un bâtiment français.

8 au 9　L'armée turque dans Navarin forme une ligne d'embossage en fer à cheval, et pendant trois jours s'occupe à rectifier cette ligne.

14 au 15　On rectifie définitivement la ligne d'embossage. Ibrahim Pacha part avec le reste de son armée qui était campée à Modon, où il ne laisse que les dépôts des hôpitaux.

17 au 18　Le 17 au matin, par la goëlette française 'l'Alcyone,' expédiée par l'Amiral De Rigny, nous recevons une sommation de la part de cet amiral de quitter le service turc, vu la situation agressive dans laquelle s'est placé la flotte en rompant l'armistice. Le même soir une frégate anglaise, le 'Dartmouth,' mouille sur la rade. Le 18 un des nôtres est envoyé à Monsr

l'amiral de Rigny dans un canot d'un bâtiment autrichien, pour l'informer que nous étions décidés à passer sur ce bâtiment neutre. La frégate anglaise, mouillée la veille, appareille à deux h^{res} de l'après-midi.

Vers 1 h^{re} $\frac{3}{4}$ environ les escadres combinées, le vais- le 20. seau l''Asia' en tête, se dirigent sur la rade de Navarin; nous étions depuis le matin retirés à bord du bâtiment autrichien, excepté Monsr Le'Tellier, qui était resté à terre malade. A 2 h^{res} les trois vaisseaux de tête étaient mouillés près des vaisseaux turcs; et des canots qui paraissaient parlementer allaient à bord du vaisseau amiral anglais et en étaient expédiés, lorsqu'une fusillade s'engagea entre les brûlots qui étaient à chaque extrémité du fer à cheval; et des embarcations qui s'en approchaient. Cela fut suivi de près par quelques coups de canon tirés des corvettes turques de la tête de la ligne, auquel il fut répondu par la 'Sirène,' qui venait mouiller en ce moment. Alors les forts tirèrent sur les vaisseaux français et russes, qui entraient successivement dans la baie, et la fumée de l'engagement général qui s'ensuivit ne nous permit plus de rien distinguer. Vers 5 h^{res} $\frac{1}{2}$ le feu se ralentit et cessa. La flotte turque était presqu'entièrement détruite. Il ne restait qu'une seule frégate égyptienne, 'Le Lion,' dont la mâture fut haute; le reste des vaisseaux et frégates était jeté à la côte, coulé et entièrement démâté; plusieurs explosions eurent lieu dans la soirée et dans la nuit.

Au jour on voyait une trentaine de bâtimens, cor- Le 21 vettes, brigs et transports, qui restaient intacts, octobre mais paraissaient abandonnés des équipages. Les explosions continuaient toujours. Les vaisseaux amiraux français et anglais paraissaient avoir beaucoup souffert; ils étaient démâtés du mât d'artimon.

Je fus prendre les ordres de l'amiral de Rigny, qui me fit passer, ainsi que les autres officiers fran- le 22 çais, sur le vaisseau la 'Provence' qui devait partir pour Toulon.

Pour extrait conforme,

BOMPAR.

Note communiquée par Monsieur Bompar, et extraite de son Journal. *

COMPOSITION DE L'ARMÉE ÉGYPTIENNE, PARTIE D'ALEXANDRIE LE 5 AOÛT 1827.

Bâtimens de Constantinople .	{ Vaisseaux	2
	Frégates	5
	Corvettes	9
Égyptiens	{ Frégates	3
	Corvettes	9
	Brigs	4
	Goëlettes	6
Transports 46	{ Brûlots	6
	Transports	35
	Idm. impériaux . .	5
Tunisiens	{ Frégates	3
	Brig	1
Ralliés à Marmorice . .	Frégate	1
Venant d'Égypte . . .	Brigs	2
	Total . . .	91

Navires qui étaient déjà dans Navarin.

Bâtimens de Constantinople sous les ordres de Tahir Pacha .	{ Vaisseaux . . .	1
	Frégates . . .	8
	Corvettes . . .	14
	Total général . .	114

From the three Admirals to the Members of the Permanent Committee of the Legislative Body.

[Page 91.]

Port of Navarin: October 24, 1827.

GENTLEMEN,—We learn with lively feelings of indignation that, while the ships of the Allied Powers have destroyed the Turkish fleet, which had refused submitting to an armistice *de facto*, the Greek cruisers continue to infest the seas; and that the Prize Court, the only tribunal recognised by the Greek Code, seeks by legal forms to justify their excesses.

Your Provisional Government appears to think that the chiefs of the allied squadrons are not agreed on the measures to be adopted for putting a stop to this system of lawless plunder. It deceives itself. We here declare to you with one voice, that we will not suffer your seeking, under false pretexts, to enlarge the theatre of war, that is to say, the circle of piracies.

We will not suffer any expedition, any cruise, any blockade to be made by the Greeks, beyond the limits of from Volo to Lepanto, including Salamina, Egina, Hydra, and Spezzia.

We will not suffer the Greeks to incite insurrection at Scio or in Albania, thereby exposing the population to be massacred by the Turks in retaliation.

* Received by Sir E. C. at a later period from Admiral De Rigny.

We will consider as void all papers given to cruisers found beyond the prescribed limits, and the ships of war of the Allied Powers will have orders to arrest them wherever they may be so found.

There remains for you no pretext.

The armistice by sea exists on the part of the Turks *de facto*. Their fleet exists no more. Take care of yours, for we will also destroy it, if need be, to put a stop to a system of robbery on the high seas, which would end in your exclusion from the law of nations.

As the present Provisional Government is as weak as it is immoral, we address these final and irrevocable resolutions to the Legislative Body.

With respect to the Prize Court which it has instituted, we declare it incompetent to judge any of our vessels without our concurrence.

(Signed by the three Admirals.)

The Council of the Greeks to their Excellencies the Admirals of the Allied Powers.

[Page 91.]

Egina: November 30, 1827.

EXCELLENCIES,—The Greek nation has seen with delight the triumphs which the naval forces of the three Allied Powers have gained over the enemies of Christianity and civilisation, and all Greece has re-echoed with acclamations which have been justly attributed to the ability and prudence of the accomplishers of this great enterprise. Prayers have been offered up to the Almighty, and blessings invoked upon the three Allied Powers and their representatives for their protection and favour to the Greek nation, and for that blood which has been freely shed for the welfare of Greece. In proportion to this feeling of gratitude so strongly imprinted on the heart of every Greek, is the severe and profound regret occasioned by the receipt of your letter of October 24, sent by you to the Greek Council; as, by that letter, the legislative body learnt how much you were displeased by the conduct of some cruisers. Without losing a moment, the Council not only obtained from the Government a renewal of the proclamation which had been previously issued for the cessation of this evil, but has also made every exertion that the strongest and most severe measures against it should be carried into effect; and the Council hopes that, through your co-operation, the Greek seas will be entirely cleared from piracy. Greece is scarcely yet emerging from slavery and the profound ignorance attendant on it, in which she has suffered for many centuries therefore she is, in consequence of the long and unequal war in which she has struggled, scarcely able to obtain sufficient forces to fight for the great enterprise of her own independence; yet she has always made, and still makes, strenuous efforts to unite herself to the great civilised world, by using every possible means in her power for the accomplishment of that glorious object. But great as these objects are, they are inadequate to place her on a par with other civilised constituted nations, and European Governments must therefore regard Greece with an indulgent and philanthropic eye. The Greek Council observes in your letter that limits are fixed by you for navigating from the Gulf of Volo on the Eastern Sea, to the Straits of Lepanto on the Western Sea; on which the Council takes the liberty of making the following observations :—

Humanity was the principal object of the Allied Powers in their undertaking to put a stop to the effusion of blood, and to the hostilities between the belligerent nations; but *beyond* those fixed limits there are some Greek troops stationed who can communicate by *sea only* with the Greek Government; and if Greek vessels are prohibited from taking the necessary assistance to such places, it follows that the Greeks who are actually there must be left exposed to the rage of their wild and savage tyrants, which is inconsistent with the humanity of the Allied Powers.

The Greek Council therefore thinks that it would be expedient that you should be pleased to allow the limits of the navigation of the Greek men-of-war from the Gulf of Salonica on the eastward, to the Gulf of Arta on the westward, including also those islands on which there are troops and Greek population.

Be pleased, Gentlemen, to comply with these just demands of the Greeks, showing always towards them the condescension and benevolence which their circumstances so justly claim for them.

The President of the Council,
REINIERIS.

Joint Instructions for the Interpreters of Great Britain, France, and Russia, dated Constantinople, October 29, 1827.

[Page 101.]

The Interpreters will repair to the Reis Effendi, and make to him the following communication in the name of the Representatives :—

By an agreement entered into between the Admirals and

Ibrahim of September 26, in the presence of the principal officers of the Ottoman fleet, as assembled at Navarin, no division of that fleet was to attempt to sail from thence, until the Porte should make known to the Vizier whether he was definitively to yield to the representations of the said Admirals, or to pay no attention to them. That engagement has been violated. The greater part of the combined fleet, under orders of Ibrahim, quitted Navarin, and the result was that the squadrons of the High Powers *were under the necessity of employing force.*

Thus has been realised the resolution which the Representatives notified to the Porte in the name of their Courts.

In this state of things, and while they renew to the Reis Effendi the expression of the sincere desire of the High Powers for the continuance of peace between them and the Sublime Porte, the Representatives demand of that Minister to be categorically informed, in the first place, what is the nature of the orders which the Government of His Highness has transmitted to Ibrahim Pacha, in answer to the report which he made to it of his agreement with the Admirals of September 26; in the second place, whether, in case these orders may have been to pay no attention to the declaration of the said Admirals, the Sublime Porte perseveres in them; and, lastly, whether it regards the recent occurrence between its fleet and the fleets of the three Great Powers as establishing a state of war between them.

The Interpreters will take care to announce to the Reis Effendi, that an evasive answer on his part will not the less place the Representatives under the necessity of adopting, without delay, such resolutions as the interests which they have to protect and to defend may prescribe to them.

STRATFORD CANNING.
COUNT GUILLEMINOT.
RIBEAUPIERRE.

Interview with the Reis Effendi at Constantinople, October 30, 1827.

M. Franchini said that he was the bearer of a message in the name of the Representatives of the Allied Powers.

' What Allies ? ' said the Reis Effendi; ' we do not know them.' ' The Allies,' answered M. Franchini, ' are Great Britain, France, and Russia.'

His Excellency then listened with the most profound attention, and with the utmost calmness, to the whole instruction.

At the passage, ' Thus has been realised the resolution which the Representatives notified to the Porte,' the Minister observed that nothing had ever been notified to him, excepting assurances that no act on the part of the three Powers should interrupt the friendship which existed.

M. Desgranges observed, that it had been announced to the Reis Effendi that the operations of the Ottoman fleet would be prevented by force. At the end of the first of the three questions his Excellency suffered these words to escape him, ' Truly this is very amusing.' He then desired M. Franchini to proceed. The Reis Effendi did not again interrupt him. These were his replies :—

'1. Whatever may be the answer returned to Ibrahim Pacha by the Sublime Porte, you have no right to interrogate us on that score. That concerns no one but Ibrahim Pacha and us ; let every one mind his own business. When your Governments give orders to their commanders, do we ask you what those orders are ? Our commanders and your commanders are officers charged with the execution of the instructions of their Courts. The Porte has not given powers to Ibrahim Pacha to sign any convention.

' The Vizier is commanded to employ all his forces, and every means at his disposal, to enforce submission on the rebellious Rayas, and to reduce them to obedience.'

' 2. We are ignorant of what has taken place between our fleets and yours. When a woman is with child which of you can tell whether she will bring forth a boy or a girl ? Knowing nothing we can say nothing.'

' 3. The Sublime Porte has always declared that it will never admit the interference of others in its affairs. The Sublime Porte does not alter its resolutions ; and, as it has already declared, so it still declares, that, till the Day of Judgment, it will refuse to admit of any foreign interference. It would be impossible that now, when, according to your repeated assurances, the Powers desire the maintenance of peace, we should presume that anything would be likely to disturb our friendship. In a word, the Sublime Porte has no new answer to give to you.'

In the last place, with respect to the declaration of their Excellencies the Representatives, as to their resolution in the event of an equivocal answer on the part of the Reis Effendi, His Excellency said, ' The Representatives can regulate their concerns in whatever way they please. Their intention, by to-day's proceeding, has, doubtless, not been to advance recriminations or complaints.

' It would be easy in such a case for us to ask to whom

belonged the right to make them, and what then might we not have to say!   But our business is to go on as heretofore, and to attend to all the affairs of your Embassies, in constant conformity with Treaties.'

The undersigned then retired.

(Signed by the three Interpreters.)

Conference of Ambassadors at Constantinople.

November 2, 1827.

The Representatives being assembled, the Interpreters, who, at the request of the Reis Effendi, had presented themselves at the Porte, reported as follows :—The Ottoman Minister, professing his entire ignorance of the event of Navarin, excepting from public rumour, had questioned them separately upon the subject.   The Interpreters confined themselves to saying, that up to that time their own information was derived from the same source, and that they had not received from the Representatives any communication which would enable them to give to His Excellency the explanations which he sought.   It was therefore resolved, that the Interpreters should return in the course of the day to the Reis Effendi, and communicate to him the contents of the annexed instruction.

STRATFORD CANNING.
COUNT GUILLEMINOT.
RIBEAUPIERRE.

Joint Instruction to the Interpreters of Great Britain, France, and Russia, dated November 2, 1827.

The Interpreters will return to the Reis Effendi, and will answer the questions which were put to them by that Minister in the following manner :—Ibrahim Pacha, as is known to the Porte, had, on September 26th, entered into an engagement with the Admirals to undertake no operation, nor to quit Navarin, until he should receive an answer from the Divan to his report of his conference with the said Admirals. This engagement was violated.   The Admirals presented themselves on October 20th in the Port of Navarin, but without committing any hostilities.   An act of aggression took place on the part of the Ottoman fleet : the battle then took place.   It appears that the fleet has been destroyed.

This is the information that has come to the knowledge of the Representatives.   They deplore the melancholy results of the necessity which compelled their squadrons to oppose force to force. May it please Heaven that the present resolutions of the Sublime Porte may be such as to prevent the recurrence of similar disasters.

STRATFORD CANNING.
COUNT GUILLEMINOT.
RIBEAUPIERRE.

None of these communications, which took place at Constantinople on hearing of the battle of Navarin, were made known to Sir Edward Codrington until long afterwards. They were published in the Parliamentary Papers from which they are now copied.

From Earl Dudley to H.R.H. the Lord High Admiral.
(Sent under a covering letter from the Admiralty.)

[Page 120.]

Foreign Office : October 15, 1827.[*]

In reference to my letter of July 13 last, I have the King's command to acquaint Your Royal Highness that it appears from the despatches of His Majesty's Ambassador at Constantinople, and from copies which His Excellency has transmitted to his Government of a letter from Admiral De Rigny to Count Guilleminot, together with Count Guilleminot's answer, that some doubts have arisen as to the application of some part of the joint Instructions conveyed to their respective Admirals by the three Allied Powers, and dated August 31. His Majesty's Government observe with satisfaction that the construction which the Ambassadors and Admirals are disposed to put upon these passages is agreeable to the spirit of the Instructions themselves, and to the intention of those by whom they were framed. Still, in order to exempt the Commanders of the fleets, entrusted with the execution of an arduous and delicate task, from the possibility of doubt or hesitation as to the precise line of their duty, it is thought proper to lay down the following rules in explanation and in confirmation of their original Instructions. I have, therefore, to signify to Your Royal Highness His Majesty's commands that the Commander of the British fleet should be directed to intercept all ships, whether of war or merchants, under the flag of Turkey, Egypt, and the States of Africa, having on board troops, arms, ammunition, stores, or provisions, for the use of the Turkish force employed, or intended to be employed, against the Greeks, either on the continent or in the islands. He

[*] Received by Sir E. C. at Malta, November 8, 1827.

will not, however, use force for such interception, unless it' shall become absolutely necessary by the commanders of those vessels persisting after having been duly warned to the contrary, to proceed to the place of their destination; and he will take care to abstain, under present circumstances, from giving any interruption to the regular commerce of neutrals with any of the ports of Turkey, or of Greece, though occupied by the Turks.

He will concert with the Commanders of the Allied Powers the most effectual mode of preventing any movements by sea on the part of the Turkish or Egyptian forces.

In the meantime the position taken up off the harbour of Navarin, appears to be well calculated for this purpose, as it watches and controls the most efficient naval force that the Porte and the Pacha of Egypt have now at sea.

It is also considered desirable that a station should be taken at the Dardanelles to prevent the egress of any Turkish naval force, or Turkish merchant ships, carrying men, arms, ammunition, stores, or provisions: but it must be left to the judgment and discretion of the Admirals to decide, in conjunction with the Ambassadors, whether any portion of this force should be so employed either off Constantinople or Alexandria. The line described in the protocol for the operations of the Greek blockade appears to be that which is best adapted to the actual situation of the contending parties. It is therefore sanctioned by the Allied Powers, subject, however, to such variations as circumstances may suggest to the Ambassadors and Admirals judging of them upon the spot as they arise.

He will concert with the Greek authorities that the whole of their naval force shall be exclusively appropriated to the blockade of the ports of Greece, now occupied by the Turkish or Egyptian forces. In that case, he will not restrain the Greek naval forces from exercising, in respect to neutrals attempting to break the blockade, all the rights belonging to a belligerent.

But with a view to prevent the continuance of the predatory warfare by the Greek cruisers, now the subject of such frequent complaints on the part of the Allies, and of all nations trading to the Levant, he will try to procure from the Greek Government their consent that any Greek vessel carrying less than *ten* guns, which may be found at sea, unless provided with a passport for some specific voyage, and from the Greek Government itself, should be liable to detention by the naval forces of the Allies. In general he will lose no opportunity of impressing upon the Greek

'Government the necessity of endeavouring earnestly, by every means they possess, to check robbery and plunder by sea, which have prevailed in the Levant since the beginning of the present troubles.

He will represent to them that though in the infancy of their power they may not possess the means of putting down this system, yet that by discountenancing it themselves, and by sanctioning active measures on our part, they will at once satisfy the Mediating Powers, and relieve their cause from a great weight of odium under which it has hitherto laboured. Upon their coming under an undertaking to this effect, and upon proof that they are in a situation to receive and send commercial agents, and to establish relations of commerce, His Majesty's Government will take measures for executing that part of the secret Article which relates to this point. His Majesty's Government will then also be ready to receive either from the Commander of the British fleet or from His Majesty's Ambassador any suggestion as to the proper moment for sending such agents, and as to the places to which they shall be sent.

I have the honor, &c.,

DUDLEY.

From Earl Dudley to H.R.H. the Lord High Admiral.
(Sent under a covering letter from the Admiralty.)

Foreign Office: October 15, 1827.

SIR,—As my letters of this date will have acquainted Your Royal Highness with the course the British Naval Commander in the Levant is required to pursue in the execution of his duty, he will be under no embarrassment as to how to act, as the Instructions founded on them will completely coincide with the explanation of the patent Instructions which had already been transmitted to him by His Majesty's Ambassador at Constantinople. It remains only to state one limitation as to the mode in which these Instructions are to be carried into effect, a limitation which will itself be subject to the discretion of the commanders of the naval forces, according to the exigencies of the case. It is thought expedient by His Majesty's Government, not only that the regular commerce of neutrals, that is, such as is not carried on in order to aid the belligerent, should proceed uninterrupted, but that the interruption should be confined to neutrals sailing under the convoy of Turkish ships-of-war.

This is to be taken as the general rule, but if any unforeseen circumstances were to arise, in which the passing of neutrals, even without convoy, would be likely to defeat the object of the Treaty, the British Admiral will then not hesitate to hinder them from proceeding to the place of their destination, always, however, preferring the mildest mode of accomplishing that object. I have to signify to Your Royal Highness His Majesty's commands that you will be pleased to issue secret instructions to the Commander of the British fleet, in conformity with the spirit of this communication.

I have the honor to be, &c.,
DUDLEY.

To H.R.H. the Lord High Admiral.
(Sent under covering letter from the Admiralty, October 16.)

Foreign Office · October 15, 1827.

SIR,—In reference to my letter to Your Royal Highness of this day's date, I have to signify to Your Royal Highness the King's commands, that the Admiral to whom the task of watching the port of Navarin shall be allotted by mutual agreement betwixt himself and his colleagues, should be instructed to hold out, in concert with them, every inducement to the Pacha of Egypt and to his son to withdraw the Egyptian ships and land forces altogether from Greece, and to assure them that every facility and protection will be given for their safe return to Alexandria. But he is on no account to enter into any stipulation for allowing the ships to return to Alexandria without the troops.

I have the honor to be, &c., &c.,
DUDLEY.

General Order.—For circulation.

[Page 271.]

' Ocean,' off Coron. May 21, 1828.

In consequence of deceptions which have been practised by the Ottoman vessels which have been permitted to approach the ports of the Morea, both as regards their entrance into them and their return from them to Alexandria; it is my direction that no vessels whatever, under any pretence, are henceforth to be permitted to approach any part of the coast under the Greek blockade, nor any vessels which are now in the ports be permitted to come away. No communication is to be had with the Ottoman forces on shore but through the senior officer of His Majesty's ships on this coast.

EDWD. CODRINGTON.

To the respective Captains and Commanders.

Protocol of Conference held at Zante by the three Admirals.
[Page 381.]
July 25, 1828.

Les amiraux alliés s'étant réunis à Zante à l'effet de constater par la communication de leurs renseignemens respectifs la situation actuelle des affaires à l'égard des troupes égyptiennes en Morée; considérant les instances à eux adressées par le comte Capodistrias pour aviser aux moyens les plus prompts de décider la retraite d'Ibrahim, à l'effet de sauver le reste du Péloponnèse d'une entière dévastation;

Ont reconnu, que déjà la sévérité du blocus avait amené la disette parmi ces troupes; que cette disette avait eu pour conséquence des révoltes partielles dans le camp d'Ibrahim, que les chefs de ses régimens avaient fait un complot afin de s'embarquer pour l'Égypte aussitôt qu'ils auraient les moyens de transport.

D'un autre côté les amiraux sont fondés à croire, d'après ce qui a été communiqué à monsieur Drovetti, Consul-Général de France, que Méhémet Ali est disposé à fournir lui-même des moyens de transport et à prendre tels arrangemens pour l'évacuation définitive.

Mais comme il pourrait se faire que, permettant la sortie de la flotte et des transports de Méhémet Ali, il n'en profitât pour faire parvenir par ruse des provisions en Morée, les amiraux, pour y obvier, ont concerté les dispositions suivantes:

1° De faciliter le départ des bâtimens égyptiens par les communications que continueront à entretenir avec eux Méhémet Ali, les consuls de France et d'Angleterre; et de donner aux commandans des bâtimens de guerre anglais et français qui croisent sur les côtes d'Égypte des ordres de suivre la flotte et de la conduire devant Navarin.

2° De continuer le blocus des forts de la Morée avec la même sévérité; de préparer et concerter avec Ibrahim les dispositions principales et les mesures locales pour l'évacuation quand les bâtimens arriveraient.

Ces dispositions ont été préalablement communiquées à LL. EE. le comte Guilleminot et sir Frederick Adam à Corfou, en l'absence de LL. EE. monsieur Stratford Canning et monsieur de Ribeaupierre, et approuvées par eux.

Les amiraux en préparant ces mesures, et n'ayant point de moyens de transport à leur disposition, comptent à la vérité sur ceux d'Égypte; si leur expérience à cet égard est déçue, ils auront fait tout ce qui était en leur pouvoir; et les choses resteront dans le même état, sans qu'aucun moment ait été perdu.

Ils ont en conséquence signé le présent protocol de leur conférence à Zante, le 25 juillet 1828.

> H. DE RIGNY, Vice-Amiral.
> LE COMTE LOUIS DE HEIDEN, Vice-Amiral.
> EDWD. CODRINGTON, Vice-Admiral.

Pour compléter et assurer les dispositions ci-dessus, tant dans un lieu que dans un autre, le comte Heiden et monsieur de Rigny ont proposé à l'amiral Codrington de vouloir bien rejoindre lui-même ses deux vaisseaux anglais, qu'il a précédemment envoyés sur les côtes d'Égypte, et de se charger dans ces parages de l'exécution des mesures concertées, en mettant sous sa direction les bâtimens français qui s'y trouvent.

> H. DE RIGNY, Vice-Amiral.
> LE COMTE L. DE HEIDEN, Vice-Amiral.

L'amiral Codrington et le comte Heiden proposent à monsieur l'amiral de Rigny de se charger des arrangemens préalables à prendre avec Ibrahim pour l'évacuation quand le moment sera arrivé, et des communications dont il sera besoin à cet effet.

> EDWD. CODRINGTON, Vice-Admiral
> LE COMTE L. DE HEIDEN, Vice-Amiral.

Note written by Sir E. Codrington on the first page of the Treaty.

[Page 400.]

' French copy of the Treaty of Alexandria—the Turkish original being presented to the British Museum by me.—E.C.'

Treaty of Alexandria.

Les divers rapports reçus successivement de la part d'Ibrahim Pacha, général en chef de l'armée égyptienne en Morée, ayant convaincu S.A. Méhémet Ali Pacha, Visir d'Égypte, de l'impossibilité absolue où était son fils de tenir plus longtems dans la position affreuse à laquelle ses troupes se trouvaient réduites par le manque total de subsistance, l'ont placé en même tems dans la douloureuse nécessité d'autoriser Ibrahim Pacha à entrer en négociation avec LL.EE. les amiraux commandant les forces navales des Puissances Alliées dans les mers du Levant, afin d'obtenir une capitulation honorable pour lui, pour son armée, et pour les intérêts de la Sublime Porte Ottomane, qu'il est chargé de soutenir et de défendre en Morée.

En vertu de cette autorisation S.E. Ibrahim Pacha a eu, le 6 juillet dernier, une conférence avec LL. EE. les amiraux de Rigny et de Heiden et monsieur le commodore Campbell. Dans cette entrevue Ibrahim Pacha déclara formellement qu'il était prêt à évacuer, mais qu'il ne s'embarquerait, lui et ses troupes, que sur des bâtimens turcs.

Il s'engagea à ne point emmener des esclaves grecs avec son armée. Il se récria contre la demande qui lui fut faite de la restitution des esclaves conduits en Égypte après la bataille de Navarin, en disant que cette condition ne dépendait pas de lui, et excédait ses pouvoirs. Nulle mention ne fut faite des places fortes occupées par les troupes égyptiennes, sur le sort desquelles on se réservait de statuer lorsque S.E. l'amiral Codrington aurait rejoint ses collègues à Corfou.

Un conseil a été tenu par LL.EE. Il en résultait la détermination que l'amiral Codrington viendrait à Alexandrie pour traiter définitivement avec S.A. Méhémet Ali Pacha des conditions déjà proposées par S.A. elle-même, qui n'avaient point été définies dans la conférence du 6 juillet, et pour s'entendre sur les mesures propres à réaliser l'évacuation.

En effet aujourd'hui, 6 août 1828, S.E. l'amiral Codrington s'étant présenté chez S.A. Méhémet Ali Pacha en audience privée, accompagné seulement de messieurs Drovetti, consul-général de S.M. Très-Chrétienne, et Barker, consul de S.M. Britannique, monsieur le commodore Campbell, monsieur le capitaine Richards, monsieur le capitaine E. Curzon, et monsieur le capitaine W. J. Codrington, après avoir longuement discuté les articles principaux de l'évacuation des places fortes occupées par les troupes égyptiennes en Morée, et de la mise en liberté des esclaves grecs transportés du Péloponnèse en Égypte après l'affaire de Navarin—dans laquelle discussion le Vizir s'est surtout attaché à démontrer l'impudence avec laquelle les journalistes d'Angleterre et de France ont exagéré le nombre de ces esclaves et les mauvais traitemens auxquels ils sont exposés en Égypte—on est convenu de l'évacuation de la Morée par les troupes égyptiennes aux conditions suivantes :—

ARTICLE 1. S.A. Méhémet Ali Pacha s'engage à restituer les esclaves grecs conduits de la Morée en Égypte après la bataille de Navarin.

Il commencera par faire mettre à la disposition de S.E. l'amiral Codrington tous ceux de ses esclaves qu'il est en son pouvoir de libérer immédiatement. Quant à ceux de ces esclaves qui seraient devenus la propriété des particuliers, S.A. promet l'emploi efficace de ses bons offices pour que messieurs les consuls des Puissances Alliées puissent en racheter le plus grand nombre, et aux meilleures conditions possibles.

De son côté S.E. l'amiral Codrington s'oblige de faire rendre à la liberté tous les soldats, ou sujets égyptiens, qui se trouvent prisonniers chez les Grecs, ainsi que les officiers et marins de la corvette égyptienne capturée par les Russes dans les eaux de Modon.

ARTICLE 2. S.A. Méhémet Ali Pacha promet de faire partir dans le plus court délai possible tous les bâtimens de guerre et transport dont il peut disposer, pour aller chercher à Navarin, et recevoir à leurs bords, toutes les troupes égyptiennes. Ces troupes devront évacuer entièrement la Morée dans le plus court délai possible.

ARTICLE 3. Les bâtimens de guerre ou de transport seront escortés par des navires anglais ou français, qui les accompagneront, et entreront avec eux dans le port de Navarin ou autres ports de la Morée aux fins ci-dessus mentionnés.

ARTICLE 4. Les mêmes bâtimens, à leur sortie de Navarin, seront également escortés jusqu'à la vue du port d'Alexandrie.

ARTICLE 5. Ni S.E. Ibrahim Pacha, ni aucun officier de sa suite ou de l'armée—enfin, aucune personne faisant partie de l'évacuation—ne pourra emmener aucun Grec, à moins qu'il ne le désire lui-même, soit homme, femme, ou enfant.

ARTICLE 6. S.E. Ibrahim Pacha, en évacuant la Morée, pourra laisser dans les places fortes de Patras, Castel-Tornèse, Modon, Coron, et Navarin une garnison suffisante à leur défense.

Fait à Alexandrie d'Égypte, le jour, mois et an que dessus.

(L.S.) Cachet de S.A. LE PACHA.

Article additionnel.

S.A. Méhémet Ali Pacha s'oblige d'ordonner à Ibrahim Pacha de former les garnisons des forteresses de Patras, Castel-Tornèse, Modon, Coron, et Navarin de manière qu'on ne puisse en aucun cas et sous aucun prétexte y laisser, comme faisant partie de ces garnisons, plus de mille deux cents soldats égyptiens.

(L.S.) Cachet de S.A. LE PACHA.

*Explanatory Reply to Lord Aberdeen's Despatch of May 1828.
From Sir E. C. to the Admiralty.**

[Page 411.]

'Asia,' off Alexandria: August 10, 1828.

SIR,—In order that no unfavorable impression should be made on the mind of His Royal Highness the Lord High Admiral by the desire expressed by His Majesty's Government that I should be superseded in this command, I gave such explanation of the charges arrayed against me in Lord Aberdeen's despatch as the hurry of the moment permitted. Since that time I have had leisure to examine with more attention the mass of papers to which they refer; and I presume to submit the observations to which that investigation has given rise to His Royal Highness's particular consideration.

The despatch in which Lord Aberdeen has announced to me the decision of His Majesty's Government grounds that decision upon the construction which they are now pleased to give to an order to my predecessor, dated February 8, 1826, and the Instructions of the Earl of Dudley of October 16, 1827. I deny altogether the interpretation both in letter and spirit which has thus been given to either of these documents.

The order of February 8, 1826, directs Sir Harry Neale to send an officer to ascertain from Ibrahim Pacha himself if the report be true of his designing to extirpate systematically the whole community of the Morea, and to re-people the country from Africa or Asia; and to demand an explicit disavowal or renunciation of it in a written document: and even if he should refuse, the officer is only empowered to tell him that 'effectual means will be taken to prevent, by the intervention of His Majesty's naval forces, the accomplishment of so unwarrantable a project,' and that 'his refusal will be forthwith reported to His Majesty.' And Sir Harry Neale is then to make a report of the result of the 'negotiation,' as Lord Bathurst terms it, or 'mission,' as it is termed in the Admiralty letter.

The despatch of Lord Aberdeen says that these instructions 'have put me in possession of the intention of His Majesty's Government that the transportation of the Greeks of the Morea to Egypt should not be permitted.' But the letter from Mr. Consul Barker to the Earl of Dudley, of May 17, shows:—

That from fifteen to twenty thousand Greeks have been

* Acknowledged September 15, 1828, and a copy sent by the Admiralty to the Foreign Office.

brought to Alexandria from the Morea since the beginning of the contest; that the mass of captives was taken at the storming of Missolonghi and Calavrita in April 1826; and that the transmission of these slaves has been carried on by regular slave merchants.

The despatch to my predecessor, of February 1826, observes—that His Majesty, in deploring the continuance of the excesses that have taken place, 'has not thought fit hitherto to interpose except in those cases in which the rights of his subjects, &c., have been clearly compromised;' and although the deportation of the mass of these captives took place subsequent to the order of February 8, 1826, yet His Majesty's Government has permitted such transmissions, and no reference has ever been made to it until it is now brought forward as a charge against me.

I say, then, that if His Majesty's Government has had the intention that such deportation should not be permitted, no indication of that wish, nor any instruction to carry that intention into effect, has been given to the Admiral in the Mediterranean command from February 8, 1826, to March 18, 1828;* and although the despatch of this latter date, with-

[All the notes to this letter were written by Sir E. C. upon the despatch.]

An officer was sent to Ibrahim Pacha by Sir H. Neale in execution of this instruction. On Ibrahim's learning the nature of his communication, he said it was a political business for which he must refer to the Sultan; and the officer then represented the matter to two Commissioners of the Porte, then in Ibrahim's camp, and who refused to give any answer on the subject. Mr. S. Canning made enquiry at Constantinople, and found that there never was such an intention as described in the despatch of the 8th February, 1826. The whole business accordingly 'dropped to the ground' (as stated by Mr. Peel, in Parliament), and the despatch was left by Sir H. Neale, marked 'The service here directed has been executed.'

Vice-Admiral Sir H. Neale, to whom this order was addressed, and by whom it was executed, has entirely the same view of it; he could not further act on it than by reporting Ibrahim Pacha's decision, and only left it for me in case a reference should be made to it again from H M. Government.

Thus the great charge of permitting the transmission of Greek slaves recoils upon the Government which did not take measures to prevent it. And the question, as far as it relates to Sir E. Codrington, is settled and put entirely at rest by the following observation made by Lord Goderich personally to him —

'As to the question of Greek slaves, which is made a charge against you,—why! you have not in the whole of your orders and instructions one word which could justify your interfering. It may be a fault in us, but the fact is, the subject never once occurred to any one of us; and if you will ask Lord Lansdowne, or any of my late colleagues, they will tell you the same.'

* In this despatch of the 18th March, of which the express object was to call upon me to account for having permitted such deportation, no reference is made to the Instruction of 8th February, 1826; but solely to the passage in the instructions of 16th October 1827 'to prevent any movements by sea on the part of the Turkish or Egyptian forces.'

out giving any authority for future interposition, imputes blame to me for not having so interfered, and notwithstanding I subsequently asked the direct question*—'If I was to release any Greek captives found on board Ottoman ships?' His Majesty's Government has neither answered that question, nor furnished me with any authority to do so. But I can refer to the whole of the instructions addressed to me for my guidance to show that I am under orders of a directly opposite tendency, and that my doing that which it is now implied that I ought to have done, would have been in direct defiance of those orders.†

I deny that what is given in Lord Aberdeen's despatch as the meaning of the Protocol of September 4, 1827, is consistent either with the wording or the spirit of that Protocol. It says:—'Les amiraux agiront dans le sens du Traité en protégeant, selon le besoin, toute portion des forces navales, grecques ou mussulmanes, qui s'engagerait à ne pas prendre part aux hostilités, et en favorisant, d'après ce principe, le retour, soit à Alexandrie, soit à Constantinople, de tout bâtiment de guerre turc et égyptien, de même que tout transport de l'une ou de l'autre nation ayant à bord des troupes retirées.'

In another part of the same Protocol, it says, 'L'utilité de faire un pareil mouvement vers Alexandrie dans le but d'accélérer la retraite de la flotte égyptienne est laissée à la décision des amiraux.' These quotations clearly show that the condition of my affording protection to ships-of-war did not depend upon their having troops on board; it was enough that they did not take part in hostilities.‡ The words 'de même que tout transport de l'une ou de l'autre

---

* In my letter to Earl Dudley of 7th April, acknowledged in London on 7th May.

† The Protocol of September 4, of the Ambassadors, was formed in consequence of the questions put to them by Admiral De Rigny and myself. These questions were put by me in my (secret) letter to Mr. S. Canning, of the 11th August, 1827, which he answered by his letter (confidential) of the 19th August, saying 'some of the questions which you do me the honor to propose for my consideration must be talked over with my colleagues,' &c.; and in another letter from him (confidential) of September 1, 1827, 'I have considered and talked over with my colleagues the several questions mentioned in your letters marked secret, as having been objects of conversation between you and Admiral De Rigny, &c.,' and his letter of September 8, accompanying and explaining the Protocol, also refers to these questions as the cause of its formation.

‡ Extract from my letter to Mr. S. Canning, of the 11th August:—'Another point in which I wish to be instructed is, whether or not we may guarantee the retirement of any of the belligerent forces as far as we have power to do so, if they propose to withdraw themselves from the contest.' This question was answered by that part of the Protocol of which an extract is made.

nation ayant à bord des troupes retirées,' were inserted at the suggestion of Mr. Stratford Canning, in order to guard the commanders of the Allied Forces from employing the means at their disposal in measures not conducive to the execution of the Treaty, by the admission of claims for protection on the part of the transports forming part of that expedition which should return without troops. The letter of Count Guilleminot of September 4, 1827, inclosed to me by Mr. Stratford Canning for my information, clearly shows the sentiments both of himself and his colleagues upon this point. After speaking of measures to be taken, 'dans le but d'attirer loin du théâtre des hostilités la flotte égyptienne,' he says, 'Enfin, mes collègues et moi nous avons été d'avis que les escadres des cours devraient protéger dans leur retraite toutes celles des forces navales et des troupes ottomanes qui témoigneraient vouloir quitter la Grèce pour retourner sans coup férir,' &c.

The despatch next refers to the instructions of October 16, 1827,* and I equally deny that the construction now put

---

* (*Extract.*)

Foreign Office, October 16.

'In reference to my letter of the 13th July last, I have the King's commands to acquaint your Royal Highness that it appears from the despatches of His Majesty's Ambassador at Constantinople, and from copies which His Excellency has transmitted to his Government, of a letter from Admiral De Rigny to Count Guilleminot, together with Count Guilleminot's answer, that some doubts have arisen as to the application of the joint instructions conveyed to their respective Admirals by the three allied Powers, and dated August 31, His Majesty's Government observe with satisfaction that the construction which the Ambassadors and Admirals are disposed to put upon these passages is agreeable to the spirit of the instructions themselves, and to the intention of those by whom they were framed.

'Still, in order to exempt the commanders of the fleets entrusted with the execution of an arduous and delicate task from the possibility of doubt or hesitation as to the precise line of their duty, it is thought proper to lay down the following rules in explanation, and in confirmation of their original instructions.

Extract from the Secret letter of the same date.

F. O., October 15, 1827.

'Sir,—As my letters of this date will have acquainted your Royal Highness with the course the British Naval Commander in the Levant is requested to pursue in the execution of his duty, he will be under no embarrassment as to how to act, as the instructions founded on them will completely coincide with the explanations of the Patent Instructions, which had already been transmitted to him by His Majesty's Ambassador at Constantinople.

'This part of the instructions of the 16th October is evidently an answer to my question to Mr. S. Canning, "If I could guarantee the retirement of any of the belligerent forces, should they propose to withdraw from the contest."

'It was a question of *protection* to be given, not of mere permission to

upon them is consistent with either the terms or the spirit of the Protocol from which they emanated,—or of the explanations given by the Ambassadors to Admiral de Rigny and myself,—or of the instructions of July 12, 1827, of which Lord Dudley and Lord Aberdeen respectively have declared them to be an 'explanation' and a 'confirmation.'

I cannot suppose it is intended by the application of the word 'altogether,' in Lord Aberdeen's despatch, that facility and protection should be afforded to the Ottoman Forces only in case of their consenting that the whole of the land and naval forces should return together, since this would be in direct contradiction to the Protocol of September 4. As to my being 'on no account to enter into any stipulation for allowing the ships to return to Alexandria without the troops,' authorizing me, as the despatch alleges, to ascertain what the ships in question contained, I cannot consider it in that light. That paragraph was inserted in confirmation of that part of the Protocol which was added at the suggestion of Mr. Stratford Canning, to prevent an improper claim to our protection, as I have before stated. It was not, and could not have been, intended that I should by so obnoxious a measure throw impediments in the way of the return 'de tout bâtiment de guerre turc ou égyptien,' &c.; a measure which I could not have exercised without an assumption of belligerent rights, which would have degenerated into hostilities.

The despatch then states that 'my fleet does not appear to have been so disposed as to have been able to prevent the movements of the Turkish and Egyptian ships, whatever they might have contained or whatever might have been their destination.'

That 'it does not appear that any ships were specifically directed to watch the ports of the Morea.'

That 'the first information received by you of the sailing of the Turkish and Egyptian fleet from Navarin appears to have been obtained when you learnt its arrival at Alexandria.'

That 'that fleet appears to have been unwatched at Navarin,' &c.

I must, in the first place, protest against this gratuitous assumption of appearances for the purpose of censuring me,

depart. I was thus authorised to protect the returning ships of war, and also the transports having on board troops; but it was also an instruction of *precaution*, that I might not be called on to stipulate for protection being claimed for empty transports.

'As to *allowing* even the empty vessels to return, it was evidently advantageous, as depriving Ibrahim of the means of carrying on a hostile movement against the islands of Greece.'

because no disposition of the ships under my orders happens to have reached the Admiralty during a certain period when all my attention was required and all my time occupied by much more important considerations.

By the term 'your fleet,' the despatch implies that I had an efficient and disposable force with which I could have controlled any movements of the Ottoman Navy, when the very returns of the disposition of the squadron, which are now brought forward in confirmation of the charges against me, show that I had no such fleet; and it is scarcely necessary for me to add that, with the small force remaining after the battle of Navarin, it was my first and imperative duty to afford to the British Consulates and mercantile establishments that protection, the want of which, at so critical a time, might have led to the most serious consequences.

I can, nevertheless, oppose facts to the assumptions above enumerated. In contradiction of the assumptions that the fleet was unwatched at Navarin, and that the first information I received of the sailing of that fleet was when it arrived at Alexandria, the fact is that the Ottoman fleet was reconnoitred by the 'Pelican' in the port of Navarin on November 15, 1827, and that she continued to watch that port, as far as weather and other circumstances permitted, until December 22, when, having actually stood in between the batteries, and, finding the fleet had sailed, she proceeded to give me the intelligence at Malta, where she arrived on December 27, five days afterwards. Although these facts, established by Commander Hamilton's letters and the 'Pelican's' log book, disprove at once the three assumptions of 'no specific orders having been given to watch the port of Navarin,' of its 'being actually unwatched,' and 'of the first information of the fleet having sailed being received by me when it arrived at Alexandria,' I have to add that the port was reconnoitred by the 'Parthian' on December 5, by 'specific orders' from Captain Hamilton, of the 'Cambrian,' who went immediately after the battle to induce the Greek Government to establish that blockade which has at length been the principal cause of Ibrahim's present difficulties and disposition to retire; that le Capitaine Pujol, of His Most Christian Majesty's brig 'la Flèche,' left Milo, 'pour aller observer les ports de Navarin et Modon, et communiquer, si les circonstances le permettaient, pour obtenir quelques renseignemens sur la situation d'Ibrahim;' and that he reported to Admiral de Rigny that, whilst the brig was lying before Modon with three anchors ahead on December 19, in a N.E. gale of wind, 'Ibrahim fit sortir les débris de sa flotte, emportant, indépendamment des équipages, des milliers de blessés—6 à 7 mille hommes appartenant à son armeé.'

It is observed in the despatch that 'that fleet might have conveyed the effective force of Ibrahim Pacha to any other point of the Morea, or to any of the islands, with the same facility with which it conveyed all the useless persons of the army to Alexandria.'

It is difficult to imagine how the word 'facility' came to be selected on such an occasion. On the 21st January, 1828, I sent home letters from Commanders Richards and Keith, descriptive of the state in which that fleet reached the coasts of Candia and Egypt; and on the 30th January I sent home a report of Capitaine Pujol of the state in which they left Navarin; and considering the minute enquiry which has been made into my official returns, and the rigid scrutiny which my conduct has undergone since the battle of Navarin, I cannot but think it very extraordinary that these particular documents should have been entirely overlooked. However, I may safely assert that, whatever may have been the motive for introducing this word facility, there is no instance on record, since the beginning of time, of ships putting to sea with such an absence of every facility whatever for preserving the existence of those who were embarked in them.*

The despatch then observes that 'no measures were taken to prevent the return of that fleet from Egypt;' and that 'it was unobserved during its passage, and would not have been adequately, if at all, opposed had it directed its course again to Navarin instead of to Candia.' This is another gratuitous assumption for which I cannot account, but which the facts will show to be without foundation. For the allied force at Alexandria when the detachment sailed, was sufficient to control the whole force which the Viceroy could send to sea. And the movement of that detachment was sanctioned by the senior French and English officers there, in consequence of the Viceroy pledging his word that they were destined for Candia and not for the Morea. The whole of this detachment, which the despatch terms 'that fleet,' thereby implying that it was composed of the whole which had left Navarin, and is said to be able to move to any other point with so much 'facility,' amounted to 2 frigates, 4 corvettes, and several brigs and transports, making in all 22 sail. And the difficulty of collecting even this force is shown by one of the frigates being in the same crippled state as she was left after the battle of Navarin; she had a jury main-mast, a fished fore-mast and bowsprit, and her shot-holes were unstopped. The 'Isis,' ' Rattle-

* See also Captain Richards' letter, Aug. 11, 1828, p. 315.

snake,' 'Zebra,' and 'Chamelion' were then at Carabusa, from whence they could have been called by signal, and 'l'Iphigénie,' double frigate, 'l'Armide,' the 'Rifleman,' and 'Musquito,' were then off Modon and Navarin.

It is then observed that the 'Warspite' did not arrive at Navarin until March 12, as if it were a fault in me that she had not been there before; when, in fact, this very circumstance is evidence, not only of the paucity of means at my disposal, but of the zealous exertions of Captain Parker in performing the duties of that station. For his own letters, which have been so closely scrutinised for grounds of accusation, state, that upon hearing of the sailing of the Ottoman detachment from Alexandria, he hastened from another very important service to prevent supplies being landed in the Morea. It is next said in the despatch that he remained there merely on account of a wish expressed by Count Guilleminot; although he himself, in the same letter from which one single sentence is thus selected, accounts for it by his 'anxiety not to leave an insufficient force there,' and by his 'determination to remain there in company with "l'Iphigénie" until he ascertains positively that the "*provisions*," &c., have been landed in Candia, and the ships of war gone to Alexandria.'

The despatch then states, by way of summary, that 'from December to March the movements of a large fleet between Egypt and the Morea seem to have been free from interruption, and not even exposed to observation.' It is thus implied that several such movements have taken place; whereas there has been only one such movement of a fleet, if this name can be given to the miserable collection of vessels, the principal part of which were destitute not only of the means of hostility, but also of common safety, and even of subsistence; and this movement, let it be observed, was from the Morea to Egypt, and, consequently, one which my instructions absolutely order me to encourage. No Ottoman fleet whatever has since arrived in the Morea.

But in order to show that I have disobeyed the orders under which I acted, in thus permitting this one movement from the Morea to Egypt, and a subsequent one from Egypt to Candia, the following passage is made as an extract from the instructions of October 16 :—' You were directed to intercept all ships, either of war or merchants, having on board troops, arms, ammunition, stores or provisions for the use of the Turkish force employed against the Greeks either on the continent or in the islands.' The extract thus made from those instructions is incorrect, inasmuch as the proper expressions are 'for the use of the Turkish force employed or *intended to be employed* against the Greeks;' and this part of my instructions, limited, however, by the secret article of the same date, I have always considered absolute, and have acted upon it in that manner.

I cannot suppose that His Majesty's Government consider the remains of the Ottoman fleet which left the Morea, and which returned to Alexandria after the battle of Navarin, as included under 'ships whether of war or merchants having on board troops, arms, ammunition, stores or provisions for the use of the Turkish force employed or intended to be employed against the Greeks either on the continent or in the islands.'

Nor can I suppose it intended by His Majesty's Government that, under this instruction, I was to prevent that movement of an Egyptian detachment which subsequently took place from Egypt to Candia—a movement which was not hostile in itself—proceeding to a port in their own possession, which was excluded from our operations by the instructions of October 16, and 'not employed or intended to be employed against the Greeks either on the continent or in the islands' included in the Protocol. That detachment returned direct to Alexandria, and, with very few exceptions, the single vessels bringing provisions and other supplies to the coast of the Morea have been stopped and turned back.

But as another ground of accusation in not having prevented the movements above referred to, the despatch extracts from my instructions of October 16 that I was directed 'to concert with the commanders of the allied fleets the most effectual mode of preventing any movements by sea on the part of the Turkish or Egyptian forces.' To show how different a construction has lately been given to these instructions, it is only necessary for me to refer to the letters from Admiral De Rigny and myself to the Ambassadors at Constantinople, and to their Protocol of September 4, which, on being sent to London, produced the instructions of October 16, 'in confirmation and explanation' of those with which we were originally furnished.

The preventing 'any movements by sea on the part of the Turkish or Egyptian forces,' is by these documents clearly shown to be in confirmation and an approval of the measure which Admiral De Rigny and myself had previously adopted, without having been actually authorised in so doing by the instructions of July 12, viz., that of preventing the Ottoman fleet then at Navarin from undertaking any movement from one port in Greece to another. But when the despatch states that 'I am to concert with the allied commanders the most effectual means of preventing any movements by sea on the part of the Turkish or Egyptian forces,'* and adds that 'the instructions on this point were absolute,' I answer that I did consult with the commanders of the Allied Powers; that they did, and do still, agree with me in this understanding of the instructions, in direct opposition to that which is now attributed to them; that they think with me, that the instructions are no less absolute in directing the encouragement of the return of all or any part of the Ottoman forces to Egypt; and they also think with me that it is quite manifest no such return could take place if the reading now given to these instructions be the correct one, viz., that of absolutely preventing any movement by sea on the part of the Turkish or Egyptian forces. In proof, however, of this being the real construction—in proof of how little it was at that time thought proper to separate these instructions from those of July 12—in proof, also, that His Majesty's Government then considered the view which we had taken of the line of our duty to be correct—no clearer language can be used than that of the instruction of October 16 itself. After saying

* *Extract of a Letter from Sir E. C. to Earl Dudley.*

'Asia,' off Navarin: September 13, 1827.

'It is not, however, clear to me that the direction to prevent supplies, &c., being thrown upon the coast of Greece, authorises a prevention of such supplies to places in the Adriatic, which, like Modon, have continued in their hands, and which, without such aid, might starve' . . . 'and as I may possibly be again so situated, I ask for your judgment on it.' . . . 'I am not yet aware of what may be the object of the Turkish Commander now that his forces have reached this, their first destination; nor am I sure that it is within my instructions, the preventing communications between this and the ports in the Gulf of Lepanto, by vessels which can certainly, by degrees, convey all the supplies they require.' . . . 'I feel much disposed to intercept all such communications. If I find my colleagues' opinion to accord with mine, I should act on it without hesitation.'

Extract from Sir E. C. to Mr. S. Canning.

Off Navarin: September 16, 1827.

'I wish to make you aware not only of my movements, but the motives by which they are guided. It is not clear that we are to prevent all supplies being sent to places absolutely Turkish and in these seas, and I should gladly have taken my colleagues' opinion' . . . 'and as the whole future events seem to me to turn upon this expedition, I decided at once on intercepting them if possible. But if the Turkish fleet should put to sea with any other purpose than to return to their own shores, I shall consider it the case contemplated in the instructions, and oppose their proceedings to the utmost of my power. If, however, any circumstances should arise to occasion their desire to quit the Morea, and return to a Turkish port, I shall protect them in such a movement from any interference on the part of the Greek navy.'

that doubts have arisen as to some part of the joint instructions conveyed to the Admirals, it declares that 'His Majesty's Government observe with satisfaction that the construction which the Ambassadors and Admirals are disposed to put upon these passages is agreeable to the spirit of the instructions themselves and to the intention of those by whom they were framed.

'Still in order to exempt the commanders of the fleets entrusted with the execution of an arduous and delicate task, from the possibility of doubt or hesitation as to the precise line of their duty, it is thought proper to lay down the following rules in explanation and in confirmation of their original instructions.'

The despatch then refers to the verbal omission of provisions in my order of March 2.*   Provisions were always from the commencement of the execution of the Treaty considered by me and the officers under my command as included under the head of supplies, &c.   Captain Hamilton, the senior officer in the Archipelago, gave express orders to that effect; and Captain Parker, as I have before stated, remained off Navarin for the same purpose.

In no instance did the service suffer by it; it was occasioned by my having taking the words of my former order, and was rectified shortly afterwards.

I will not presume to comment on an important omission in a despatch coming from His Majesty's Government; but a material error has been made in taking the latter part of a sentence in my instructions, as general, when the former part of the same sentence expressly mentions the conditions on which, and on which only, I am to give effect to the measure therein contemplated.

The despatch of June 4, observes: 'By the same instructions you were directed not to restrain the Greek naval forces from exercising, in respect to neutrals attempting to break the blockade, all the rights of a belligerent,' leaving out the preceding part of the same sentence from which this quotation is selected; for the extract from the instruction of October 16 is, 'He will concert with the Greek authorities that the whole of their naval force shall be exclusively appropriated to the blockade of the ports of Greece now occupied by the Turkish or Egyptian forces.

* This observation implies that owing to the omission of the *word*, provisions were introduced into the Morea; although all the ships on that coast had continually stopped provisions, as the Government knew by the receipt of Captain Parker's letters from the 3rd March to the 5th April, in which he mentioned the several vessels which he had turned back because they were laden with those supplies.

'*In that case* he will not restrain the Greek naval forces from exercising, in respect to neutrals attempting to break the blockade, all the rights of a belligerent.'

Now, that case contemplated by the instructions, and mentioned as the particular condition of those orders to be given by me, had not then arrived. The Greek blockade was not established. The President of Greece distinctly informed me in his letter, accompanying a copy of the orders to Admiral Sactouris, of the $\frac{6}{18}$ March 1828, that the force under his orders waited my sanction to publish the act of blockade and put those orders into execution. That sanction was not given until April 7; and it was made known to His Majesty's Government by my letter of April 11, acknowledged in London on May 7. Admiral Sactouris was at that time, as Captain Parker states in his letter, on his way to Dragomestre with troops; it was only preparatory to the meditated blockade, without the legal notification of which such a measure cannot be exercised even in war, and consequently the Greek cruisers could not be allowed to capture the Ionian boats and neutral vessels which were then trafficking in the ports of the Morea.

Fault is imputed to me for not comprehending what is meant by the word 'blockade' whenever it has been used. The blockade mentioned in the protocol of September 4, and in the instructions of October 16, refers solely to a blockade by the Greeks with all the rights of belligerents. As the Allies were not belligerents, the term 'blockade' was never applied to the operations of their squadrons, until it was made a fault in me by the despatch of March 18, that the forts of the Morea had been 'free from blockade,' and that I did not prevent that return of the Ottoman ships to Alexandria which I found myself by the same instructions expressly ordered to facilitate and protect. I therefore could but understand it in its most extended sense. On the other hand, the principle laid down for my guidance by the Earl

---

* ' J'ai enjoint à l'antinavarque Sacturis d'expédier immédiatement à Malte, à bord d'un des bâtimens de sa division, M. Latris, etc. etc, pour porter à Votre Excellence mes dépêches, et d'attendre son retour avant de publier les actes du blocus. . . . Je le répète, cependant, Monsr. l'Amiral, je ne procéderai pas à la publication des actes avant de connoître que les mesures que j'ai jugé nécessaires de prendre ont obtenu votre approbation et celle de votre collègue Monsr. le comte Heiden. . . . Je place sous vos auspices un paquet pour Monsr. le général Adam, et V.E. aura peut-être l'extrême bonté de la faire parvenir à sa destination du moment qu'elle aura honoré de son suffrage les décrets du blocus.

(Signé)   'J. CAPODISTRIAS.'

Dudley * in his note to Prince Esterhazy, is, that England not being a belligerent we could not institute a blockade.

In this difficulty I requested an explanation of my instructions, and asked the direct questions, the answers to which I had hoped would have clearly pointed out the line of my duty.

In the meantime, however, I received the despatch from Mr. Huskisson of the 6th April. By this I was directed ' to appropriate all the naval forces at my disposal, not wanted for other indispensable services, to strictly watching and blockading, according to the tenor of those instructions, the ports of Greece occupied by the Turks or Egyptians, from the Gulf of Volo to the western side of the Isthmus of Corinth ; and to a like blockade of the port of Alexandria.

The first part of this order had long been carried into effect; the ports of Greece so occupied had already been closely watched, and the orders for intercepting supplies had been strictly enforced.

I must, however, acknowledge that I did not understand what was the intention of His Majesty's Government conveyed by this expression. I could not conceive that the only directions for so complicated an operation would be conveyed in such terms; and as I also considered it impossible to establish ' a like blockade of Alexandria' to those measures in force on the coast of the Morea, I felt it my duty not to undertake a measure of so much importance without a clear understanding both of the intention of His Majesty's Government and the orders under which I was to act.† It was in this view that I awaited the answers to my letter of April 7,‡ rather than expose the service in which I was engaged to those difficulties which the misunderstanding of my instruc-

---

* *Extract from a Note to Prince Esterhazy from Earl Dudley.*

F. O., November 28, 1827.

'It is perfectly clear that His Majesty, not being at war with the Porte, cannot claim the exercise of belligerent rights. It is equally clear that blockade is one of those rights that even in case of war could not be exercised without notification. This is a principle that has been strictly attended to in the instructions that have been furnished by His Majesty's commands to his Admiral.'

† 'And it is of importance that you should have a perfect knowledge of the object proposed by the Powers, and the means on which they reckon to effect it.'—See second instructions to Admirals.

‡ The questions asked in my letter of the 7th April, were :—'If I am henceforth to consider myself empowered to establish blockades; If I am to prevent the return of any Turkish or Egyptian forces from Greece; and in case the return of such forces should be permitted, If I am to examine the ships containing it, and release any Greek captives which may be found on board them.

tions attributed to me in the Earl of Dudley's despatch of March 18 would certainly have produced.

I have still to reply to the observation, 'that it was not till April 19 that I stationed three of His Majesty's ships between Egypt and Candia, for the purpose of watching and intercepting the movements of any Ottoman ships carrying supplies from Alexandria to the Morea.'

I assert distinctly, in the first place, that, excepting single vessels, whose arrival it was sometimes impossible to prevent, no supplies whatever were conveyed from Alexandria to the Morea.

If it is meant, however, that my having placed ships on the coast of Candia on April 19 was the first measure I had taken to prevent supplies being received by the Egyptian army, I may refer, in refutation of this charge, to the orders to those very ships, and the directions previously given to the English squadron on the coast of the Morea, composed of all the force under my orders which was not required for other duties, and supported by considerable detachments of both French and Russian ships.

But if it is meant by this observation that those measures should have been put in force on the coast of Candia which were already in force on the coast of the Morea, I have to state that, by the Protocol of September 4, I was not authorised to take any measures respecting that island; that Candia is not mentioned as the theatre of operations, either in the instructions of October 16, 1827, or in the only instructions I have since received, dated March 23 and April 6, 1828.

I nevertheless took upon myself the responsibility of intercepting supplies and provisions on the coast of Candia, when I found that island made use of as a means of defeating the object of the Treaty. His Majesty's Government was made acquainted with this measure, and my reason for adopting it, in my letter of April 30, 1828.

I believe I have now adverted to every accusation and every imputation upon which, according to the Earl of Aberdeen's despatch, my supersession is grounded. It is not for me to judge whether the explanations I have now given would have prevented that decision or not, if I had been afforded the opportunity of making them. My present object is to convince His Royal Highness the Lord High Admiral that I have done nothing to forfeit the protection and the confidence with which he has honoured me.

I can appeal to the manly avowal of my colleagues to show that they have always understood our joint instructions in the same sense as I have myself. I can appeal to facts to prove that every object embraced in those instructions has now been fulfilled; and, however unpleasant to speak of myself personally, I feel called upon to mention in recapitulation of those facts, that—

By my resistance of the movements of Ibrahim Pacha and his four assisting Admirals off the Gulf of Lepanto, with only the 'Asia,' the 'Dartmouth,' and the 'Talbot' (the 'Zebra' being despatched for assistance), when opposed to 5 double 60-gun frigates, 5 single frigates, 13 corvettes, and 30 brigs and transports; and subsequently by entering the harbour of Navarin with the Allied squadron, all the hostile attacks were prevented for which that fleet was so industriously prepared, and a stop was put to the ravages under which Greece was till then suffering.

By the measures adopted by my colleagues and myself, aided by the President Count Capodistrias at my instance, piracy is no longer heard of.

No hostile operation whatever has taken place against Greece since I received instructions to prevent them.

At my instance the Greek blockade of the Morea has been regularly established, and the means of subsistence for the Ottoman Army efficiently cut off.

And to conclude—I have ratified a convention with the Pacha of Egypt for the evacuation of the Morea by his troops, an event which it was the principal object of my instructions to accomplish, and which was considered as the first measure for giving a practical execution to the Treaty of London.

I am, &c.,
EDWD. CODRINGTON, Vice-Admiral.

Having received no answer to his explanatory letter of August 10, 1828, sent through the Admiralty to the Secretary of State, Lord Aberdeen, Sir E. C. wrote to the Admiralty on December 22, 1828, asking 'if any disapprobation attaches to my conduct during the time I had the honour of commanding His Majesty's ships and vessels on the Mediterranean station,' adding,—

'The question of my supersession involves that professional reputation which I value as my existence; and there is no sacrifice which I am not ready to make in its defence. I trust indeed their Lordships will see that the elucidation of my conduct on this occasion is due to my brother officers liable to be similarly situated; that it is due to the brave men who so zealously served with and so gallantly supported

me through difficulties of no ordinary nature; that it is due
to my personal friends, my family, myself, and my countrymen in general; and I hope I may be permitted to add,
with the grateful respect which emanates from a heart
sensibly impressed by the kindness and generosity with which
my conduct in the battle of Navarin was so highly honoured,
that it is scarcely less due to my Sovereign and his illustrious
brother, the late Lord High Admiral.   I therefore respectfully, but earnestly, entreat the favour of an early and
explicit answer to my request.'

The Admiralty, on December 30, 1828, wrote to Sir E. C.
that his letter of the 22nd had been sent to the Secretary of
State for Foreign Affairs, and enclosed his answer of the
same date (30th), in which Mr. Backhouse, directed by Lord
Aberdeen, stated, that ' upon the professional conduct of Sir
E. Codrington, His Majesty's Government do not feel themselves called upon to express an opinion.   Forming their
judgment upon the communications from Sir E. Codrington
in their possession at the time, and upon his declared conception of the instructions under which he was acting, they
felt it to be their painful duty to advise that he should be
relieved from his command in the Mediterranean; and I am
to add that the impression under which His Majesty's
Government acted in taking that step has not been altered
by the communications subsequently received from Sir E.
Codrington.

' If Lord Aberdeen does not think it necessary to enter into
a detailed examination of the various statements contained
in Sir E. C.'s letter of August 10, transmitted to this department by your letter of September 17, he desires that it
may not be inferred that His Majesty's Government acquiesce
in all those statements, or in the conclusions which Sir E.
Codrington has founded on them.

' With respect to the observation of Sir E. C., that he was
superseded in a sudden and unusual manner, without waiting
for the explanation of the errors imputed to him, Lord Aberdeen directs me to remark that Sir E. Codrington was not
relieved from his command without waiting for the explanation received from him; nor until after the receipt of his
despatch of April 7, in answer to that addressed to him on
March 18 by Lord Dudley; as well as of that of April 30 in
answer to Mr. Secretary Huskisson's despatch of the 6th of
that month.

' I am, &c.,
'J. BACKHOUSE.'

Sir Edward Codrington then wrote the following letter to the Admiralty :—

Windsor : January 11, 1829.

SIR,—However much I lament it on my own account, as well as on account of my brother officers, that the Lords Commissioners of the Admiralty should have declined to give an explicit opinion on my professional conduct under the peculiar circumstances of the case, my respect for the high office which their Lordships fill prevents my further pressing that question. But as their Lordships seem to have withheld their judgment on account of my being placed under the more immediate direction of His Majesty's Government, and of my explanations having specially referred to a despatch which had not passed through their office, I consider it my duty to send their Lordships copies of all those documents which I received from His Majesty's Government during the time I was so placed under their direction, except a secret despatch from Mr. Huskisson, which does not appear to affect my conduct in either way. Being, however, thus left to defend my professional character in the best way I can against the errors imputed to me, I feel necessarily called upon to refer to Mr. Backhouse's letter of the 13th of last December.

In this letter it is said that His Majesty's Government ' formed their judgment upon the communications in their possession at the time, and upon his declared conception of the instructions under which he was acting.' In consequence of this declaration, I have re-examined minutely all those communications, including my letter to the Earl Dudley of April 7, to which I am led to suppose Lord Aberdeen particularly refers for my ' declared understanding of the instructions under which I was acting.'

In order to explain more fully the conception I then had, and still have, of the true meaning of these instructions, I beg to submit to their Lordships' consideration the enclosed memorandum,* which I have drawn up for the purpose of elucidating the two passages in the instructions of October 16, to which reference has been more particularly made. It was not choice that led me to differ with Lord Dudley as to the true meaning of an instruction of the Lord High Admiral, founded on a letter from his Lordship's office. I was impelled to it in self-defence, against an attack upon my professional conduct, implying that a neglect of duty on my

* See explanation of the instructions of October 16.

part had given rise to an event 'calculated to excite the most painful feelings throughout the country.'

The despatch of Lord Dudley of March 18, in direct opposition to my understanding of my instructions, implied that I ought to have prevented the return of the Ottoman fleet from Navarin to Alexandria; and, as authority for my so doing, quoted from my instructions, that I was to prevent ' any movements by sea on the part of the Turkish or Egyptian forces.' In answer to this observation, I explained in my letter of April 7, that to have so prevented ' any movements,' on the part of the Turkish or Egyptian forces, I must have previously consulted the Ambassadors;—because such a proceeding would have been directly contrary to the Protocol of September 4, as well as to that very instruction of October 16;— both of which order me to facilitate, and even to protect, the retirement of any portion of the Turkish or Egyptian forces from Greece. My meaning was, that if under the term of ' any movements,' I was to prevent the return of the Ottoman forces to Egypt, in contradiction to the instruction to encourage 'every' such movement,—in that case it would have been necessary that the sanction of the Ambassadors should authorise such a deviation from my orders. It would now, however, seem, by Mr. Backhouse's letter, that His Majesty's Government construed this explanation into an understanding on my part that I did not consider myself authorised to act upon these instructions, even under my own view of them, without the decision of the Ambassadors; when, in fact, the expression alluded to had reference merely to the interpretation of them given by Lord Dudley, and not to my own conception of them.

Considering myself justified in supposing that His Majesty's Government have so misunderstood the expressions used by me, and that it was on account of such supposed misconception on my part that they directed me to be superseded, I beg leave to refer their Lordships to the following communications, by which it will be seen that such could not possibly have been my conception of the instructions; and to press particularly upon their Lordships' attention that these were among the communications from me in possession of the Government at the time, and upon which they formed their judgment:—To my letter to yourself of March 24, acknowledged on April 19, enclosing Captain Parker's detail of proceedings from the 3rd to the 10th March 1828, in the execution of my orders:—My letter to Lord Dudley of April 7, acknowledged May 7, stating 'that my arrangements have been made for preventing the arrival

of men, arms, &c., destined against Greece, &c., and enclosing my general order of March 2 (in addition to that of
September 8), for the interception of supplies on the coast
of the Morea, and my letter to Colonel Cradock on January 22,
stating that I felt myself authorised so to intercept supplies:—
My letter to you of April 11 (acknowledged May 7,) on the
establishment of the Greek blockade, and enclosing two
letters from Captain Parker of 17th and 30th March, which
show that he went off Navarin for the express purpose of
intercepting the Egyptian convoy from Alexandria, and that
he had actually intercepted the first vessel which attempted
to convey provisions from Candia to the Morea, upon which
I grounded my restrictions on that island:—My letter to you
of April 18 (acknowledged May 23), enclosing two letters
from Captain Parker of 4th and 5th April, which detailed his
further interception of supplies on the coast of the Morea:—
My letter to Mr. Huskisson of April 30, with its several
enclosures, among which are—extracts of two letters from
Captain Parker of 4th and 5th April, before mentioned—my
orders of April 19 to the ' Dartmouth ' and ' Glasgow,' in
extension of my previous orders on the same subject of intercepting supplies,—and my general order of April 30, by
which I took upon myself the responsibility of including
Candia within the line of our operations, in further execution
of the instructions of October 16. The whole of these communications were received before May 23, 1828, the despatch
from Lord Aberdeen bearing date June 4, 1828. And I submit them to their Lordships' consideration as proofs—and as
· proofs before His Majesty's Government at the date of Lord
Aberdeen's despatch—that I had a proper conception of the
instructions furnished to me for my guidance.

I now beg leave to advert to the observation in Mr. Back-
house's letter, ' that Sir Edward Codrington was not relieved
from his command without waiting for the explanation received from him ; nor until after the receipt of his despatch of
April 7, in answer to that addressed to him March 18, by
Lord Dudley ; as well as of that of April 30, in answer to
Mr. Secretary Huskisson's despatch of the 6th of that month.
In support of the remark in my letter of December 22
last, against this direct contradiction given in the name of
Lord Aberdeen, I submit to their Lordships' attention that,
although my answers to Lord Dudley and Mr. Huskisson
were received before my recall was directed, the despatch of
June 4 contains the following additional charges, on points
independent of these answers, upon which I feel justified in
repeating that I had no opportunity of explaining myself,

since these charges were first made known to me in the despatch announcing my supersession :—

The not having considered the order of February 8, 1826, as showing 'the intention of His Majesty's Government that the transportation of the Greeks of the Morea to Egypt should not be permitted:'—upon which I have since explained, that the 'mission' therein mentioned being fulfilled, there remained no order to act upon ; the wording of which order itself, coupled with the strong injunctions to avoid hostilities, and to favour the return of the Egyptian forces to Alexandria, marks clearly an intention that I should not have interfered on such an occasion :— Misconception of my instructions, founded on a reference to the Protocol of September 4, and on an extract from the instructions of October 16, 'that I was not to enter into any stipulation for allowing the ships to return to Alexandria without the troops'—a charge which I have since shown to have arisen from an erroneous view of the object of that passage, and inconsistent with the origin of its formation :— 'That no measures appear to have been taken to prevent the return of the Egyptian fleet from Alexandria'—a movement which I have shown that I had a force ready to control, if it had come within the limits of our operations :—That Captain Parker remained off Navarin, not in consequence of my instructions, 'but because General Guilleminot seemed desirous that the port should be closely watched;' directly contradicted by Captain Parker himself, in his letter to me of September 5 :—'That the movements of a large fleet between Egypt and the Morea were free from interruption,' &c., when, as I have shown, there was only one such movement of a fleet, and that from the Morea to Egypt, which it was my duty to facilitate :—'Having omitted to give the officers under my command authority to intercept provisions destined for the Turkish force'—my subsequent explanation having shown that His Majesty's Government, at the time that charge was made, had in their possession letters detailing the actual interception of provisions by the ships under my orders :—'Not having allowed the Greek naval forces to exercise, in respect to neutrals attempting to break the blockade all the rights of a belligerent,'—my subsequent explanation having shown that such a charge could only have been founded on that passage in the instructions, by the omission of part of the same sentence :—The implication that by stationing three ships off Candia on April 19 I had not taken any previous measures for intercepting supplies from Alexandria to the Morea,—which orders of April 19 I have since shown were an extension of my former measures for the interception of supplies on the coast of the Morea.

I confidently refer their Lordships to the various documents to establish the fact that, whatever opinion may have been formed by the receipt of my answers to the despatches of Lord Dudley and Mr. Huskisson, I was not heard upon the several charges now enumerated, previous to my supersession being decided upon. I would readily offer an apology for the trouble I am now giving their Lordships, if I did not trust that, as guardians of the profession over which they preside, they require no apology for an earnest endeavour on the part of an officer placed in so unusual a situation, to preserve his professional character against reflections which he feels confident he does not deserve.

During the time I held the command of His Majesty's ships and vessels on the Mediterranean station, I can conscientiously assure their Lordships that I had not a wish or a thought which did not incline to the correct execution of the very complicated and important services which I was called upon to perform. I devoted myself to my duty, with the proud feeling that the honour of the country was in some measure entrusted to me; and I persevered in the firm resolution that that honour should not be tarnished in my hands.

Concluding my command with the Treaty of Alexandria, I may venture to say their Lordships have practical proof before them of the successful execution of every object contemplated in their orders and instructions.

That His Majesty's Government should, notwithstanding, have attributed to me a line of conduct which could justify so harsh a measure as directing my supersession, without consulting my professional judges, is a circumstance I must ever lament.

Their Lordships will, however, see that the feeling which excited my endeavour to perform my duty, and the consciousness that I deserved a different treatment, imperiously call upon me to defend my character by all the means in my power, and to show to my Sovereign and my countrymen that I am not unworthy of the approbation which my previous conduct had disposed them to confer on me.

I have the honour, &c.,
EDWD. CODRINGTON, Vice-Admiral.

From the Admiralty to Sir E. C., closing his communications
with the Board upon the subject of his supersession.

Admiralty Office: January 12, 1829.

SIR,—I have received your two letters of the 10th and
11th inst., with their several enclosures, and I have laid the
same before my Lords Commissioners of the Admiralty.

I am, Sir, &c., &c.,

J. W. CROKER.

Further correspondence took place between Sir E. Codrington and the Admiralty and Lord Aberdeen on the subject
of his recall from the Mediterranean, in the course of which
was sent the following—

Explanation of the Instructions of October 16, 1827, elucidated
by quotations from the papers to which they refer.

[See p. 440.]

The instructions of July 12, sent to the Admirals, direct
them ' to intercept all supplies of men, arms, vessels, and
warlike stores destined against Greece, and coming either
from Turkey or Africa in general.' Upon receiving directions
from Constantinople to act upon these instructions, Sir
Edward Codrington proceeded towards the Morea, and, on
arriving off Navarin, found the Turco-Egyptian fleet at
anchor in that port. Consequently, the interception of supplies, &c., coming from Turkey, &c., could not take place.
It therefore became a question whether or not the Allied
Admirals could consider themselves justified in preventing
supplies of men, arms, &c., going from one Turkish port in
Greece to another Turkish port in Greece.

This was a case not contemplated by the instructions of
July 12. In consequence of this, in a letter dated December
13, 1827 (acknowledged to have been received before October
16), Sir Edward Codrington wrote thus to Earl Dudley :—

' It is not, however, clear to me that the direction to prevent supplies, &c., being thrown upon the coast of Greece
authorises a prevention of such supplies to places in the
Adriatic (Ionian seas), which, like Modon, have continued in
their hands, and which, without such aid, might starve. .
. . And, as I may possibly be again so situated, I ask for
your judgment on it. . . . I am not yet aware of what
may be the object of the Turkish commander now that his
forces have reached this their first destination; nor am I
sure that it is within my instructions, the preventing com-

munications between this and the Gulf of Lepauto, and which can certainly by degrees convey all the supplies they require.

. . . .

'I feel much disposed to interrupt all such communications, and, if I find my colleagues' opinion to accord with mine, I should act on it without hesitation.'

The judgment which was thus asked by Sir Edward Codrington was given by Lord Dudley in his instructions of October 16. The first sentence of the instruction says:— 'It appears that some doubts have arisen in the minds of the Ambassadors and Admirals as the application of some part of the joint "instructions" (those of July 12).' 'His Majesty's Government observe with satisfaction that the construction which the Ambassadors and Admirals are disposed to put upon these passages, is agreeable to the spirit of the instructions themselves and to the intention of those by whom they were framed. Still, in order to exempt the commanders of the Allied Forces, entrusted with the execution of an arduous and delicate task, from the possibility of doubt or hesitation as to the precise line of their duty, it is thought proper to lay down the following rules in explanation and in confirmation of their original instructions.' One of these rules is : 'He will concert with the Allied commanders the most effectual mode of preventing any movements by sea on the part of the Turkish or Egyptian naval forces;' thus giving the judgment that was asked by Sir E. Codrington on the 'preventing any movements of the Turkish or Egyptian forces from one port in Greece to another port in Greece.' As the evacuation of the Morea by the return of the Egyptian fleet and army to Alexandria, was one of the first objects of all his instructions, it is manifestly impossible that the Admirals were positively 'to prevent any movements by sea on the part of the Turkish or Egyptian forces;' and clearly shows that this order was never meant to be, and could not be, obeyed *in letter*, but that the movements contemplated were the movements of the Egyptian fleet then at Navarin 'going from one port in Greece to another port in Greece;' at the same time that the Admiral was authorised by his original instructions ' to intercept all supplies destined against Greece and coming from Turkey or Africa.'

In the same manner the original instructions of July 12 did not contemplate the voluntary retirement of the belligerent forces from the theatre of war, and therefore on August 11, 1827, Sir E. Codrington wrote to Mr. S. Canning (whose directions he was ordered to obey) saying, ' another point on which I wish to be instructed is, whether or not we may guarantee the retirement of any of the belligerent forces, as far as we have power to do so, if they propose to withdraw themselves from the contest.' To which Mr. S. Canning answered on September 8, 'I have communicated with my colleagues,' &c. 'Some of the questions to which I advert are too delicate to be definitively settled by us. But as it is not in your power to keep them back until the decision of His Majesty's Government can reach you, a knowledge of our opinions upon them may be of use to you in the interval. The opinions on which we have agreed are recorded in the Protocol of our last Conference.'

This Protocol of September 4, 1827, enclosed by Mr. S. Canning for Sir E. Codrington's guidance, says (in answer to his question about 'guaranteeing the retirement of any belligerent force') :—'The Admirals will act in the spirit of the Treaty by protecting as requisite every portion of the Greek or Mussulman naval forces which would engage not to take part in hostilities; and by favouring, according to that principle, the return either to Constantinople or to Alexandria of every Turkish or Egyptian ship-of-war, as well as every transport having on board retiring troops.'

And Count Guilleminot (the French Ambassador) writing at the same time to Admiral De Rigny, and whose letter was sent for Sir E. Codrington's information, says :—' Lastly, my colleagues and myself are of opinion that the squadrons of the Allied Courts should protect in their retirement all such of the Ottoman naval forces and of the Ottoman troops which should show a desire to quit Greece, in order to return without striking a blow, either to the Dardanelles or to Alexandria.' These extracts from the instructions of the English and French Ambassadors are therefore in answer to the question put by Sir E. Codrington to Mr. S. Canning, 'if he might guarantee the retirement of any of the belligerent forces.' It was a question to what ships and vessels he might extend his *guarantee* and protection; and it was thus determined by the Ambassadors that he might so *protect* and *guarantee* the retirement to Alexandria of all Turkish and Egyptian ships of war; that this same *protection* and *guarantee* might also be given to the transports which should have retiring troops on board; but that his protection and guarantee were to be *confined* to these, and not to be given to the transports returning without troops. Any vessels might be *allowed* to go; it was not that any vessels whatever were to be *prevented* leaving the Morea to return to Alexandria, for it was evidently an advantage that even the empty transports should return, and be even encouraged to return, in order to deprive Ibrahim Pacha of his means of attack against the Greek islands, then the particular object of the expedition from Egypt.

Now, as the instructions of October 16 were formed ' in consequence of these communications between the Ambassadors and Admirals, and in confirmation and in explanation' of those of July 12, and as the instructions of October 16 further say :—' These instructions will completely coincide with the explanation of the Patent Instructions already transmitted to the Admiral by His Majesty's Ambassador at Constantinople,' it is quite clear that the question by Sir Edward Codrington about ' protecting the return of any of the belligerent forces,' and the decision of the Ambassadors respecting it, produced the following passage in the instructions of October 16, ' to completely coincide with the explanations transmitted by the Ambassador to the British Admiral.' 'He is to hold out every inducement to the Pacha of Egypt and to his son to withdraw the Egyptian ships and land forces altogether from Greece, and to assure them that every facility and protection would be given for their safe return to Alexandria.   But he is on no account to enter into any stipulations for allowing the ships to return without the troops to Alexandria.' This extract from instructions, declared to be ' in confirmation and in explanation' of those of July 12, and ' to completely coincide with the explanations of those instructions by His Majesty's Ambassador at Constantinople,' means therefore to confirm and coincide with the opinions of the Ambassadors in the Protocol of September 4 and their letters, viz., that the Egyptian ships and land forces were to be protected, and every facility afforded them in withdrawing altogether (i.e. entirely, ' without engaging in any hostile operation in the way') from Greece ; but that the Admiral was on no account to enter into any stipulation by which he should bind himself to give that protection and facility to the ships returning to Alexandria without the troops.   This coincides in the opinion given ' by His Majesty's Ambassador.' It was, again, no question of preventing the return of any vessels whatever, or that the condition of allowing them to depart should be the having troops on board, for this would naturally have brought on the search of ships-of-war as well as others—a measure which would have been very much opposed to ' facilitating the retirement of the Ottoman naval forces from the Morea' ; and so obnoxious and insulting a proceeding towards the ships-of-war of an independent nation would have also been in direct opposition to that part of the instructions which says : 'Most particular care is to be taken that the measures adopted against the Ottoman navy do not degenerate into hostilities.'

Narrative of the Proceedings of Vice-Admiral Sir E. Codrington, during his command of His Majesty's Ships and Vessels on the Mediterranean Station, from February 28, 1827, until August 22, 1828. (Written February, 1829.)
[See p 443.]

Two strong motives impel me to draw up a narrative of my proceedings during the time I held the command of His Majesty's ships and vessels in the Mediterranean.

First to show my friends, and all others who are desirous of forming a just judgment of my conduct, that I am not undeserving of their good opinion; and, secondly, that whatever misrepresentations may have been raised against me, may be contradicted by a fair statement of the truth.

Upon receiving the command from Vice-Admiral Sir Harry Neale, in February 1827, I opened a correspondence with all the ambassadors and consuls within the limits of my station.* And after a personal interview and extended communication with the Lord High Commissioner of the Ionian Islands, at Corfu, I proceeded into the Archipelago, and devoted myself particularly to the state of affairs in Greece, upon which the commercial interests of Europe in those seas seemed entirely to depend.

The position of the Provisional Government, and the condition of the country at that period, excited fears that whenever the expected Treaty for its pacification should arrive, there would be no sufficient authority for carrying it into execution. There was a Lord High Admiral and a Generalissimo, each having authority to act without previous communication with the Government; which, instead of. being able to resist any abuse of that power, was shut up within the walls of Nauplia, under the control of rival chiefs, fighting with each other for their own mercenary purposes.†

Several vessels, Ionian as well as others, charged with illegal trading, were there waiting the judgment of a marine tribunal, which was under similar constraint.

Foreign intrigue, which had before contributed to the fall of Athens, was very busy in fomenting these quarrels, and the consequent destruction of this important fortress, which would have put an end to the Greek cause altogether.

* June 23rd to 27th, 1827.
† The forts began to fire on each other on July 10, 1827.

In anticipation of the Treaty of London, I considered it my duty to counteract this injurious interference.*

After various communications, both on board the 'Asia' and on shore, with the several chiefs who were in possession of the different batteries, each of whom evinced much anxiety for my support; and after many addresses to separate bodies of the armed populace as to the consequences of the factions proceedings in which they were taking part, I succeeded in withdrawing some thousands of the women, children, and other peaceable inhabitants, from the plunder and misery to which they were exposed by a sanguinary civil warfare, and also in getting the members of the Provisional Government and the Legislative body out of the town, and from under the control of the combatants.

Having effected this object,† and the Government having decided on removing to Egina, I hastened to Smyrna to communicate with Mr. Stratford Canning at Constantinople; and to enable him, in contradiction of other reports industriously spread, to declare on my authority that there was still a properly authorised representation of the Greek nation, ready to act under the Treaty whenever it might be received by the allied Ambassadors.

Whilst at Smyrna,‡ I used the influence which my position gave me for disposing the Pacha to preserve an advantageous neutrality in case of a rupture with the Porte; and to weigh well the consequences to the town of Smyrna of any ill-treatment of the Franks. I at the same time pressed upon the Viceroy of Egypt, through Mr. Consul-General Salt, my earnest hope that he would not risk the disastrous consequences which would attend his imprudently placing his fleet in collision with ours; expressing the great unwillingness of the British Government to do anything which might interrupt the commerce of Alexandria, and the harmony then prevailing with His Highness.

On the night of August 10-11, I received the Treaty and the instructions emanating from it, officially; and on the 17th, I was again at Nauplia, accompanied by Admiral de Rigny, preparing the Greeks, according to the instructions of the ambassadors, to assent to the mediation which the Treaty proposed. This point being satisfactorily arranged, I returned to Smyrna,§ in order to meet directions from Mr.

* On July 17, Mr. Elliot informed Sir E. Codrington that the Treaty was signed. The Treaty itself was in the 'Times' newspaper of July 12, 1827.
† July 19, 1827. ‡ Arrived on July 24, 1827.
§ Arrived on August 21, 1827.

S. Canning for carrying the Treaty into full execution. But hearing that the great Egyptian expedition had sailed from Alexandria, and fearing it might reach Hydra, its understood destination, I lost no time in placing the English squadron off that island,[*] in readiness to impede its operations, leaving a despatch vessel to follow with my instructions the moment they should arrive.

These instructions having reached me on September 7, I immediately took a more advanced position off Cape Angelo. And on the 10th, hearing that the expedition had passed on towards the western coast, I proceeded round Cape Matapan, accompanied by the 'Genoa,' the 'Albion,' and the 'Dartmouth' frigate towards Navarin,[†] where I found that it had already anchored on the 9th.

My instructions held out that I should have a force competent, in the opinion of His Majesty's Government, to awe the Ottoman fleet into submission. But the French squadron had not joined me from Paros, where it waited Admiral de Rigny's orders; and that of Russia had not been heard of in the Mediterranean.

Thus, before I was enabled to execute my instructions to arrest the progress of this long-expected expedition on its way to Greece, and before I was joined by the force calculated upon by the Allied Governments for inducing its commander to abandon the purpose for which it was intended without offering resistance, it had already reached its first destination, and was preparing to carry that purpose into execution. Moreover, the instructions only directed the prevention of supplies coming from Asia or Africa to Greece; and did not contemplate hostile movements from one port of Greece to another port in Greece, both in Turkish possession.

I therefore wrote immediately to Mr. S. Canning,[‡] to whom I was directed to look for instructions, describing the situation in which I found myself, and informing him of my disposition, in the absence of instructions on this head, to consider myself as acting in the true spirit of the Treaty by preventing any such movements as far as the small force then with me would enable me. And I took advantage of having been put into official communication with Lord Dudley on one particular event,[§] to give him a narrative of all my proceedings, describing the difficulty I was then under, and the line I proposed to adopt, and asking his judgment

* Arrived on September 3, 1827.   † Arrived on September 12, 1827.
‡ By letter of September 16, 1827.
§ On the Greek Acceptance of the Treaty.

on it.* I may here observe that these communications, with others from Admiral de Rigny, gave rise to the instructions of October 16, 1827.

Observing a movement in the Ottoman fleet, and being still without the support of either of my colleagues, I addressed a letter† to the Ottoman Admiral in command of the fleet, and sent it by the 'Dartmouth' frigate, informing him of my being ordered to prevent any movement hostile to the Greeks, and urging him to relinquish all such operations. And upon the arrival of Admiral de Rigny, we wrote a joint letter to the same effect in French,‡ which I requested my colleague, who well knew Ibrahim, and had reason to think he had an influence over him, would himself take into Navarin, accompanied by the Honourable Colonel Cradock, who was just arrived from Alexandria, where he had been sent on a similar mission by the English Government.

Ibrahim Pacha assumed the appearance of, and perhaps really had, a particular desire to act as we required, and he discussed with Admiral de Rigny, in private, the manner in which it was to be effected upon his fleet putting to sea. At his earnest request, I subsequently went into the harbour myself in the 'Asia,'§ accompanied by Admiral de Rigny in 'La Syrène;' and the armistice consequent on my interview with him,‖ was agreed upon in the presence of his chiefs assembled for the purpose at my particular desire.

Many ships of the Turkish division of his fleet were at this time outside of the harbour. But they were permitted to come in again, upon his agreeing that both the land and sea forces should remain inactive in Navarin until he should receive answers from the Porte and from his father, which could not arrive within twenty days. And he was at all events to give us notice if the agreement should not be ratified by them, or if any change should take place.

In expectation therefore of having to convey part of the fleet to the Dardanelles, the English ships were sent to Malta to replenish their stores and provisions; and the French ships accompanied their Admiral to Cervi Bay, where they had a store-ship in readiness, and where they would have an opportunity of intercepting any hostile movement towards Hydra, &c. Anxious to be at hand in case of any unexpected occurrence, and fearing small detachments might be secretly sent into the Gulf of Lepanto, to destroy a few Greek vessels

* In letter dated September 13, 1827.   † September 19, 1827.
† Of September 22, 1827.   § On September 24, 1827.
‖ On September 25.   Vide letters to the Admiralty, Lord Dudley, and to Mr. Stratford Canning of September 25, 1827.

there under Captain Hastings; and for the further purpose of preventing an operation meditated by Lord Cochrane on the coast of Albania beyond the theatre of the war, injurious to the Greeks themselves, and in violation of Ionian neutrality, I myself proceeded to Zante in the 'Asia,' accompanied by the 'Talbot' and the 'Zebra;' the 'Dartmouth' on my part, and 'l'Armide' on that of Admiral de Rigny, being left to watch the ports of Navarin and Modon.

On the night of my arrival at Zante,* and of the sixth day after the armistice, at about eight o'clock, Captain Fellowes of the 'Dartmouth' came on board the 'Asia' and informed me of some forty and odd sail of the Ottoman fleet having put to sea shortly after our having left Navarin, and that they were at some distance astern of the 'Dartmouth,' coming to the northward.†

In spite of very great difficulty, occasioned by the variable winds of a thunder storm, and a heavy swell setting directly into the bay—the 'Asia,' 'Talbot' and 'Zebra' were got out to sea,—kept a short distance ahead of the Ottoman fleet during the remainder of the night, and at daylight were drawn up in preparation for battle betwixt them and the Gulf of Patras, for which they were steering.‡

I sent Captain Spencer of the 'Talbot' to inform the senior of the two admirals under whose command this fleet was acting, that as they had broken the word of honour given in their presence on the 25th instant, I was not inclined to treat them with much ceremony, and that I should fire into the first ship that might attempt to pass the 'Asia's' broadside; and that in case of a single shot being fired in return at the British flag, I would sink their whole fleet if I could.

The Rear-Admiral was then sent by his superior to wait upon me, and to ask permission to go to Patras, according to his orders.   And after a parley of considerable length, in which his Italian interpreter was afraid of explaining fully what I said ; and after my giving him in writing the decision which I before sent him verbally, he returned to his ship, and the whole of them began to trace back their steps.§

Some of these ships persevered until fired at. But at length, when the whole had proceeded under our direction nearly as far as the southernmost end of Zante on the 3rd of October, Ibrahim himself, with two other admirals carrying flags at the main and fourteen ships and vessels of war, came in sight betwixt Zante and Cephalonia ; and upon his making a signal

---

* On October 1, 1827.   † See letter to Admiralty of October 2, 1827.
‡ October 2, 1827.
§ See letter to Mustapha Bey of October 2, 1827, and his answer.

and firing a gun, the whole of the first division bore up to join him. The English ships were at this time considerably to the southward of the others, in order to prevent their again getting into Navarin ; and the ' Zebra ' being sent the preceding night in search of assistance, my own little force was diminished, whilst that of the Ottomans was very much increased.

Nevertheless, considering the fatal consequences which might attend the successful performance of Ibrahim's meditated purpose, I made the signal for the ' Dartmouth ' and ' Talbot ' to prepare for battle ; and with the crew of the ' Asia ' at their quarters, ran down to enforce that obedience to the armistice, by the breach of which the Pacha had forfeited all claim to delicacy on my part. As we approached, the Vice-Admiral to whom I had sent my decision in writing, was observed to go on board Ibrahim's ship. I therefore waited the result of this interview ; which terminated by a signal from Ibrahim's ship, and the whole Ottoman fleet making sail back to the southward, although the wind was still fair for Patras.

After dark, when most of the fleet had passed to the southward of Zante Bay, the ' Asia ' and ' Talbot ' anchored at its entrance in order to get coals, water, and other supplies of which they were much in want, leaving the ' Dartmouth ' under sail to watch the movements of the Ottomans.

At dawn of day on the 4th, the ship of Ibrahim Pacha, those of the four other admirals, and several others of the largest class, were seen at anchor in the Gulf of Patras ; having as we afterwards learned, taken advantage of a heavy squall of wind and rain at midnight to bear away for that fortress.

The ' Asia ' and ' Talbot ' weighed their anchors immediately, and proceeded towards them under all sail prepared for battle. As if sensible of the persevering duplicity of their chief, the Turkish vessels, contrary to their custom of carrying their colours when other ships would not, persisted in not showing them as we passed, even when shot were fired across their bows. Shot were therefore fired into them by each of our ships as we closed with them, until they hoisted their ensigns and hove to : thus evincing that hostile determination on our part by which I hoped to shake the resolution of this treacherous Commander detected in his breach of faith.

This mode of proceeding had the desired effect. Awed by our firing upon that portion of his fleet with which we had already come in contact, I learned by the ' Philomel,' which joined me the next day from within the Gulf of Lepanto, that Ibrahim had profited by the coming darkness and the strong wind which had prevented his nearer approach to Patras, to make the best of his way out to sea.

The wind had increased during the night to a perfect hurricane; and in order to save the masts and sails from any accident which might have disabled us from making any effectual opposition to the meditated enterprise of a force so numerically superior, the 'Asia' took in all her sails and was let to go before the wind until the gale abated.

At daylight we were again pushing forward towards Patras; when between twenty and thirty of the largest of the Ottoman ships were seen from the masthead running off under a press of sail, between the islands of Zante and Cephalonia.

Although it was evident that Ibrahim himself had given up his enterprise, many of the scattered ships were still steering for Patras. And as I thought it probable he might have left a force sufficient to destroy the little Greek detachment in the Gulf of Lepanto, I persevered in proceeding in that direction. At nine o'clock at night on the 4th we reached Cape Papa, and found ourselves surrounded by about twenty of the Ottoman fleet which were not aware of their Admiral's hasty retreat. All these we were eventually enabled to turn back, either by persuasion or coercion; although with partial injury to several, and considerable damage to one Turkish brig, the obstinate perseverance of which brought her under the fire both of the ships and the armed boats before we obtained our object.

We were joined by the Russian squadron when again off Zante on the 13th of October,; and also by the French ships from Cervi Bay, and the English ships from Malta. And upon resuming our position off Navarin, we found the whole Ottoman fleet re-assembled in the harbour, the troops disembarked and pursuing a systematic plan of devastation.

It appeared as if Ibrahim,* angry at being thus foiled at sea by a mere tithe of the force which he now saw collected, whilst waiting the chance of a gale of wind driving us out of his way,—had adopted that brutal destruction by land which it was one object of the Treaty to prevent. One division of his army was sent to enter Maina; but by sending the 'Cambrian'† to guard the pass of Armyro in the Gulf of Coron, its progress was stopped, and its purpose defeated.

But as the Pacha would not receive a warning letter‡ from my colleagues and myself,—and as we must have committed

---

* Representations of a deputation from Maina.
† Letter from Captain Hamilton.   ‡ Dated October 17, 1827.

hostilities in the execution of our orders if we had fallen in with his fleet at sea,—it was unanimously agreed between us, that the only way of saving the inhabitants of the Morea from destruction, and the best chance of executing the Treaty without a battle, was to take the Allied fleet into the port of Navarin and, under the awe of its presence there, renew our proposals for the return of the Ottoman fleet to Egypt.

After submitting to be driven before so comparatively small a force as I had with me off Patras, we had no reason to expect that Ibrahim would oppose the Allied squadrons united. But he was well aware that we had no other means left us for fulfilling the objects of the Treaty; and with the able assistance of Monsieur Letellier, he had made such preparations for our reception,* as he thought would enable him to effect our entire destruction. And it was in this confidence that his fleet made that attack on ours which brought down upon him the annihilation of his means of further aggression.

Thus, the act of hostility with which the Treaty must have been enforced sooner or later, and of which my instructions evinced so much apprehension, was transferred to Ibrahim himself; whilst the object of paralysing his future attempts to commit barbarity, was effectually accomplished.

There no longer existed a force sufficient to excuse the Greeks from blockading their enemies in the Morea. They were therefore urged by the Allied Admirals† to adopt this measure at once, as one to which they were adequate, during the absence and temporary disability of the ships of the Allies. By adopting this measure under our protection against foreign interruption, a prospect would be opened of effectually cutting off the supplies, and reducing the Ottoman force to the necessity of evacuating the country. It is evident that this was also the readiest way of checking the piracy which it was one of the principal objects of the Alliance to suppress.

Captain Hamilton, of the 'Cambrian,' was sent to urge the Greek Government to the execution of this arrangement;‡ and such of our ships as were available were stationed to watch the proceedings of all the parties.

---

* Letellier was three days placing the ships in the form of a horse-shoe, and it was further rectified subsequently. See 'Le Journal de Mons. Bompar,' p. 543.

† Letter of the three Admirals of October 24, 1827, to the Greek Legislative body, p. 546.

‡ Sir E. Codrington's order of October 16, 1827.

The remainder of the Allied fleet in a fit state for service was employed in protecting the Embassies, the Consulates, and the different Christian establishments extending along the coast of the Mahomedan dominions, and which were exposed to the ebullition of a barbarian populace, only to be kept under control by the fear of meeting a just retribution from the Allied ships of war.

The arrival of His Majesty's ship 'Isis' at this critical period, when British subjects were flying from Tripoli,—when the Consul had removed his own family for safety and had claimed my assistance,—enabled me to check any attempts of this sort at once. I despatched Commodore Sir Thomas Staines with a letter strongly expressive of my sentiments, to which the Bey deemed it prudent to pay marked attention. Other vessels were sent to the smaller settlements; and shortly afterwards the family of the Consul and other refugees returned to their situations. So that it may fairly be attributed to the precautionary measures thus early adopted, that in an instance which had excited such alarm for contrary consequences, there has been a remarkable abstinence from the barbarities usually practised on such occasions. I am not aware of the life of one single individual having been taken away in this manner in consequence of the battle of Navarin. Even at Constantinople more attention was paid by the Reis Effendi to the representations of our Ambassador after the result of the battle was known, than had been done before.

Ibrahim, foreseeing the consequences to his army and himself which would follow the loss of his fleet, meditated evacuating the Morea whenever he could procure the means. It was with this view that he sent away the sick, the wounded, the harems, and such others as the ships remaining in his possession, and those he could collect together, were capable of receiving.* And but for the peremptory orders subsequently received from his father and from the Porte, there is little doubt but he would have then made proposals for his own retirement and that of his army.

Fear for the consequences of the Sultan's anger prevented the acquiescence of Mehemet Ali in this earnest desire of his son. Sending positive orders for Ibrahim to remain, he awaited that necessity arising from privation in which he might at length find a justification for withdrawing his troops from the Morea.

---

* On December 19, 1827, the vessels remaining after the battle put to sea.

The means of effective hostility to the Greeks being cut off from the Turco-Egyptian army, and having taken measures for the security of the Christian inhabitants against Mussulman irritation and violence, my attention was next given to the destruction of piracy.

The island of Carabusa, which had been captured by the Greeks from the Turks, is admirably situated for the interception of all vessels either going into or coming out of the Archipelago. It has an anchorage well adapted for securing the small pirate vessels fitted either for rowing or sailing as required; but it is dangerous for larger ships. And the fort on the rocky summit of the island in the hands of the most desperate pirate leaders, had set us at defiance by actually firing upon our ships of war. No less than 28 of these pirate vessels made this their place of refuge.

In determining to destroy this nest of rapine, much circumspection was required, since it was to be expected that ruffians like these would make a desperate resistance.*

The only prospect of destroying the fort, in which the pirates themselves lived and stored their plunder, was from a height on the contiguous land of Candia. My colleagues were to be consulted and made parties; the Turks who coveted re-possession of the fortress were to be reconciled to its demolition from Turkish ground; whilst the enterprise was to be made palatable to the Greeks, who were proud of its capture, profited by the abuses to which it was applied, and valued it as the future medium of obtaining possession of Candia.

Time, and extensive communications, formed a necessary preliminary to the undertaking. And it is perhaps jointly owing to the evident determination to take it at whatever cost, and the decisive conduct and ability of Sir T. Staines and his supporters, that its capture was accomplished at so early a period. Several of the principal culprits were sent in irons to be placed at the disposal of the Greek Government, and a large mass of plundered property was conveyed to Malta, subject to the claims of its rightful owners. The opportune arrival of Count Capodistrias, enabled me to procure a simultaneous attack on the system in the upper part of the Archipelago, under Admiral Miaulis, which, coupled with this important capture, has put an end to any further piracy in those seas.

I had been ordered by the Government to send one of His Majesty's vessels of war to receive Count Capodistrias at An-

---

* Order to Sir T. Staines of November 27, 1827.

cona, and convey him to his destination. Seeing in this order a desire to show that he had our strong support, and hoping by its execution to secure a direct English influence with him and his countrymen in the just execution of the Treaty of London, I requested Captain Parker, whom I had entrusted with the duties of the Ionian Seas, to receive him in the 'Warspite;' and as my daily expectation of further Instructions, and the other most important points of my duty, confined me to Malta, I expressed my wish for a personal interview there with the President, in his way to assume the Government.*

I embraced the opportunity which our meeting gave me of urging him to devote himself at as early a period as possible to the destruction of piracy, and to the strict confinement of all the Greek cruisers to the blockade of the Morea.

I pointed out to him that, although I could not assume the belligerent right of blockading, my Instructions empowered me to support a blockade by the Greeks, against interruption; by which means I hoped to starve Ibrahim out of the country: and that thus the great objects of the Treaty of London, by which we were mutually bound, and from which neither of us could swerve with impunity, would be the more readily and thoroughly fulfilled.

Hitherto, for want of authority to prevent it, the Morean army had been supplied by Ionian as well as other Neutral vessels, although I had made frequent representations of it.† In fact, the Pacha of Egypt had an agent and even a storehouse at Zante for the purpose; whilst, on the other hand, piracy found some encouragement in the failure of the trials at Malta, and in the liberation by orders from England‡ of a vessel taken into Zante by His Majesty's sloop 'Zebra,' which had plundered an English brig then at anchor in that bay, and whose master was ready to swear to the bales of his goods found in her.

Notwithstanding these impediments, the capture of §Carabusa, and the expedition of Admiral Miaulis, put down piracy; and the interception of money and other supplies upon the larger scale from Egypt, placed the army of Ibrahim under severe privations, which, by the establishment of the Greek blockade at my instance, were increased to a state of starvation.

* He arrived on January 9, 1828, and sailed on the 14th.
† Sir F. Adam's letters to Government on this subject were received on February 22, 1828; remained unnoticed up to March 18, 1828
‡ In a letter of October 11, 1827, to Sir F. Adam, I enquired the cause; he said that he did not know, the order to liberate her being unaccompanied by any explanation.
§ Never published.

In consequence of two small vessels laden with Ibrahim's troops having fired upon an English boat sent to warn them against proceeding, I ordered that not even a boat should thenceforth be permitted to go in or come out.[*] And the distress inflicted upon Ibrahim and his army by thus taking advantage of the Greek blockade, led to a belief that he would at the head of his army seize all the harvest of the Morea and starve the inhabitants.

The anxiety of the President on this head induced him to suggest the expedient of admitting conditionally for the use of the Ottoman army an equivalent proportion of provisions.[†]

Although my colleagues were disposed to accede to this proposal, I held a very different opinion of its policy, feeling confident that in case of necessity the Pacha would profit by the relaxation, and still reap the harvest. I therefore took advantage of the arrival of the 'Ocean' from England, to proceed myself in that ship off Navarin, where I warned him by letter[‡] against the adoption of so destructive a measure, and showed him the consequences to himself and his army, whenever the time should come, as it shortly must, of their being left at the mercy of the Allies. And I have the authority of Count Capodistrias himself, and also of my colleagues and other competent judges, that from the time of His Highness's receiving that letter, he did not take anything whatever without paying for it; that he released eight hundred Greeks then in his possession; and that after patiently undergoing himself privations he had never before endured, he solicited us to send one of his agents to give that account of the misery which his army was suffering, which occasioned his father's acceding to the evacuation proposed by me, and signing the Treaty of the 6th of August at Alexandria.

Finding Ibrahim was ready to retire to Egypt with his army if his father's sanction could be obtained for it, notwithstanding the orders of the Porte to force his way into Roumelia, I held a conference with my colleagues at Zante on the 25th of July, as to the most effectual means of gaining this most important object, and thereby preventing the necessity of the French army coming to enforce it.

In order to ensure success, my colleagues deemed it advisable[§] that I should myself undertake a mission to the Pacha of Egypt for the purpose; and their request being recorded

* See Orders of May 21 and 24, 1828, p. 281.
† See Captain Parker's letter of May 20, 1828, and my answer of June 1, 1828, p. 290.
‡ Sir E. Codrington's letter to Ibrahim of May 23, 1828, p. 280.
§ Protocol of July 25, 1828.

in the Protocol of our conference, I proceeded immediately to Alexandria and anchored the 'Asia' off the Pacha's palace, where I had already collected a strong force under Commodore Campbell in the ' Ocean.'

My arrival being announced by telegraph, the Pacha set out from Cairo immediately, and arrived at Alexandria on the 4th of August.

Judging by the conference with Ibrahim at Modon on the 6th of July, that Mehemet Ali was anxious for the return of his army, I at once declined meeting him unless he would agree to the evacuation of the Morea being the basis of our conference. He consented to this preliminary, under a stipulation that his honour should be saved by his being allowed to leave garrisons in the fortresses ; and accordingly I went on shore to his palace on the 6th of August, accompanied by Commodore Campbell and several officers of the fleet, and by the French and English Consuls.

After an extended discussion upon the subject of the fortresses and the garrisons to be left in them, which I prolonged by bringing forward various objections in order to found a stronger claim on his restoration of Greek slaves, the substance of the conditions was agreed upon.

During the delay in getting the Treaty prepared both in the Turkish and French languages, a tatar arrived from Constantinople, at which place the account of the conference at Modon had already been received. This tatar is supposed to have brought the Sultan's orders not to sanction Ibrahim's meditated retirement, since it was immediately upon his arrival that the Pacha started fresh demands.

Difficulties of this sort, occasioned by the arrival of a second tatar, after my having, partly by persuasion and partly by strong language, overcome the objections consequent on the despatches received by the first, protracted the final signature and exchange of the copies of the Treaty until the 9th. In fact, the agreement was at one time entirely broken off by the Pacha's insisting upon leaving an undefined number of troops in the fortresses.

At length, however, he proposed to limit the number of Egyptians to twelve hundred, if I would permit it to be so specified by a separate document; equally to be authenticated by his signet, but which by that means he could avoid sending to the Porte.

Being satisfied by this, and by his enumerating Castle Tornese with the other fortresses although it was a deserted heap of ruins, that it was put forth merely to palliate his disobedience of the Sultan's orders, I gave my consent.

The Treaty being thus concluded,* the Pacha expressed a wish that he might again see me before my departure from Alexandria. I replied that he should do so whenever his ships might be anchored on the outside of the harbour, where the English ships were then lying. Accordingly, having seventeen sail of his frigates and brigs of war commanded by a rear-admiral, under our control, I made him another visit, which he prolonged beyond an hour by his enquiries into our customs and institutions.

I then returned on board and made sail for Navarin to meet my successor, Sir Pulteney Malcolm, to whom I delivered up my command on the 22nd of August, according to the desire of His Majesty's Government through His Royal Highness the Lord High Admiral.

EDWARD CODRINGTON.

Eaton Square, Feb. 1829.

From H.R.H. the Duke of Clarence to the Duke of Wellington.

Admiralty : February 10, 1828.†

DEAR DUKE,—The enclosed Memorial from Sir Edward Codrington reached me at the moment of the dissolution of the late Government, on which account I then kept it back. Since that time I was not inclined to trouble your Grace, because I clearly saw the many and conflicting difficulties which existed in the arrangement of the present Administration, which I trust in God is now formed. Under this persuasion, I now send your Grace the Memorial of Sir Edward Codrington, in behalf of himself and his brave companions in arms at the battle of Navarin, for head-money, and also stating the value of the loss of ships and vessels to the Turkish Empire. Though I, had the good fortune to agree with your Grace in every sentiment expressed in the House of Lords by yourself respecting the Grand Seignior being the ancient and natural ally of Great Britain, I must call your Grace's attention to the Memorial, and earnestly entreat a favourable consideration of this extraordinary and novel case, where His Majesty's officers and men have conducted themselves with such honour to their King and country, and with such credit to themselves. . . . .

I remain, dear Duke, yours truly,

WILLIAM.

---

* Dated August 6, 1828, but signed August 9.
† Despatches of Duke of Wellington, vol. iv., page 260.

[Page 449.]

To the King's Most Excellent Majesty in Council.

The Humble Memorial of

Vice-Admiral Sir Edward Codrington, on behalf of himself, and the officers, seamen, and royal marines, who contributed under his command to the victory gained by the Allied squadrons of England, France, and Russia, over the Ottoman fleet, in the Port of Navarin, on October 20, 1827.

May it please your Majesty,—

Your Memorialist begs leave humbly and respectfully to state that, according to the commands with which your Majesty was graciously pleased to honour him, he sent home, in the care of Vice-Admiral Sir John Gore, a Memorial requesting that pecuniary gratuity might be awarded to himself, the officers, seamen, and royal marines, who contributed to the victory of Navarin.

That the said Memorial was delivered at the Admiralty by Vice-Admiral Sir John Gore on January 3, 1328, and particular attention called to it, as being one of two important documents which he was specially charged by your Majesty to bring back with him from Malta.

That upon your Memorialist making enquiry, subsequent to his return to England, as to the result of his application, no trace of the Memorial could be found, either at the Admiralty, the Council Office, or the Treasury.

That on February 19, 1830, your Memorialist enclosed to the Secretary to the Admiralty, as a duplicate, the original copy of the said Memorial, which your Majesty was graciously pleased to give up for that purpose, accompanied by a statement of the opposing Ottoman force.

That a letter from the Lords Commissioners of the Treasury, dated May 28, 1830, was sent to your Memorialist through the Admiralty, purporting,—'That there did not appear to their Lordships to be any sufficient grounds for departing from the established rules which make the grant of head-money dependent on a previous declaration of war.'

That upon receipt of this decision of their Lordships, your Memorialist, in a letter of June 2, 1830, submitted three instances, selected from three separate periods, in which pecuniary gratuity was awarded without any previous declaration of war, with such further explanations as he hoped might lead to a more favourable decision; but to which he has had no reply which he can justly consider satisfactory.

That, under these circumstances, your Memorialist ventures,

with most unfeigned respect, to place before your Majesty in Council a copy of his said letter, in order that your Majesty may see the grounds upon which the claims of himself and the other parties concerned now rest.

That the most recent of the cases referred to—the battle of Algiers—appears to your Memorialist to be parallel in its origin, progress, and results; and he therefore prays that a similar gratuity to that which was given to those engaged at Algiers, may be bestowed upon those who fought under his command at Navarin.

That your Memorialist is fully sensible that no one is more competent than your Majesty to judge of the ill-effect that might possibly arise from withholding from one division of your Majesty's naval service the rewards granted to others similarly situated; and that no one can know better than your Majesty what is due to people who have so sustained the honour of the British flag when opposed to a numerically superior force.

That your Memorialist therefore feels the greatest satisfaction in being permitted to commit to your Majesty's paternal care the claims of men who, by their attention to discipline and devotion to their duty, under your Majesty's fostering protection of their profession, had the good fortune to obtain your Majesty's full and spontaneous approbation of their conduct in successful battle.

EDWARD CODRINGTON, Vice-Admiral.

Eaton Square, December 21, 1831.

[Page 77.]

OTTOMAN NAVARIN FLEET.

1st Turkish Division, commanded by the Capitan Bey, sailed from Alexandria, August 5, 1827.

Gen. No.	Ships	Guns	Men	Remarks
1	1 Ship-of-the-line, Capitan Bey's flag	84	800	Dismasted and driven on shore.
2	2　Ditto　.　.	74	730	Destroyed with all the crew on board.
3	1 Frigate (razée)　.	54	500	Destroyed.
4	2　Ditto　.　.	52	450	Ditto.
5	3　Ditto　.　.	44	360	Ditto.
6	4 Pedroni Bey*　.	52	450	Driven on shore, but got off; arrived at Alexandria Dec. 1827.
7	5　Ditto　.　.	52	450	Dismasted and driven on shore, but afterwards got off; arrived at Alexandria Dec. 1827, *unserviceable.*
8	6　Ditto　.　.	52	450	Ditto, ditto, ditto, ditto.

* The Pedroni Bey sailed from Alexandria in this frigate, but is said to have shifted his flag (at the fore) to No. 2, a 74 in the same division.

OTTOMAN NAVARIN FLEET—*continued.*

Gen. No.	Ships	Guns	Men	Remarks
9	1 Corvette . .	28	200	Destroyed.
10	2 Ditto . .	26	180	Ditto.
11	3 Ditto . .	26	180	Ditto.
12	4 Ditto . .	26	180	Dismasted and driven on shore; afterwards got off; returned to Alexandria Dec. 1827; since repaired, Aug. 1828.
13	5 Ditto . .	26	180	Ditto, ditto, ditto, laid up.
14	6 Ditto . .	24	180	Ditto, ditto, returned to Alexandria in a sinking state, and totally unserviceable.
15	7 Ditto . .	24	180	Destroyed.
16	8 Ditto . .	24	180	Ditto.
17	9 Ditto . .	24	100	Ditto.
18	10 Ditto . .	22	180	Ditto.
19	11 Ditto . .	22	180	Ditto.
20	12 Ditto . .	24	180	Ditto.
21	1 Guerrienne Moharem Bey .	60	500	Ditto.
22	2 'Diana' . .	58	500	Ditto.
23	3 Frigate . .	58	500	Ditto.
24	4 'Leone'* . .	60	500	Dismasted; returned to Alexandria Dec. 1827; since refitted.
25	1 'Navarin' . .	22	150	Destroyed.
26	2 'Lion' . .	26	160	*a.* Returned to Alexandria Dec. 1827.
27	3 'Lion' . .	22	150	*a.* Returned to Alexandria Dec. 1827.
28	4 Ditto . .	22	150	*a.* Ditto. ditto.
29	5 Ditto . .	24	150	Disabled, ditto.
30	6 Ditto . .	22	150	Ditto, and driven on shore; returned to Alexandria Dec. 1827; since repaired.
31	7 Ditto . .	24	150	Destroyed.
32	8 Ditto . .	24	150	Ditto.
33	9 Ditto . .	22	150	Ditto.
34	10 Ditto . .	22	150	Ditto.
35	11 Ditto . .	22	150	Ditto.
36	1 Brig . . .	22	130	Ditto.
37	2 'Washington' .	22	120	Not in the battle.
38	3 Ditto . .	20	120	Destroyed.
39	4 Ditto . .	20	120	Ditto.
40	5 Ditto . .	18	120	Ditto.
41	6 'Satalia' . .	22	120	Returned to Alexandria Dec. 1827.
42	7 Ditto . .	18	120	*a.* Ditto, ditto.
43	8 Ditto . .	18	120	*a.* Ditto, ditto.
44	9 Ditto . .	18	120	Disabled and driven on shore, ditto,
45	10 Ditto . .	18	120	Ditto, ditto, ditto, ditto.
46	11 Ditto . .	18	120	Ditto, returned to Alexandria, Dec. 1827.
47	12 Ditto . .	16	110	Ditto, ditto, ditto.
48	13 Brig . . .	14	100	Destroyed.
49	14 Ditto . . .	18	120	Ditto.
50	15 Ditto . . .	14	90	Ditto.
51	16 Ditto . . .	22	120	Ditto.

* The 'Leone' did not leave Alexandria with the division, but joined it at Navarin.

OTTOMAN NAVARIN FLEET—*continued.*

Gen. No.	Ships	Guns	Men	Remarks
52	17 Brig . . .	18	120	Destroyed.
53	18 Ditto . . .	16	110	Ditto.
54	19 Ditto . . .	14	100	Ditto.
55	20 Ditto . . .	14	100	Disabled; returned to Alexandria Dec. 1827.
56	21 Ditto . . .	20	120	Destroyed.
57	1 Schooner . .	18	120	
58	2 Ditto . .	16	80	*
59	3 Ditto . .	14	80	*
60	4 Ditto . .	14	80	*
61	5 Ditto . .	14	80	*
62	1 Fire Brig . .	4	15	Destroyed.
63	2 Ditto . .	4	15	Ditto.
64	3 Ditto . .	4	15	Ditto.
65	4 Ditto . .	4	15	Ditto.
66	5 Ditto . .	4	15	Ditto.
67	6 Ditto . .	4	15	Driven on shore; returned to Alexandria Dec. 1827.
	Tunisian Division.			
68	1 Frigate, Tunisian Admiral .	42	350	Destroyed.
69	2 Ditto . .	32	300	Ditto.
70	1 Brig . . .	18	120	Ditto.
	2nd Turkish Division, commanded by Tahir Pacha, from Constantinople direct to Navarin.			
71	1 Ship-of-the-line, ' Tahir Pacha '.	60	550	Dismasted and driven on shore; arrived at Alexandria.
72	1 Frigate . .	50	350	Destroyed.
73	2 Ditto . .	48	350	Ditto.
74	3 Ditto . .	44	350	Dismasted and driven on shore; arrived at Alexandria Dec. 1827.
75	4 Ditto . .	44	350	Destroyed.
76	5 Ditto . .	44	350	Ditto.
77	6 Ditto . .	44	350	Ditto.
78	1 Corvette . .	28	150	Ditto.
79	2 Ditto . .	26	150	Ditto.
80	3 Ditto . .	26	150	Ditto.
81	4 Ditto . .	24	150	Ditto.
82	5 Ditto . .	24	150	Ditto.
83	6 Ditto . .	24	150	Ditto.
84	7 Ditto . .	24	150	Ditto.
85	1 Brig . . .	18	120	Ditto.
86	2 Ditto . .	18	120	Ditto.
87	3 Ditto . .	18	120	Ditto.
88	4 Ditto . .	18	120	Ditto.
89	5 Ditto . .	18	120	Ditto.
90	6 Ditto . .	18	120	Ditto.

* These four schooners are said to have remained afloat after the battle, but as they never appeared at Alexandria, it may be supposed they perished.

OTTOMAN NAVARIN FLEET—*continued.*

Line	Double Frigates	Frigates	Corvettes	Brigs	Schooners	Fire Brigs	Transports		Total	Remarks
							Aust.	Turk.		
2	0	5	12	0	0	0	0	0	19	Captain Bey's division from Alexandria.
0	4	0	11	21	5	6	8	33	88	Moharem Bey's ditto, ditto.
0	0	2	0	1	0	0	0	0	3	Tunisian division, ditto.
1	0	6	7	6	0	0	0	0	20	Tahir Pacha's ditto, from Constantinople.
3	4	13	30	28	5	6	8	33	130	Total, Transports included.
1	3	9	22	19	1	5	0	0	60	Destroyed.
2	1	4	8	9	4	1	0	0	29	Remain, besides Transports.

Thus it appears that sixty vessels of war were totally destroyed, and the remainder driven on shore in a shattered condition, with the exception of the 'Leone' (dismasted), four corvettes, six brigs, and four schooners, which alone remained afloat after the battle. Of those which were afterwards got off, at least one ship-of-the-line, two 52-gun frigates, and one, if not two, of the corvettes are too much damaged to be repaired. The Austrian transports had sailed from Navarin previous to October 20, and at least nine or ten of the Turkish armed transports having received the remnant of the crews of some of the destroyed vessels, hoisted pendants, and were reported as brigs of war, on their return to Alexandria in December 1827. The three corvettes and two brigs marked *a*, are said to have been present on October 20; but as they had not the slightest mark of having been engaged, it is probable they were the vessels said to have been at Patras, Modon, &c., &c. The 'Washington' returned to Alexandria with despatches after the affair of Patras, and was kept by Mehemet Ali for the purpose of carrying his instructions to Ibrahim on the subject of his forcing his way through the Allied squadrons as directed by the Porte. The loss in killed and wounded is stated at 3,000 of the former, and 1,109 of the latter.*

PETER RICHARDS,
Commander of H. M. Sloop 'Pelorus.'

The prayer of the above Memorial was refused by the Treasury, as 'the grant of head-money was dependent on a previous declaration of war.'

* This account was furnished to Capt. Richards by M. Letellier, the French Instructor of the Egyptian Navy; but the number of the wounded is evidently incorrect.

MEMORANDUM OF THE SERVICES OF ADMIRAL

ACTIVE SERVICE.				On what Station chiefly Employed.	SUMMARY Of the length and nature of the Services performed in the several Ranks. Stating also the nature of any Wound or Hurt received, and if in the receipt of a Pension.
Several Bearings and Ranks.	Names of the several Ships.	Date of Entry.	Date of Discharge.		
Midshipman .	'Augusta,' Yacht.	July 1783.	—	Home Station.	Midshipman and Mate about 10 years, of which 3 were on the North American Station,
Ditto .	'Brisk' .	July 1785.	Sept. 1785.	Halifax Station.	
Ditto .	'Assistance,' Flag ship of Admiral Sawyer.	Sept. 1785.	August 1786.	Ditto.	3 were in the Mediterranean, 2 on the Home & Channel Stations with Lord Howe, 1 as Acting Lieutenant.
Ditto .	'Leander,' Flag ship of Admiral Sawyer.	August 1786.	Sept. 1788.	Ditto.	
Ditto .	'Leander,' Flag ship of Admiral Peyton (recommis²ᵈ).	Sept. 1788.	April 1790.	Mediterranean.	
Acting Lieutenant.	'Ambuscade' .	April 1790.	—	Ditto.	
Ditto .	'Assistance' .	January 1791.	—	From Mediterranean to England.	
Midshipman .	'Formidable,' Flag ship of Admiral Leveson Gower.	1791.	—	Home Station.	
Ditto .	'Queen Charlotte,' Lord Howe's Flag ship.	Feb. 1793.	—	Channel Fleet.	Served 1½ year as Lieutenant under Lord Howe in the Channel Fleet, mostly in his Flagship; selected by Lord Howe, and sent into 'Pegasus' to repeat his signals.
Lieutenant .	'Santa Margueritta.'	1793.	—	Ditto.	As Lieutenant of the 'Queen Charlotte' was present in the battles of May 28 and 29, and June 1, 1794; sent home by Lord Howe with the Duplicate Despatches of the safe arrival of the Fleet and Prizes off Dunnose.
Ditto .	'Pegasus,' repeating frigate	3 July 1793.	—	Ditto.	
Ditto .	'Queen Charlotte,' Lord Howe's Flag ship.	1793.	—	Ditto.	Continued to serve as 1st Lieutenant of 'Queen Charlotte' at Lord Howe's request, instead of being promoted at the general promotion after June 1, 1794, on the understanding that it should be considered as Commander's time.
Commander .	'Comet,' fire ship.	7 Oct. 1794.	13 April 1795.	Ditto.	Served seven months as Commander of the 'Comet' fire ship in the Channel Fleet, under Lord Howe.
Captain .	'Babet' .	April 1795.	—	Ditto.	As Captain of the 'Babet,' was present at and assisted in Lord Bridport's action off L'Orient, when three line-of-battle ships were captured.
Ditto .	'Druid' .	July 1795.	—	Lisbon and Irish Station.	As Captain of the 'Druid,' assisted at the capture of a French ship 'Armé en Flute,' part of General Hoche's squadron for the invasion of Ireland.
Ditto .	'Orion,' 74 guns	24 May 1805.	—	Channel and the blockade of Cadiz.	Commanded the 'Orion,' 74, under Lord Nelson, in the Battle of Trafalgar. Served 1½ years in command of 'Orion' in the Channel Squadron, and in the Blockade of Cadiz, under Lord Collingwood.
Ditto .	'Blake,' 74 guns	17 Nov. 1808.	—	North Sea, Walcheren, Cadiz, & Mediterranean.	Commanded the 'Blake,' 74, at the Blockade of the North Sea, during the Walcheren expedition; the bombardment of Flushing; blockade of the Texel; in the defence of Cadiz when besieged by the French; conducted four Spanish line-of-battle ships to Mahon; joined in the blockade of Toulon.

Date of passing for Lieutenant.	Whether passed through the 'Excellent,' and the date.	Whether studied for steam, and where.	Age on the 1st January, 1846.	Letters or Reports of Superior Officers, or of other Official Persons (specifying the Name and Rank of the Writer), in which such good services are noticed.	Date of Letter or Report.	This Column to be left Blank.
—	No.	No.	75 years and 8 months.			
—	—	—	—	Selected by Lord Howe and sent into 'Pegasus' to repeat his signals.		
—	—	—	—	Selected by Lord Howe to take his Duplicate Despatches after the battle of June 1, 1794. Included in the Vote of Thanks of Parliament for the battles of May 28 and 29, and June 1, 1794 (as Lieutenant of 'Queen Charlotte').		
—	—	—	—	Included in the Vote of Thanks of Parliament for Lord Bridport's action, 1795 (as Captain of 'Babet').		
—	—	—	—	Included in the Vote of Thanks of Parliament for the Battle of Trafalgar, and received the Naval Medal for it, October 21, 1805, as Captain of H.M.S. 'Orion,' 74.		
—	—	—	—	Commended by Admiral Sir Richard Strachan, and Rear-Admiral Lord Gardner for conduct in the Walcheren expedition, and at the Bombardment of Flushing.		
—	—	—	—	Letters of approbation from Admiral Sir Richard Keats, for services in conveying four Spanish line-of-battle ships from Cadiz to Mahon; and in the assistance of Spanish Patriots on the coast.		

MEMORANDUM OF THE SERVICES OF ADMIRAL SIR

ACTIVE SERVICE.				On what Station chiefly Employed.	SUMMARY Of the length and nature of the Services performed in the several Ranks. Stating also the nature of any Wound or Hurt received, and if in the receipt of a Pension.
Several Bearings and Ranks.	Names of the several Ships.	Date of Entry.	Date of Discharge.		
Colonel of Marines.	—	Commission dated 4 Dec. 1813.	—	—	As Senior Officer in command of an English Squadron, was actively employed for 3½ years in continual co-operation with the Spanish Patriots against the French Armies on the East Coast of Spain, Tarragona, &c.
Commodore and Captain of the Fleet.	Went out with his broad pennant in the 'Forth' frigate.	Commission dated 5 May 1814.	—	Coast of America	* Served as Captain of the Fleet under Vice-Admiral Sir Alexander Cochrane in the operations on the Coast of America, in 1813 to 1814; including the Chesapeake, the Patuxunt (capture of Washington), the Potowmac, the Patapsco (Baltimore), and New Orleans.
Rear - Admiral and Captain of the Fleet.	'Tonnant,' Sir Alexr. Cochrane's Flag ship.	4 June, 11 June, 1814.	—	Ditto.	*In 1813 served with other Naval Officers, and Artillery Officers on a Committee appointed by the Admiralty to enquire into the carronade system, and into some alterations proposed in it for the Naval Service.
Made K.C.B. .	—	January 1815.	—	—	Served on a Committee which re-arranged the scheme for the Allowance of Provisions to the Navy.
Rear-Admiral .	'Havannah' frigate on return to England.	1815.	—	New Orleans to England.	Returned to England on the Cessation of Hostilities between England and America.
Rear-Admiral— Red.	—	12 Aug. 1819.	—	—	
Vice-Admiral— Blue.	—	27 May 1825.	—	—	In 1826 (from May to October) served with several other flag officers on a committee which revised and altered the Signal Books of the Navy to their present form.
Do., and Commander-in-Chief.	'Asia,' 84 Flag ship.	Commission dated 11 Sept. 1826.	Oct. 1828.	Mediterranean.	Commander-in-Chief of the Mediterranean Station from 11th Sept. 1826 to Oct. 1828. Was in command of the combined English, French, and Russian squadrons employed in the pacification of Greece; and at the battle of Navarin, 20th October 1827.
Made G.C.B. .	—	13 Nov. 1827.	—	—	
Vice - Admiral of the White, commanding Channel Squadron.	'Caledonia,' 120, Flag ship.	22 July 1830.	—	—	Commanded the evolutionary squadron in the Channel in 1831.
Admiral of the Blue.	—	10 Jan. 1837.	—	—	—
(Admiral of the Blue) Commander-in-Chief.	'Britannia,' 'Queen,' 'St. Vincent,' Flag ships.	22 Nov. 1839.	31 Dec. 1842.	Portsmouth.	Commander-in-Chief on the Portsmouth station.
Admiral of the White.	—	23 Nov. 1841.	—	Ditto.	—

NO PENSION WHATEVER.

On the 25th February, 1847, was granted a pension of £300, on the death of Admiral Sir Willoughby T. Lake.

DWARD CODRINGTON, G.C.B., &c., &c.,&c.—*continued.*

Date of passing for Lieutenant.	Whether passed through the 'Excellent,' and the date.	Whether studied for steam, and where.	Age on the 1st January, 1846.	Letters or Reports of Superior Officers, or of other Official Persons (specifying the Name and Rank of the Writer), in which such good services are noticed.	Date of Letter or Report.	This Column to be left Blank.
—	—	—	—	Letters of approbation from Admiral Sir Charles Cotton, Commander-in-Chief, for services on the East Coast of Spain, in co-operation with the Spanish Patriots in the affairs of Figueras, siege of Tarragona, capture of the Medas Islands, &c.		
				Letters of approbation from the Admiralty on the same subjects.		
				Commendation of General Contreras, Governor of Tarragona, in his official account of the siege.		
				Letter of approbation from Admiral Sir E. Pellew, Commander-in-Chief, for various services of a similar nature on the East Coast of Spain.		
				Thanked by the Admiralty for his services and those of his Squadron on that Coast.	30 March 1813.	
				Letter from the Spanish Government to Sir H. Wellesley, British Ambassador at Cadiz.	8 March 1813.	
				Letter from Sir H. Wellesley, British Ambassador in Spain, to Viscount Castlereagh.	9 March 1813.	
				Letter from Conde de Fernan Nunez, Spanish Minister, to Viscount Castlereagh.	9 April 1813.	
				Included in the Vote of Thanks of Parliament for the capture of Washington, and the operations on the Coast of America.		
				Letter of thanks from Vice-Admiral Sir Alext. Cochrane to Sir E. Codrington, for his services under his command.	January 1815.	
—	—	—	—	Letters of commendation of Sir E. Codrington's services as Captain of the fleet, addressed by Vice-Admiral Sir A. Cochrane to the Admiralty.	January 1815.	
—	—	—	—	Made K.C.B. in January, 1815, for his services.		
—	—	—	—	Promoted to G.C.B., for his conduct as Admiral of the Allied English, French, and Russian squadrons at the battle of Navarin, 20th October, 1827.		

EDWD. CODRINGTON, Adml.,
92, Eaton Square, London,
23rd May, 1846.

Chronique de la Bataille de Navarin d'après Froissart.

Or oncques plus ne voulons différer de escripre et chrononiser l'histoire de cette grande et belle bataille qui fut à Navarin, laquelle avint le vingtième jour du mois d'octobre l'an mil huit cent vingt-sept de notre Seigneur; car mémoire passe avec tems qui toujours vole et oncques pour nulle chose ne s'arrête. Et à cette intente la voulons escripre fidèlement pour ce que moult à été commentée faussement et en malice par mauvaises et envieuses gens pour en tolir la gloire et l'honneur à ceux qui si vaillamment combattirent pour servir leur patrie et obéir aux ordres de icelle. Or en ce tems étoit le beau pays de Grèce en dure subjection à Turquie; et sont Turquois felles et crueuses gens, et moult oppressoient ce pauvre peuple, faisant de eux esclaves que traitoient durement, et massacrant sans nulle merci iceux qui se vouloient délivrer: et étoient toutes les nations de l'Europe courroussées de voir si bel pays comme étoit Grèce (qui classique contrée étoit, et qui en ancien tems si haute fâme avoit eue de abileté en toutes sciences, belles et hautes apertises d'armes, et sagesse pardessus toute autre nation) couru, gâté, et exilé par tel mauvais peuple que sont Turquois.

Ci les trois plus grandes nations de Europe, anglesche, françoise, et russe, firent une ligue et un traité pour impêtrer la délivrance de ce pour peuple; et à cette intente manda chacune de icelles une navie moult bien fretée et appareillée et commandée par un Amiral de mer que cuidoit digne de fiance. Et étoit l'amiral anglois le chef des trois, pour ce que Angleterre fut de tout tems reine de la mer, et sera à toujours mais. Or vous raconterons tant bien comme pourrons de la manière et du semblant de eux que bien connoissons par accointance et par renommée: ci étoit l'amiral anglois que on clamoit Messire Edouard Codrington, grand, droit, de belle contenance et affable et démontrant toute habileté et bon conseil. À ce tems étoit sa tête nue et dépourvue de cheveux; mais toutefois avoit un air moult noble, et étoit de belle apparence. Gracieuses manières avoit et courtoises, et étoit orné de toutes qualités qui à gentil chevalier appartiennent. Et étoit le Comte de Heiden l'amiral de mer pour la Russie, bon homme que oncques ne fut de meilleur; avec bon cœur et physionomie lie et aimable et manières affables et franches qui inspiroient amour et fiance, et faisoient que chacun lui aimoit. Moult étoit prisé et considéré de son Empereur qui avoit toute fiance en l'habileté de lui; et bien fit voir l'amiral par la suite, que avoit mérité telle opinion. Jà ne pouvons justement vous raconter quel semblant ni quelles manières avoit le chevalier De Rigny, qui amiral étoit du Roi de France ; car oncques ne le vîmes, laquelle chose moult nous vint à déplaisance ; mais renommée qui vole vite et loin a conté partout que vaillant et prud'-homme étoit, et chevalereux durement. Ci eut l'amiral anglois vent à volonté, et cingla tant par mer, que arriva dans les mers qui gissent au Levant de la Méditerranée ; et là ouit que Ibrahim Baquin s'étoit retraist et bouté dans une place forte que on clâmoit Navarin. Sitôt que cette nouvelle eut ouie, se conseilla et dit à soi-mesme, 'Or, comme est jà entré dans Navarin ce Baquin, amender ne le puis ; mais ci l'y veuillé-je tenir si bien que point n'en issira par mer, fort que pour se retraire à Alexandrie.' Et étoit ce Ibrahim Baquin fils à Méhémet Ali, Baquin d'Egypte, qui allié et subject étoit du Grand Sultan, et ci avoit cet Ali mandé son fils pour conquèter la Morée pour le susdit Sultan. Ci fit voile l'amiral anglois pour Navarin, et alla seul, pour ce que l'amiral russe point encore arrivé étoit (car Russie lointain pays est), et l'amiral françois cingloit par les mers, si bien que nullui ne savoit où. Ci eut l'amiral Codrington une con-férence avec le Baquin ; et tant fit et impêtra que promit Ibrahim Baquin de envoyer un héraut au Sultan, pour en-quérir de lui ce qui mestier lui étoit de faire (lequel retourner devoit dedans l'espace de vingt jours), et en outre promit que ce terme pendant, y auroit cessation de toute persécution contre Grequois ; et que ni lui ni gens à lui appartenant, ne issiroient pour oncques raison du havre de Navarin.

Ce conclus, s'en alla l'amiral à Zante, île moult voisine de là, pour ne point montrer nul semblant de défiance au Ba-quin, et pour ce que mestier lui étoit de rafraîchir sa nef. Mie longtems n'y séjourna que vint à lui la 'Dartemoutte,' frégate que stationnée avoit devant Navarin pour observer que feroit Ibrahim ; et lui avertit par signaux, que issoient les Egyptiens du havre, et cheminoient devers le Nord. Or considéra l'amiral que chose peu loyale étoit de ainsi rompre parole et traité, et alla à l'encontre de cette flotte pour eux réprimander durement ; et tant fit par menaces et dures pa-roles, que promit l'amiral turquois de retourner en arrière, mais dans la nuit, qui fut si vilaine durement et tempestu-euse, que furent toutes les nefs boutées loin et dispersées, ce mauvais Baquin que il-mesme avoit joint sa flotte, cuidant que point ne le sauroit l'amiral anglois, cingla devers le Nord, pour tâcher de ravitailler et bouter pourvéances dedans la ville de Patras, à laquelle grand mestier étoit de ce faire. Or regardez quel manque de foi et d'honneur étoit, et vilaine chose que fit ce déloyal Baquin ; et en ce bien démontra que étoit faux, mauvais et traître, et point digne de fiance.

Mais faillit à son intente, car le suivit l'amiral anglois, et le rejoignit à Patras, car jà étoit arrivé dans le Golfe que on clâme Lépante. Et à ce tems avoit l'amiral en sa compagnie quatre nefs tant seulement, les noms desquels vous dirons, pour ce que dignes sont de être recordés, pour la prouesse de eux en cette encontre. Et tout premièrement l'‘Asie,’ grande et belle nef, et noblement frêtée, que montoit l'amiral il-mesme et flottoit bel pavillon bleu à mont du mât de mizaine, et étoit pavillon de l'amiral ; et grande et belle batterie étoit cette nef, car portoit 84 gros canons : ci là commandoit le capitaine Curzon. Puis la ‘Dartemoutte,’ frégate forte et belle, la mesme que avons ci-dessus nommée, et étoit messire Thomas Fellowes capitaine de icelle. Tiercement, le ‘Talbot,’ petite frégate, mais dure et forte ; et clâmoit-on le commandeur de icelle messire Frédéric de Spensier, de famille noble et moult distinguée dans la marine ; et quartement le brick que on clâmoit ‘Zèbre,’ petit brick et gentil, et commandé par messire Charles Cotton, moult jeune capitaine, mais vaillant, et moult désireux de acquérir gloire et de lui avancer.

Et vous dis que belle et noble chose, et de hardie emprise étoit, que avec ces quatre nefs, et mie plus, de ainsi soi présenter devant la flotte de ce Ibrahim, qui ne montoit à mie moins qu'à 60 nefs. Et démontra l'amiral en cette encontre que bien à lui appartènoit de porter telle hardie devise que étoit la sienne, ‘Vultus in hostem,’ qui en notre langue signifie, ‘Face à l'ennemi ;’ car bien que non étoit ennemi déclaré, ci à peu de chose tenoit que Ibrahim ne détruisît ces quatre nefs. Ci lui envoya l'amiral anglois message dur et menaçant, et lui dit que traîtreuse et déloyale chose avoit faite que de ainsi rompre sa parole ; et lui ordonna de retourner à Navarin, en lui menaçant que si tiroit un coup de canon tant seulement encontre la bannière anglêsche, ci le détruiroit et couleroit à fond, lui et toute sa flotte.

Ci étonné et ébahi de telle hardiesse, ce couard Baquin, avec ses trois amiraux et toute sa navie, se retraist et retourna devant ces quatre nefs anglêsches. Or regardez quelle grand' vergogne et couardise étoit de s'en r'aller, ainsi que firent, comme troupeau de moutons chassés par loups !

Et en aient grand honneur cet amiral et ces quatre nefs ; car belle et noble chose firent à ce jour, qui fut·le 4ième de octobre, l'an de grâce mil huit cent vingt-sept.

Or quand Ibrahim Baquin retourné fut à Navarin, ci commença, comme fel et cruel étoit, à courir, gâter, et exiler le pays ; et tant robba et pilla, que pauvres Grequois mouroient de faim, et contraints étoient de manger herbe. Or comme à ce tems étoient jà arrivés les deux amiraux de France et Russie, eurent ces trois amiraux une conférence ensemble, et ci se conseillèrent et avisèrent l'un à l'autre ; et regardèrent que chose peu convenable étoit que de ce permettre, et envoyèrent les amiraux à Ibrahim Baquin lettre signée des trois, et scellée de leurs scels, pour lui remontrer cette chose. Mais Ibrahim, comme rusé étoit, point ne lisit ni ouvrit la lettre ; mais la remanda sans rompre les scels, disant son Drugman que nullui ne savoit où se tenoit le Baquin. Or tinrent les amiraux cette conduite à vilaine et impudente, et se retraient tous les trois à bord de l'‘ Asie,’ pour eux conseiller et prendre résolution comment mettre fin à cette cruelle dévastation que faisoit Ibrahim de Grèce, et mieux ouvrer en l'exécution du Traité de Londres. Et devisèrent entre eux trois moyens pour ce faire, et des trois se accordèrent à un que cuidèrent le meilleur ; et fut de entrer dedans le port de Navarin, les trois amiraux et leurs trois navies, et là parlementer de par eux-mesmes au Baquin, en lui requérant la raison de telle conduite. Mais ains que de entrer dedans le port, se ordonnèrent toutes les nefs à tous méchefs et fâcheuses encontres qui à eux pourroient avenir ; et étoit chacun marronnier en son lieu, ainsi que pour bataille, et chacun canon appareillé de balles et poudre ; et ce firent pour deux causes lesquelles vous dirons pour ce que moult fut blâmé l'amiral anglois qui chef étoit des trois de ainsi faire en tems de paix : et premièrement que escript est dans les ordonnances de marine, que oncque vessel ne approche nef estranière sans se ainsi appareiller ; et secondement que nulle fiance ne pouvoit ni ne devoit avoir en la foi de si déloyal et traître homme que étoit ce Baquin : mais devez savoir et regarder que ainçois de entrer dedans le port, manda lettres à tous ses capitaines pour eux ordonner que non tirassent un coup de canon tant seulement ains que de être attaqués par Turquois. Et étoient ses ordres concis, bien escripts, et devisés pour toutes encontres ; et étoit la fin de icelles, ‘ En cas que avienne bataille, ci vous veuillé-je rementever en les paroles de l'amiral Nelson de bonne et glorieuse mémoire, que “ ne peut faillir de bien faire, icelui qui adressera sa nef encontre celle d'un ennemi ; ” ’ et vous dis que moult bien consuivirent cet ordre.

Et étoit à ce jour le tems bel et clair, et le vent léger et à point ; et or vous dirai de l'ordonnance et du convenant

comment entrèrent dans le port. Tout premièrement l'' Asie,'
cette belle et gracieuse nef, qui noblement et en bel arroi
conduisit ; et fut suivie de l''Albion,' et du ' Genoa,' deux
grandes nefs, dont étoient capitaines messire Jean Acvorte
Ommannie, et messire Gautier Battourste ; et puis la ' Dartemoutte,' et le ' Talbot,' les deux frégates que vous avons nom-
mées, et portoient la ' Dartemoutte ' 42 canons, et le ' Talbot '
28 canons. Ensuite la ' Rose,' corvette de 18 canons, et étoit
commandeur de icelle messire Louis Davis ; et puis les trois
petits et gentils bricks que on clâmoit la ' Philomèle,' le
' Brisk,' et le ' Mosquito,' desquels étoient commandeurs et
patrons, messire Charles Talbot, vicomte de Ingestrie, messire
Guillaume Anson, et messire George Bohun Martin.   Un
petit après des autres, vinrent les deux frégates ' Cambrian,'
de 48 canons, et le ' Glasgow,' de 50 canons ; et com-
mandoient icelles, messire Guillaume Gawen Hamilton, et
messire Jean Alexandre Maude.   Et point ne convient taire
et oublier que entra en compagnie avec l'amiral une toute
petite nef, moult bien ordonnée et appareillée ; petit cotter,
que on clâmoit ' Hind,' et étoit commandeur de icelle un
lieutenant moult brave, qui avoit nom messire Jean Robb.
Lors vinrent en bel ordre les navies françoise et russe, et
tout premièrement la ' Sirène,' nef de 60 canons, qui portoit
pavillon de l'amiral françois ; et se clâmoient les autres
naves françoises, ' Scipion,' ' Breslau,' ' Trident,' ' Armide,'
' Alcione,' et ' Daphné,' desquels trois étoient grandes naves
que on clâme de ligne, et deux frégates, et étoient ' Daphné '
et ' Alcione ' deux petits messages schooners pour porter messages de
l'amiral. Or vous dirai des Russes : étoit le pavillon de l'amiral
russe flottant à bord de l'' Azoff,' et le capitaine se clâmoit
Lazareffe ; et puis Ezékiel, Hanhoud, et Alexandre Newsky,
et ces quatre étoient grandes nefs de ligne ; et étoient les
frégates ' Provornoy,' ' Constantin,' ' Héléna,' et ' Castor.'
Et vous dis que merveilleuse chose et belle, et de grand'
plaisance étoit à voir et à regarder ces navies de trois
nations qui oncques mais n'avoient servi ensemble, or réunies
en telle harmonie et ordonnance ainsi que une seule flotte !
Et étoient ces trois flottes et ces trois amiraux bon exemple
de cette belle et renommée devise du noble Ordre du Bain
(dont étoit chevalier messire Edouard) laquelle est, ' Tria
juncta in uno ; ' car ainsi que étoient les trois flottes comme
une, sembloient les trois amiraux n'avoir que un cœur et un
bras.
Ci au moment que l'' Asie ' passoit de lez le fort qui gît
à l'entrée du havre, chemina devers elle à force de rames un
batel turquois, avec message de part le commandant, à

l'intente que Ibrahim Baquin point n'avoit donné permission
de laisser entrer la navie alliée. Mais pour tant ne fut mie
détourné messire Edouard de son avis; et ci répondit, que
point n'étoit venu pour recevoir ordres, mais pour en donner;
et que si tiroit un seul coup de canon encontre la flotte
alliée, seroit la flotte turquoise détruite !

Et étoit la flotte turquoise placée dedans le port en forme
ainsi que de croissant, et avoient Turquois placé six nefs que
on clâme brûlots qui malement étoient dangereuses, à
l'entrée du port, de laquelle part souffloit le vent, ainsi que pour
ardoir les nefs alliées; et montroient semblant les Turquois
de eux ordonner pour combattre. La 'Dartemoutte,' qui
stationnée étoit avec les quatre bricks de lez les brûlots, pour
eux garder et empêcher, voyant que un de iceux se appareilloit
pour ardoir, envoya un batel avec pavillon de paix, pour eux
pourchasser que voulsissent se retraire un petit plus loin
pour non lui endommager: mais ains que put arriver le batel
de lez le brûlot, tirèrent ces fels gens coups de fusils devers
le batel, et occirent le lieutenant commandeur de icelui que
on clâmoit Fitz Roy. Ce voyant, fut contraint la 'Dartemoutte' de tirer coups de fusils pour son batel défendre: la
'Sirène' fit de même; après quoi tira une nef égyptienne
coups de gros canons encontre la dite 'Sirène,' et lors se
joignit chacun au hutin, et devint la bataille générale de
cette part. Le terme pendant que passoit cette chose, la nef
'Asie' ancra en mie des naves turquoises de telle manière
que avoit les deux grandes nefs qui portoient les pennons des
deux amiraux turquois et égyptien de chacun lez; et vous
dis que lieu fel et périlleux étoit, car outre ces deux naves
grandes et fortes, y avoit-il derrière eux, qui eux soutenoient,
deux autres rangs de naves qui aussi faisoient feu de grand
random.

Moharem Baquin, lequel étoit amiral de mer des Egyptiens,
se retint lui et sa nave de non attaquer les Alliés, et manda
messages et assurances devers l'amiral anglois que non
feroit feu; et pour ce dura quelque tems sans que n'y eût
hutin entre eux, et cannona l''Asie' avec Capitaine Baquin,
amiral de mer turquois, qui avoit lui attaqué. Mais par
l'espace de une demi-heure, quand l'Amiral Codrington
manda batel avec un sien lieutenant pour porter message
devers Moharem pour lui démontrer le grand désir que avoit
de non verser sang, fut traîtreusement navré à mort messire
Pietre Michel, piloteur de l''Asie,' lequel avoit mandé pour
interprêter le sien message; et chéit en arrière dedans le
batel, occis. Et d'autant plus felle et vilaine chose étoit,
que levé étoit dans le batel bannière de paix; et le firent

pour ce que il étoit Grequois, et tous Grequois avoient les Turquois en grand' haine et mautalent.

Après ce, commença Moharem à cannoner, ce dont fut si durement puni par l''Asie,' que lui, ainsi que son compaing amiral de l'autre lez, fut mis hors d'état de mie davantage guerroyer. Ci avint que une balle de une nave anglêsche ayant coupé la corde souveraine par laquelle ancrée étoit une des frégates égyptiennes, icelle quitta son lieu, et comme le vent souffloit de cette part, il la bouta du lez où gissoit l''Asie ;' ci quand arriva tout encontre de l''Asie,' sauta en l'air par effet de poudre : et vous dis que étoit moment de grand danger pour cette belle nef, car petit espace y avoit entre les deux. Lors ordonna l'Amiral à tous ceux qui là étoient, de descendre ; car bien que moult grand étoit le danger, n'y pouvoit nul pourvoir remède : et n'y resta nullui fort tant que il-mesme, qui pour oncque chose ne voulsit descendre. Lors monta grosse fûme, et si durement épaisse, que en fut l''Asie' toute enveloppée. Et cuidèrent toutes les naves alliées que étoit l''Asie' elle-mesme qui sauté avoit en l'air; laquelle chose telle consternation causa, que s'arrêta chacun de guerroyer. Mais après un tantinet, se dissipa cette fûme, et lors vit-on la belle 'Asie' toute sauve, et qui noblement tenoit son lieu ; et put chacun distinguer le preux amiral debout sur la poupe lui tant seulement. Adonc s'éleva dans la nef plus voisine, un haut cri pour exprimer leur grande joie, et lors que l'entendirent les autres, ci se communiqua à eux cette joie, et se joignit chacun au cri. Et vous dis que belle et touchante chose étoit à voir et à entendre, que ce hutin qui marquoit telle accord-ance d'amour et de joie. Lors se renouvela le combat ; et là fut bataille crueuse, forte, et fière, grand hutin et toulis, et dures encontres et périlleuses. Et ci avint que en mie de cette grande bataille, furent maintes belles appertises.

Ci fut la ' Sirène,' nave amirale, en grand danger de être arse par un de ces batels que on clâme brûlots ; mais fut sauvée par l'aide des batels de la nave 'Dartemoutte ;' et vous dis que fut à bonne cause que fut rengrâcié le capitaine de icelle par l'amiral françois !

Et à ce tems que vous recorde, fut navré à mort messire Gautier Battourste qui capitaine étoit du ' Genoa ;' et ci fut piteuse et mérancolieuse chose, et en furent tout courroucés et décomfortés tous ceux qui là étoient : et plus douloureuse chose étoit, pour ce que avoit dame que moult àmoit, et ci devenoit-elle veuve ! Et quand gissoit féri en sa cabine, ci fut apporté à son lez un sien officier navré durement, et ci dit en lui adressant :—'Mon ami, telle est fortune de

guerre.' Ce terme pendant, voyant le commandeur du
brick la ' Rose,' que étoit l''Armide' en péril d'un brûlot qui
trop étoit proche de elle, alla hardiment à la rescousse de
icelle ; ci entrementes que montoit à mont du brûlot pour
parlementer, sauta une partie en l'air, et chéit le dit capitaine jus en son propre batel, qui par spéciale providence là
étoit! et lors fut rescous. Lors quand vit le capitaine
Hugon que plus ne pouvoit aider ni guerroyer là où gissoit,
leva ancre et nagea devers l'autre lez du havre au lieu où
étoit le ' Talbot,' lequel soutenu avoit jusqu'alors dur assaut
encontre trois grandes nefs turquoises de celles que on
clâme frégates, mais qui du long combat étoit durement
travaillé et lassé. Tant fit et si appertemente manéria, que
vint parmi de eux, et délivra le 'Talbot' d'un de ses ennemis.

Ci mie ne dura longtems que la dite nef turquoise baissa
pavillon devant lui, et lors fit ce Capitaine Hugon gracieuse et
courtoise action, car fit hisser à·mont du mât de la nef
vaincue, les deux pavillons d'Angleterre et de France, et
l'anglêsche par dessus ; laquelle chose fit pour démontrer
à chacun que l'honneur de telle prise étoit dû au ' Talbot,'
pour ce que avoit longtems guerroyé cette nef ains que il ne
vint. Ci la petite nef ' Hind,' bien que moult étoit petite,
point ne faillit à guerroyer de tout son pouvoir ; et vous dis
que n'y eut oncques canons dans tout le havre, qui mieux
furent administrés que les six petits canons que elle portoit.
Mais de la petitesse de icelle lui avint grand péril, car bouta
aventureusement le sien arcboutant dans la fenestre de
l'arrière de la nef de Moharem Baquin ! Ci quand la virent
les Turquois en telle mauvaise encontre, prirent avantage de
cet arcboutant pour passer dessus comme pont, et entrer
dedans icelle—mais non purent ; car dure et felle résistance
y trouvèrent, pour ce que eussent été le commandeur et ses
vingt-quatre hommes tous morts ains que de laisser entrer
un Turquois en leur vessel ! Ci moult fut grevée et endommagée cette petite nef, car eut occis et navrés la moitié de
ses gens, et reçut grande foison de balles, si que merveille.
Mais aussi en eut, comme bien appartenoit, grand honneur et
renom. Fut aussi l''Asie' durement endommagée des balles
des naves turquoises. Chéit son mât de mizaine par force de
blessures en travers de la poupe, et tous ses cordages avec,
dans lesquels se tenoient deux marronniers, qui cependant par
bonne aventure trouvèrent moyen de eux sauver—et à cet
instant marchoit l'amiral de long en large sur la poupe ! et
faillit peu que ne chéit sur lui le mât ; mais par grande providence passa l'instant avant que ne chéit !

Et fut l''Asie' durement grevée, non pas seulement en

un lieu, mais en toutes les parties de icelle, si que quasi ne
pouvoit-on montrer endroit que n'y fut trou.

Or avint que au fort du hutin, fut occis un moult brave
homme que on clâmoit Guillaume Smith, qui patron étoit de
l''Asie;' ci avint cette occision en le moment que lui donnoit
ordre le capitaine de tourner la nef en autre position—et
vous dis que le tinrent les siens compaigns à trop grand
meschef et dommage; et quand fut mort sentit chacun qui
à lui étoit accointé que avoit perdu un sien ami; car l'àmoit
chacun pour son franc caractère, ses manières douces et
amiables, et l'appertise de lui en son état. Et or imaginez le
déconfort et la piteuse situation de la pauvre veuve de lui,
et de ses six enfans devenus orphelins!

Or quand eut jà duré le combat trois heures, fut navré
durement le main-né fils de l'amiral anglois, qui étoit en
service de marine dans la nef du sien père! Gentil garçon
étoit, et grand durement; mais moult jeune, car mie n'avoit
encore de barbe; et eut au mesme moment trois navrures,
une au col, une autre qui lui traversa en mie la jambe, et une
tierce en la cuisse, où la balle demeura. Son sire de père
point ne le vit férir, mais après un espace de tems, quand
tourna pour le chercher, plus le ne trouva; et lors jugez que
devoit sentir, quand point n'osoit demander à nullui que étoit
devenu son fils! Et maintes périlleuses aventures eut l'amiral il-mesme; fut le sien habit déchiré en cinq endroits, et son
chapeau féri d'un coup de balle: fut la montre que il tenoit
dedans sa poche rompue et endommagée par un coup moult
fel, lequel lui auroit occis, si point ne l'eut sauvé cette ma-
chine. Et à une fois, dans le moment que parloit à un marronnier, vint une balle qui navra à mort le dit marronnier,
et chéit devant lui sur le pont! Mais de tous ces périls
échappa-t-il sans nul dommage, bien que fut plus exposé que
les autres, car avint que deux fois la bataille durant, demeura,
lui, un homme tant seulement, debout sur la poupe! Et en
ce peut-on voir que spéciale Providence veilloit à lui, car si
ce n'eut été, comment fut-il sauvé, quand gissoient autour de
lui telle foison de morts et de navrés! Mais Dieu, qui pouvoir
a de détruire et de sauver, avoit ordonné que point n'auroit
meschef, et lors balles et poudre faillirent à lui endommager.

Et vous dis que en cette journée, tous, François, Russes, et
Anglois, guerroyèrent, que un, que autre, à leur loyal pouvoir;
et si bien combattirent tous, que 'ne sais à dire à la vérité,
"c'ils se maintinrent le mieux," ou "c'ils le firent le mieux;"
ni n'en ouis oncques nul priser plus avant que autre.

Ci dura cette felle bataille l'espace de quatre heures et
demie, et vous dis que glorieuse bataille fut, et durement bien

combattue ; et là y eut grande occision, et grande foison d'hommes furent morts et navrés ; ci dans la nef opposée à l'"Asie' tant seulement, gissoient sur les ponts six cent et cinquante Turquois !

Et pour tant étoient Turquois grandement les plus forts, car avoient quatre-vingt et neuf nefs, lesquelles portoient jusqu'à deux mille deux cent et quarante canons ; ci ne comptoient les navies alliées que trente-six nefs, et mille trois cent et vingt-quatre canons tant seulement ; or voyez quelle différence !

Que vous ferai-je long conte ! En ce jour et en cette bataille fut détruite toute la navie turquoise. Les aucuns vessels turquois sautoient en l'air par effet de poudre, les aucuns effondroient pour ce que étoient troués et pertuisés, et la yaue entroit à grand random dedans ; et d'autres étoient arses par les Turquois mesmes, pour ce que mie plus ne pouvoient guerroyer. Et ci le lendemain à soleil levant, quand virent les alliés la grande déconfiture de leurs ennemis, et les corps morts qui dans le havre flottoient, ainsi que les débris des naves détruites, musèrent et ' considérèrent adonc plus parfaitement le grand péril où ils avoient été.'

Lors se retrairent tant bien comme purent les flottes alliées chacune en son lieu, la françoise à Toulon, et l'anglêsche et la russe à Malte. Or nous tairons nous de plus escripre ; car maintenant que avons recordé cette belle et glorieuse bataille, le restant n'est mie plaisant à chroniquer ni à recorder.

Or, courtois lecteur, si cuidez que trop longue avons fait cette relation, vous devez vous ramenter que si noble et hardie emprise ne fait mie à escripre légèrement ; et que si avons longuement commenté tous détails et minutieuses circonstances, l'avons fait ' pour tous jeunes bacheliers encourager et exemplier.'

FIN.

Escript et chroniqué par les moult aimantes et affectionnées filles de icelui preux amiral de mer, Jeanne, Marie, et Emma Codrington, en le mois de septembre, l'an de grâce mil huit cent vingt-huit.

LONDON: PRINTED BY
SPOTTISWOODE AND CO., NEW-STREET SQUARE
AND PARLIAMENT STREET